Garfield by the pound

BY: JIM DAVIS

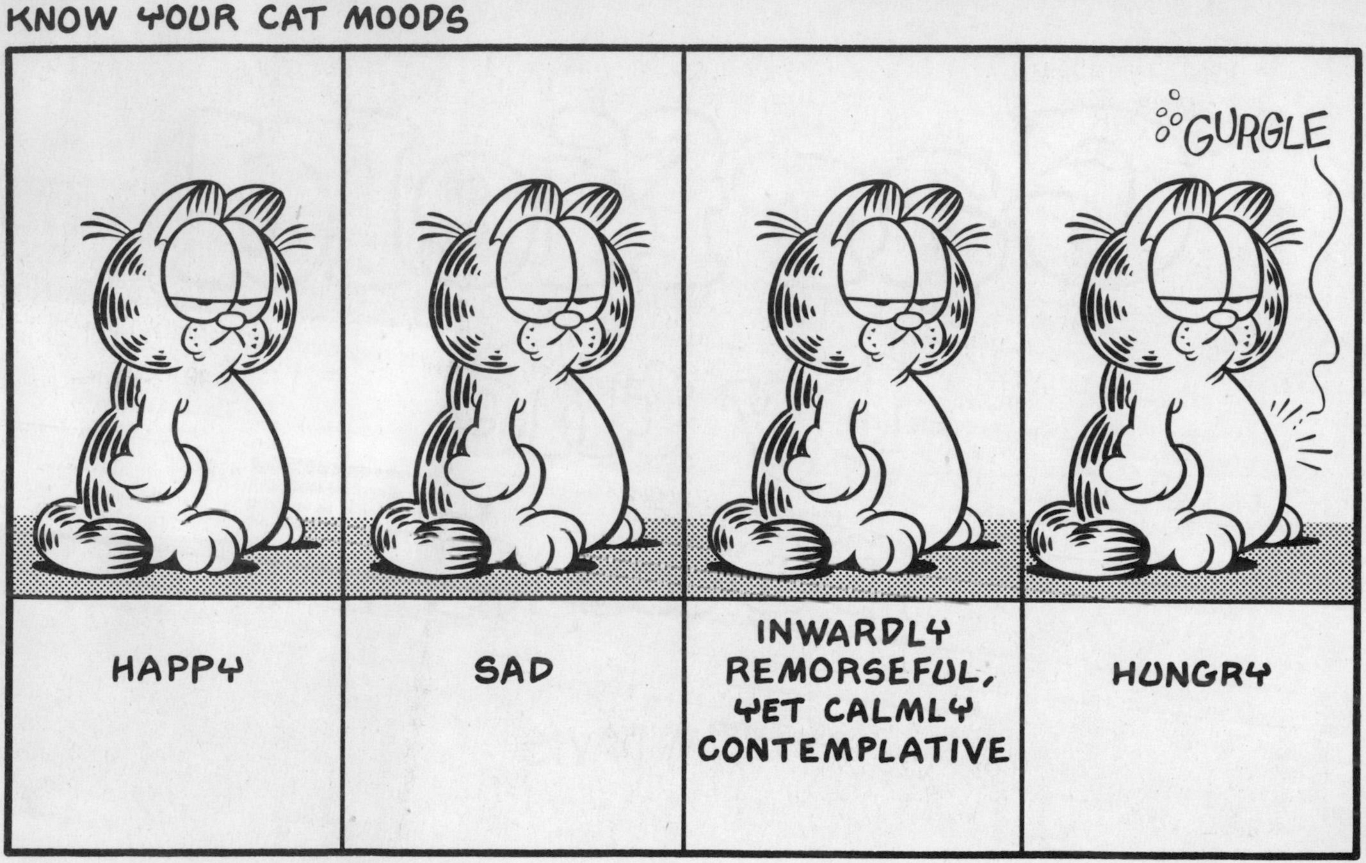
KNOW YOUR CAT MOODS
GURGLE
HAPPY
SAD
INWARDLY REMORSEFUL, YET CALMLY CONTEMPLATIVE
HUNGRY

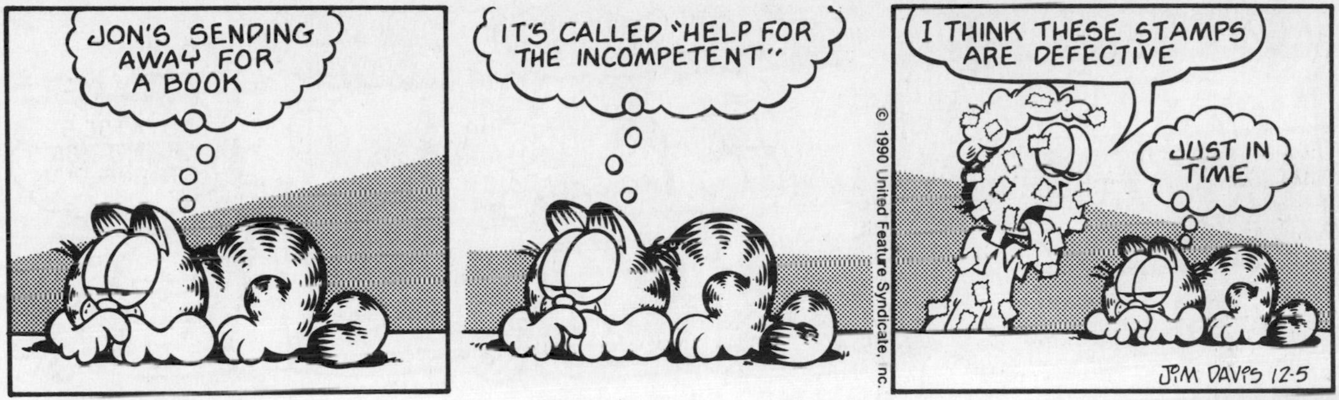
JON'S SENDING AWAY FOR A BOOK
IT'S CALLED "HELP FOR THE INCOMPETENT"
I THINK THESE STAMPS ARE DEFECTIVE
JUST IN TIME
JIM DAVIS 12-5
© 1990 United Feature Syndicate, Inc.

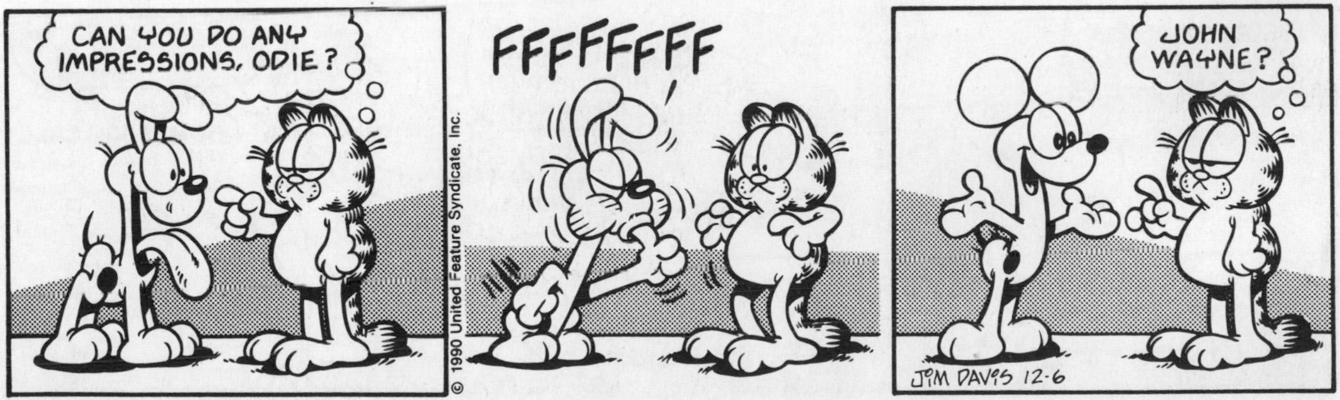
CAN YOU DO ANY IMPRESSIONS, ODIE?
FFFFFFFF
JOHN WAYNE?
JIM DAVIS 12-6
© 1990 United Feature Syndicate, Inc.

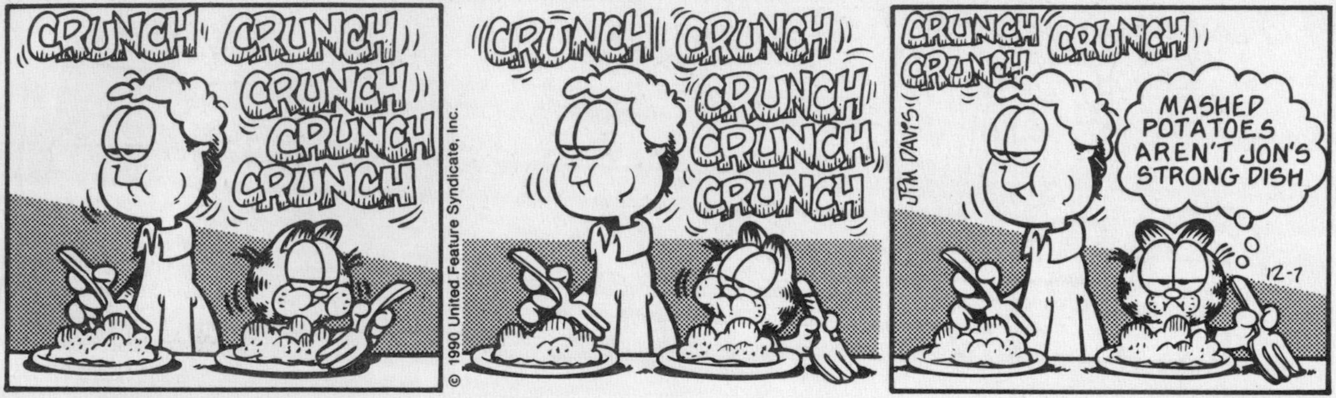
CRUNCH CRUNCH
CRUNCH
CRUNCH
CRUNCH
CRUNCH CRUNCH
CRUNCH
CRUNCH
CRUNCH
CRUNCH CRUNCH
CRUNCH
MASHED POTATOES AREN'T JON'S STRONG DISH
JPM DAVPS
12-7
© 1990 United Feature Syndicate, Inc.

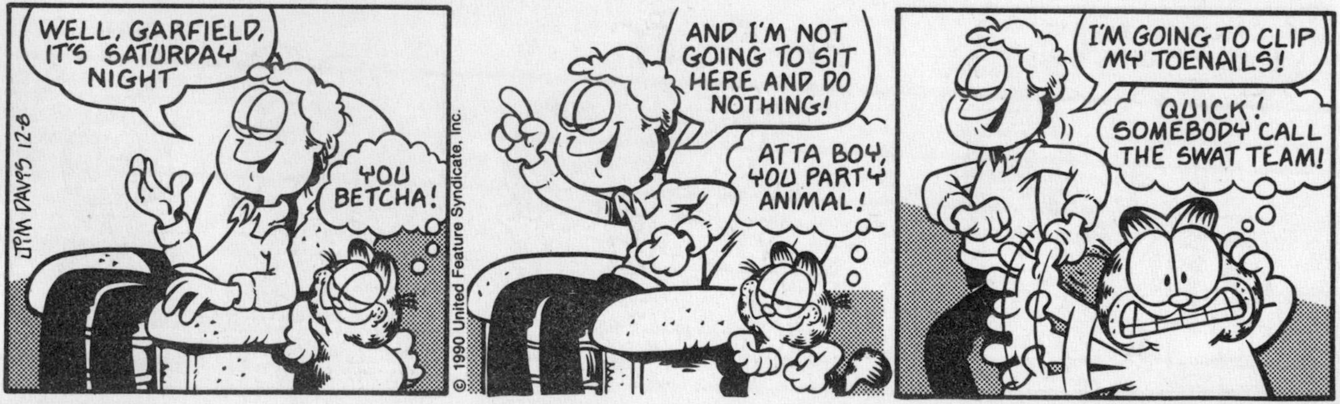
WELL, GARFIELD, IT'S SATURDAY NIGHT
YOU BETCHA!
JPM DAVPS 12-8
© 1990 United Feature Syndicate, Inc.
AND I'M NOT GOING TO SIT HERE AND DO NOTHING!
ATTA BOY, YOU PARTY ANIMAL!
I'M GOING TO CLIP MY TOENAILS!
QUICK! SOMEBODY CALL THE SWAT TEAM!

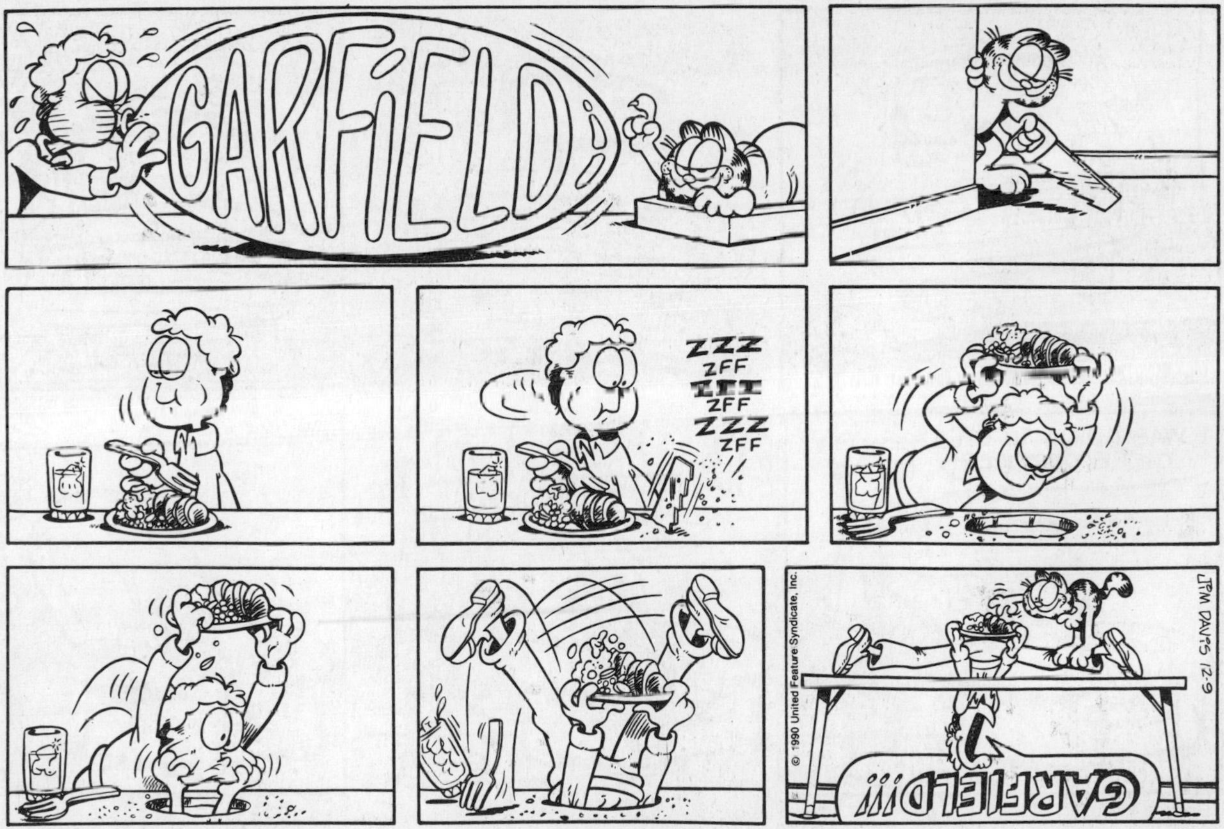
GARFIELD
ZZZ
ZFF
ZZZ
ZFF
ZZZ
ZFF
GARFIELD!!!
JIM DAVIS 12-9
© 1990 United Feature Syndicate, Inc.

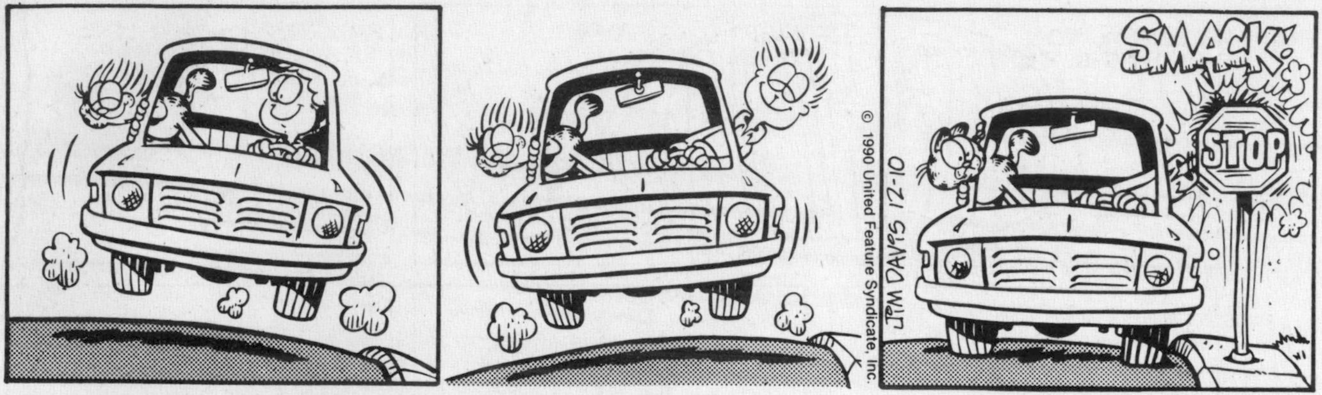
SMACK!
STOP
JIM DAVIS 12-10
© 1990 United Feature Syndicate, Inc.

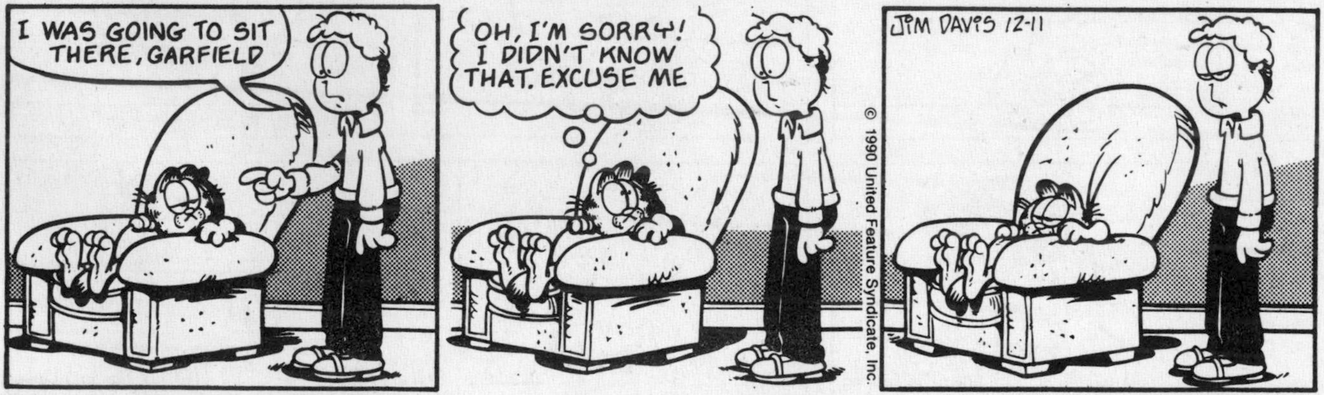
I WAS GOING TO SIT THERE, GARFIELD
OH, I'M SORRY! I DIDN'T KNOW THAT. EXCUSE ME
JIM DAVIS 12-11
© 1990 United Feature Syndicate, Inc.

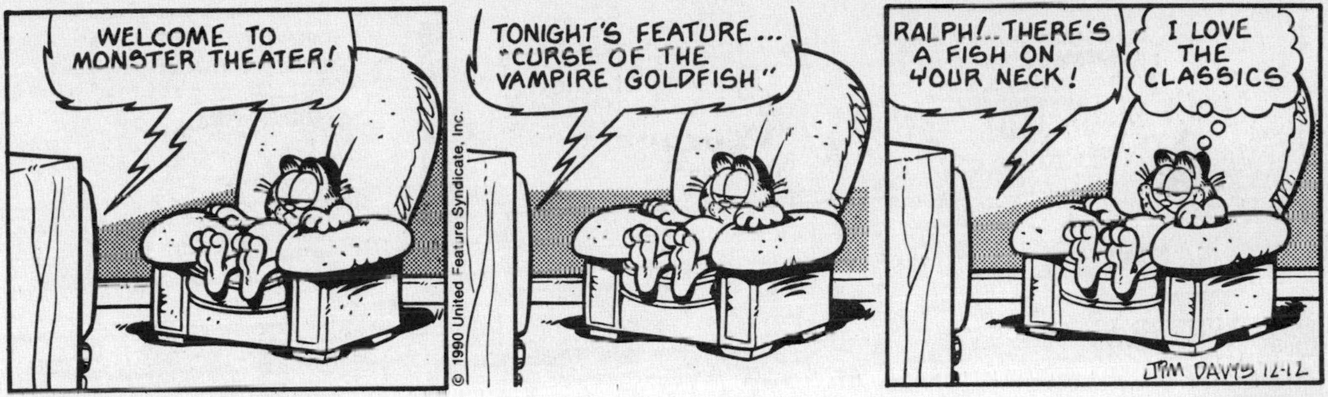
WELCOME TO MONSTER THEATER!
TONIGHT'S FEATURE... "CURSE OF THE VAMPIRE GOLDFISH"
RALPH!..THERE'S A FISH ON YOUR NECK!
I LOVE THE CLASSICS
© 1990 United Feature Syndicate, Inc.
JIM DAVIS 12-12

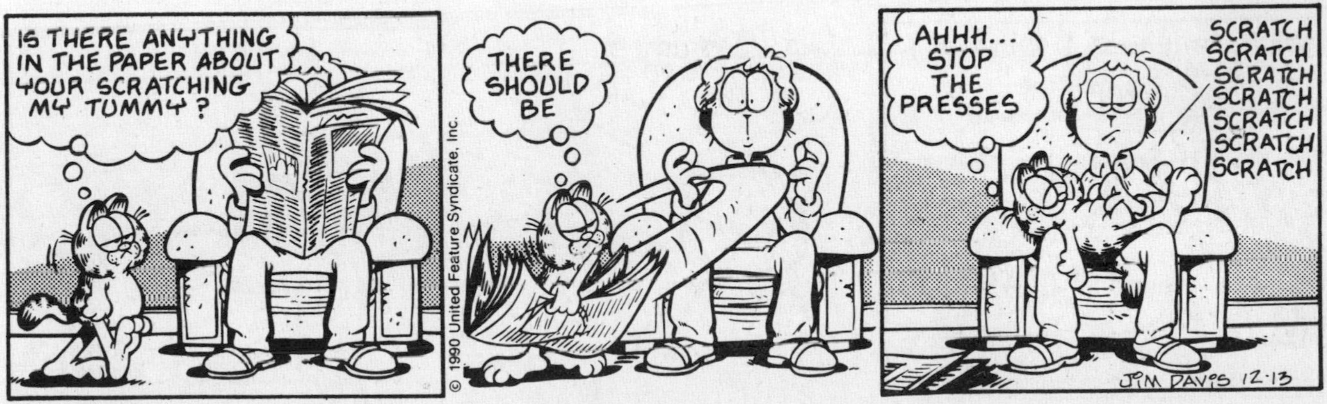
IS THERE ANYTHING IN THE PAPER ABOUT YOUR SCRATCHING MY TUMMY?
THERE SHOULD BE
AHHH... STOP THE PRESSES
SCRATCH SCRATCH SCRATCH SCRATCH SCRATCH SCRATCH SCRATCH
© 1990 United Feature Syndicate, Inc.
JIM DAVIS 12-13

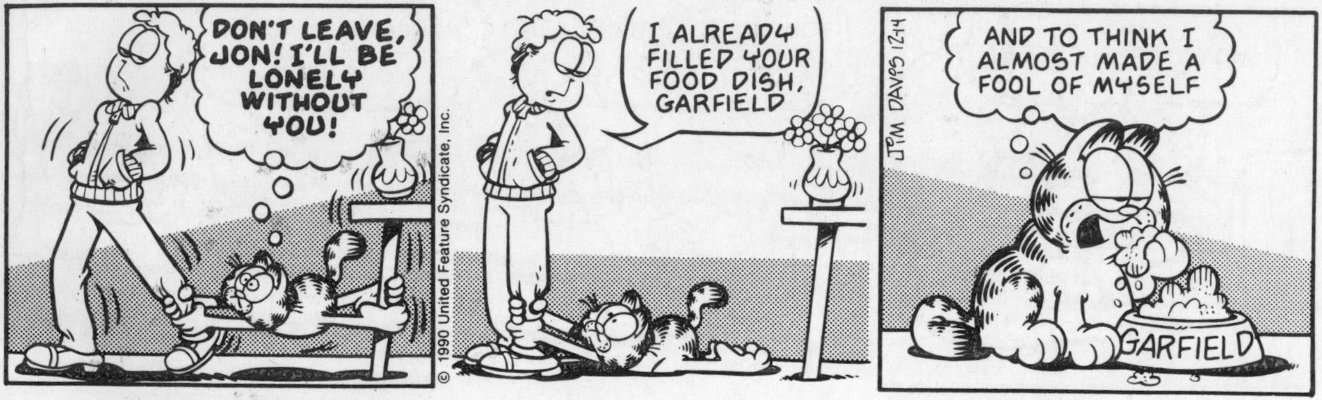
DON'T LEAVE, JON! I'LL BE LONELY WITHOUT YOU!
© 1990 United Feature Syndicate, Inc.
I ALREADY FILLED YOUR FOOD DISH, GARFIELD
JIM DAVIS 12-14
AND TO THINK I ALMOST MADE A FOOL OF MYSELF
GARFIELD

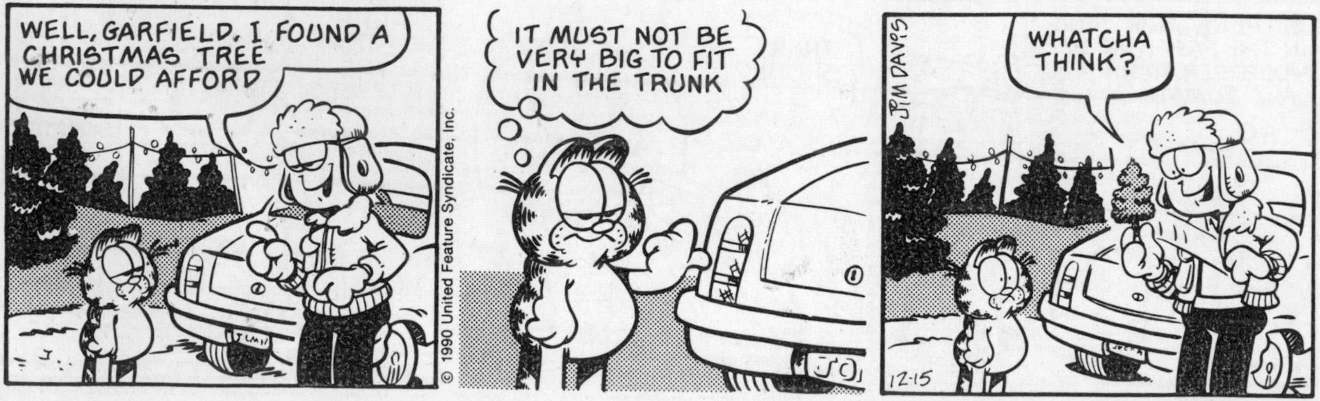
WELL, GARFIELD, I FOUND A CHRISTMAS TREE WE COULD AFFORD
© 1990 United Feature Syndicate, Inc.
IT MUST NOT BE VERY BIG TO FIT IN THE TRUNK
JIM DAVIS
WHATCHA THINK?
12-15

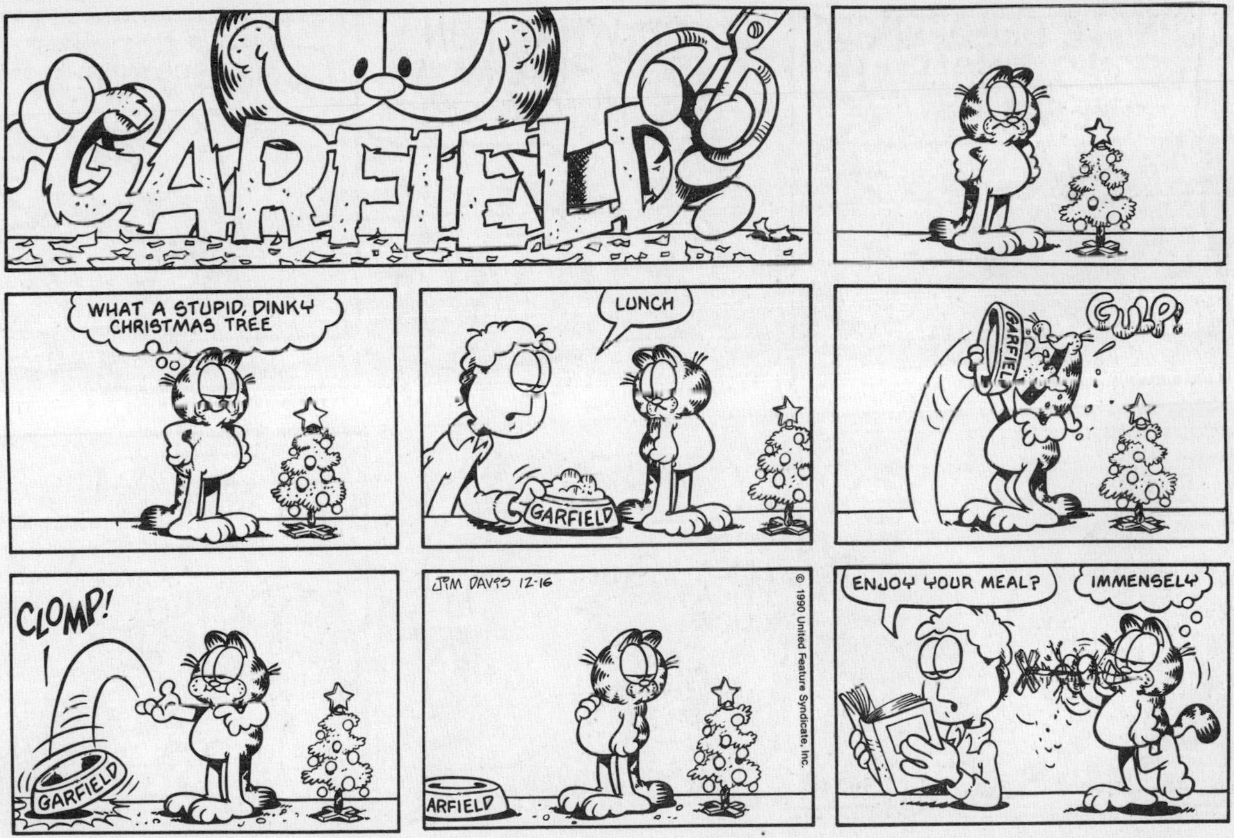
GARFIELD
WHAT A STUPID, DINKY CHRISTMAS TREE
LUNCH
GARFIELD
GARFIEL
GULP!
CLOMP!
GARFIELD
JIM DAVIS 12-16
© 1990 United Feature Syndicate, Inc.
ARFIELD
ENJOY YOUR MEAL?
IMMENSELY

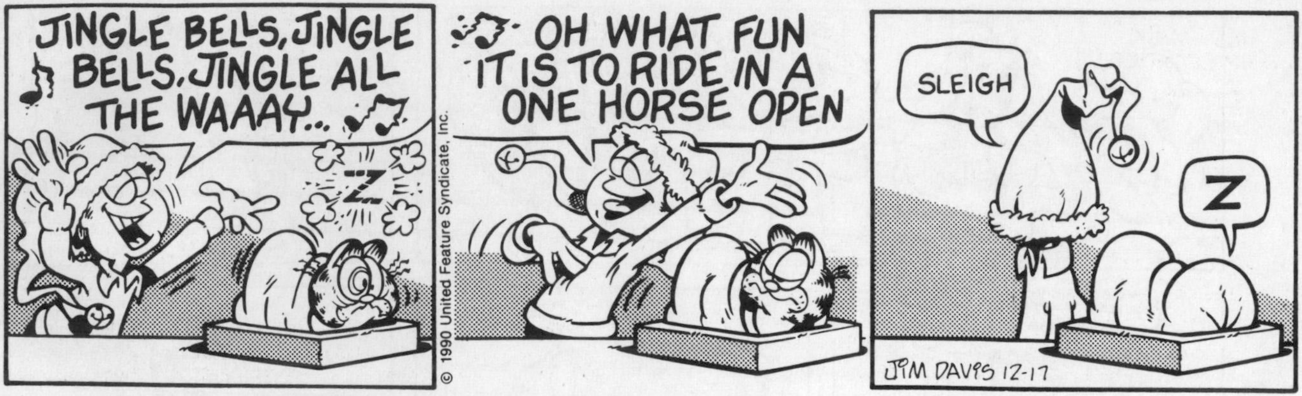
JINGLE BELLS, JINGLE BELLS, JINGLE ALL THE WAAAY...
Z
© 1990 United Feature Syndicate, Inc.
OH WHAT FUN IT IS TO RIDE IN A ONE HORSE OPEN
SLEIGH
Z
JIM DAVIS 12-17

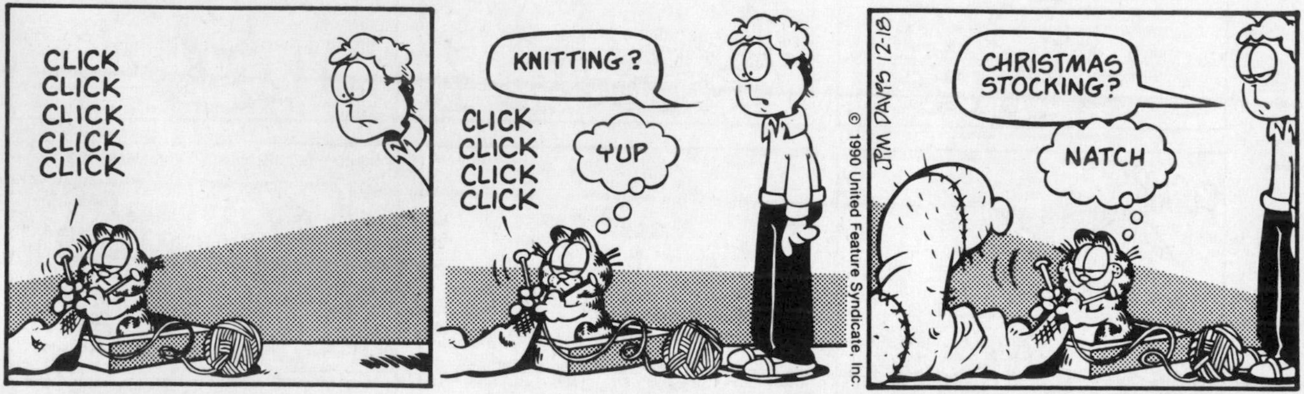
CLICK CLICK CLICK CLICK CLICK
KNITTING?
CLICK CLICK CLICK CLICK
YUP
© 1990 United Feature Syndicate, Inc.
JIM DAVIS 12-18
CHRISTMAS STOCKING?
NATCH

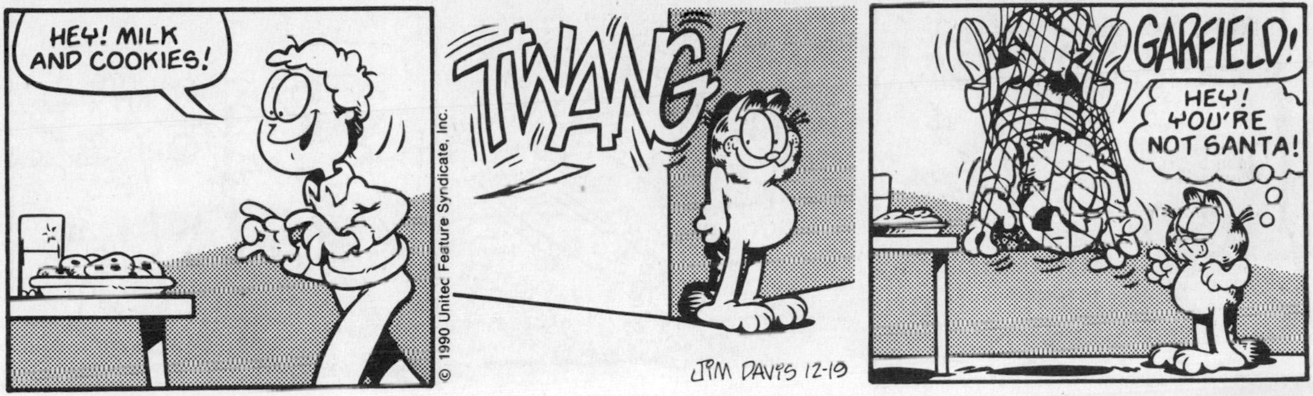
HEY! MILK AND COOKIES!
© 1990 United Feature Syndicate, Inc.
TWANG!
JIM DAVIS 12-19
GARFIELD!
HEY! YOU'RE NOT SANTA!

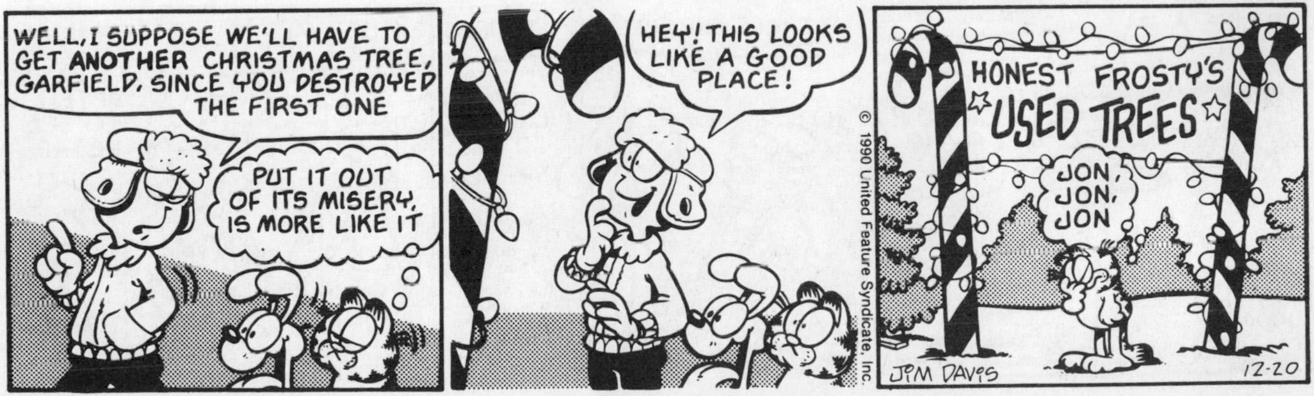
WELL, I SUPPOSE WE'LL HAVE TO GET ANOTHER CHRISTMAS TREE, GARFIELD, SINCE YOU DESTROYED THE FIRST ONE
PUT IT OUT OF ITS MISERY, IS MORE LIKE IT
HEY! THIS LOOKS LIKE A GOOD PLACE!
© 1990 United Feature Syndicate, Inc.
HONEST FROSTY'S
USED TREES
JON, JON, JON
JIM DAVIS
12-20

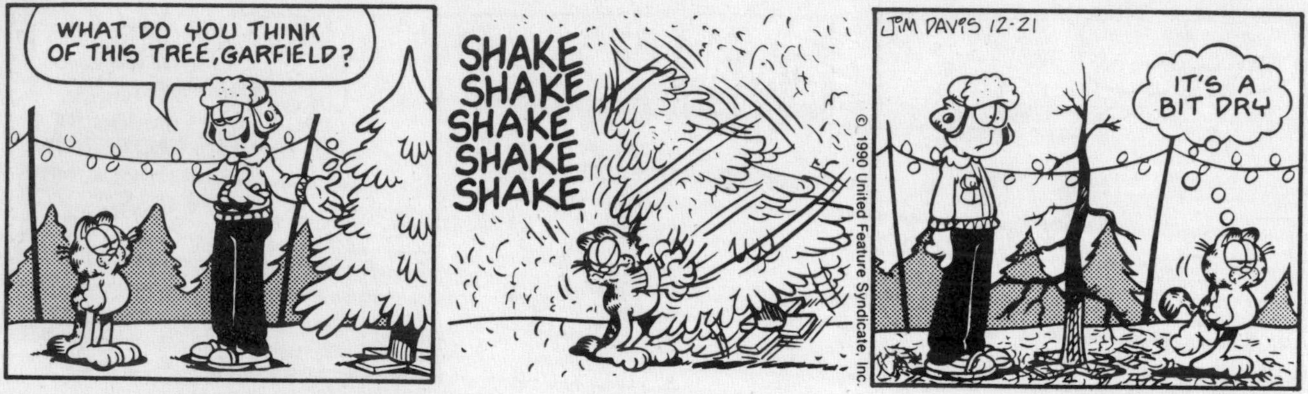
WHAT DO YOU THINK OF THIS TREE, GARFIELD?
SHAKE SHAKE SHAKE SHAKE SHAKE
© 1990 United Feature Syndicate, Inc.
JIM DAVIS 12-21
IT'S A BIT DRY

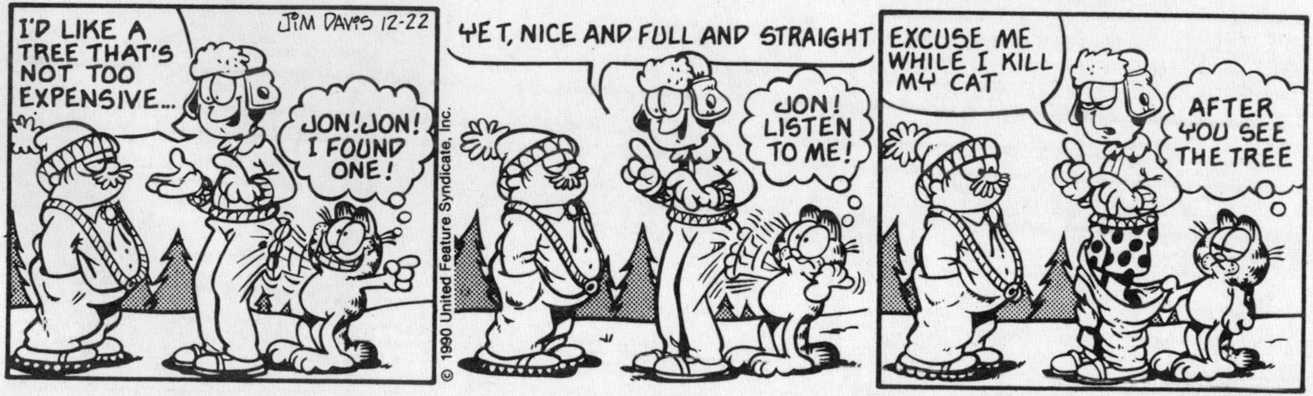
JIM DAVIS 12-22
I'D LIKE A TREE THAT'S NOT TOO EXPENSIVE...
JON! JON! I FOUND ONE!
© 1990 United Feature Syndicate, Inc.
YET, NICE AND FULL AND STRAIGHT
JON! LISTEN TO ME!
EXCUSE ME WHILE I KILL MY CAT
AFTER YOU SEE THE TREE

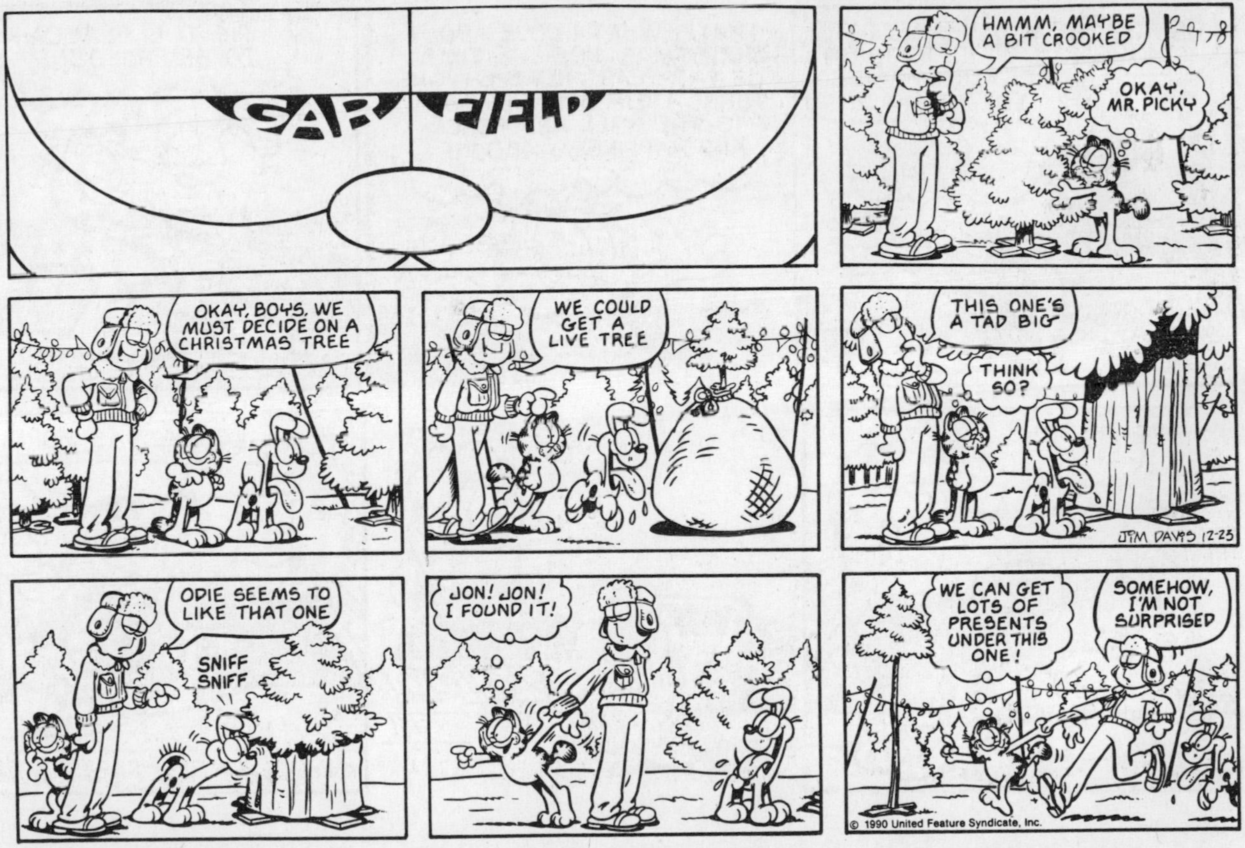
GARFIELD
HMMM, MAYBE A BIT CROOKED
OKAY, MR. PICKY
OKAY, BOYS, WE MUST DECIDE ON A CHRISTMAS TREE
WE COULD GET A LIVE TREE
THIS ONE'S A TAD BIG
THINK SO?
JIM DAVIS 12-25
ODIE SEEMS TO LIKE THAT ONE
SNIFF SNIFF
JON! JON! I FOUND IT!
WE CAN GET LOTS OF PRESENTS UNDER THIS ONE!
SOMEHOW, I'M NOT SURPRISED
© 1990 United Feature Syndicate, Inc.

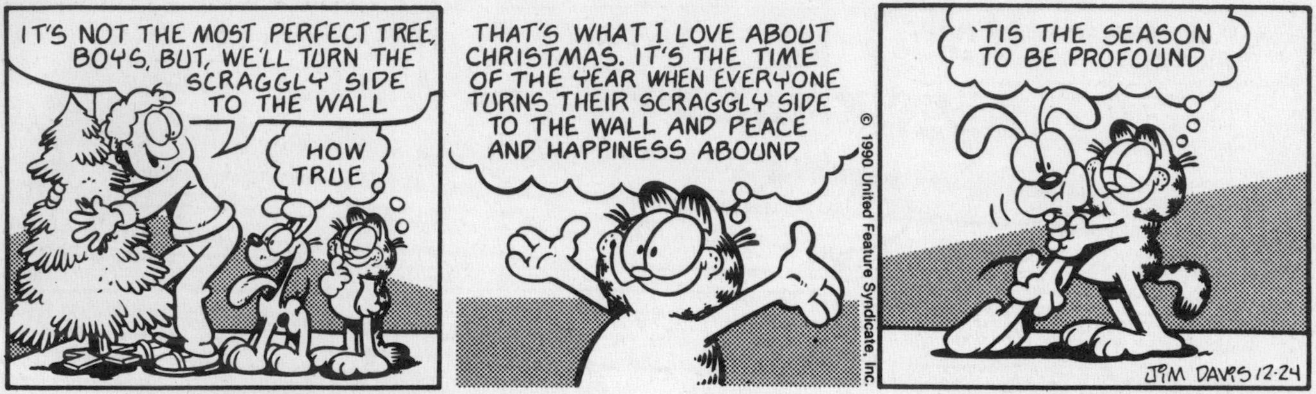
IT'S NOT THE MOST PERFECT TREE, BOYS, BUT, WE'LL TURN THE SCRAGGLY SIDE TO THE WALL
HOW TRUE
THAT'S WHAT I LOVE ABOUT CHRISTMAS. IT'S THE TIME OF THE YEAR WHEN EVERYONE TURNS THEIR SCRAGGLY SIDE TO THE WALL AND PEACE AND HAPPINESS ABOUND
© 1990 United Feature Syndicate, Inc.
'TIS THE SEASON TO BE PROFOUND
JIM DAVIS 12-24

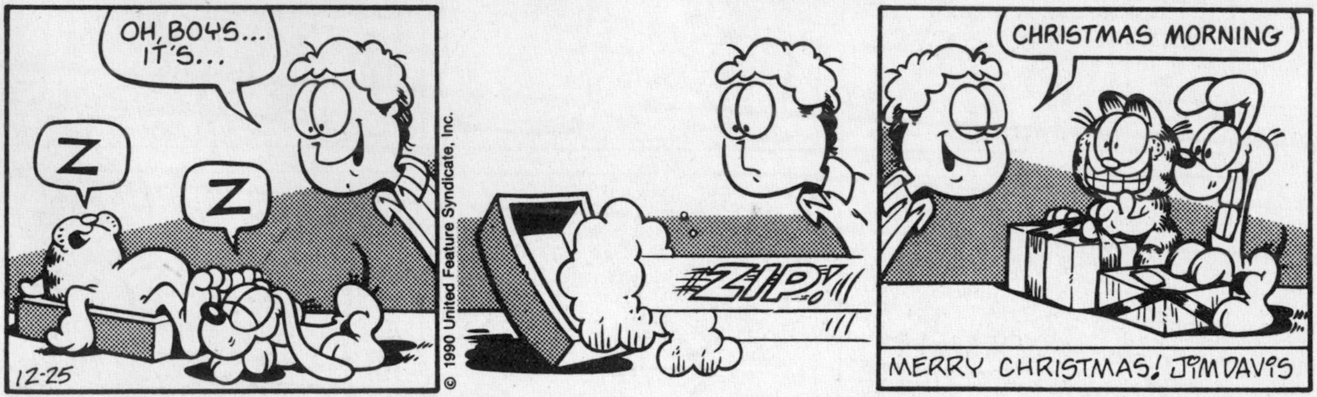
OH, BOYS... IT'S...
Z
Z
12-25
© 1990 United Feature Syndicate, Inc.
ZIP!
CHRISTMAS MORNING
MERRY CHRISTMAS! JIM DAVIS

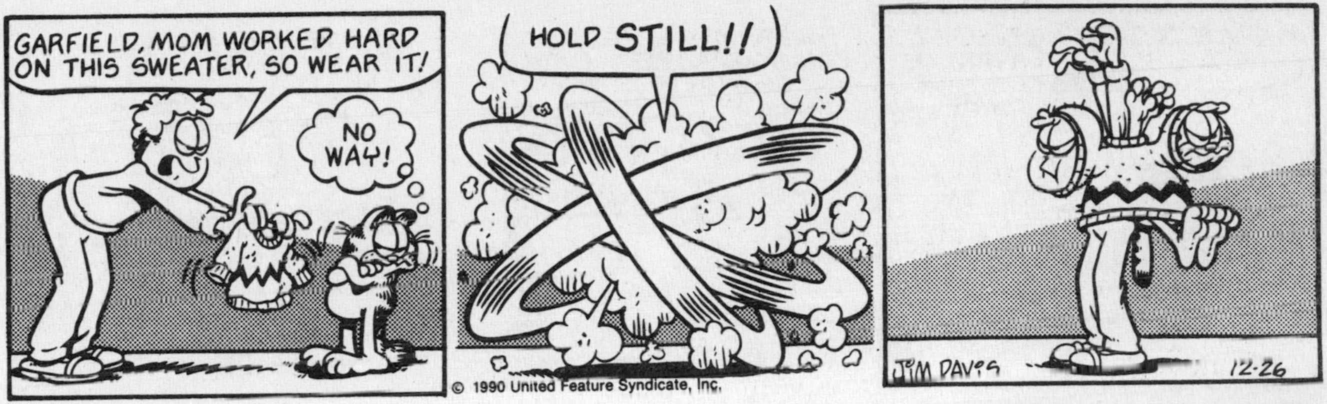
GARFIELD, MOM WORKED HARD ON THIS SWEATER, SO WEAR IT!
NO WAY!
HOLD STILL!!
© 1990 United Feature Syndicate, Inc.
JIM DAVIS 12-26

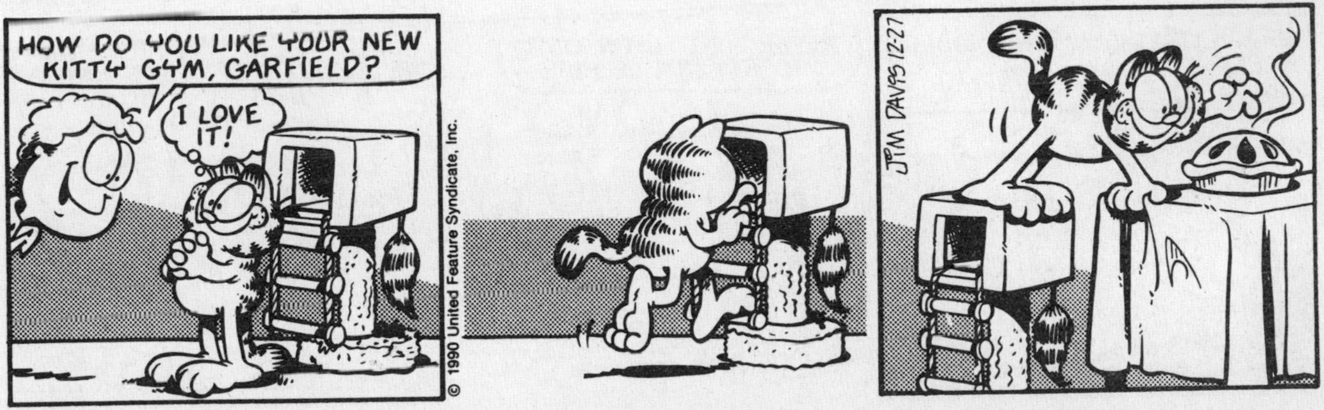
HOW DO YOU LIKE YOUR NEW KITTY GYM, GARFIELD?
I LOVE IT!
© 1990 United Feature Syndicate, Inc.
JIM DAVIS 12-27

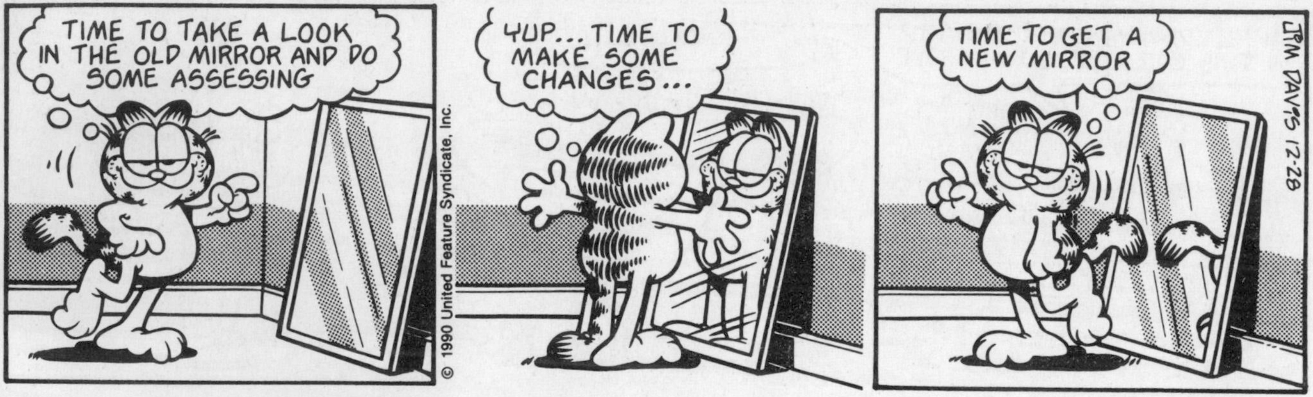
TIME TO TAKE A LOOK IN THE OLD MIRROR AND DO SOME ASSESSING
YUP... TIME TO MAKE SOME CHANGES...
TIME TO GET A NEW MIRROR
JIM DAVIS 12-28
© 1990 United Feature Syndicate, Inc.

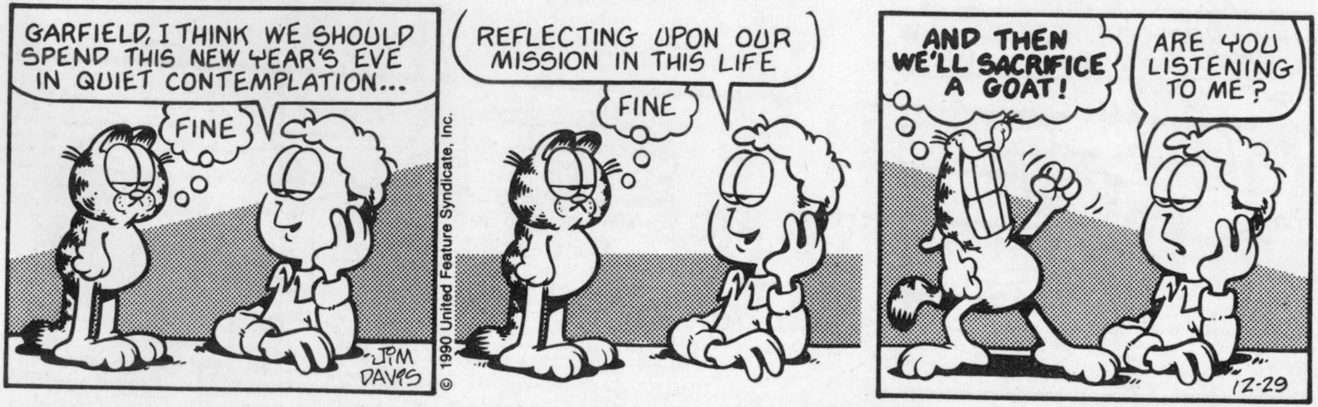
GARFIELD, I THINK WE SHOULD SPEND THIS NEW YEAR'S EVE IN QUIET CONTEMPLATION...
FINE
JIM DAVIS
REFLECTING UPON OUR MISSION IN THIS LIFE
FINE
AND THEN WE'LL SACRIFICE A GOAT!
ARE YOU LISTENING TO ME?
12-29
© 1990 United Feature Syndicate, Inc.

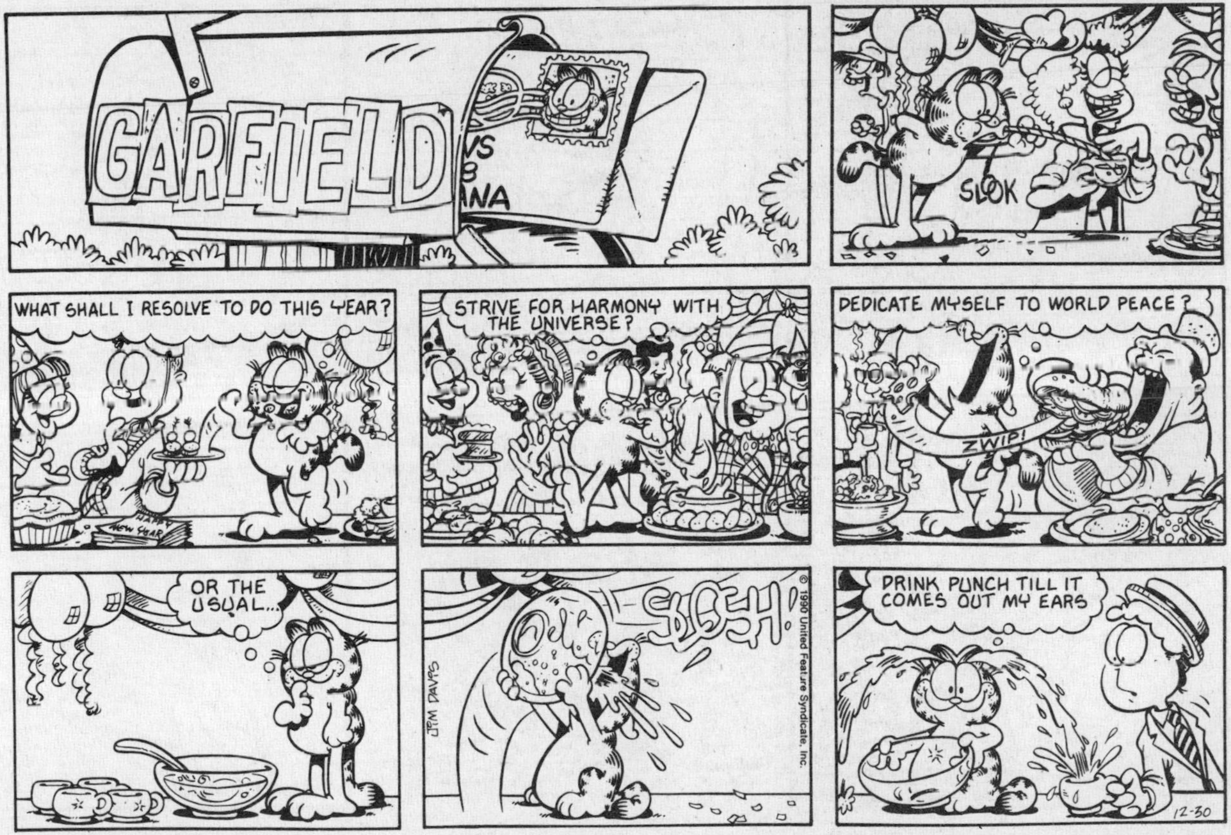
GARFIELD
SLOK
WHAT SHALL I RESOLVE TO DO THIS YEAR?
HAPPY NEW YEAR
STRIVE FOR HARMONY WITH THE UNIVERSE?
DEDICATE MYSELF TO WORLD PEACE?
ZWIP!
OR THE USUAL...
JIM DAVIS
SLOSH!
© 1990 United Feature Syndicate, Inc.
DRINK PUNCH TILL IT COMES OUT MY EARS
12-30

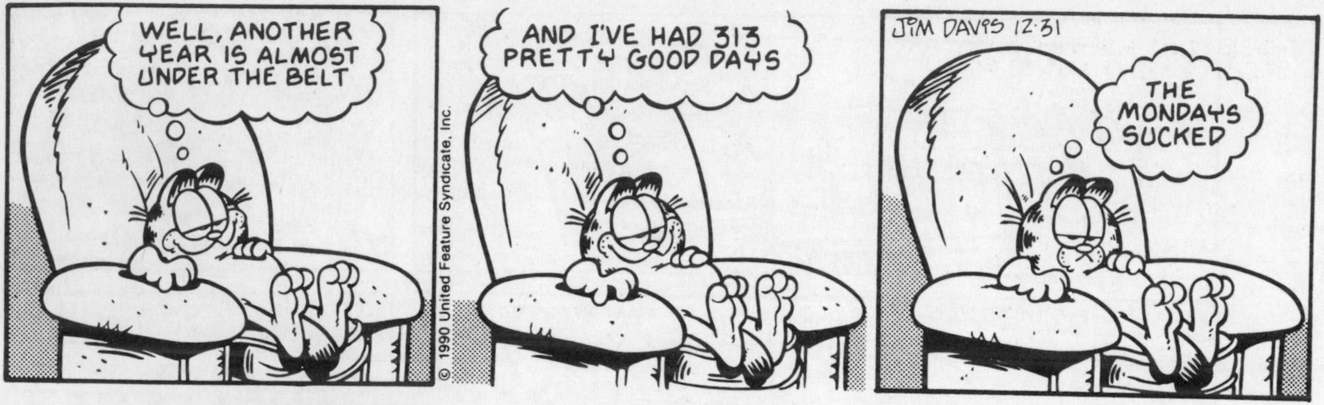
WELL, ANOTHER YEAR IS ALMOST UNDER THE BELT
© 1990 United Feature Syndicate, Inc.
AND I'VE HAD 313 PRETTY GOOD DAYS
JIM DAVIS 12·31
THE MONDAYS SUCKED

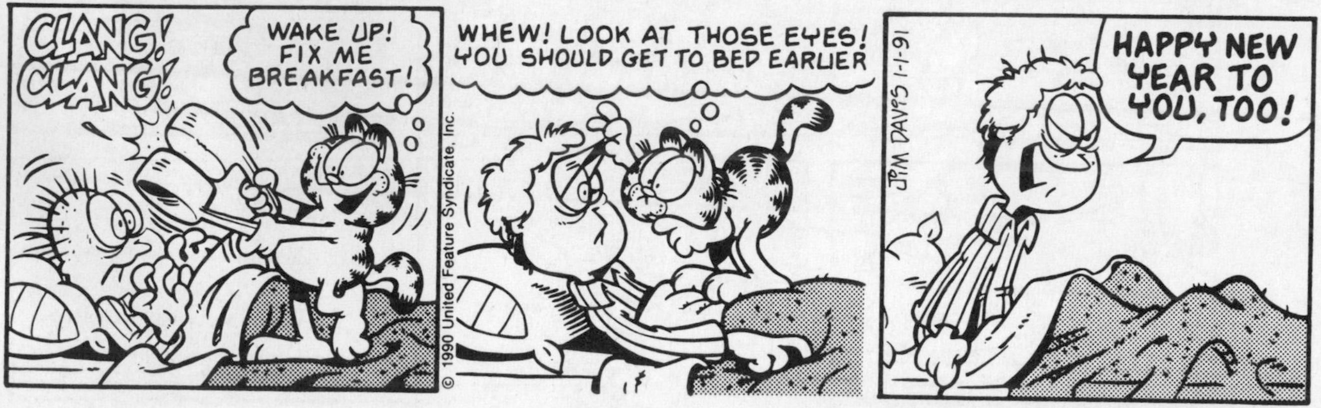
CLANG! CLANG!
WAKE UP! FIX ME BREAKFAST!
© 1990 United Feature Syndicate, Inc.
WHEW! LOOK AT THOSE EYES! YOU SHOULD GET TO BED EARLIER
JIM DAVIS 1-1-91
HAPPY NEW YEAR TO YOU, TOO!

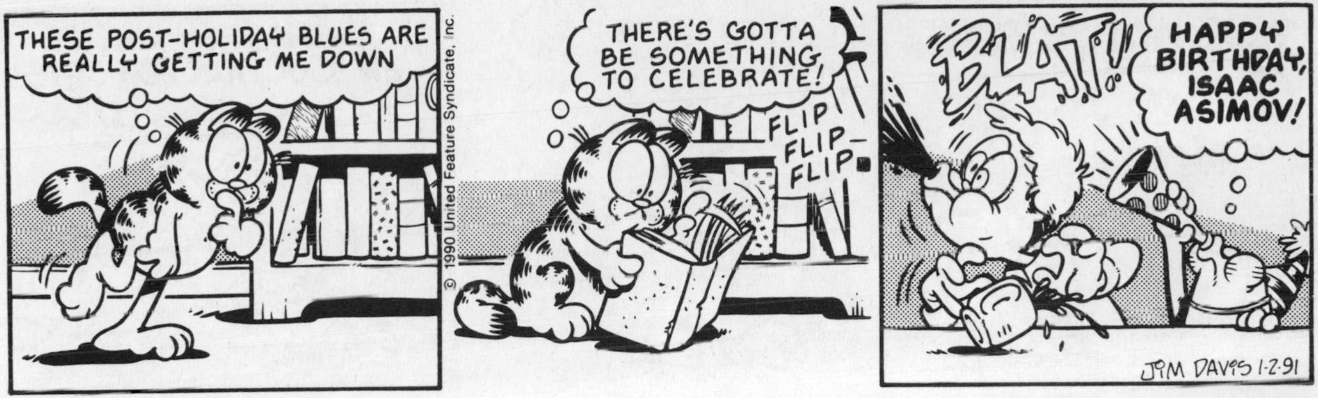
THESE POST-HOLIDAY BLUES ARE REALLY GETTING ME DOWN
© 1990 United Feature Syndicate, Inc.
THERE'S GOTTA BE SOMETHING TO CELEBRATE!
FLIP FLIP FLIP
BLAT!
HAPPY BIRTHDAY, ISAAC ASIMOV!
JIM DAVIS 1-2-91

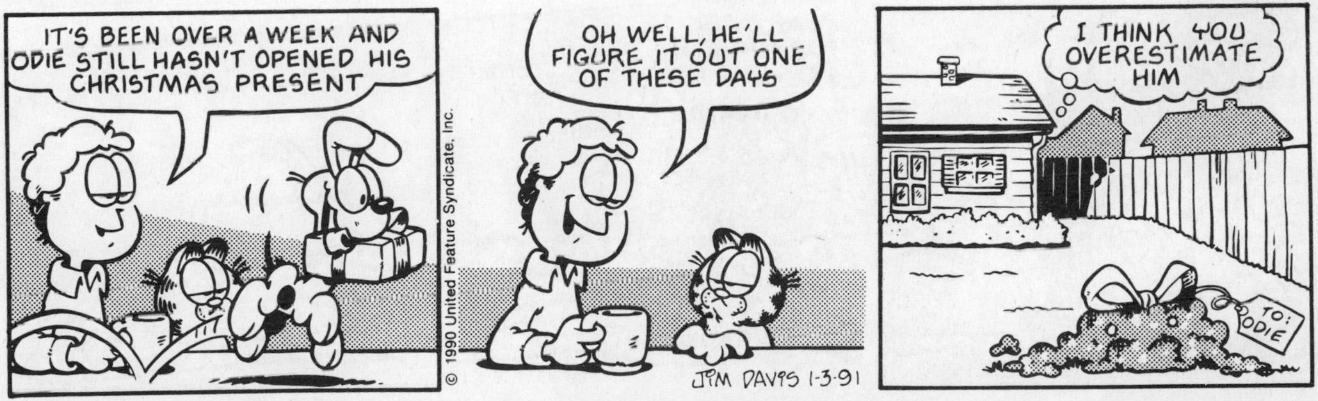
IT'S BEEN OVER A WEEK AND ODIE STILL HASN'T OPENED HIS CHRISTMAS PRESENT
© 1990 United Feature Syndicate, Inc.
OH WELL, HE'LL FIGURE IT OUT ONE OF THESE DAYS
JIM DAVIS 1-3-91
I THINK YOU OVERESTIMATE HIM
TO: ODIE

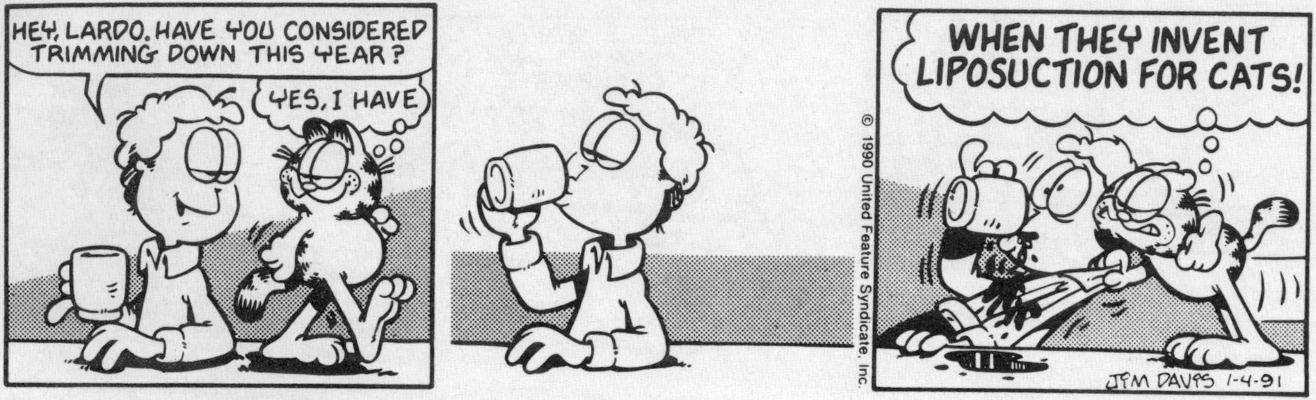
HEY, LARDO. HAVE YOU CONSIDERED TRIMMING DOWN THIS YEAR?
YES, I HAVE
WHEN THEY INVENT LIPOSUCTION FOR CATS!
© 1990 United Feature Syndicate, Inc.
JIM DAVIS 1-4-91

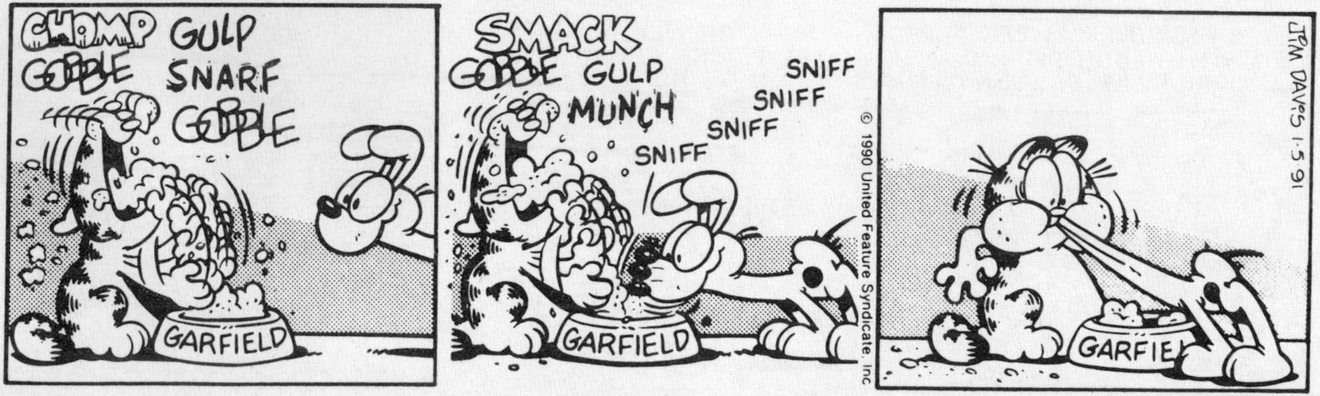
CHOMP GULP
GOBBLE SNARF
GOBBLE
SMACK
GOBBLE GULP
MUNCH
SNIFF
SNIFF
SNIFF
SNIFF
GARFIELD
GARFIELD
GARFIE
© 1990 United Feature Syndicate, Inc.
JIM DAVIS 1-5-91

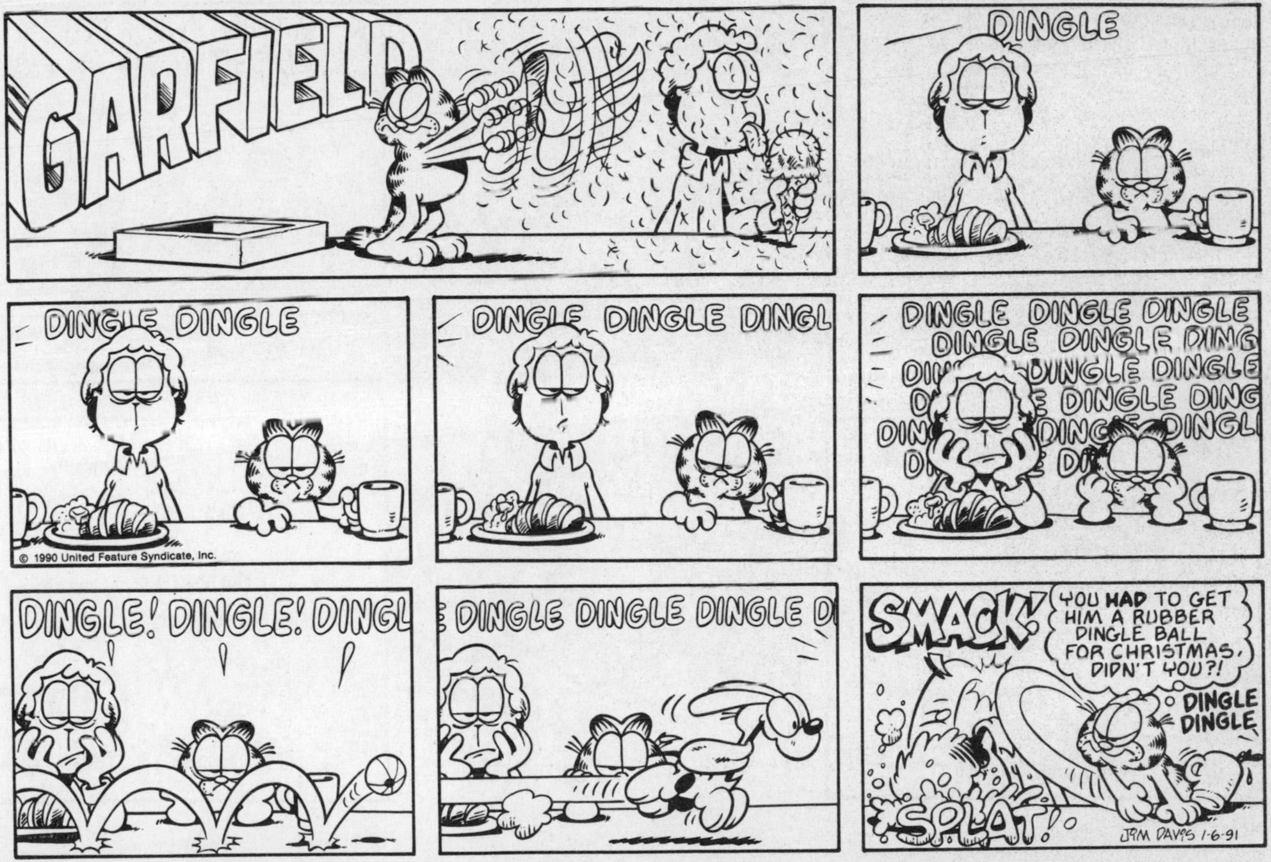

GARFIELD
DINGLE
DINGLE DINGLE
© 1990 United Feature Syndicate, Inc.
DINGLE DINGLE DINGL
DINGLE DINGLE DINGLE
DINGLE DINGLE DING
DINGLE DINGLE
DINGLE DING
DINGLE DINGL
DINGLE! DINGLE! DINGL
E DINGLE DINGLE DINGLE D
SMACK!
YOU HAD TO GET HIM A RUBBER DINGLE BALL FOR CHRISTMAS, DIDN'T YOU?!
DINGLE DINGLE
SPLAT!
JIM DAVIS 1-6-91

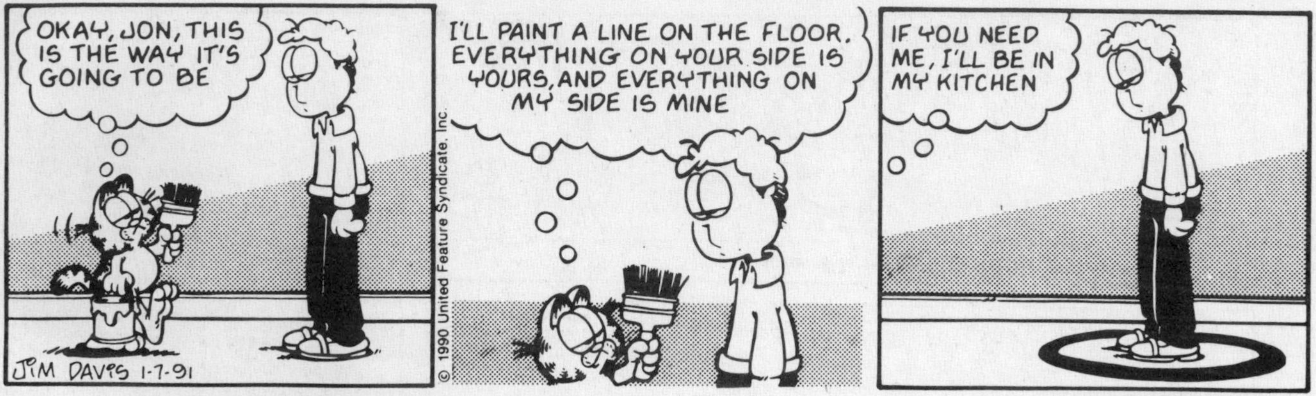
OKAY, JON, THIS IS THE WAY IT'S GOING TO BE
JIM DAVIS 1-7-91
© 1990 United Feature Syndicate, Inc.
I'LL PAINT A LINE ON THE FLOOR. EVERYTHING ON YOUR SIDE IS YOURS, AND EVERYTHING ON MY SIDE IS MINE
IF YOU NEED ME, I'LL BE IN MY KITCHEN

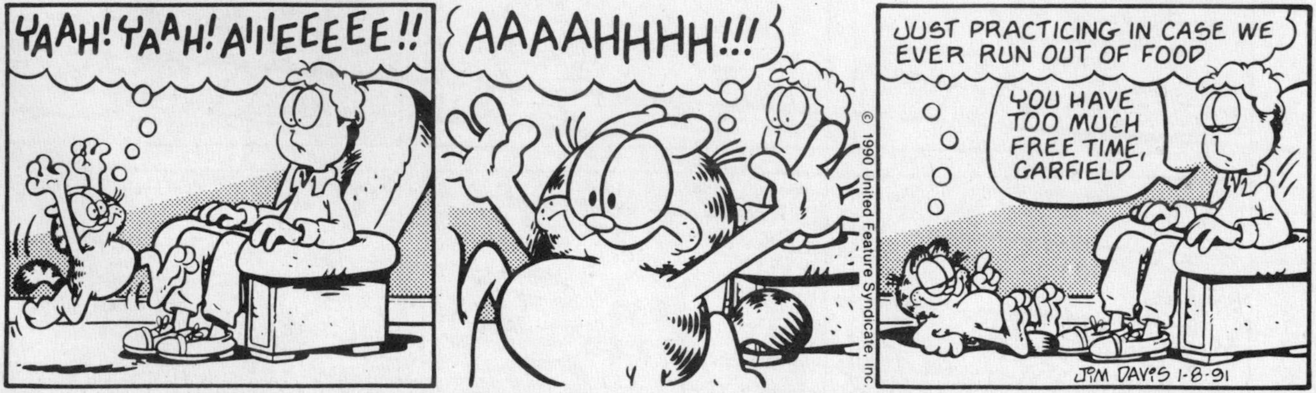
YAAH! YAAH! AIIEEEEEE!!
AAAAHHHH!!!
© 1990 United Feature Syndicate, Inc.
JUST PRACTICING IN CASE WE EVER RUN OUT OF FOOD
YOU HAVE TOO MUCH FREE TIME, GARFIELD
JIM DAVIS 1-8-91

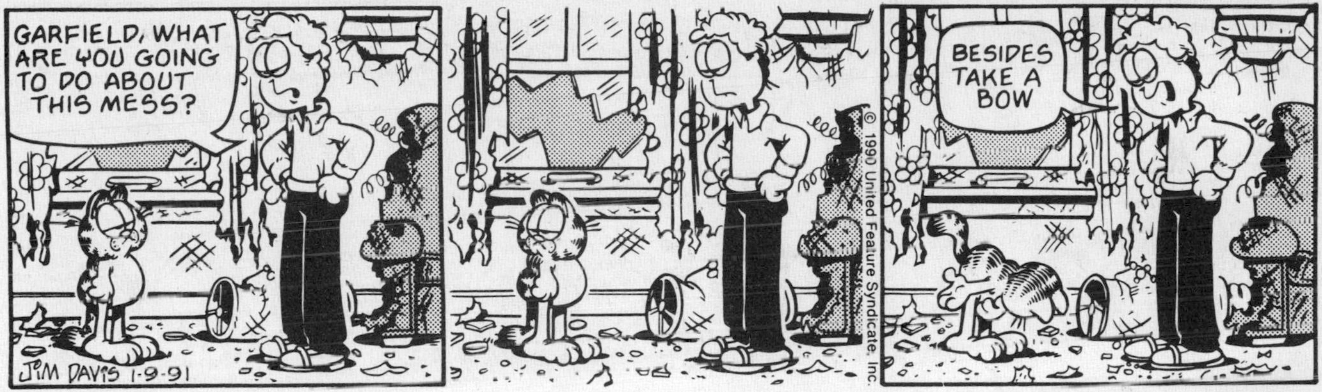
GARFIELD, WHAT ARE YOU GOING TO DO ABOUT THIS MESS?
BESIDES TAKE A BOW
JIM DAVIS 1-9-91

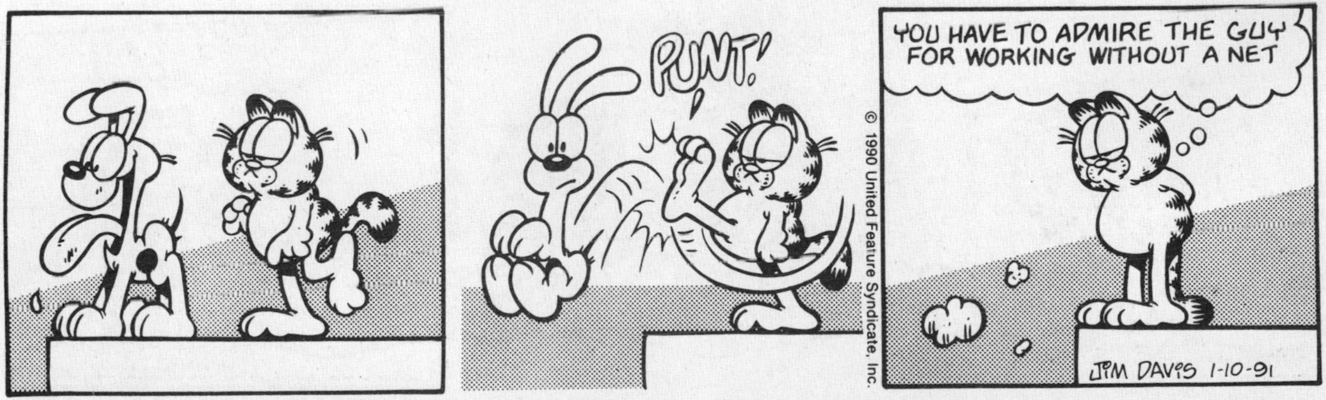
PUNT!
YOU HAVE TO ADMIRE THE GUY FOR WORKING WITHOUT A NET
JIM DAVIS 1-10-91

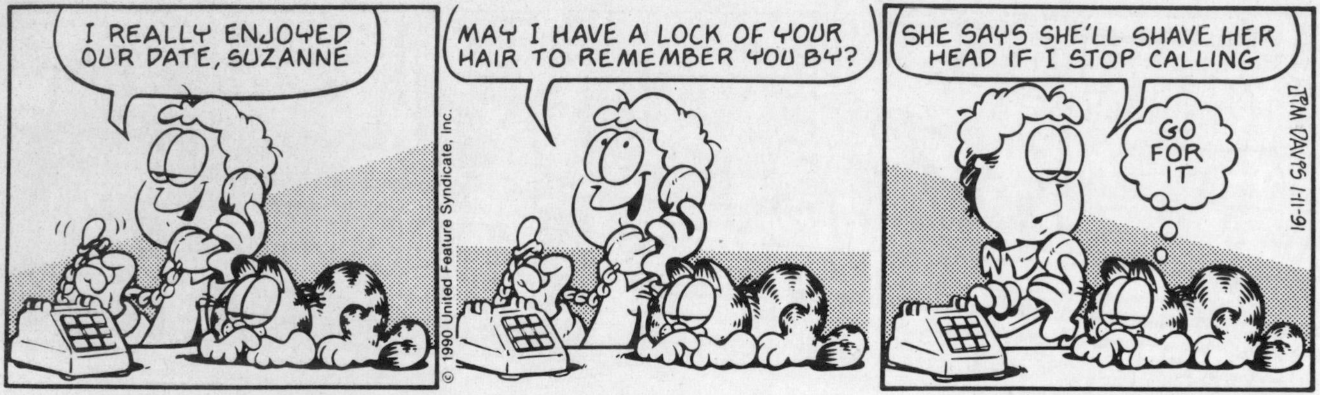
I REALLY ENJOYED OUR DATE, SUZANNE
MAY I HAVE A LOCK OF YOUR HAIR TO REMEMBER YOU BY?
SHE SAYS SHE'LL SHAVE HER HEAD IF I STOP CALLING
GO FOR IT
JIM DAVIS 1-11-91
© 1990 United Feature Syndicate, Inc.

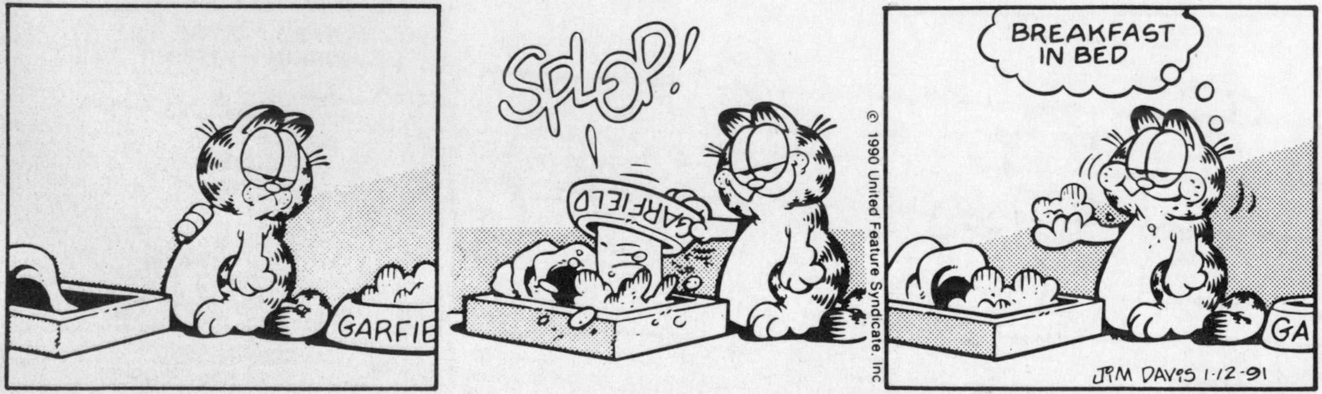
GARFIE
SPLOP!
GARFIELD
BREAKFAST IN BED
GA
JIM DAVIS 1-12-91
© 1990 United Feature Syndicate, Inc.

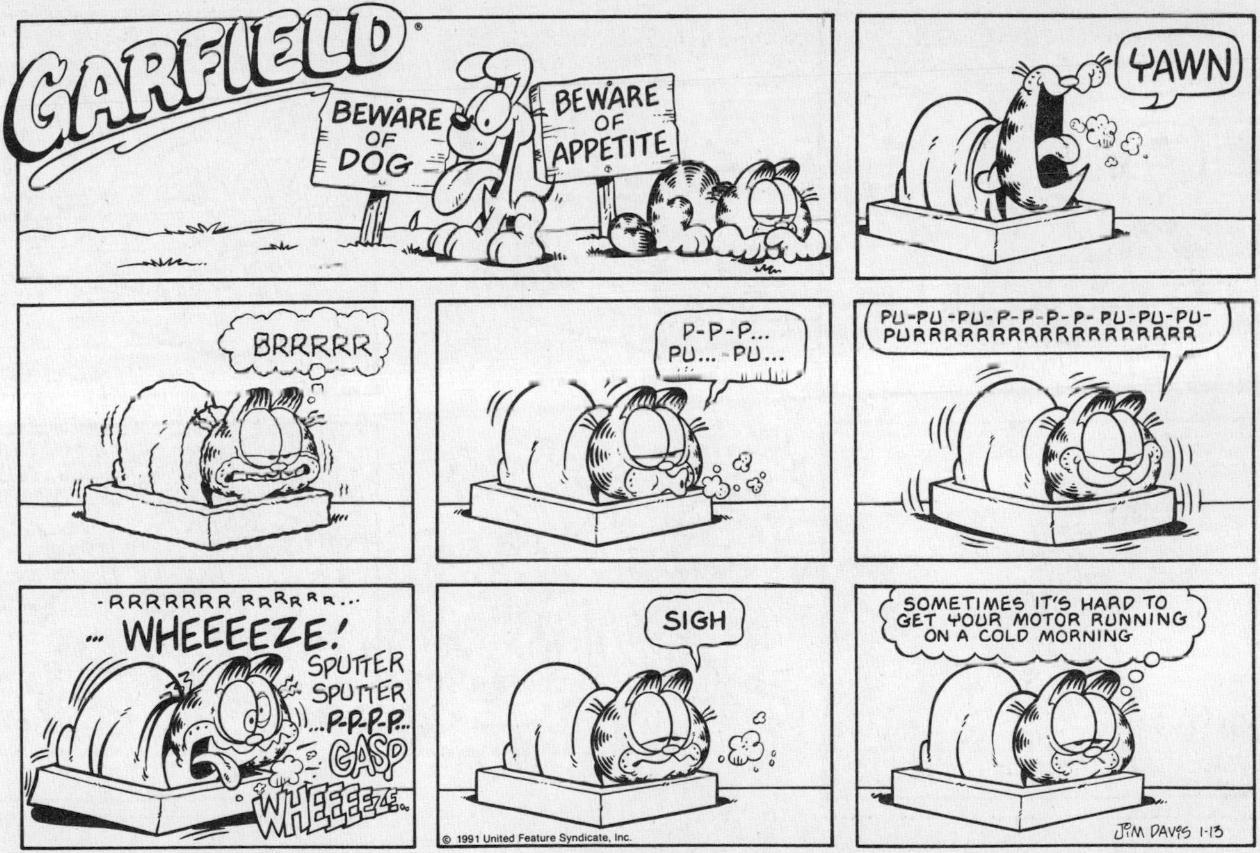
GARFIELD
BEWARE OF DOG
BEWARE OF APPETITE
YAWN
BRRRRR
P-P-P... PU... -PU...
PU-PU-PU-P-P-P-P-PU-PU-PU-PURRRRRRRRRRRRRRRRRR
-RRRRRRR RRRRRR...
... WHEEEEZE!
SPUTTER
SPUTTER
...P-P-P-P...
GASP
WHEEEEZE
SIGH
SOMETIMES IT'S HARD TO GET YOUR MOTOR RUNNING ON A COLD MORNING
© 1991 United Feature Syndicate, Inc.
JIM DAVIS 1-13

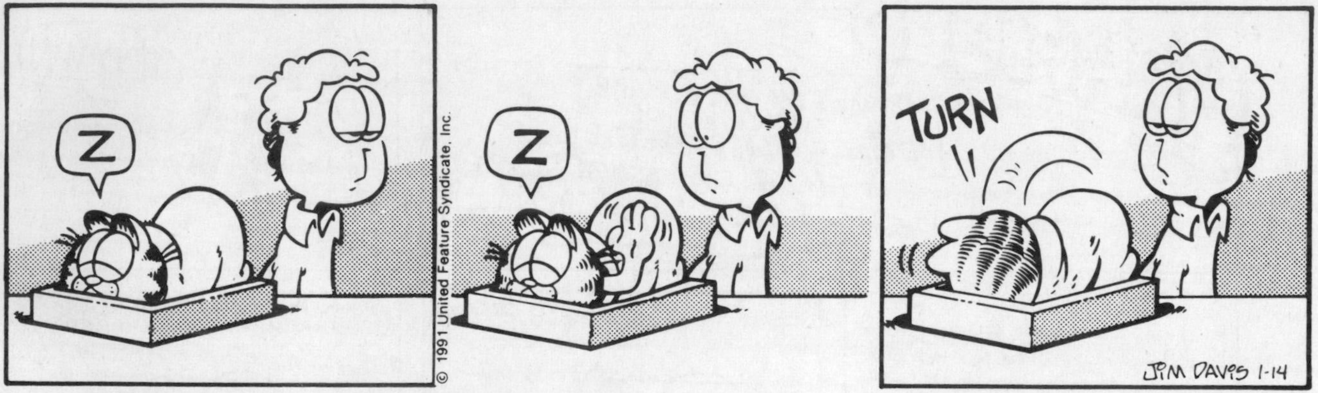
Z
Z
© 1991 United Feature Syndicate, Inc.
TURN
JIM DAVIS 1-14

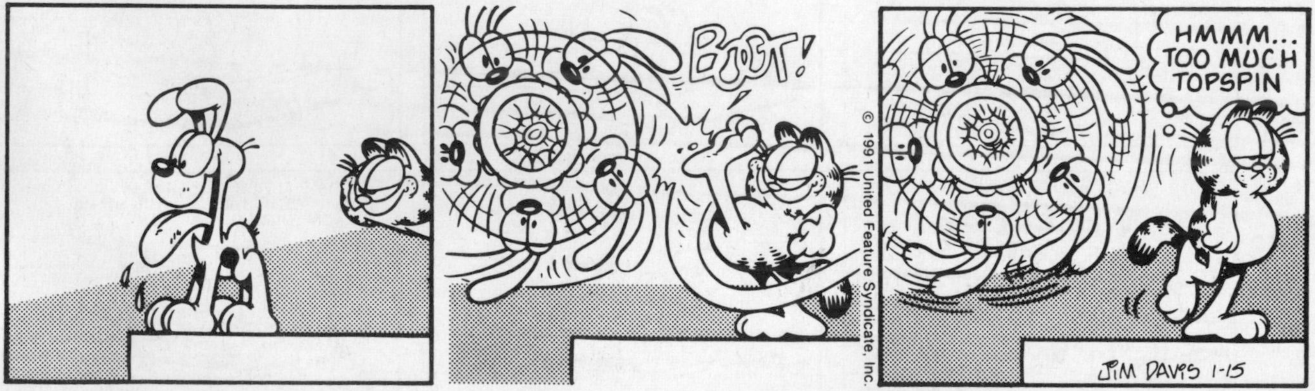
BOOT!
© 1991 United Feature Syndicate, Inc.
HMMM... TOO MUCH TOPSPIN
JIM DAVIS 1-15

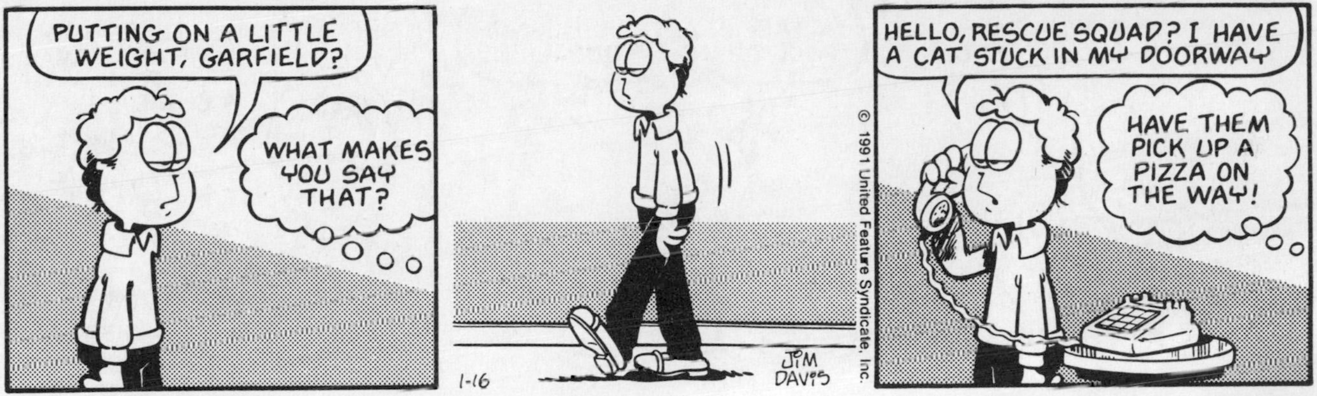
PUTTING ON A LITTLE WEIGHT, GARFIELD?
WHAT MAKES YOU SAY THAT?
HELLO, RESCUE SQUAD? I HAVE A CAT STUCK IN MY DOORWAY
HAVE THEM PICK UP A PIZZA ON THE WAY!
1-16
JIM DAVIS

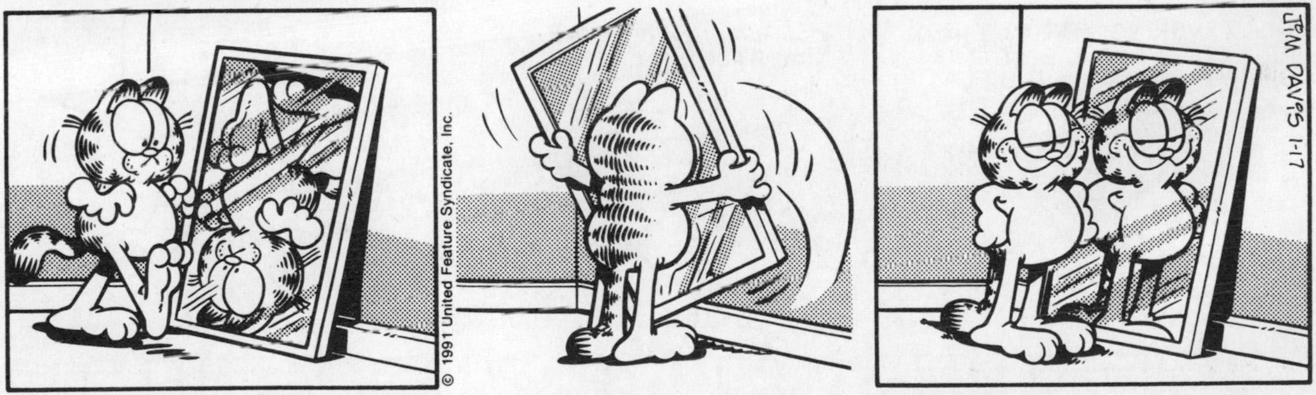
JIM DAVIS 1-17

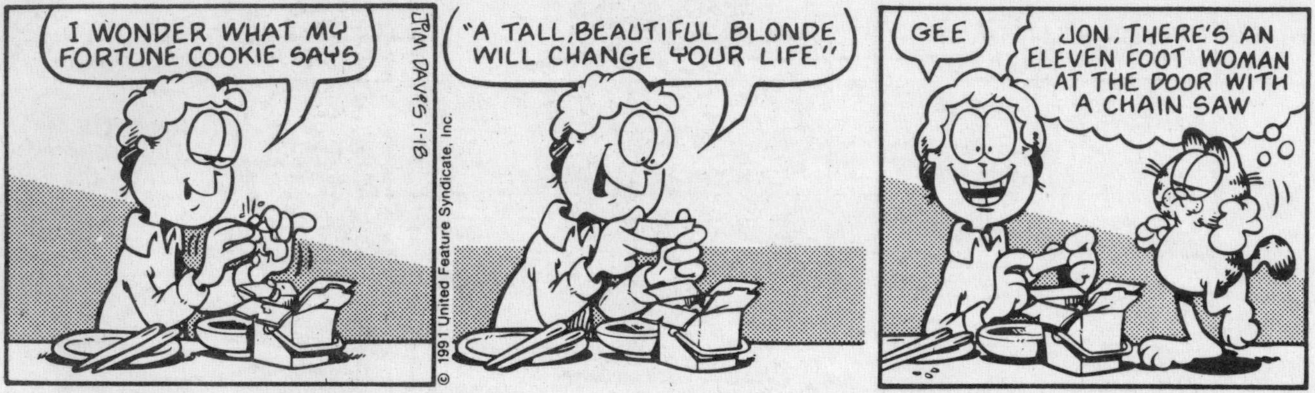
I WONDER WHAT MY FORTUNE COOKIE SAYS
JIM DAVIS 1-18
© 1991 United Feature Syndicate, Inc.
"A TALL, BEAUTIFUL BLONDE WILL CHANGE YOUR LIFE"
GEE
JON, THERE'S AN ELEVEN FOOT WOMAN AT THE DOOR WITH A CHAIN SAW

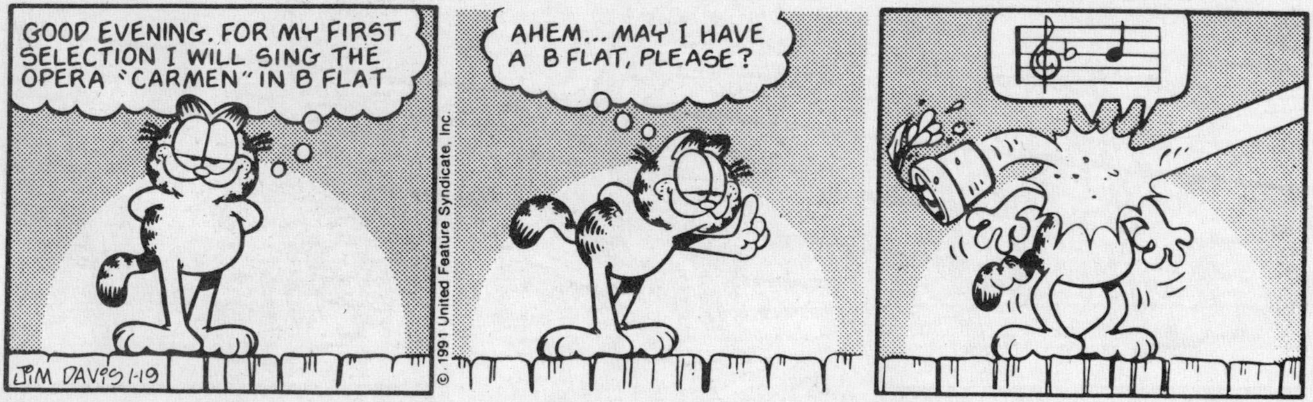
GOOD EVENING. FOR MY FIRST SELECTION I WILL SING THE OPERA "CARMEN" IN B FLAT
JIM DAVIS 1-19
© 1991 United Feature Syndicate, Inc.
AHEM... MAY I HAVE A B FLAT, PLEASE?

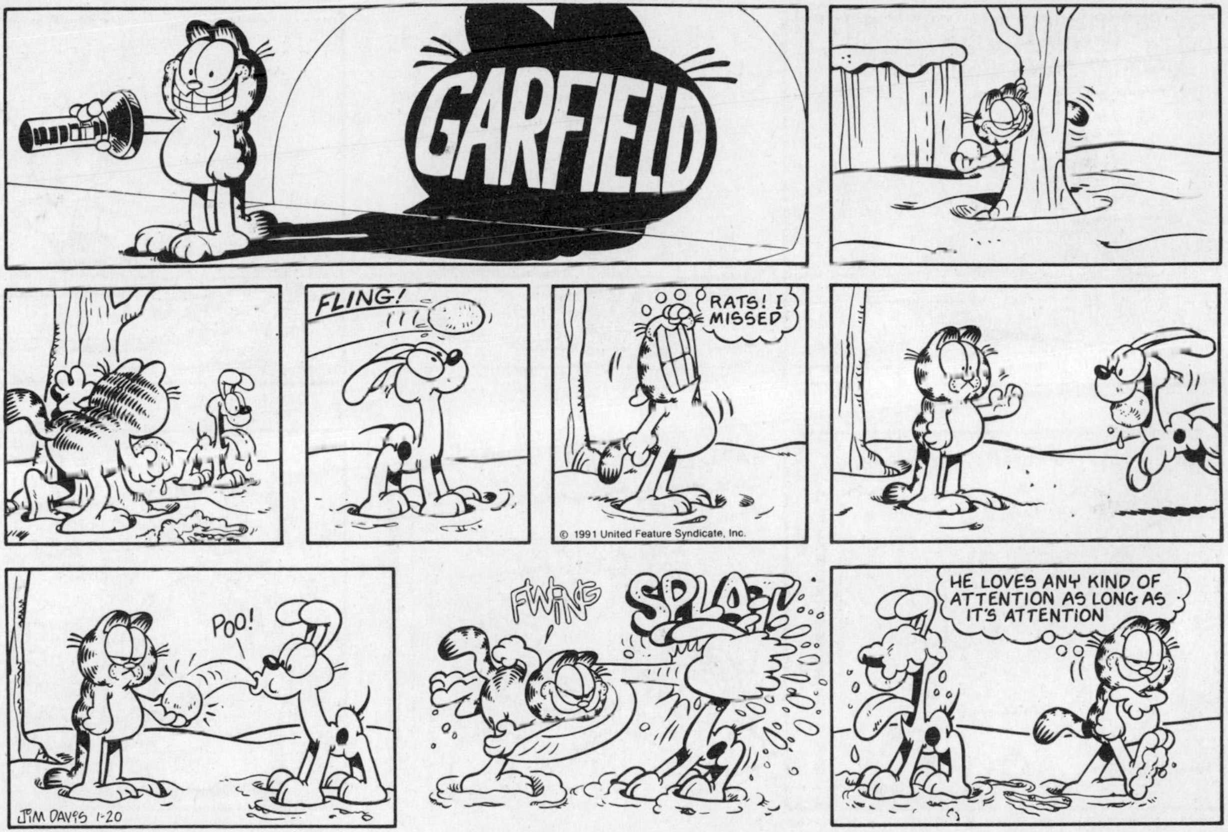
GARFIELD
FLING!
RATS! I MISSED
© 1991 United Feature Syndicate, Inc.
POO!
JIM DAVIS 1-20
FWING
SPLAT!
HE LOVES ANY KIND OF ATTENTION AS LONG AS IT'S ATTENTION

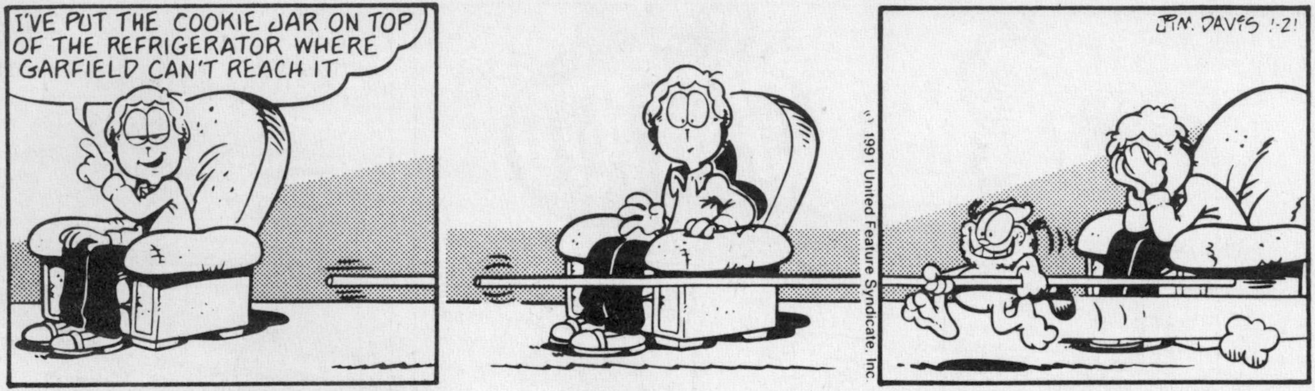
I'VE PUT THE COOKIE JAR ON TOP OF THE REFRIGERATOR WHERE GARFIELD CAN'T REACH IT
JIM DAVIS 1-21
© 1991 United Feature Syndicate, Inc.

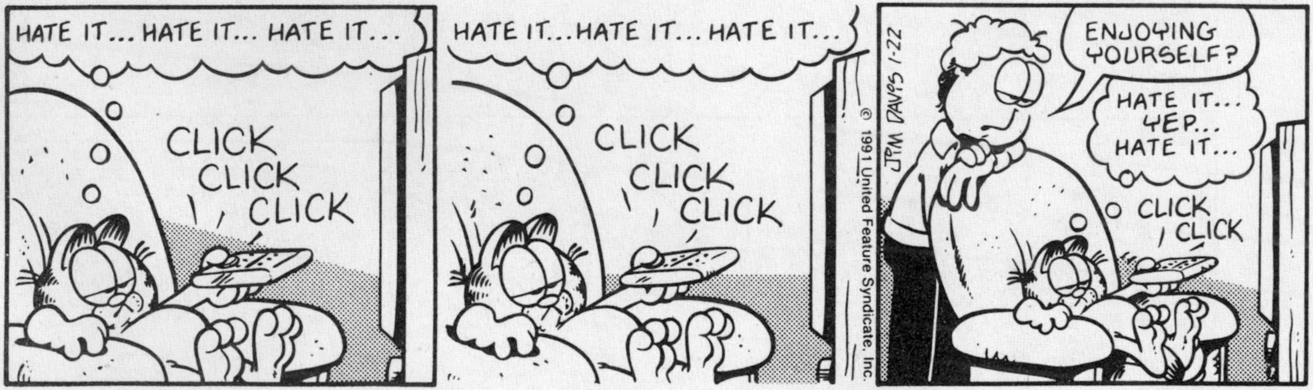
HATE IT... HATE IT... HATE IT...
CLICK
CLICK
CLICK
HATE IT...HATE IT... HATE IT...
CLICK
CLICK
CLICK
JIM DAVIS 1-22
© 1991 United Feature Syndicate, Inc.
ENJOYING YOURSELF?
HATE IT... YEP... HATE IT...
CLICK
CLICK

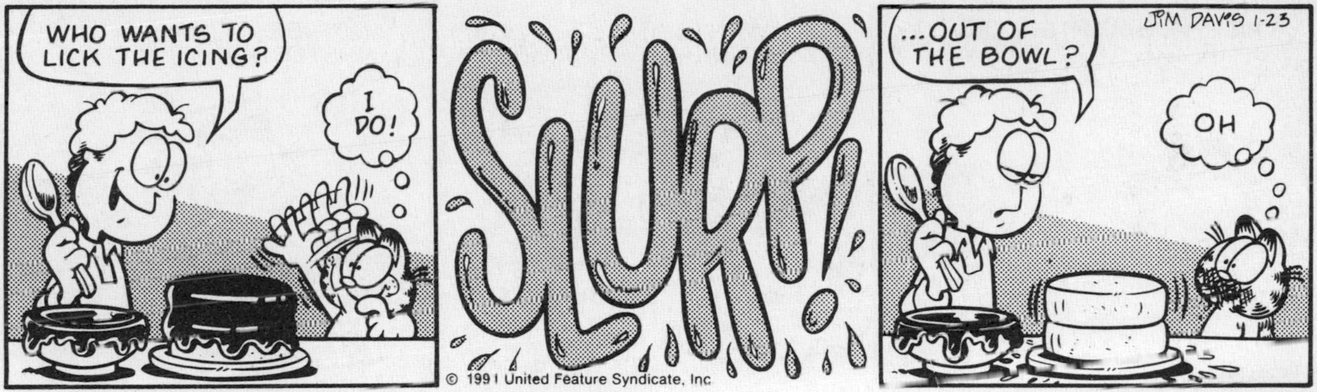
WHO WANTS TO LICK THE ICING?
I DO!
SLURP!
© 1991 United Feature Syndicate, Inc
JIM DAVIS 1-23
...OUT OF THE BOWL?
OH

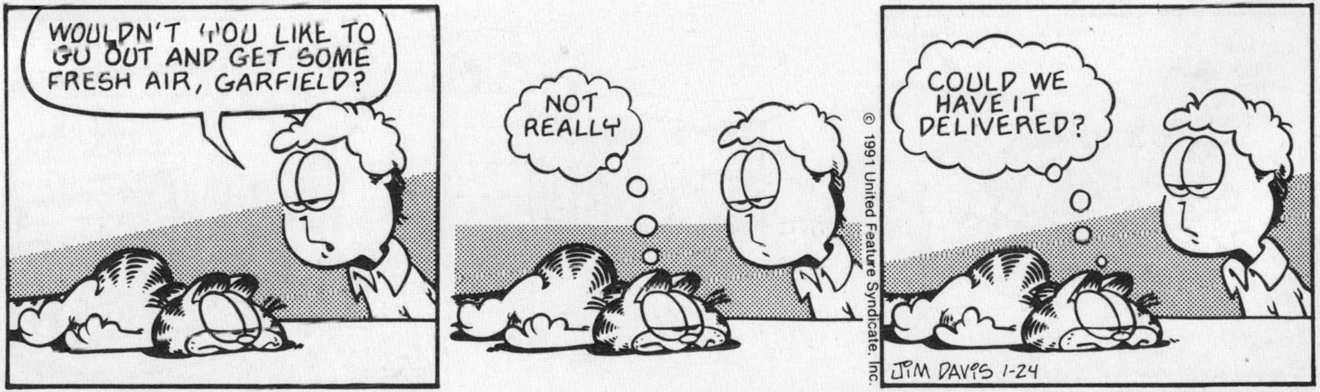
WOULDN'T YOU LIKE TO GO OUT AND GET SOME FRESH AIR, GARFIELD?
NOT REALLY
© 1991 United Feature Syndicate, Inc.
COULD WE HAVE IT DELIVERED?
JIM DAVIS 1-24

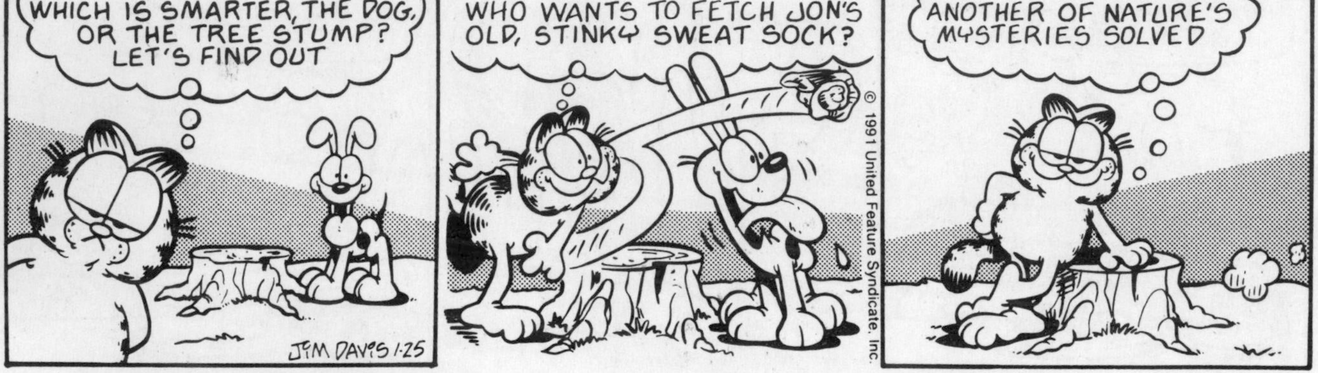
WHICH IS SMARTER, THE DOG, OR THE TREE STUMP? LET'S FIND OUT
JIM DAVIS 1-25
WHO WANTS TO FETCH JON'S OLD, STINKY SWEAT SOCK?
© 1991 United Feature Syndicate, Inc.
ANOTHER OF NATURE'S MYSTERIES SOLVED

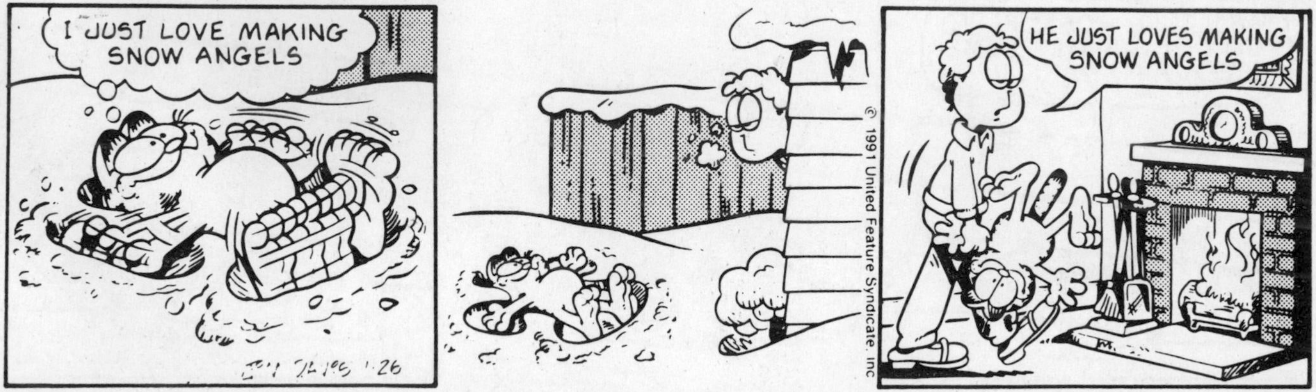
I JUST LOVE MAKING SNOW ANGELS
© 1991 United Feature Syndicate, Inc.
HE JUST LOVES MAKING SNOW ANGELS

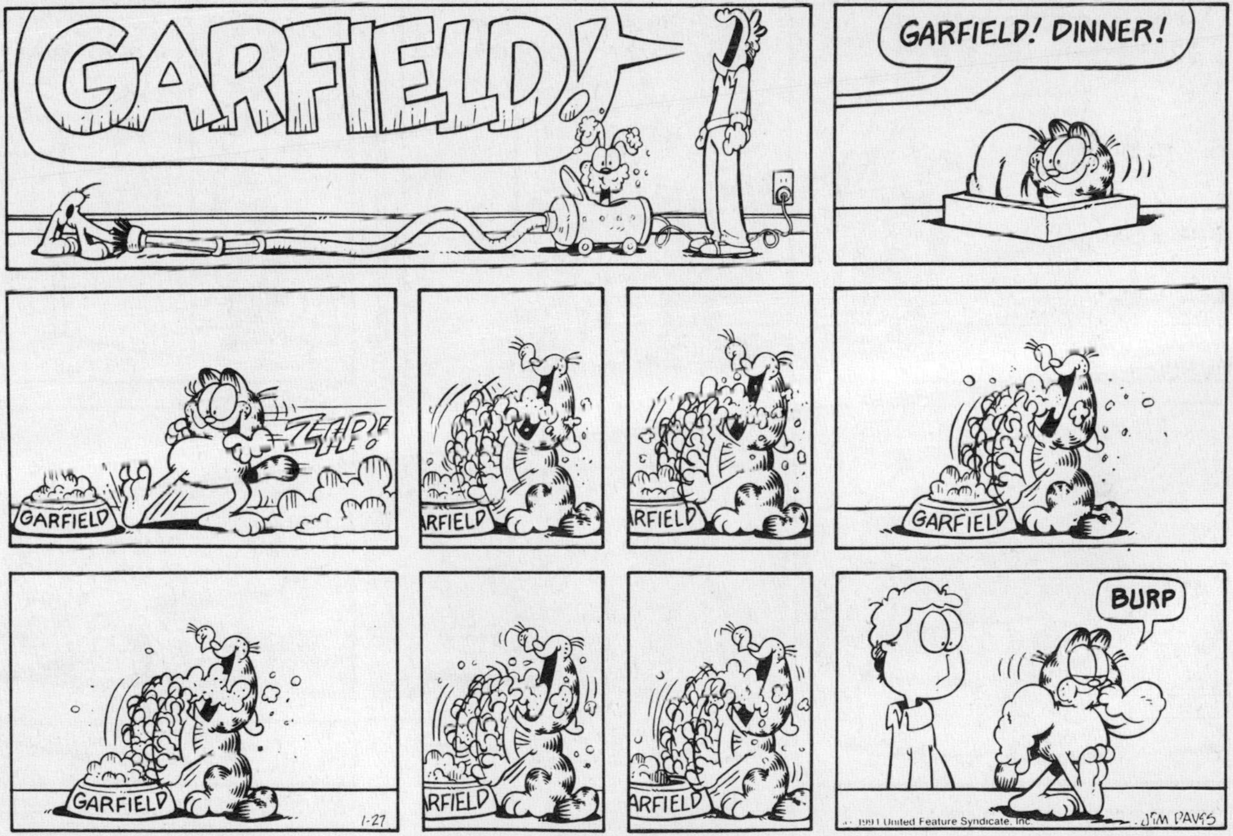
GARFIELD!
GARFIELD! DINNER!
ZZAP!!
GARFIELD
ARFIELD
ARFIELD
GARFIELD
GARFIELD
ARFIELD
ARFIELD
BURP
1-27
1991 United Feature Syndicate, Inc.
JIM DAVIS

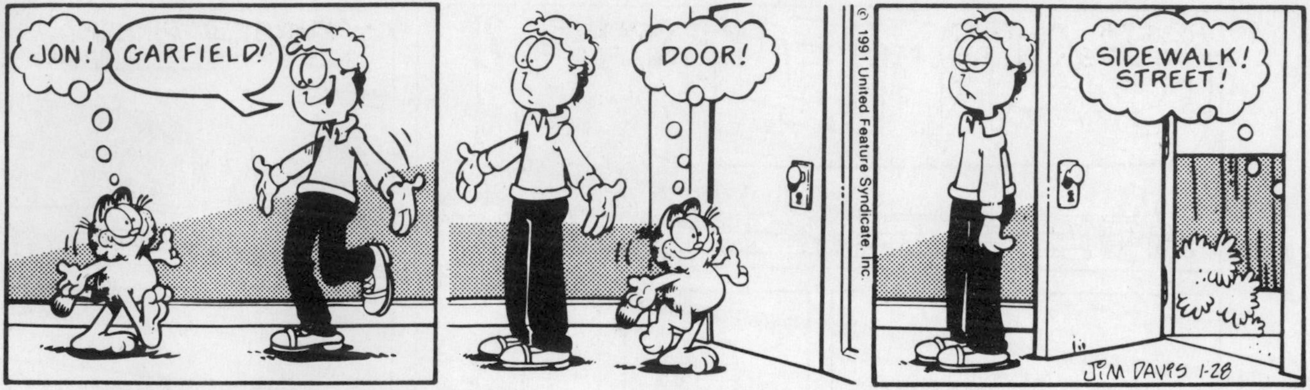
JON!
GARFIELD!
DOOR!
SIDEWALK! STREET!
© 1991 United Feature Syndicate, Inc.
JIM DAVIS 1-28

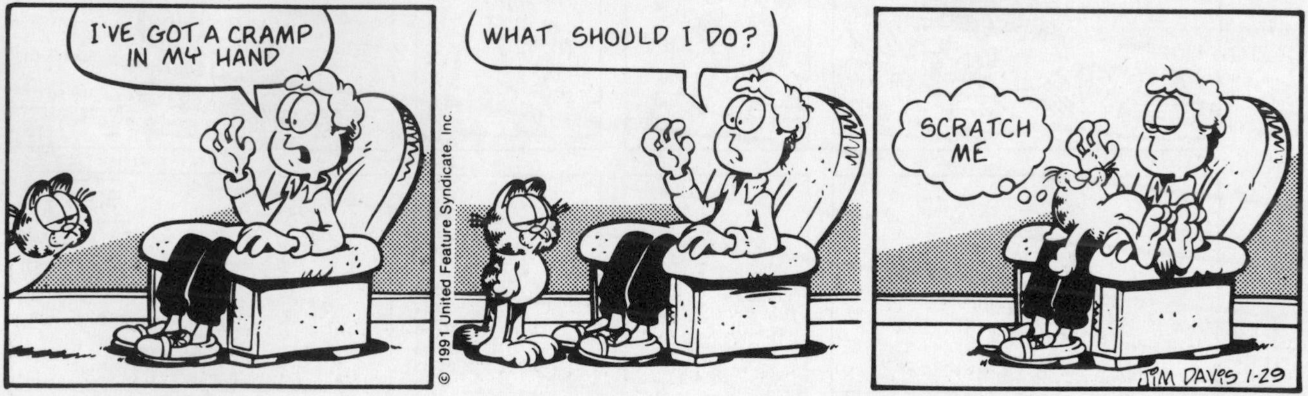
I'VE GOT A CRAMP IN MY HAND
WHAT SHOULD I DO?
SCRATCH ME
© 1991 United Feature Syndicate, Inc.
JIM DAVIS 1-29

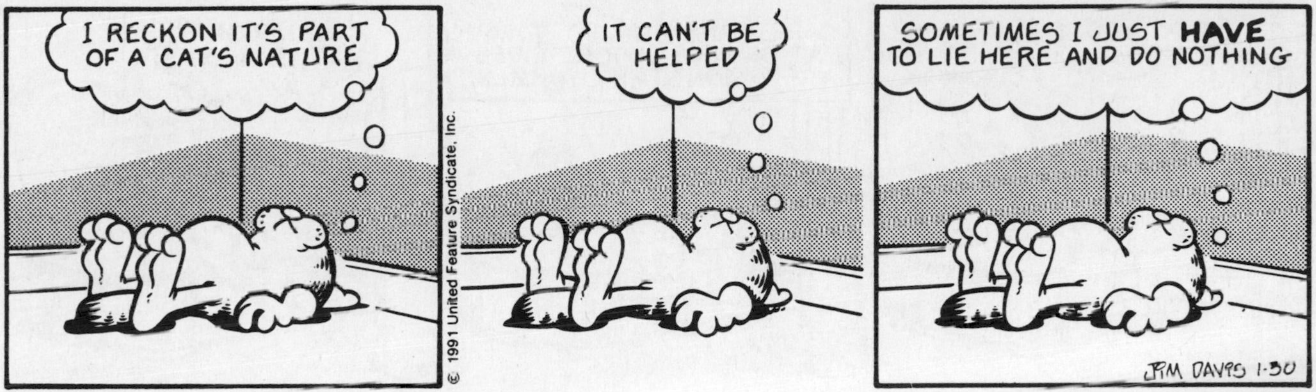
I RECKON IT'S PART OF A CAT'S NATURE
IT CAN'T BE HELPED
SOMETIMES I JUST **HAVE** TO LIE HERE AND DO NOTHING
© 1991 United Feature Syndicate, Inc.
JIM DAVIS 1-30

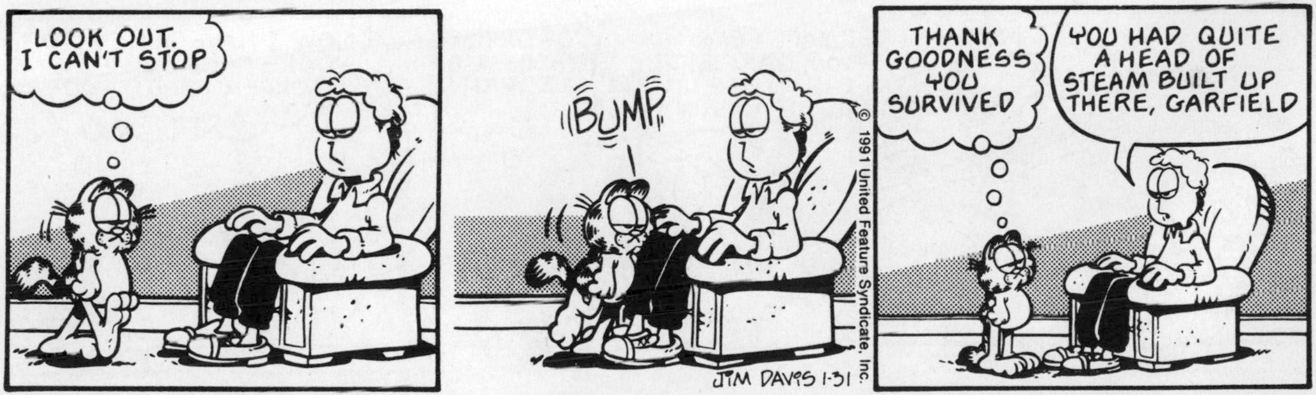
LOOK OUT. I CAN'T STOP
BUMP
THANK GOODNESS YOU SURVIVED
YOU HAD QUITE A HEAD OF STEAM BUILT UP THERE, GARFIELD
© 1991 United Feature Syndicate, Inc.
JIM DAVIS 1-31

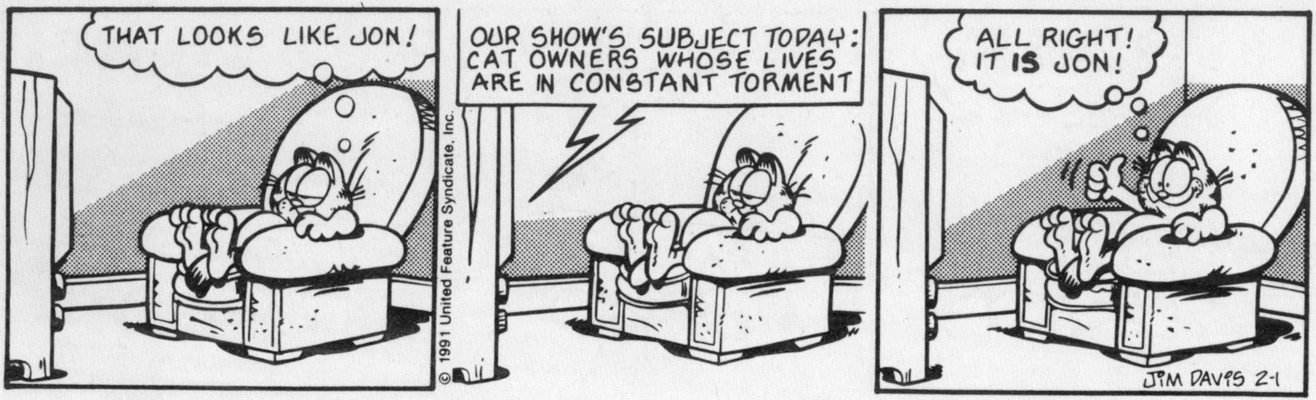
THAT LOOKS LIKE JON!
© 1991 United Feature Syndicate, Inc.
OUR SHOW'S SUBJECT TODAY: CAT OWNERS WHOSE LIVES ARE IN CONSTANT TORMENT
ALL RIGHT! IT **IS** JON!
JIM DAVIS 2-1

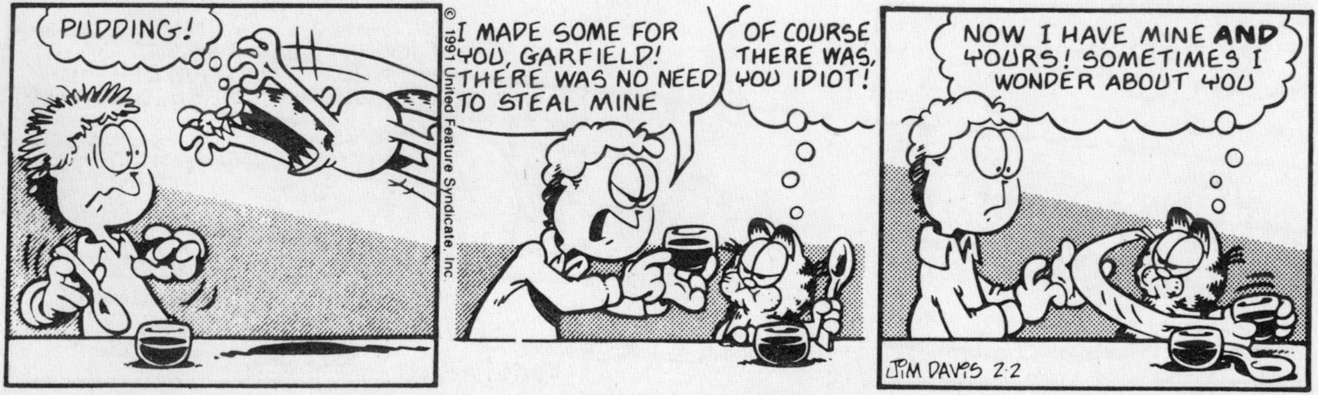
PUDDING!
© 1991 United Feature Syndicate, Inc.
I MADE SOME FOR YOU, GARFIELD! THERE WAS NO NEED TO STEAL MINE
OF COURSE THERE WAS, YOU IDIOT!
NOW I HAVE MINE **AND** YOURS! SOMETIMES I WONDER ABOUT YOU
JIM DAVIS 2-2

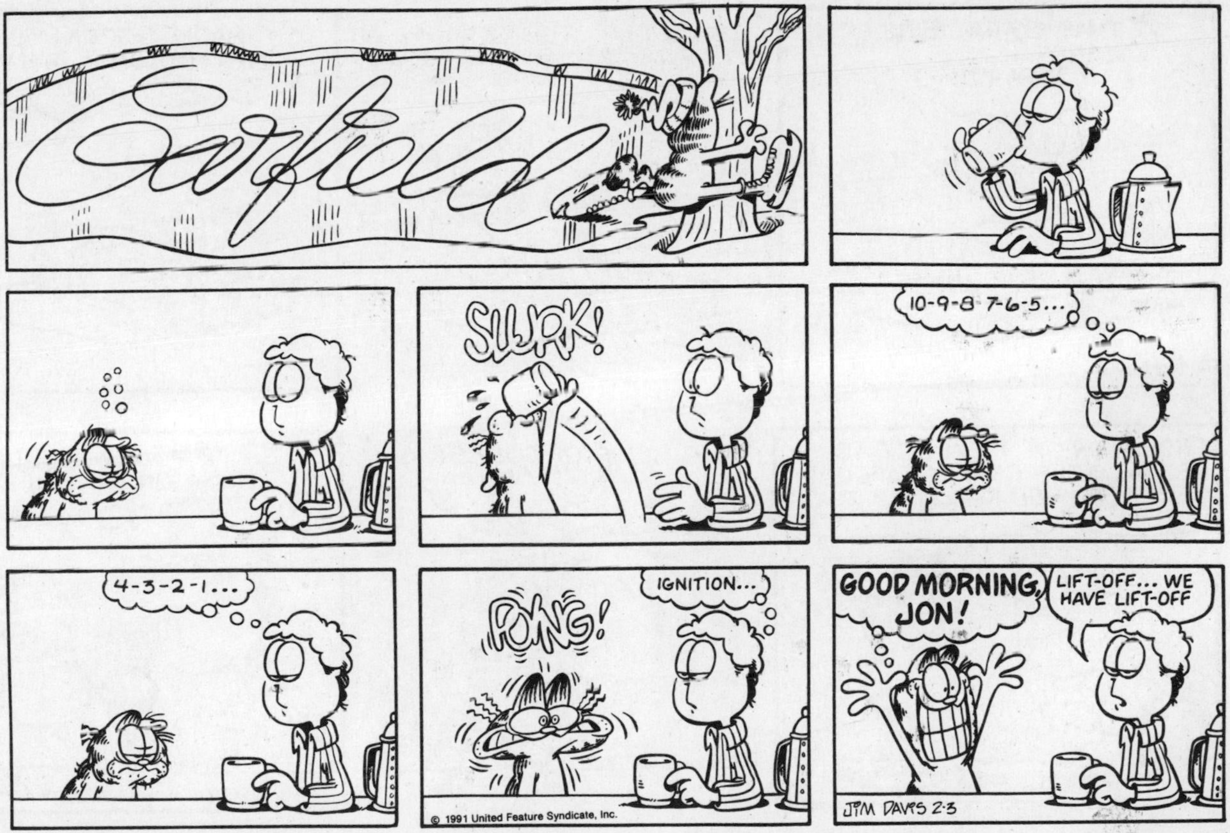
Garfield
SLURK!
10-9-8-7-6-5...
4-3-2-1...
IGNITION...
PONG!
GOOD MORNING, JON!
LIFT-OFF... WE HAVE LIFT-OFF
© 1991 United Feature Syndicate, Inc.
JIM DAVIS 2-3

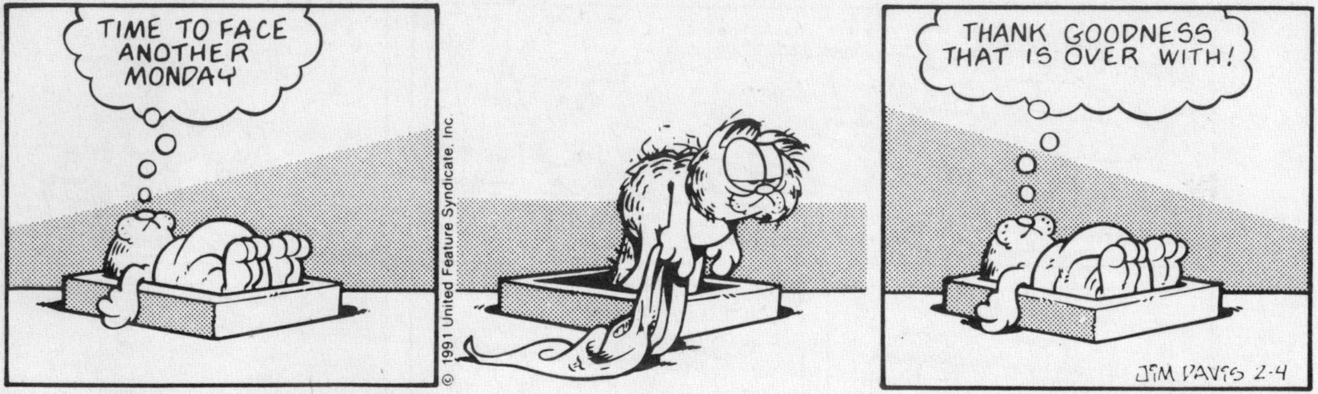
TIME TO FACE ANOTHER MONDAY
© 1991 United Feature Syndicate, Inc.
THANK GOODNESS THAT IS OVER WITH!
JIM DAVIS 2-4

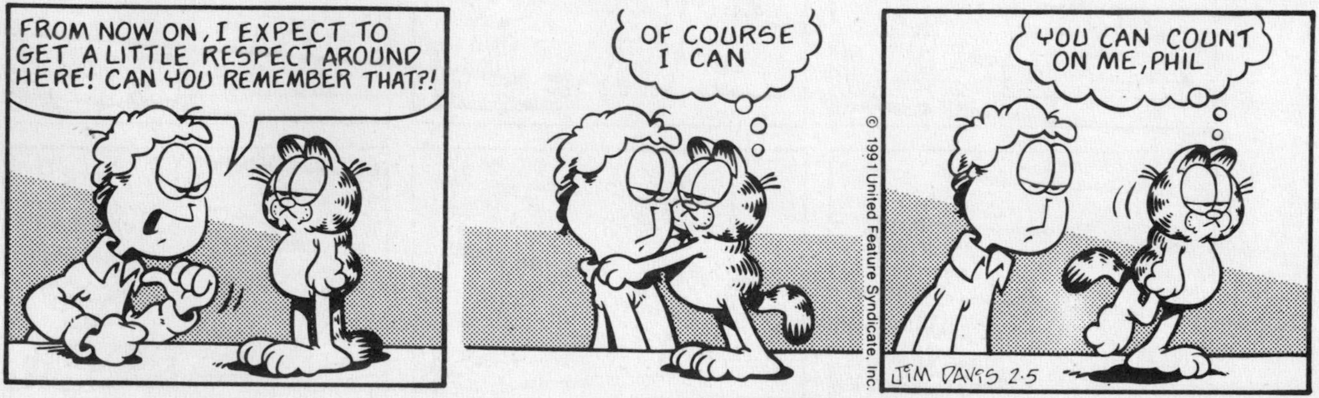
FROM NOW ON, I EXPECT TO GET A LITTLE RESPECT AROUND HERE! CAN YOU REMEMBER THAT?!
OF COURSE I CAN
© 1991 United Feature Syndicate, Inc.
YOU CAN COUNT ON ME, PHIL
JIM DAVIS 2-5

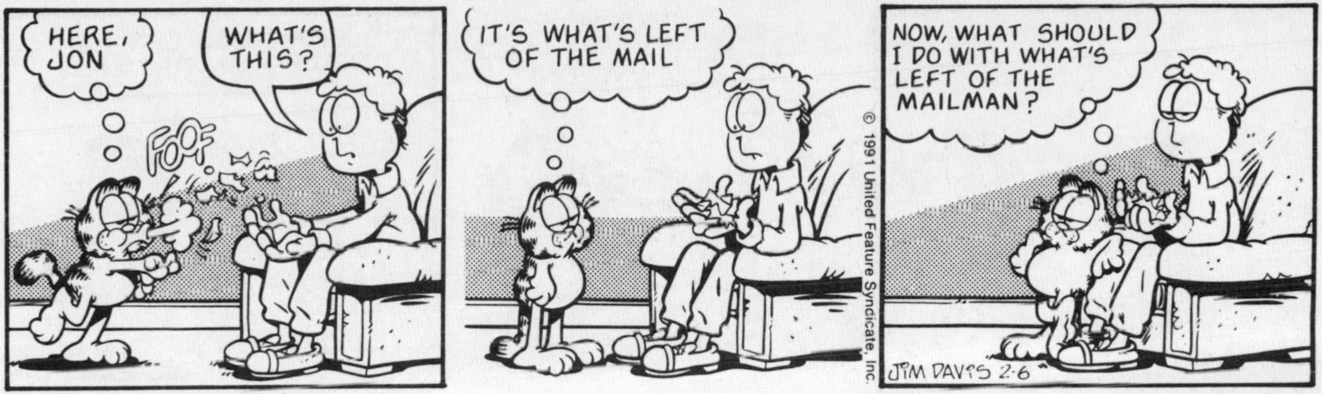
HERE, JON
FOOF
WHAT'S THIS?
IT'S WHAT'S LEFT OF THE MAIL
NOW, WHAT SHOULD I DO WITH WHAT'S LEFT OF THE MAILMAN?
JIM DAVIS 2-6
© 1991 United Feature Syndicate, Inc.

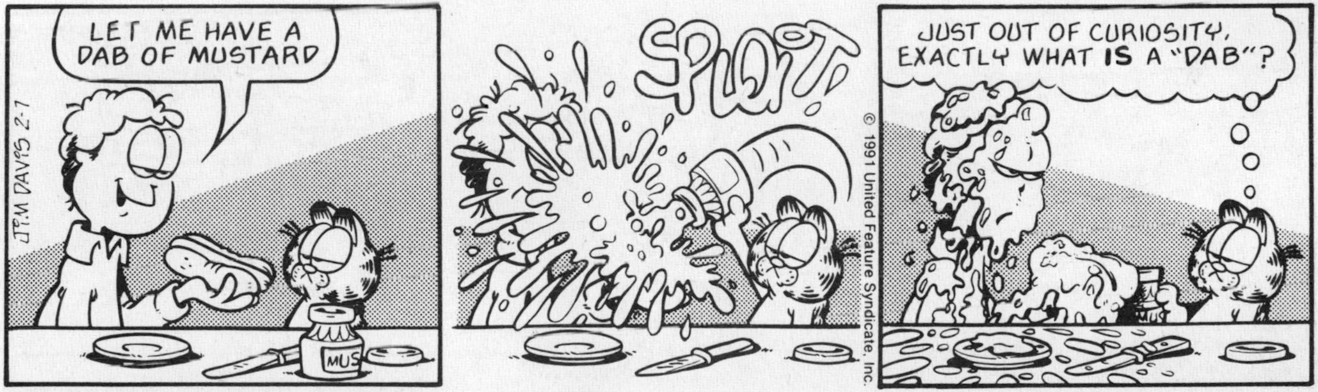
LET ME HAVE A DAB OF MUSTARD
JIM DAVIS 2-7
MUS
SPLOIT
JUST OUT OF CURIOSITY, EXACTLY WHAT **IS** A "DAB"?
© 1991 United Feature Syndicate, Inc.

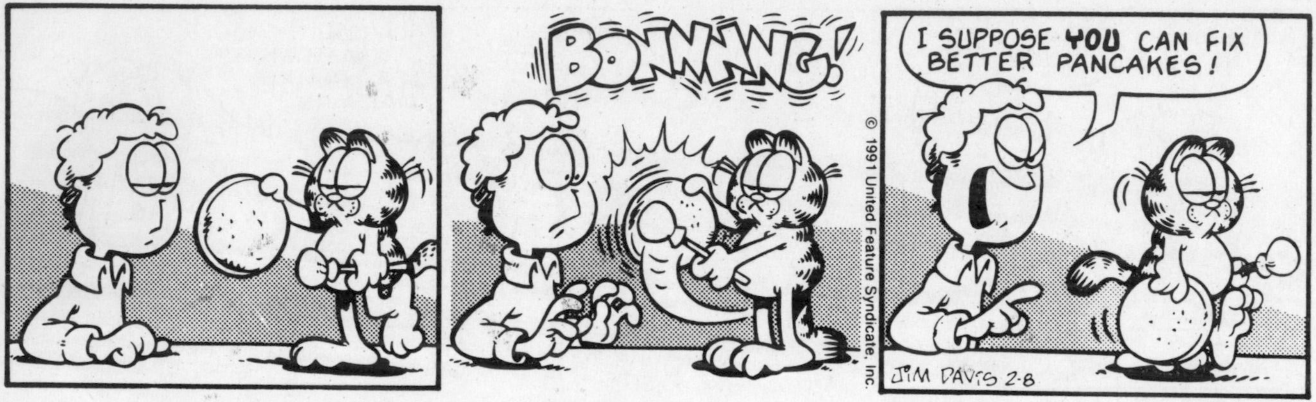
BONNNG!
© 1991 United Feature Syndicate, Inc.
I SUPPOSE YOU CAN FIX BETTER PANCAKES!
JIM DAVIS 2-8

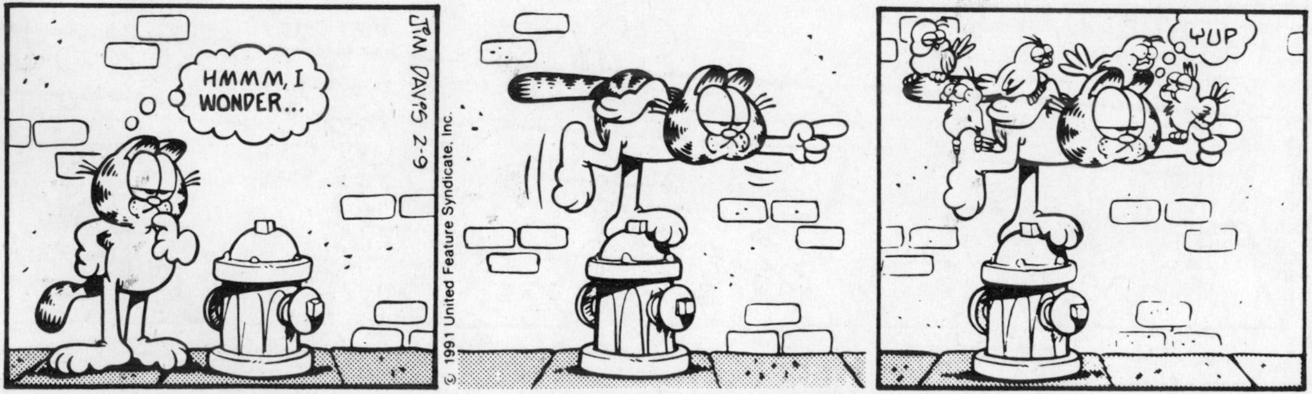
HMMM, I WONDER...
JIM DAVIS 2-9
© 1991 United Feature Syndicate, Inc.
YUP

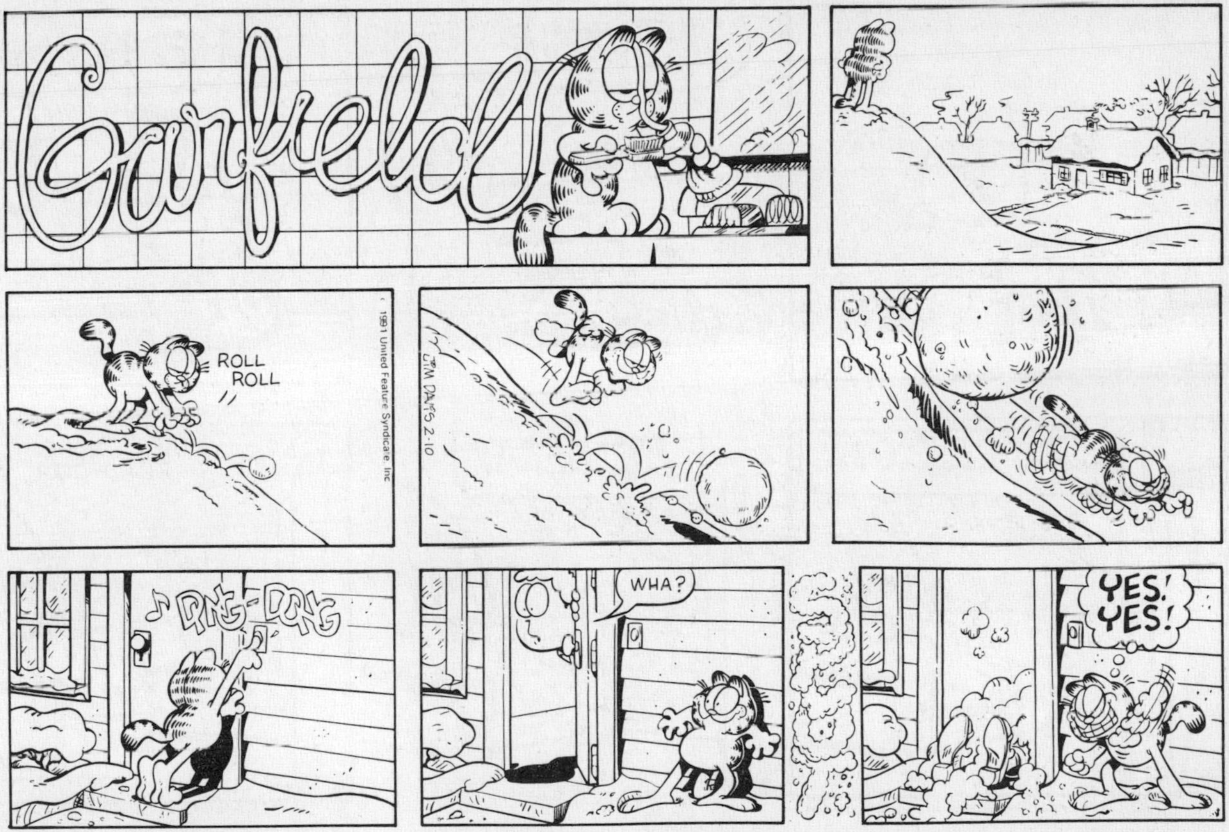
Garfield
ROLL ROLL
© 1991 United Feature Syndicate, Inc.
JIM DAVIS 2-10
DING-DONG
WHA?
YES! YES!

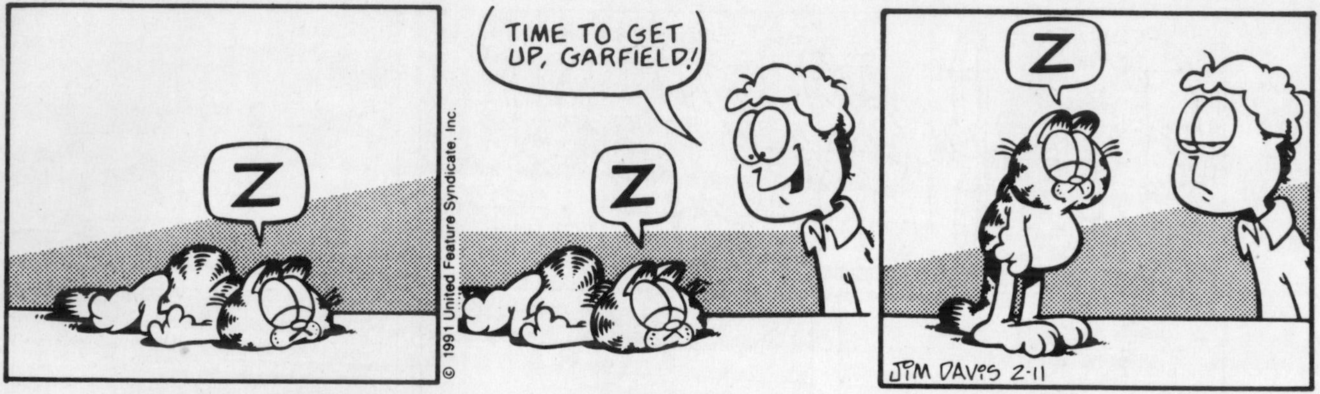
Z
TIME TO GET UP, GARFIELD!
Z
Z
JIM DAVIS 2-11
© 1991 United Feature Syndicate, Inc.

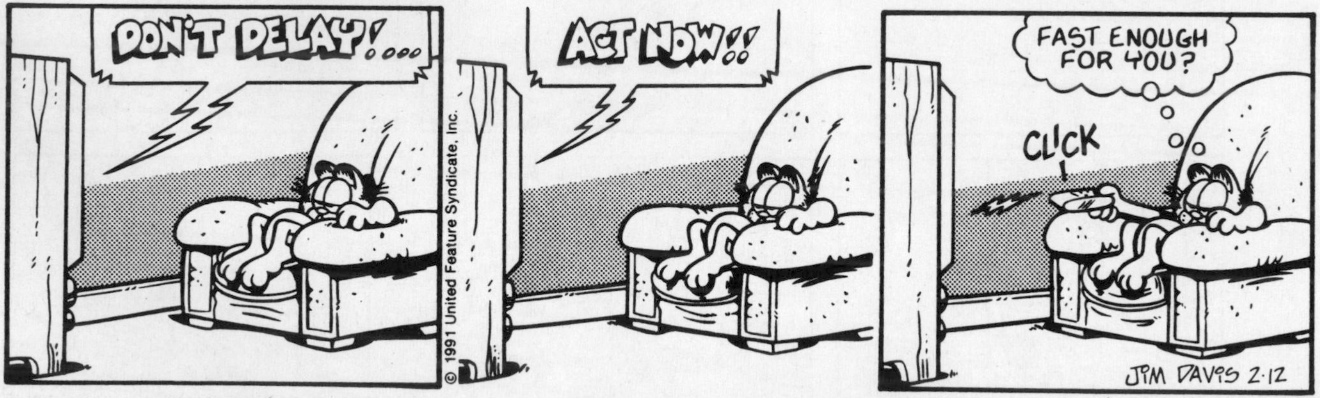
DON'T DELAY!....
ACT NOW!!
FAST ENOUGH FOR YOU?
CLICK
JIM DAVIS 2-12
© 1991 United Feature Syndicate, Inc.

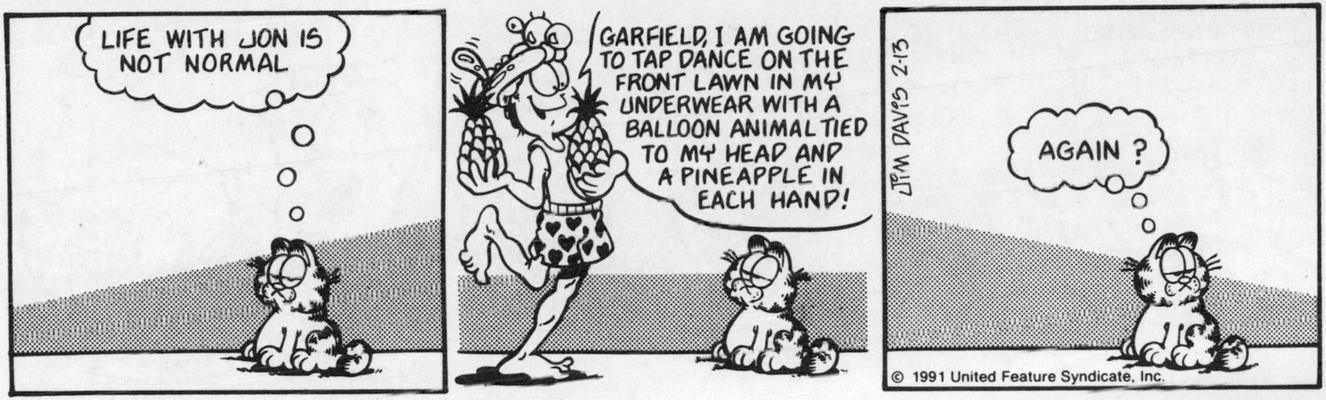
LIFE WITH JON IS NOT NORMAL
GARFIELD, I AM GOING TO TAP DANCE ON THE FRONT LAWN IN MY UNDERWEAR WITH A BALLOON ANIMAL TIED TO MY HEAD AND A PINEAPPLE IN EACH HAND!
JIM DAVIS 2-13
AGAIN ?
© 1991 United Feature Syndicate, Inc.

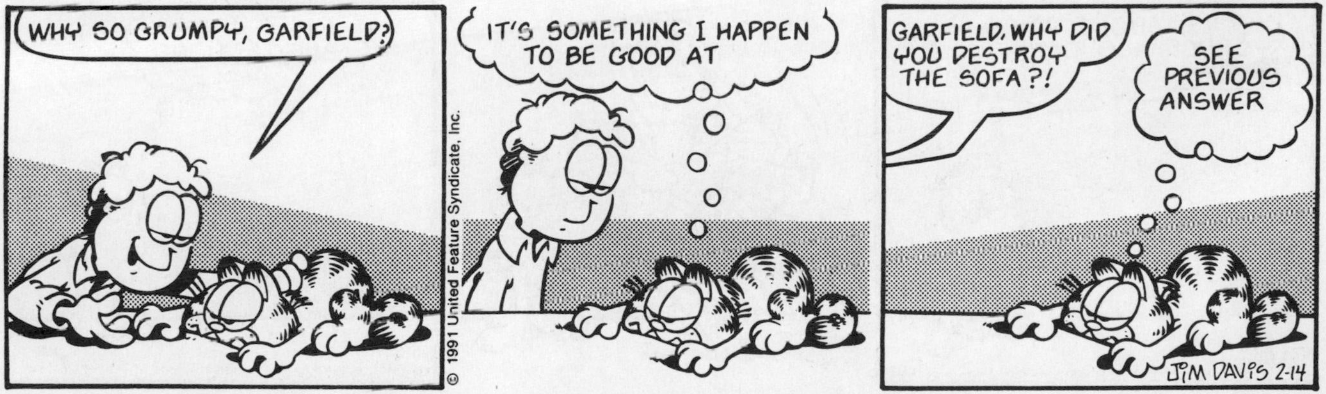
WHY SO GRUMPY, GARFIELD?
© 1991 United Feature Syndicate, Inc.
IT'S SOMETHING I HAPPEN TO BE GOOD AT
GARFIELD, WHY DID YOU DESTROY THE SOFA?!
SEE PREVIOUS ANSWER
JIM DAVIS 2-14

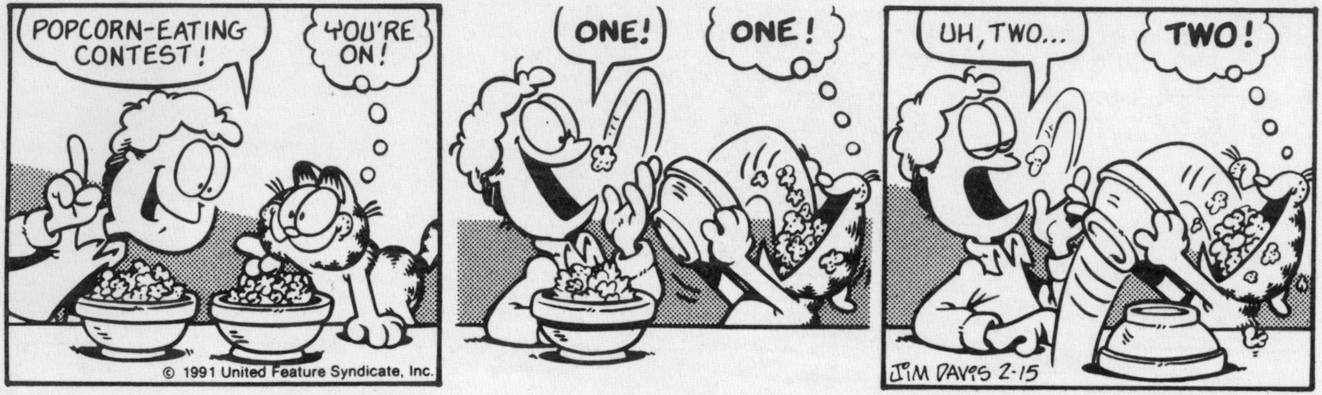
POPCORN-EATING CONTEST!
YOU'RE ON!
© 1991 United Feature Syndicate, Inc.
ONE!
ONE!
UH, TWO...
TWO!
JIM DAVIS 2-15

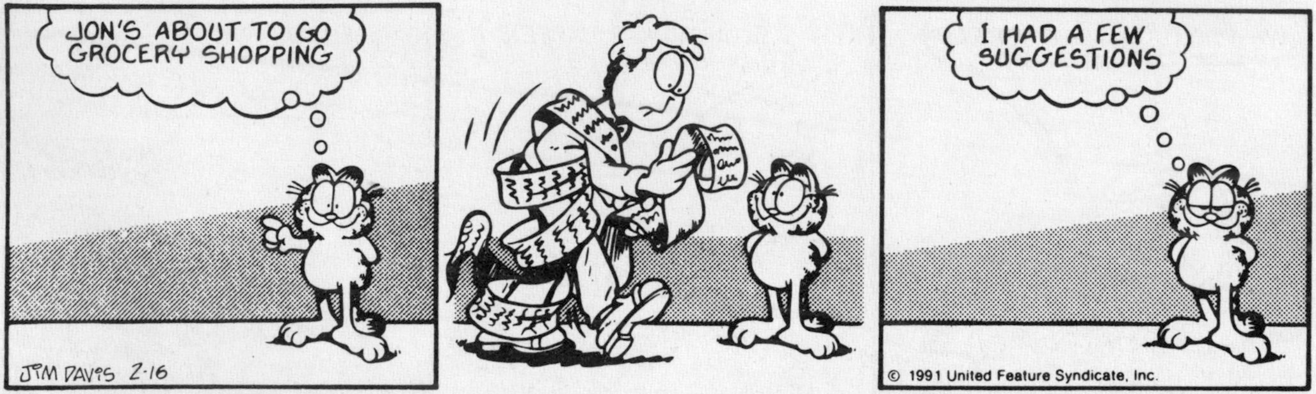
JON'S ABOUT TO GO GROCERY SHOPPING
JIM DAVIS 2-16
I HAD A FEW SUGGESTIONS
© 1991 United Feature Syndicate, Inc.

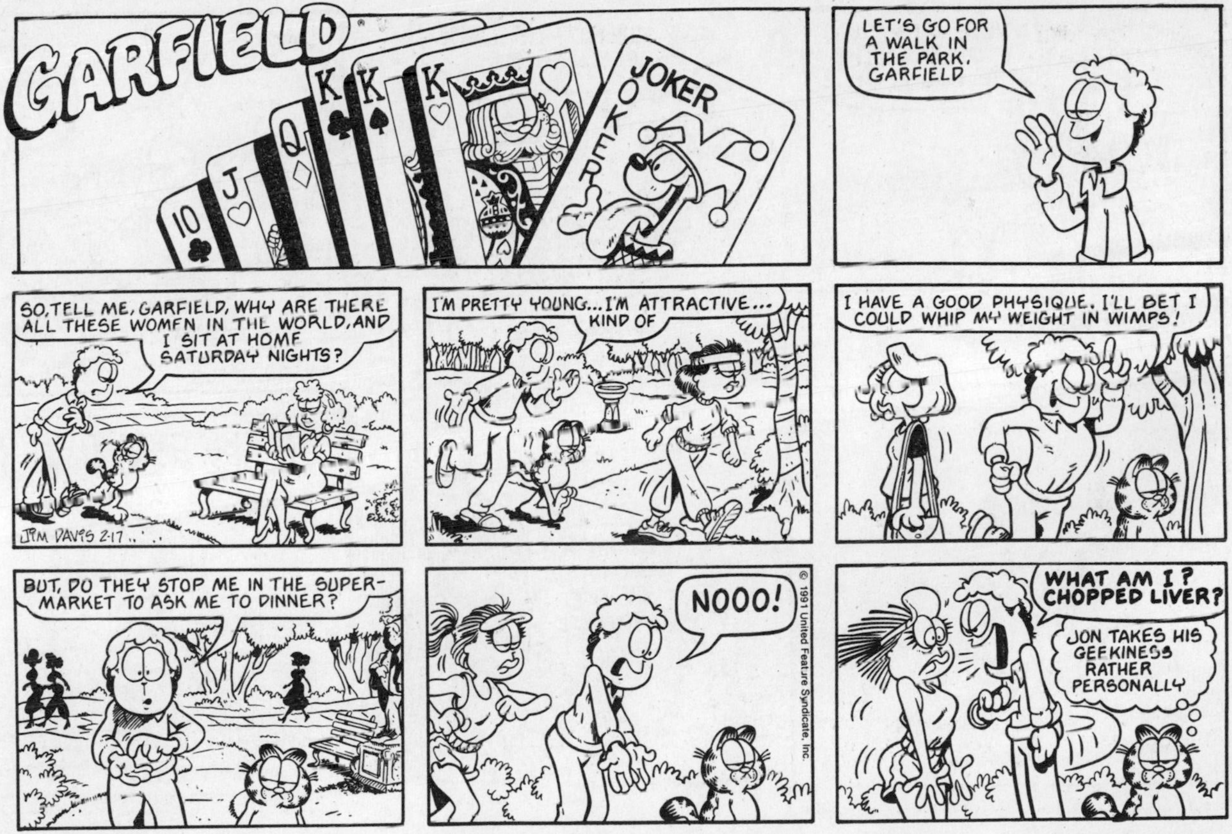
GARFIELD®
K
K
K
Q
J
10
JOKER
JOKER
LET'S GO FOR A WALK IN THE PARK, GARFIELD
SO, TELL ME, GARFIELD, WHY ARE THERE ALL THESE WOMEN IN THE WORLD, AND I SIT AT HOME SATURDAY NIGHTS?
JIM DAVIS 2-17
I'M PRETTY YOUNG... I'M ATTRACTIVE... KIND OF
I HAVE A GOOD PHYSIQUE. I'LL BET I COULD WHIP MY WEIGHT IN WIMPS!
BUT, DO THEY STOP ME IN THE SUPER-MARKET TO ASK ME TO DINNER?
NOOO!
© 1991 United Feature Syndicate, Inc.
WHAT AM I? CHOPPED LIVER?
JON TAKES HIS GEEKINESS RATHER PERSONALLY

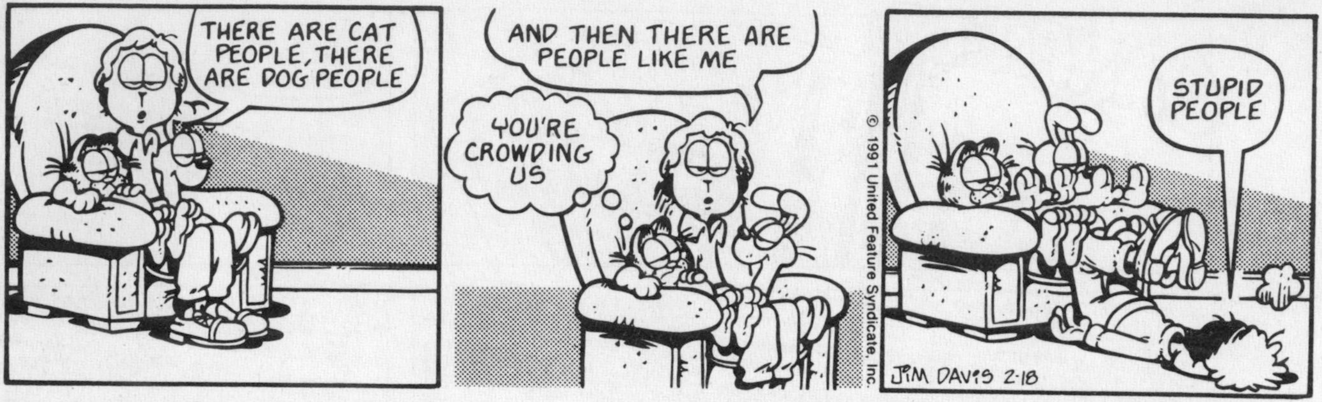
THERE ARE CAT PEOPLE, THERE ARE DOG PEOPLE
AND THEN THERE ARE PEOPLE LIKE ME
YOU'RE CROWDING US
STUPID PEOPLE
© 1991 United Feature Syndicate, Inc.
JIM DAVIS 2-18

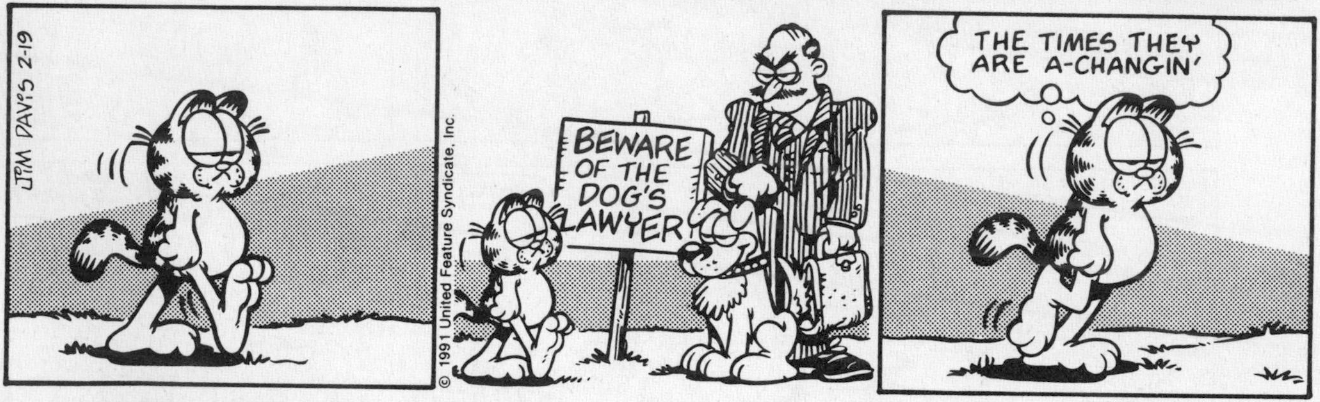
JIM DAVIS 2-19
© 1991 United Feature Syndicate, Inc.
BEWARE OF THE DOG'S LAWYER
THE TIMES THEY ARE A-CHANGIN'

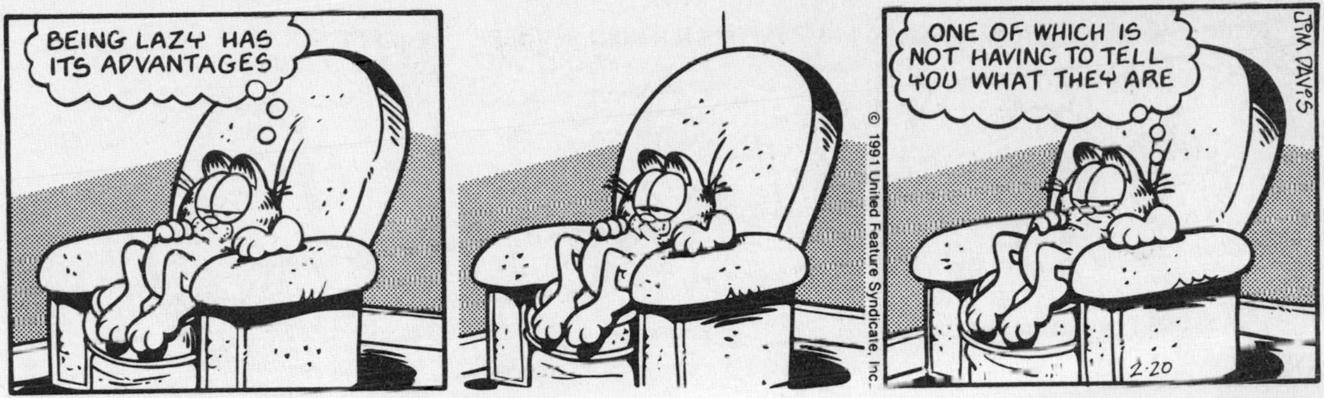
BEING LAZY HAS ITS ADVANTAGES
ONE OF WHICH IS NOT HAVING TO TELL YOU WHAT THEY ARE
JIM DAVIS
2-20
© 1991 United Feature Syndicate, Inc.

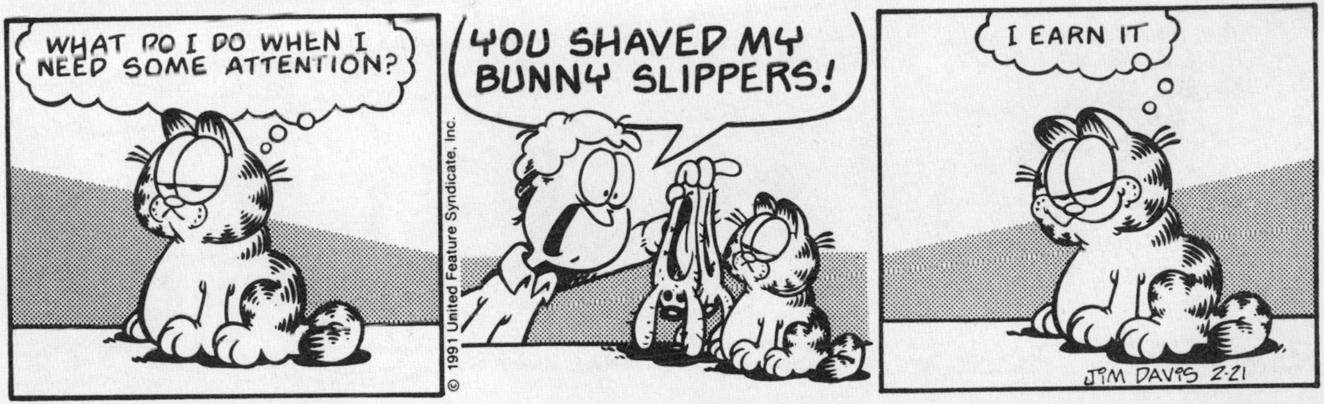
WHAT DO I DO WHEN I NEED SOME ATTENTION?
YOU SHAVED MY BUNNY SLIPPERS!
I EARN IT
JIM DAVIS 2-21
© 1991 United Feature Syndicate, Inc.

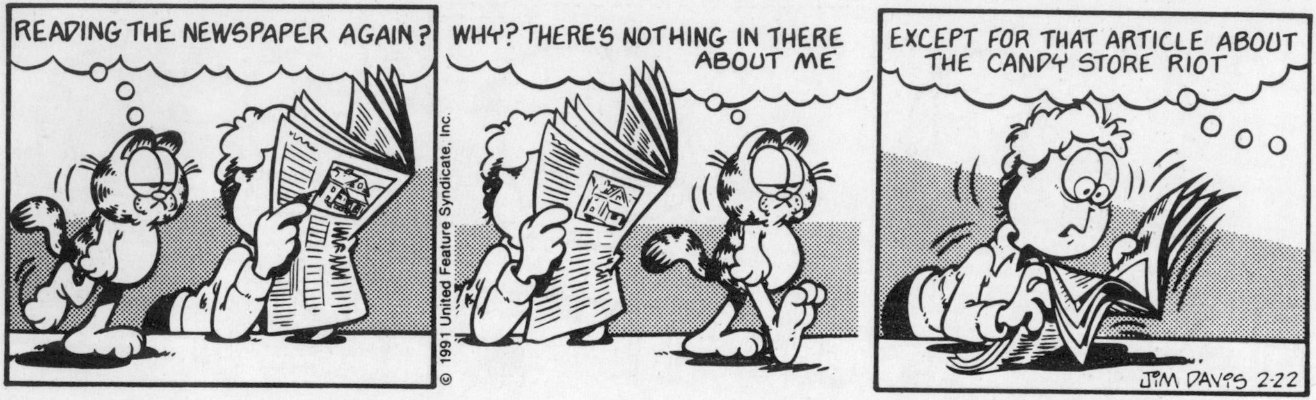
READING THE NEWSPAPER AGAIN?
WHY? THERE'S NOTHING IN THERE ABOUT ME
EXCEPT FOR THAT ARTICLE ABOUT THE CANDY STORE RIOT
JIM DAVIS 2-22
© 1991 United Feature Syndicate, Inc.

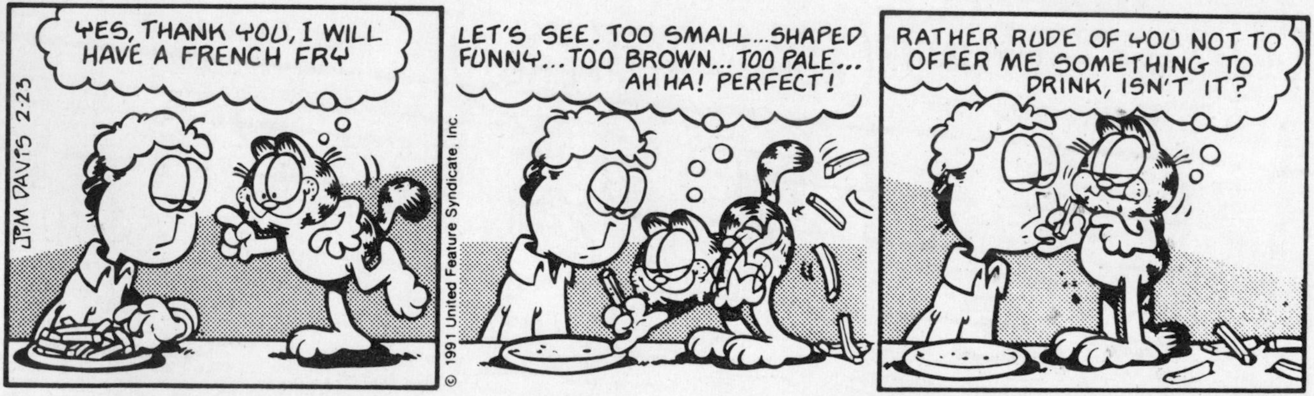
YES, THANK YOU, I WILL HAVE A FRENCH FRY
JIM DAVIS 2-23
LET'S SEE. TOO SMALL...SHAPED FUNNY... TOO BROWN... TOO PALE... AH HA! PERFECT!
RATHER RUDE OF YOU NOT TO OFFER ME SOMETHING TO DRINK, ISN'T IT?
© 1991 United Feature Syndicate, Inc.

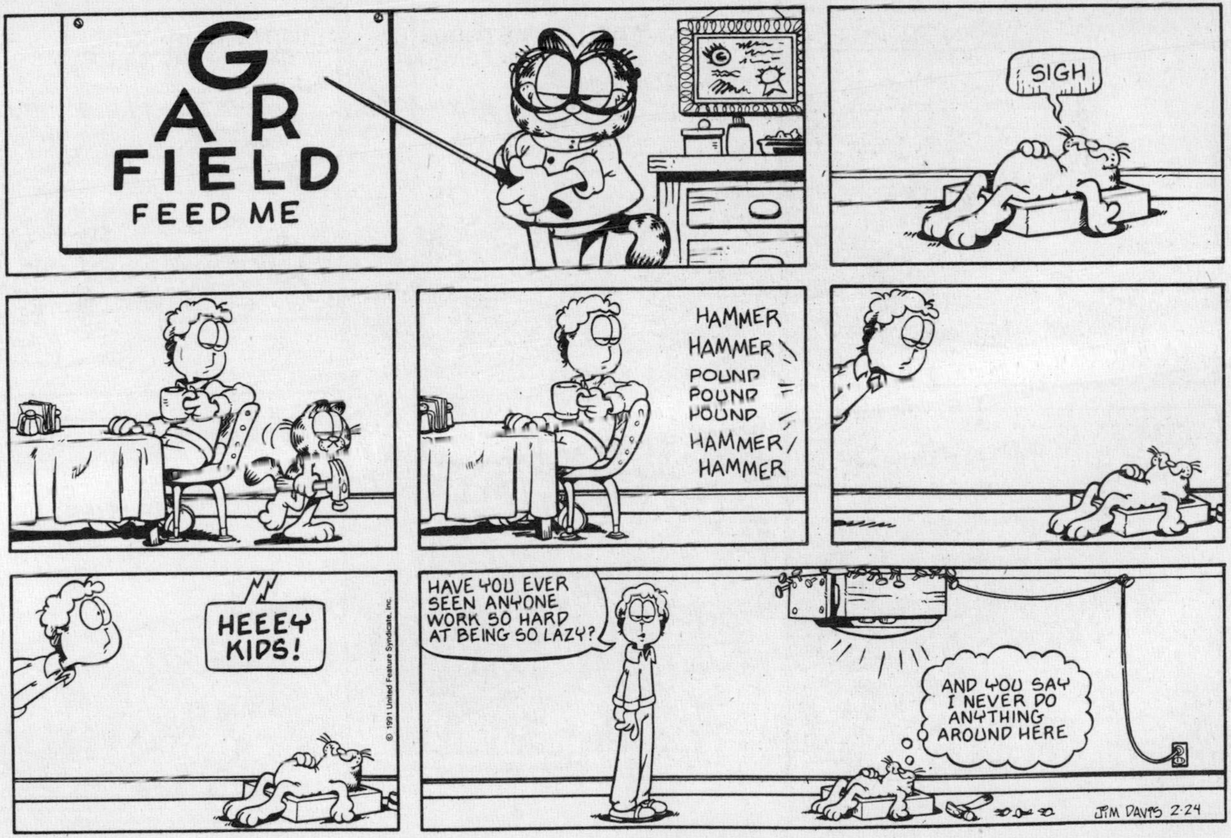
GARFIELD
FEED ME
SIGH
HAMMER
HAMMER
POUND
POUND
POUND
HAMMER
HAMMER
HEEEY KIDS!
HAVE YOU EVER SEEN ANYONE WORK SO HARD AT BEING SO LAZY?
AND YOU SAY I NEVER DO ANYTHING AROUND HERE
JIM DAVIS 2-24
© 1991 United Feature Syndicate, Inc.

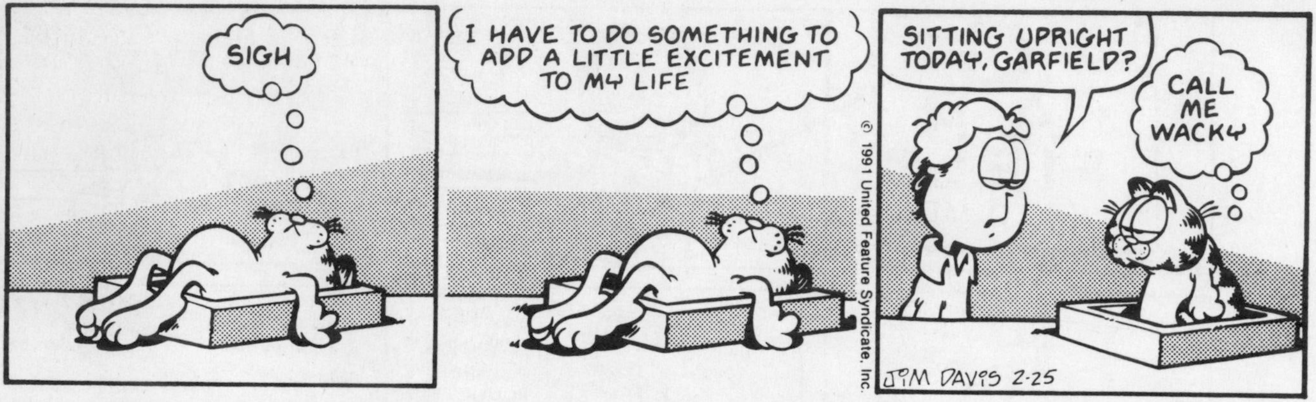
SIGH
I HAVE TO DO SOMETHING TO ADD A LITTLE EXCITEMENT TO MY LIFE
SITTING UPRIGHT TODAY, GARFIELD?
CALL ME WACKY
© 1991 United Feature Syndicate, Inc.
JIM DAVIS 2-25

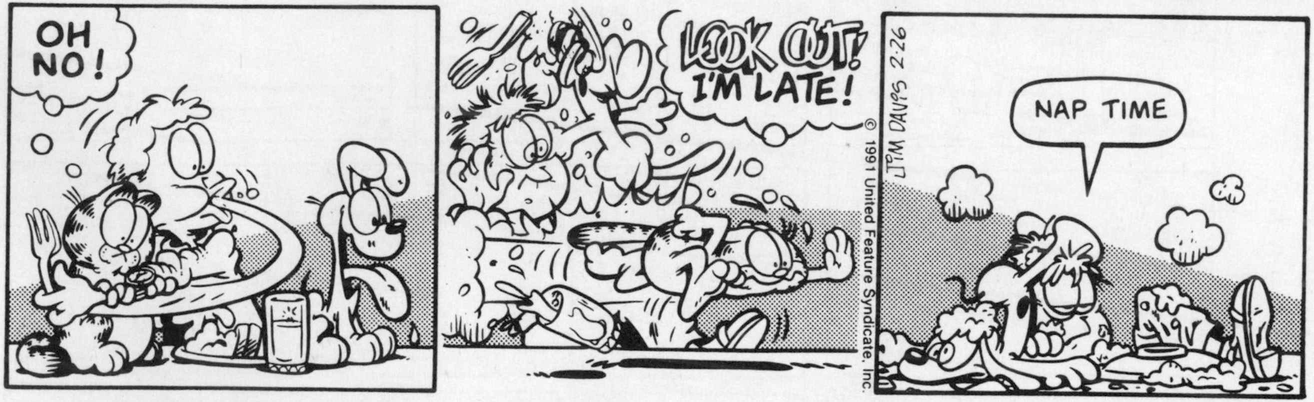
OH NO!
LOOK OUT! I'M LATE!
NAP TIME
© 1991 United Feature Syndicate, Inc.
JIM DAVIS 2-26

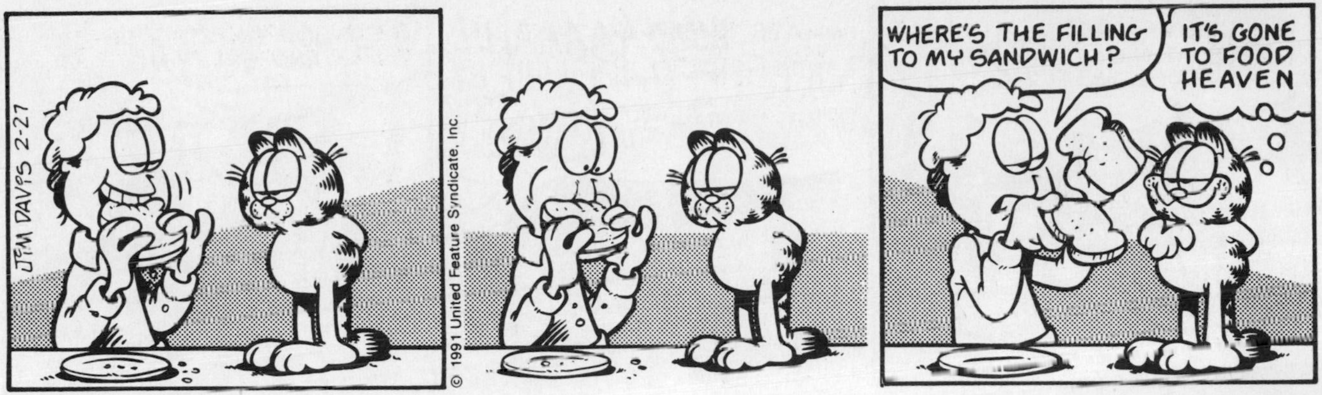
JIM DAVIS 2-27
© 1991 United Feature Syndicate, Inc.
WHERE'S THE FILLING TO MY SANDWICH?
IT'S GONE TO FOOD HEAVEN

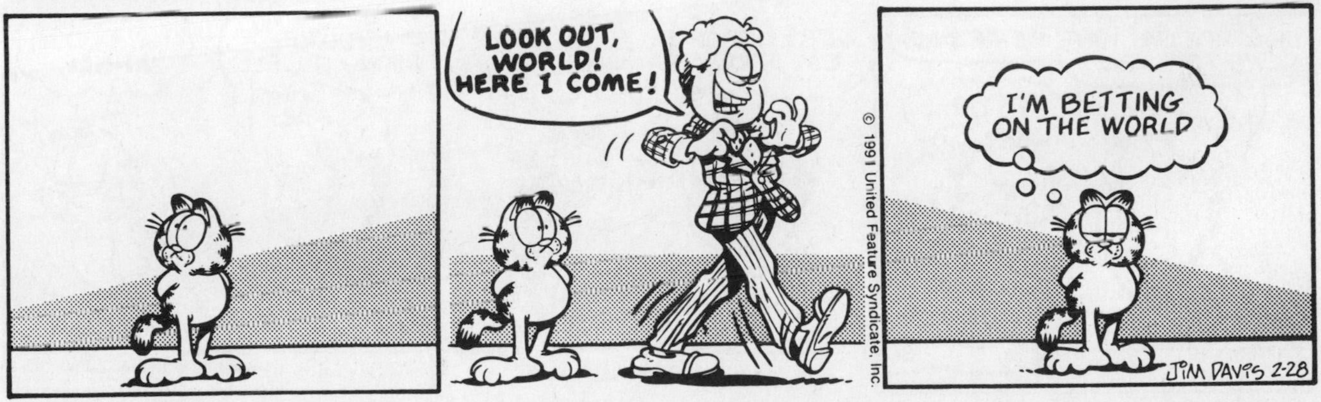
LOOK OUT, WORLD! HERE I COME!
© 1991 United Feature Syndicate, Inc.
I'M BETTING ON THE WORLD
JIM DAVIS 2-28

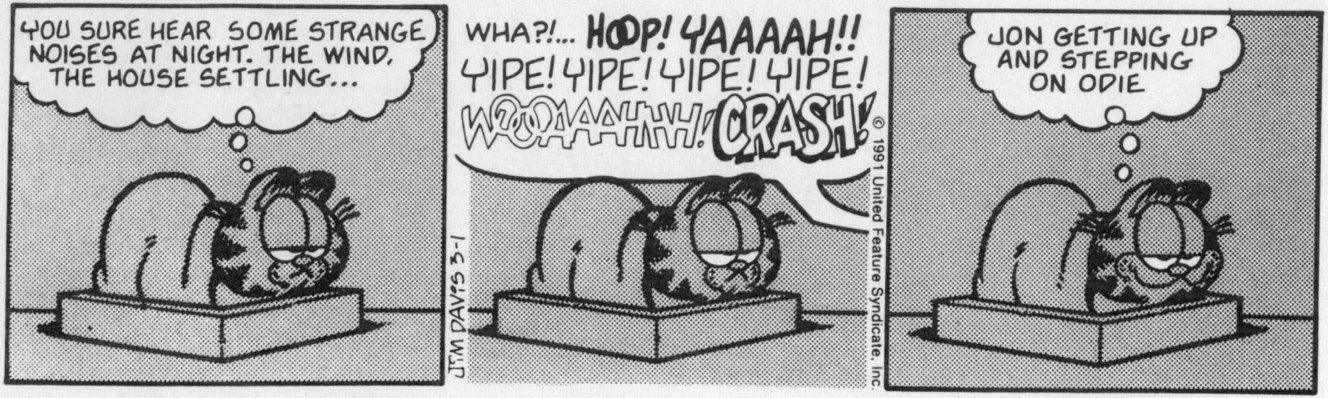
YOU SURE HEAR SOME STRANGE NOISES AT NIGHT. THE WIND, THE HOUSE SETTLING...
JIM DAVIS 3-1
WHA?!... HOOP! YAAAAH!!
YIPE! YIPE! YIPE! YIPE!
WOOOAAAHHH! CRASH!
© 1991 United Feature Syndicate, Inc.
JON GETTING UP AND STEPPING ON ODIE

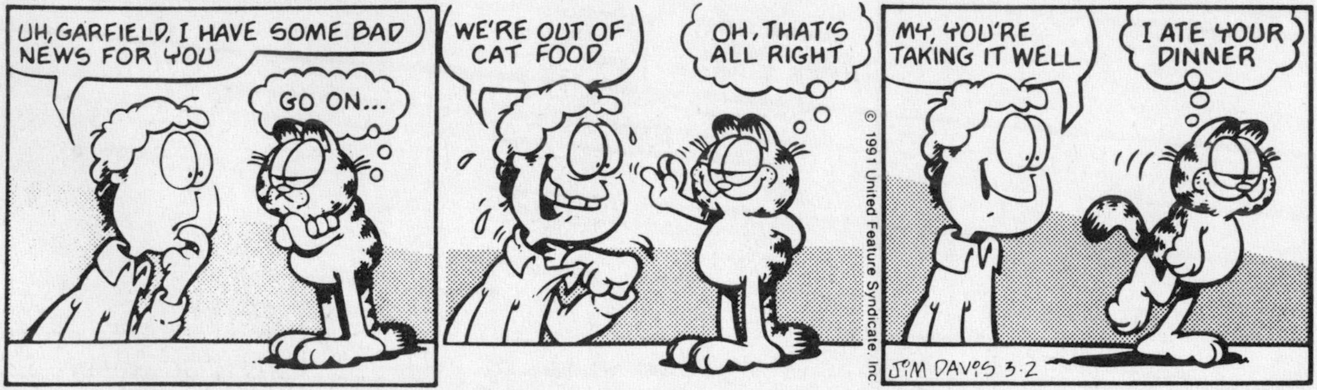
UH, GARFIELD, I HAVE SOME BAD NEWS FOR YOU
GO ON...
WE'RE OUT OF CAT FOOD
OH, THAT'S ALL RIGHT
© 1991 United Feature Syndicate, Inc.
MY, YOU'RE TAKING IT WELL
I ATE YOUR DINNER
JIM DAVIS 3-2

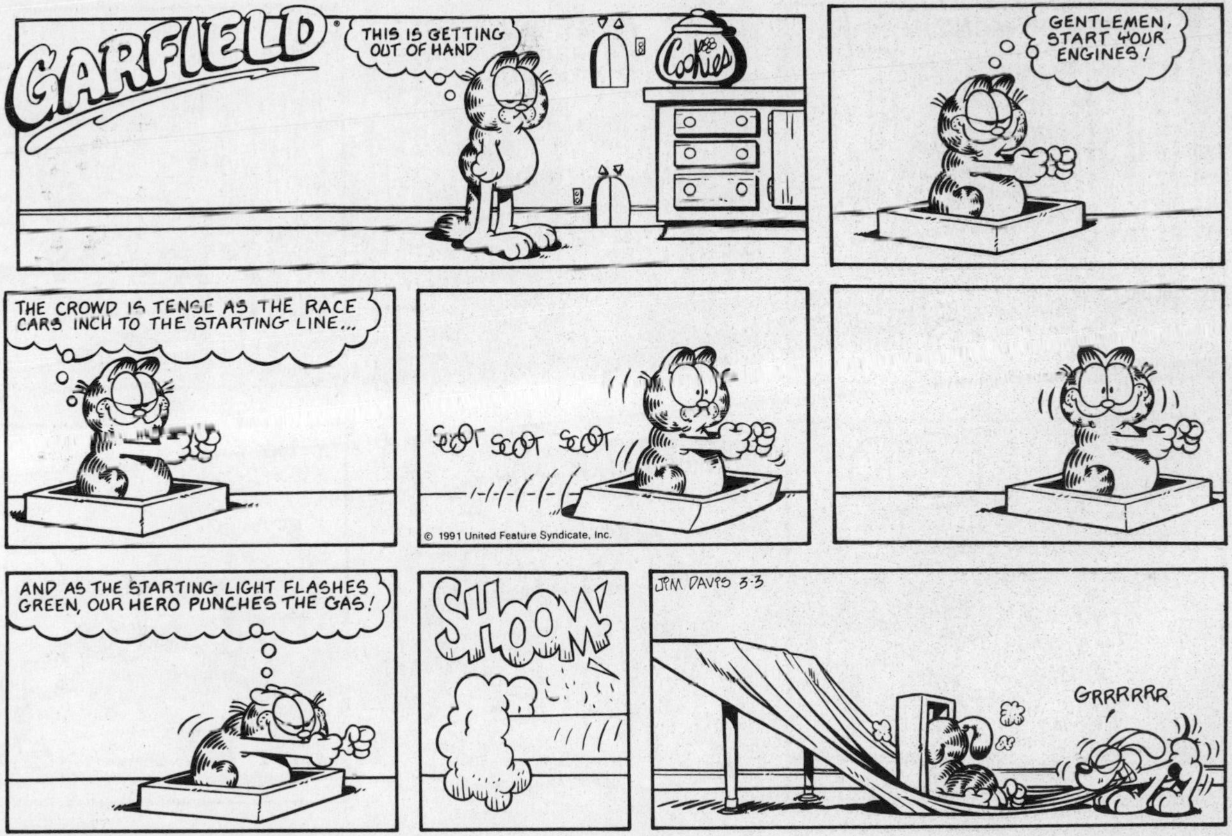
GARFIELD
THIS IS GETTING OUT OF HAND
Cookies
GENTLEMEN, START YOUR ENGINES!
THE CROWD IS TENSE AS THE RACE CARS INCH TO THE STARTING LINE...
SCOOT SCOOT SCOOT
© 1991 United Feature Syndicate, Inc.
AND AS THE STARTING LIGHT FLASHES GREEN, OUR HERO PUNCHES THE GAS!
SHOOM!
JIM DAVIS 3-3
GRRRRRR

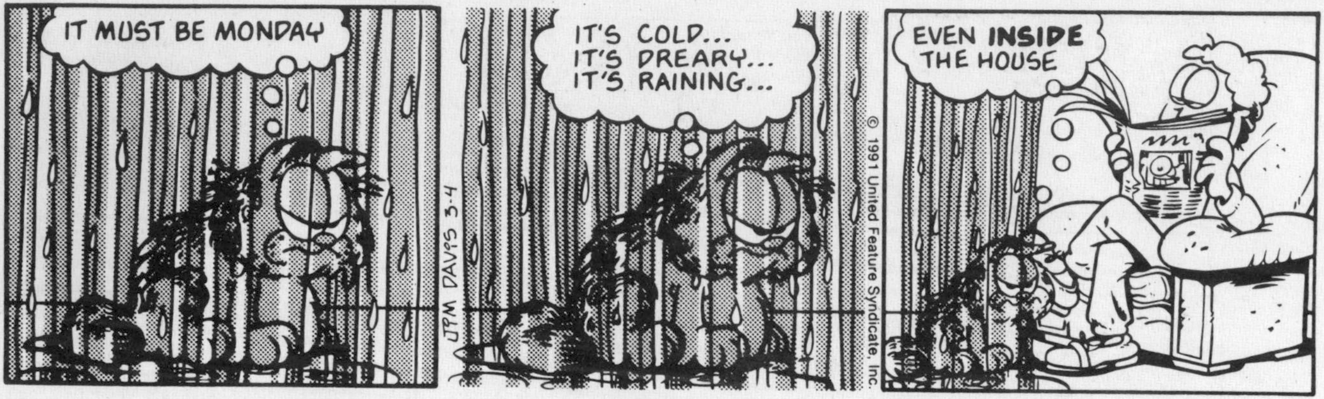
IT MUST BE MONDAY
IT'S COLD... IT'S DREARY... IT'S RAINING...
EVEN INSIDE THE HOUSE
JIM DAVIS 3-4
© 1991 United Feature Syndicate, Inc.

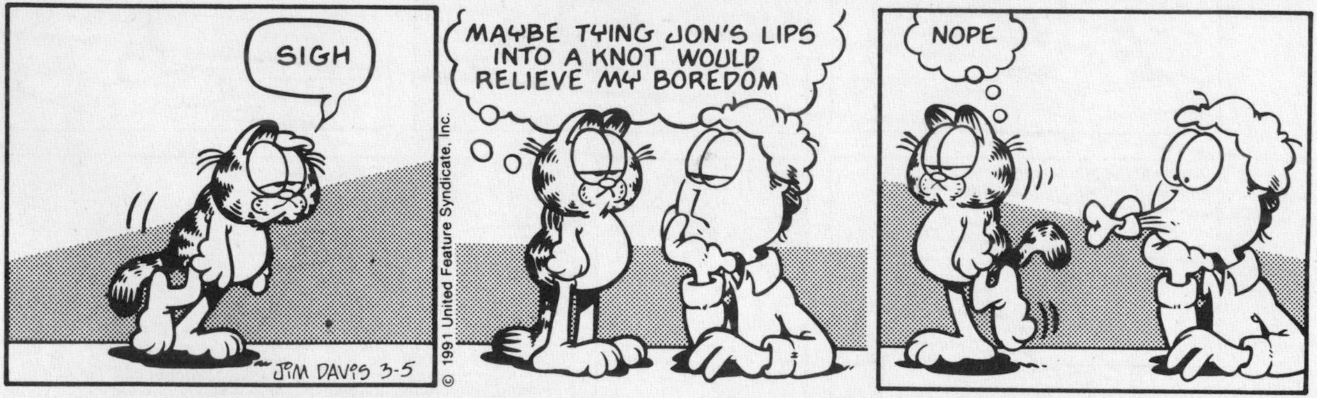
SIGH
MAYBE TYING JON'S LIPS INTO A KNOT WOULD RELIEVE MY BOREDOM
NOPE
JIM DAVIS 3-5
© 1991 United Feature Syndicate, Inc.

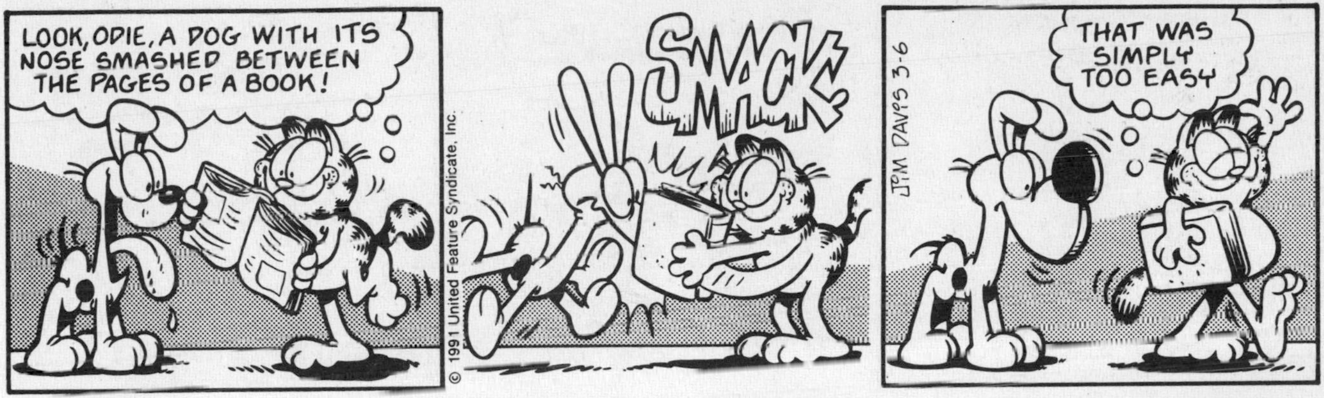
LOOK, ODIE, A DOG WITH ITS NOSE SMASHED BETWEEN THE PAGES OF A BOOK!
© 1991 United Feature Syndicate, Inc.
SMACK
JIM DAVIS 3-6
THAT WAS SIMPLY TOO EASY

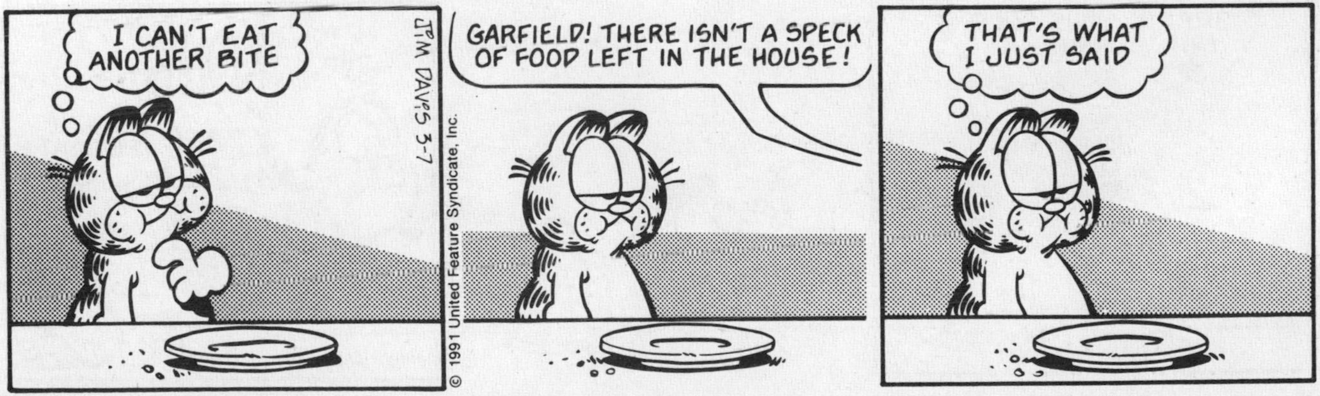
I CAN'T EAT ANOTHER BITE
JIM DAVIS 3-7
© 1991 United Feature Syndicate, Inc.
GARFIELD! THERE ISN'T A SPECK OF FOOD LEFT IN THE HOUSE!
THAT'S WHAT I JUST SAID

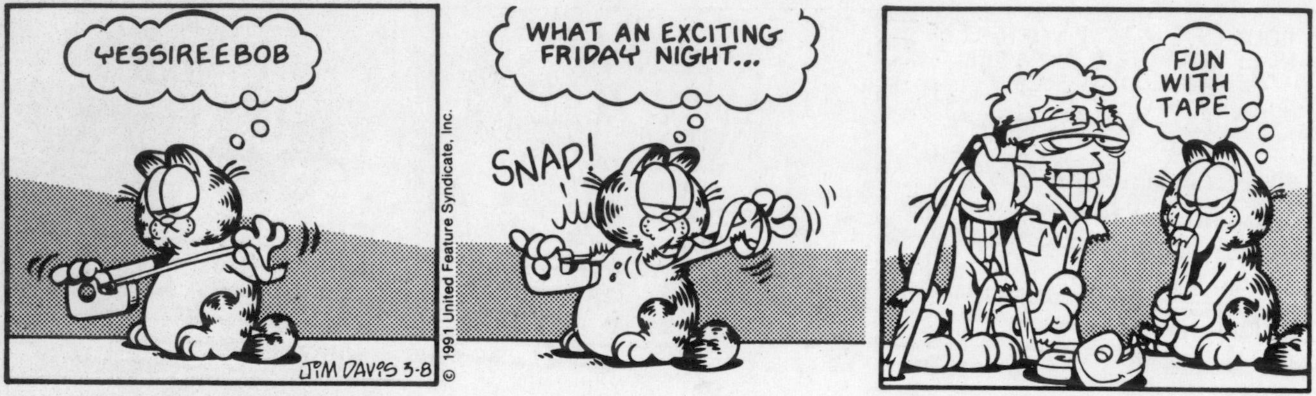
YESSIREEBOB
JIM DAVIS 3-8
© 1991 United Feature Syndicate, Inc.
WHAT AN EXCITING FRIDAY NIGHT...
SNAP!
FUN WITH TAPE

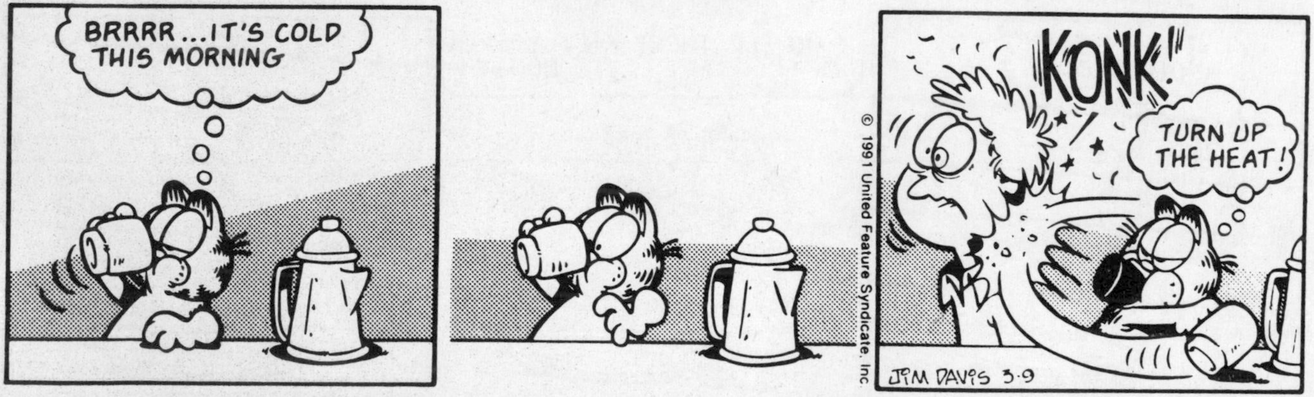
BRRRR...IT'S COLD THIS MORNING
© 1991 United Feature Syndicate, Inc.
KONK!
TURN UP THE HEAT!
JIM DAVIS 3-9

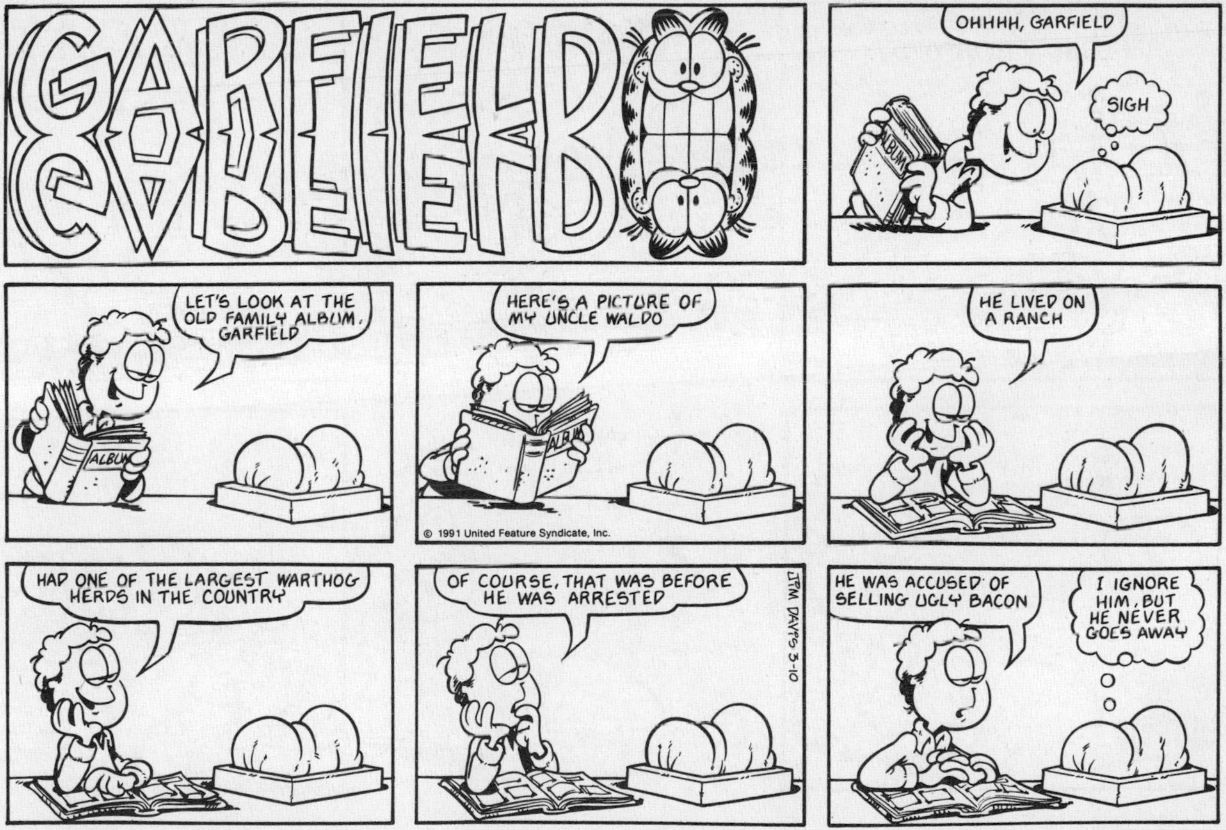
GARFIELD
OHHHH, GARFIELD
SIGH
LET'S LOOK AT THE OLD FAMILY ALBUM, GARFIELD
ALBUM
HERE'S A PICTURE OF MY UNCLE WALDO
ALBUM
© 1991 United Feature Syndicate, Inc.
HE LIVED ON A RANCH
HAD ONE OF THE LARGEST WARTHOG HERDS IN THE COUNTRY
OF COURSE, THAT WAS BEFORE HE WAS ARRESTED
JIM DAVIS 3-10
HE WAS ACCUSED OF SELLING UGLY BACON
I IGNORE HIM, BUT HE NEVER GOES AWAY

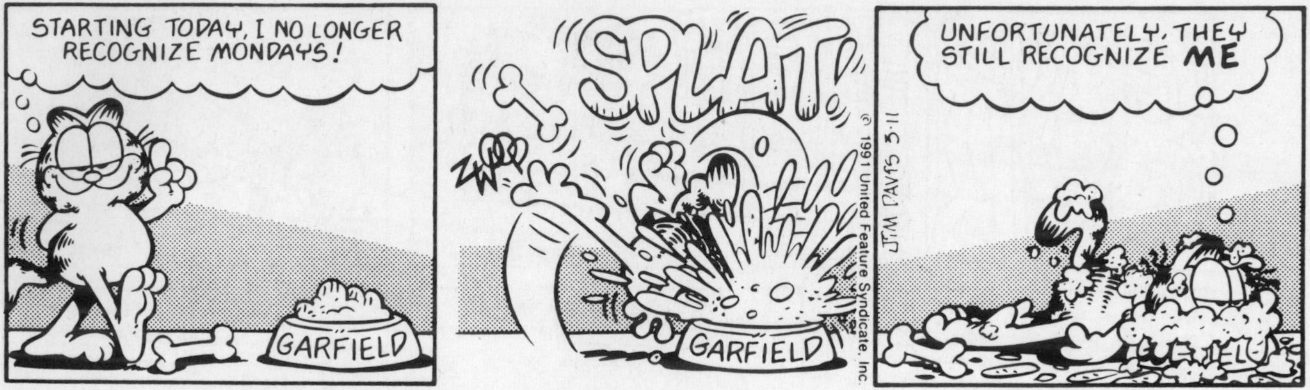
STARTING TODAY, I NO LONGER RECOGNIZE MONDAYS!
SPLAT!
UNFORTUNATELY, THEY STILL RECOGNIZE ME
GARFIELD
© 1991 United Feature Syndicate, Inc.
JIM DAVIS 3-11

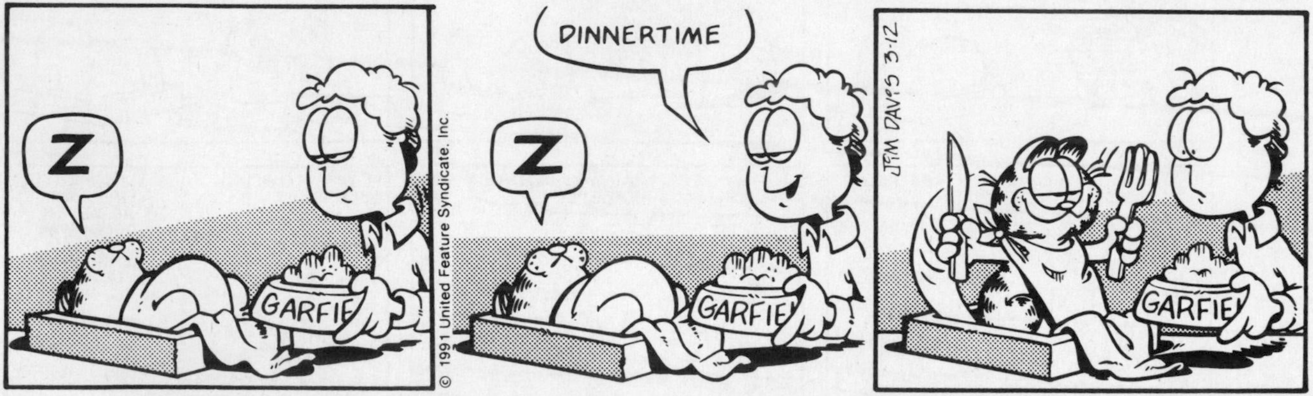
Z
Z
DINNERTIME
© 1991 United Feature Syndicate, Inc.
JIM DAVIS 3-12

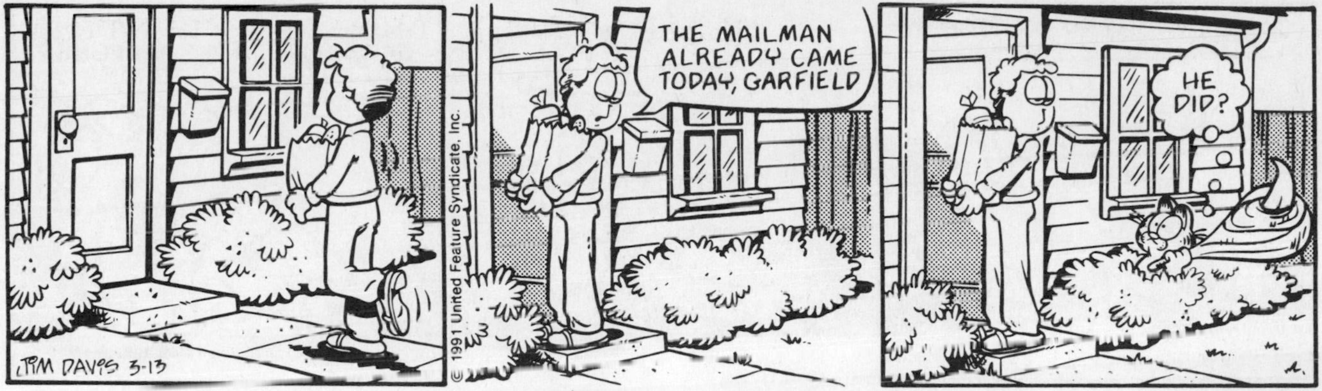
JIM DAVIS 3-13
© 1991 United Feature Syndicate, Inc.
THE MAILMAN ALREADY CAME TODAY, GARFIELD
HE DID?

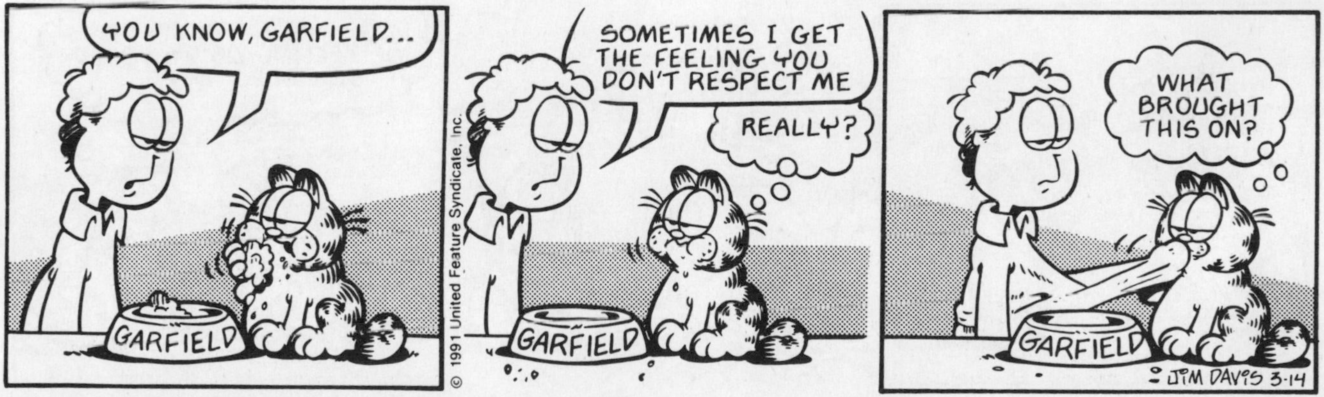
YOU KNOW, GARFIELD...
GARFIELD
© 1991 United Feature Syndicate, Inc.
SOMETIMES I GET THE FEELING YOU DON'T RESPECT ME
REALLY?
GARFIELD
WHAT BROUGHT THIS ON?
GARFIELD
JIM DAVIS 3-14

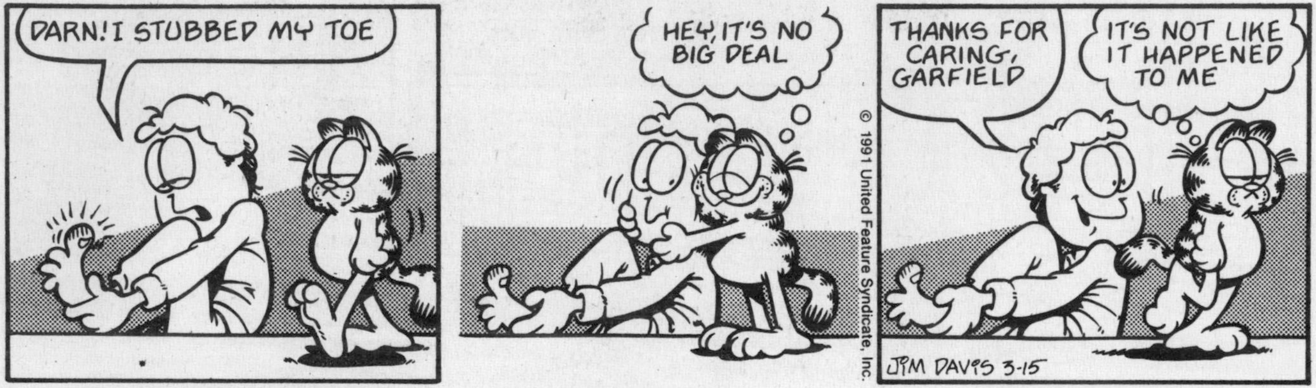
DARN! I STUBBED MY TOE
HEY, IT'S NO BIG DEAL
THANKS FOR CARING, GARFIELD
IT'S NOT LIKE IT HAPPENED TO ME
JIM DAVIS 3-15
© 1991 United Feature Syndicate, Inc.

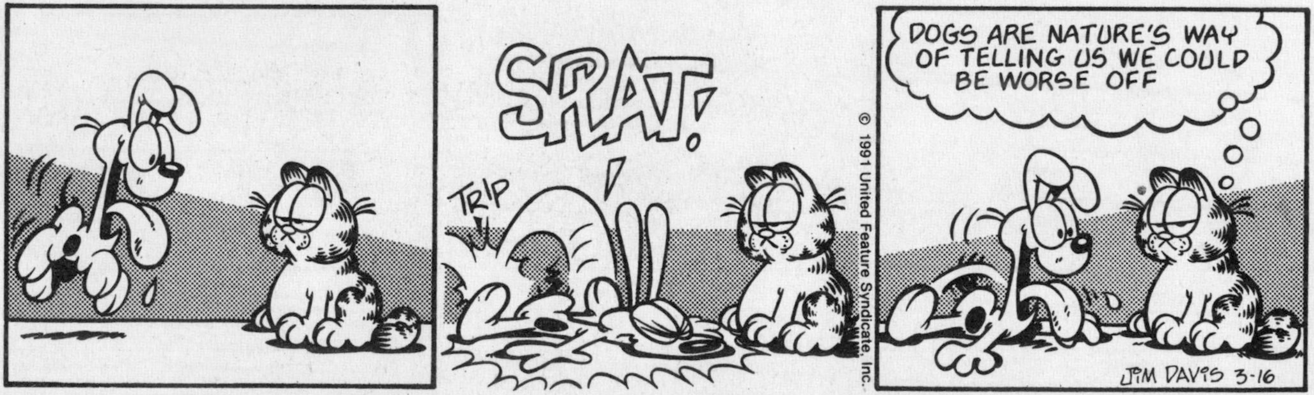
TRIP
SPLAT!
DOGS ARE NATURE'S WAY OF TELLING US WE COULD BE WORSE OFF
JIM DAVIS 3-16
© 1991 United Feature Syndicate, Inc.

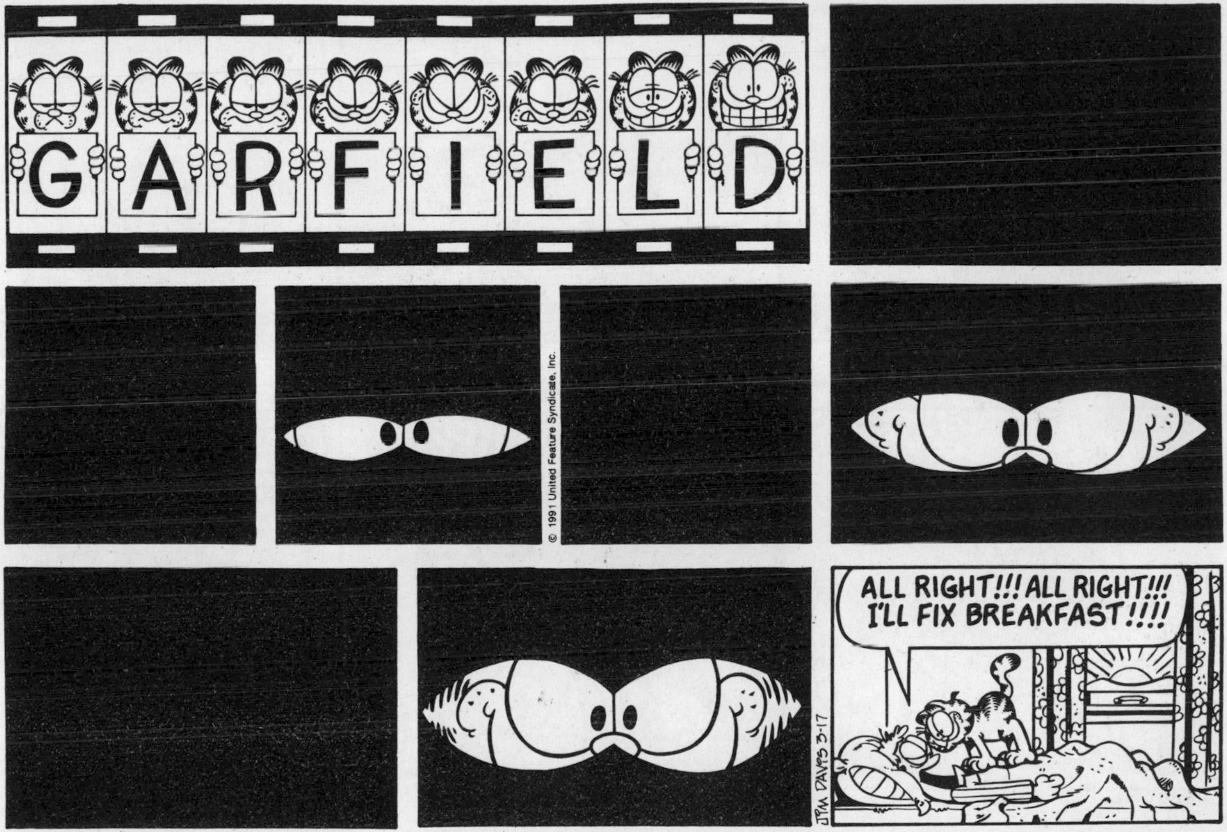
GARFIELD
© 1991 United Feature Syndicate, Inc.
JIM DAVIS 3-17
ALL RIGHT!!! ALL RIGHT!!! I'LL FIX BREAKFAST!!!!

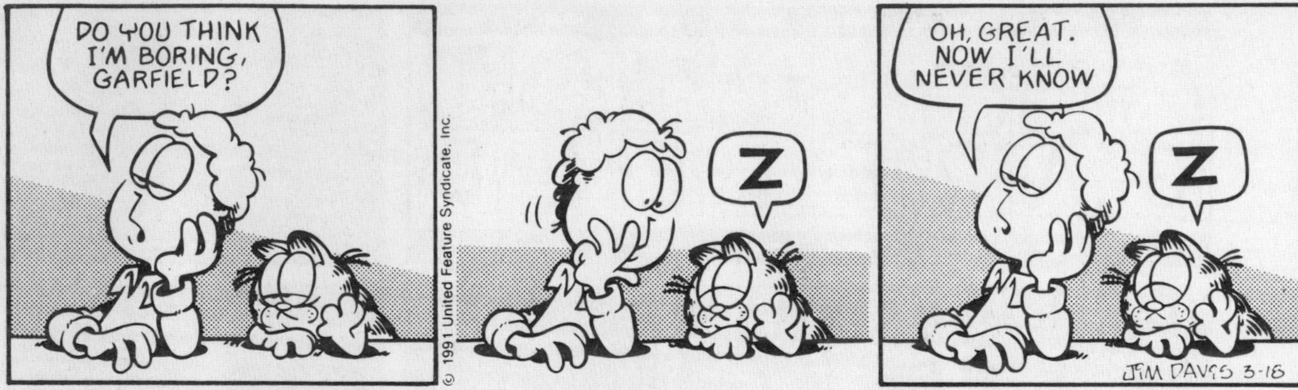
DO YOU THINK I'M BORING, GARFIELD?
Z
OH, GREAT. NOW I'LL NEVER KNOW
JIM DAVIS 3-18
© 1991 United Feature Syndicate, Inc.

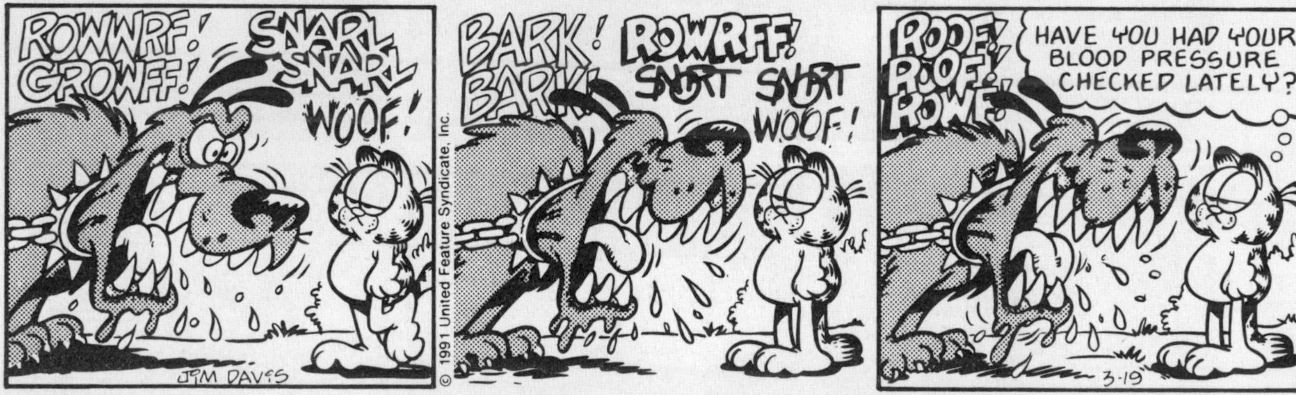
ROWWRF! GROWFF!
SNARL SNARL
WOOF!
JIM DAVIS
BARK! BARK!
ROWRFF!
SNORT SNORT
WOOF!
ROOF! ROOF! ROWF!
HAVE YOU HAD YOUR BLOOD PRESSURE CHECKED LATELY?
3-19
© 1991 United Feature Syndicate, Inc.

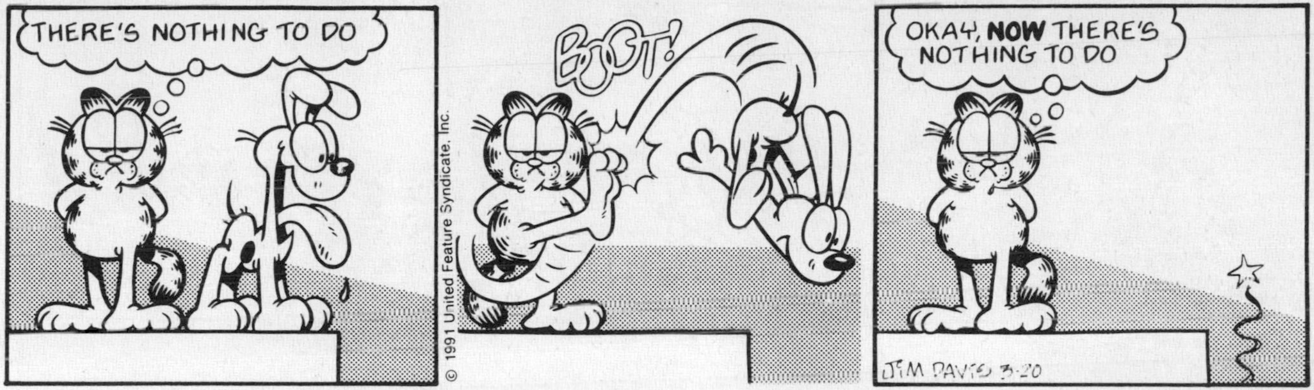
THERE'S NOTHING TO DO
BOOT!
© 1991 United Feature Syndicate, Inc.
OKAY, **NOW** THERE'S NOTHING TO DO
JIM DAVIS 3-20

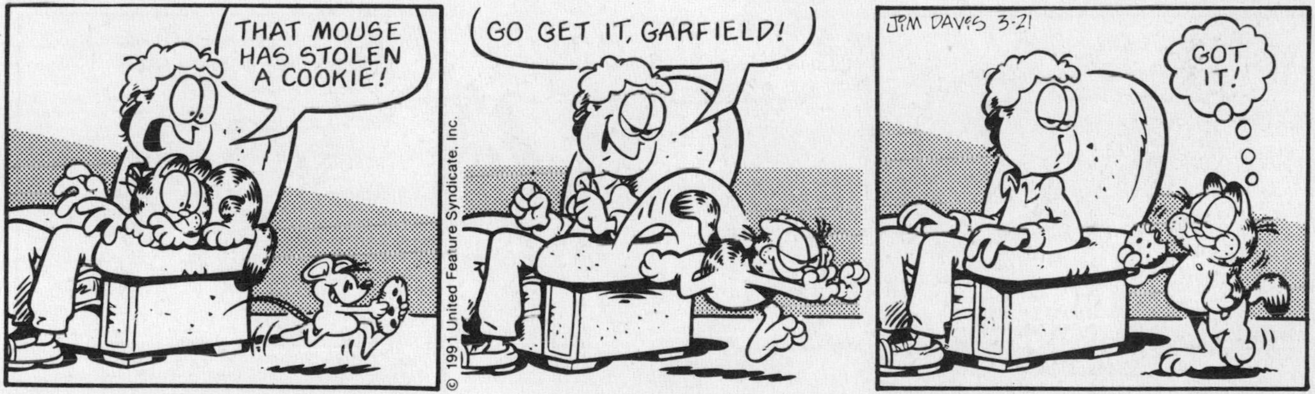
THAT MOUSE HAS STOLEN A COOKIE!
© 1991 United Feature Syndicate, Inc.
GO GET IT, GARFIELD!
JIM DAVIS 3-21
GOT IT!

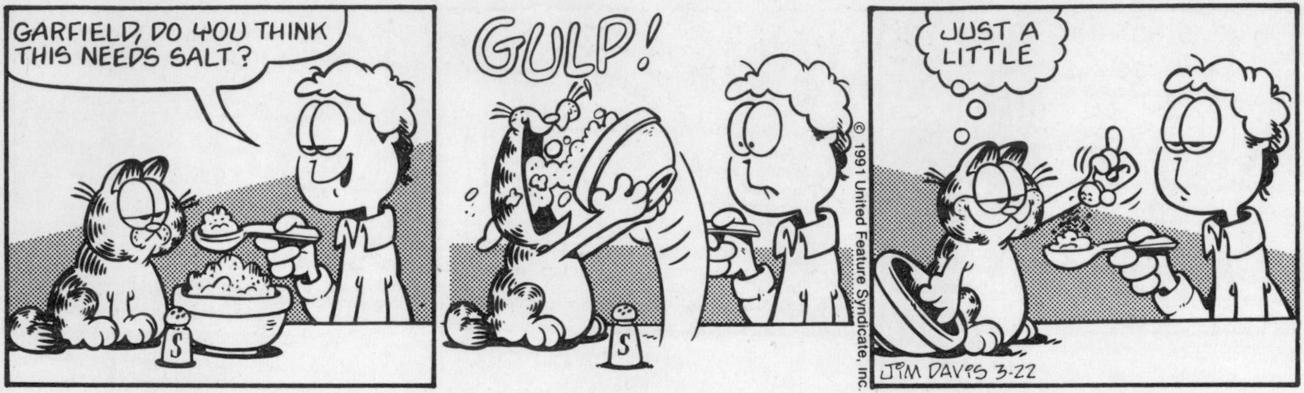
GARFIELD, DO YOU THINK THIS NEEDS SALT?
GULP!
JUST A LITTLE
S
© 1991 United Feature Syndicate, Inc.
JIM DAVIS 3-22

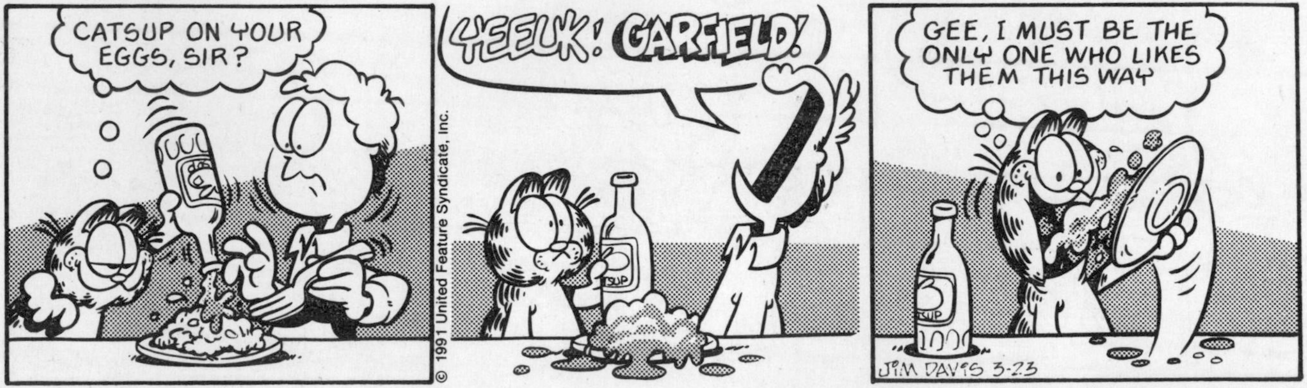
CATSUP ON YOUR EGGS, SIR?
YEEUK! GARFIELD!
GEE, I MUST BE THE ONLY ONE WHO LIKES THEM THIS WAY
© 1991 United Feature Syndicate, Inc.
JIM DAVIS 3-23

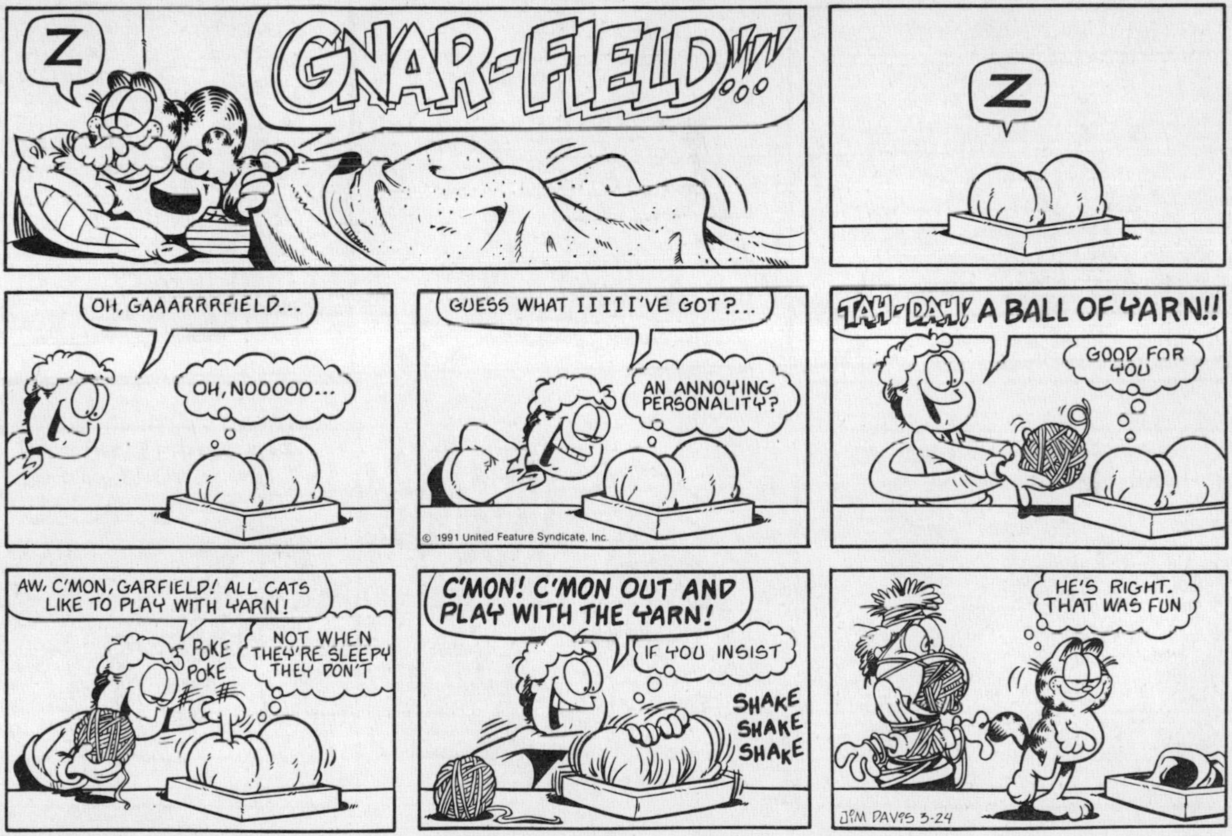
Z
GNAR-FIELD!!!
Z
OH, GAAARRRFIELD...
OH, NOOOOO...
GUESS WHAT IIIII'VE GOT?...
AN ANNOYING PERSONALITY?
© 1991 United Feature Syndicate, Inc.
TAH-DAH! A BALL OF YARN!!
GOOD FOR YOU
AW, C'MON, GARFIELD! ALL CATS LIKE TO PLAY WITH YARN!
POKE POKE
NOT WHEN THEY'RE SLEEPY THEY DON'T
C'MON! C'MON OUT AND PLAY WITH THE YARN!
IF YOU INSIST
SHAKE SHAKE SHAKE
HE'S RIGHT. THAT WAS FUN
JIM DAVIS 3-24

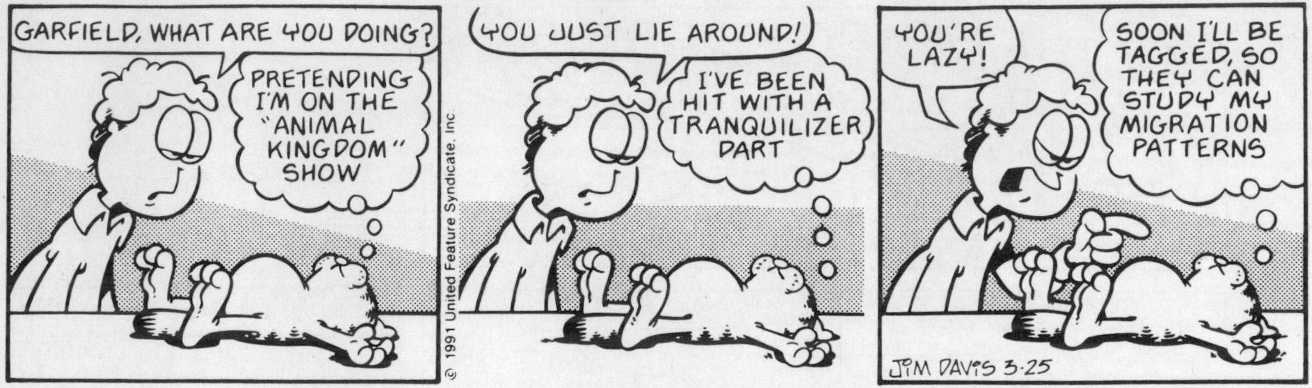
GARFIELD, WHAT ARE YOU DOING?
PRETENDING I'M ON THE "ANIMAL KINGDOM" SHOW
YOU JUST LIE AROUND!
I'VE BEEN HIT WITH A TRANQUILIZER DART
YOU'RE LAZY!
SOON I'LL BE TAGGED, SO THEY CAN STUDY MY MIGRATION PATTERNS
JIM DAVIS 3-25

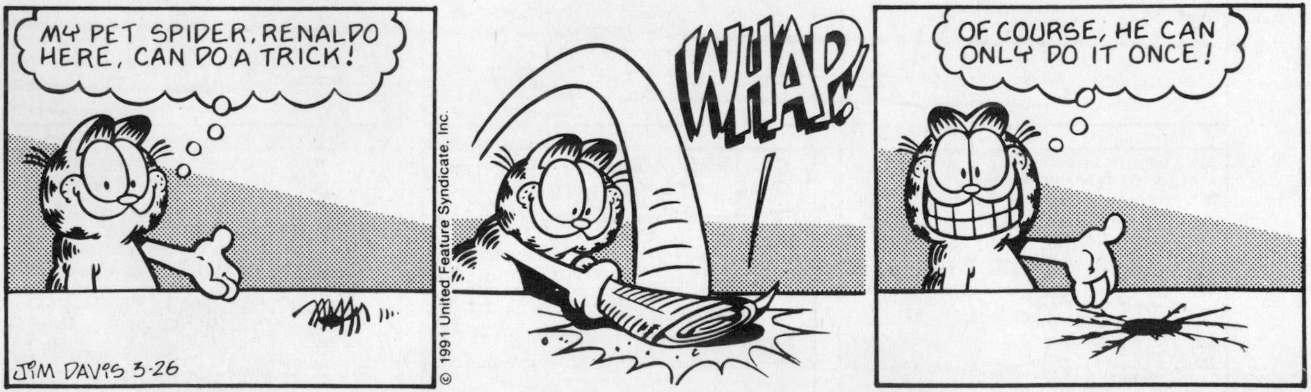
MY PET SPIDER, RENALDO HERE, CAN DO A TRICK!
JIM DAVIS 3-26
WHAP!
OF COURSE, HE CAN ONLY DO IT ONCE!

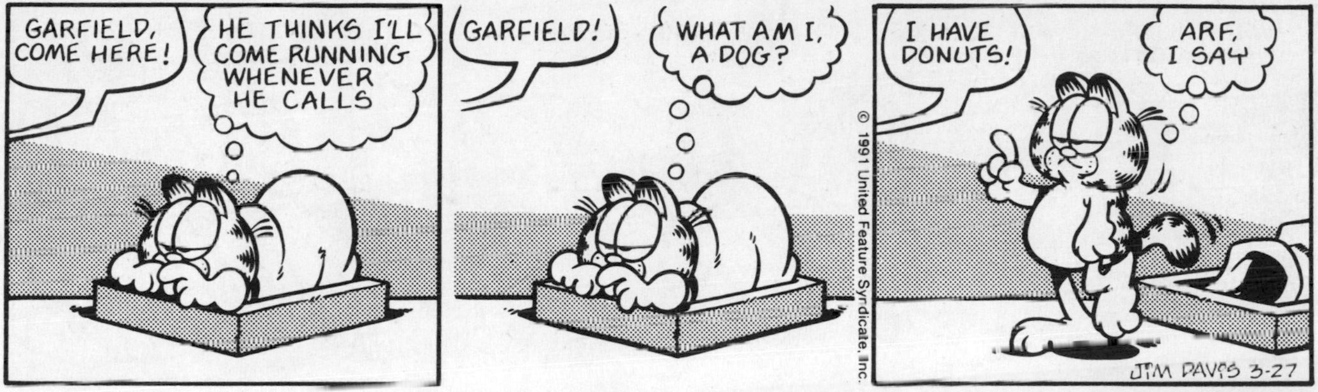
GARFIELD, COME HERE!
HE THINKS I'LL COME RUNNING WHENEVER HE CALLS
GARFIELD!
WHAT AM I, A DOG?
I HAVE DONUTS!
ARF, I SAY
JIM DAVIS 3-27
© 1991 United Feature Syndicate, Inc.

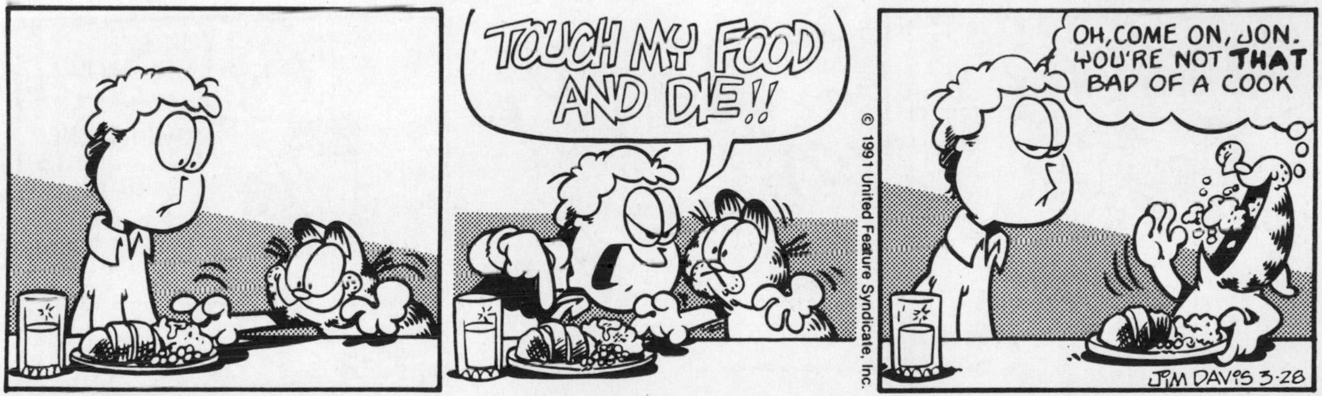
TOUCH MY FOOD AND DIE!!
OH, COME ON, JON. YOU'RE NOT THAT BAD OF A COOK
JIM DAVIS 3-28
© 1991 United Feature Syndicate, Inc.

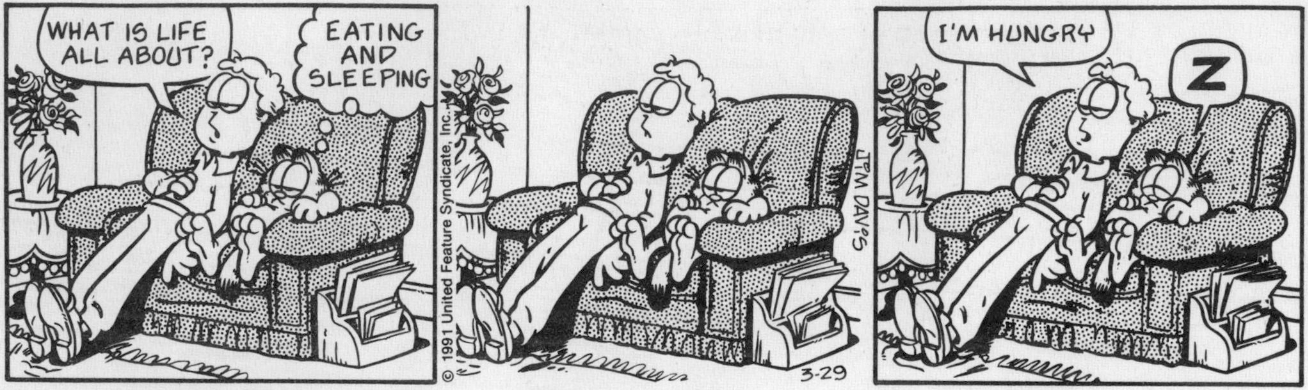
WHAT IS LIFE ALL ABOUT?
EATING AND SLEEPING
© 1991 United Feature Syndicate, Inc.
JIM DAVIS
3-29
I'M HUNGRY
Z

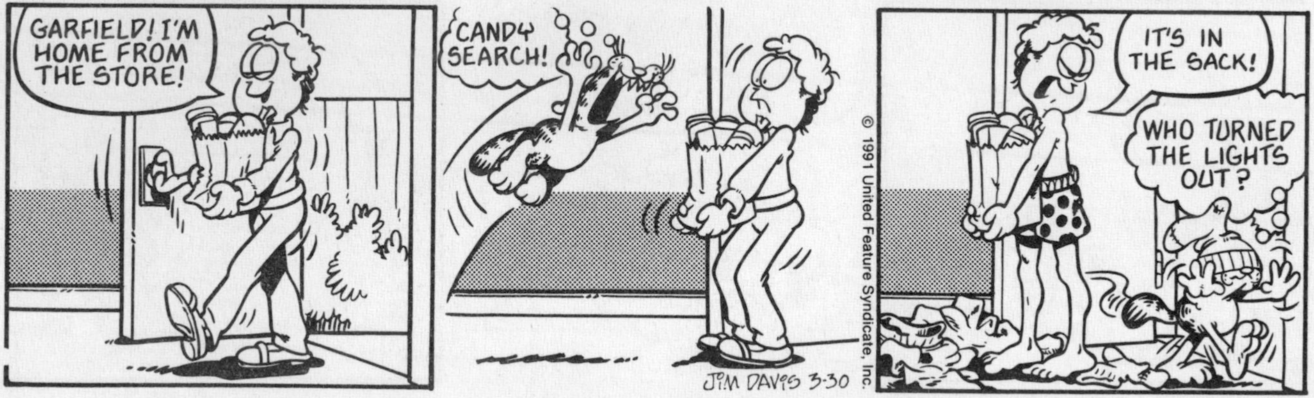
GARFIELD! I'M HOME FROM THE STORE!
CANDY SEARCH!
JIM DAVIS 3-30
© 1991 United Feature Syndicate, Inc.
IT'S IN THE SACK!
WHO TURNED THE LIGHTS OUT?

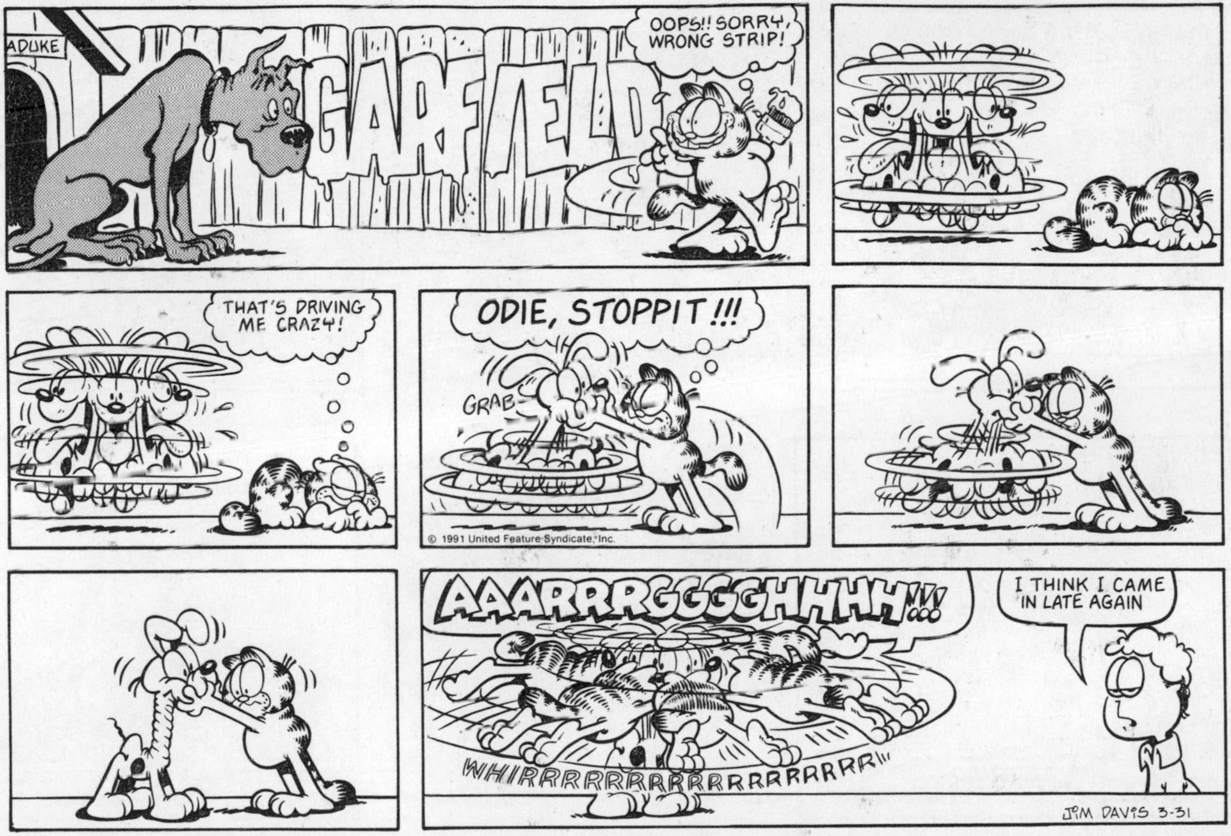
ADUKE
GARFIELD
OOPS!! SORRY, WRONG STRIP!
THAT'S DRIVING ME CRAZY!
ODIE, STOPPIT!!!
GRAB
© 1991 United Feature Syndicate, Inc.
AAARRRGGGGHHHH!!!
I THINK I CAME IN LATE AGAIN
WHIRRRRRRRRRRRRRRRRRR
JIM DAVIS 3-31

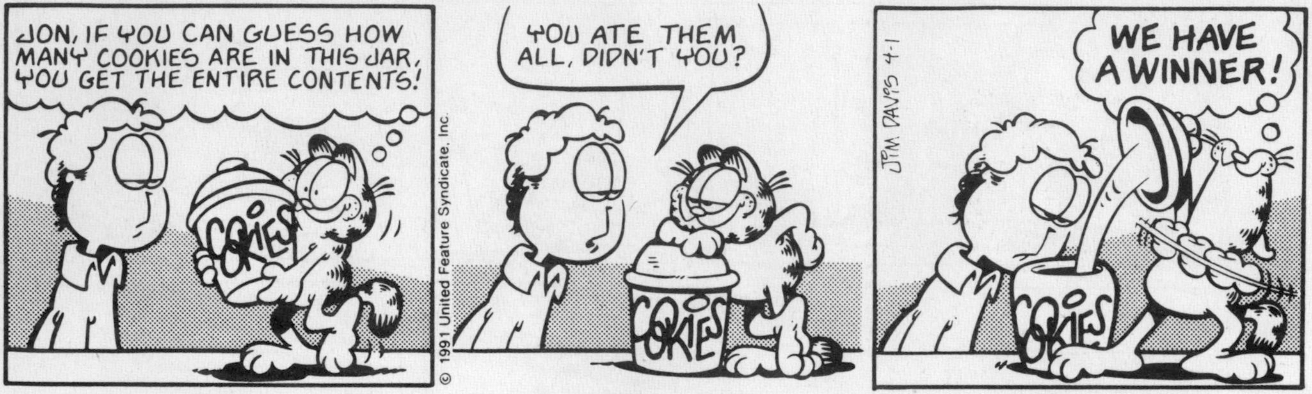
JON, IF YOU CAN GUESS HOW MANY COOKIES ARE IN THIS JAR, YOU GET THE ENTIRE CONTENTS!
COOKIES
YOU ATE THEM ALL, DIDN'T YOU?
COOKIES
WE HAVE A WINNER!
COOKIES
JIM DAVIS 4-1

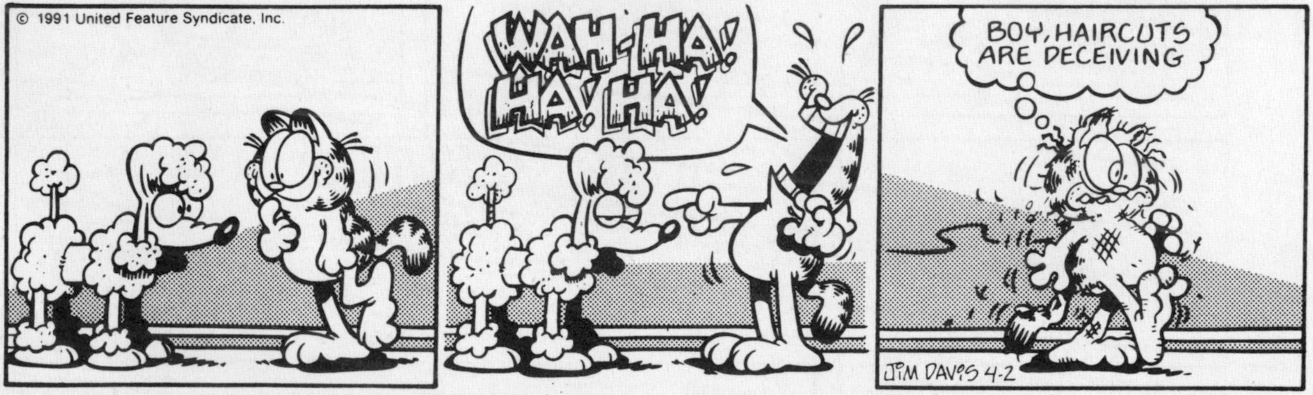
WAH-HA! HA! HA!
BOY, HAIRCUTS ARE DECEIVING
JIM DAVIS 4-2

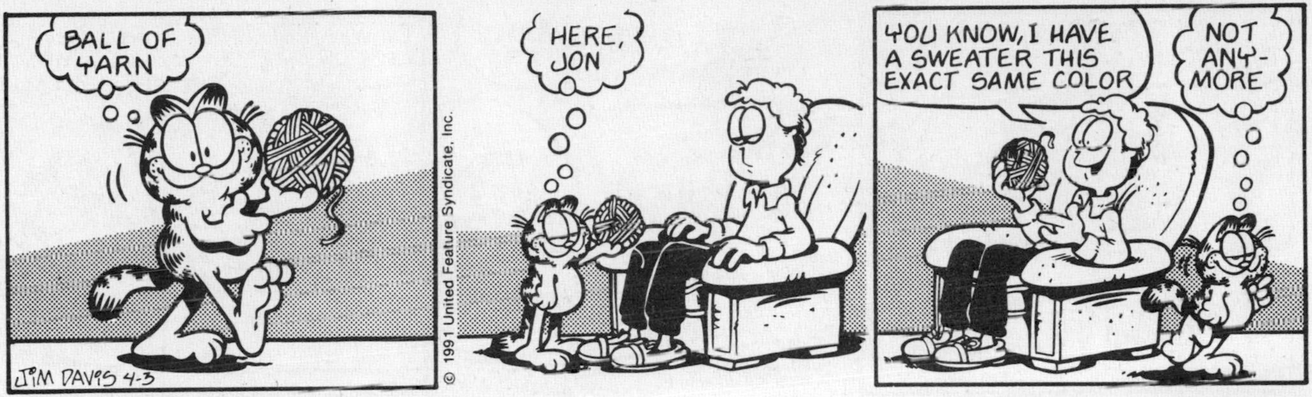
BALL OF YARN
JIM DAVIS 4-3
© 1991 United Feature Syndicate, Inc.
HERE, JON
YOU KNOW, I HAVE A SWEATER THIS EXACT SAME COLOR
NOT ANY-MORE

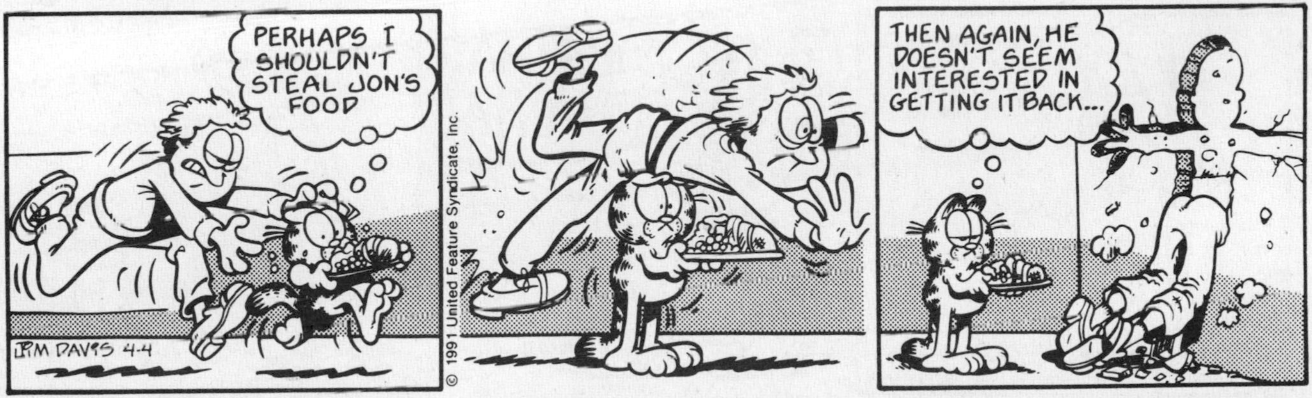
PERHAPS I SHOULDN'T STEAL JON'S FOOD
JIM DAVIS 4-4
© 1991 United Feature Syndicate, Inc.
THEN AGAIN, HE DOESN'T SEEM INTERESTED IN GETTING IT BACK...

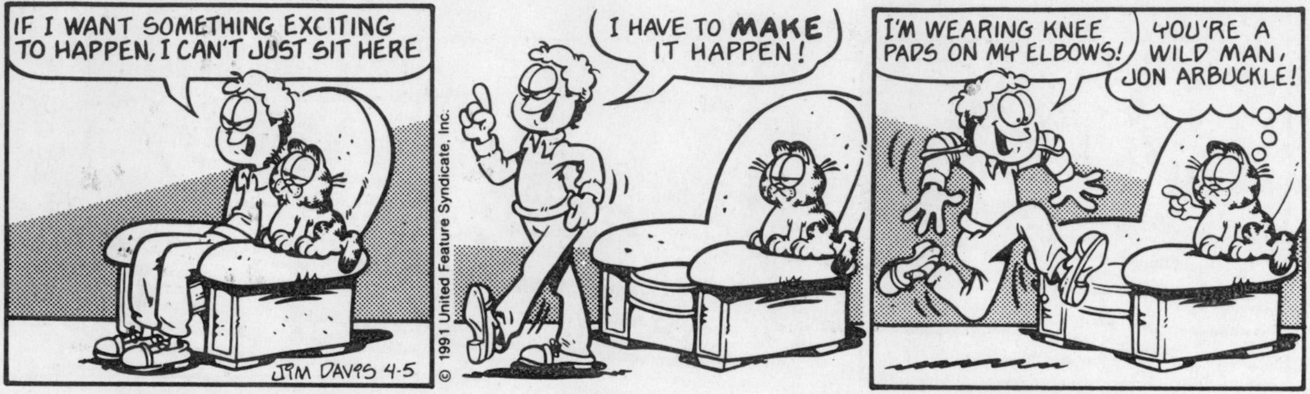
IF I WANT SOMETHING EXCITING TO HAPPEN, I CAN'T JUST SIT HERE
JIM DAVIS 4-5
© 1991 United Feature Syndicate, Inc.
I HAVE TO **MAKE** IT HAPPEN!
I'M WEARING KNEE PADS ON MY ELBOWS!
YOU'RE A WILD MAN, JON ARBUCKLE!

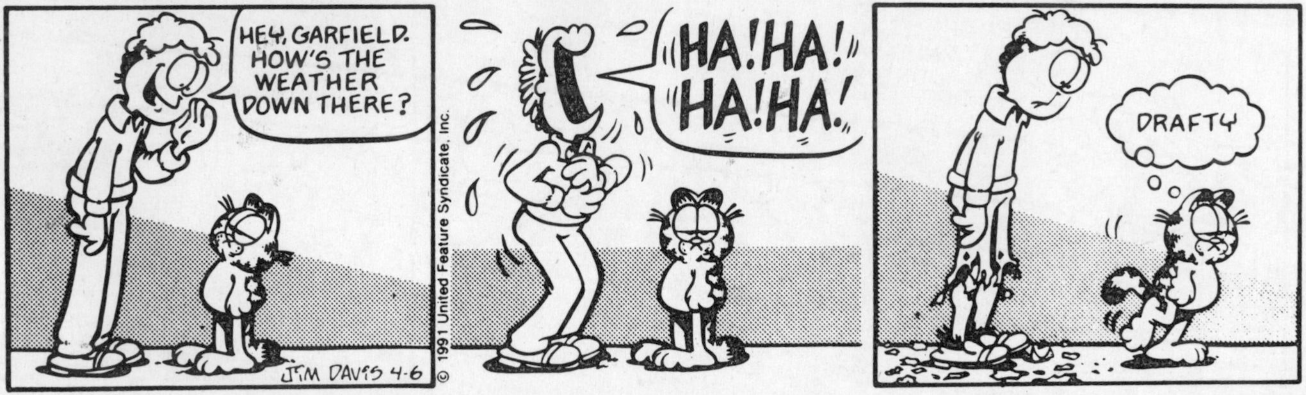
HEY, GARFIELD. HOW'S THE WEATHER DOWN THERE?
JIM DAVIS 4-6
© 1991 United Feature Syndicate, Inc.
HA! HA! HA! HA!
DRAFTY

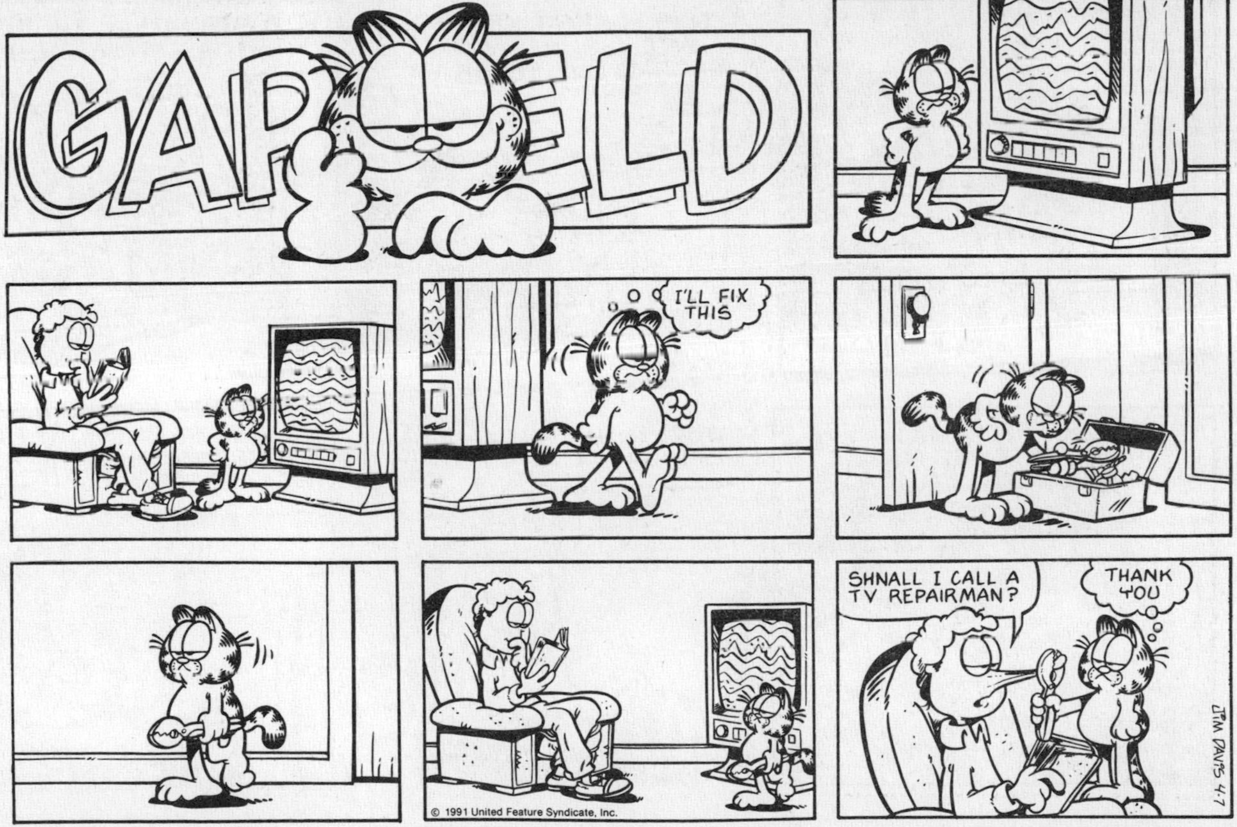
GARFIELD
I'LL FIX THIS
SHNALL I CALL A TV REPAIRMAN?
THANK YOU
JIM DAVIS 4-7
© 1991 United Feature Syndicate, Inc.

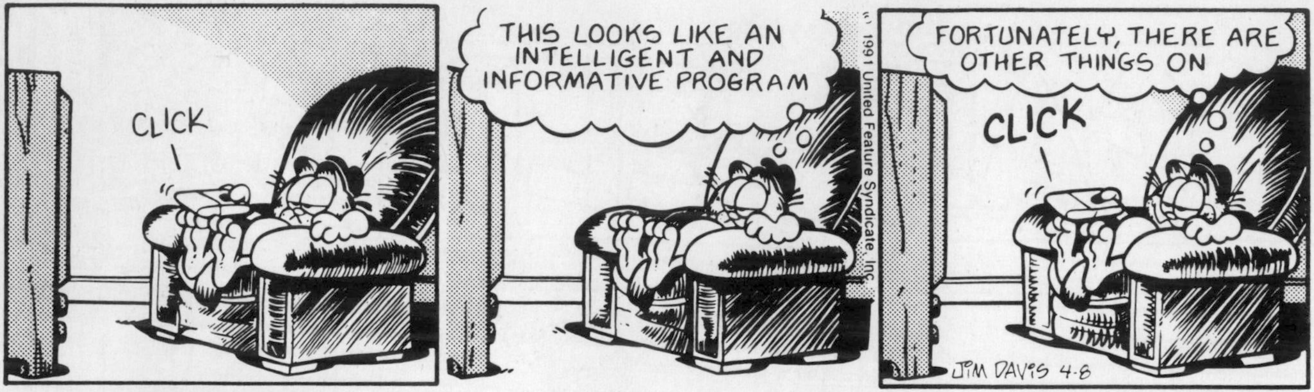
CLICK
THIS LOOKS LIKE AN INTELLIGENT AND INFORMATIVE PROGRAM
FORTUNATELY, THERE ARE OTHER THINGS ON
CLICK
JIM DAVIS 4-8
© 1991 United Feature Syndicate, Inc.

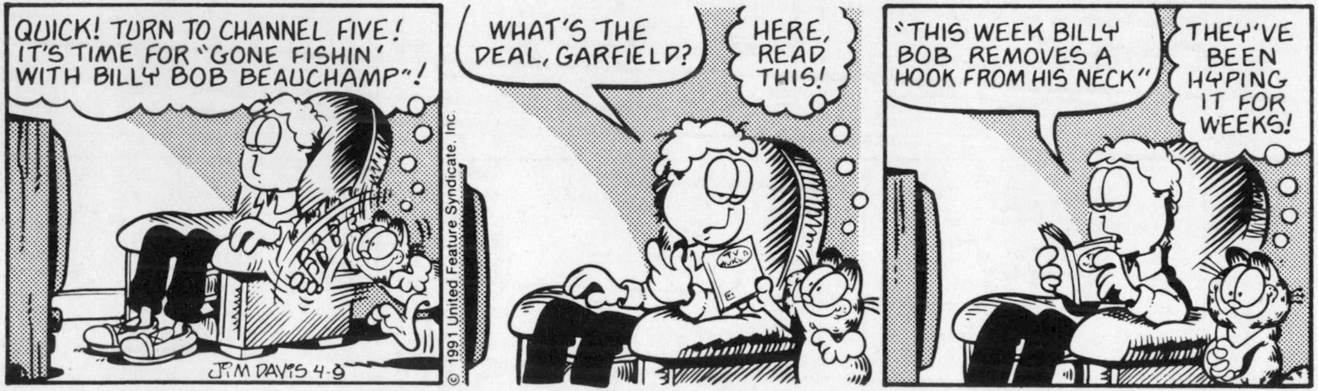
QUICK! TURN TO CHANNEL FIVE! IT'S TIME FOR "GONE FISHIN' WITH BILLY BOB BEAUCHAMP"!
JIM DAVIS 4-9
© 1991 United Feature Syndicate, Inc.
WHAT'S THE DEAL, GARFIELD?
HERE, READ THIS!
"THIS WEEK BILLY BOB REMOVES A HOOK FROM HIS NECK"
THEY'VE BEEN HYPING IT FOR WEEKS!

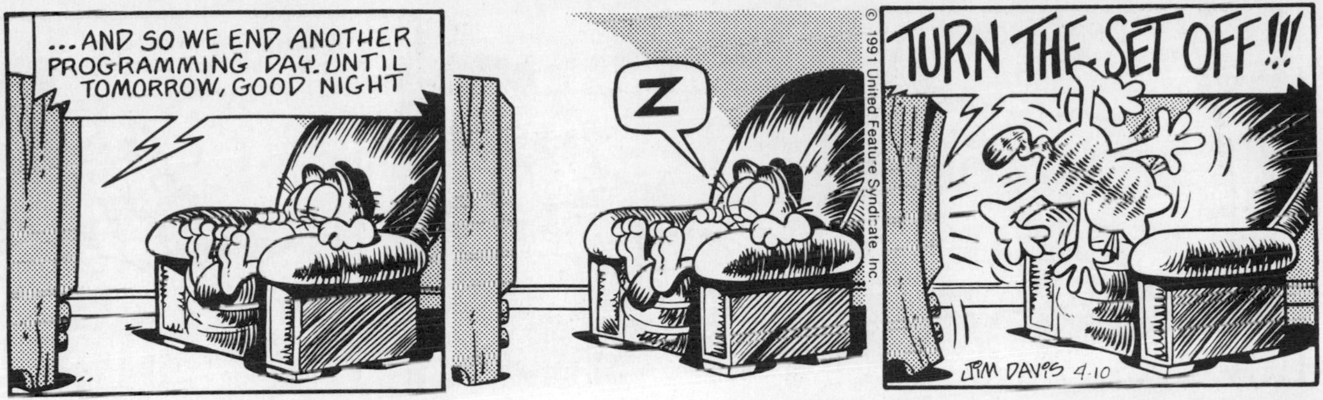
...AND SO WE END ANOTHER PROGRAMMING DAY. UNTIL TOMORROW, GOOD NIGHT
Z
TURN THE SET OFF!!!
© 1991 United Feature Syndicate, Inc.
JIM DAVIS 4-10

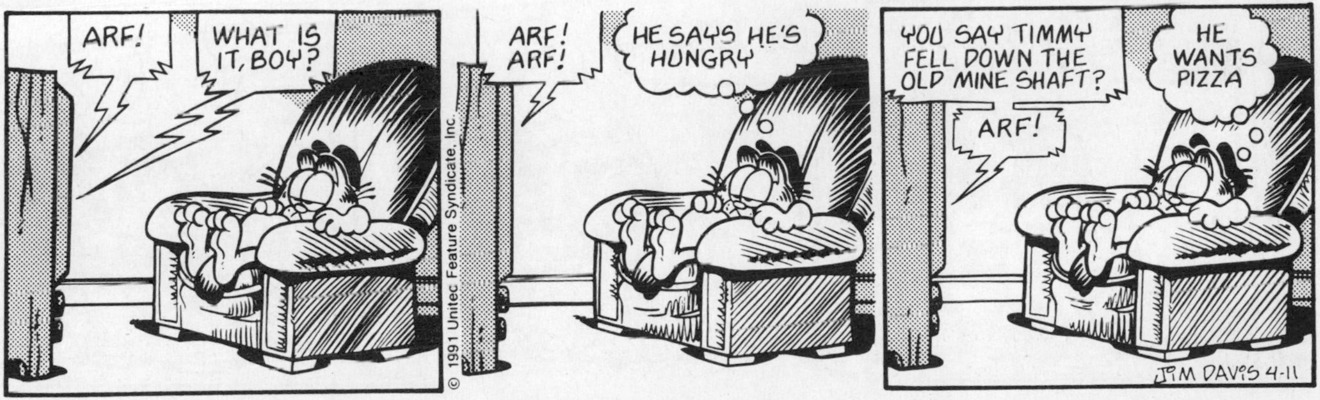
ARF!
WHAT IS IT, BOY?
ARF! ARF!
HE SAYS HE'S HUNGRY
YOU SAY TIMMY FELL DOWN THE OLD MINE SHAFT?
ARF!
HE WANTS PIZZA
© 1991 United Feature Syndicate, Inc.
JIM DAVIS 4-11

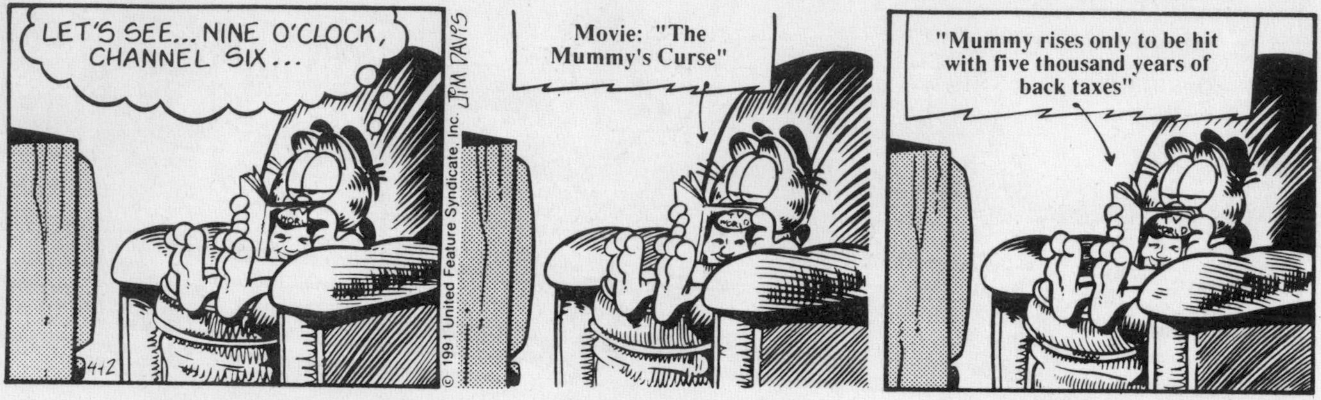
LET'S SEE... NINE O'CLOCK, CHANNEL SIX...
Movie: "The Mummy's Curse"
"Mummy rises only to be hit with five thousand years of back taxes"
© 1991 United Feature Syndicate, Inc.
JPM DAVIS
4-12

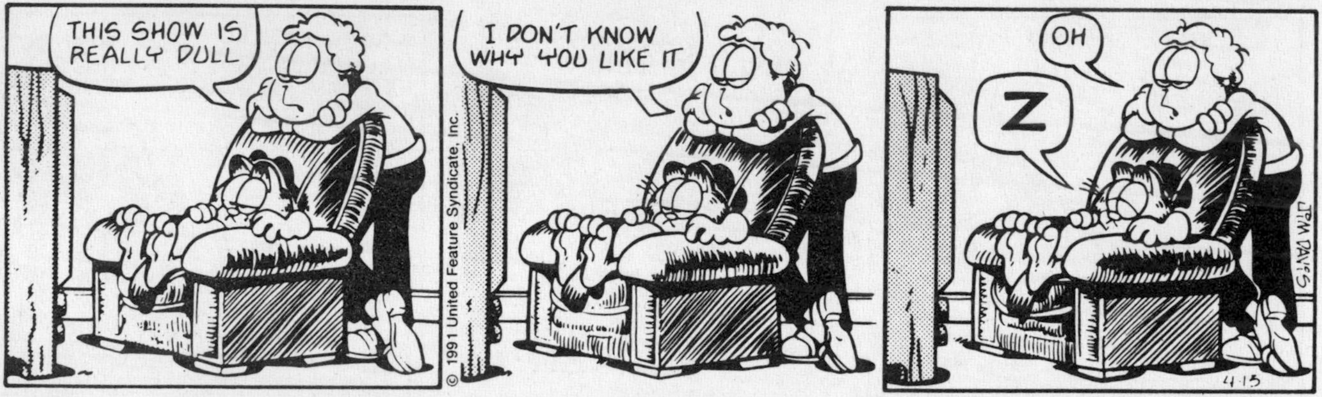
THIS SHOW IS REALLY DULL
I DON'T KNOW WHY YOU LIKE IT
Z
OH
© 1991 United Feature Syndicate, Inc.
JPM DAVIS
4-13

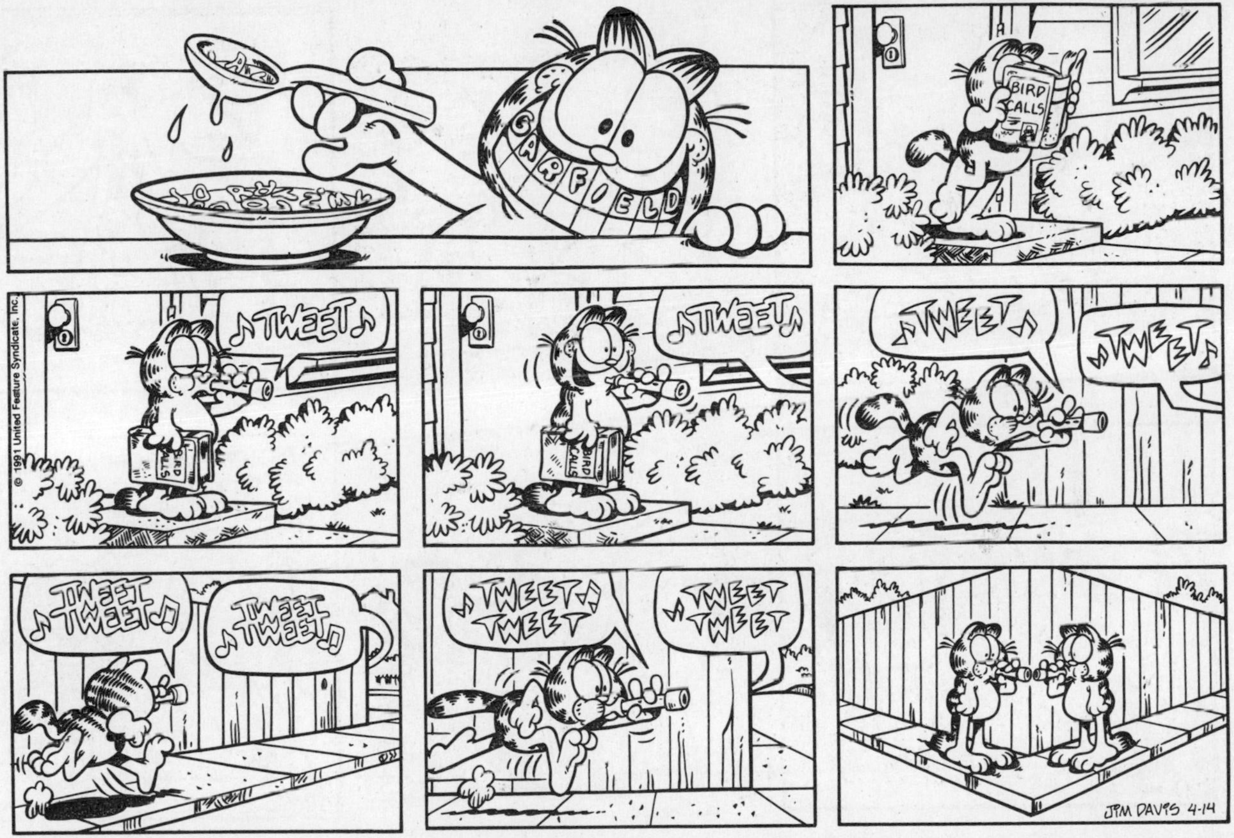

GARFIELD
BIRD CALLS
♪TWEET♪
© 1991 United Feature Syndicate, Inc.
BIRD CALLS
♪TWEET♪
BIRD CALLS
♪TWEET♪
♪TWEET♪
TWEET TWEET♪
♪TWEET TWEET♪
♪TWEET♪ TWEET
♪TWEET TWEET
JIM DAVIS 4-14

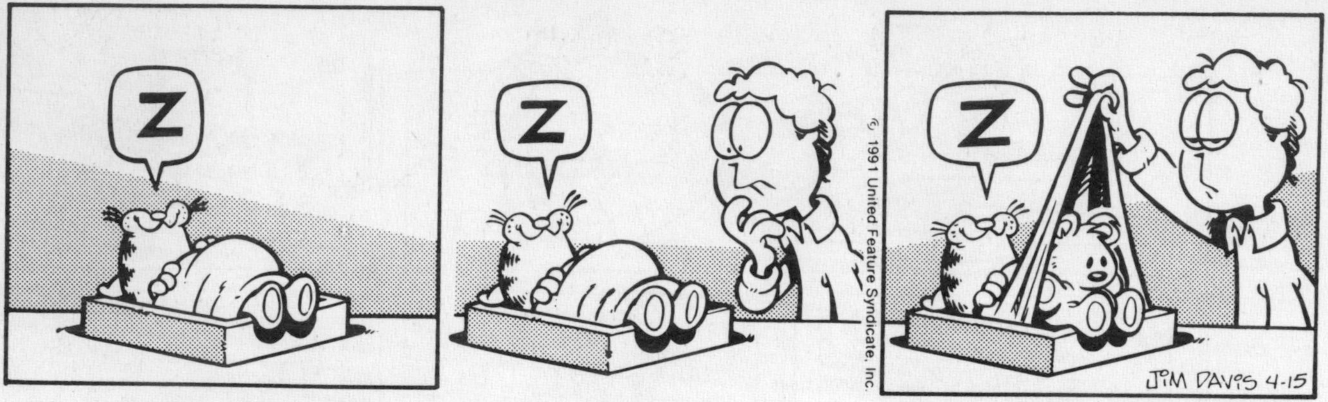
Z
Z
Z
© 1991 United Feature Syndicate, Inc.
JIM DAVIS 4-15

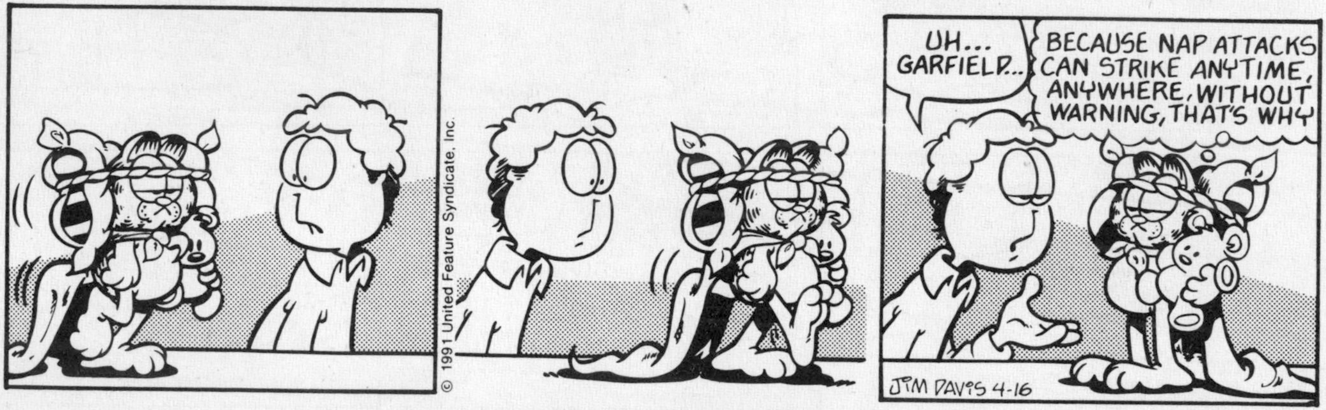
© 1991 United Feature Syndicate, Inc.
UH... GARFIELD...
BECAUSE NAP ATTACKS CAN STRIKE ANYTIME, ANYWHERE, WITHOUT WARNING, THAT'S WHY
JIM DAVIS 4-16

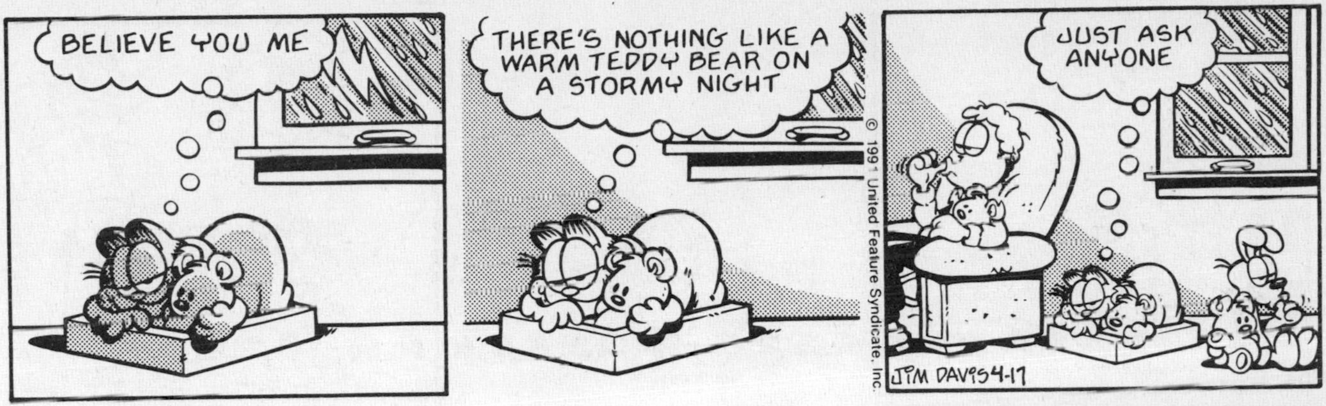
BELIEVE YOU ME
THERE'S NOTHING LIKE A WARM TEDDY BEAR ON A STORMY NIGHT
© 1991 United Feature Syndicate, Inc.
JUST ASK ANYONE
JIM DAVIS 4-17

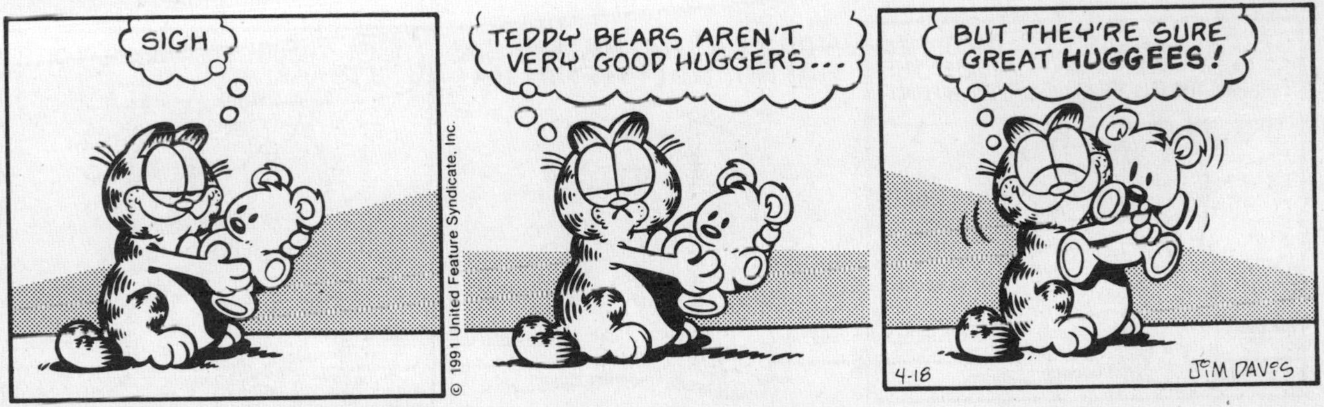
SIGH
© 1991 United Feature Syndicate, Inc.
TEDDY BEARS AREN'T VERY GOOD HUGGERS...
BUT THEY'RE SURE GREAT **HUGGEES!**
4-18
JIM DAVIS

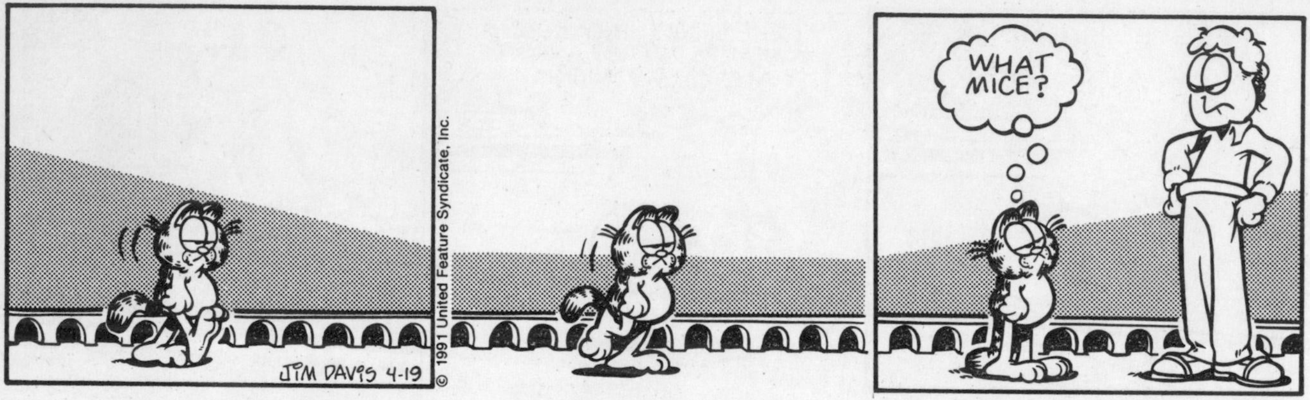
WHAT MICE?
JIM DAVIS 4-19
© 1991 United Feature Syndicate, Inc.

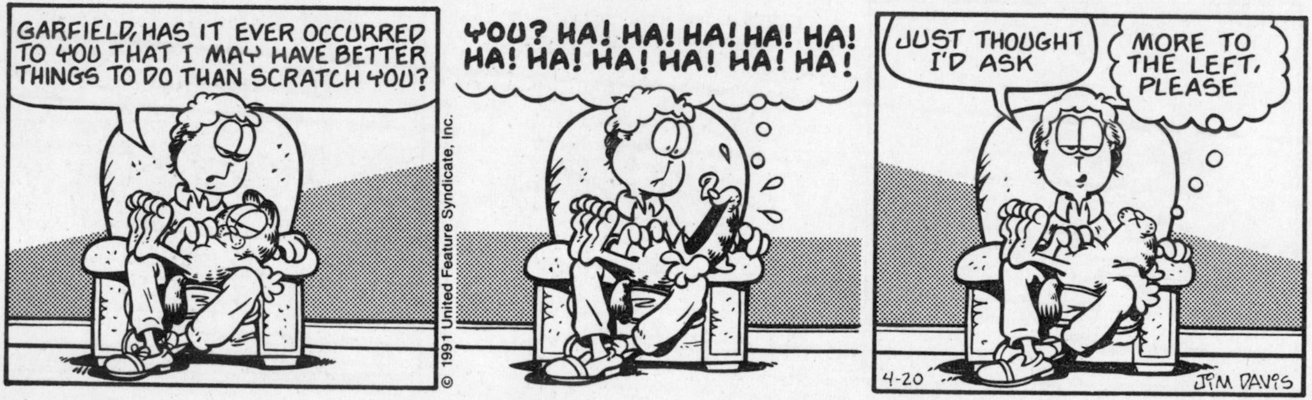
GARFIELD, HAS IT EVER OCCURRED TO YOU THAT I MAY HAVE BETTER THINGS TO DO THAN SCRATCH YOU?
YOU? HA! HA! HA! HA! HA! HA! HA! HA! HA! HA! HA!
JUST THOUGHT I'D ASK
MORE TO THE LEFT, PLEASE
4-20
JIM DAVIS
© 1991 United Feature Syndicate, Inc.

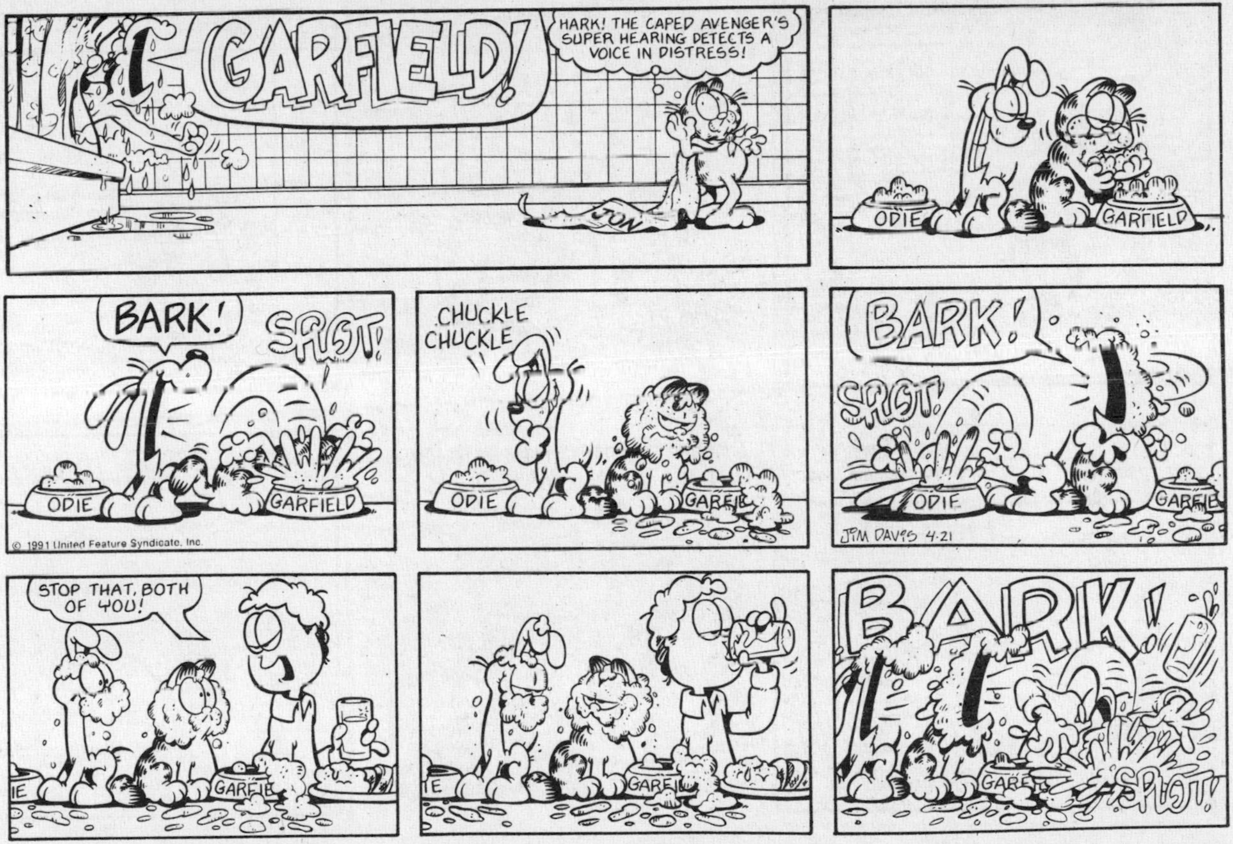
GARFIELD!
HARK! THE CAPED AVENGER'S SUPER HEARING DETECTS A VOICE IN DISTRESS!
JON
ODIE
GARFIELD
BARK!
SPLOT!
ODIE
GARFIELD
© 1991 United Feature Syndicate, Inc.
CHUCKLE CHUCKLE
ODIE
BARK!
SPLOT!
ODIE
JIM DAVIS 4-21
STOP THAT, BOTH OF YOU!
BARK!
SPLOT!

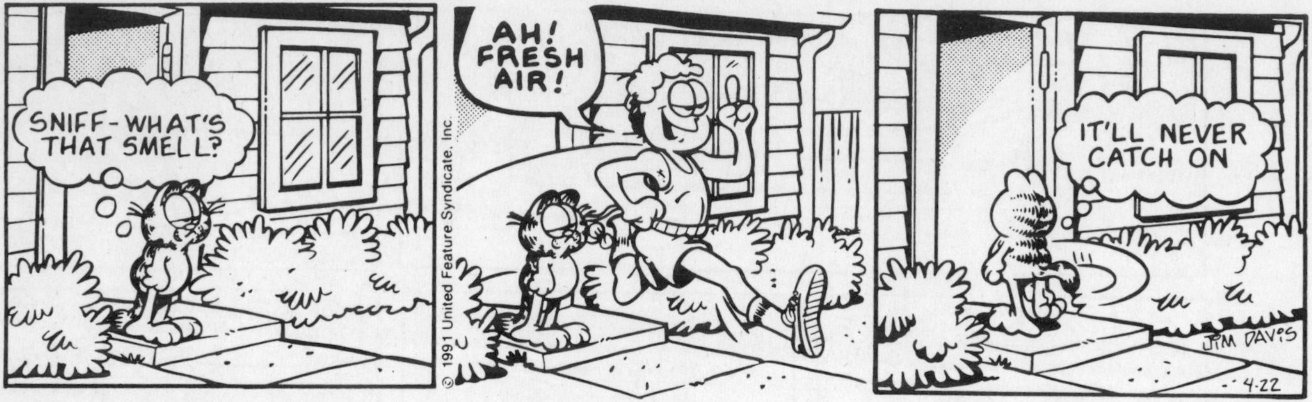
SNIFF-WHAT'S THAT SMELL?
AH! FRESH AIR!
IT'LL NEVER CATCH ON
© 1991 United Feature Syndicate, Inc.
JIM DAVIS
4-22

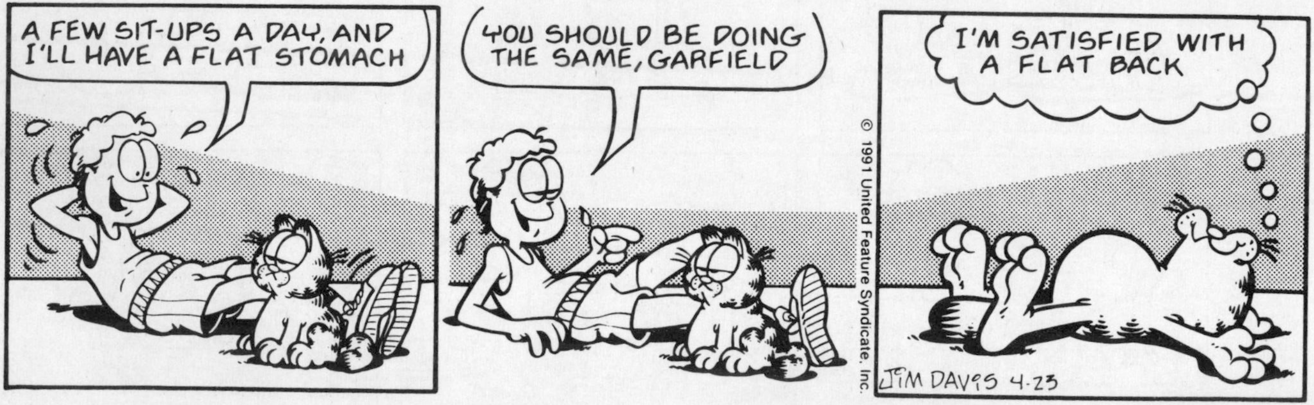
A FEW SIT-UPS A DAY, AND I'LL HAVE A FLAT STOMACH
YOU SHOULD BE DOING THE SAME, GARFIELD
I'M SATISFIED WITH A FLAT BACK
© 1991 United Feature Syndicate, Inc.
JIM DAVIS 4-23

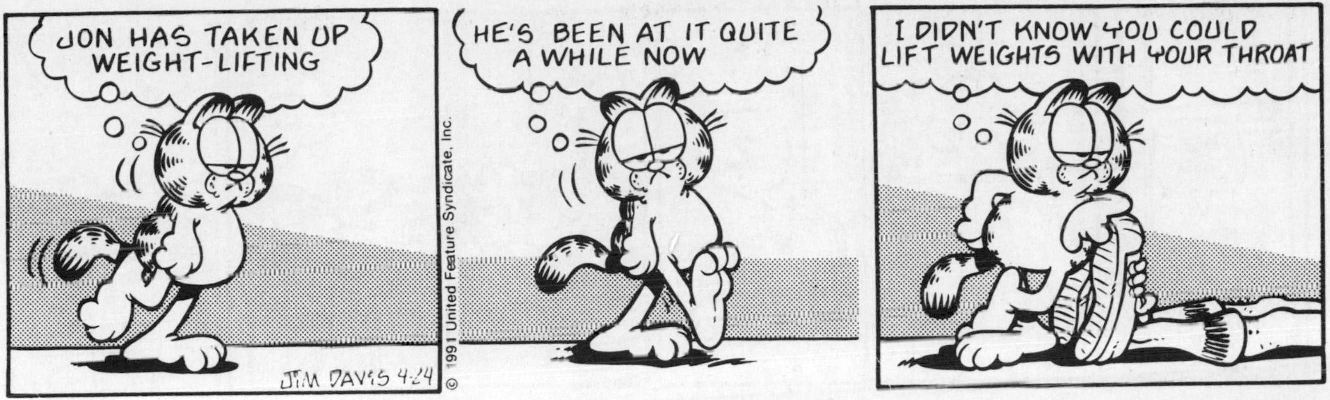
JON HAS TAKEN UP WEIGHT-LIFTING
JIM DAVIS 4-24
© 1991 United Feature Syndicate, Inc.
HE'S BEEN AT IT QUITE A WHILE NOW
I DIDN'T KNOW YOU COULD LIFT WEIGHTS WITH YOUR THROAT

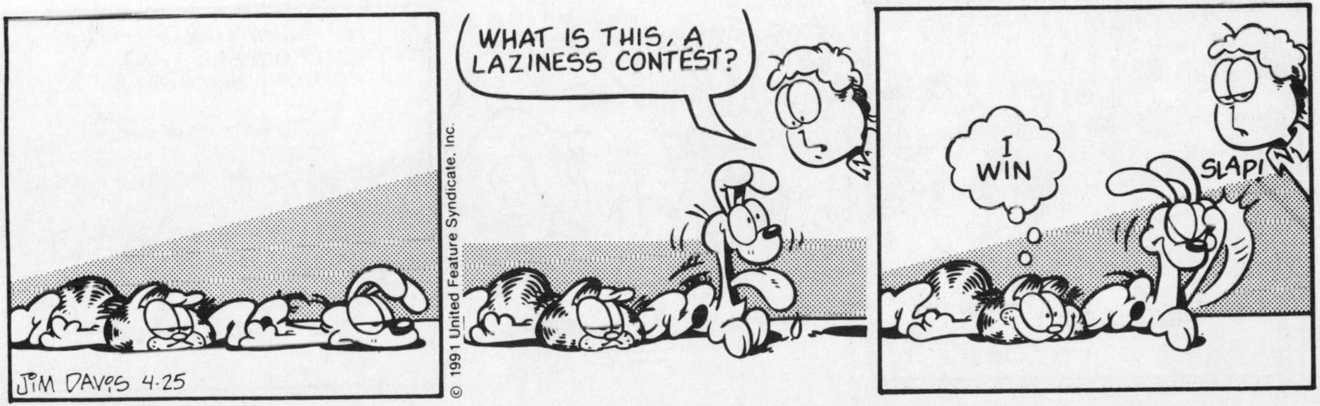
JIM DAVIS 4-25
© 1991 United Feature Syndicate, Inc.
WHAT IS THIS, A LAZINESS CONTEST?
I WIN
SLAP!

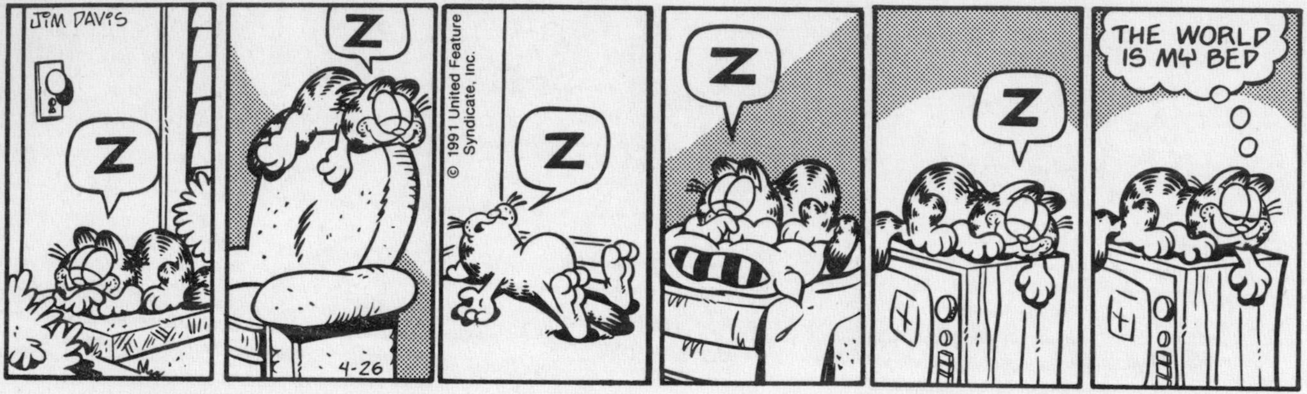
JIM DAVIS
Z
Z
4-26
© 1991 United Feature Syndicate, Inc.
Z
Z
Z
THE WORLD IS MY BED

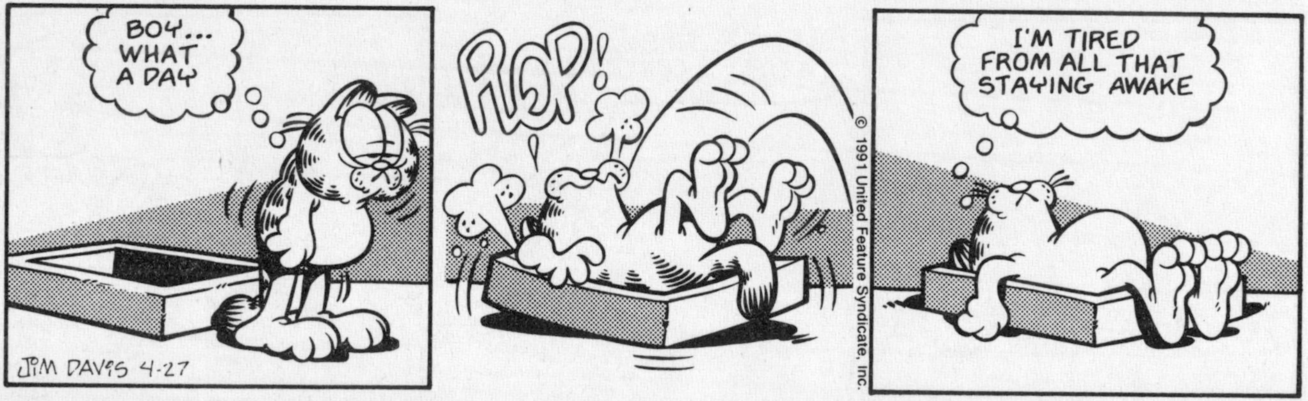
BOY... WHAT A DAY
JIM DAVIS 4-27
PLOP!
© 1991 United Feature Syndicate, Inc.
I'M TIRED FROM ALL THAT STAYING AWAKE

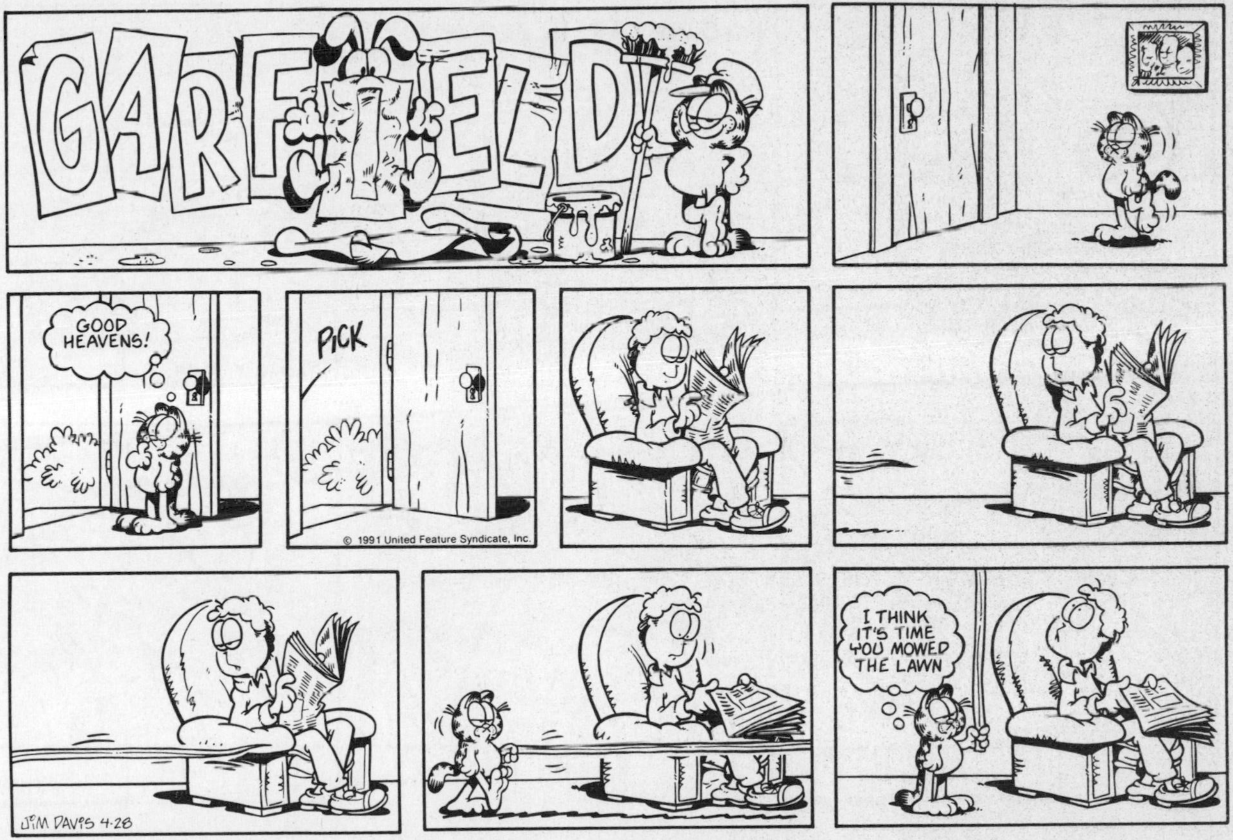
GARFIELD
GOOD HEAVENS!
PICK
© 1991 United Feature Syndicate, Inc.
I THINK IT'S TIME YOU MOWED THE LAWN
JIM DAVIS 4-28

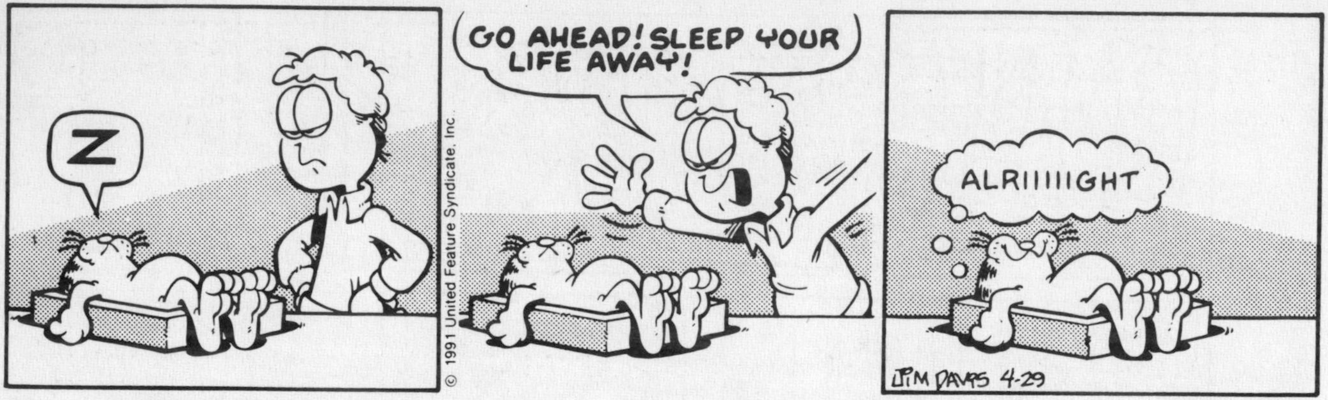
Z
GO AHEAD! SLEEP YOUR LIFE AWAY!
ALRIIIIIGHT
JIM DAVIS 4-29
© 1991 United Feature Syndicate, Inc.

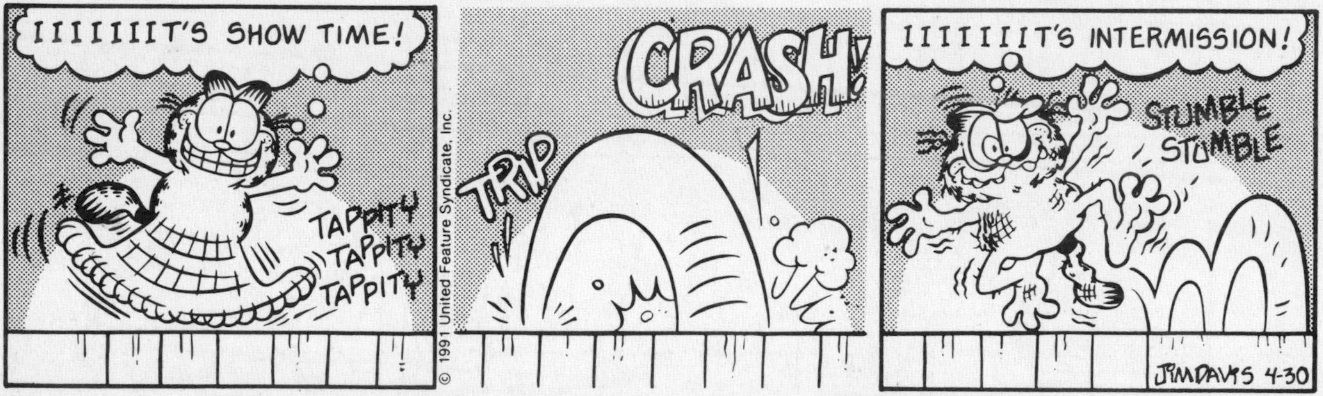
IIIIIIIT'S SHOW TIME!
TAPPITY
TAPPITY
TAPPITY
TRIP
CRASH!
IIIIIIIT'S INTERMISSION!
STUMBLE
STUMBLE
JIM DAVIS 4-30
© 1991 United Feature Syndicate, Inc.

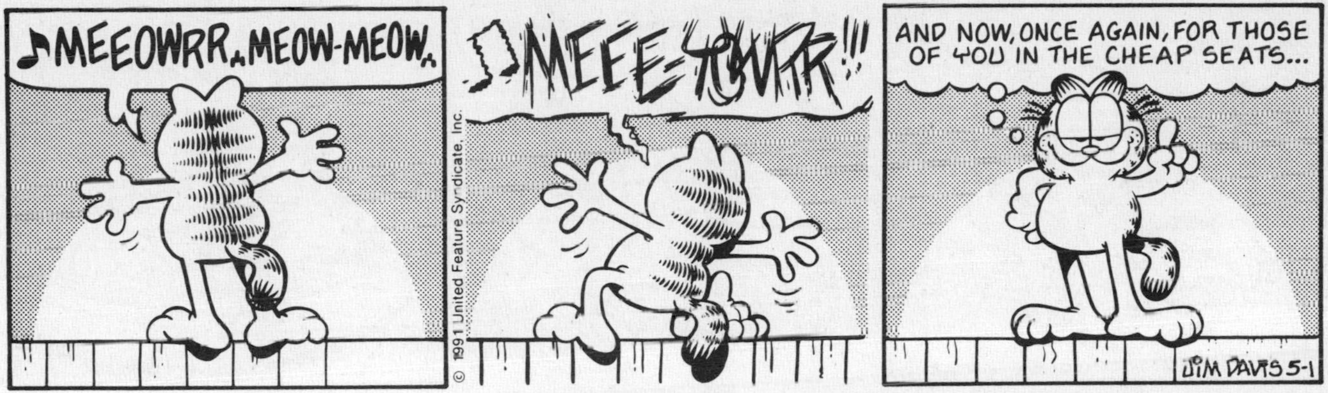
♪MEEOWRR, MEOW-MEOW,
♪MEEE-YOWRR!!
AND NOW, ONCE AGAIN, FOR THOSE OF YOU IN THE CHEAP SEATS...
JIM DAVIS 5-1

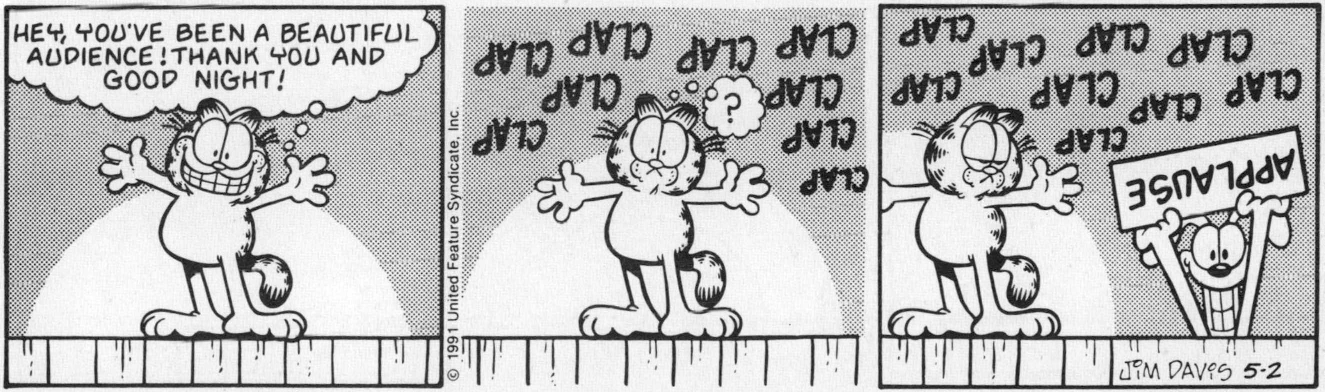
HEY, YOU'VE BEEN A BEAUTIFUL AUDIENCE! THANK YOU AND GOOD NIGHT!
CLAP CLAP CLAP CLAP CLAP CLAP CLAP CLAP CLAP
?
CLAP CLAP CLAP CLAP CLAP CLAP CLAP CLAP CLAP
APPLAUSE
JIM DAVIS 5-2

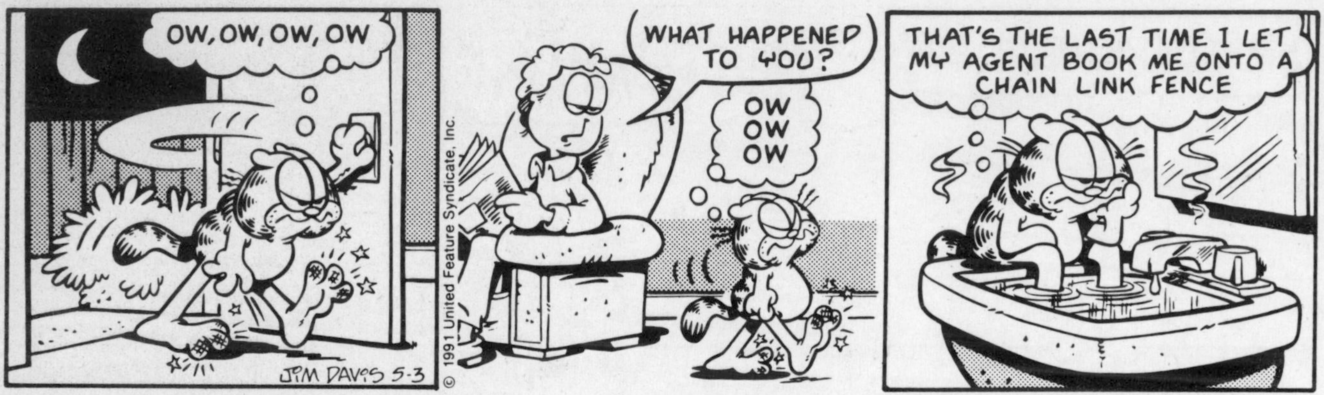
OW, OW, OW, OW
JIM DAVIS 5-3
© 1991 United Feature Syndicate, Inc.
WHAT HAPPENED TO YOU?
OW OW OW
THAT'S THE LAST TIME I LET MY AGENT BOOK ME ONTO A CHAIN LINK FENCE

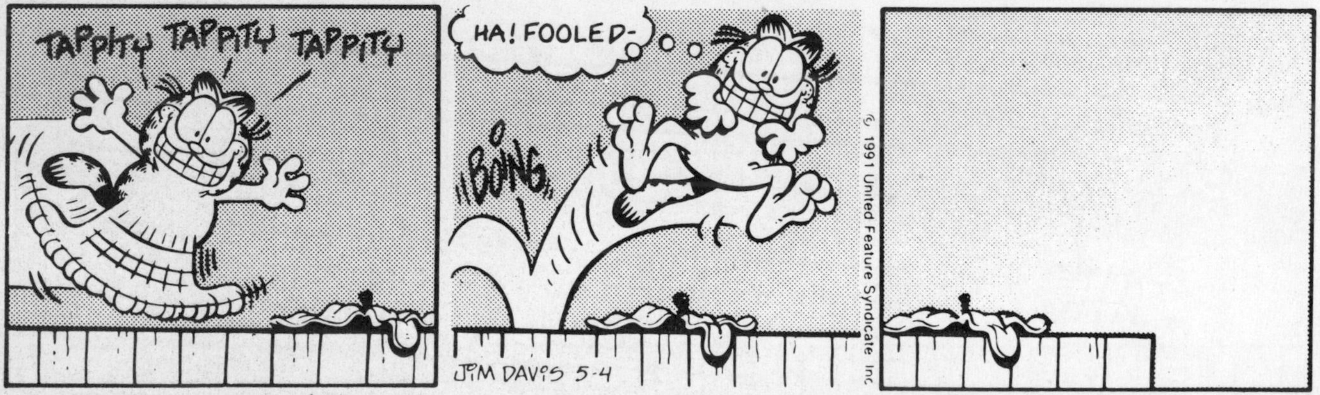
TAPPITY TAPPITY TAPPITY
BOING
HA! FOOLED-
JIM DAVIS 5-4
© 1991 United Feature Syndicate Inc.

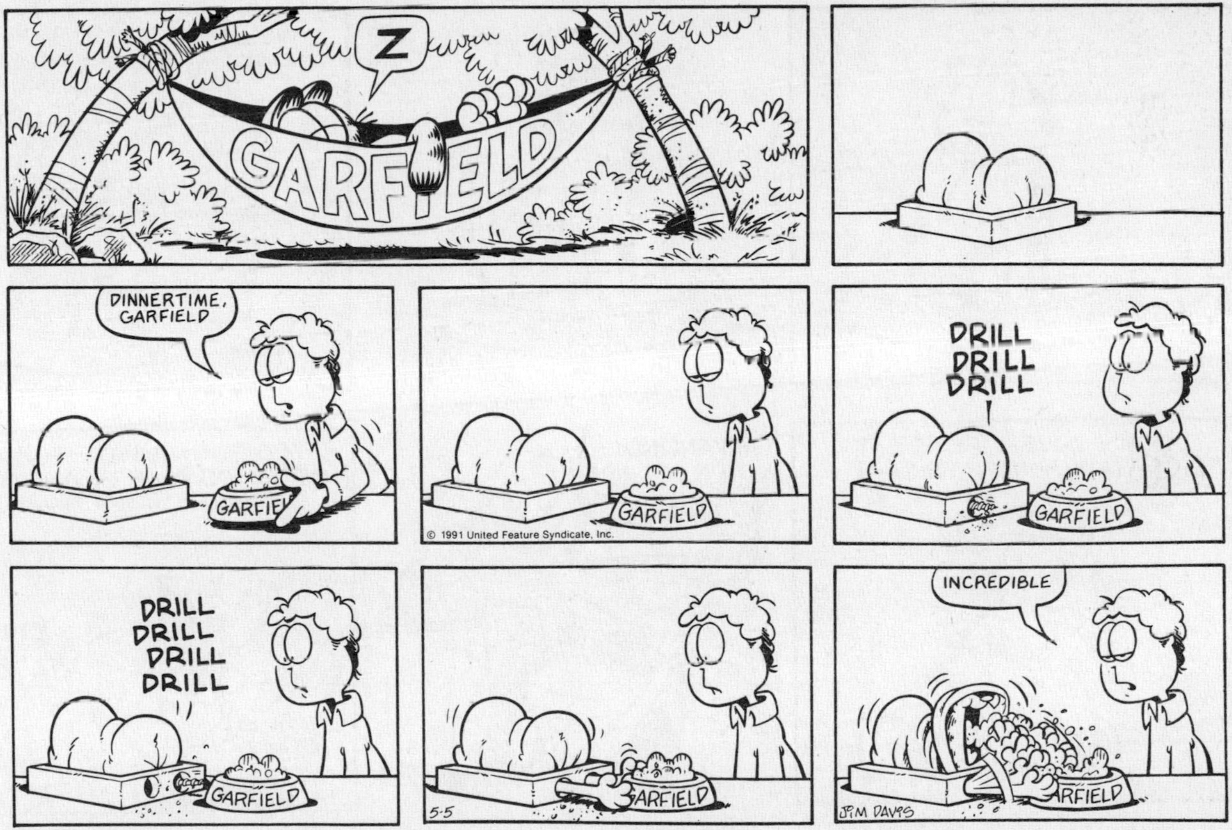
Z
GARFIELD
DINNERTIME, GARFIELD
GARFIELD
GARFIELD
© 1991 United Feature Syndicate, Inc.
DRILL DRILL DRILL
GARFIELD
DRILL DRILL DRILL DRILL
GARFIELD
5-5
ARFIELD
INCREDIBLE
ARFIELD
JIM DAVIS

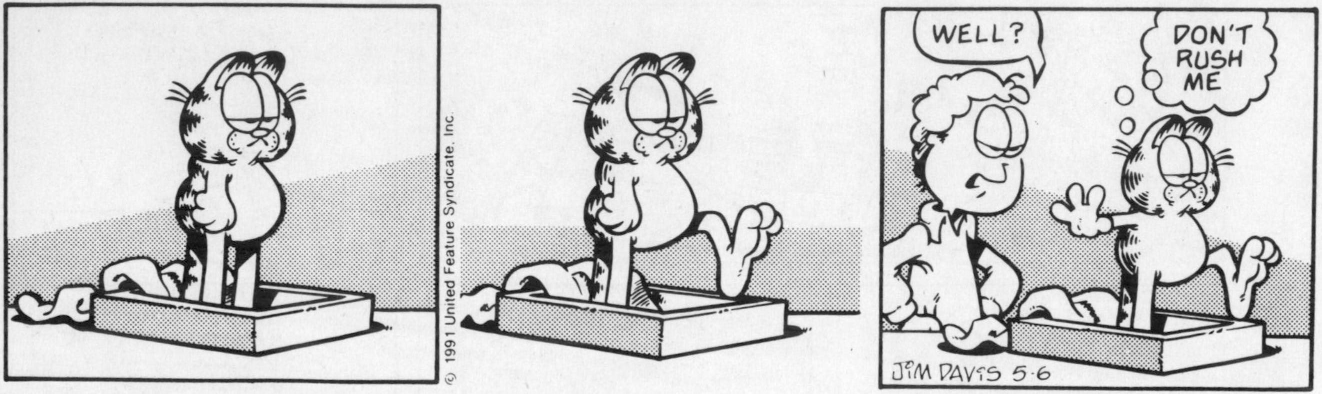
© 1991 United Feature Syndicate, Inc.
WELL?
DON'T RUSH ME
JIM DAVIS 5-6

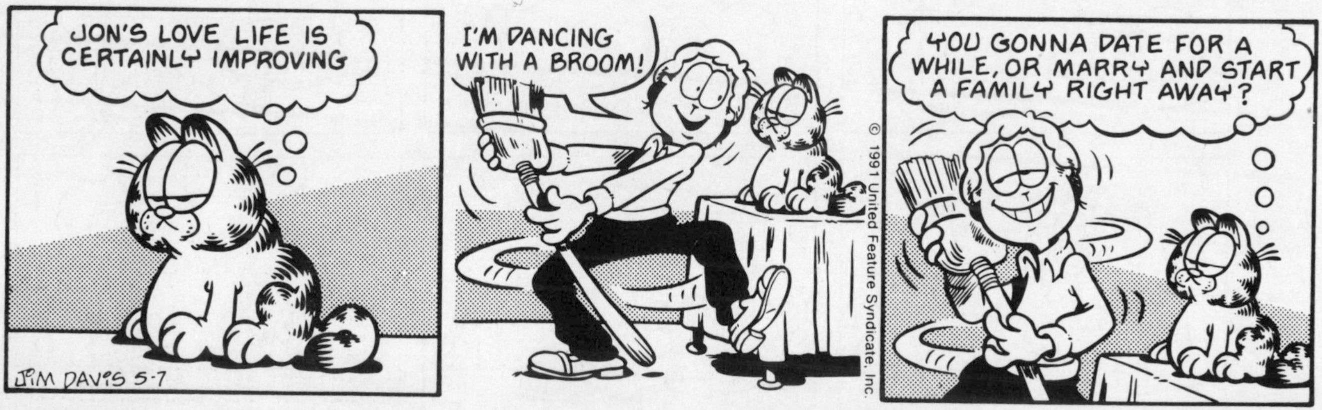
JON'S LOVE LIFE IS CERTAINLY IMPROVING
JIM DAVIS 5-7
I'M DANCING WITH A BROOM!
© 1991 United Feature Syndicate, Inc.
YOU GONNA DATE FOR A WHILE, OR MARRY AND START A FAMILY RIGHT AWAY?

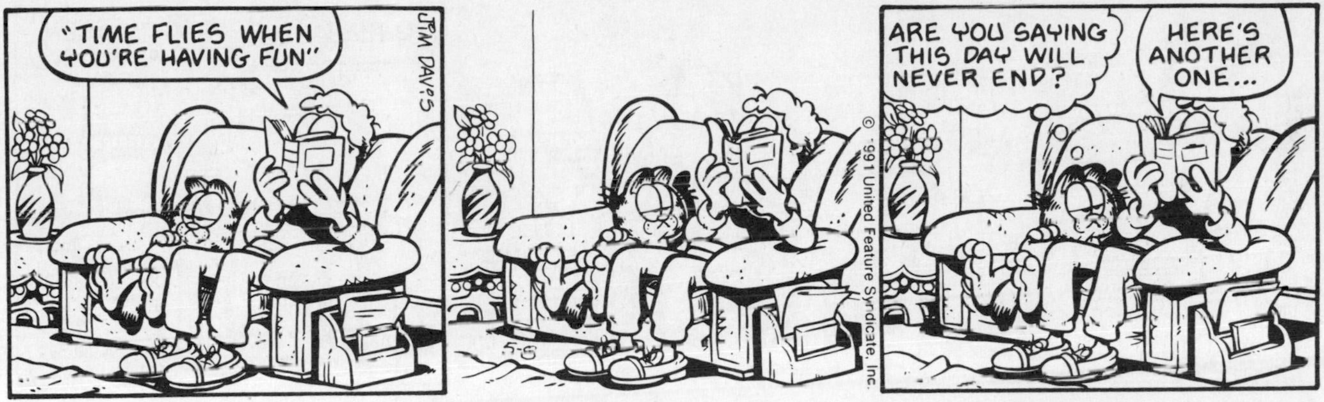
"TIME FLIES WHEN YOU'RE HAVING FUN"
ARE YOU SAYING THIS DAY WILL NEVER END?
HERE'S ANOTHER ONE...

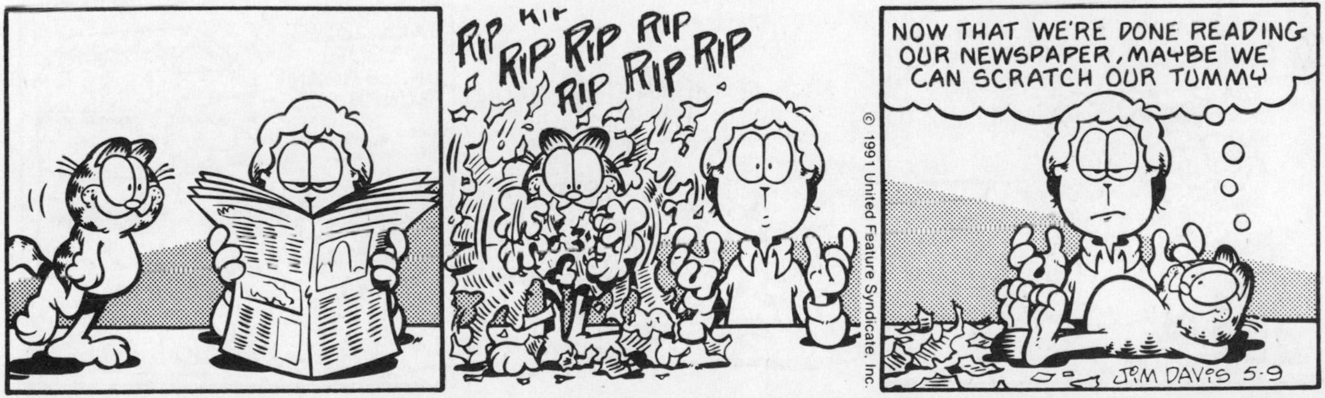
RIP
RIP RIP RIP
RIP RIP RIP
NOW THAT WE'RE DONE READING OUR NEWSPAPER, MAYBE WE CAN SCRATCH OUR TUMMY

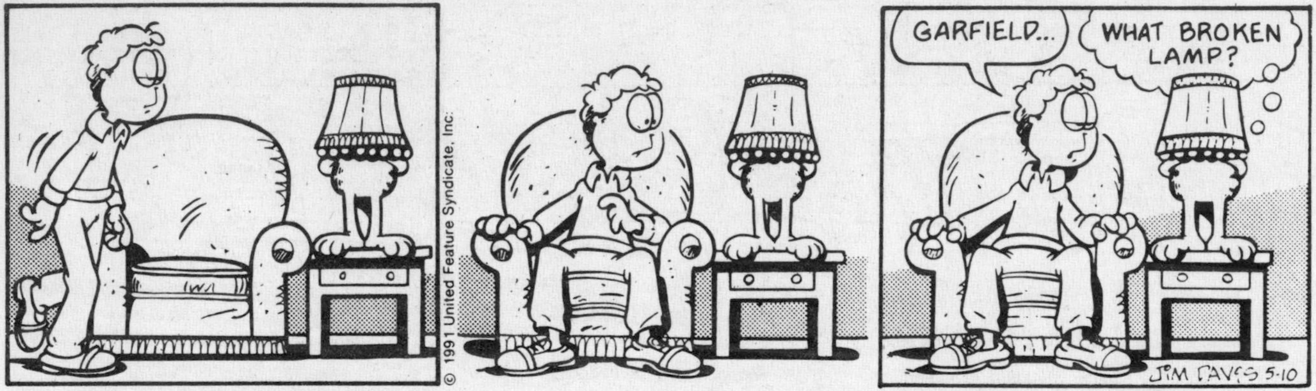
GARFIELD...
WHAT BROKEN LAMP?
JIM DAVIS 5-10
© 1991 United Feature Syndicate, Inc.

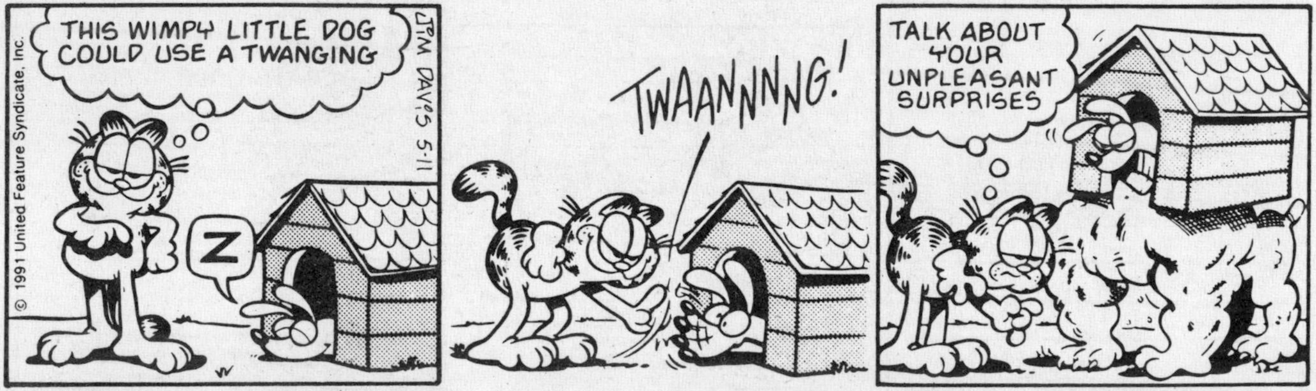
© 1991 United Feature Syndicate, Inc.
JIM DAVIS 5-11
THIS WIMPY LITTLE DOG COULD USE A TWANGING
Z
TWAANNNNG!
TALK ABOUT YOUR UNPLEASANT SURPRISES

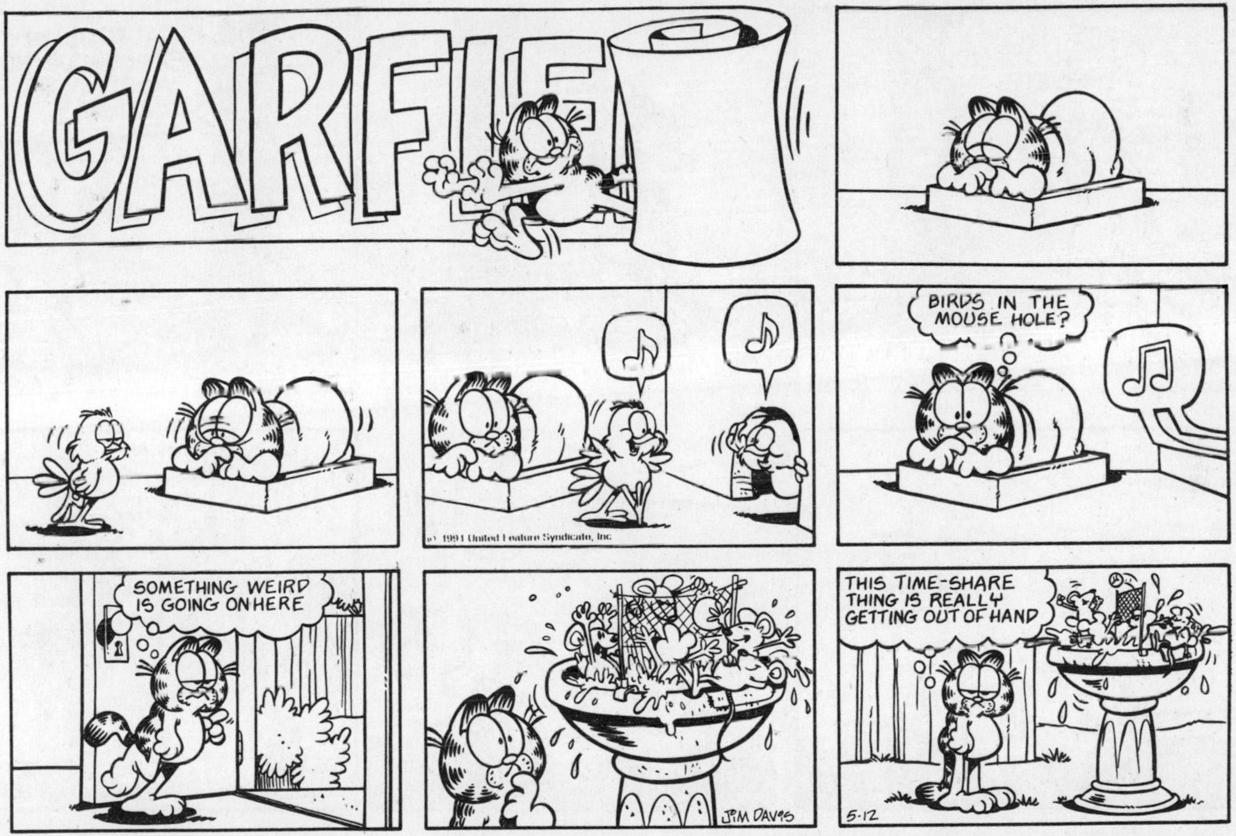
GARFIELD
BIRDS IN THE MOUSE HOLE?
© 1991 United Feature Syndicate, Inc.
SOMETHING WEIRD IS GOING ON HERE
JIM DAVIS
THIS TIME-SHARE THING IS REALLY GETTING OUT OF HAND
5-12

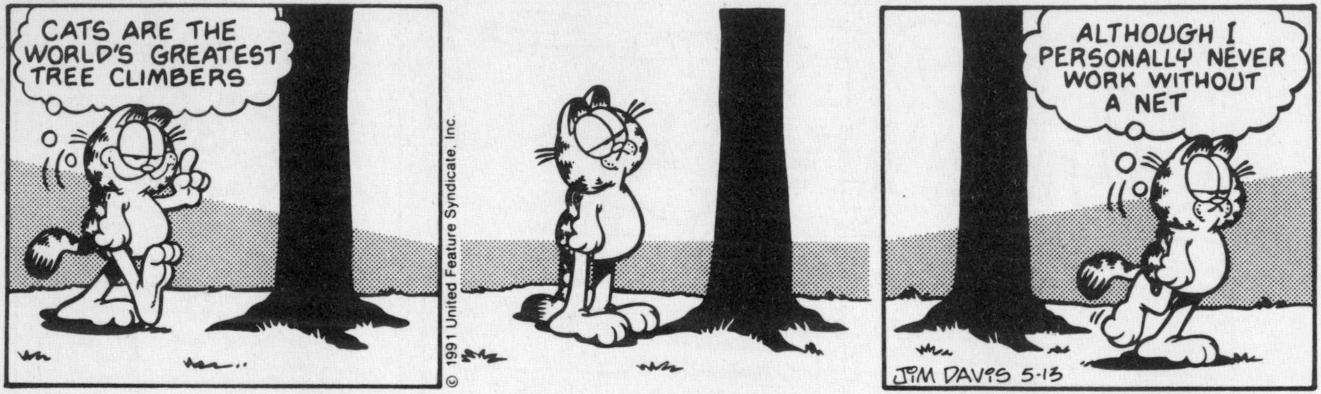
CATS ARE THE WORLD'S GREATEST TREE CLIMBERS
ALTHOUGH I PERSONALLY NEVER WORK WITHOUT A NET
JIM DAVIS 5-13
© 1991 United Feature Syndicate, Inc.

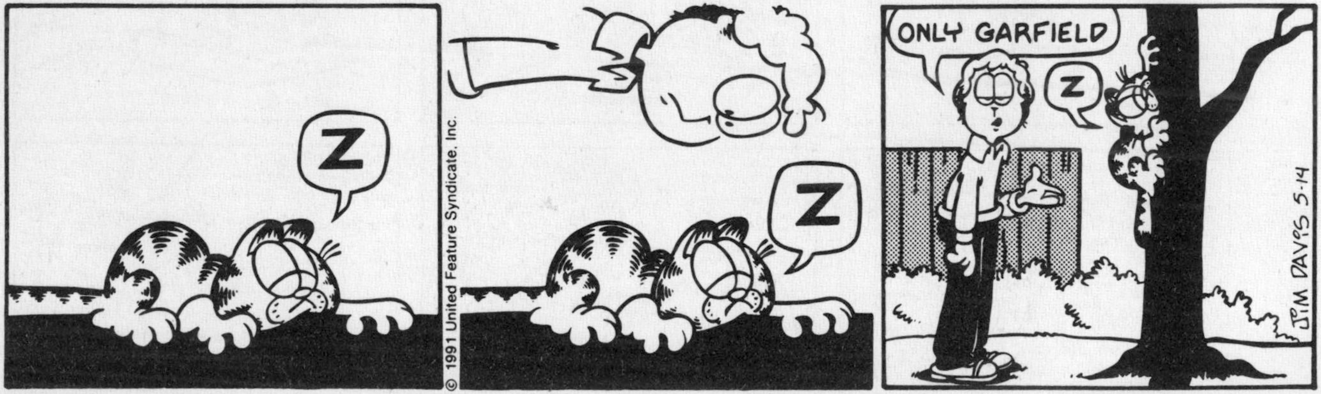
Z
Z
ONLY GARFIELD
Z
JIM DAVIS 5-14
© 1991 United Feature Syndicate, Inc.

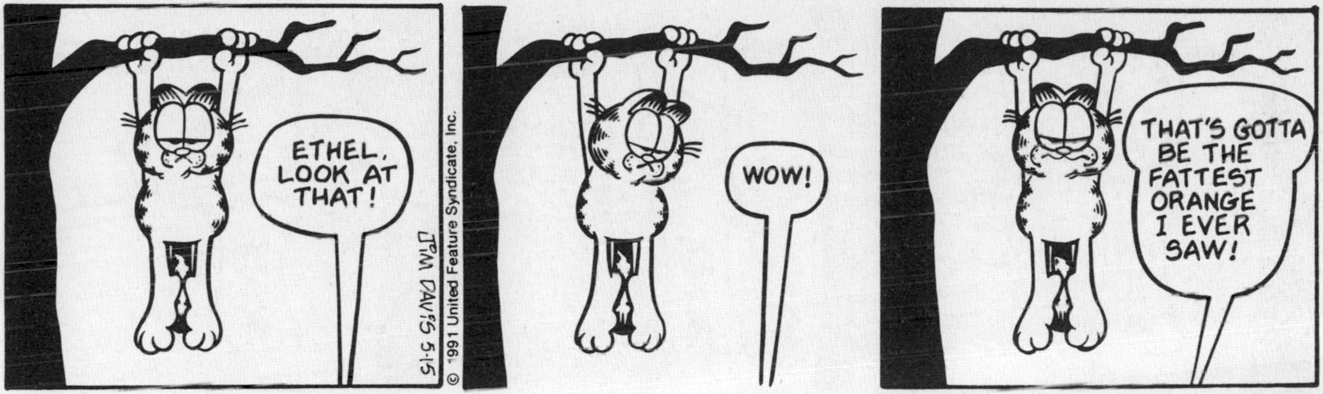
ETHEL, LOOK AT THAT!
JIM DAVIS 5-15
© 1991 United Feature Syndicate, Inc.
WOW!
THAT'S GOTTA BE THE FATTEST ORANGE I EVER SAW!

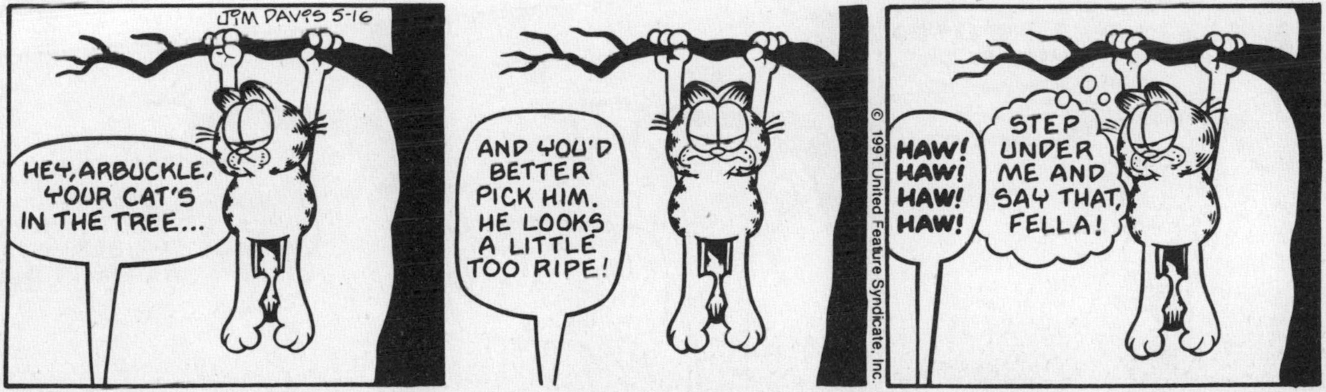
JIM DAVIS 5-16
HEY, ARBUCKLE, YOUR CAT'S IN THE TREE...
AND YOU'D BETTER PICK HIM. HE LOOKS A LITTLE TOO RIPE!
© 1991 United Feature Syndicate, Inc.
HAW! HAW! HAW! HAW!
STEP UNDER ME AND SAY THAT, FELLA!

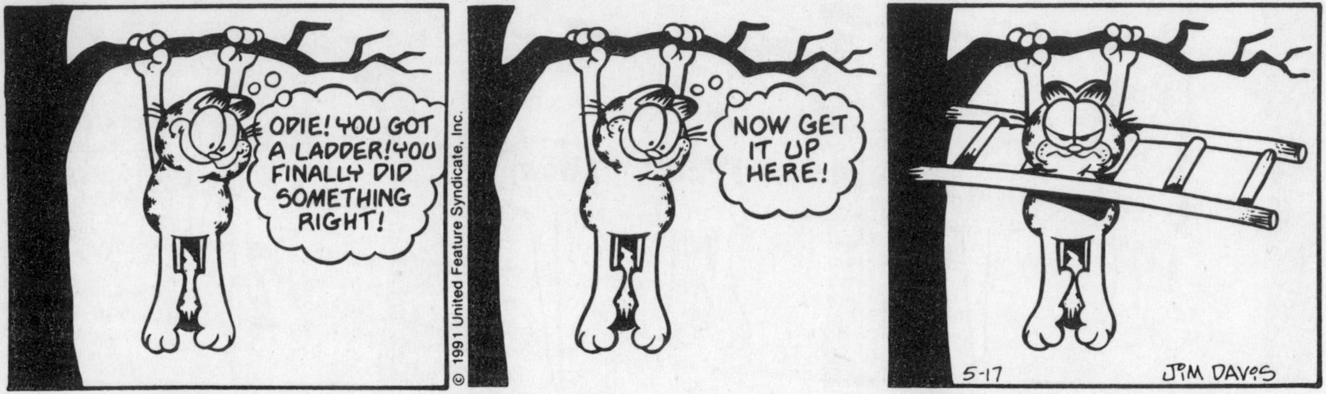
ODIE! YOU GOT A LADDER! YOU FINALLY DID SOMETHING RIGHT!
© 1991 United Feature Syndicate, Inc.
NOW GET IT UP HERE!
5-17
JIM DAVIS

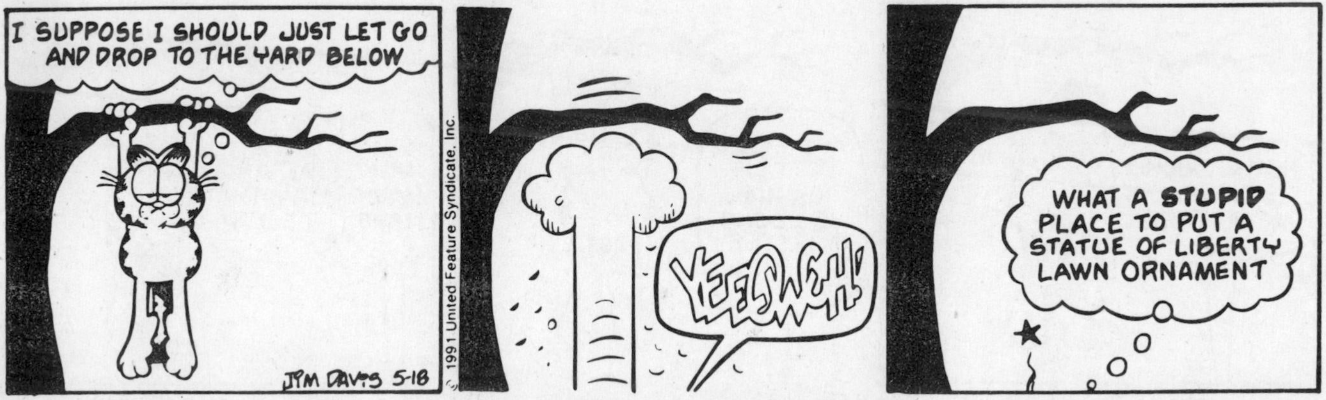
I SUPPOSE I SHOULD JUST LET GO AND DROP TO THE YARD BELOW
JIM DAVIS 5-18
© 1991 United Feature Syndicate, Inc.
YEEOWCH!
WHAT A STUPID PLACE TO PUT A STATUE OF LIBERTY LAWN ORNAMENT

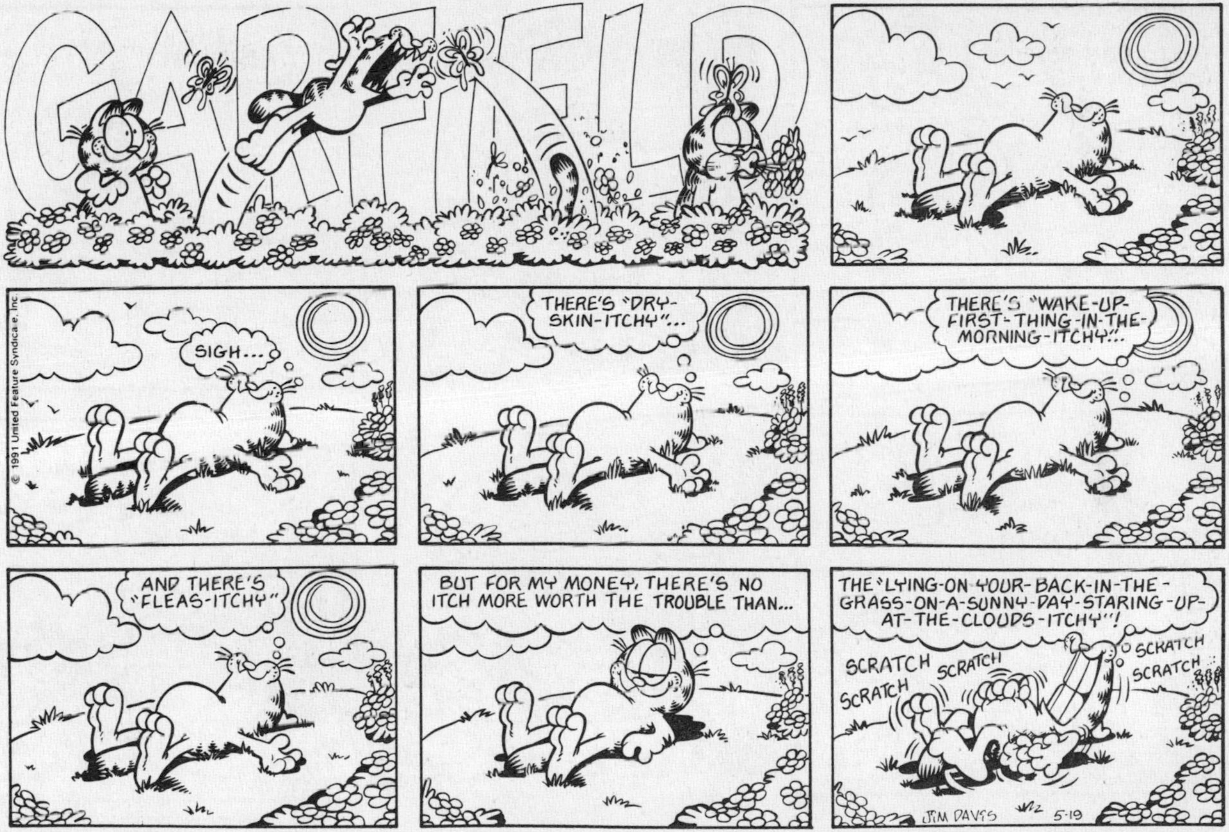
GARFIELD
© 1991 United Feature Syndicate, Inc.
SIGH...
THERE'S "DRY-SKIN-ITCHY"...
THERE'S "WAKE-UP-FIRST-THING-IN-THE-MORNING-ITCHY"...
AND THERE'S "FLEAS-ITCHY"
BUT FOR MY MONEY, THERE'S NO ITCH MORE WORTH THE TROUBLE THAN...
THE "LYING-ON-YOUR-BACK-IN-THE-GRASS-ON-A-SUNNY-DAY-STARING-UP-AT-THE-CLOUDS-ITCHY"!
SCRATCH
SCRATCH
SCRATCH
SCRATCH
SCRATCH
JIM DAVIS 5-19

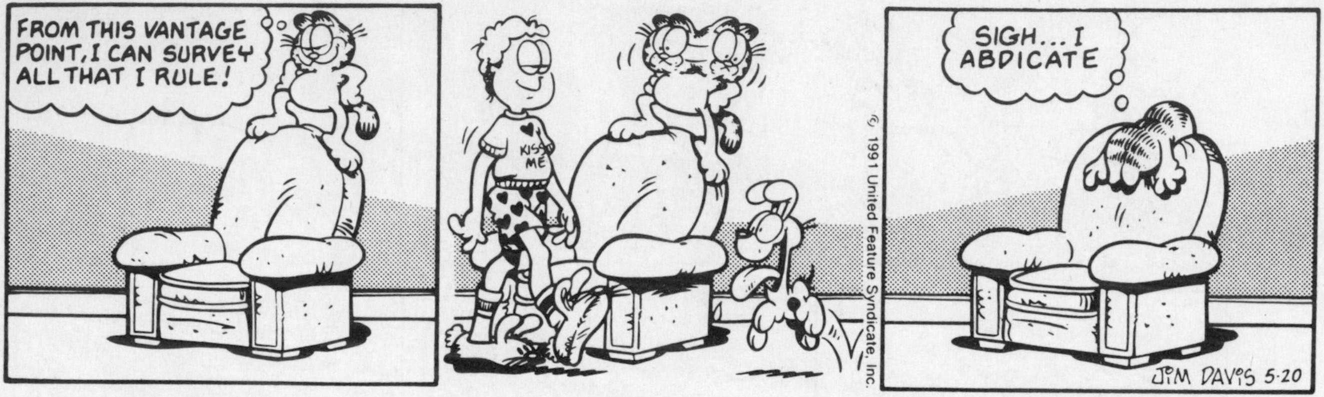
FROM THIS VANTAGE POINT, I CAN SURVEY ALL THAT I RULE!
KISS ME
© 1991 United Feature Syndicate, Inc.
SIGH... I ABDICATE
JIM DAVIS 5·20

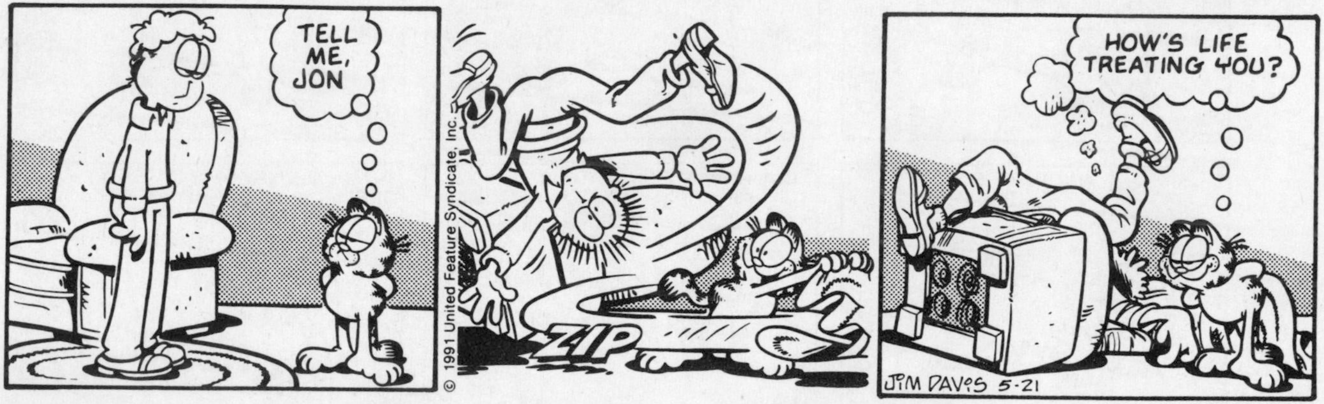
TELL ME, JON
© 1991 United Feature Syndicate, Inc.
ZIP
HOW'S LIFE TREATING YOU?
JIM DAVIS 5·21

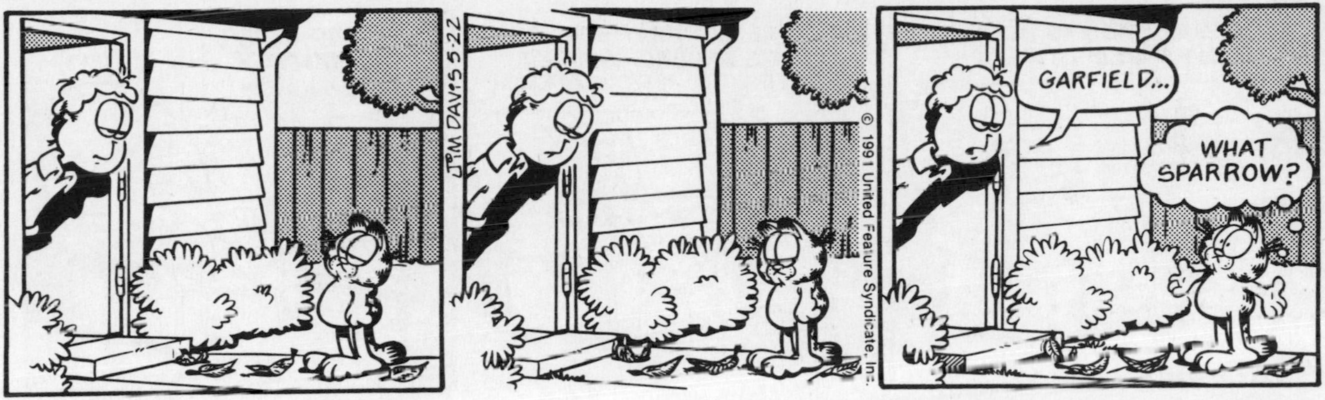
JIM DAVIS 5-22
© 1991 United Feature Syndicate, Inc.
GARFIELD...
WHAT SPARROW?

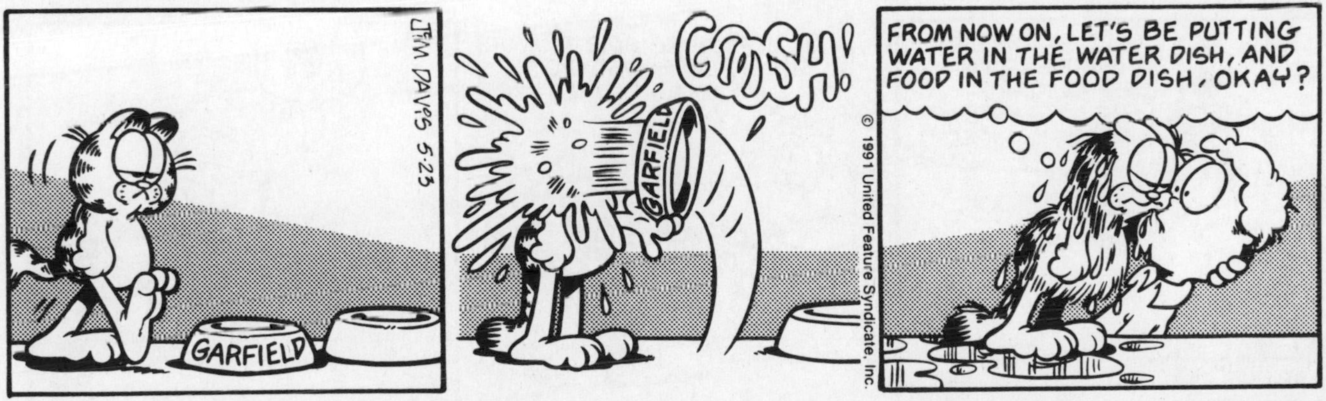
JIM DAVIS 5-23
GARFIELD
GOOSH!
GARFIELD
© 1991 United Feature Syndicate, Inc.
FROM NOW ON, LET'S BE PUTTING WATER IN THE WATER DISH, AND FOOD IN THE FOOD DISH, OKAY?

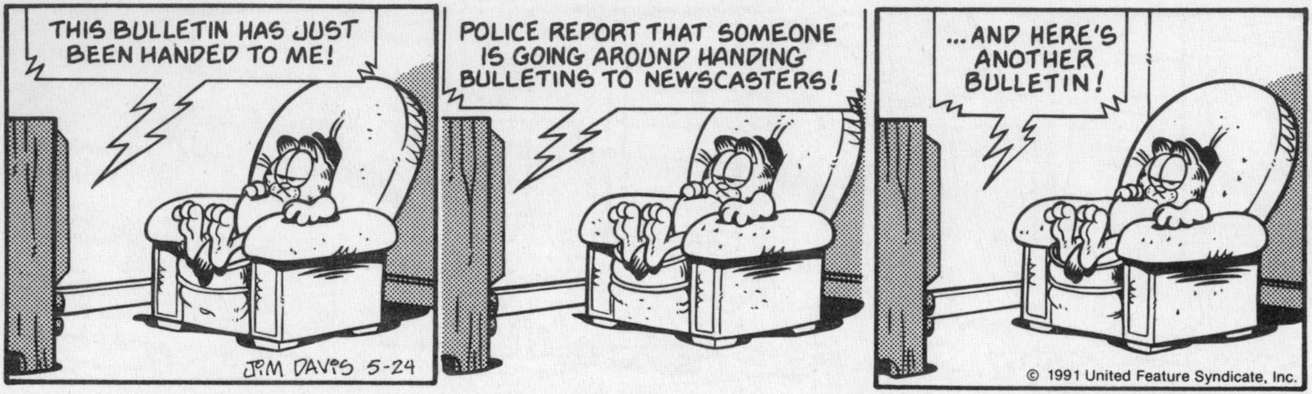
THIS BULLETIN HAS JUST BEEN HANDED TO ME!
POLICE REPORT THAT SOMEONE IS GOING AROUND HANDING BULLETINS TO NEWSCASTERS!
...AND HERE'S ANOTHER BULLETIN!
JIM DAVIS 5-24
© 1991 United Feature Syndicate, Inc.

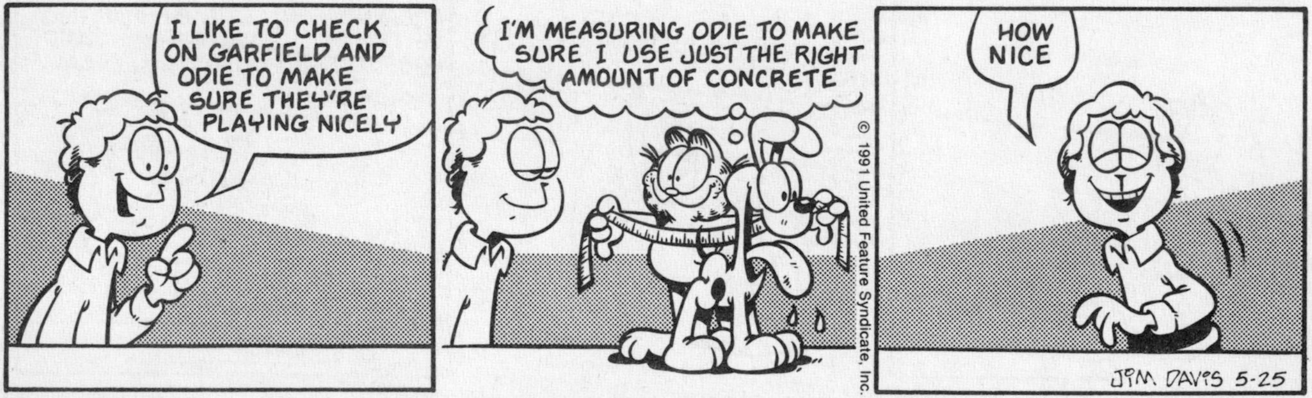
I LIKE TO CHECK ON GARFIELD AND ODIE TO MAKE SURE THEY'RE PLAYING NICELY
I'M MEASURING ODIE TO MAKE SURE I USE JUST THE RIGHT AMOUNT OF CONCRETE
HOW NICE
JIM DAVIS 5-25
© 1991 United Feature Syndicate, Inc.

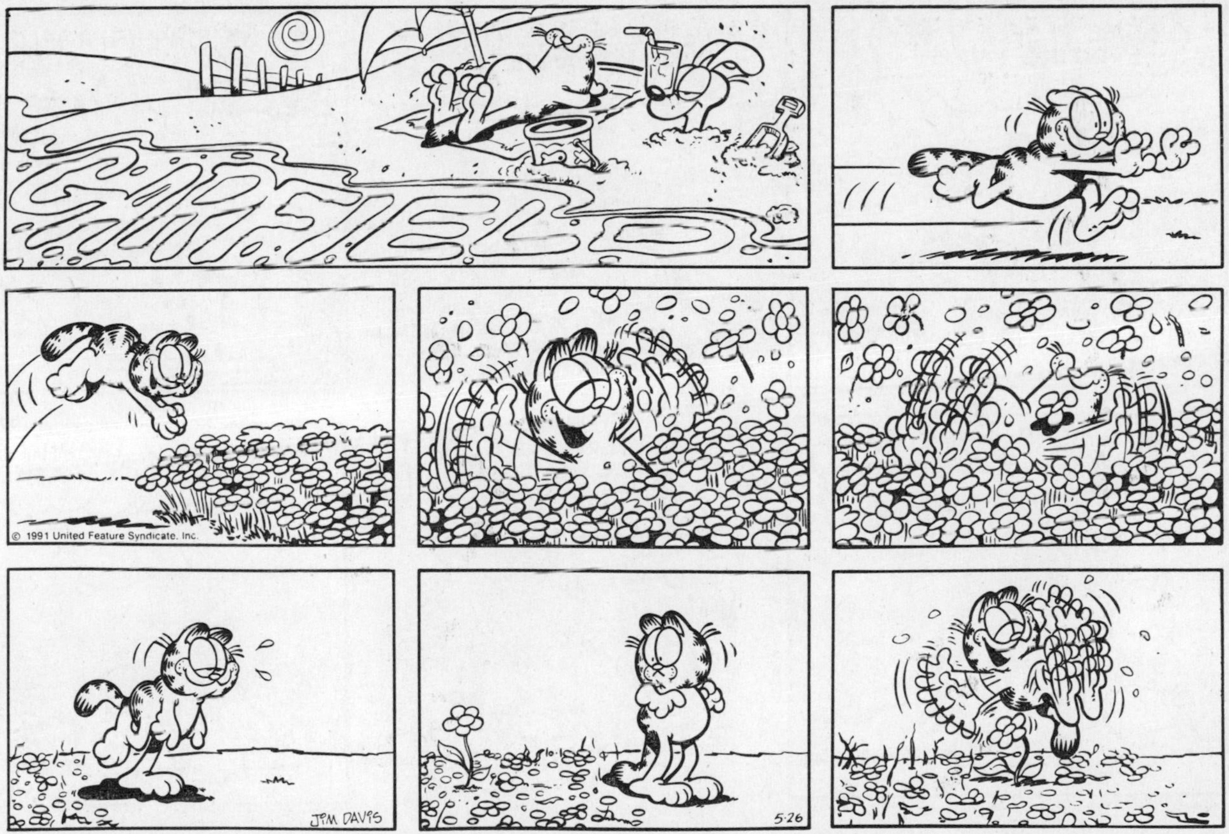
GARFIELD
© 1991 United Feature Syndicate, Inc.
JIM DAVIS
5-26

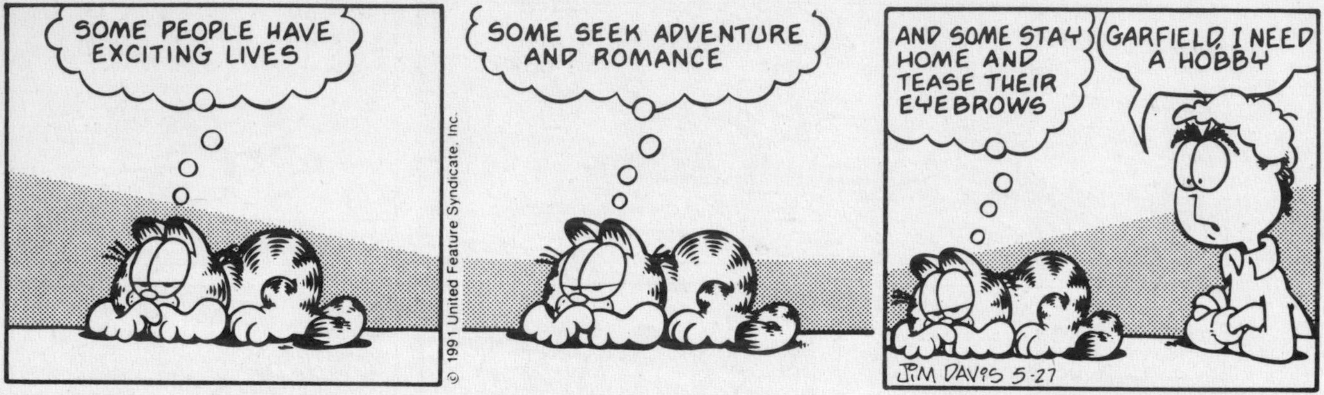
SOME PEOPLE HAVE EXCITING LIVES
SOME SEEK ADVENTURE AND ROMANCE
AND SOME STAY HOME AND TEASE THEIR EYEBROWS
GARFIELD, I NEED A HOBBY
JIM DAVIS 5-27

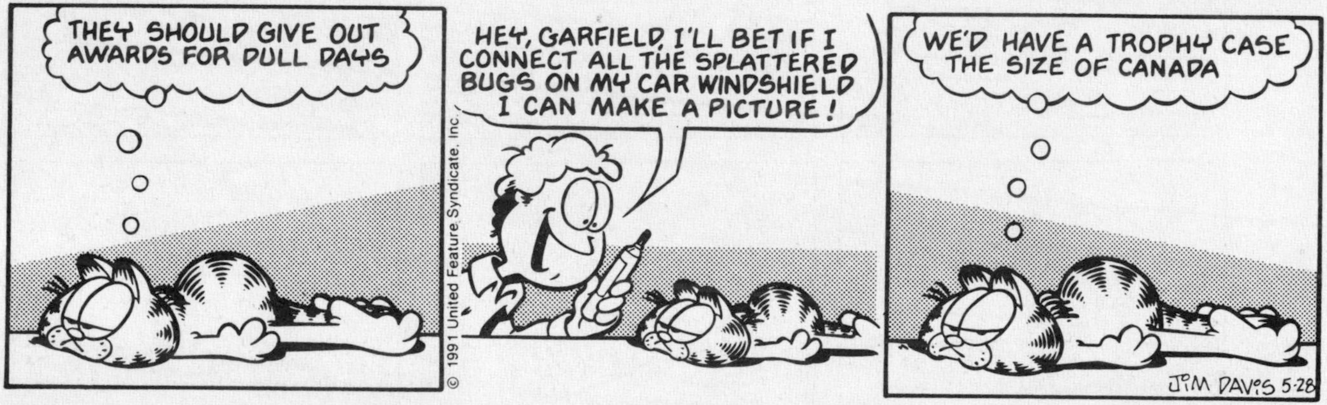
THEY SHOULD GIVE OUT AWARDS FOR DULL DAYS
HEY, GARFIELD, I'LL BET IF I CONNECT ALL THE SPLATTERED BUGS ON MY CAR WINDSHIELD I CAN MAKE A PICTURE!
WE'D HAVE A TROPHY CASE THE SIZE OF CANADA
JIM DAVIS 5-28

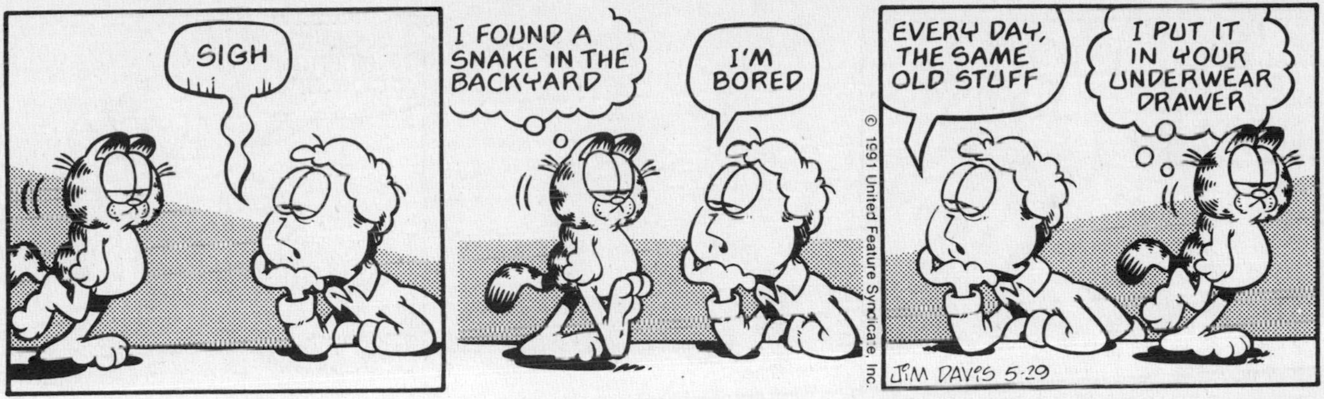
SIGH
I FOUND A SNAKE IN THE BACKYARD
I'M BORED
© 1991 United Feature Syndicate, Inc.
EVERY DAY, THE SAME OLD STUFF
I PUT IT IN YOUR UNDERWEAR DRAWER
JIM DAVIS 5-29

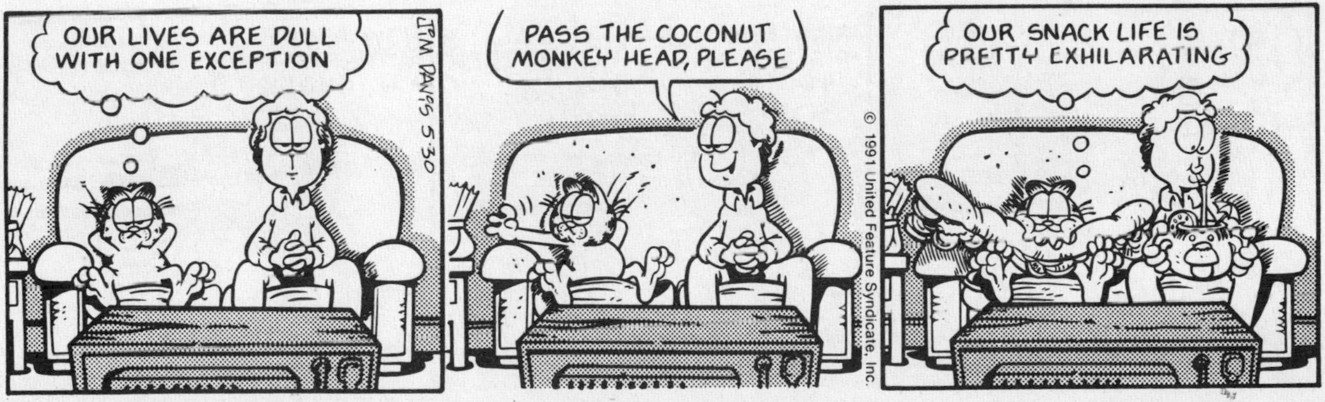
OUR LIVES ARE DULL WITH ONE EXCEPTION
JIM DAVIS 5-30
PASS THE COCONUT MONKEY HEAD, PLEASE
© 1991 United Feature Syndicate, Inc.
OUR SNACK LIFE IS PRETTY EXHILARATING

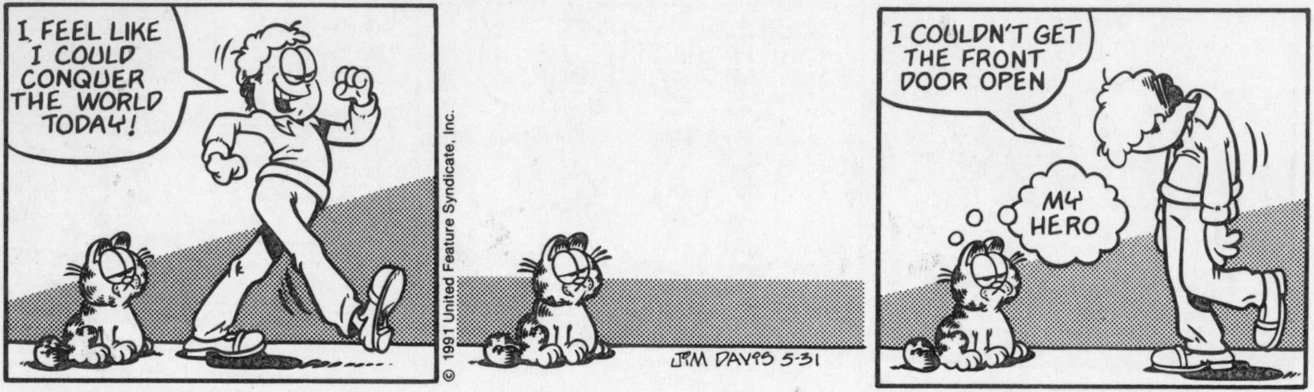
I FEEL LIKE I COULD CONQUER THE WORLD TODAY!
© 1991 United Feature Syndicate, Inc.
JIM DAVIS 5-31
I COULDN'T GET THE FRONT DOOR OPEN
MY HERO

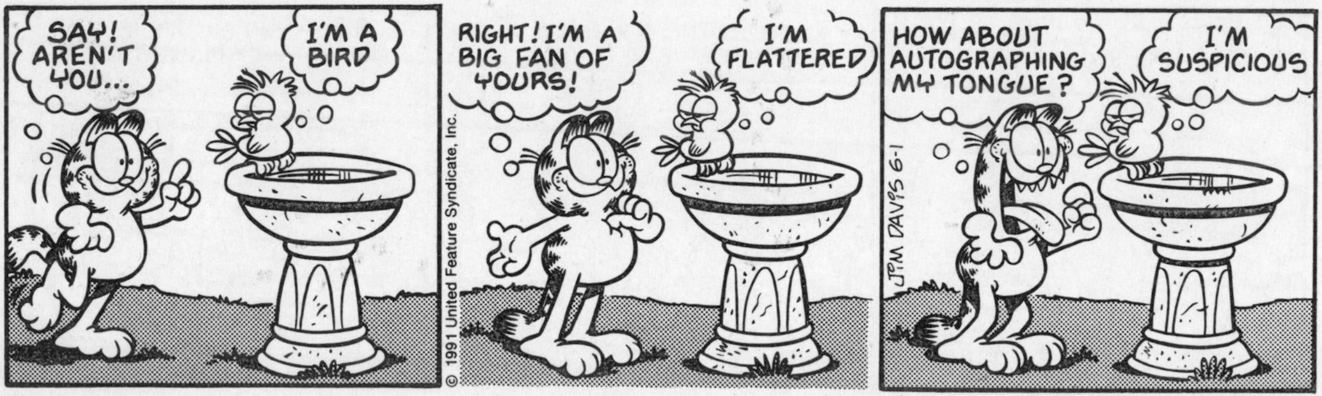
SAY! AREN'T YOU...
I'M A BIRD
© 1991 United Feature Syndicate, Inc.
RIGHT! I'M A BIG FAN OF YOURS!
I'M FLATTERED
HOW ABOUT AUTOGRAPHING MY TONGUE?
I'M SUSPICIOUS
JIM DAVIS 6-1

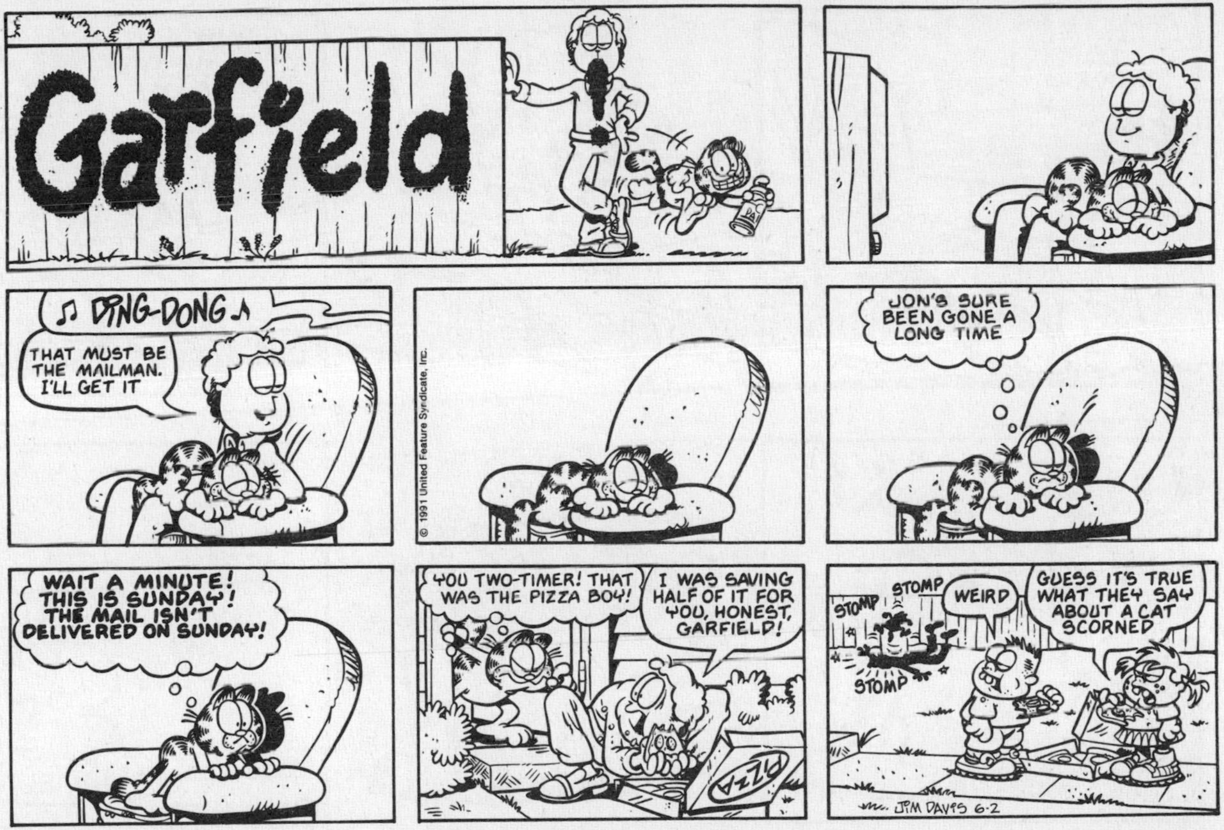
Garfield
PAINT
♫ DING-DONG ♪
THAT MUST BE THE MAILMAN. I'LL GET IT
JON'S SURE BEEN GONE A LONG TIME
WAIT A MINUTE! THIS IS SUNDAY! THE MAIL ISN'T DELIVERED ON SUNDAY!
YOU TWO-TIMER! THAT WAS THE PIZZA BOY!
I WAS SAVING HALF OF IT FOR YOU, HONEST, GARFIELD!
PIZZA
STOMP
STOMP
STOMP
WEIRD
GUESS IT'S TRUE WHAT THEY SAY ABOUT A CAT SCORNED
JIM DAVIS 6-2
© 1991 United Feature Syndicate, Inc.

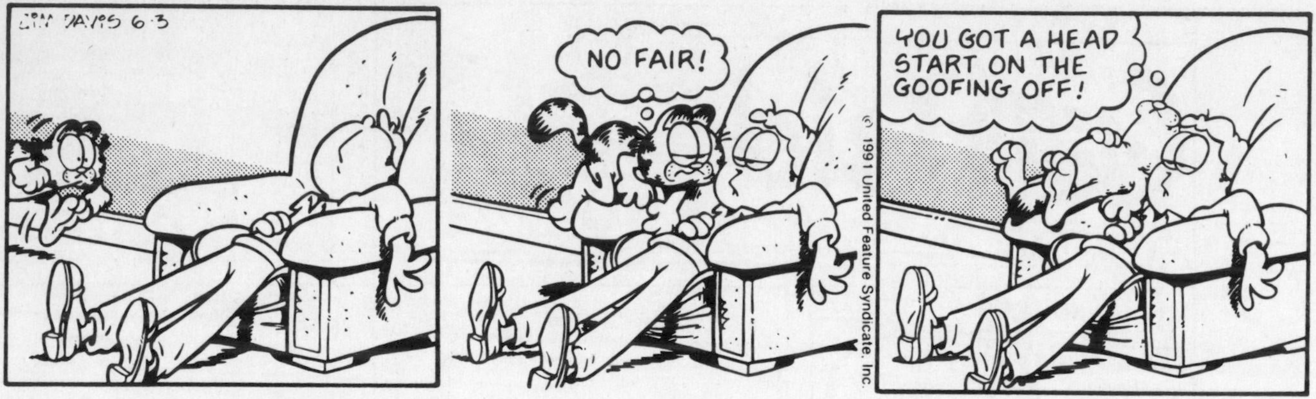
JIM DAVIS 6-3
NO FAIR!
YOU GOT A HEAD START ON THE GOOFING OFF!

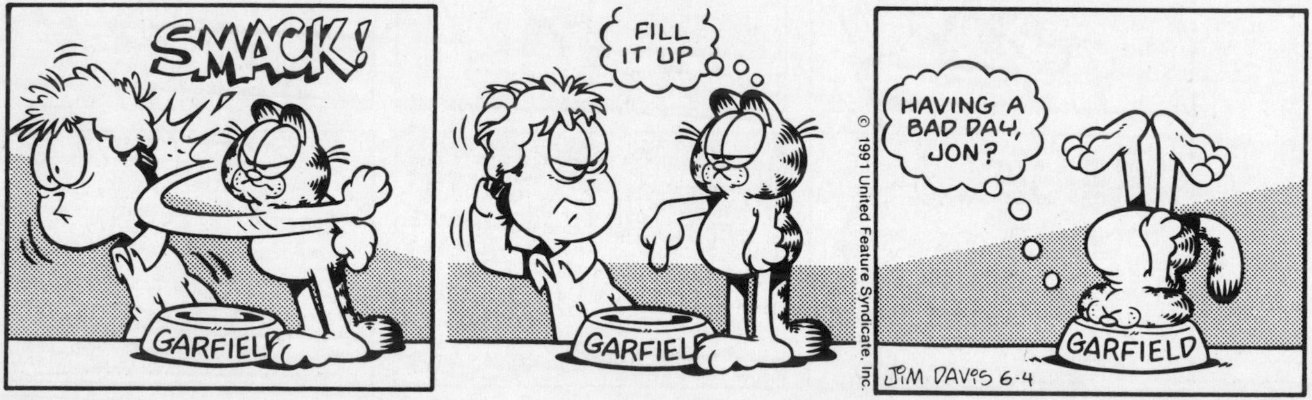
SMACK!
GARFIEL
FILL IT UP
GARFIEL
HAVING A BAD DAY, JON?
GARFIELD
JIM DAVIS 6-4

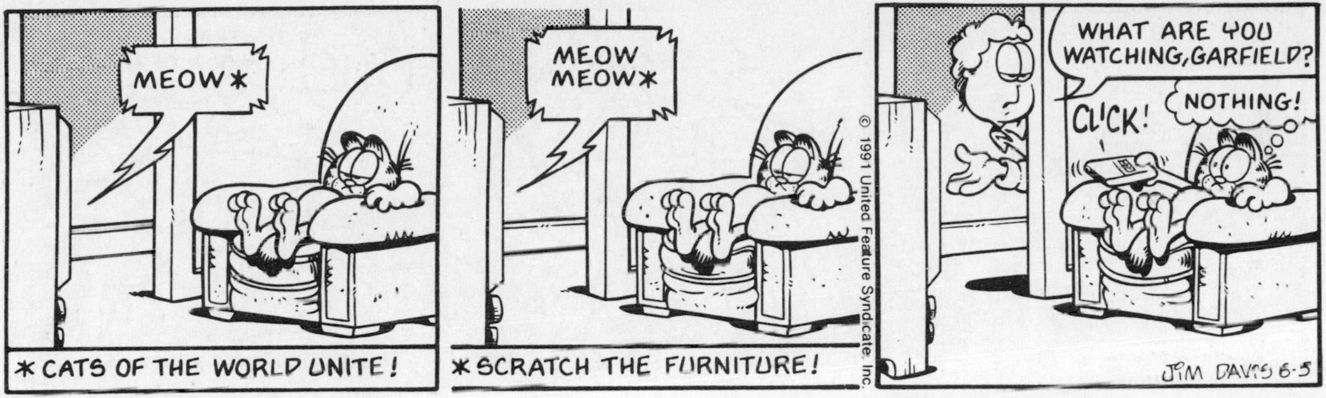
MEOW*
*CATS OF THE WORLD UNITE!
MEOW MEOW*
*SCRATCH THE FURNITURE!
© 1991 United Feature Syndicate, Inc.
WHAT ARE YOU WATCHING, GARFIELD?
CLICK!
NOTHING!
JIM DAVIS 6-5

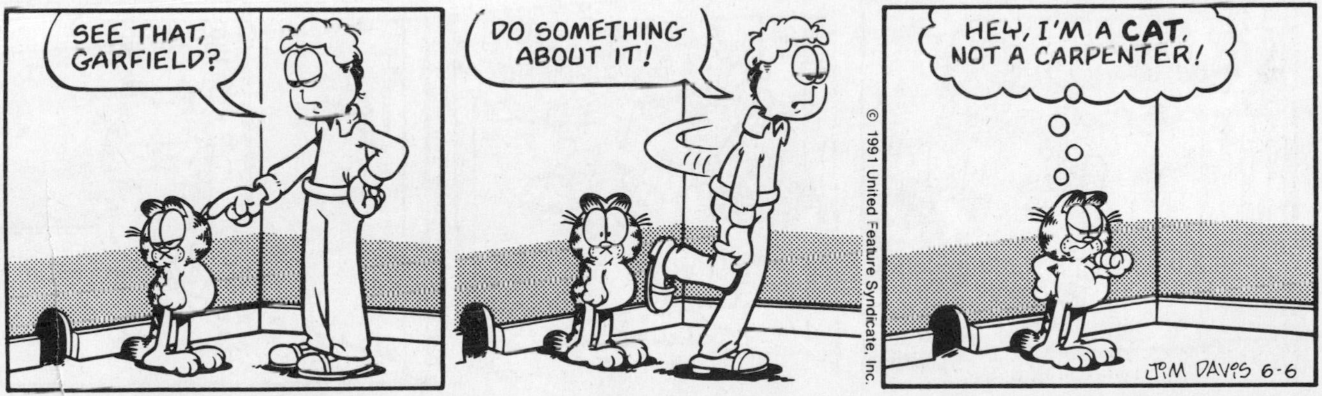
SEE THAT, GARFIELD?
DO SOMETHING ABOUT IT!
© 1991 United Feature Syndicate, Inc.
HEY, I'M A CAT, NOT A CARPENTER!
JIM DAVIS 6-6

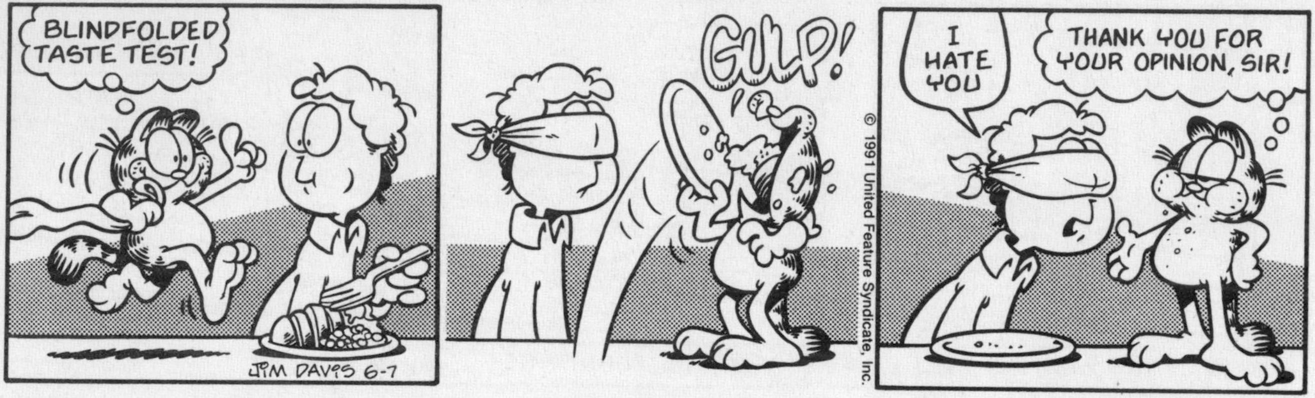
BLINDFOLDED TASTE TEST!
JIM DAVIS 6-7
GULP!
I HATE YOU
THANK YOU FOR YOUR OPINION, SIR!
© 1991 United Feature Syndicate, Inc.

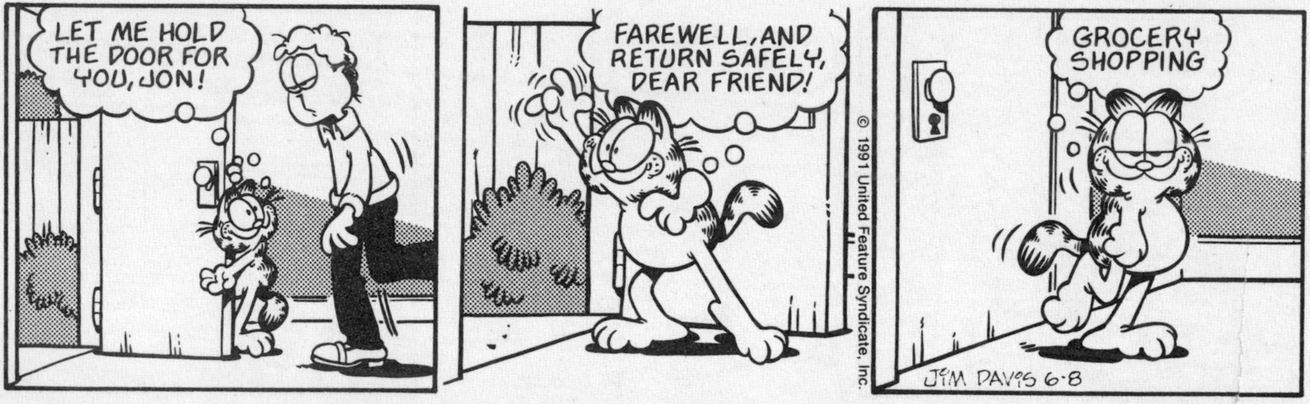
LET ME HOLD THE DOOR FOR YOU, JON!
FAREWELL, AND RETURN SAFELY, DEAR FRIEND!
GROCERY SHOPPING
JIM DAVIS 6-8
© 1991 United Feature Syndicate, Inc.

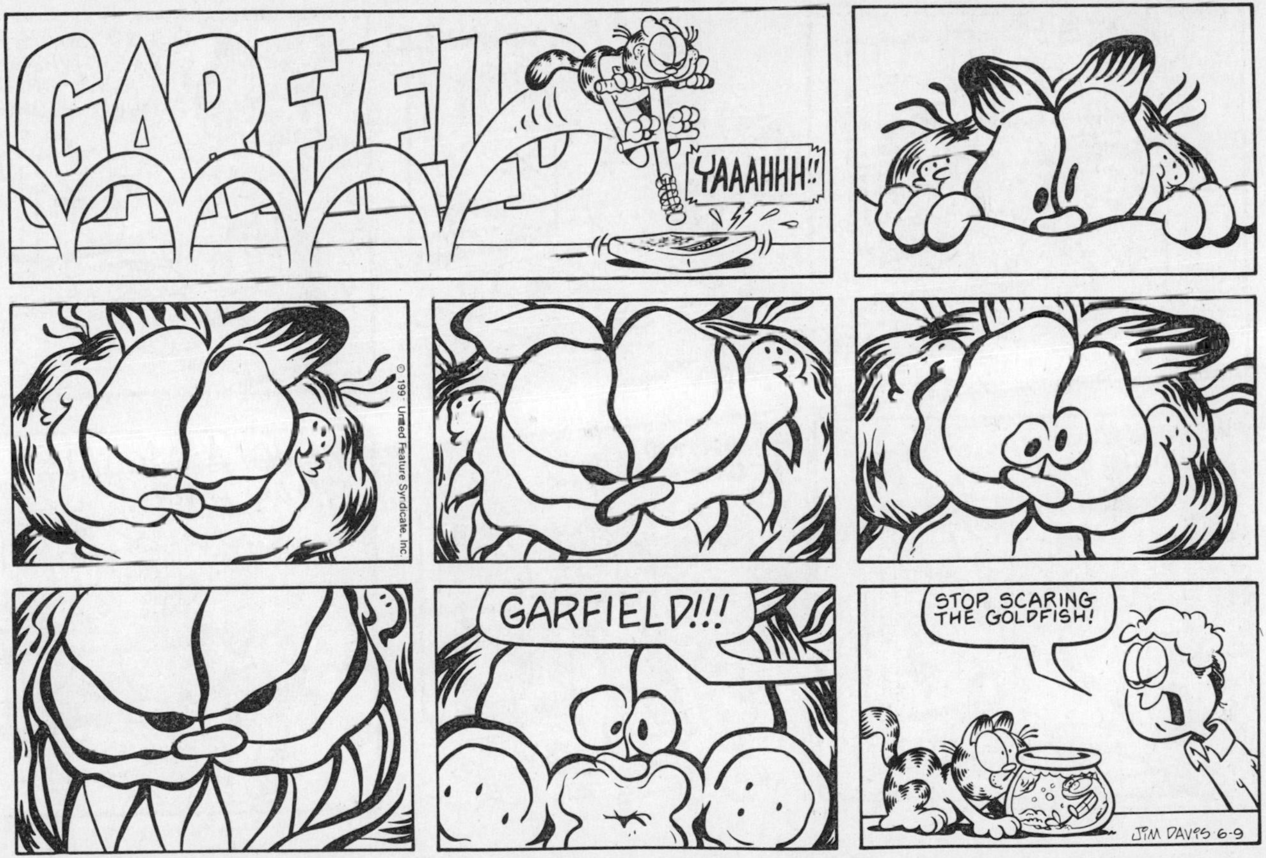
GARFIELD
YAAAHHH!!
© 199 United Feature Syndicate, Inc.
GARFIELD!!!
STOP SCARING THE GOLDFISH!
JIM DAVIS 6-9

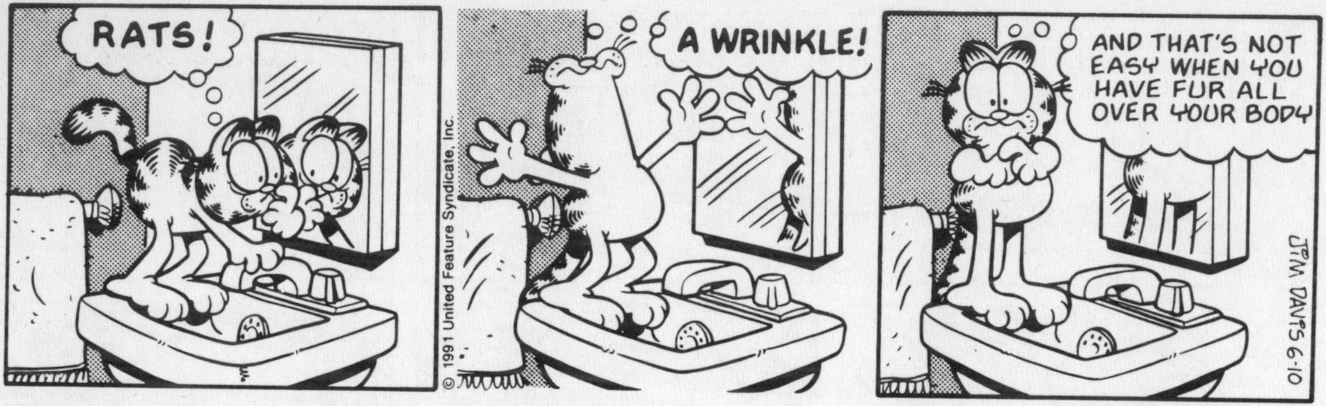
RATS!
A WRINKLE!
AND THAT'S NOT EASY WHEN YOU HAVE FUR ALL OVER YOUR BODY
© 1991 United Feature Syndicate, Inc.
JIM DAVIS 6-10

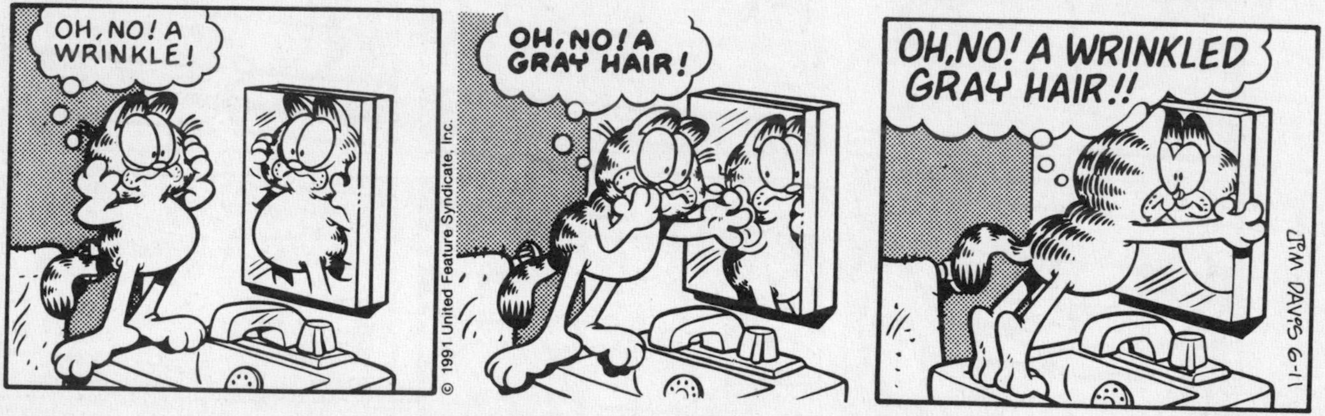
OH, NO! A WRINKLE!
OH, NO! A GRAY HAIR!
OH, NO! A WRINKLED GRAY HAIR!!
© 1991 United Feature Syndicate, Inc.
JIM DAVIS 6-11

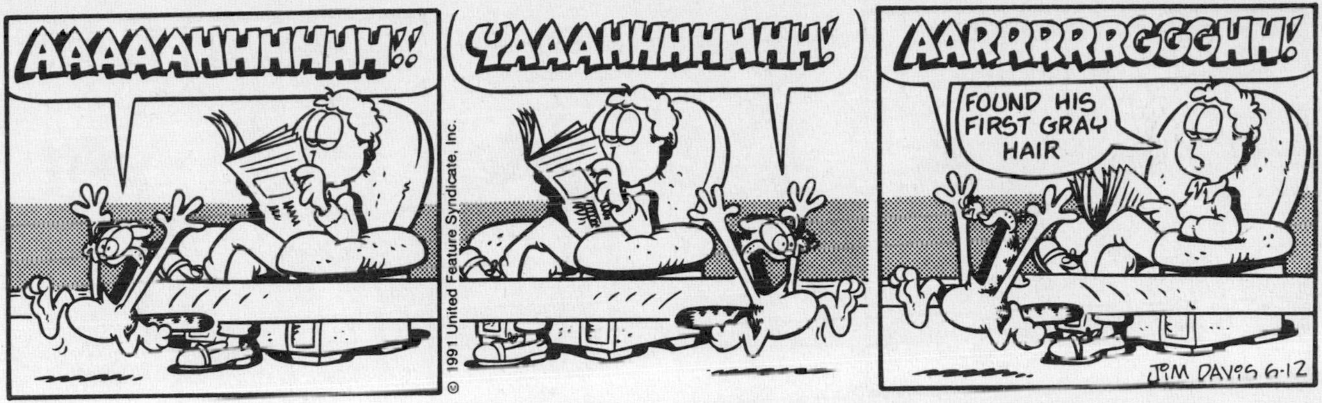
AAAAAHHHHHH!!
© 1991 United Feature Syndicate, Inc.
YAAAHHHHHHH!
AARRRRRRGGGHH!
FOUND HIS FIRST GRAY HAIR
JIM DAVIS 6-12

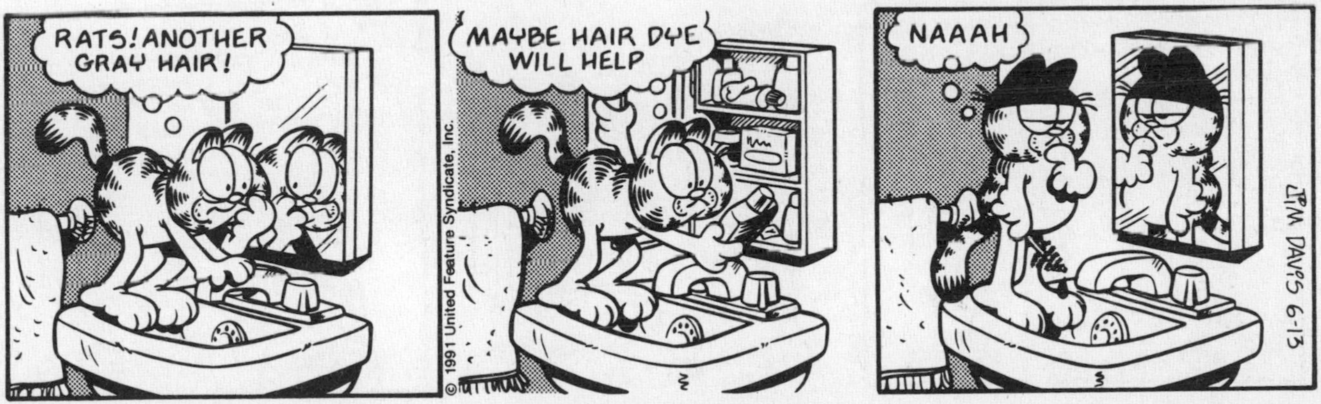
RATS! ANOTHER GRAY HAIR!
© 1991 United Feature Syndicate, Inc.
MAYBE HAIR DYE WILL HELP
NAAAH
JIM DAVIS 6-13

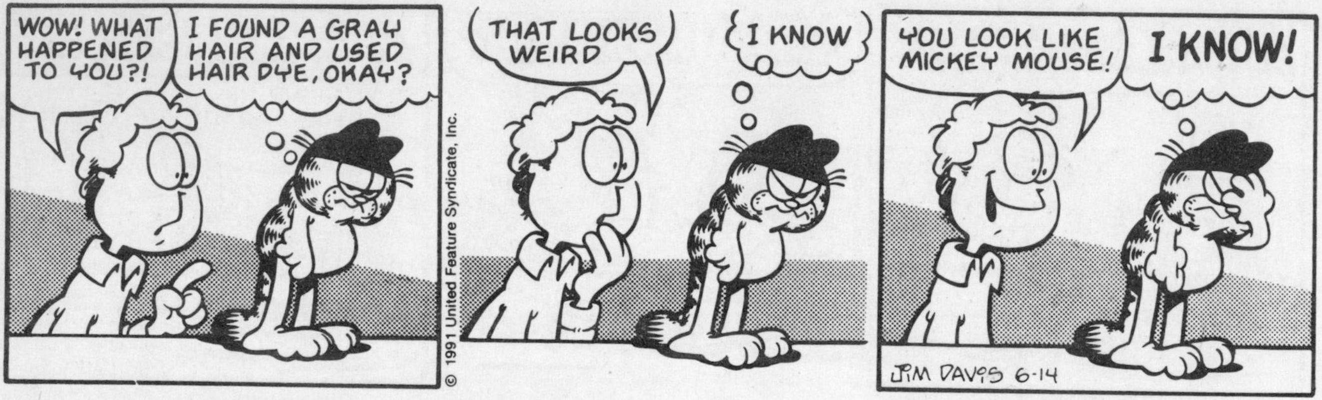
WOW! WHAT HAPPENED TO YOU?!
I FOUND A GRAY HAIR AND USED HAIR DYE, OKAY?
THAT LOOKS WEIRD
I KNOW
YOU LOOK LIKE MICKEY MOUSE!
I KNOW!
JIM DAVIS 6-14

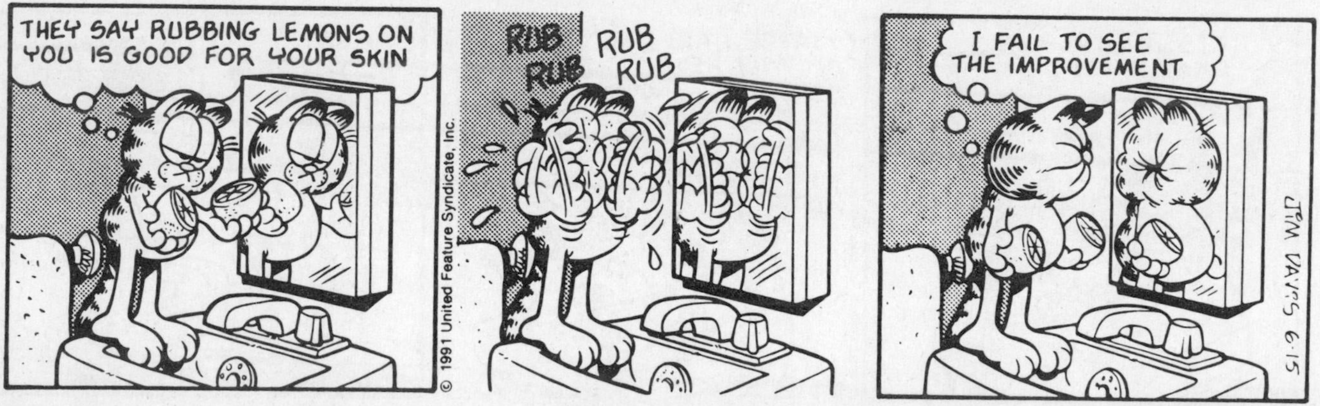
THEY SAY RUBBING LEMONS ON YOU IS GOOD FOR YOUR SKIN
RUB RUB
RUB RUB
I FAIL TO SEE THE IMPROVEMENT
JIM DAVIS 6-15

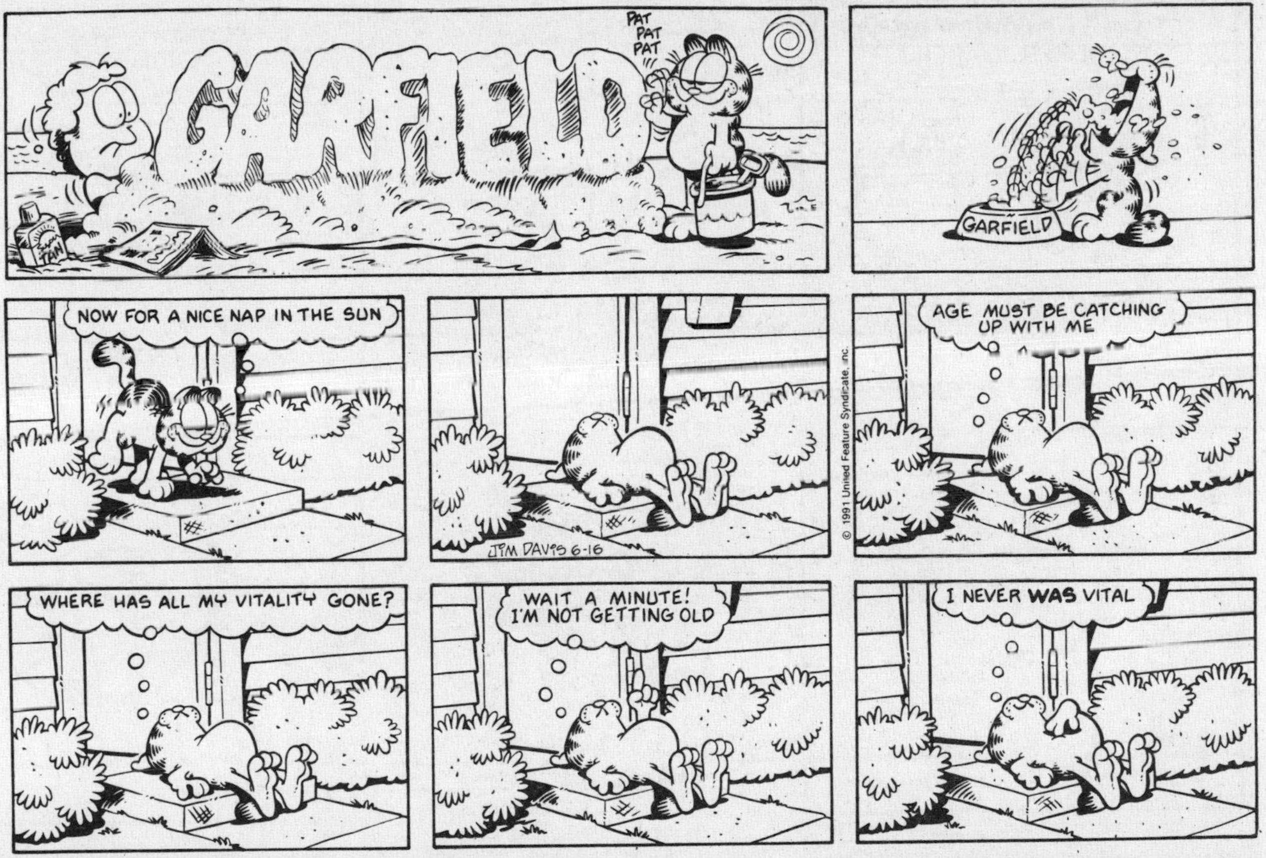

GARFIELD
PAT PAT PAT
GARFIELD
NOW FOR A NICE NAP IN THE SUN
JIM DAVIS 6-16
© 1991 United Feature Syndicate, Inc.
AGE MUST BE CATCHING UP WITH ME
WHERE HAS ALL MY VITALITY GONE?
WAIT A MINUTE! I'M NOT GETTING OLD
I NEVER WAS VITAL

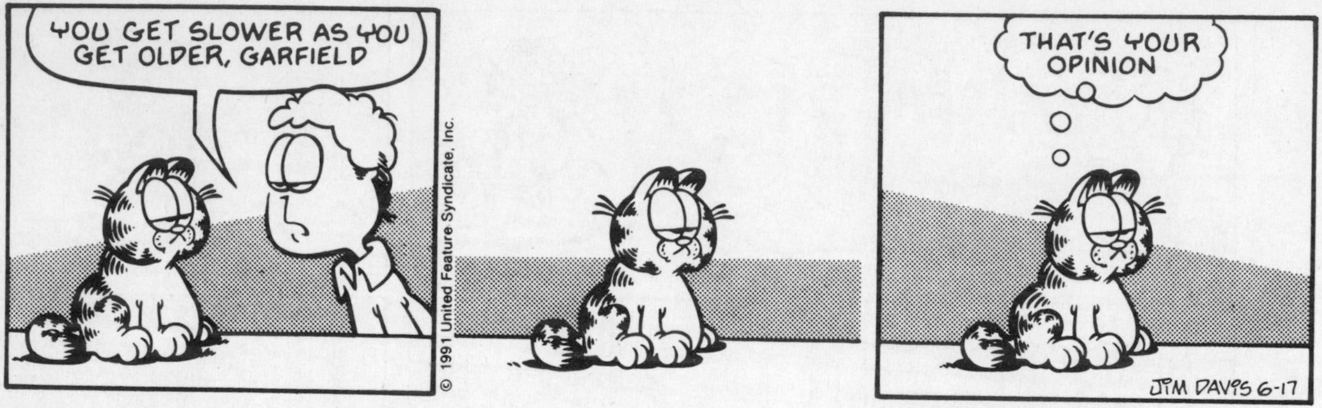
YOU GET SLOWER AS YOU GET OLDER, GARFIELD
© 1991 United Feature Syndicate, Inc.
THAT'S YOUR OPINION
JIM DAVIS 6-17

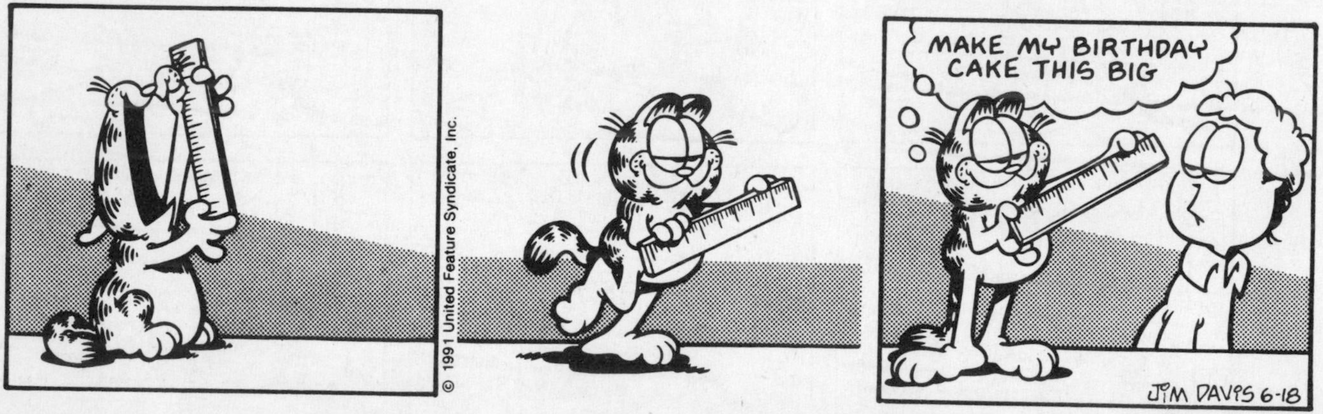
© 1991 United Feature Syndicate, Inc.
MAKE MY BIRTHDAY CAKE THIS BIG
JIM DAVIS 6-18

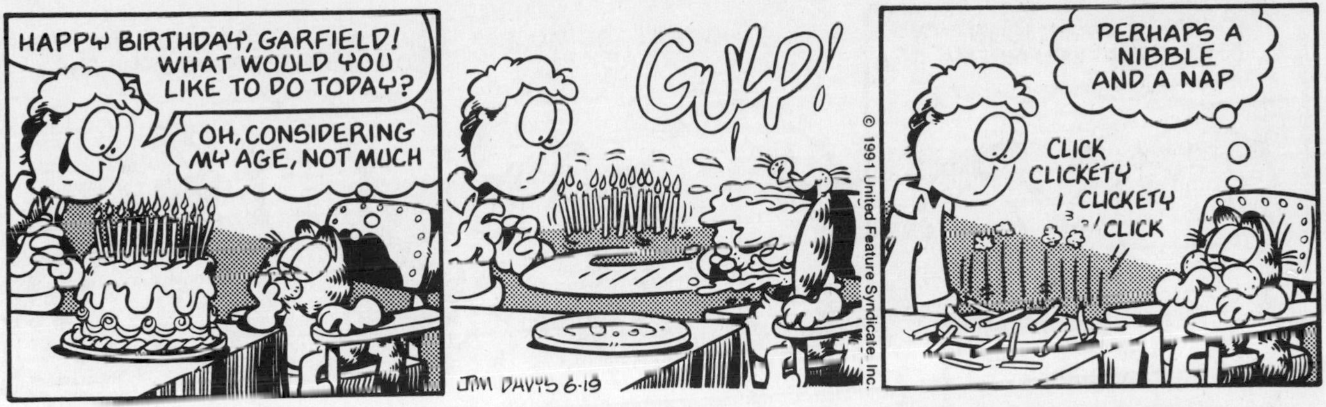
HAPPY BIRTHDAY, GARFIELD! WHAT WOULD YOU LIKE TO DO TODAY?
OH, CONSIDERING MY AGE, NOT MUCH
GULP!
JIM DAVIS 6-19
© 1991 United Feature Syndicate, Inc.
PERHAPS A NIBBLE AND A NAP
CLICK CLICKETY CLICKETY CLICK

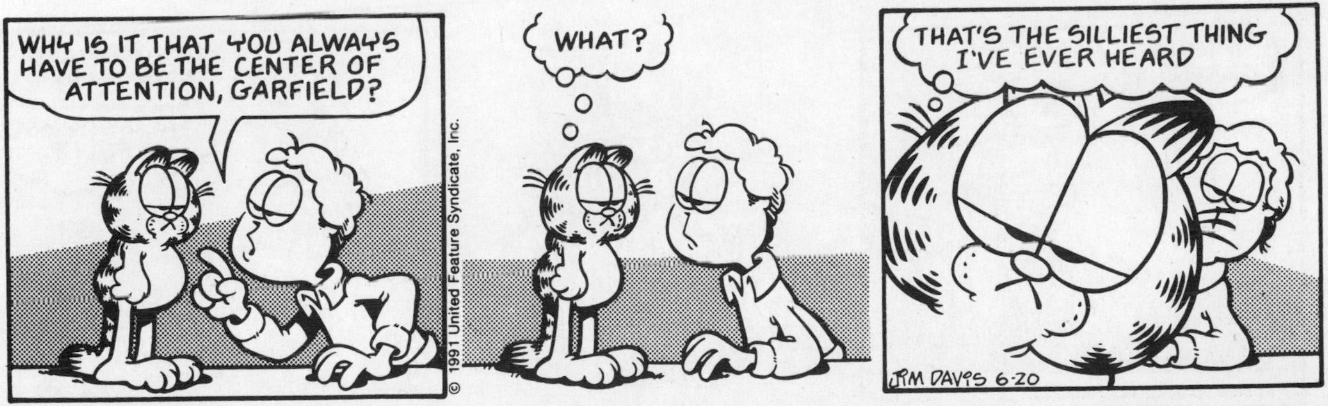
WHY IS IT THAT YOU ALWAYS HAVE TO BE THE CENTER OF ATTENTION, GARFIELD?
© 1991 United Feature Syndicate, Inc.
WHAT?
THAT'S THE SILLIEST THING I'VE EVER HEARD
JIM DAVIS 6-20

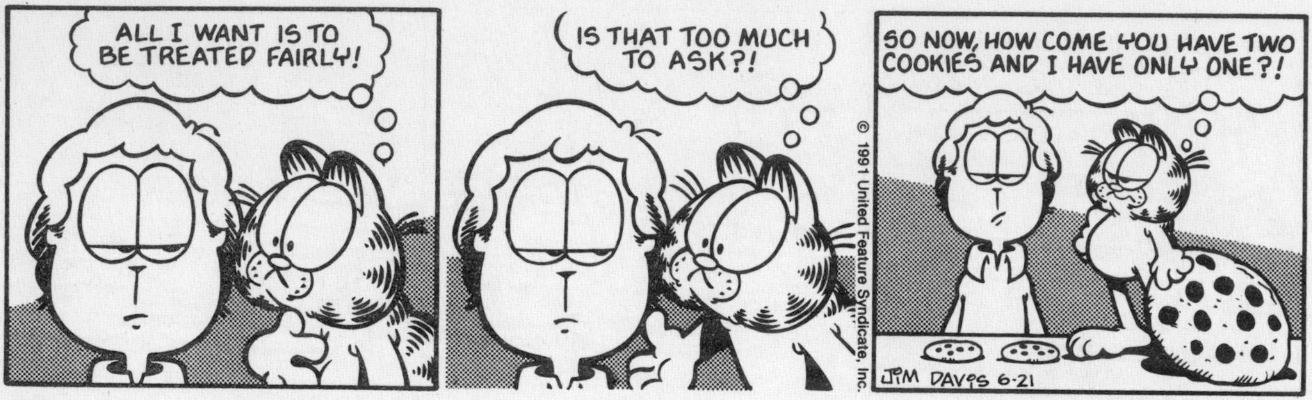
ALL I WANT IS TO BE TREATED FAIRLY!
IS THAT TOO MUCH TO ASK?!
© 1991 United Feature Syndicate, Inc.
SO NOW, HOW COME YOU HAVE TWO COOKIES AND I HAVE ONLY ONE?!
JIM DAVIS 6-21

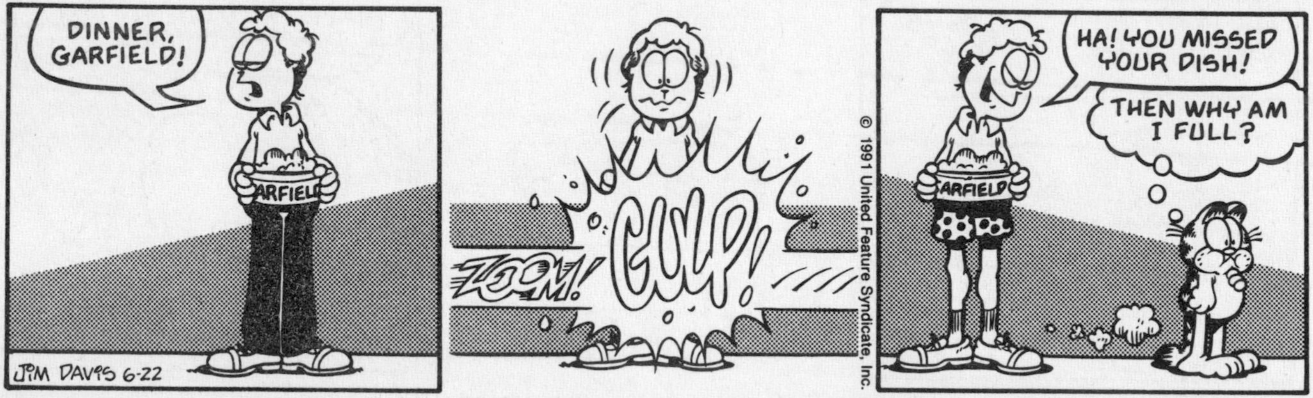
DINNER, GARFIELD!
GARFIELD
JIM DAVIS 6-22
ZOOM!
GULP!
© 1991 United Feature Syndicate, Inc.
HA! YOU MISSED YOUR DISH!
THEN WHY AM I FULL?
ARFIELD

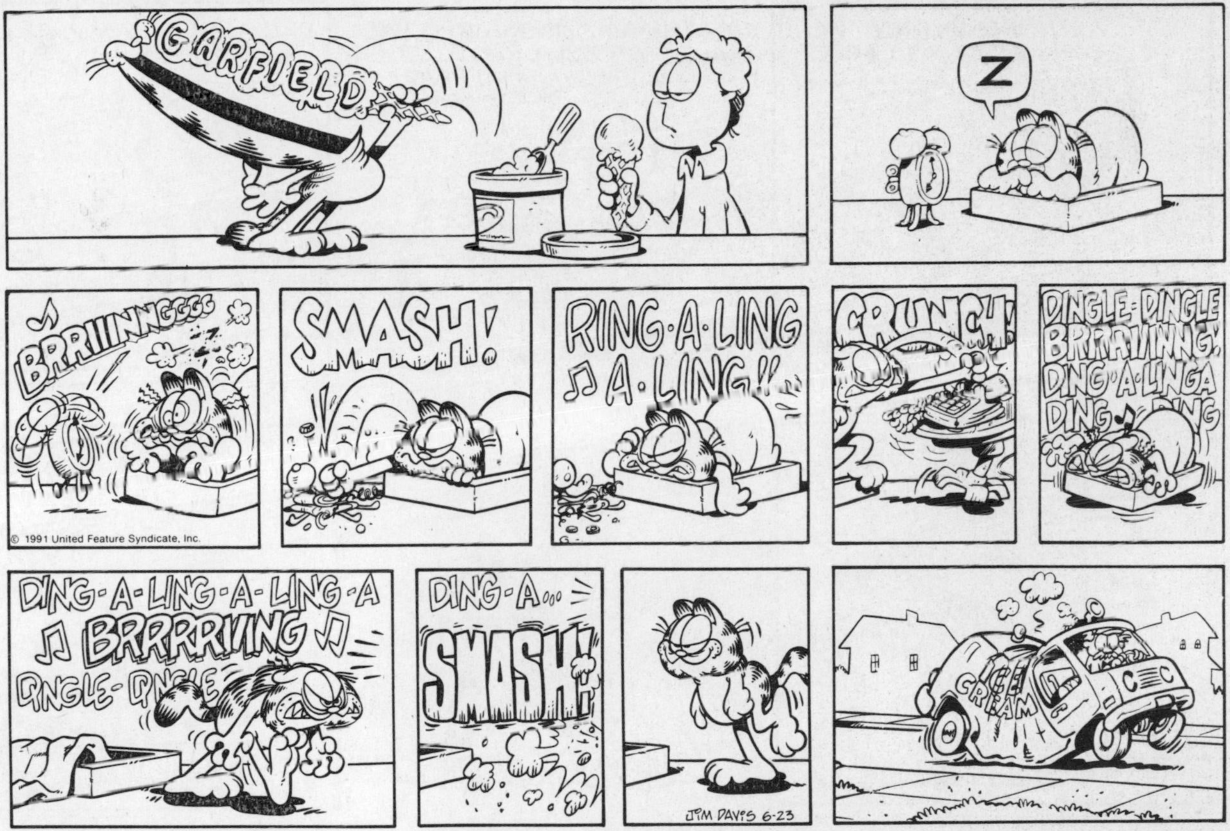
GARFIELD
Z
BRRIIINNGGGG
SMASH!
RING-A-LING
A-LING!!
CRUNCH!
DINGLE-DINGLE
BRRRRIIINNG!
DING-A-LINGA
DING
DING-A-LING-A-LING-A
BRRRRIIING
DINGLE-DINGLE
DING-A...
SMASH!
ICE CREAM
© 1991 United Feature Syndicate, Inc.
JIM DAVIS 6-23

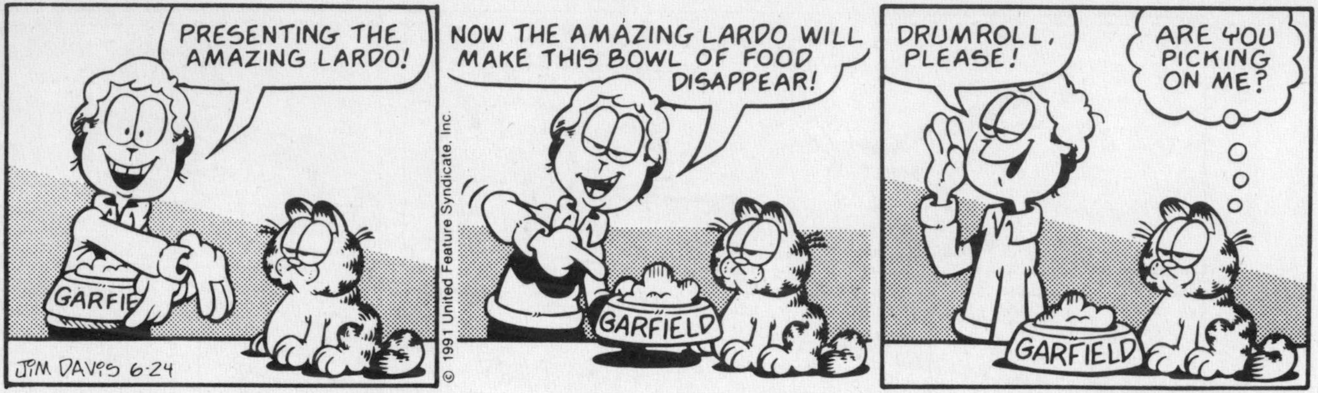
PRESENTING THE AMAZING LARDO!
NOW THE AMAZING LARDO WILL MAKE THIS BOWL OF FOOD DISAPPEAR!
DRUMROLL, PLEASE!
ARE YOU PICKING ON ME?
JIM DAVIS 6-24

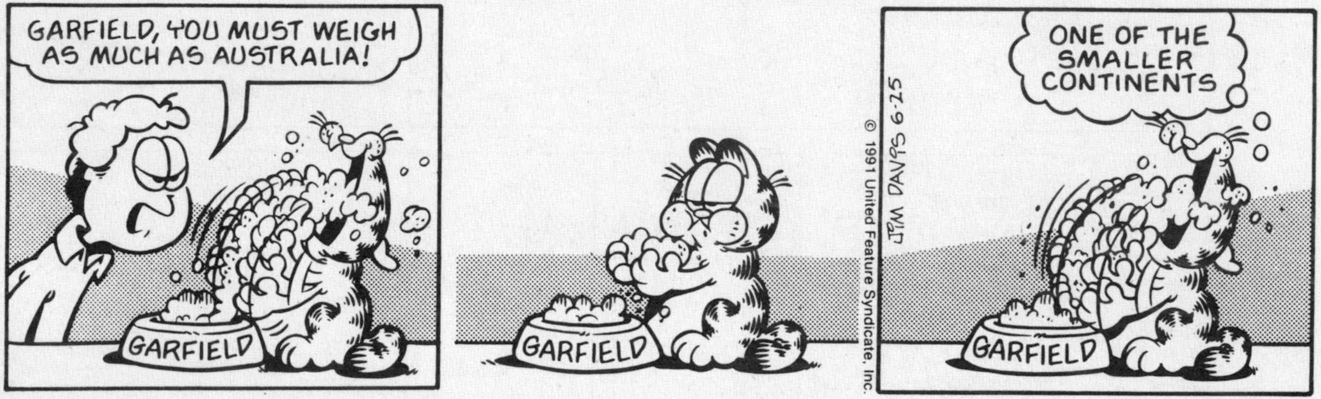
GARFIELD, YOU MUST WEIGH AS MUCH AS AUSTRALIA!
ONE OF THE SMALLER CONTINENTS
JIM DAVIS 6-25

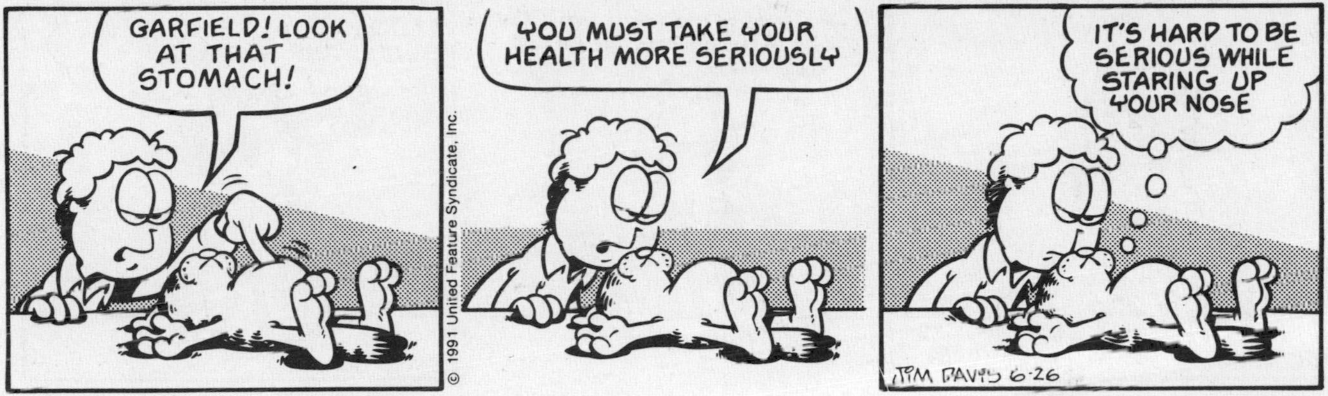
GARFIELD! LOOK AT THAT STOMACH!
YOU MUST TAKE YOUR HEALTH MORE SERIOUSLY
IT'S HARD TO BE SERIOUS WHILE STARING UP YOUR NOSE
© 1991 United Feature Syndicate, Inc.
JIM DAVIS 6-26

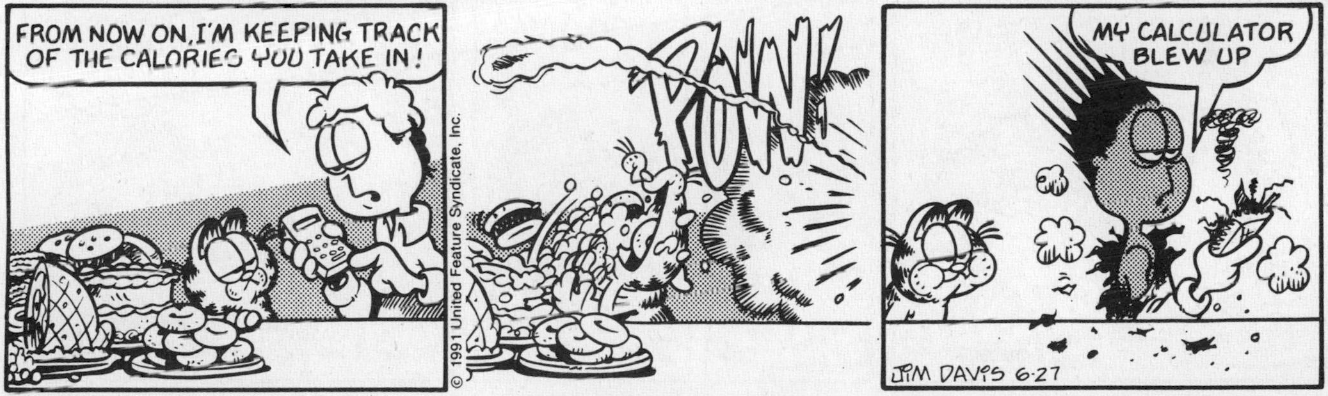
FROM NOW ON, I'M KEEPING TRACK OF THE CALORIES YOU TAKE IN!
POW!
MY CALCULATOR BLEW UP
© 1991 United Feature Syndicate, Inc.
JIM DAVIS 6-27

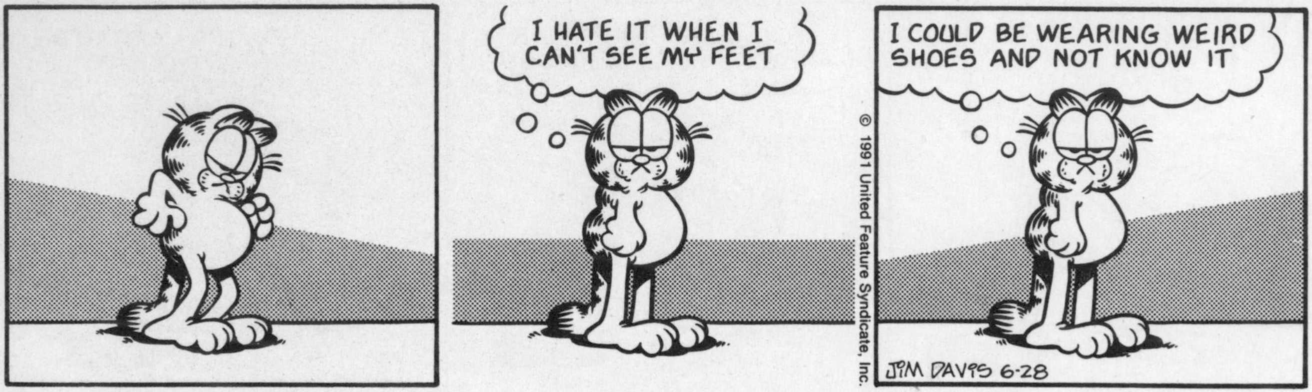
I HATE IT WHEN I CAN'T SEE MY FEET
I COULD BE WEARING WEIRD SHOES AND NOT KNOW IT
JIM DAVIS 6-28
© 1991 United Feature Syndicate, Inc.

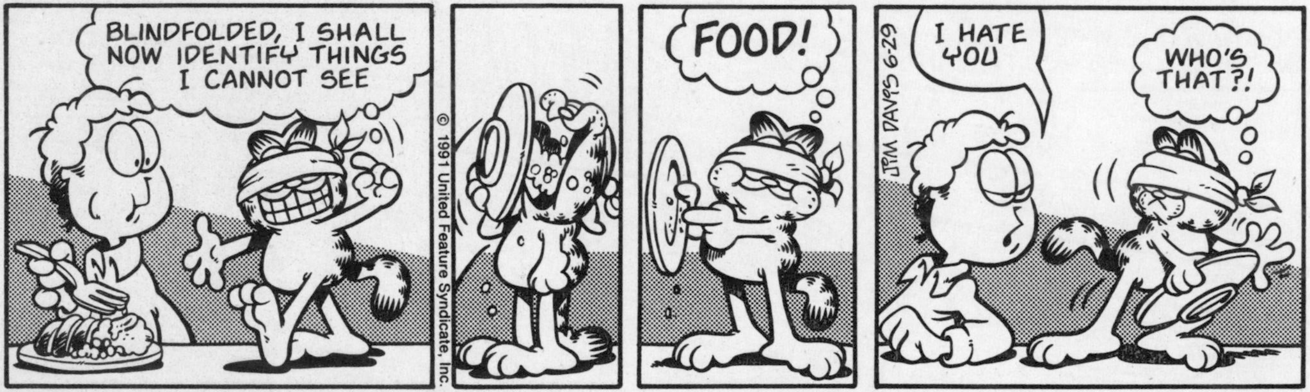
BLINDFOLDED, I SHALL NOW IDENTIFY THINGS I CANNOT SEE
© 1991 United Feature Syndicate, Inc.
FOOD!
JIM DAVIS 6-29
I HATE YOU
WHO'S THAT?!

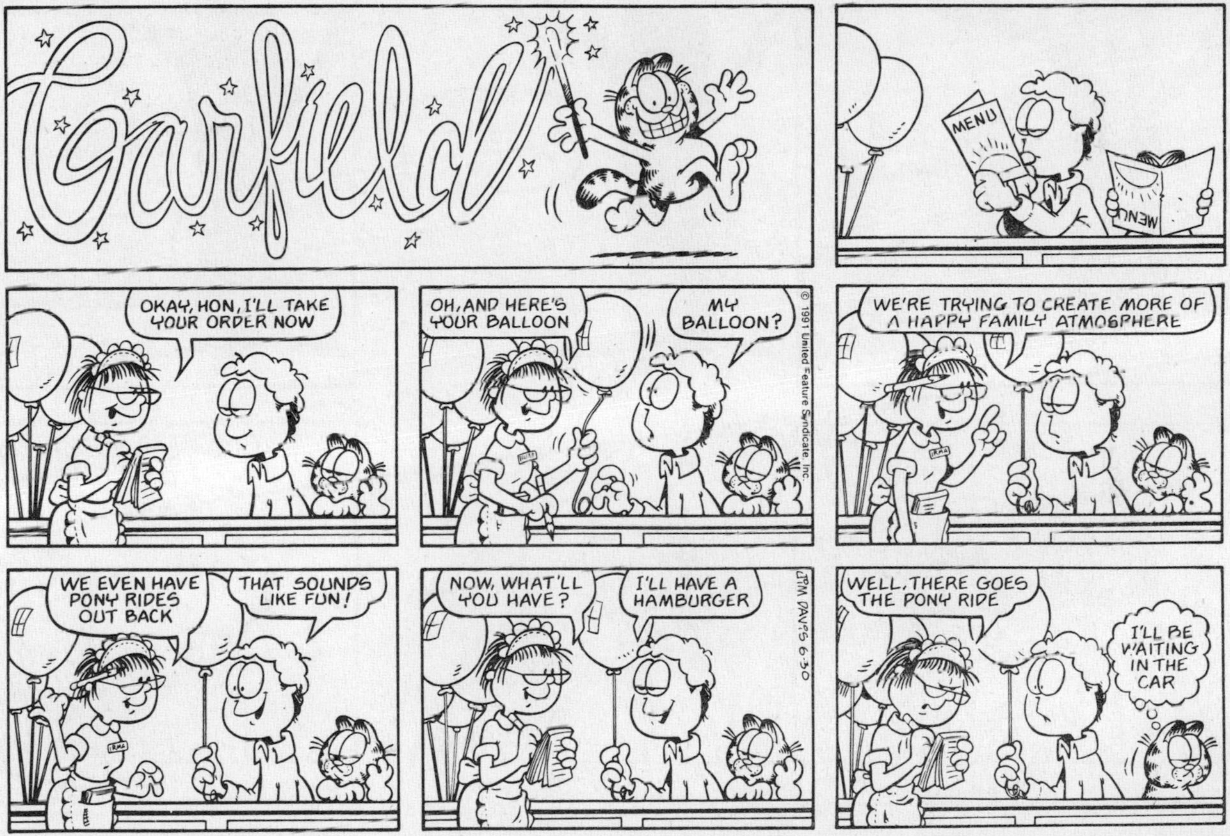
Garfield
MENU
MENU
OKAY, HON, I'LL TAKE YOUR ORDER NOW
OH, AND HERE'S YOUR BALLOON
MY BALLOON?
© 1991 United Feature Syndicate, Inc.
WE'RE TRYING TO CREATE MORE OF A HAPPY FAMILY ATMOSPHERE
WE EVEN HAVE PONY RIDES OUT BACK
THAT SOUNDS LIKE FUN!
NOW, WHAT'LL YOU HAVE?
I'LL HAVE A HAMBURGER
JPM DAVIS 6-30
WELL, THERE GOES THE PONY RIDE
I'LL BE WAITING IN THE CAR

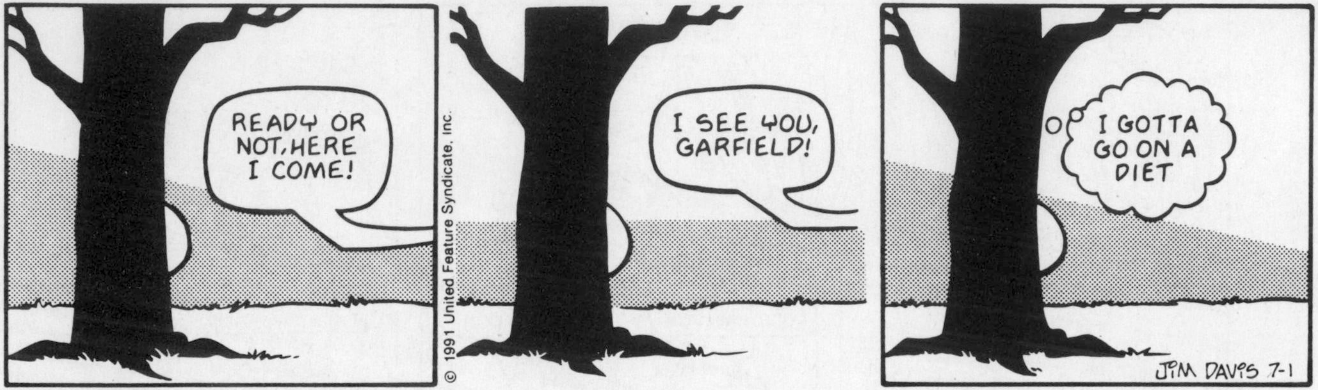
READY OR NOT, HERE I COME!
I SEE YOU, GARFIELD!
I GOTTA GO ON A DIET
JIM DAVIS 7-1

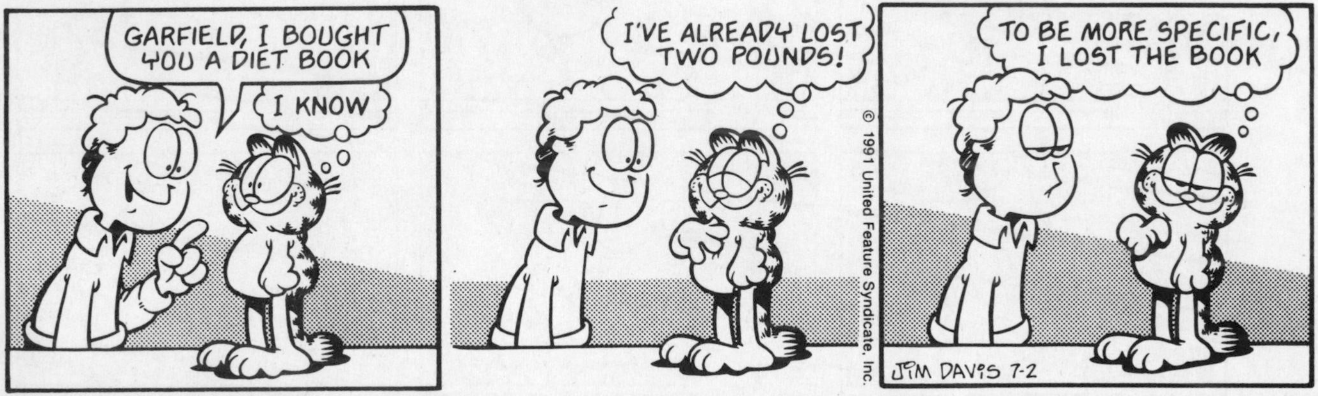
GARFIELD, I BOUGHT YOU A DIET BOOK
I KNOW
I'VE ALREADY LOST TWO POUNDS!
TO BE MORE SPECIFIC, I LOST THE BOOK
JIM DAVIS 7-2

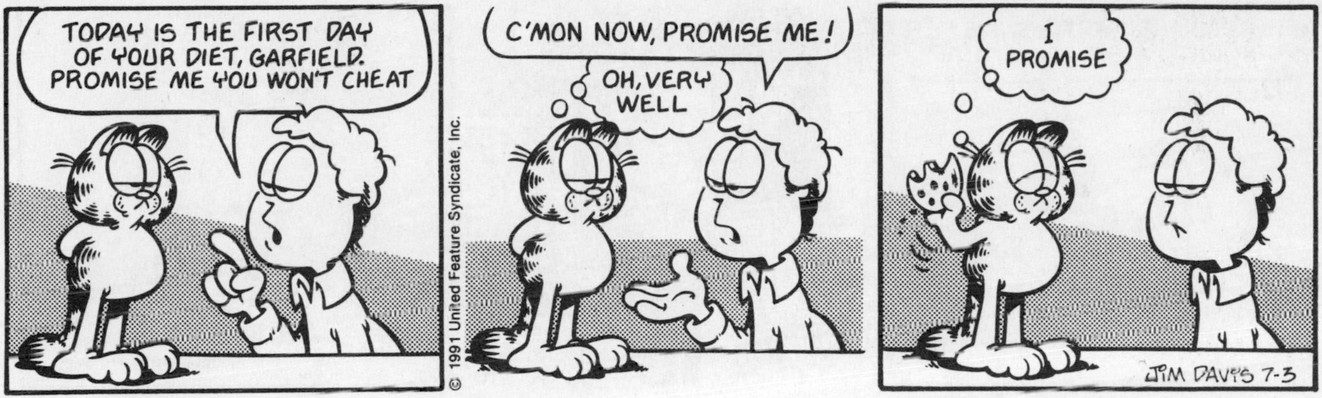
TODAY IS THE FIRST DAY OF YOUR DIET, GARFIELD. PROMISE ME YOU WON'T CHEAT
C'MON NOW, PROMISE ME!
OH, VERY WELL
I PROMISE
JIM DAVIS 7-3
© 1991 United Feature Syndicate, Inc.

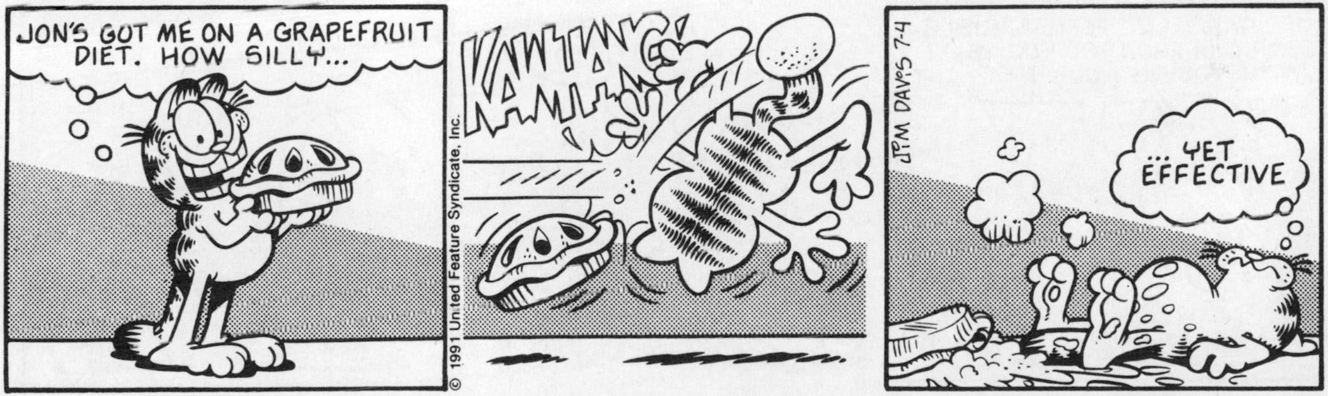
JON'S GOT ME ON A GRAPEFRUIT DIET. HOW SILLY...
KAWHANG!
... YET EFFECTIVE
JIM DAVIS 7-4
© 1991 United Feature Syndicate, Inc.

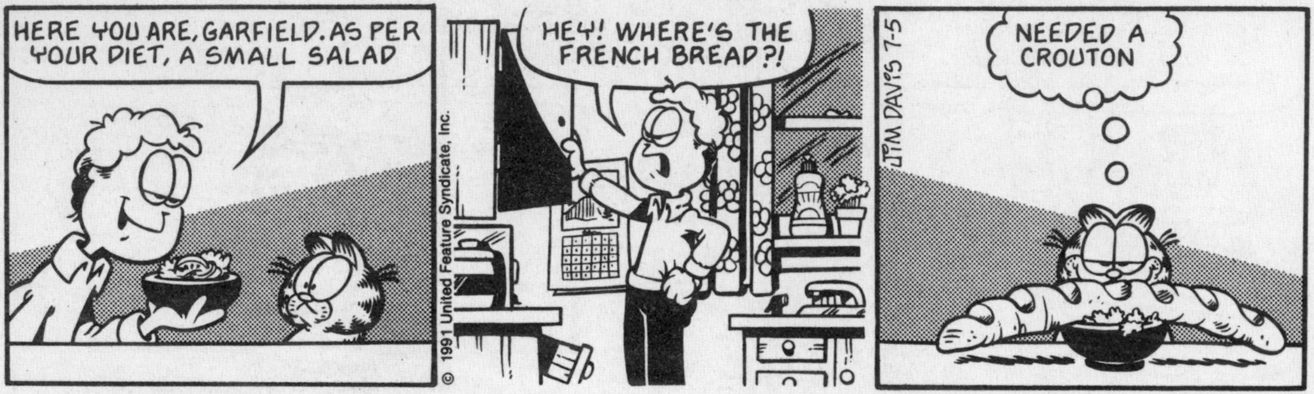
HERE YOU ARE, GARFIELD. AS PER YOUR DIET, A SMALL SALAD
© 1991 United Feature Syndicate, Inc.
HEY! WHERE'S THE FRENCH BREAD?!
JIM DAVIS 7-5
NEEDED A CROUTON

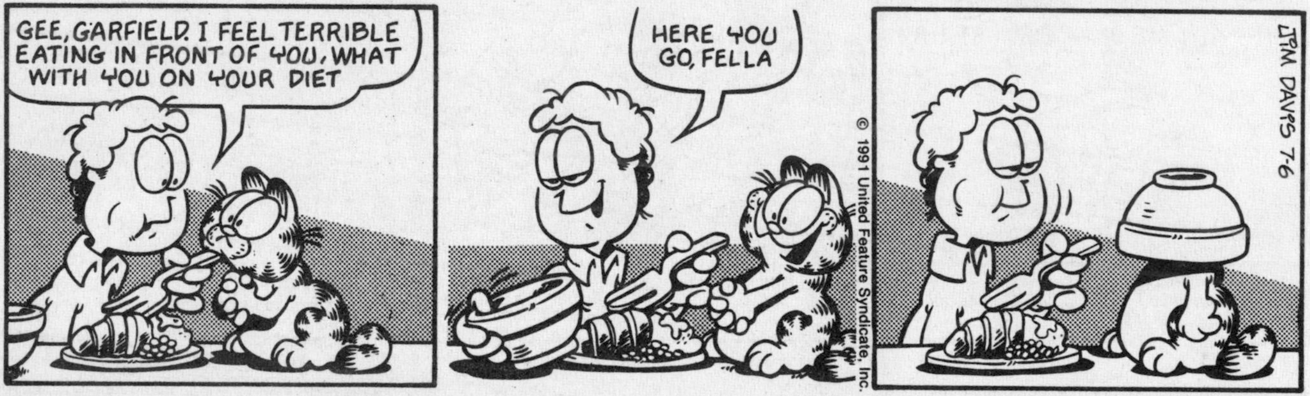
GEE, GARFIELD. I FEEL TERRIBLE EATING IN FRONT OF YOU, WHAT WITH YOU ON YOUR DIET
HERE YOU GO, FELLA
© 1991 United Feature Syndicate, Inc.
JIM DAVIS 7-6

Sometime in the 21st century...

GARFIELD PREDICTS

Days will be made longer so cats can get more sleep

France will officially change its name to "The Francster"

Scientists will develop a disposable dog

A large burp will devastate parts of Siberia

Astronomers will discover a huge flea collar encircling Pluto

Jon will be inducted into the "Geek Hall of Fame"

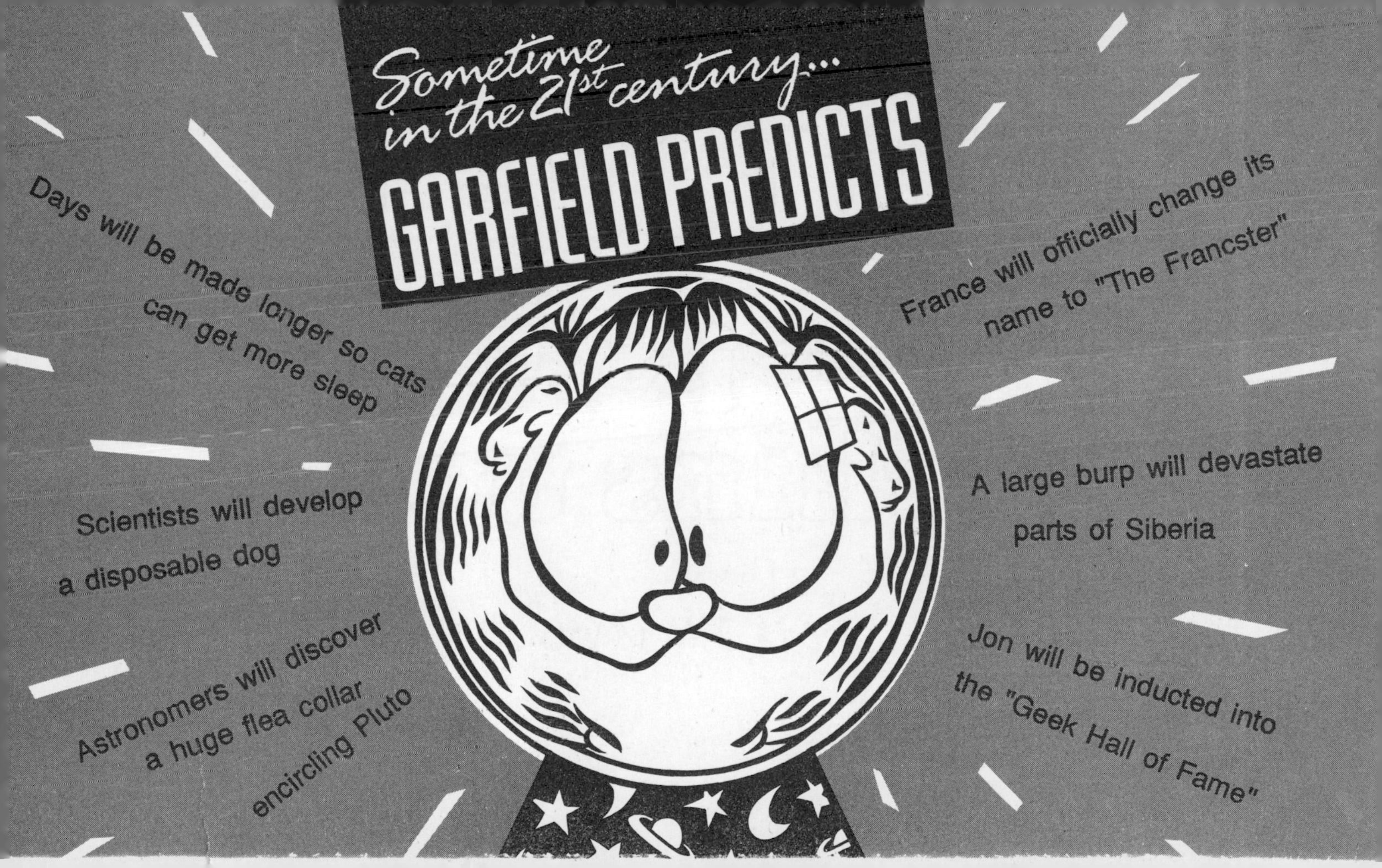

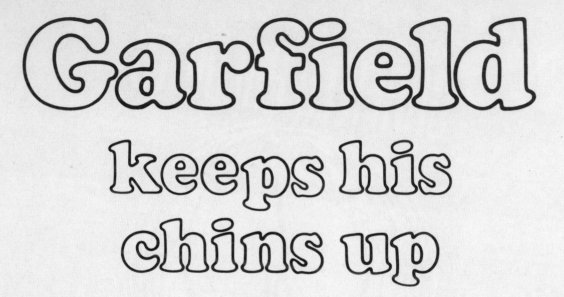

Garfield keeps his chins up

BY: JIM DAVIS

YOU KNOW YOU'RE GETTING FAT WHEN...

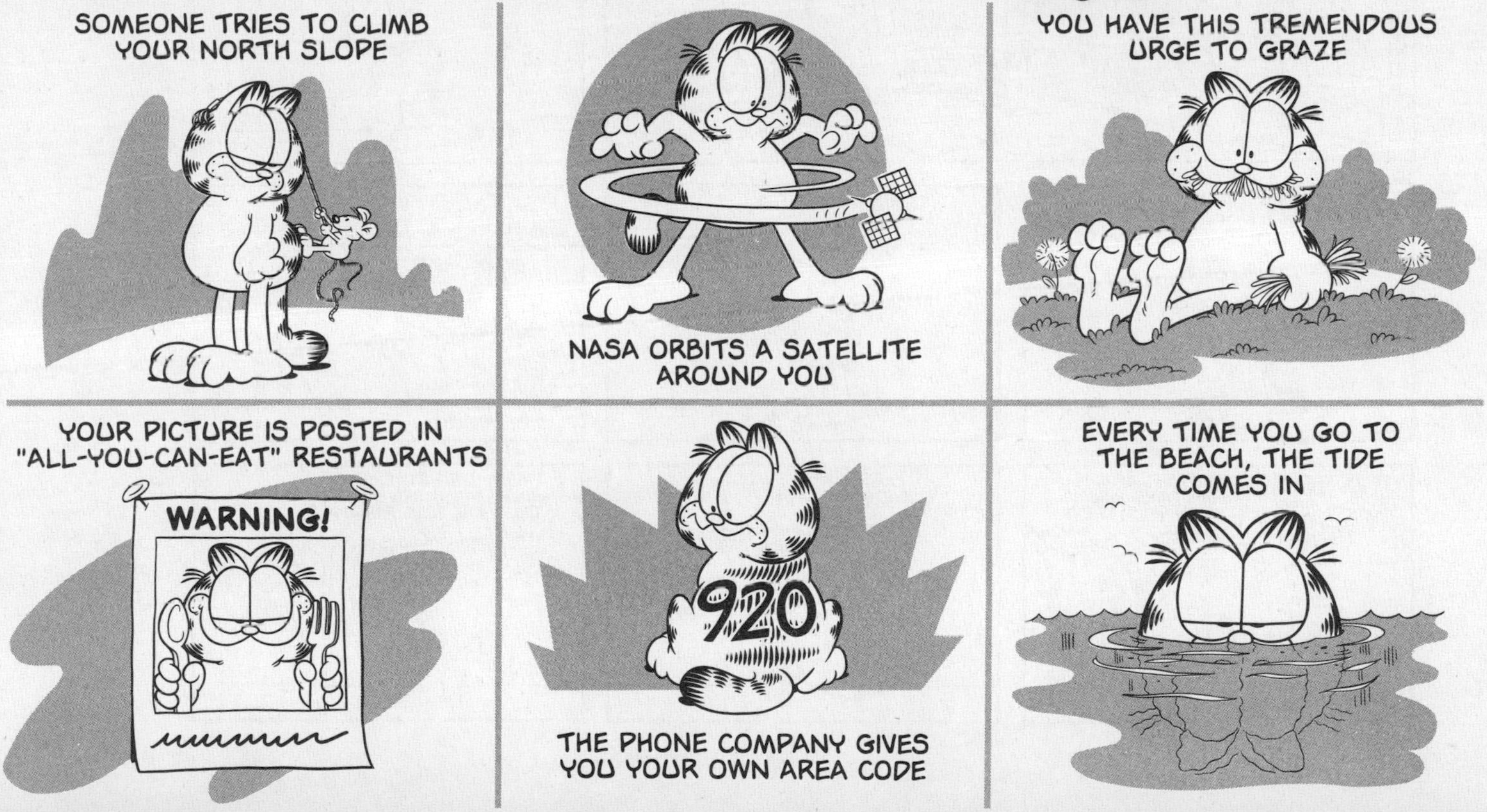
SOMEONE TRIES TO CLIMB YOUR NORTH SLOPE
NASA ORBITS A SATELLITE AROUND YOU
YOU HAVE THIS TREMENDOUS URGE TO GRAZE
YOUR PICTURE IS POSTED IN "ALL-YOU-CAN-EAT" RESTAURANTS
WARNING!
920
THE PHONE COMPANY GIVES YOU YOUR OWN AREA CODE
EVERY TIME YOU GO TO THE BEACH, THE TIDE COMES IN

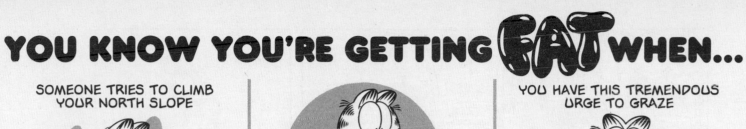

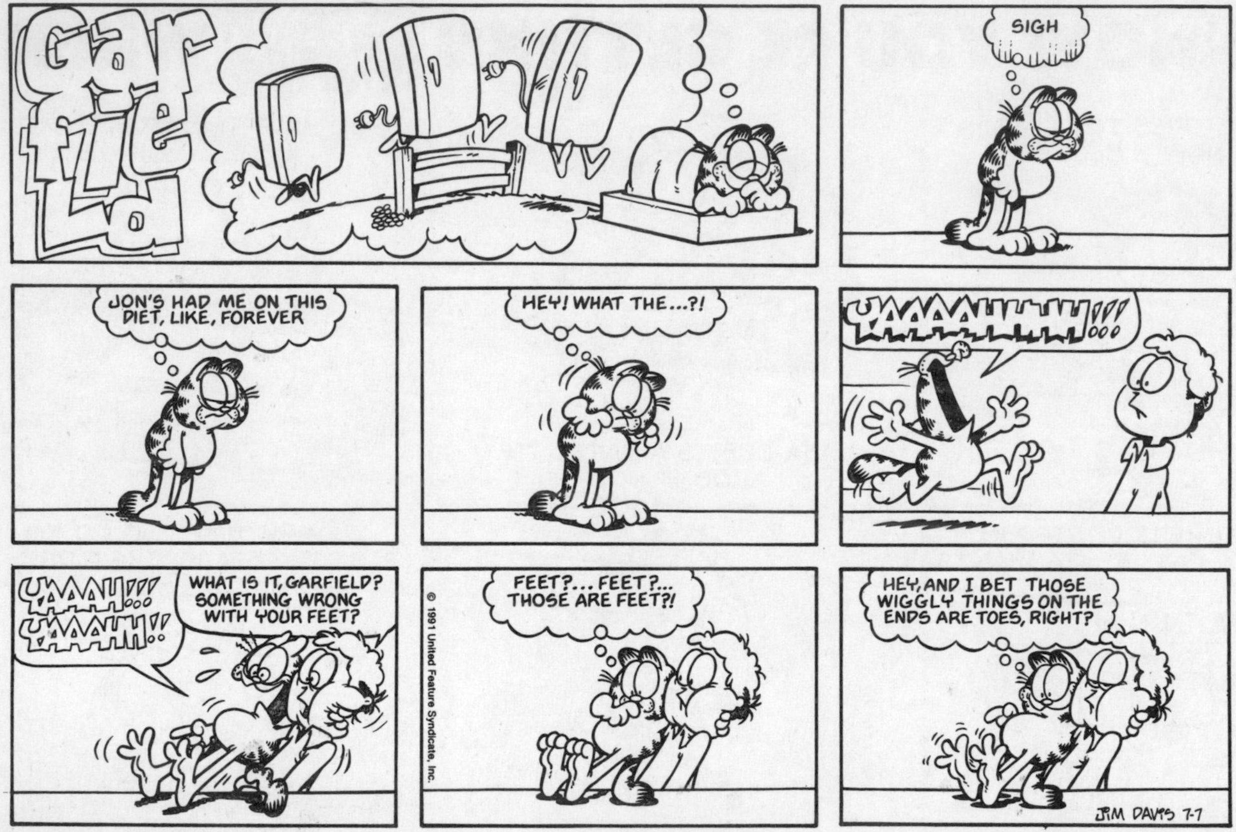

GARFIELD
SIGH
JON'S HAD ME ON THIS DIET, LIKE, FOREVER
HEY! WHAT THE...?!
YAAAAHHHH!!!
YAAAH!!!
YAAAHH!!
WHAT IS IT, GARFIELD? SOMETHING WRONG WITH YOUR FEET?
© 1991 United Feature Syndicate, Inc.
FEET?... FEET?... THOSE ARE FEET?!
HEY, AND I BET THOSE WIGGLY THINGS ON THE ENDS ARE TOES, RIGHT?
JIM DAVIS 7-7

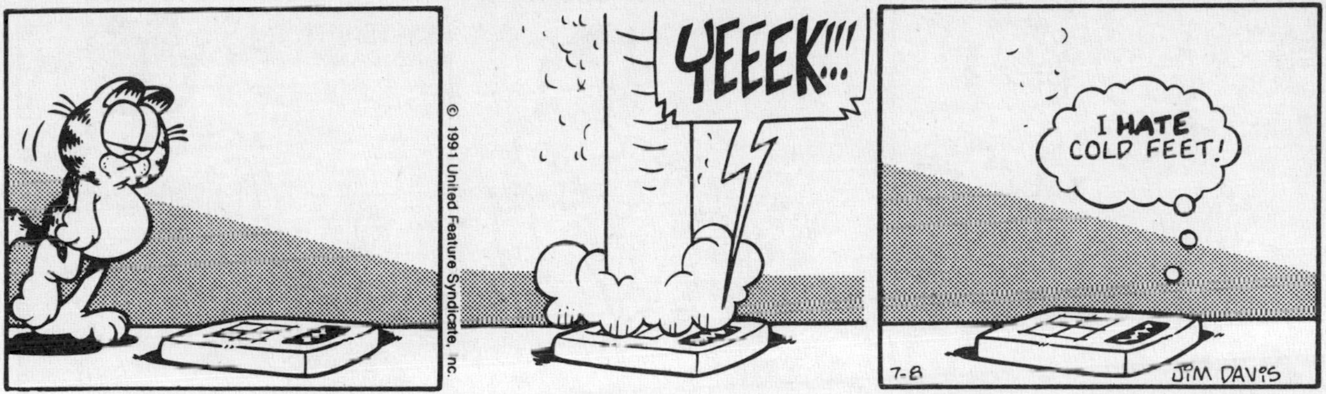
YEEEK!!!...
I HATE COLD FEET!
7-8
JIM DAVIS
© 1991 United Feature Syndicate, Inc.

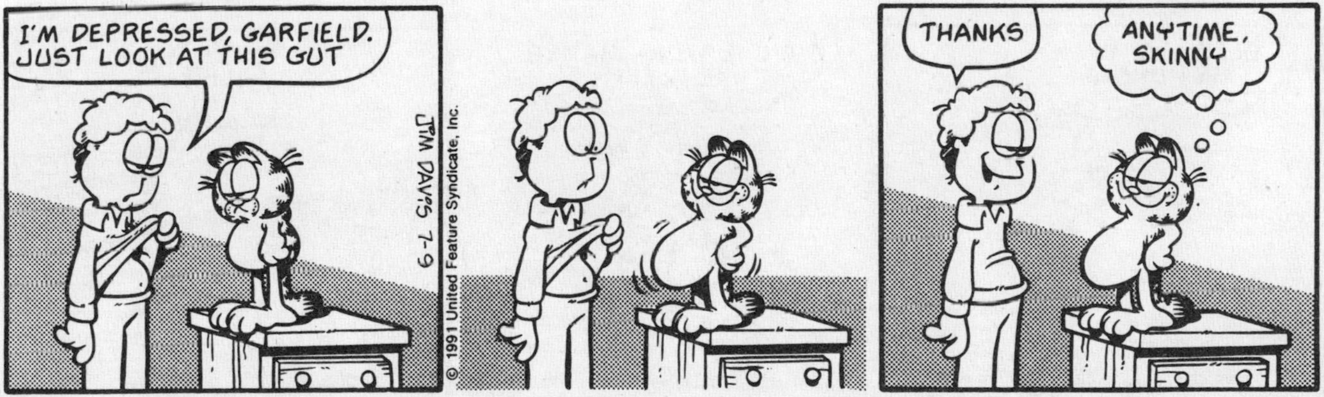
I'M DEPRESSED, GARFIELD. JUST LOOK AT THIS GUT
THANKS
ANYTIME, SKINNY
JIM DAVIS 7-9
© 1991 United Feature Syndicate, Inc.

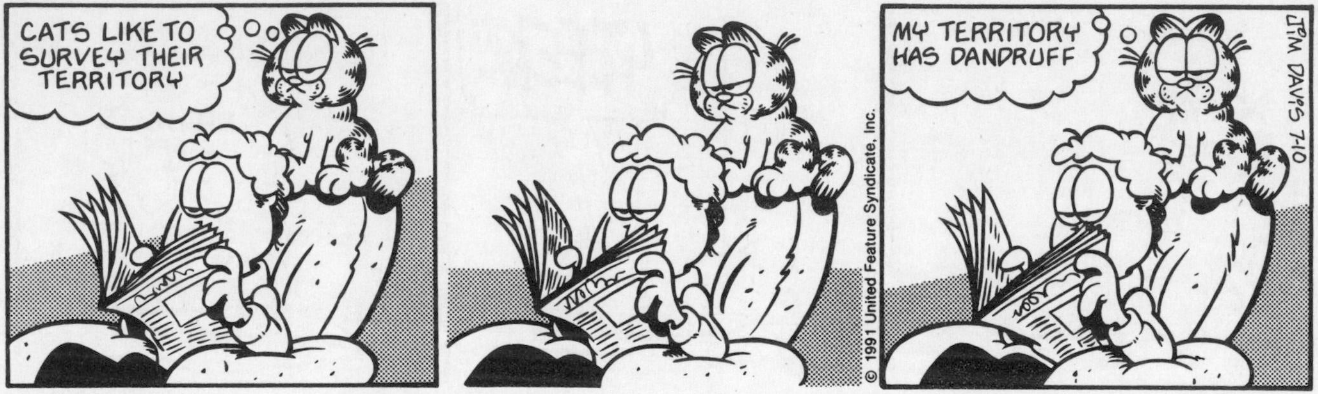
CATS LIKE TO SURVEY THEIR TERRITORY
MY TERRITORY HAS DANDRUFF
JIM DAVIS 7-10
© 1991 United Feature Syndicate, Inc.

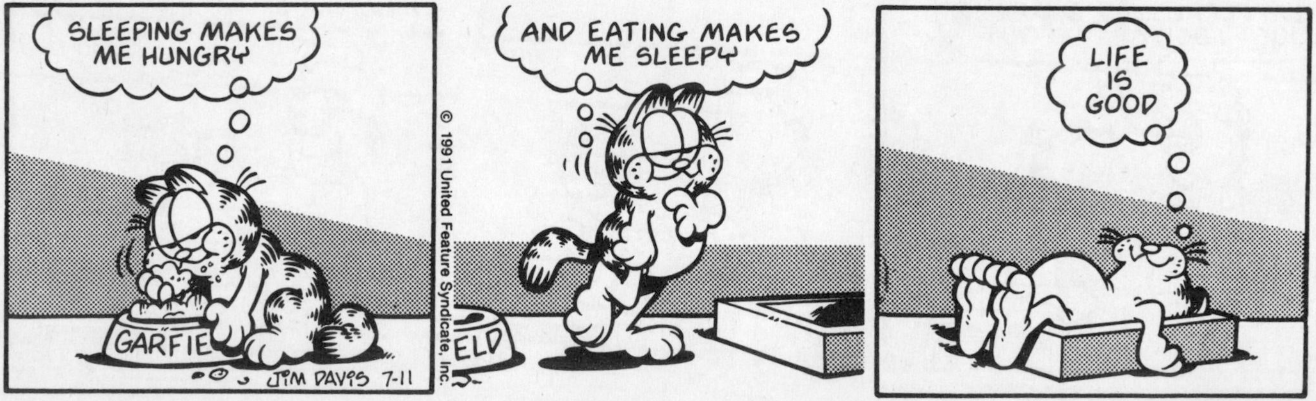
SLEEPING MAKES ME HUNGRY
GARFIE
JIM DAVIS 7-11
© 1991 United Feature Syndicate, Inc.
AND EATING MAKES ME SLEEPY
ELD
LIFE IS GOOD

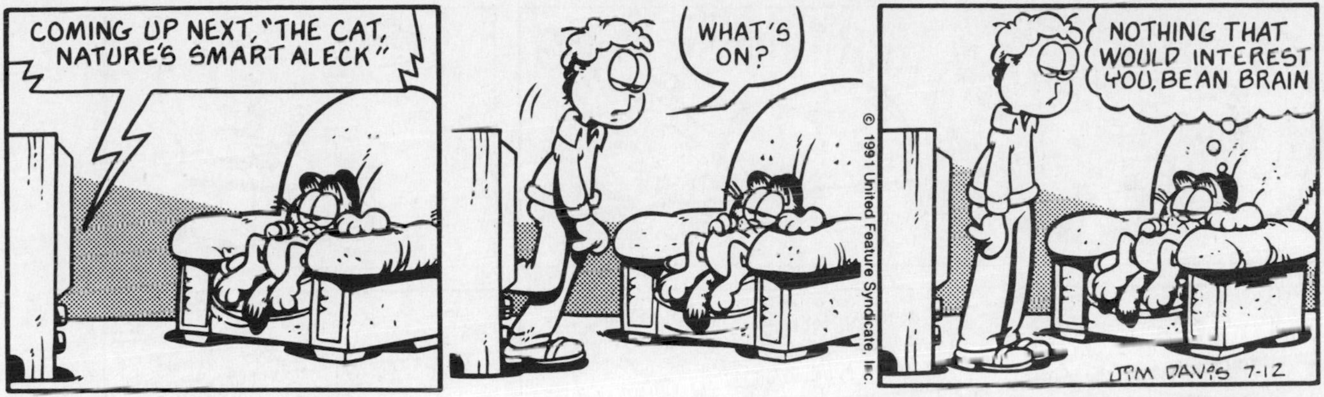
COMING UP NEXT, "THE CAT, NATURE'S SMART ALECK"
WHAT'S ON?
NOTHING THAT WOULD INTEREST YOU, BEAN BRAIN
JIM DAVIS 7-12

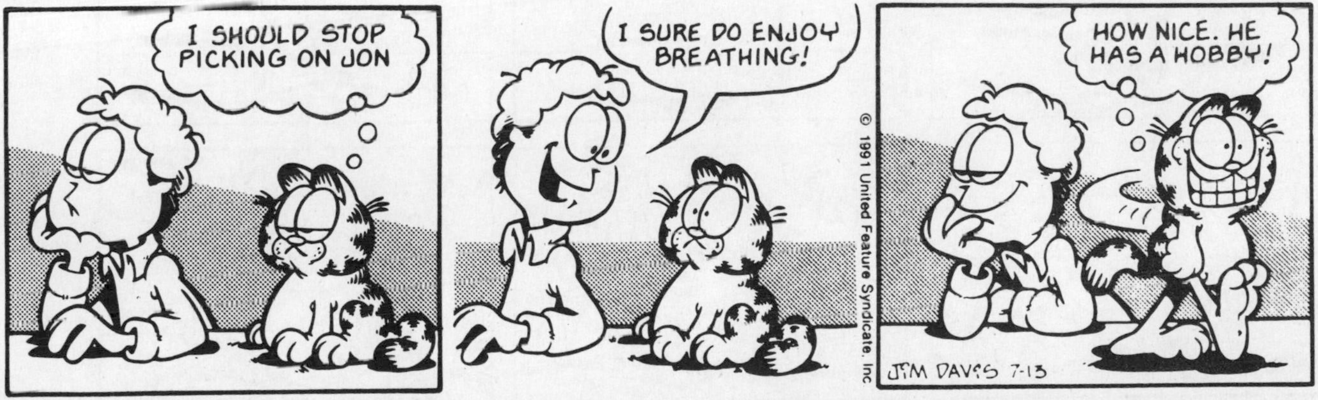
I SHOULD STOP PICKING ON JON
I SURE DO ENJOY BREATHING!
HOW NICE. HE HAS A HOBBY!
JIM DAVIS 7-13

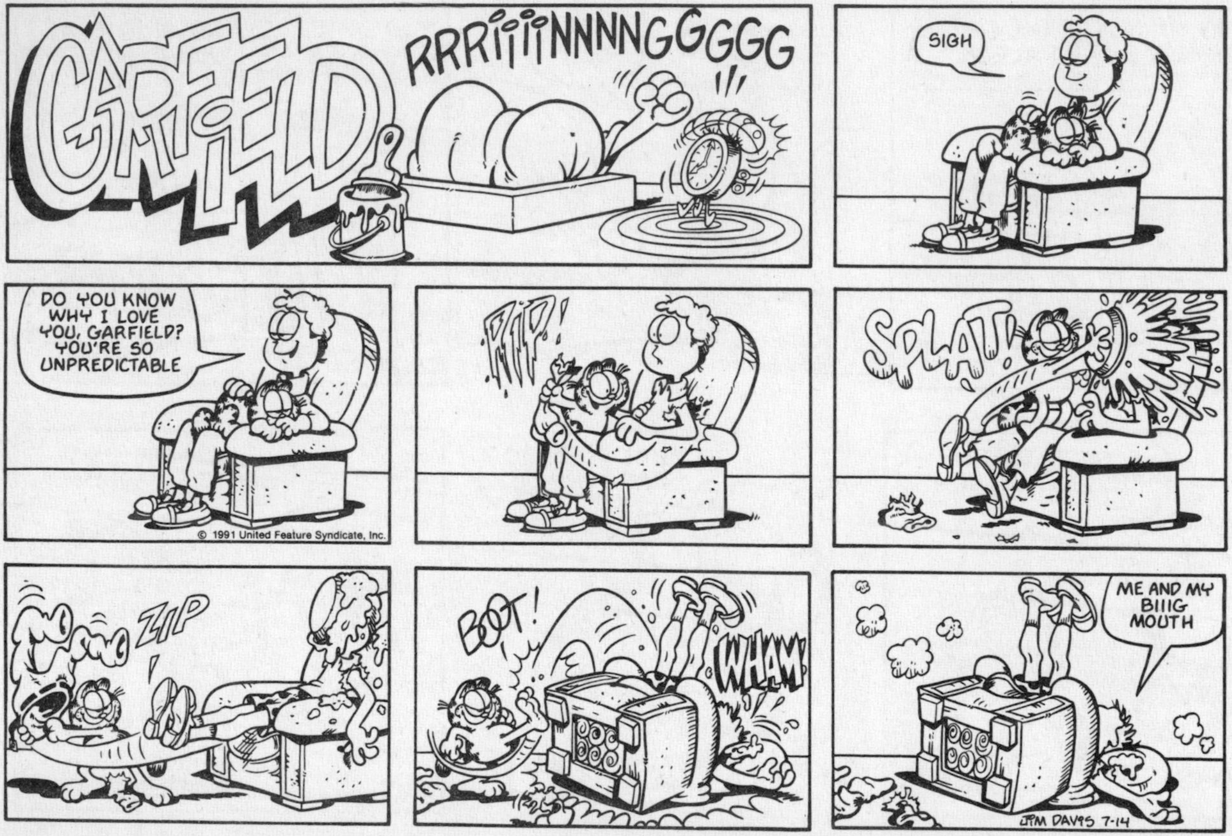
GARFIELD
RRRiiiiNNNNGGGGG
SIGH
DO YOU KNOW WHY I LOVE YOU, GARFIELD? YOU'RE SO UNPREDICTABLE
© 1991 United Feature Syndicate, Inc.
RIP!
SPLAT!
ZIP
BOOT!
WHAM
ME AND MY BIIIG MOUTH
JIM DAVIS 7-14

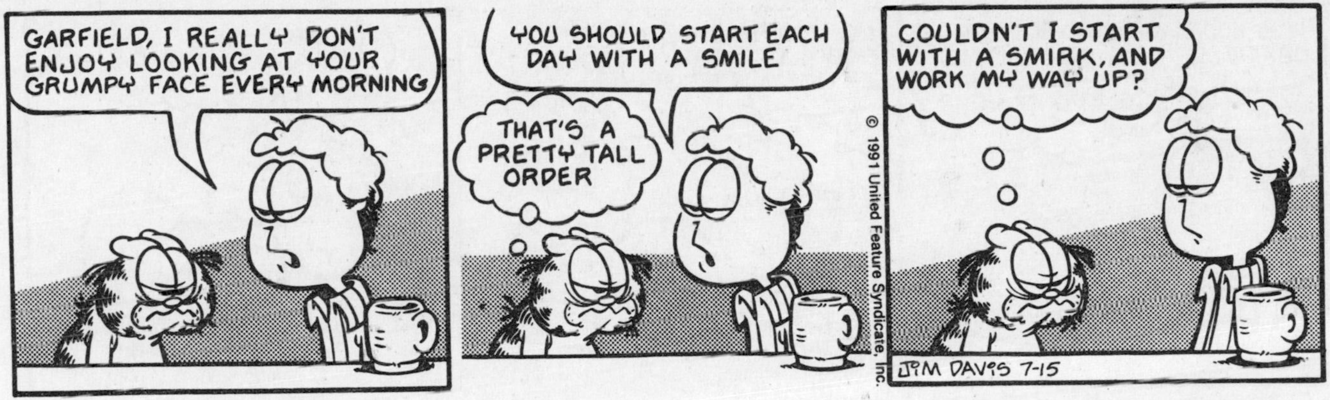
GARFIELD, I REALLY DON'T ENJOY LOOKING AT YOUR GRUMPY FACE EVERY MORNING
YOU SHOULD START EACH DAY WITH A SMILE
THAT'S A PRETTY TALL ORDER
© 1991 United Feature Syndicate, Inc.
COULDN'T I START WITH A SMIRK, AND WORK MY WAY UP?
JIM DAVIS 7-15

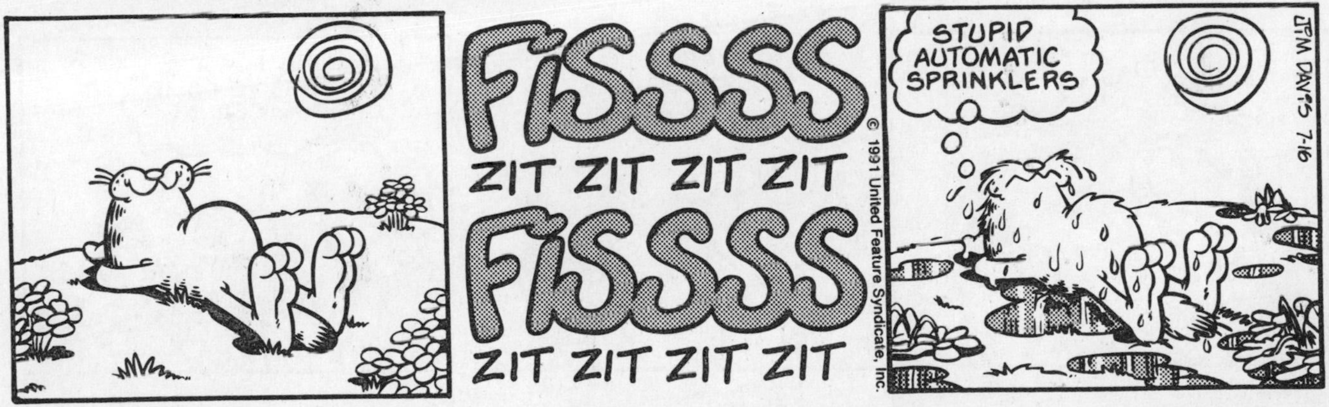
FISSSS
ZIT ZIT ZIT ZIT
FISSSS
ZIT ZIT ZIT ZIT
© 1991 United Feature Syndicate, Inc.
STUPID AUTOMATIC SPRINKLERS
JIM DAVIS 7-16

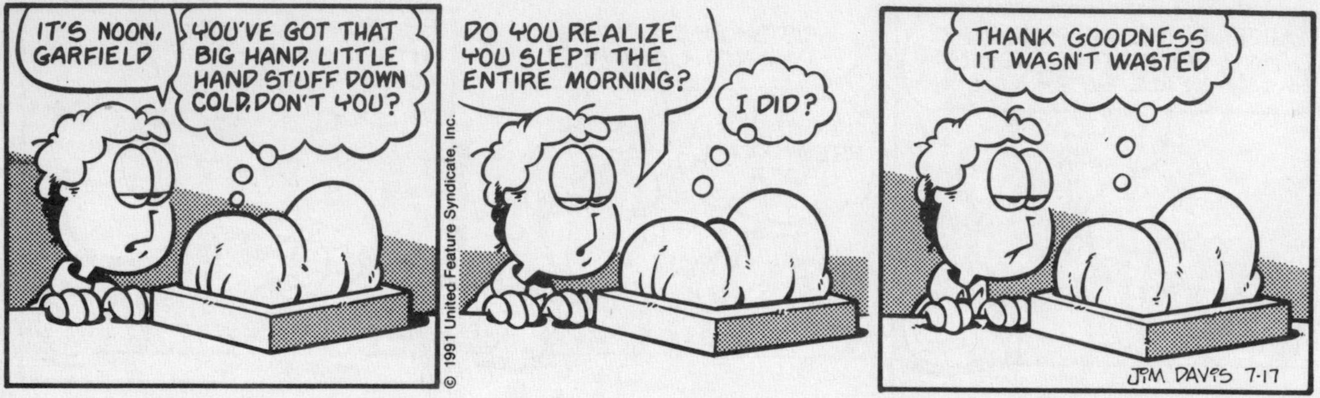
IT'S NOON, GARFIELD
YOU'VE GOT THAT BIG HAND, LITTLE HAND STUFF DOWN COLD, DON'T YOU?
DO YOU REALIZE YOU SLEPT THE ENTIRE MORNING?
I DID?
THANK GOODNESS IT WASN'T WASTED
© 1991 United Feature Syndicate, Inc.
JIM DAVIS 7-17

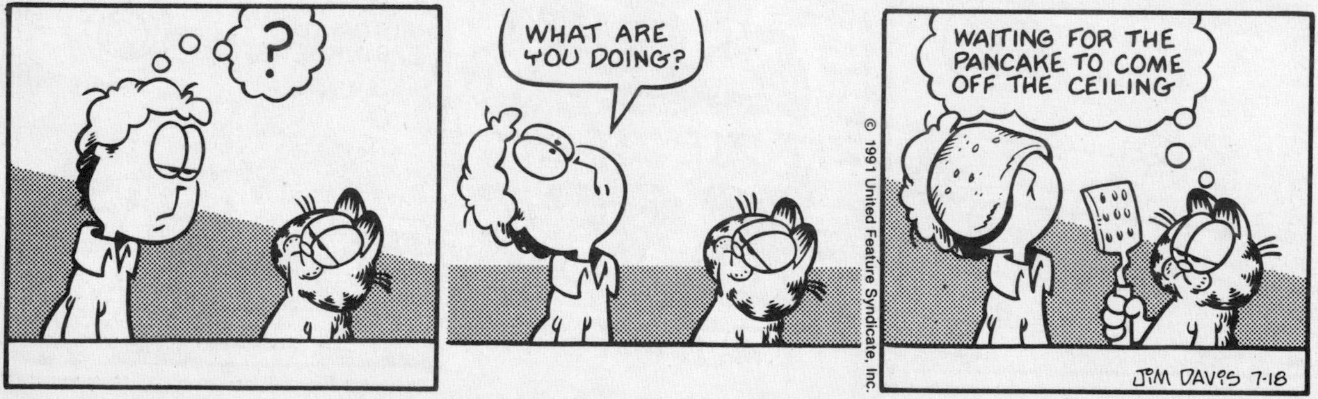
?
WHAT ARE YOU DOING?
WAITING FOR THE PANCAKE TO COME OFF THE CEILING
© 1991 United Feature Syndicate, Inc.
JIM DAVIS 7-18

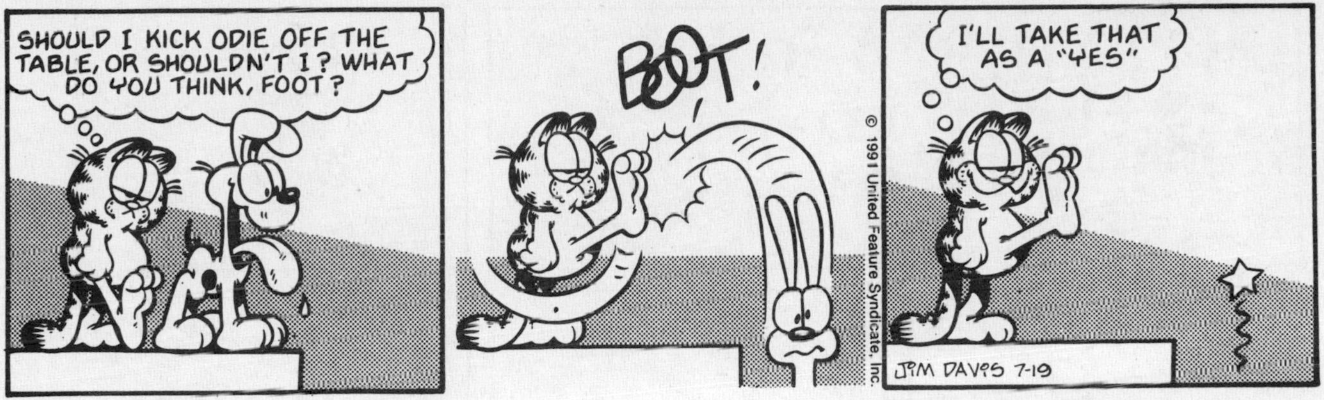
SHOULD I KICK ODIE OFF THE TABLE, OR SHOULDN'T I? WHAT DO YOU THINK, FOOT?
BOOT!
© 1991 United Feature Syndicate, Inc.
I'LL TAKE THAT AS A "YES"
JIM DAVIS 7-19

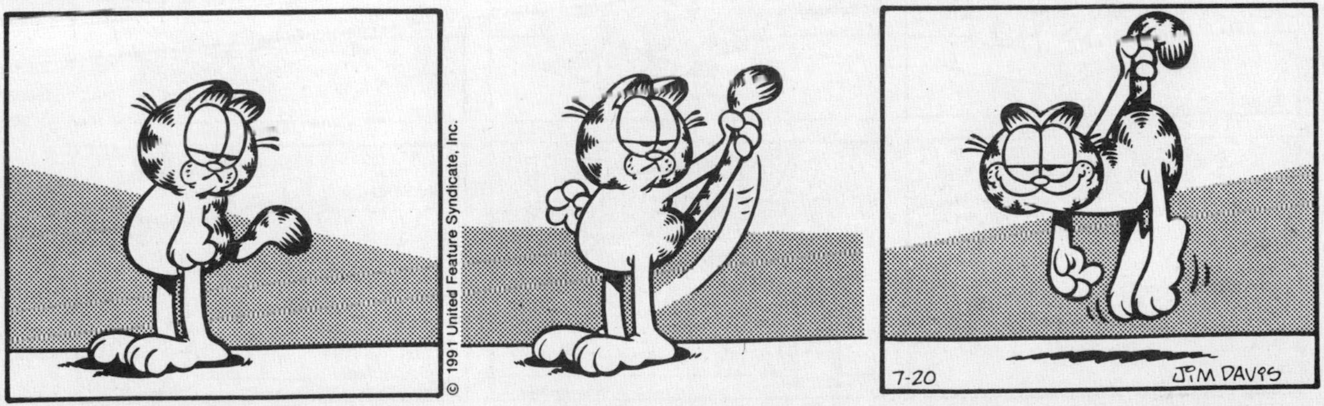
© 1991 United Feature Syndicate, Inc.
7-20
JIM DAVIS

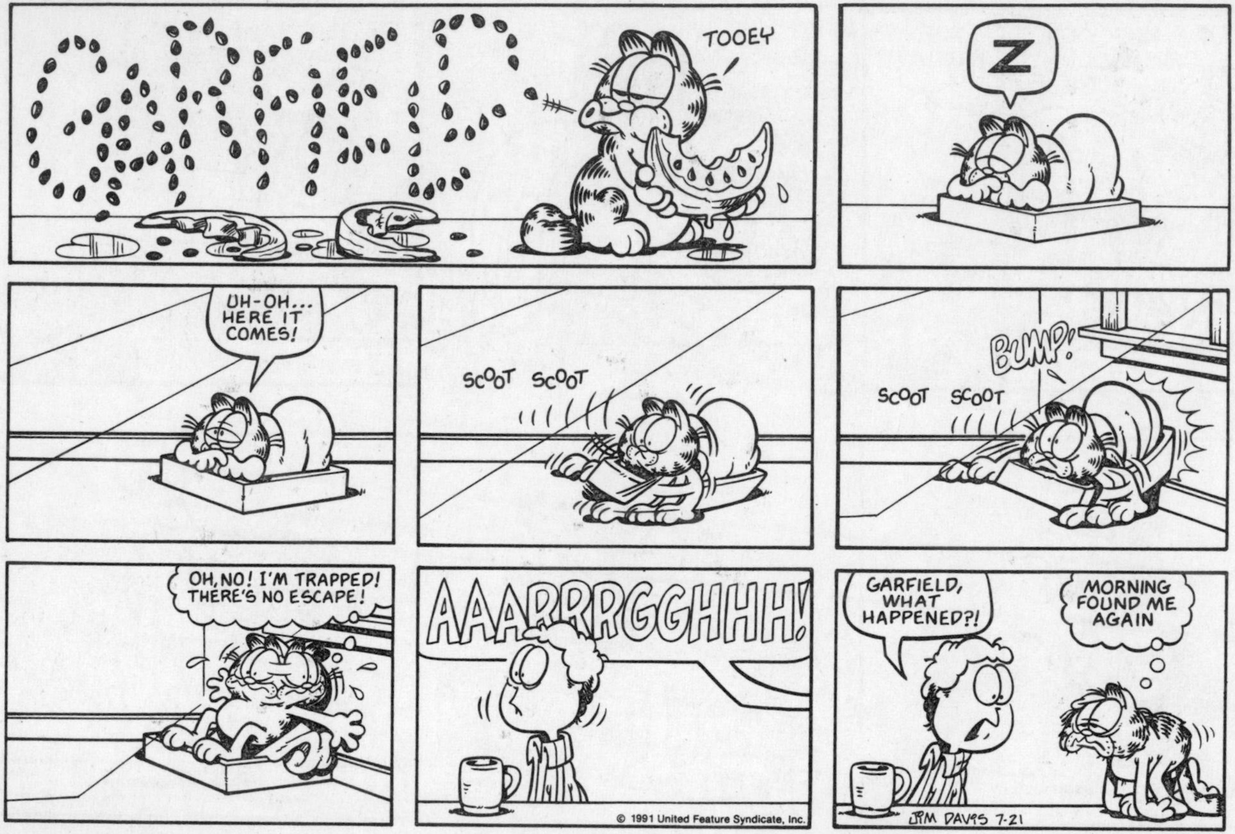
TOOEY
Z
UH-OH... HERE IT COMES!
SCOOT SCOOT
SCOOT SCOOT
BUMP!
OH, NO! I'M TRAPPED! THERE'S NO ESCAPE!
AAARRRGGHHH!
GARFIELD, WHAT HAPPENED?!
MORNING FOUND ME AGAIN
© 1991 United Feature Syndicate, Inc.
JIM DAVIS 7-21

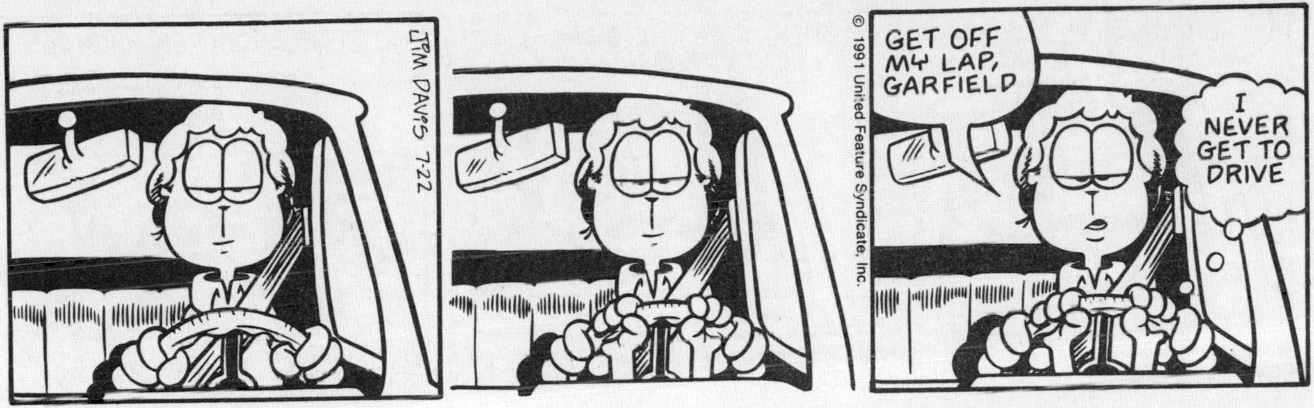
JIM DAVIS 7-22
GET OFF MY LAP, GARFIELD
I NEVER GET TO DRIVE
© 1991 United Feature Syndicate, Inc.

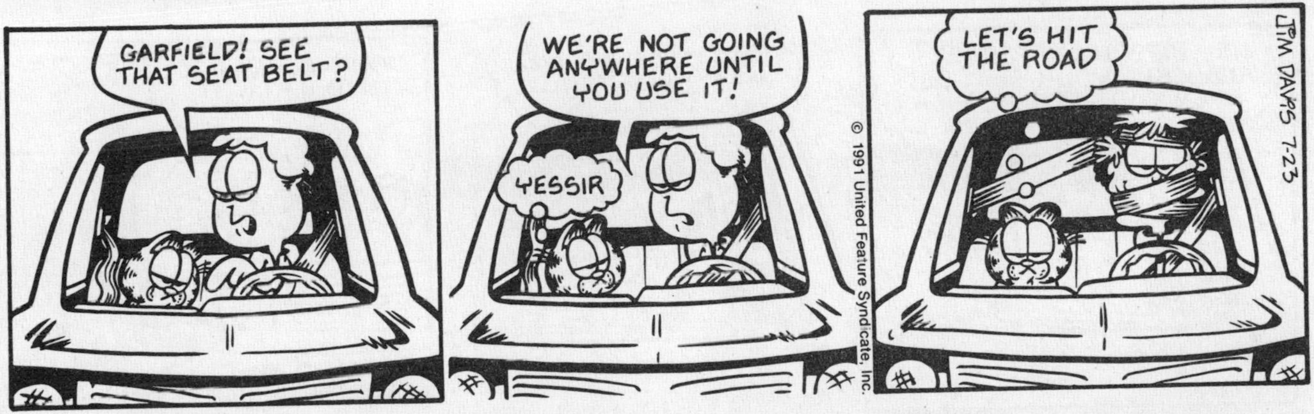
GARFIELD! SEE THAT SEAT BELT?
WE'RE NOT GOING ANYWHERE UNTIL YOU USE IT!
YESSIR
LET'S HIT THE ROAD
JIM DAVIS 7-23
© 1991 United Feature Syndicate, Inc.

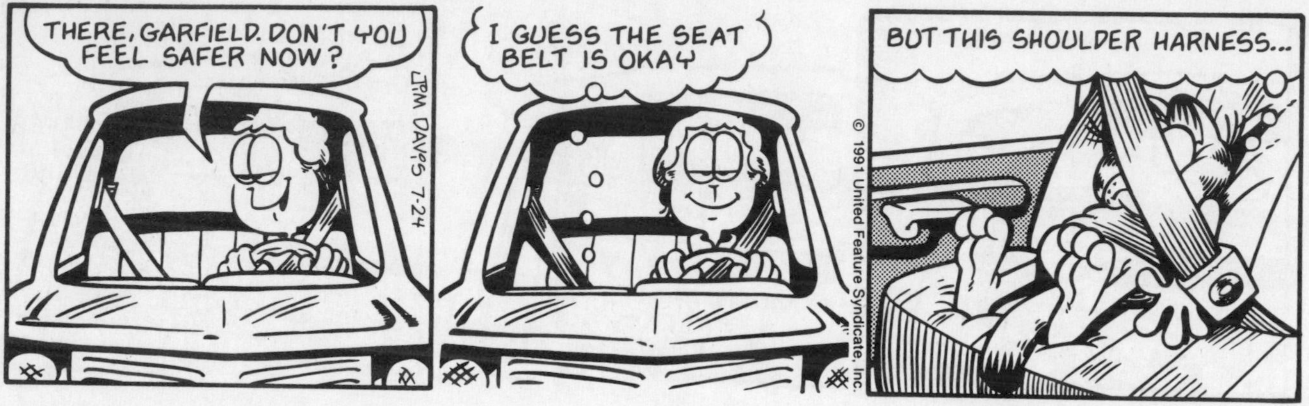
THERE, GARFIELD. DON'T YOU FEEL SAFER NOW?
JIM DAVIS 7-24
I GUESS THE SEAT BELT IS OKAY
© 1991 United Feature Syndicate, Inc.
BUT THIS SHOULDER HARNESS...

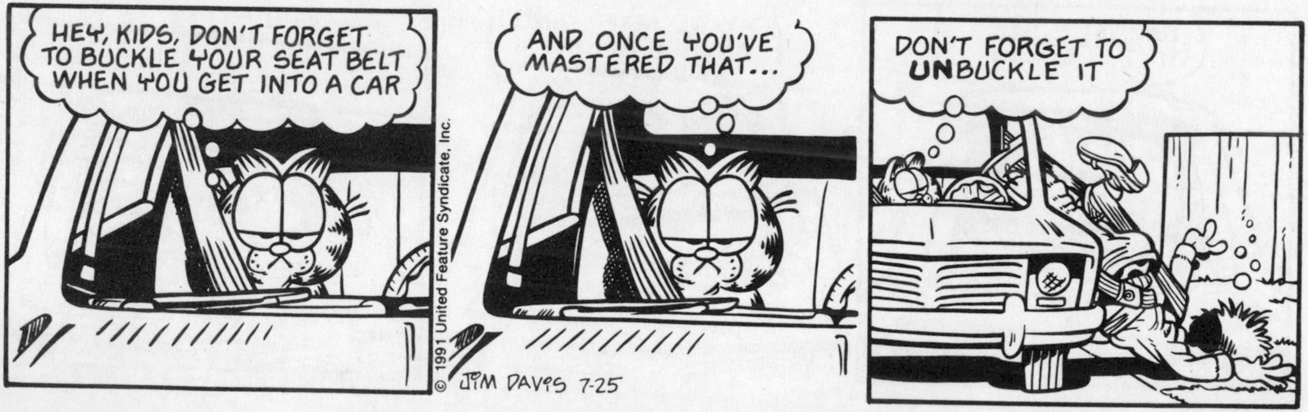
HEY, KIDS, DON'T FORGET TO BUCKLE YOUR SEAT BELT WHEN YOU GET INTO A CAR
© 1991 United Feature Syndicate, Inc.
AND ONCE YOU'VE MASTERED THAT...
JIM DAVIS 7-25
DON'T FORGET TO **UN**BUCKLE IT

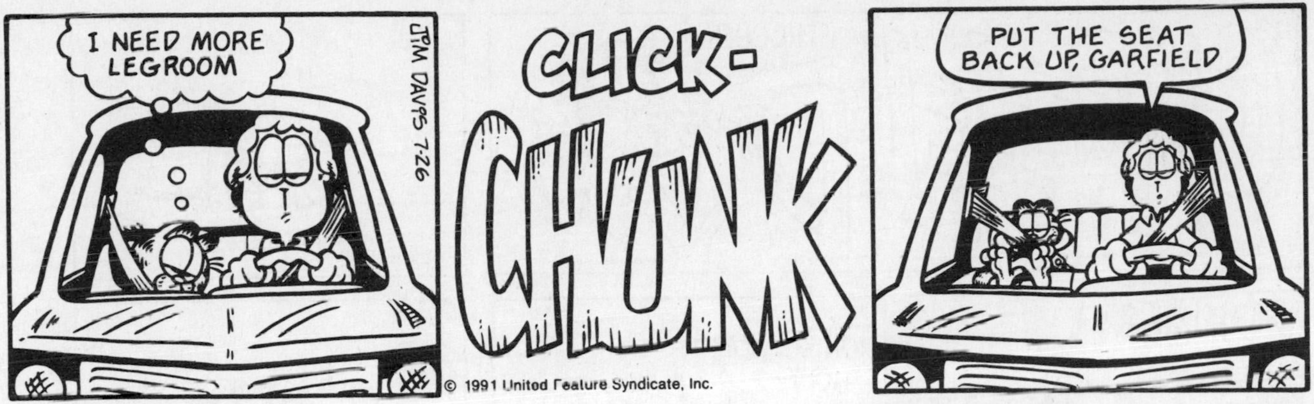
I NEED MORE LEGROOM
JIM DAVIS 7-26
CLICK-CHUNK
PUT THE SEAT BACK UP, GARFIELD
© 1991 United Feature Syndicate, Inc.

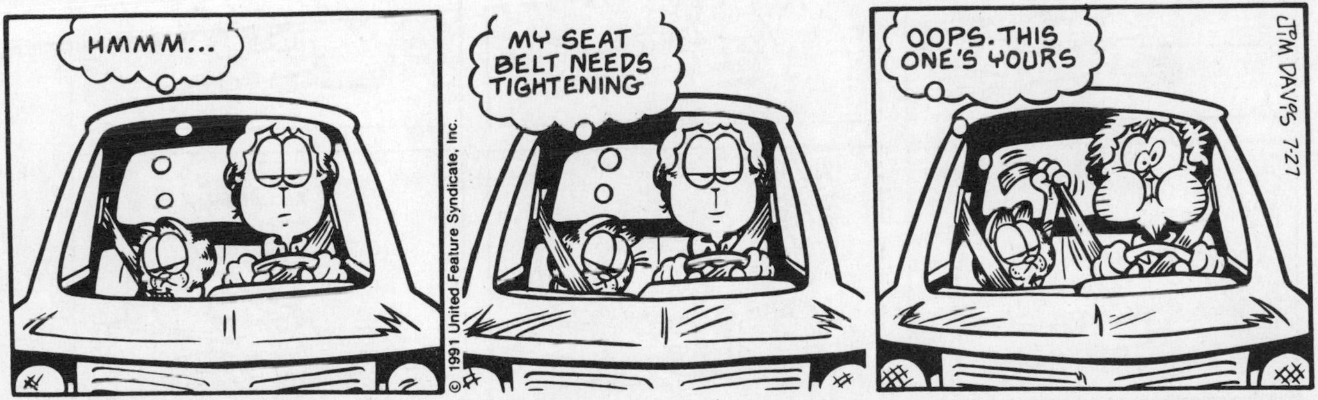
HMMM...
MY SEAT BELT NEEDS TIGHTENING
OOPS. THIS ONE'S YOURS
JIM DAVIS 7-27
© 1991 United Feature Syndicate, Inc.

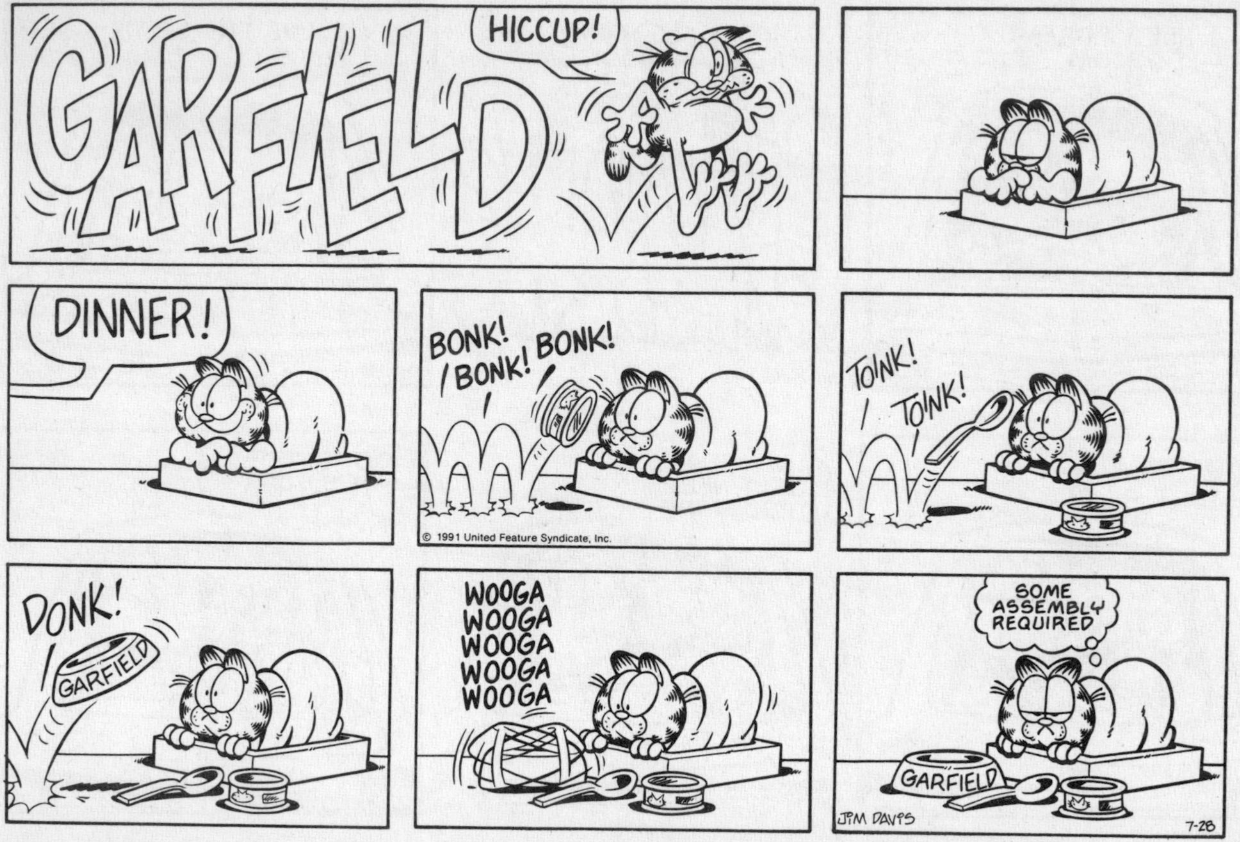
GARFIELD
HICCUP!
DINNER!
BONK!
BONK!
BONK!
© 1991 United Feature Syndicate, Inc.
TOINK!
TOINK!
DONK!
GARFIELD
WOOGA
WOOGA
WOOGA
WOOGA
WOOGA
WOOGA
SOME ASSEMBLY REQUIRED
GARFIELD
JIM DAVIS
7-28

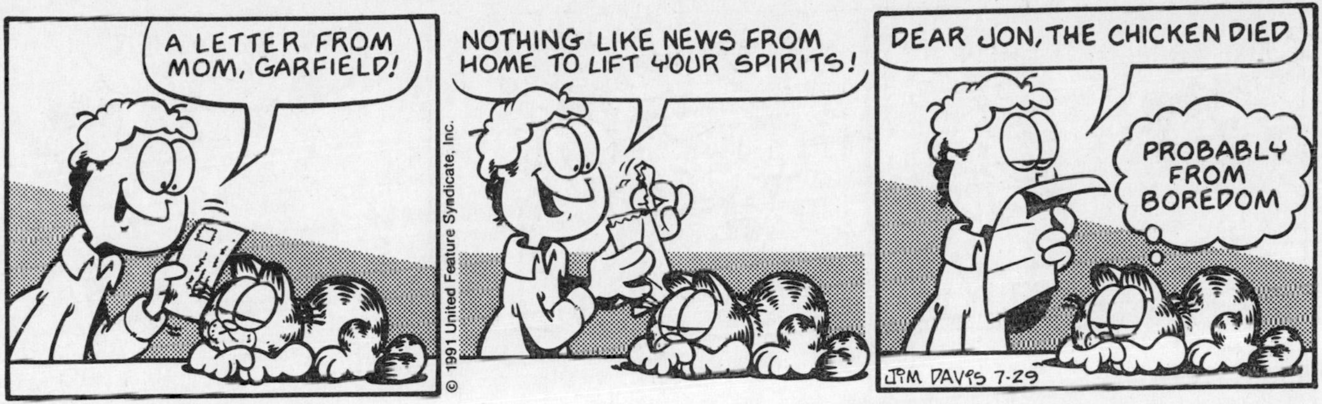
A LETTER FROM MOM, GARFIELD!
NOTHING LIKE NEWS FROM HOME TO LIFT YOUR SPIRITS!
DEAR JON, THE CHICKEN DIED
PROBABLY FROM BOREDOM
JIM DAVIS 7-29

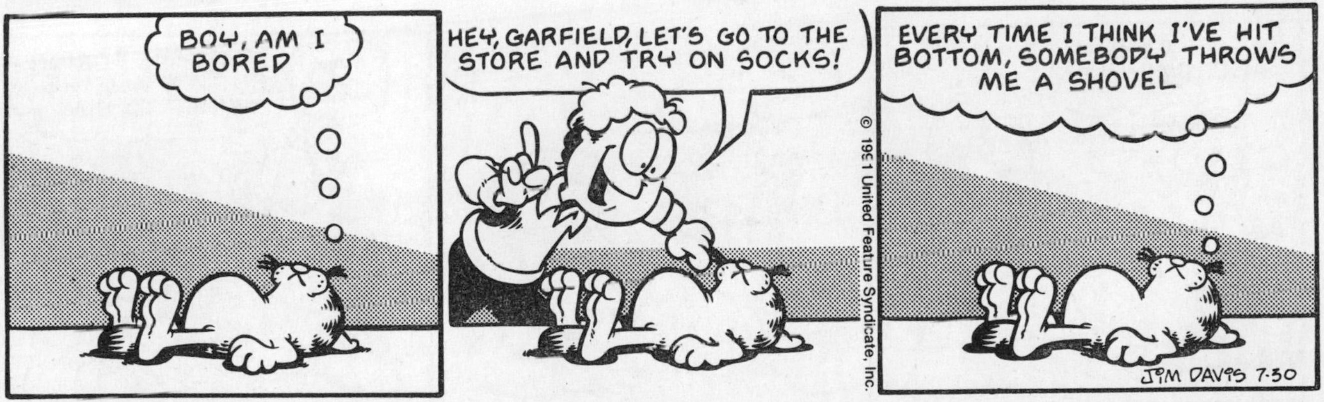
BOY, AM I BORED
HEY, GARFIELD, LET'S GO TO THE STORE AND TRY ON SOCKS!
EVERY TIME I THINK I'VE HIT BOTTOM, SOMEBODY THROWS ME A SHOVEL
JIM DAVIS 7-30

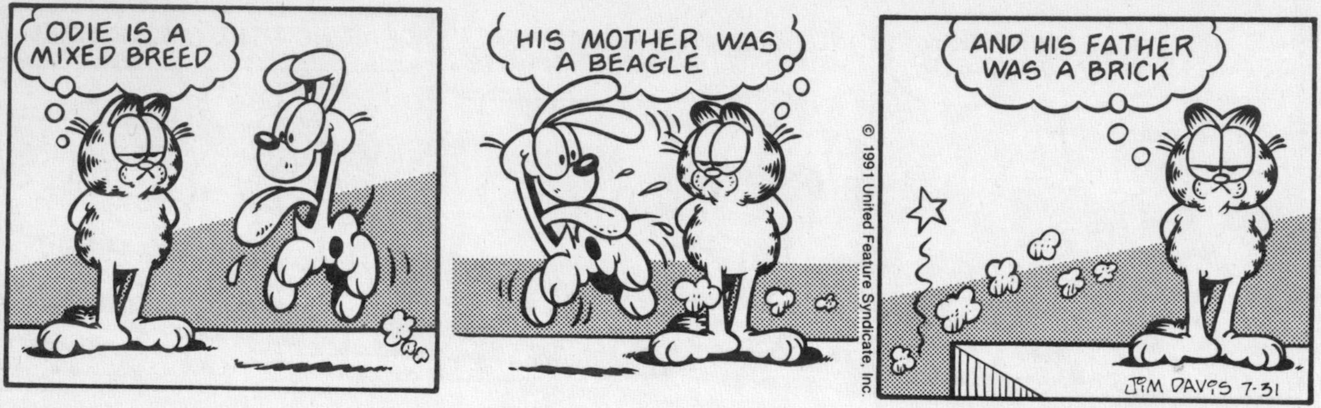
ODIE IS A MIXED BREED
HIS MOTHER WAS A BEAGLE
AND HIS FATHER WAS A BRICK
JIM DAVIS 7-31

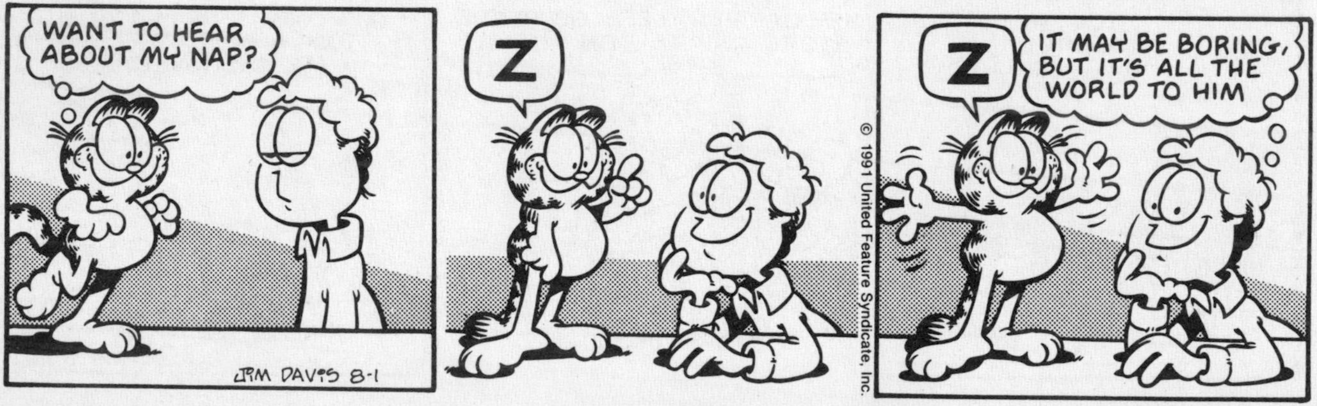
WANT TO HEAR ABOUT MY NAP?
JIM DAVIS 8-1
Z
Z
IT MAY BE BORING, BUT IT'S ALL THE WORLD TO HIM

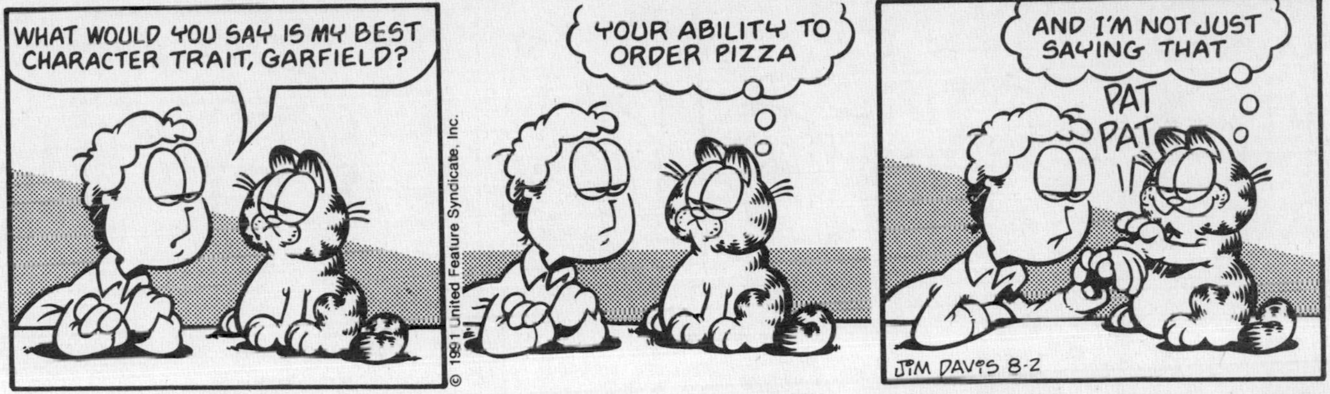
WHAT WOULD YOU SAY IS MY BEST CHARACTER TRAIT, GARFIELD?
YOUR ABILITY TO ORDER PIZZA
AND I'M NOT JUST SAYING THAT
PAT PAT
JIM DAVIS 8-2
© 1991 United Feature Syndicate, Inc.

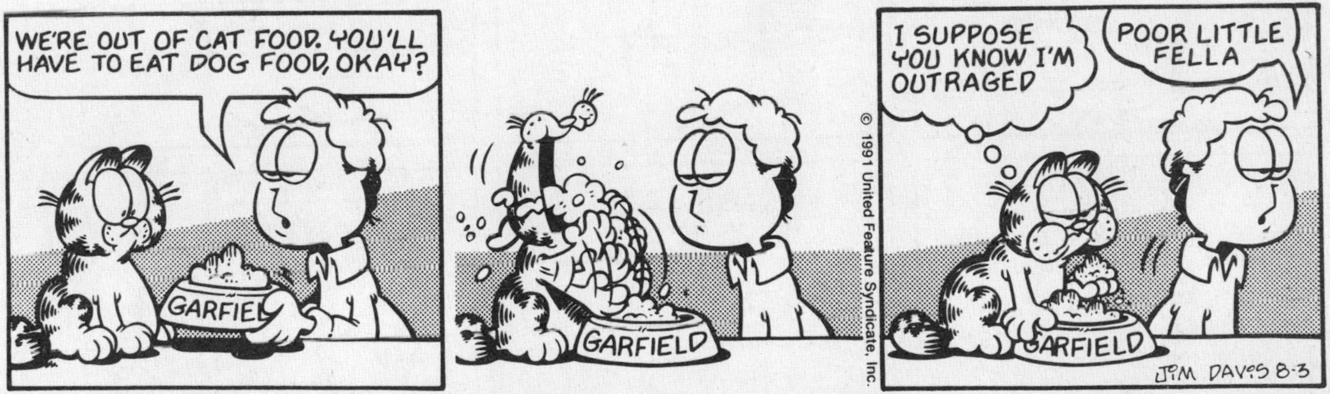
WE'RE OUT OF CAT FOOD. YOU'LL HAVE TO EAT DOG FOOD, OKAY?
GARFIEL
GARFIELD
I SUPPOSE YOU KNOW I'M OUTRAGED
POOR LITTLE FELLA
ARFIELD
JIM DAVIS 8-3
© 1991 United Feature Syndicate, Inc.

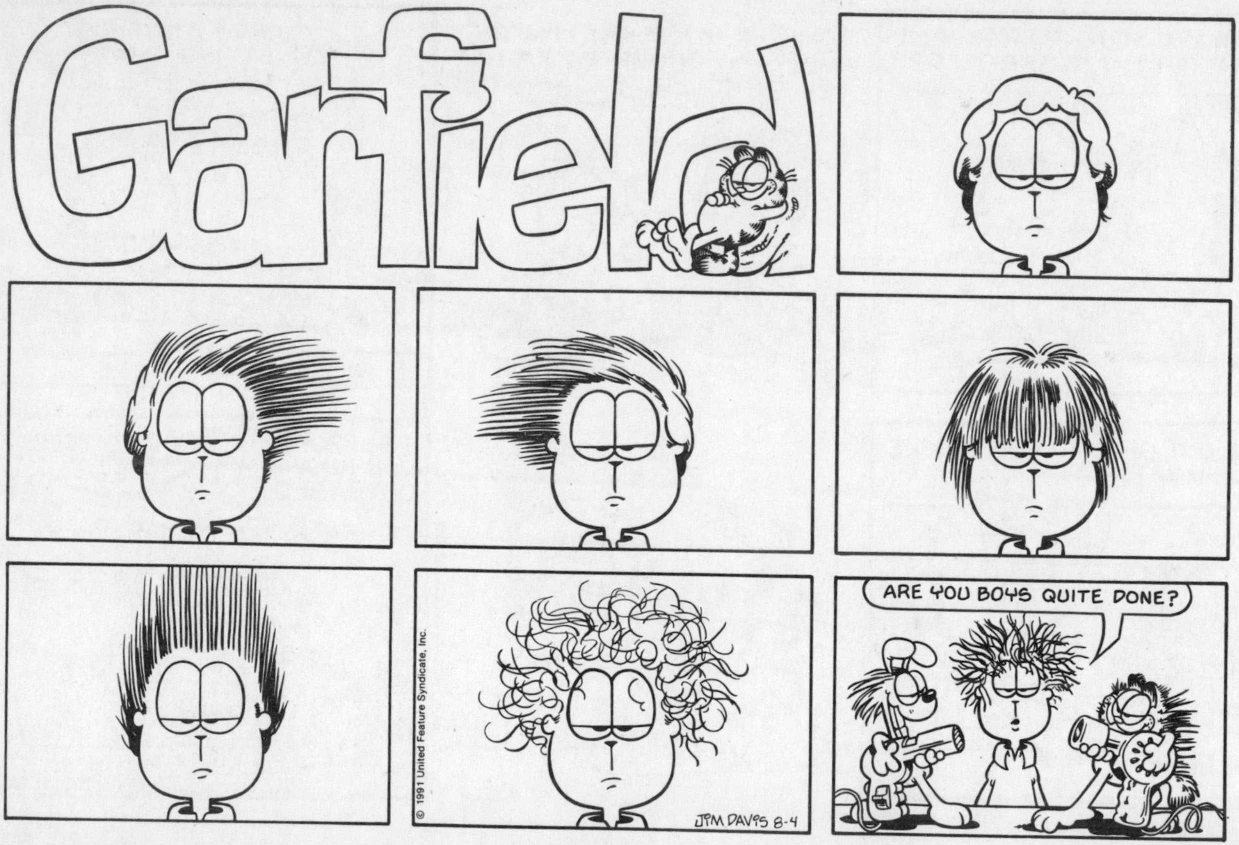
Garfield
ARE YOU BOYS QUITE DONE?
© 1991 United Feature Syndicate, Inc.
JIM DAVIS 8-4

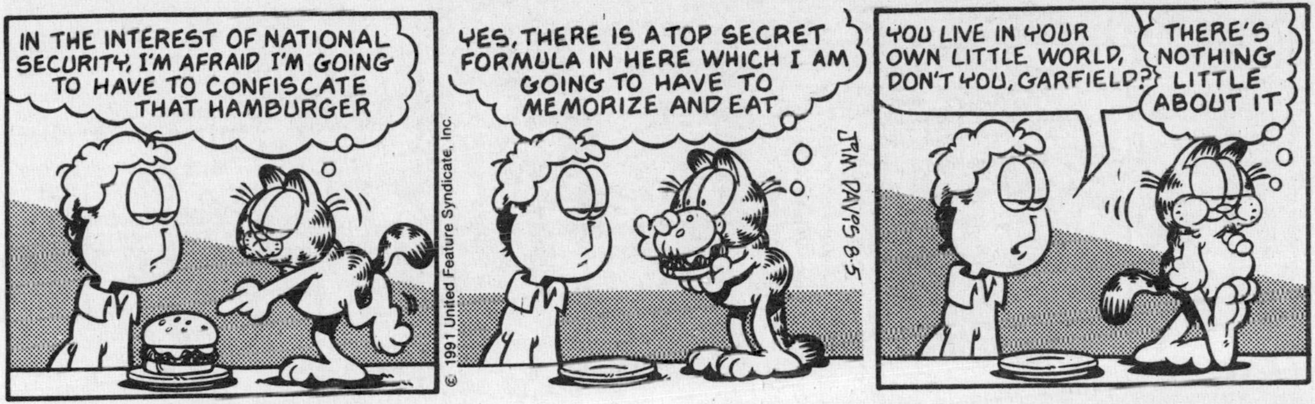
IN THE INTEREST OF NATIONAL SECURITY, I'M AFRAID I'M GOING TO HAVE TO CONFISCATE THAT HAMBURGER
YES, THERE IS A TOP SECRET FORMULA IN HERE WHICH I AM GOING TO HAVE TO MEMORIZE AND EAT
YOU LIVE IN YOUR OWN LITTLE WORLD, DON'T YOU, GARFIELD?
THERE'S NOTHING LITTLE ABOUT IT
© 1991 United Feature Syndicate, Inc.
JIM DAVIS 8-5

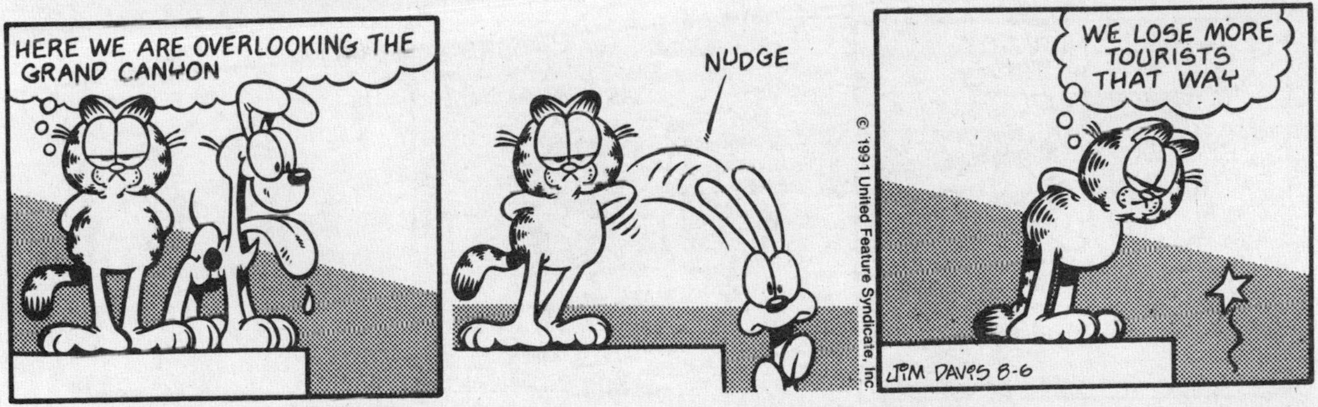
HERE WE ARE OVERLOOKING THE GRAND CANYON
NUDGE
WE LOSE MORE TOURISTS THAT WAY
© 1991 United Feature Syndicate, Inc.
JIM DAVIS 8-6

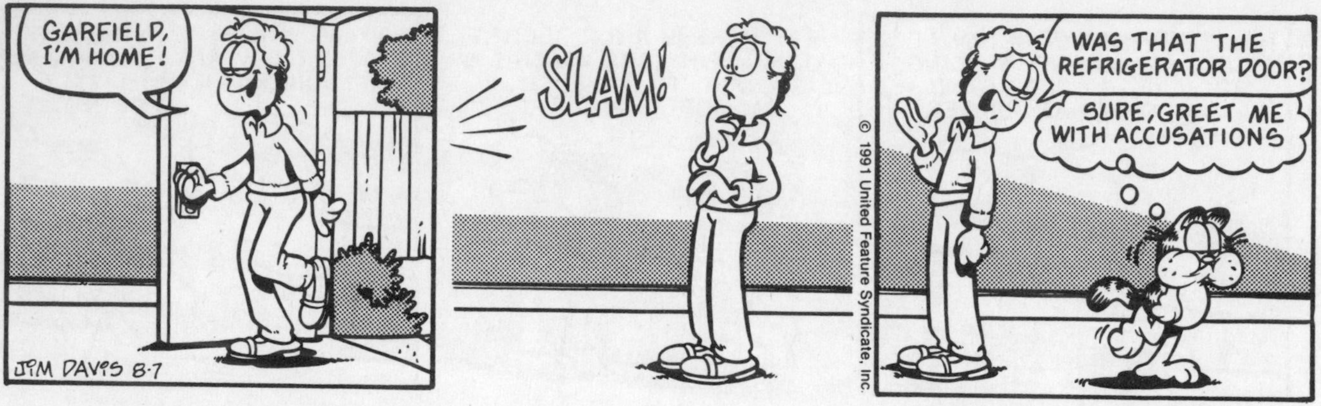
GARFIELD, I'M HOME!
JIM DAVIS 8-7
SLAM!
© 1991 United Feature Syndicate, Inc.
WAS THAT THE REFRIGERATOR DOOR?
SURE, GREET ME WITH ACCUSATIONS

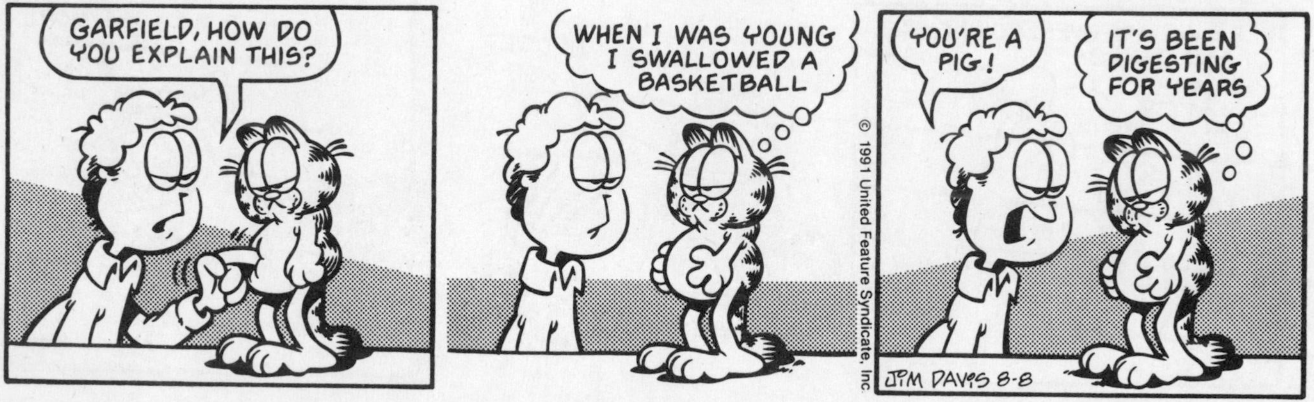
GARFIELD, HOW DO YOU EXPLAIN THIS?
WHEN I WAS YOUNG I SWALLOWED A BASKETBALL
© 1991 United Feature Syndicate, Inc.
YOU'RE A PIG!
IT'S BEEN DIGESTING FOR YEARS
JIM DAVIS 8-8

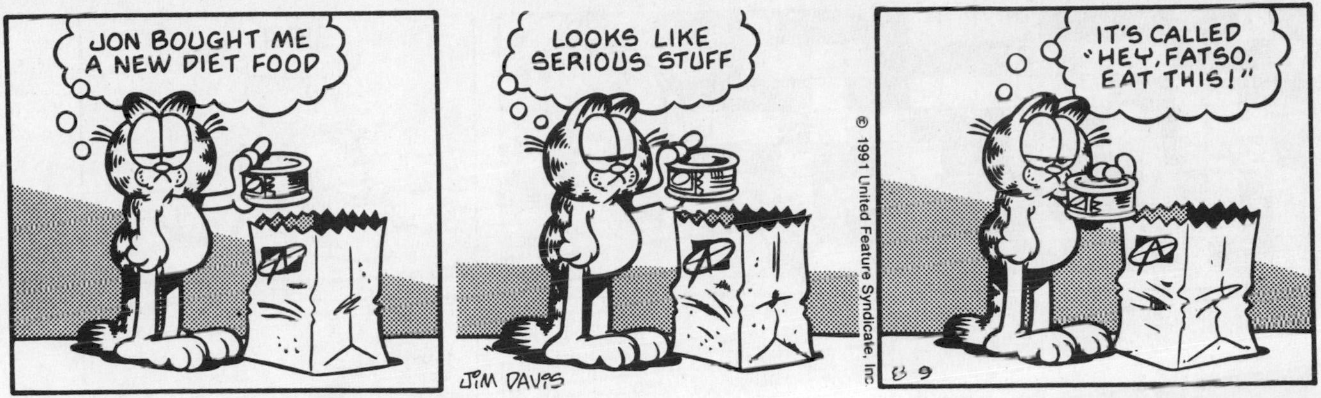
JON BOUGHT ME A NEW DIET FOOD
LOOKS LIKE SERIOUS STUFF
IT'S CALLED "HEY, FATSO. EAT THIS!"
JIM DAVIS
8-9
© 1991 United Feature Syndicate, Inc.

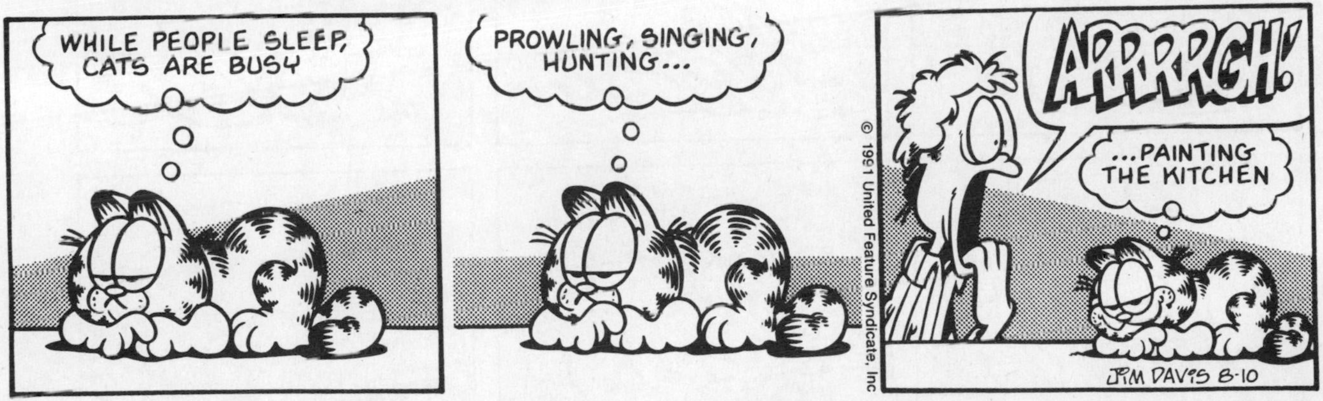
WHILE PEOPLE SLEEP, CATS ARE BUSY
PROWLING, SINGING, HUNTING...
AARRRGH!
...PAINTING THE KITCHEN
JIM DAVIS 8-10
© 1991 United Feature Syndicate, Inc.

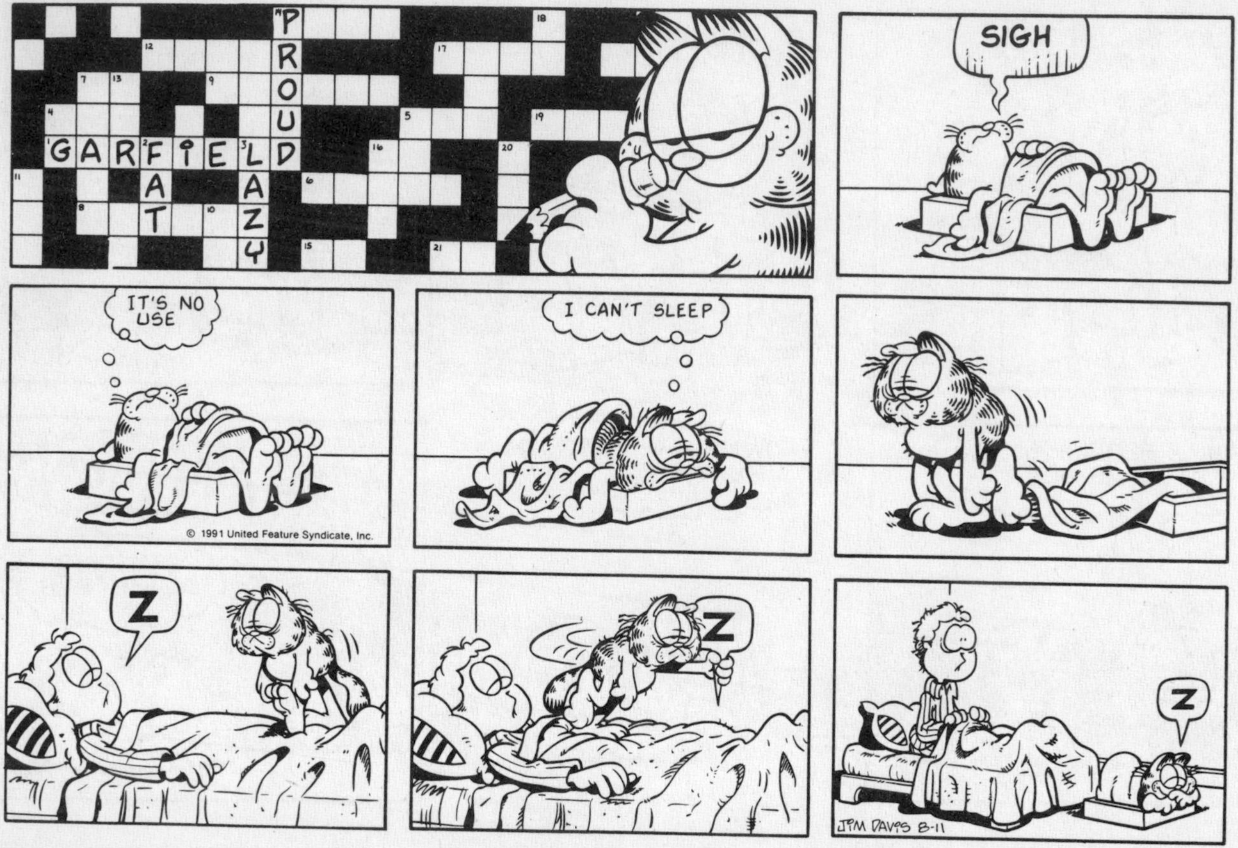
GARFIELD
PROUD
FAT
LAZY
SIGH
IT'S NO USE
© 1991 United Feature Syndicate, Inc.
I CAN'T SLEEP
Z
Z
Z
JIM DAVIS 8-11

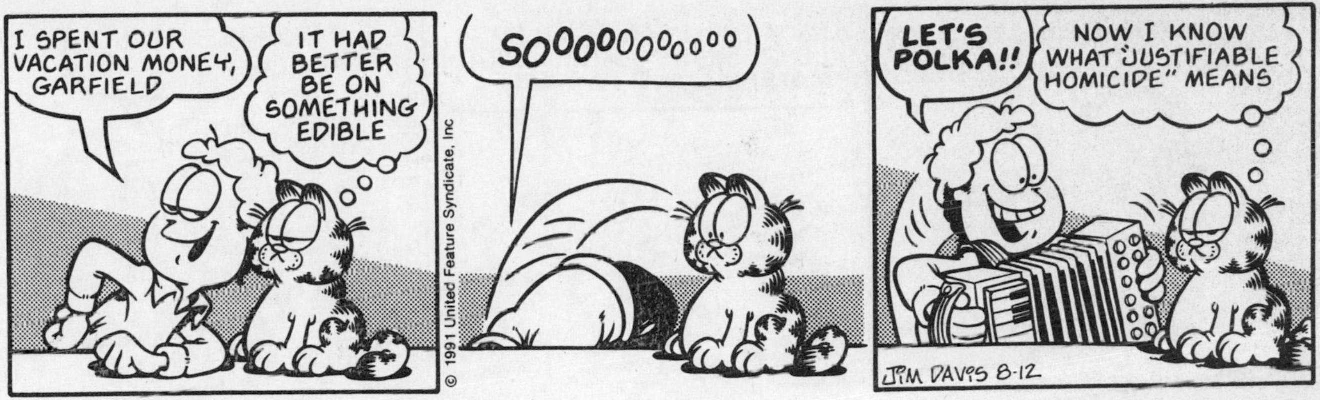
I SPENT OUR VACATION MONEY, GARFIELD
IT HAD BETTER BE ON SOMETHING EDIBLE
© 1991 United Feature Syndicate, Inc
SOOOOOOOOOOO
LET'S POLKA!!
NOW I KNOW WHAT "JUSTIFIABLE HOMICIDE" MEANS
JIM DAVIS 8-12

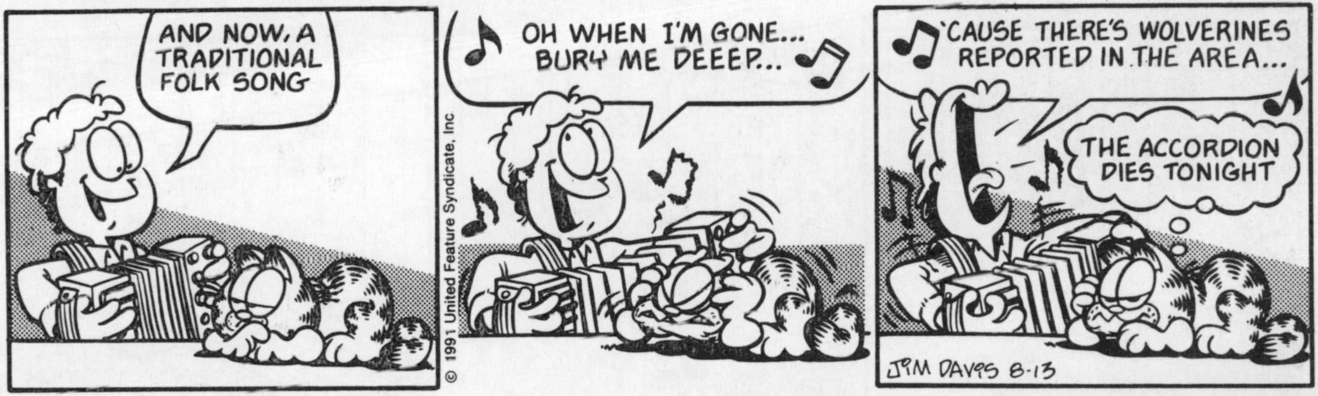
AND NOW, A TRADITIONAL FOLK SONG
© 1991 United Feature Syndicate, Inc
OH WHEN I'M GONE... BURY ME DEEEP...
'CAUSE THERE'S WOLVERINES REPORTED IN THE AREA...
THE ACCORDION DIES TONIGHT
JIM DAVIS 8-13

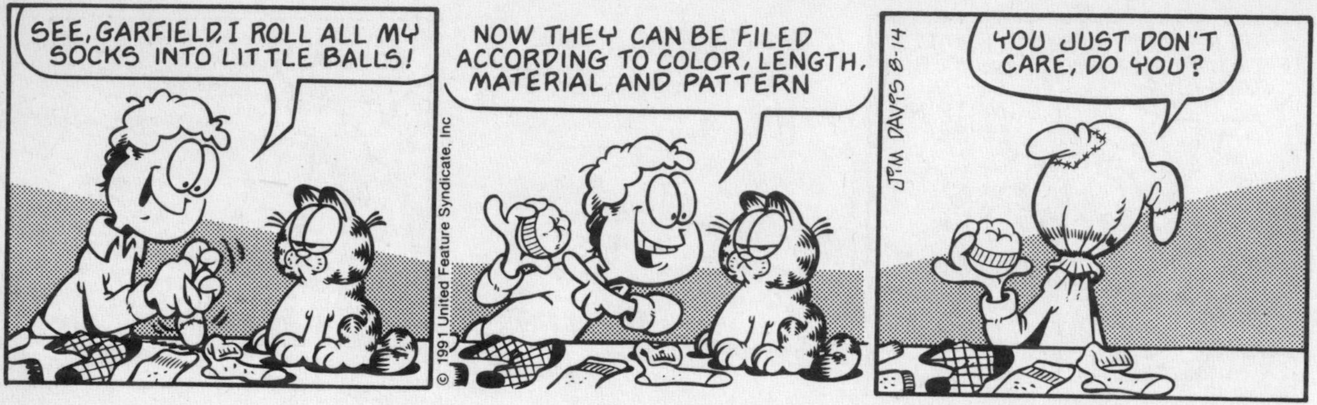
SEE, GARFIELD, I ROLL ALL MY SOCKS INTO LITTLE BALLS!
© 1991 United Feature Syndicate, Inc
NOW THEY CAN BE FILED ACCORDING TO COLOR, LENGTH, MATERIAL AND PATTERN
JIM DAVIS 8-14
YOU JUST DON'T CARE, DO YOU?

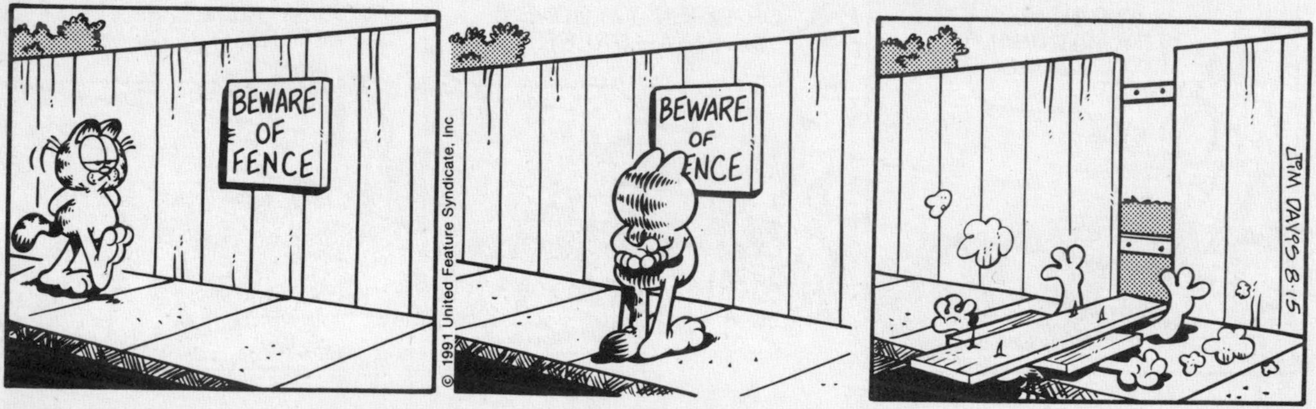
BEWARE OF FENCE
© 1991 United Feature Syndicate, Inc
BEWARE OF
ENCE
JIM DAVIS 8-15

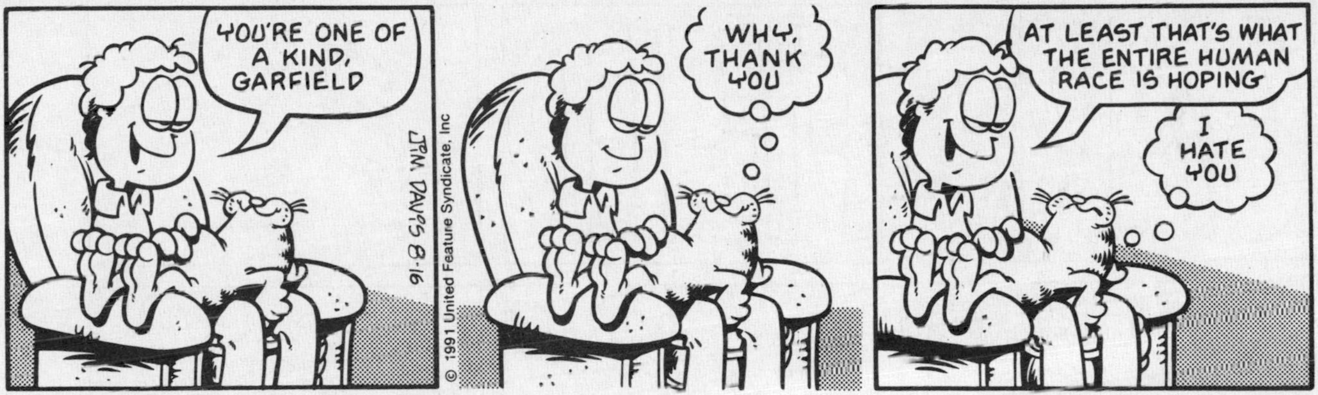
YOU'RE ONE OF A KIND, GARFIELD
JIM DAVIS 8-16
© 1991 United Feature Syndicate, Inc
WHY, THANK YOU
AT LEAST THAT'S WHAT THE ENTIRE HUMAN RACE IS HOPING
I HATE YOU

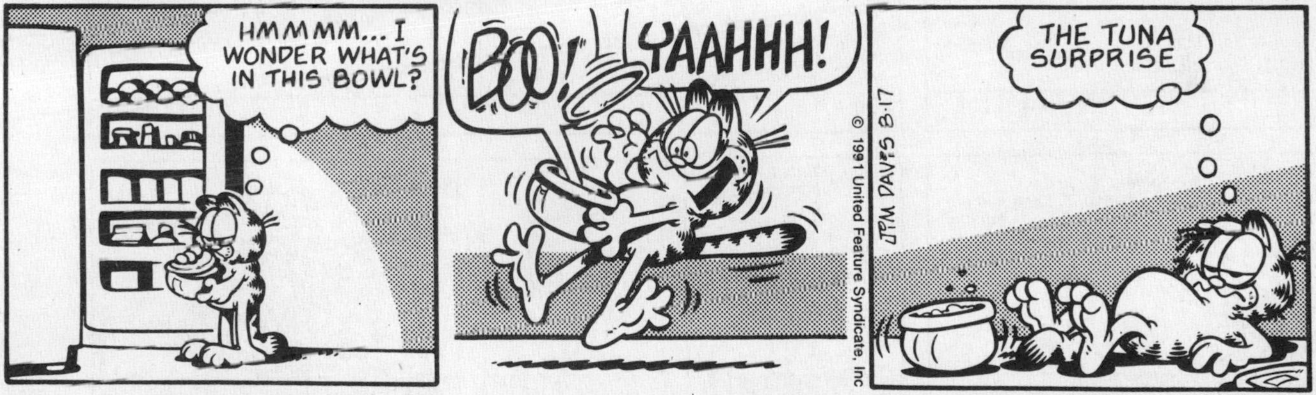
HMMMM... I WONDER WHAT'S IN THIS BOWL?
BOO!
YAAHHH!
© 1991 United Feature Syndicate, Inc
JIM DAVIS 8-17
THE TUNA SURPRISE

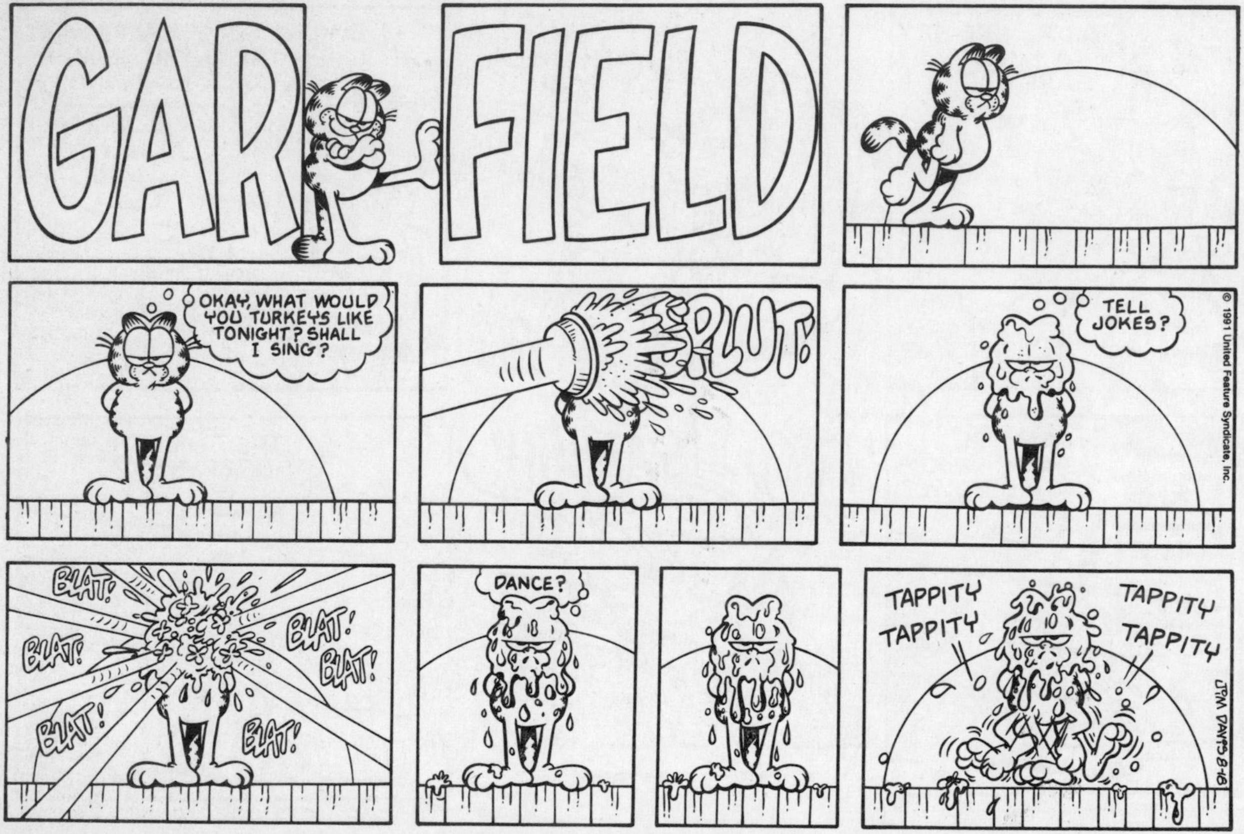
GARFIELD
OKAY, WHAT WOULD YOU TURKEYS LIKE TONIGHT? SHALL I SING?
SPLUT!
TELL JOKES?
BLAT!
BLAT!
BLAT!
BLAT!
BLAT!
BLAT!
DANCE?
TAPPITY TAPPITY
TAPPITY TAPPITY
JPM DAVPS 8-18
© 1991 United Feature Syndicate, Inc.

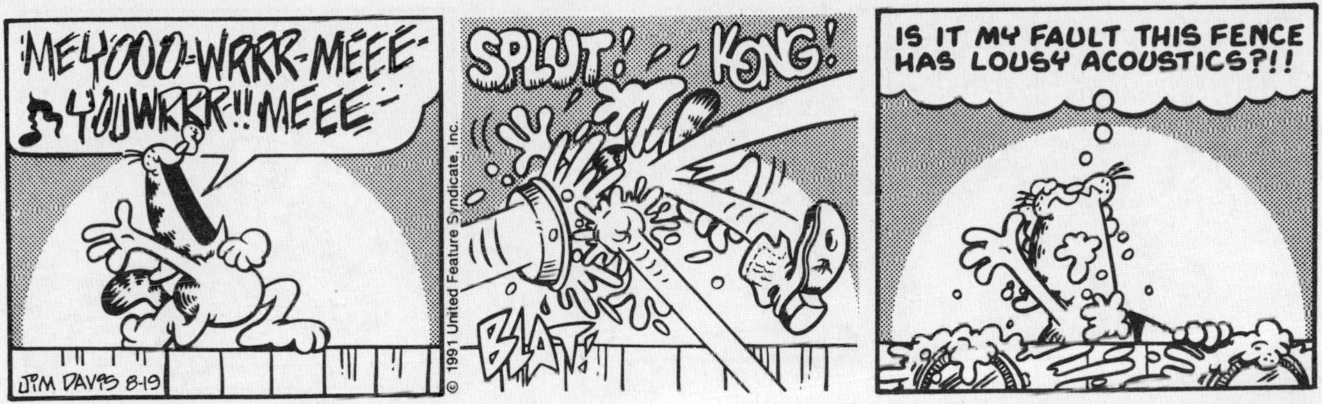
MEYOOO-WRRR-MEEE-
YOUWRRR!! MEEE
SPLUT!
KONG!
BLAT!
IS IT MY FAULT THIS FENCE HAS LOUSY ACOUSTICS?!!
JIM DAVIS 8-19
© 1991 United Feature Syndicate, Inc.

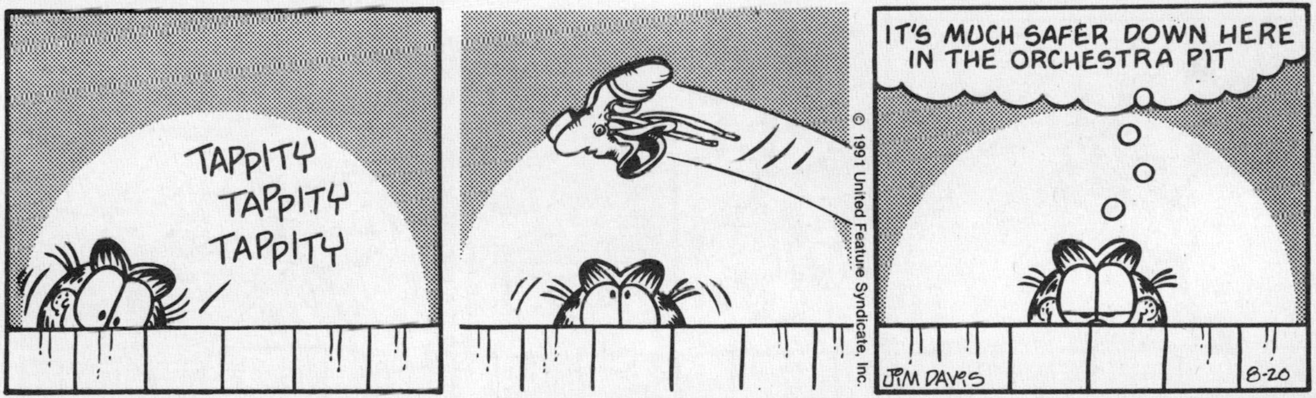
TAPPITY
TAPPITY
TAPPITY
IT'S MUCH SAFER DOWN HERE IN THE ORCHESTRA PIT
JIM DAVIS 8-20
© 1991 United Feature Syndicate, Inc.

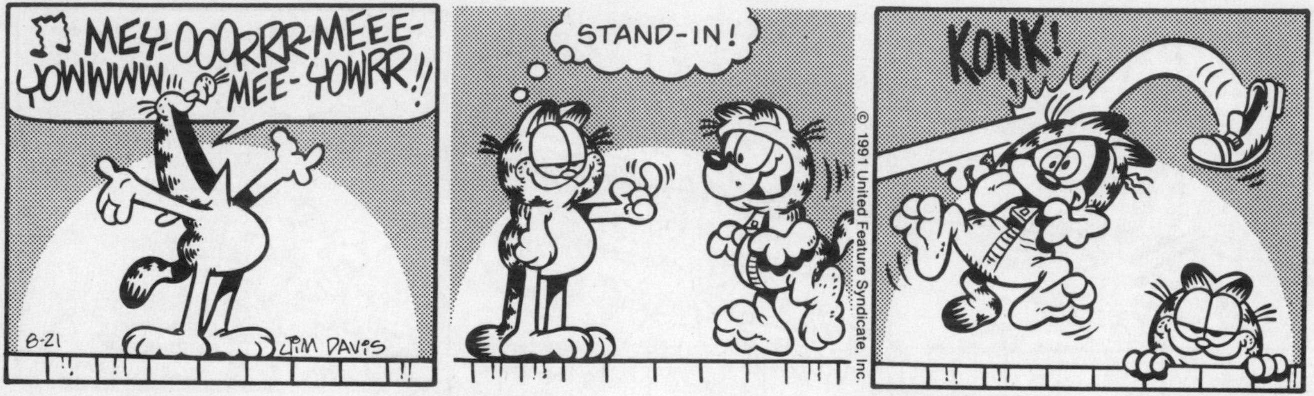
MEY-OOORRR-MEEE-YOWWWW MEE-YOWRR!!
STAND-IN!
© 1991 United Feature Syndicate, Inc.
KONK!
8-21
JIM DAVIS

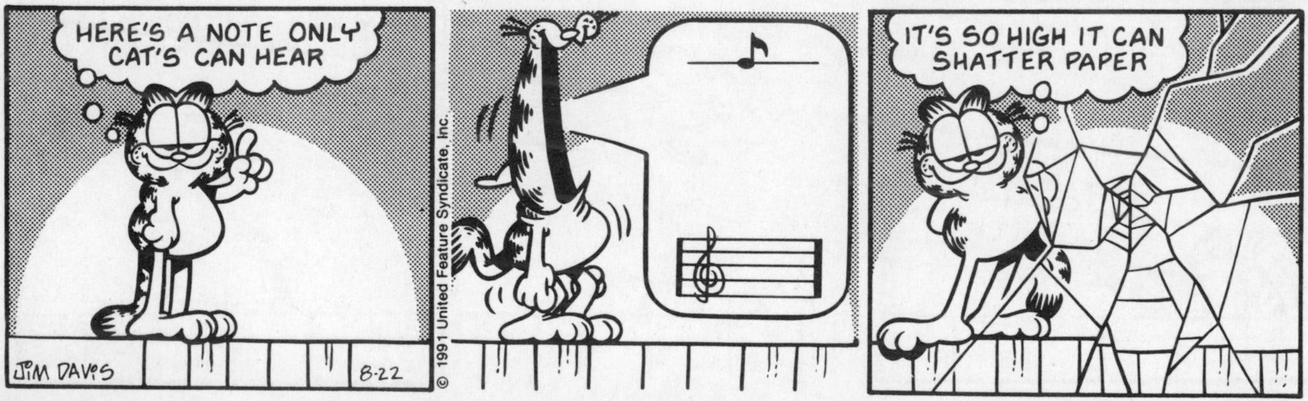
HERE'S A NOTE ONLY CAT'S CAN HEAR
JIM DAVIS
8-22
© 1991 United Feature Syndicate, Inc.
IT'S SO HIGH IT CAN SHATTER PAPER

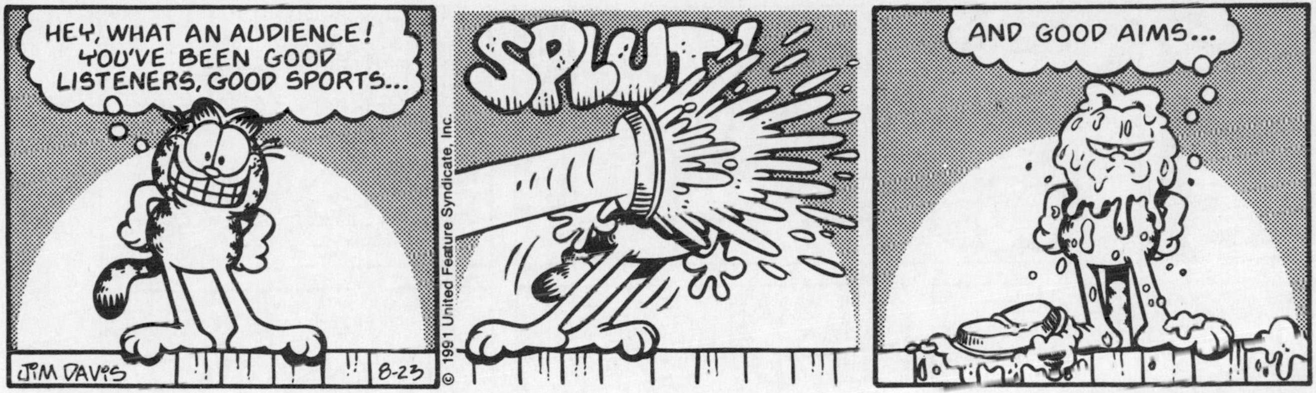
HEY, WHAT AN AUDIENCE! YOU'VE BEEN GOOD LISTENERS, GOOD SPORTS...
JIM DAVIS
8-23
SPLUT!
© 1991 United Feature Syndicate, Inc.
AND GOOD AIMS...

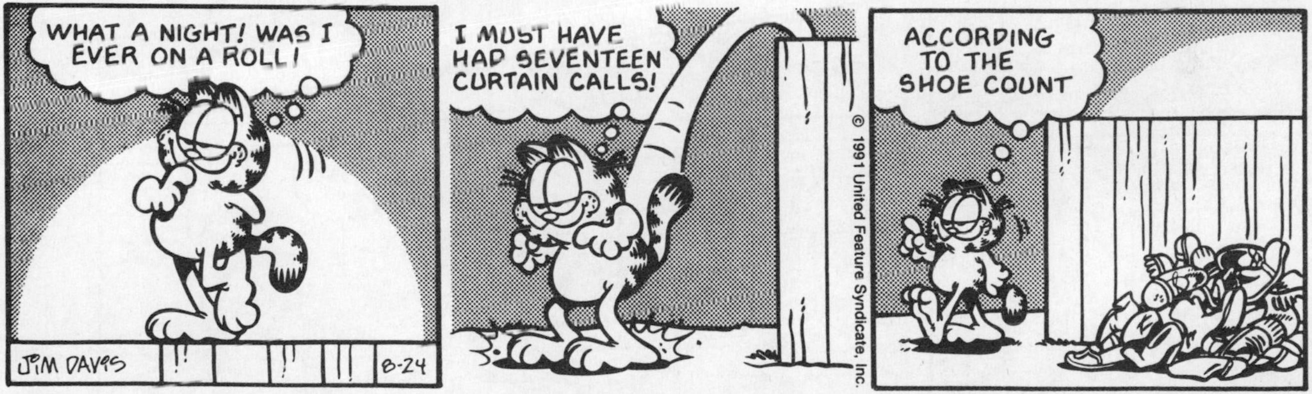
WHAT A NIGHT! WAS I EVER ON A ROLL!
JIM DAVIS
8-24
I MUST HAVE HAD SEVENTEEN CURTAIN CALLS!
© 1991 United Feature Syndicate, Inc.
ACCORDING TO THE SHOE COUNT

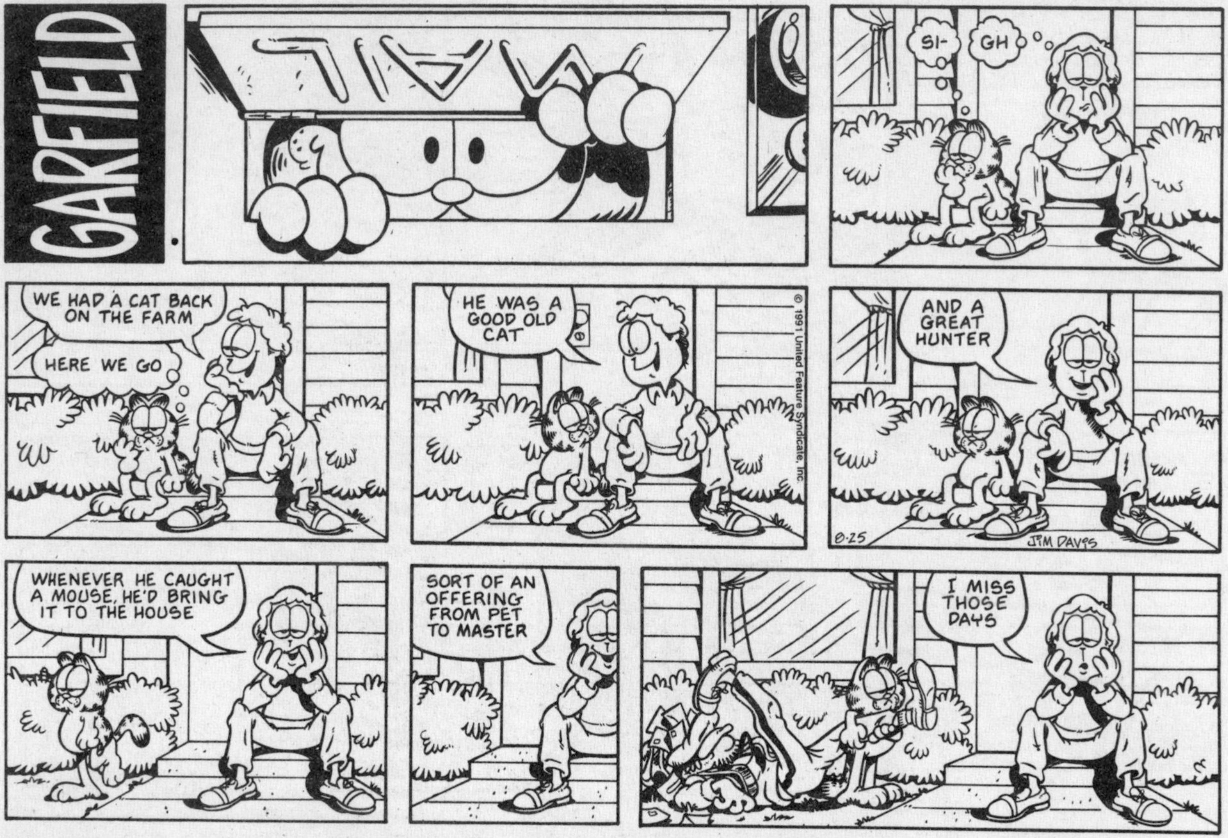
GARFIELD
SI-
GH
WE HAD A CAT BACK ON THE FARM
HERE WE GO
HE WAS A GOOD OLD CAT
© 1991 United Feature Syndicate, Inc.
AND A GREAT HUNTER
8·25
JIM DAVIS
WHENEVER HE CAUGHT A MOUSE, HE'D BRING IT TO THE HOUSE
SORT OF AN OFFERING FROM PET TO MASTER
I MISS THOSE DAYS

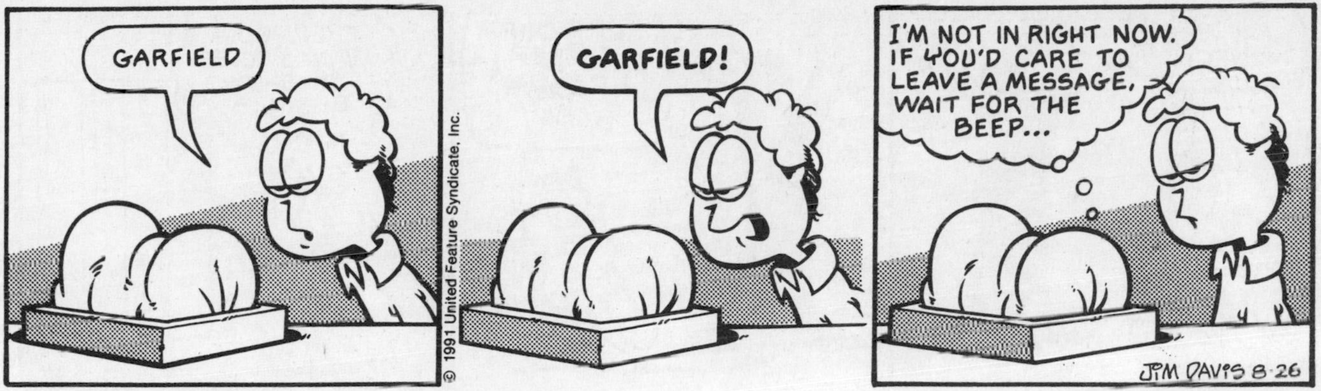
GARFIELD
GARFIELD!
I'M NOT IN RIGHT NOW. IF YOU'D CARE TO LEAVE A MESSAGE, WAIT FOR THE BEEP...
© 1991 United Feature Syndicate, Inc.
JIM DAVIS 8-26

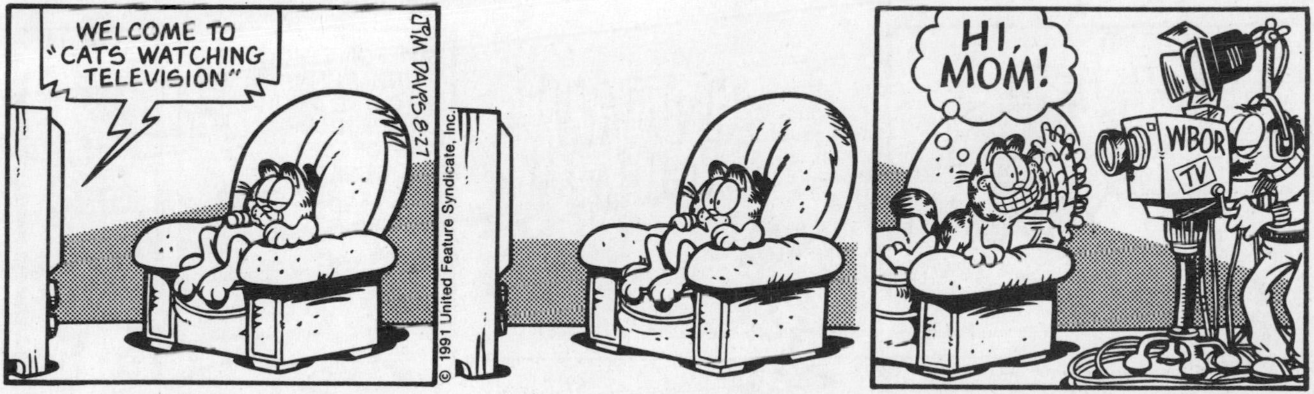
WELCOME TO "CATS WATCHING TELEVISION"
HI, MOM!
WBOR
TV
© 1991 United Feature Syndicate, Inc.
JIM DAVIS 8-27

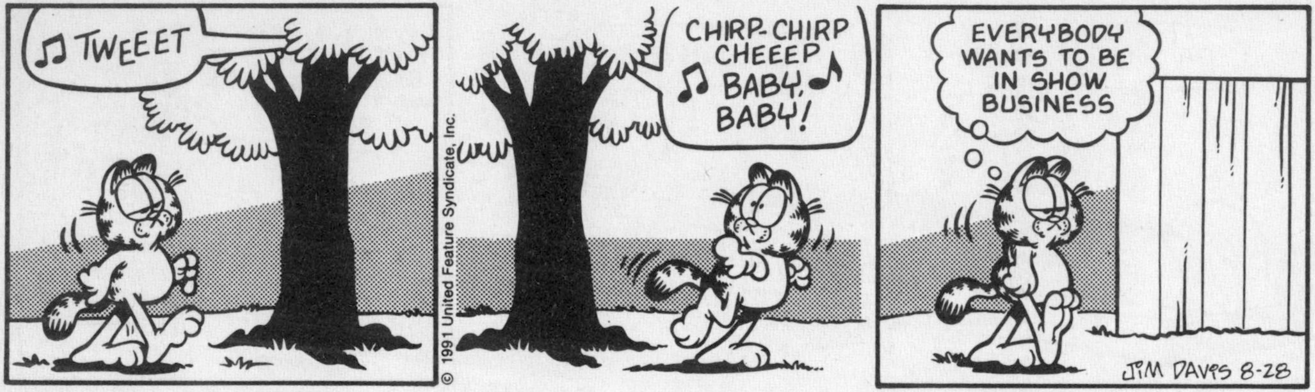
♫ TWEEET
CHIRP-CHIRP CHEEEP ♫ BABY, BABY! ♪
© 1991 United Feature Syndicate, Inc.
EVERYBODY WANTS TO BE IN SHOW BUSINESS
JIM DAVIS 8-28

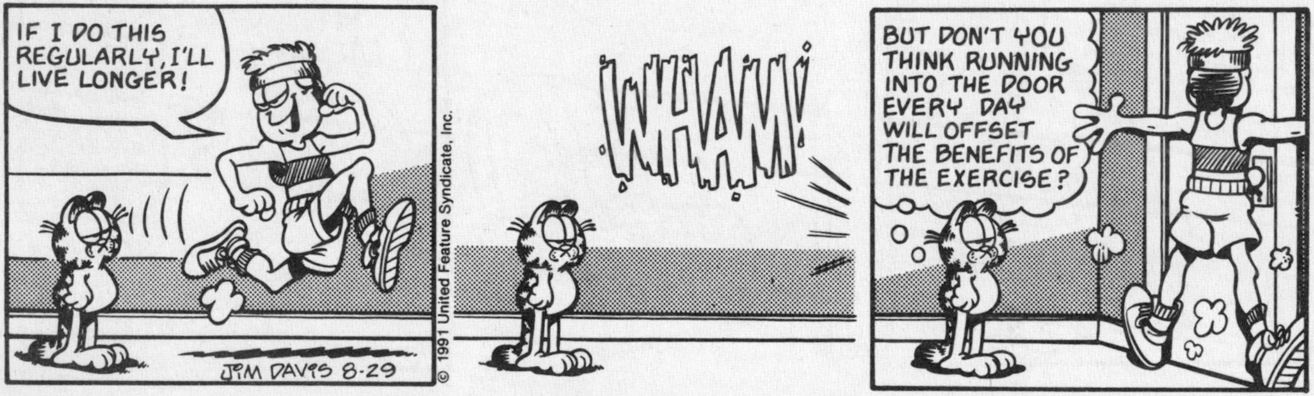
IF I DO THIS REGULARLY, I'LL LIVE LONGER!
JIM DAVIS 8-29
© 1991 United Feature Syndicate, Inc.
WHAM!
BUT DON'T YOU THINK RUNNING INTO THE DOOR EVERY DAY WILL OFFSET THE BENEFITS OF THE EXERCISE?

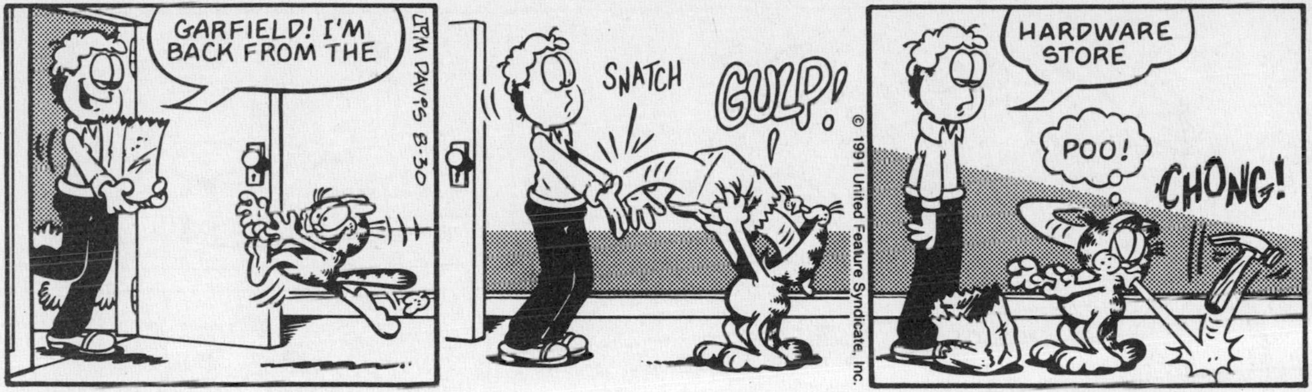
GARFIELD! I'M BACK FROM THE
JIM DAVIS 8-30
SNATCH
GULP!
HARDWARE STORE
POO!
CHONG!
© 1991 United Feature Syndicate, Inc.

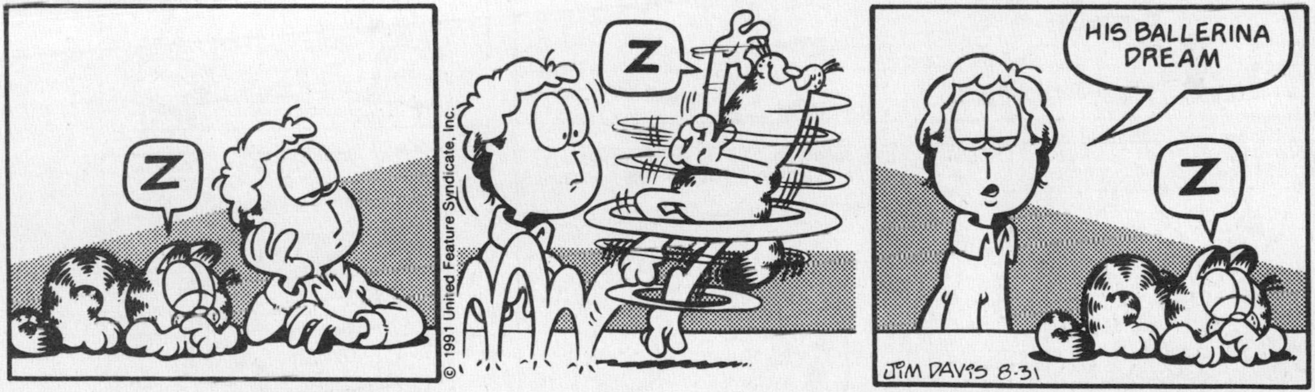
Z
© 1991 United Feature Syndicate, Inc.
Z
HIS BALLERINA DREAM
Z
JIM DAVIS 8-31

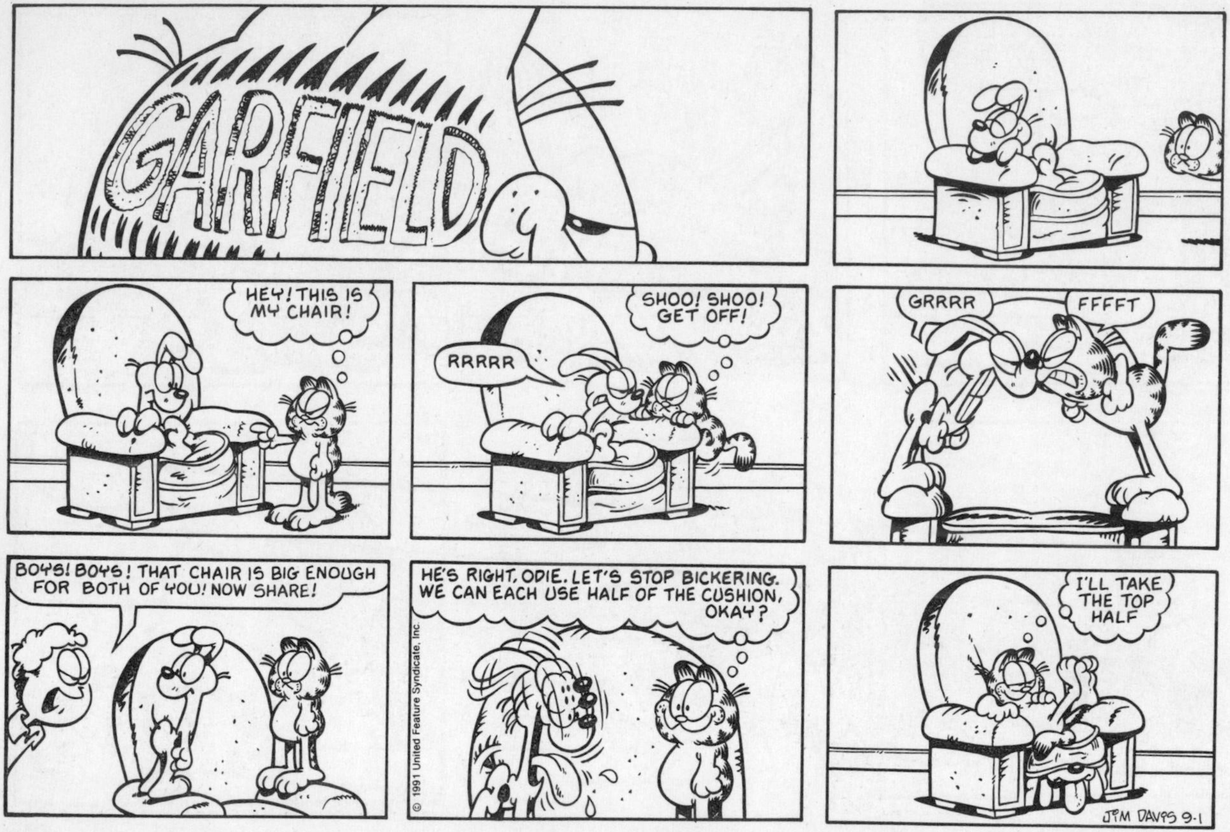
GARFIELD
HEY! THIS IS MY CHAIR!
RRRRR
SHOO! SHOO! GET OFF!
GRRRR
FFFFT
BOYS! BOYS! THAT CHAIR IS BIG ENOUGH FOR BOTH OF YOU! NOW SHARE!
HE'S RIGHT, ODIE. LET'S STOP BICKERING. WE CAN EACH USE HALF OF THE CUSHION, OKAY?
I'LL TAKE THE TOP HALF
© 1991 United Feature Syndicate, Inc.
JIM DAVIS 9-1

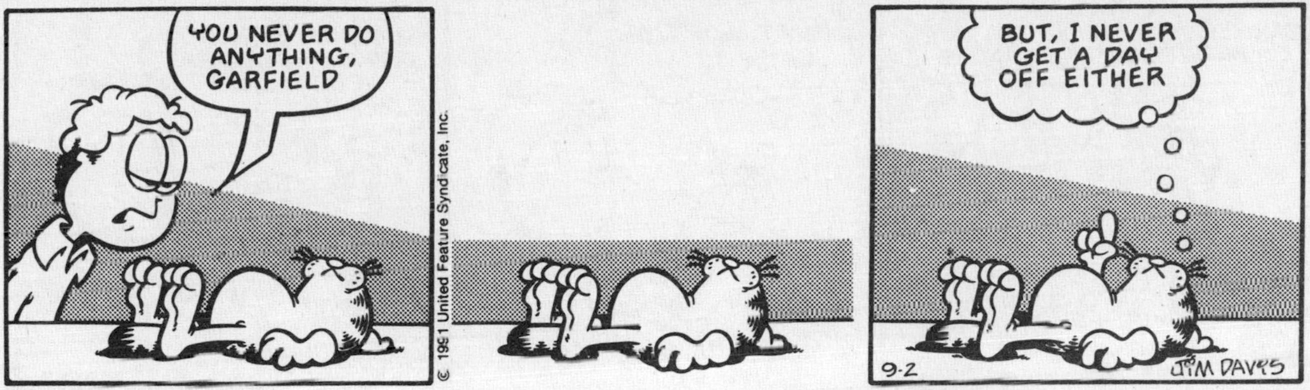
YOU NEVER DO ANYTHING, GARFIELD
BUT, I NEVER GET A DAY OFF EITHER
9-2
JIM DAVIS

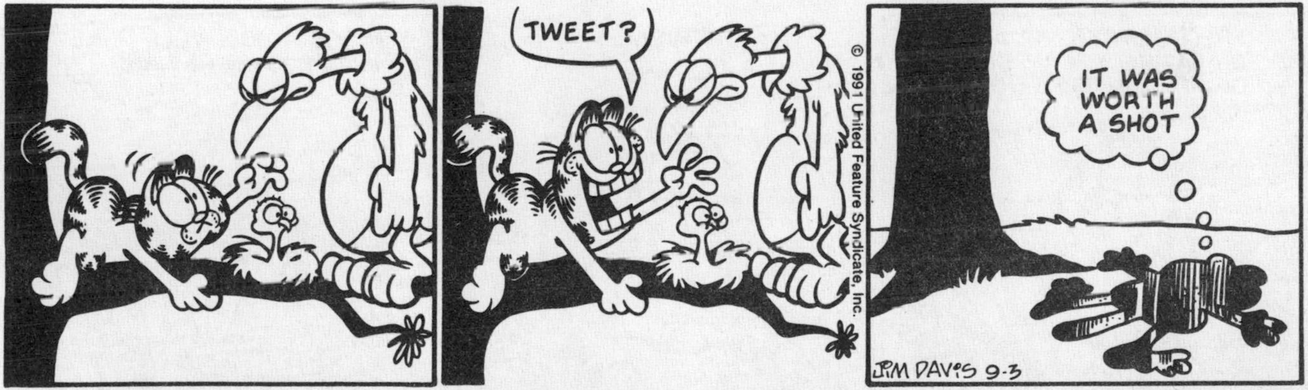
TWEET?
IT WAS WORTH A SHOT
JIM DAVIS 9-3

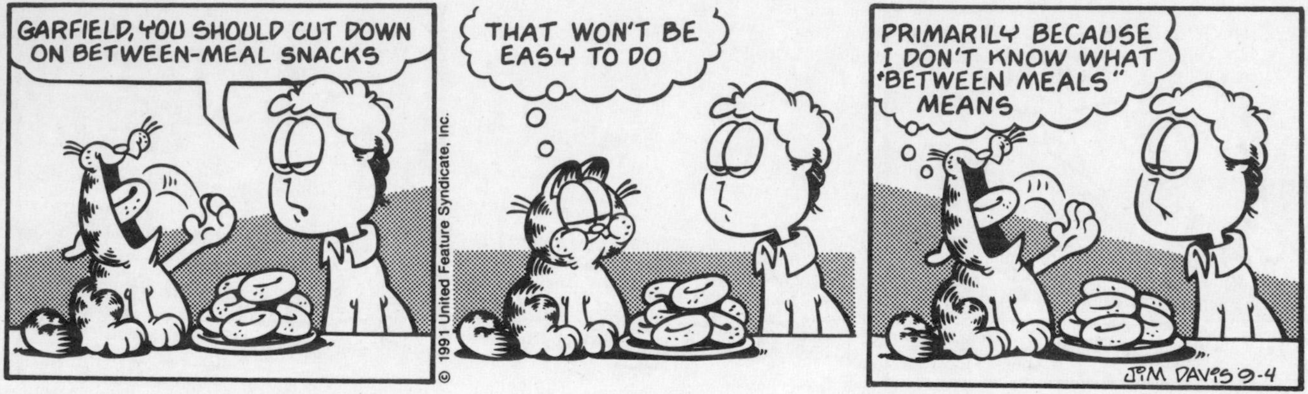
GARFIELD, YOU SHOULD CUT DOWN ON BETWEEN-MEAL SNACKS
© 1991 United Feature Syndicate, Inc.
THAT WON'T BE EASY TO DO
PRIMARILY BECAUSE I DON'T KNOW WHAT "BETWEEN MEALS" MEANS
JIM DAVIS 9-4

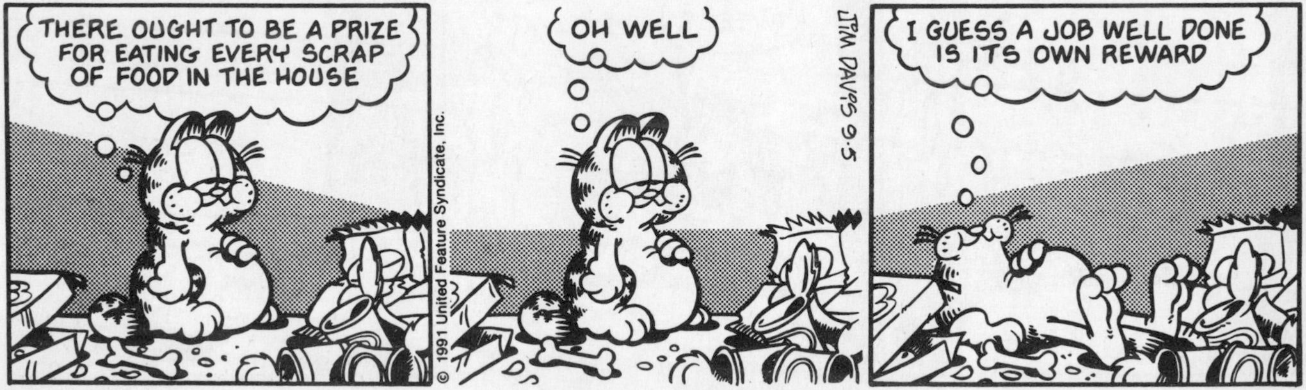
THERE OUGHT TO BE A PRIZE FOR EATING EVERY SCRAP OF FOOD IN THE HOUSE
© 1991 United Feature Syndicate, Inc.
OH WELL
JIM DAVIS 9-5
I GUESS A JOB WELL DONE IS ITS OWN REWARD

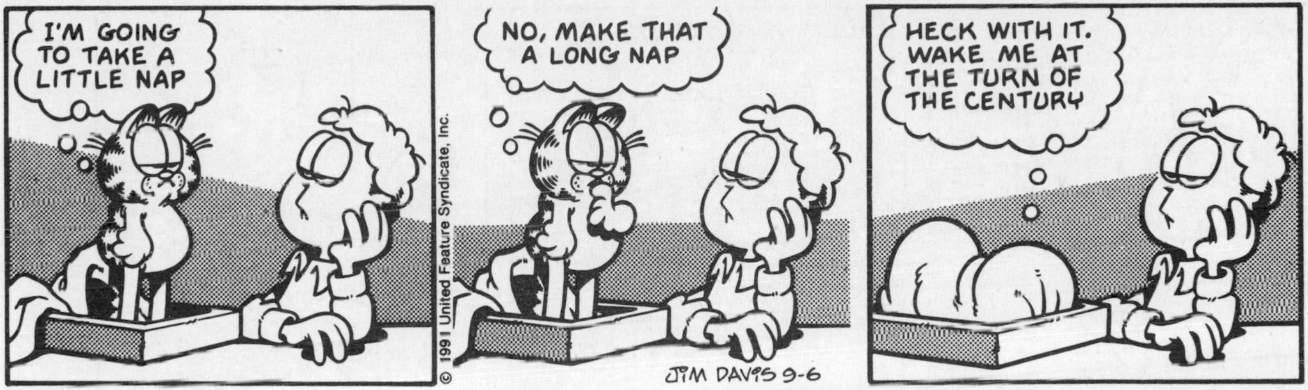
I'M GOING TO TAKE A LITTLE NAP
NO, MAKE THAT A LONG NAP
HECK WITH IT. WAKE ME AT THE TURN OF THE CENTURY
© 1991 United Feature Syndicate, Inc.
JIM DAVIS 9-6

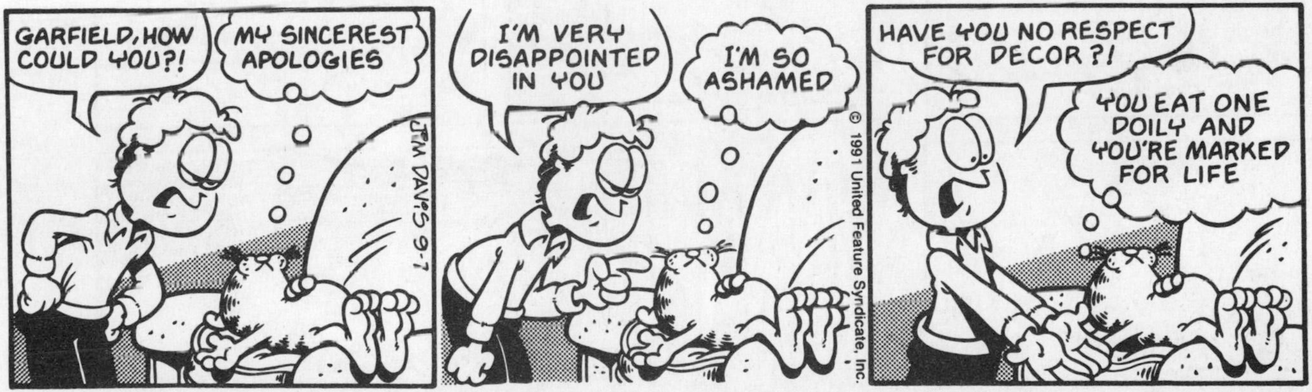
GARFIELD, HOW COULD YOU?!
MY SINCEREST APOLOGIES
JIM DAVIS 9-7
I'M VERY DISAPPOINTED IN YOU
I'M SO ASHAMED
© 1991 United Feature Syndicate, Inc.
HAVE YOU NO RESPECT FOR DECOR?!
YOU EAT ONE DOILY AND YOU'RE MARKED FOR LIFE

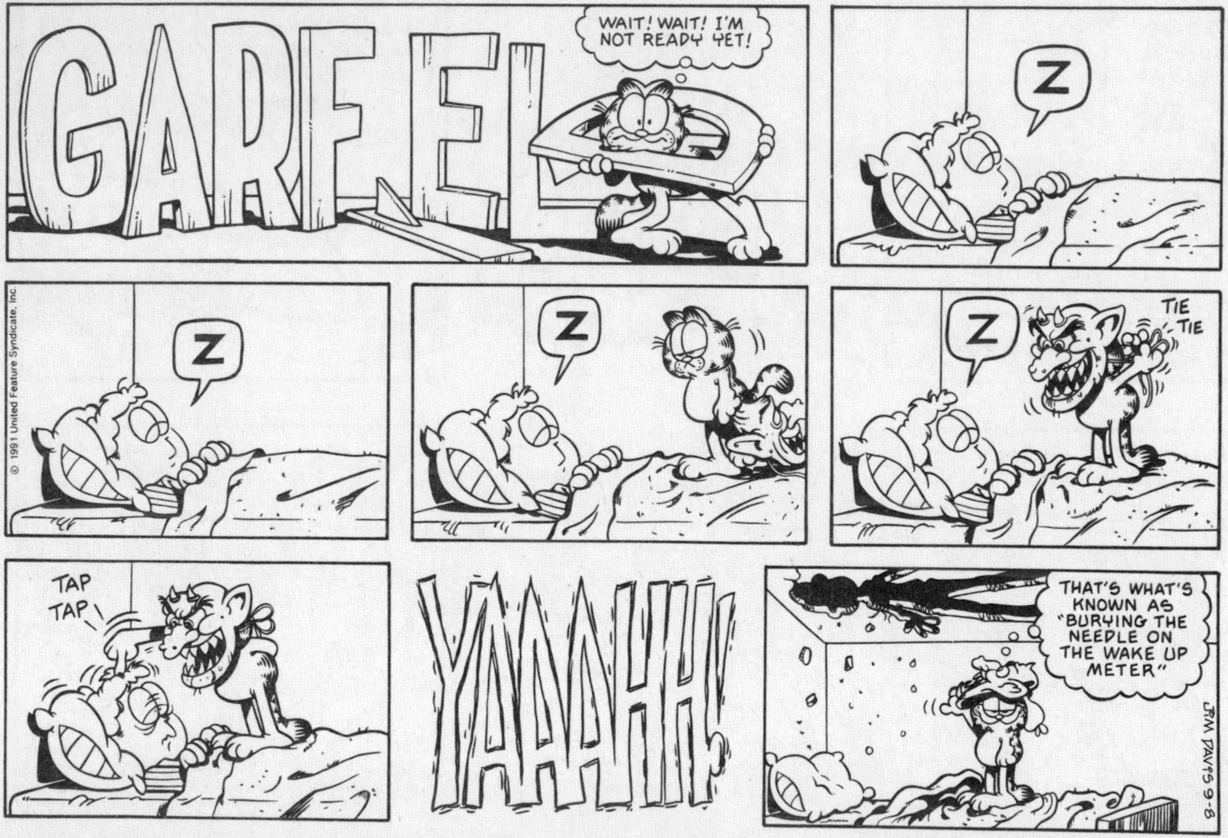
GARFIELD
WAIT! WAIT! I'M NOT READY YET!
Z
Z
Z
Z
TIE TIE
TAP TAP
YAAAHH!
THAT'S WHAT'S KNOWN AS "BURYING THE NEEDLE ON THE WAKE UP METER"
JIM DAVIS 9-8
© 1991 United Feature Syndicate, Inc.

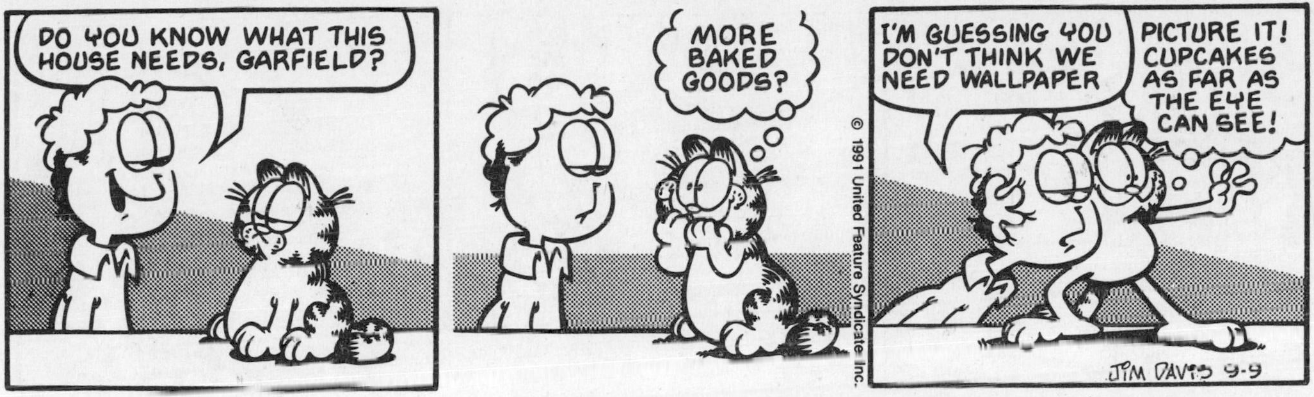
DO YOU KNOW WHAT THIS HOUSE NEEDS, GARFIELD?
MORE BAKED GOODS?
I'M GUESSING YOU DON'T THINK WE NEED WALLPAPER
PICTURE IT! CUPCAKES AS FAR AS THE EYE CAN SEE!
© 1991 United Feature Syndicate, Inc.
JIM DAVIS 9-9

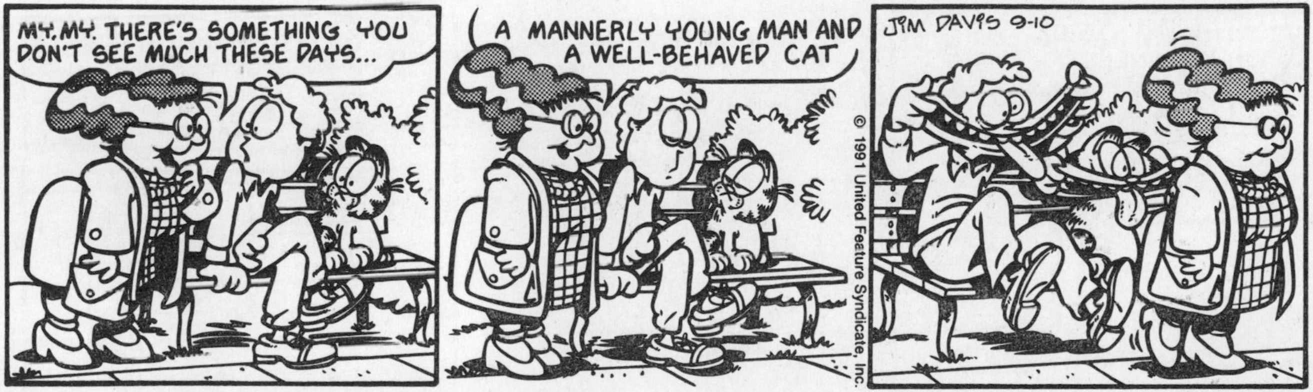
MY, MY. THERE'S SOMETHING YOU DON'T SEE MUCH THESE DAYS...
A MANNERLY YOUNG MAN AND A WELL-BEHAVED CAT
© 1991 United Feature Syndicate, Inc.
JIM DAVIS 9-10

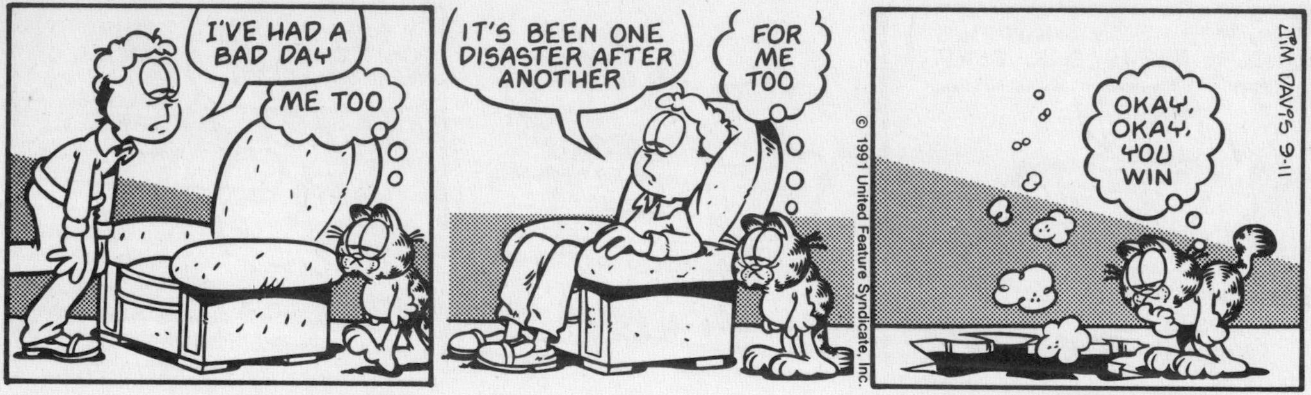
I'VE HAD A BAD DAY
ME TOO
IT'S BEEN ONE DISASTER AFTER ANOTHER
FOR ME TOO
OKAY, OKAY, YOU WIN
JIM DAVIS 9-11
© 1991 United Feature Syndicate, Inc.

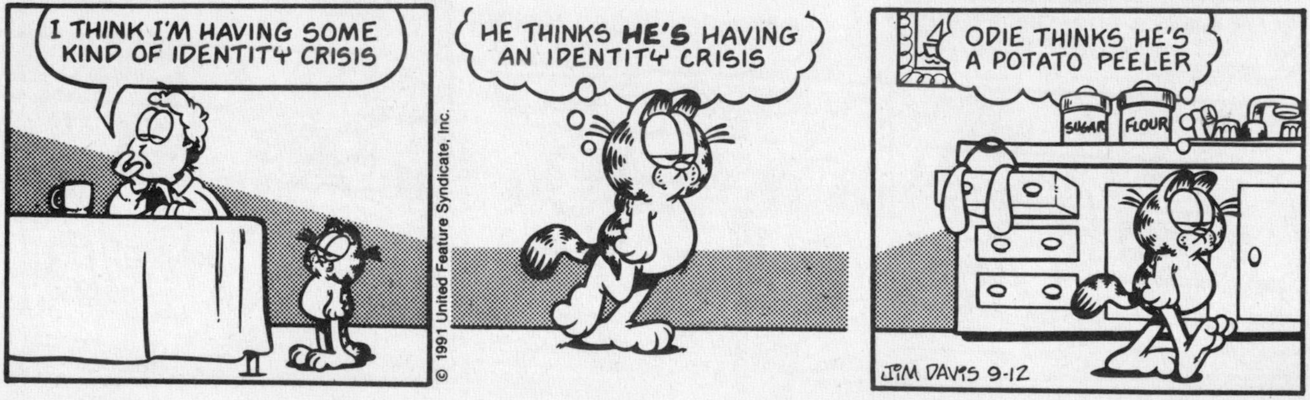
I THINK I'M HAVING SOME KIND OF IDENTITY CRISIS
© 1991 United Feature Syndicate, Inc.
HE THINKS **HE'S** HAVING AN IDENTITY CRISIS
ODIE THINKS HE'S A POTATO PEELER
SUGAR
FLOUR
JIM DAVIS 9-12

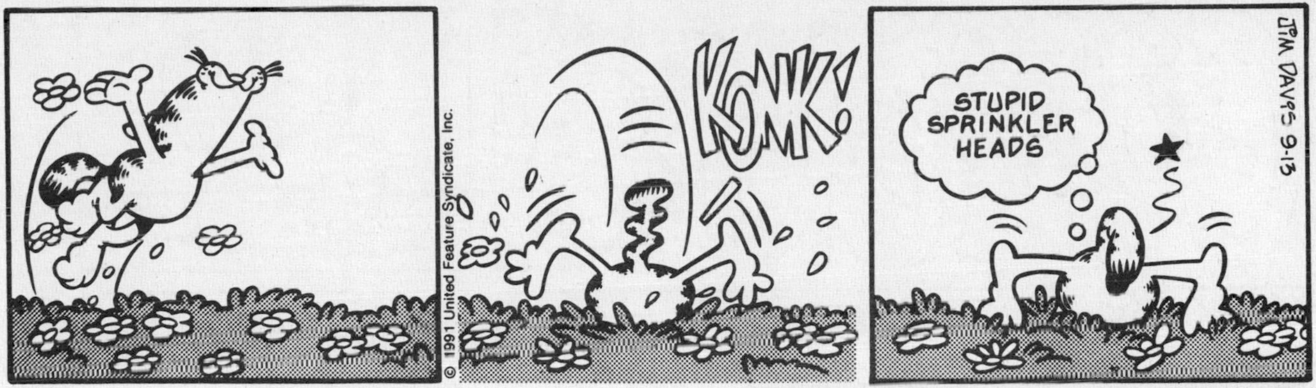
© 1991 United Feature Syndicate, Inc.
KONK!
STUPID SPRINKLER HEADS
JIM DAVIS 9-13

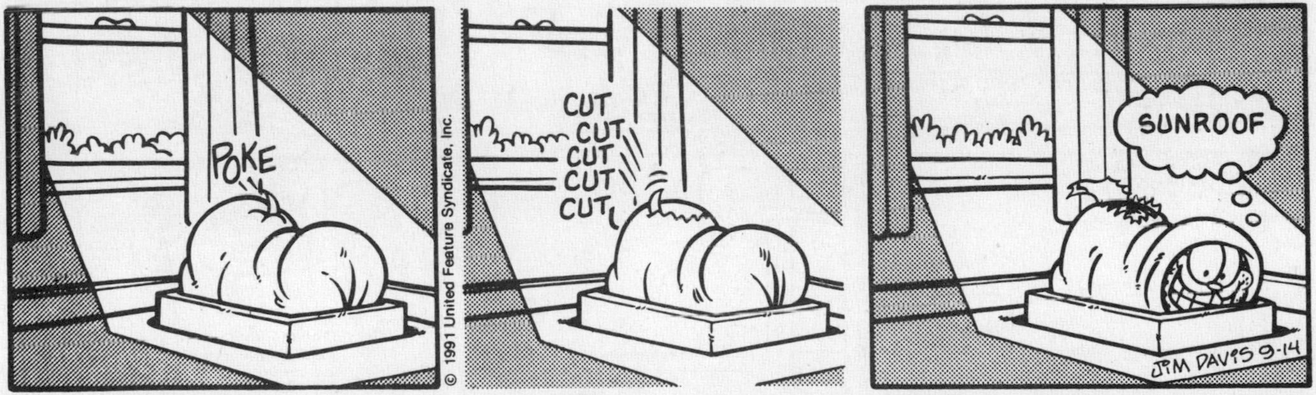
POKE
© 1991 United Feature Syndicate, Inc.
CUT
CUT
CUT
CUT
CUT
SUNROOF
JIM DAVIS 9-14

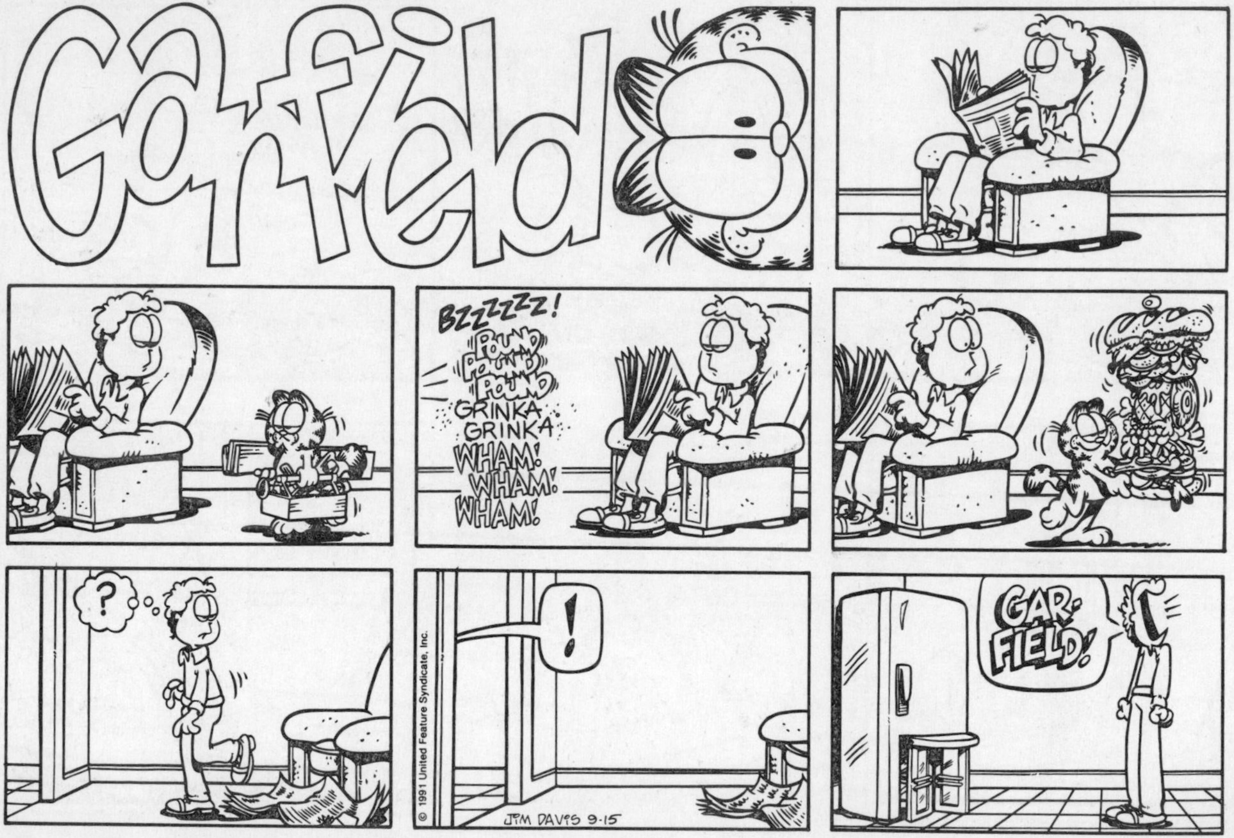
GARFIELD
BZZZZZZ!
POUND POUND POUND
GRINKA GRINKA
WHAM! WHAM! WHAM!
?
!
GAR-FIELD!
© 1991 United Feature Syndicate, Inc.
JIM DAVIS 9-15

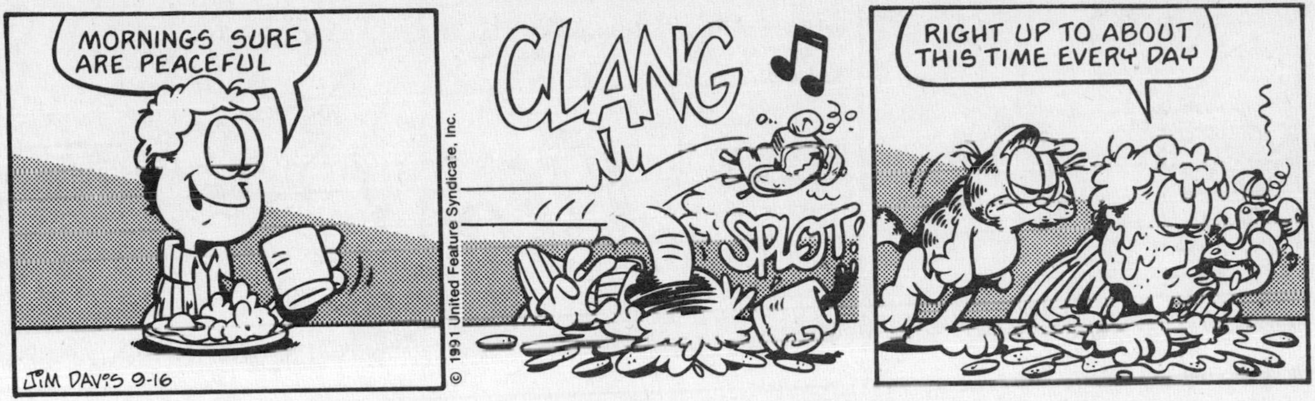
MORNINGS SURE ARE PEACEFUL
JIM DAVIS 9-16
© 1991 United Feature Syndicate, Inc.
CLANG
SPLOT!
RIGHT UP TO ABOUT THIS TIME EVERY DAY

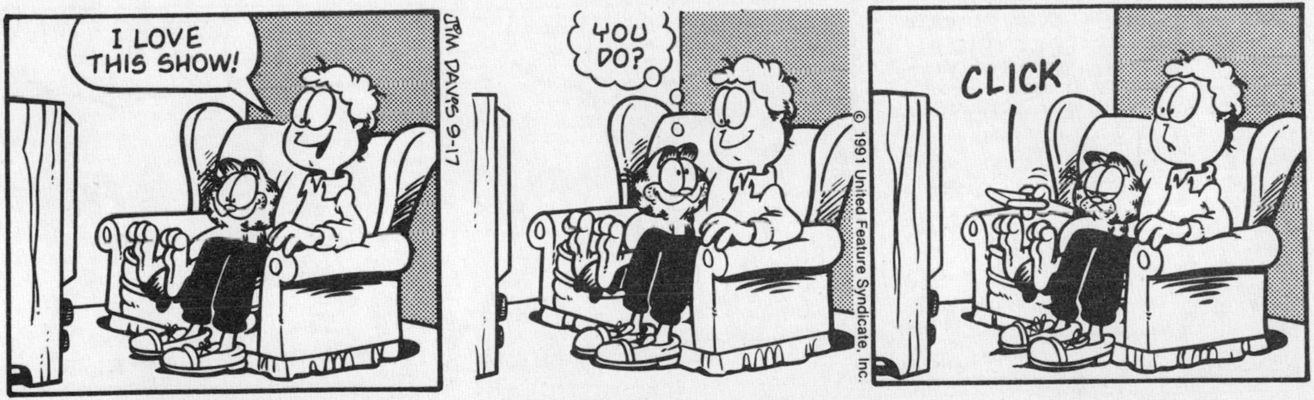
I LOVE THIS SHOW!
JIM DAVIS 9-17
YOU DO?
© 1991 United Feature Syndicate, Inc.
CLICK

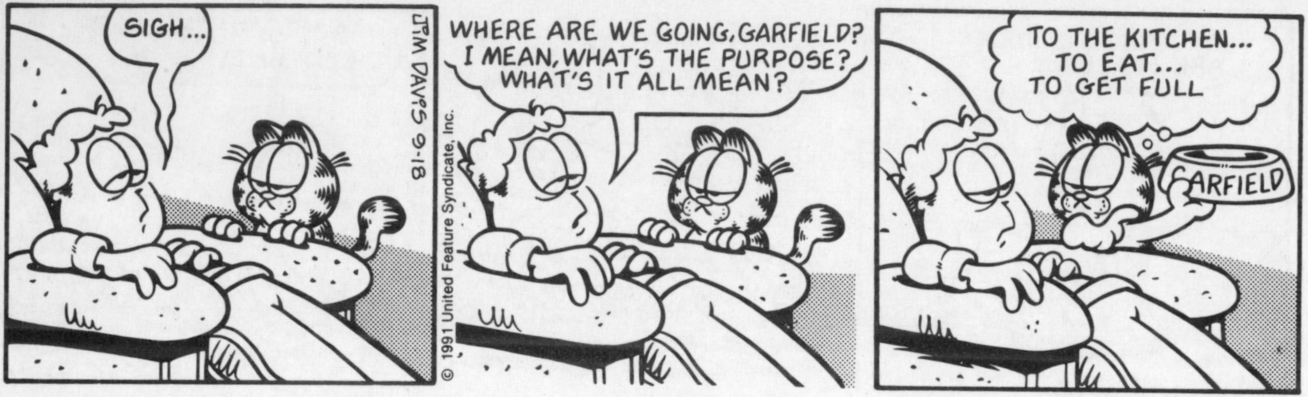
SIGH...
JIM DAVIS 9-18
© 1991 United Feature Syndicate, Inc.
WHERE ARE WE GOING, GARFIELD? I MEAN, WHAT'S THE PURPOSE? WHAT'S IT ALL MEAN?
TO THE KITCHEN... TO EAT... TO GET FULL
GARFIELD

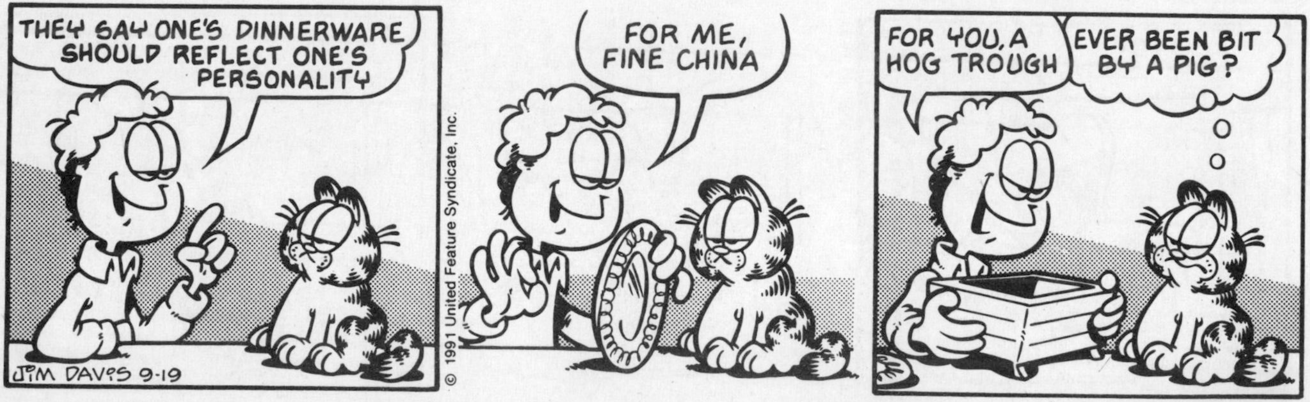
THEY SAY ONE'S DINNERWARE SHOULD REFLECT ONE'S PERSONALITY
JIM DAVIS 9-19
© 1991 United Feature Syndicate, Inc.
FOR ME, FINE CHINA
FOR YOU, A HOG TROUGH
EVER BEEN BIT BY A PIG?

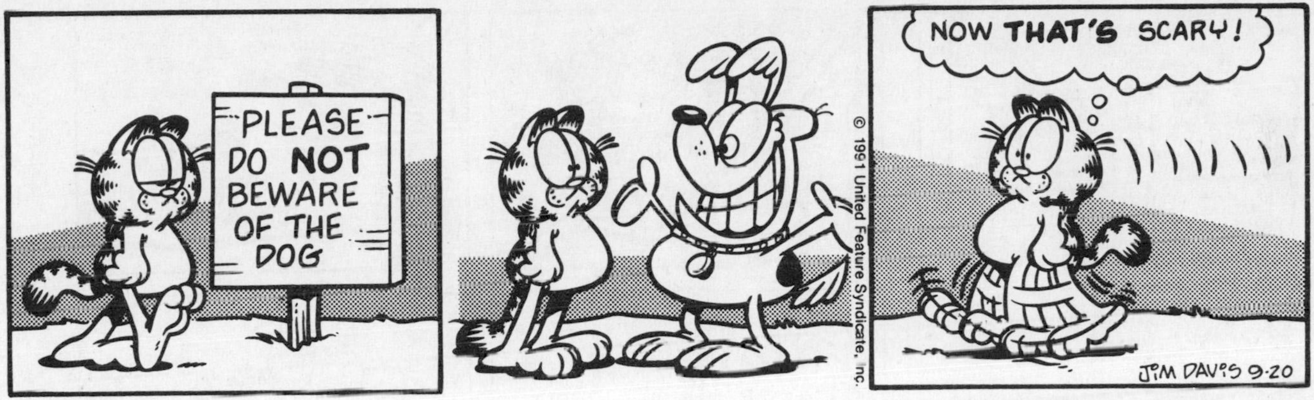
PLEASE DO NOT BEWARE OF THE DOG
NOW THAT'S SCARY!
© 1991 United Feature Syndicate, Inc.
JIM DAVIS 9-20

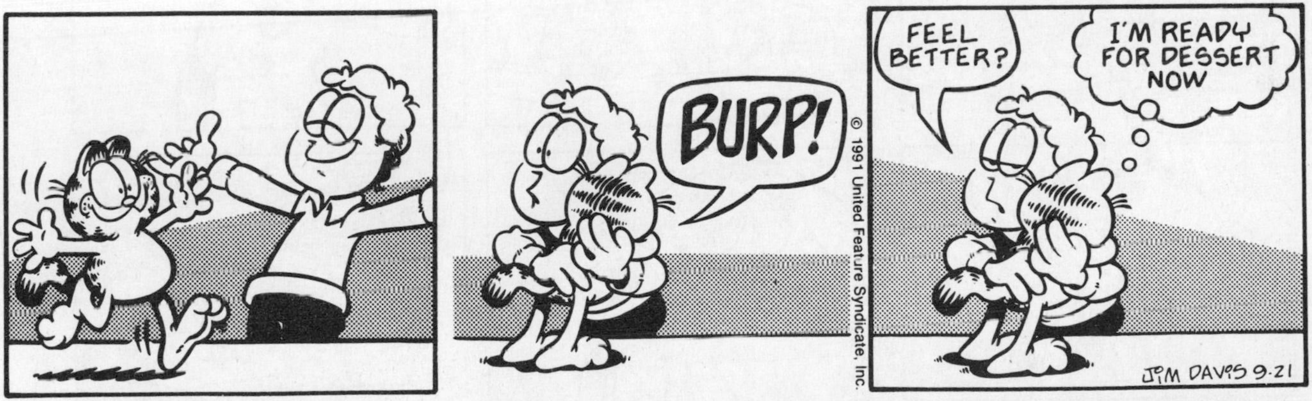
BURP!
FEEL BETTER?
I'M READY FOR DESSERT NOW
© 1991 United Feature Syndicate, Inc.
JIM DAVIS 9-21

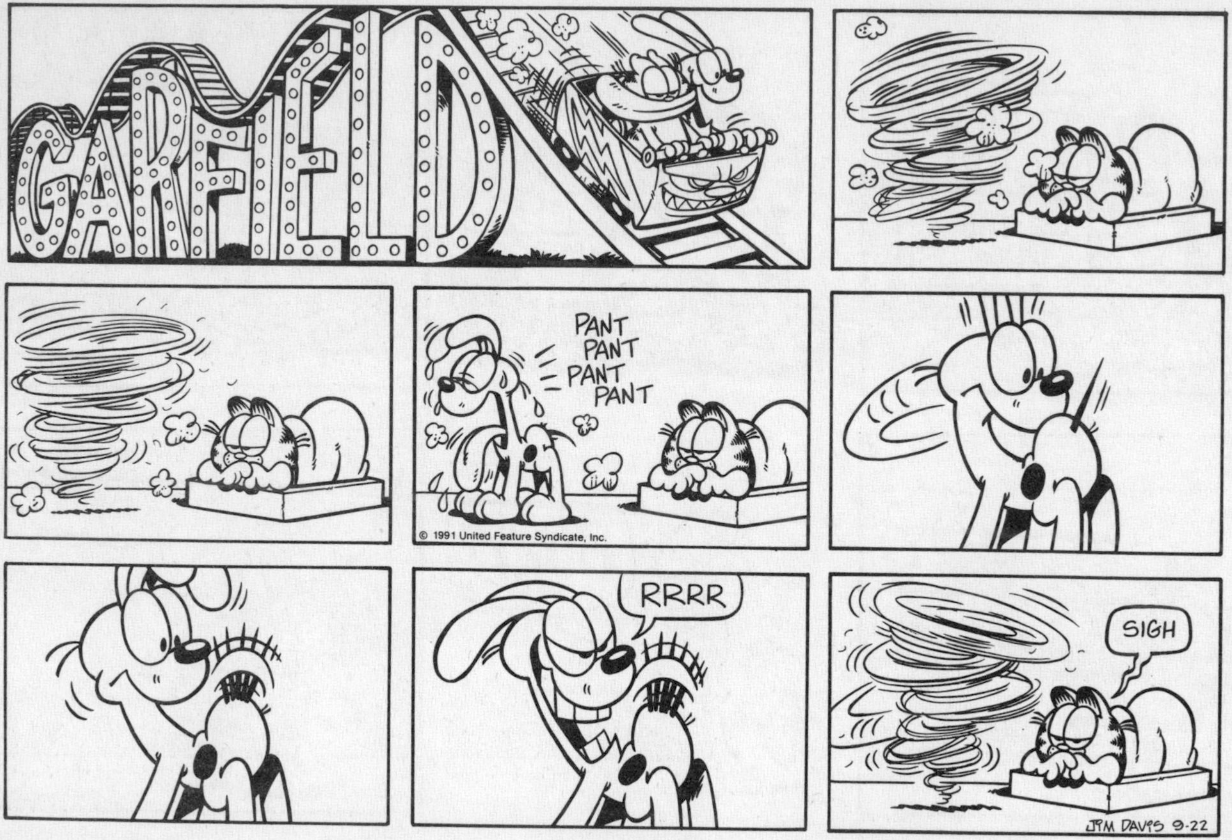
GARFIELD
PANT
PANT
PANT
PANT
© 1991 United Feature Syndicate, Inc.
RRRR
SIGH
JIM DAVIS 9-22

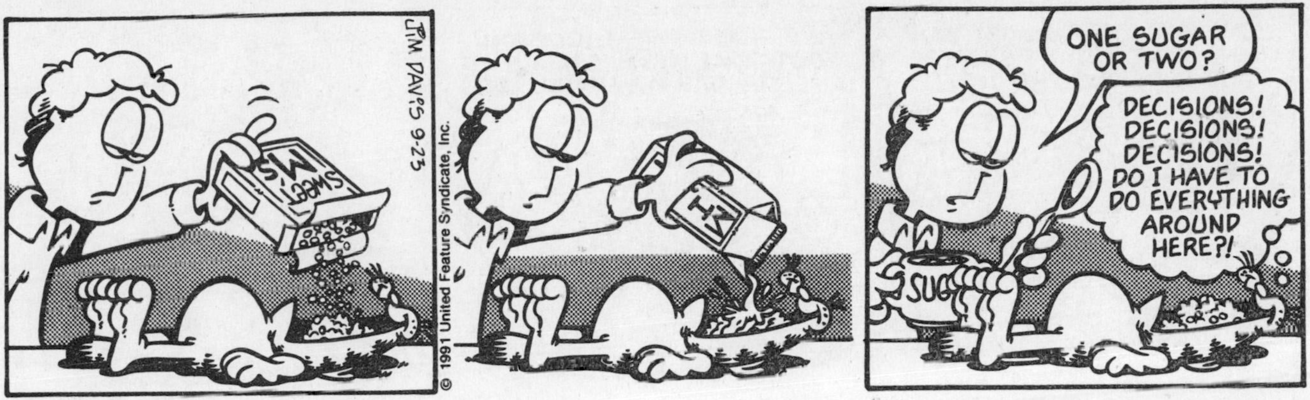
JIM DAVIS 9-23
SWEET MS
© 1991 United Feature Syndicate, Inc.
ONE SUGAR OR TWO?
DECISIONS! DECISIONS! DECISIONS! DO I HAVE TO DO EVERYTHING AROUND HERE?!
SUG

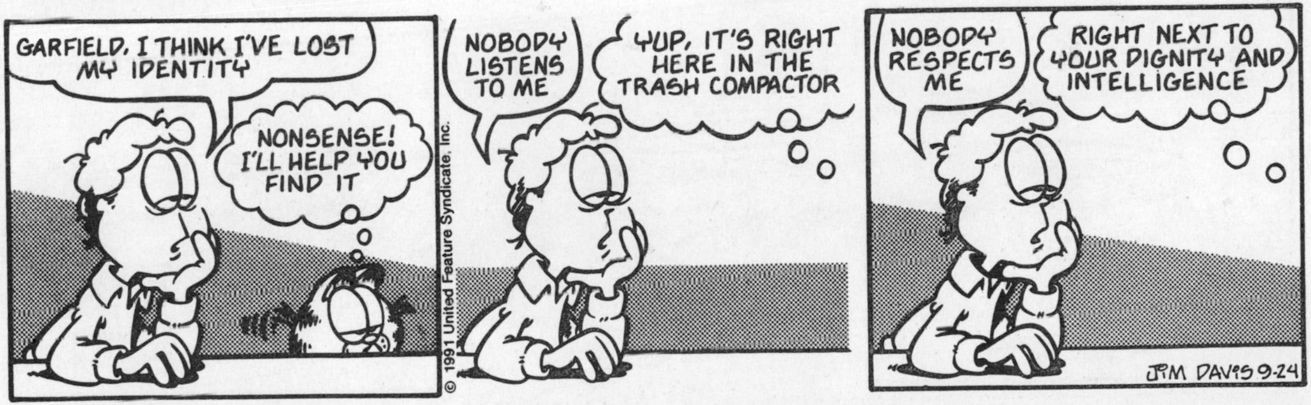
GARFIELD, I THINK I'VE LOST MY IDENTITY
NONSENSE! I'LL HELP YOU FIND IT
© 1991 United Feature Syndicate, Inc.
NOBODY LISTENS TO ME
YUP, IT'S RIGHT HERE IN THE TRASH COMPACTOR
NOBODY RESPECTS ME
RIGHT NEXT TO YOUR DIGNITY AND INTELLIGENCE
JIM DAVIS 9-24

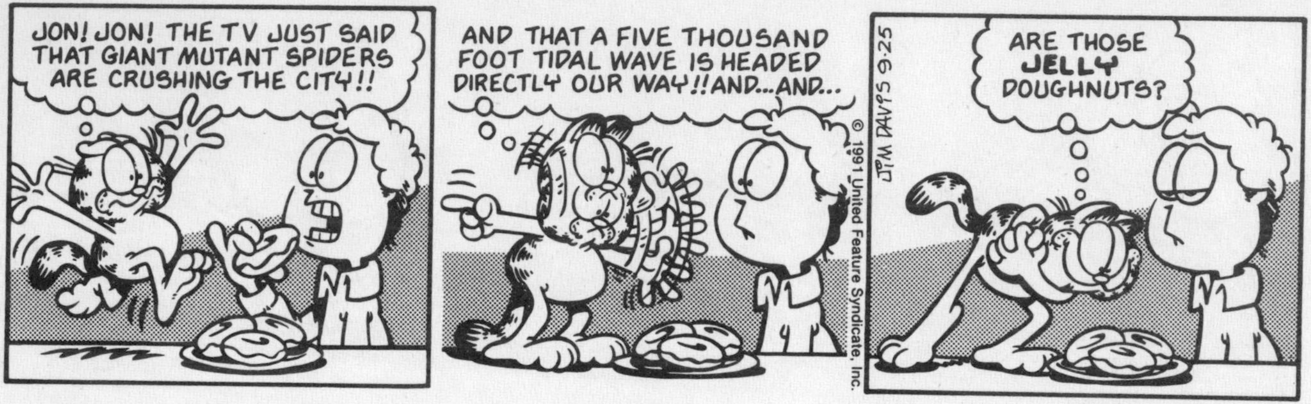
JON! JON! THE TV JUST SAID THAT GIANT MUTANT SPIDERS ARE CRUSHING THE CITY!!
AND THAT A FIVE THOUSAND FOOT TIDAL WAVE IS HEADED DIRECTLY OUR WAY!! AND...AND...
© 1991 United Feature Syndicate, Inc.
JIM DAVIS 9-25
ARE THOSE JELLY DOUGHNUTS?

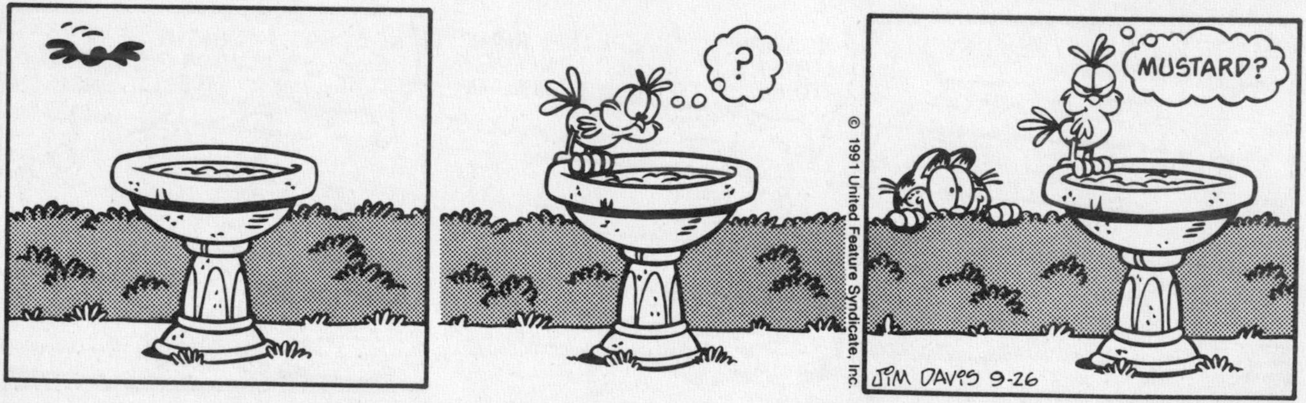
?
© 1991 United Feature Syndicate, Inc.
MUSTARD?
JIM DAVIS 9-26

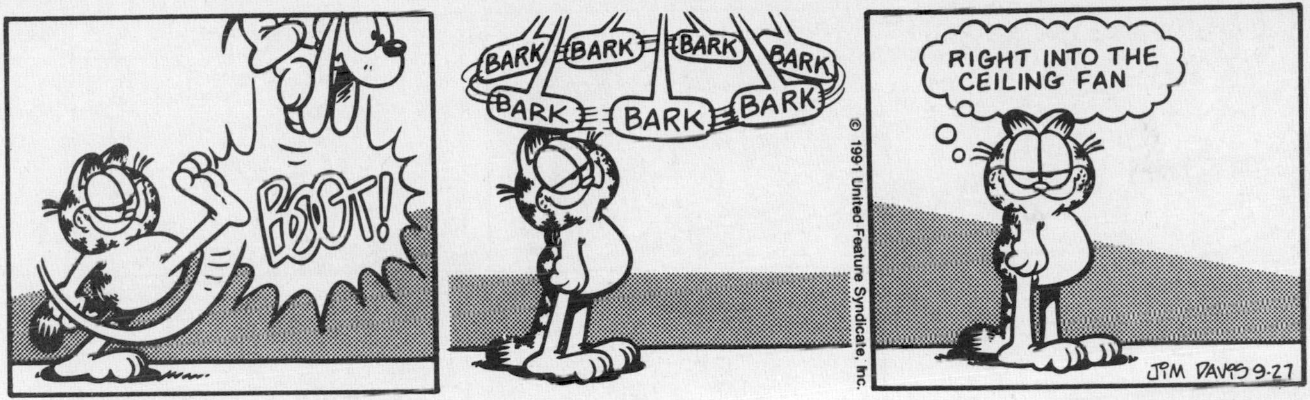
BOOT!
BARK BARK BARK BARK BARK BARK BARK
RIGHT INTO THE CEILING FAN
© 1991 United Feature Syndicate, Inc.
JIM DAVIS 9-27

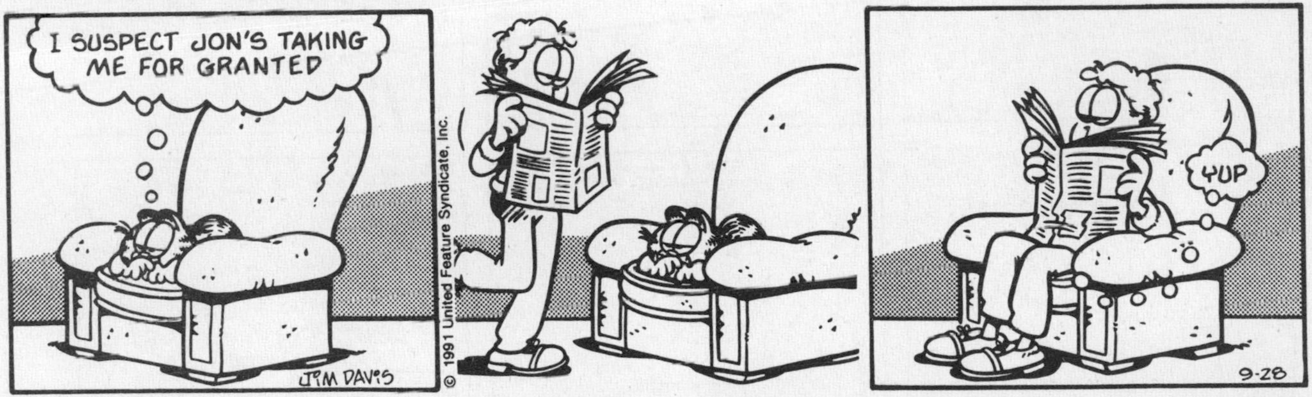
I SUSPECT JON'S TAKING ME FOR GRANTED
JIM DAVIS
© 1991 United Feature Syndicate, Inc.
YUP
9-28

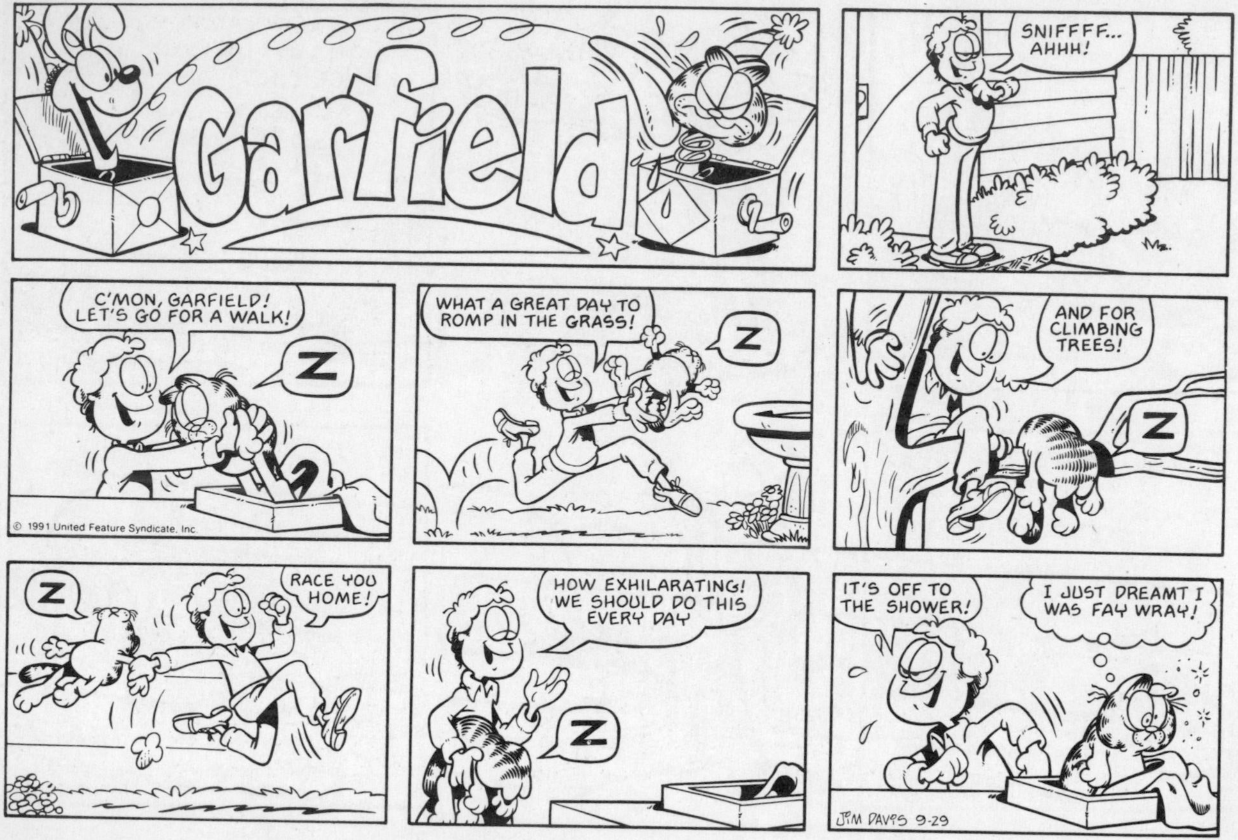
Garfield
SNIFFFF... AHHH!
C'MON, GARFIELD! LET'S GO FOR A WALK!
Z
© 1991 United Feature Syndicate, Inc.
WHAT A GREAT DAY TO ROMP IN THE GRASS!
Z
AND FOR CLIMBING TREES!
Z
Z
RACE YOU HOME!
HOW EXHILARATING! WE SHOULD DO THIS EVERY DAY
Z
IT'S OFF TO THE SHOWER!
I JUST DREAMT I WAS FAY WRAY!
JIM DAVIS 9-29

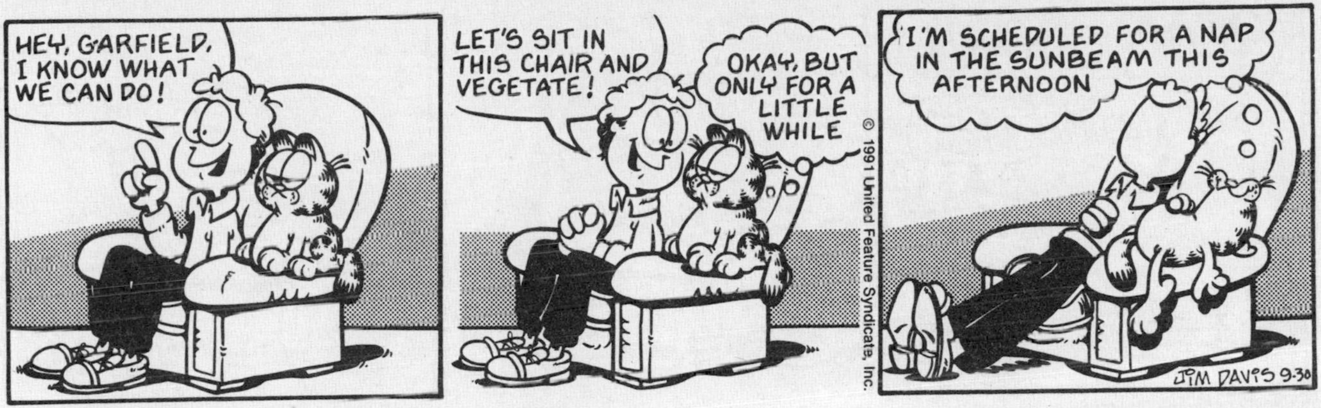
HEY, GARFIELD, I KNOW WHAT WE CAN DO!
LET'S SIT IN THIS CHAIR AND VEGETATE!
OKAY, BUT ONLY FOR A LITTLE WHILE
I'M SCHEDULED FOR A NAP IN THE SUNBEAM THIS AFTERNOON
JIM DAVIS 9-30
© 1991 United Feature Syndicate, Inc.

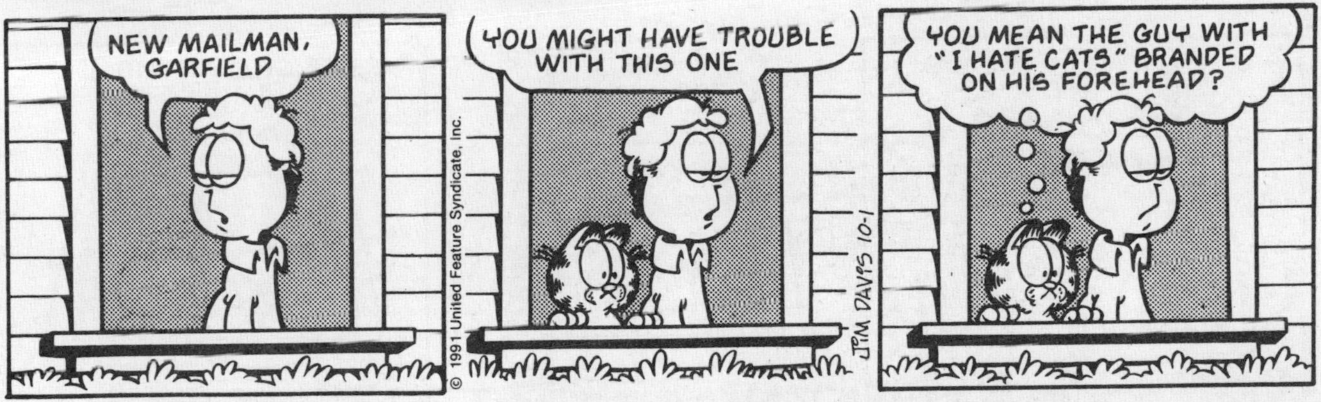
NEW MAILMAN, GARFIELD
YOU MIGHT HAVE TROUBLE WITH THIS ONE
YOU MEAN THE GUY WITH "I HATE CATS" BRANDED ON HIS FOREHEAD?
JIM DAVIS 10-1
© 1991 United Feature Syndicate, Inc.

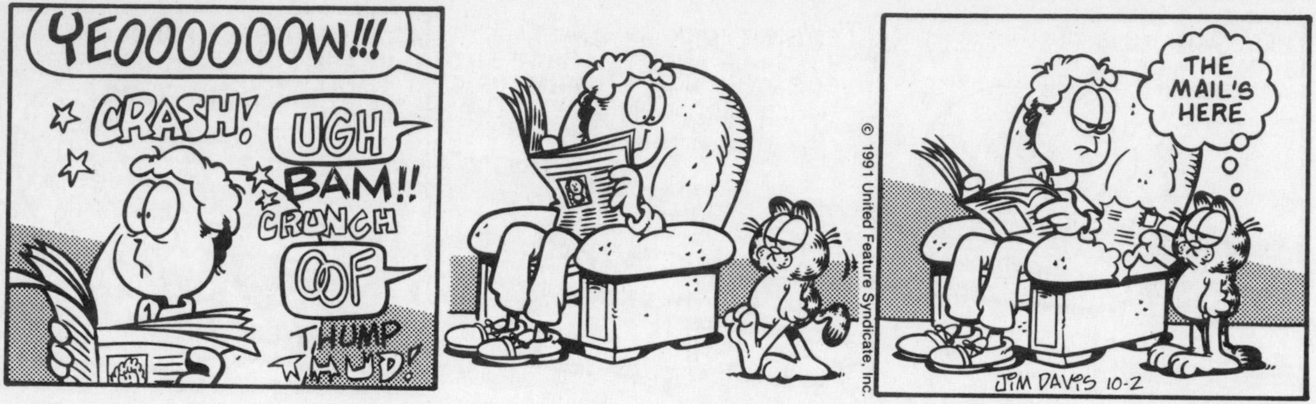
YEOOOOOOW!!!
CRASH!
UGH
BAM!!
CRUNCH
OOF
THUMP
THUD!
© 1991 United Feature Syndicate, Inc.
THE MAIL'S HERE
JIM DAVIS 10-2

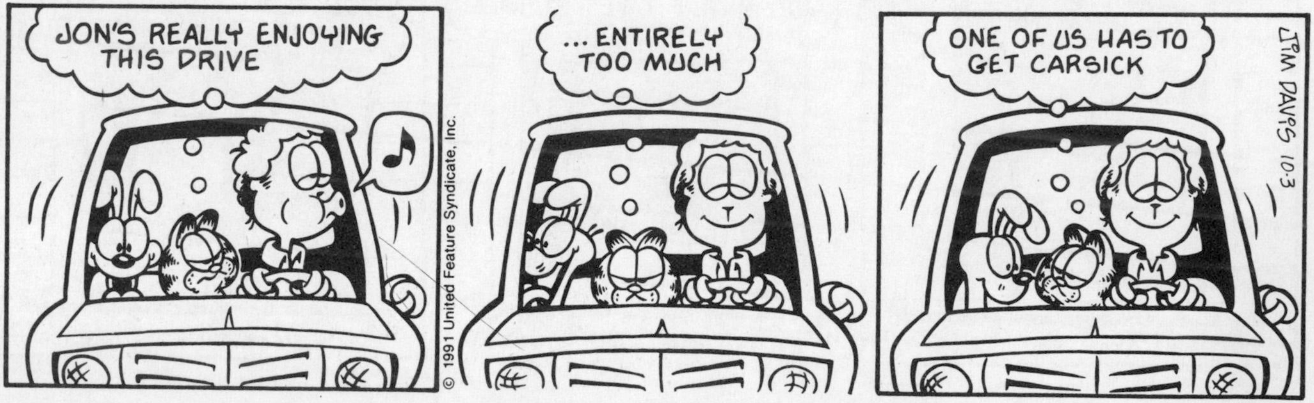
JON'S REALLY ENJOYING THIS DRIVE
© 1991 United Feature Syndicate, Inc.
... ENTIRELY TOO MUCH
ONE OF US HAS TO GET CARSICK
JIM DAVIS 10-3

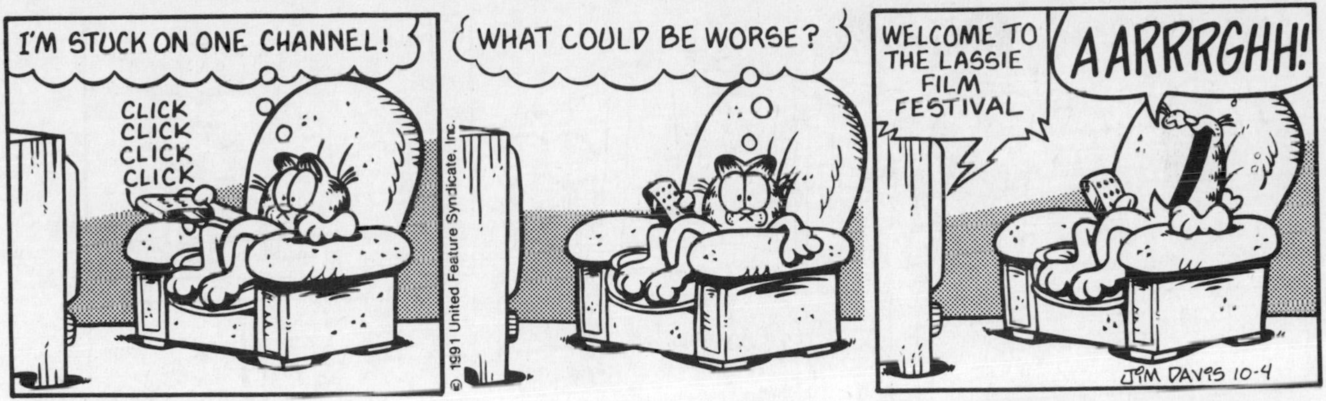
I'M STUCK ON ONE CHANNEL!
CLICK CLICK CLICK CLICK
WHAT COULD BE WORSE?
WELCOME TO THE LASSIE FILM FESTIVAL
AARRRGHH!
© 1991 United Feature Syndicate, Inc.
JIM DAVIS 10-4

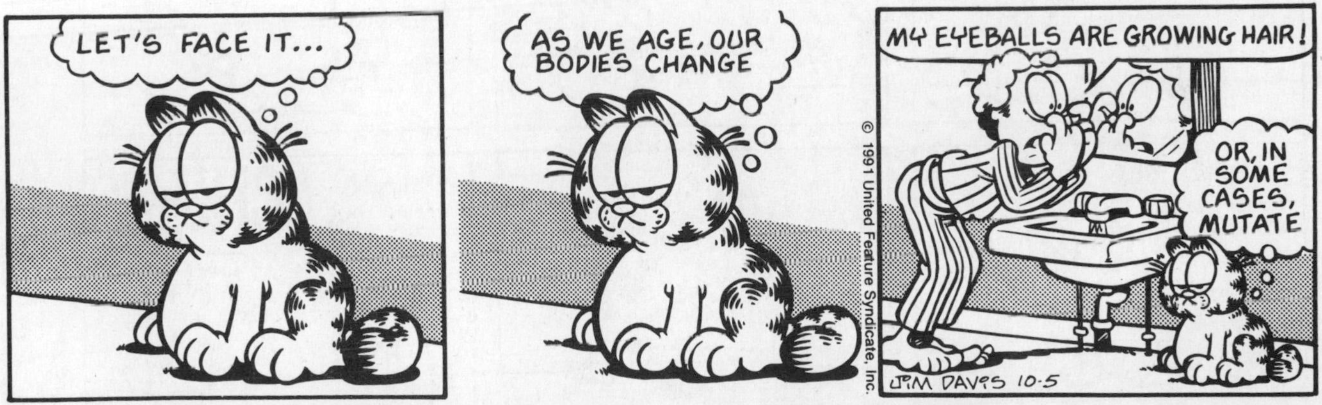
LET'S FACE IT...
AS WE AGE, OUR BODIES CHANGE
MY EYEBALLS ARE GROWING HAIR!
OR, IN SOME CASES, MUTATE
© 1991 United Feature Syndicate, Inc.
JIM DAVIS 10-5

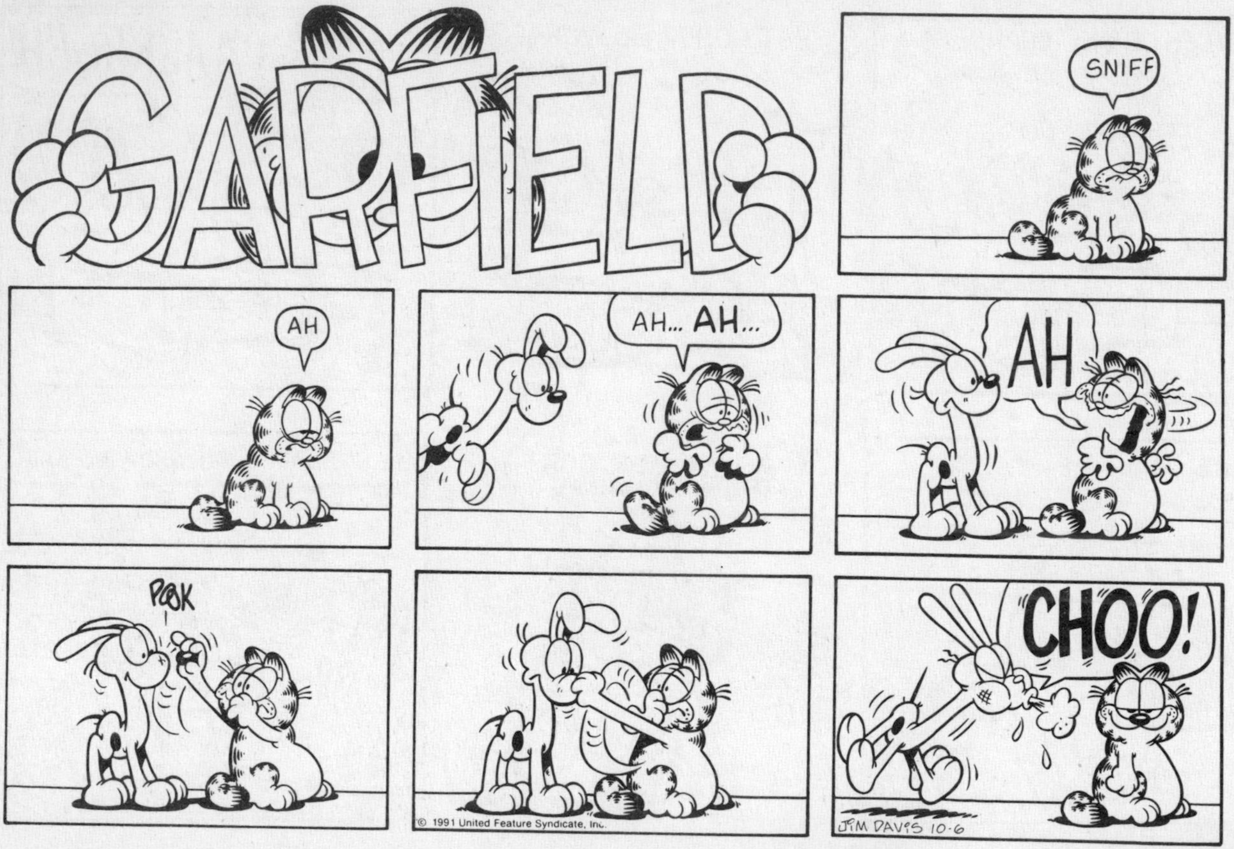
GARFIELD
SNIFF
AH
AH... AH...
AH
POOK
CHOO!
© 1991 United Feature Syndicate, Inc.
JIM DAVIS 10·6

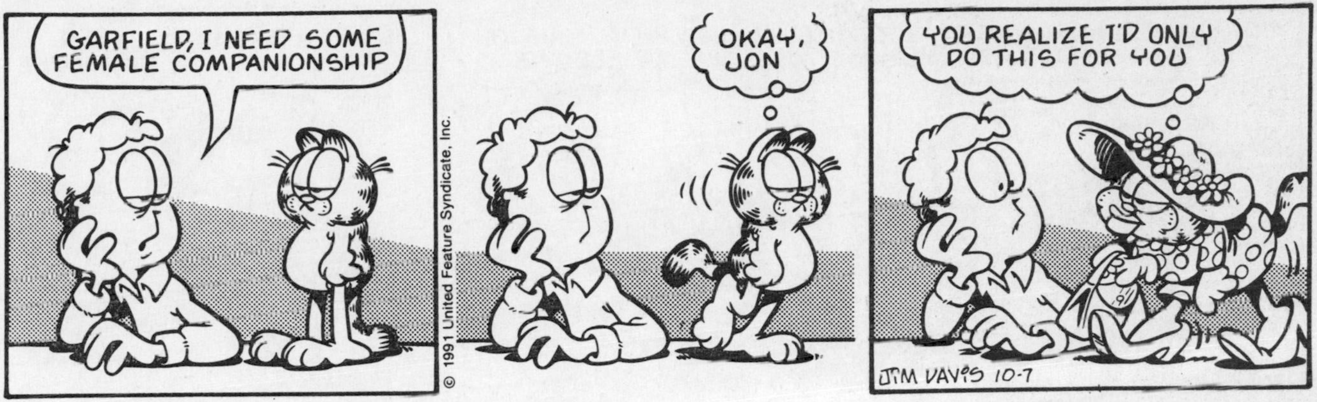
GARFIELD, I NEED SOME FEMALE COMPANIONSHIP
OKAY, JON
YOU REALIZE I'D ONLY DO THIS FOR YOU
© 1991 United Feature Syndicate, Inc.
JIM DAVIS 10-7

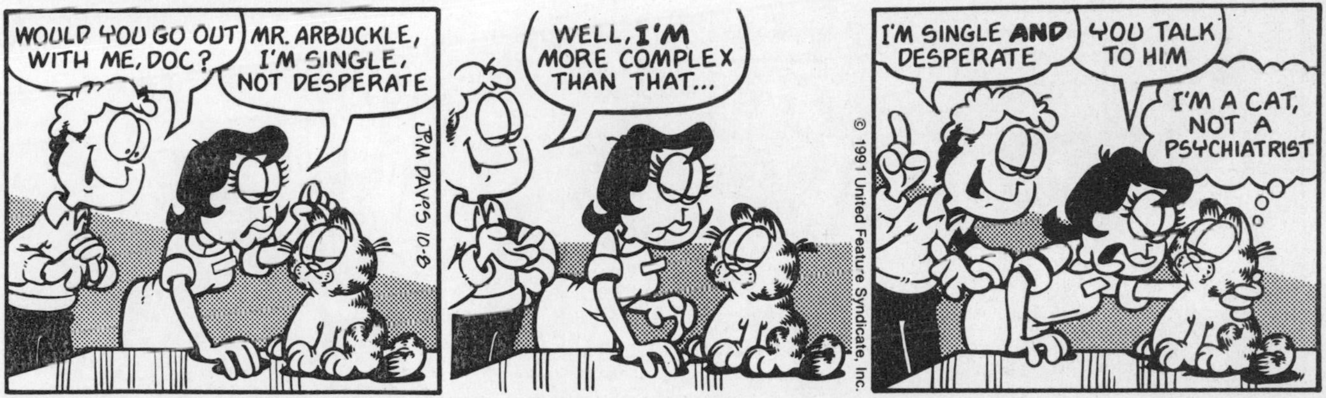
WOULD YOU GO OUT WITH ME, DOC?
MR. ARBUCKLE, I'M SINGLE, NOT DESPERATE
JIM DAVIS 10-8
WELL, **I'M** MORE COMPLEX THAN THAT...
I'M SINGLE **AND** DESPERATE
YOU TALK TO HIM
I'M A CAT, NOT A PSYCHIATRIST
© 1991 United Feature Syndicate, Inc.

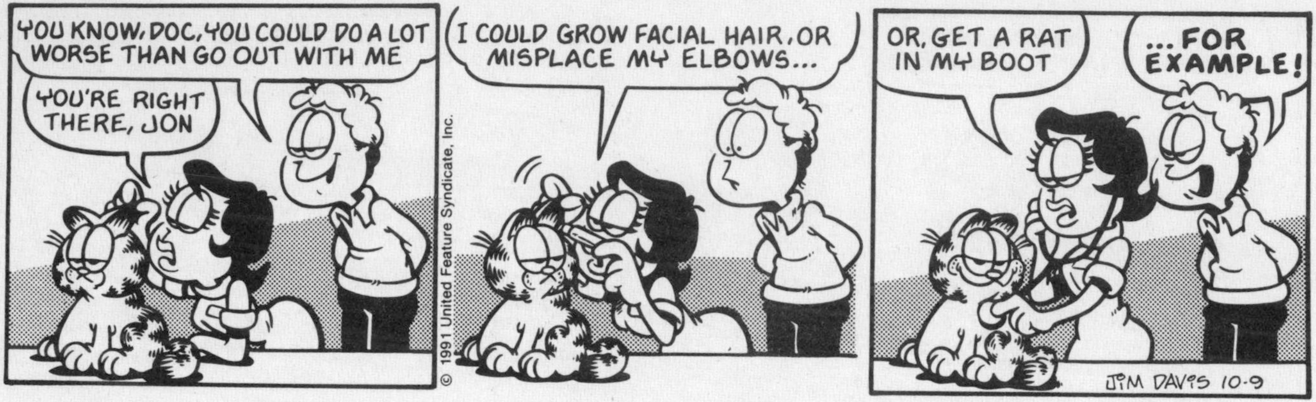
YOU KNOW, DOC, YOU COULD DO A LOT WORSE THAN GO OUT WITH ME
YOU'RE RIGHT THERE, JON
I COULD GROW FACIAL HAIR, OR MISPLACE MY ELBOWS...
OR, GET A RAT IN MY BOOT
...FOR EXAMPLE!
© 1991 United Feature Syndicate, Inc.
JIM DAVIS 10-9

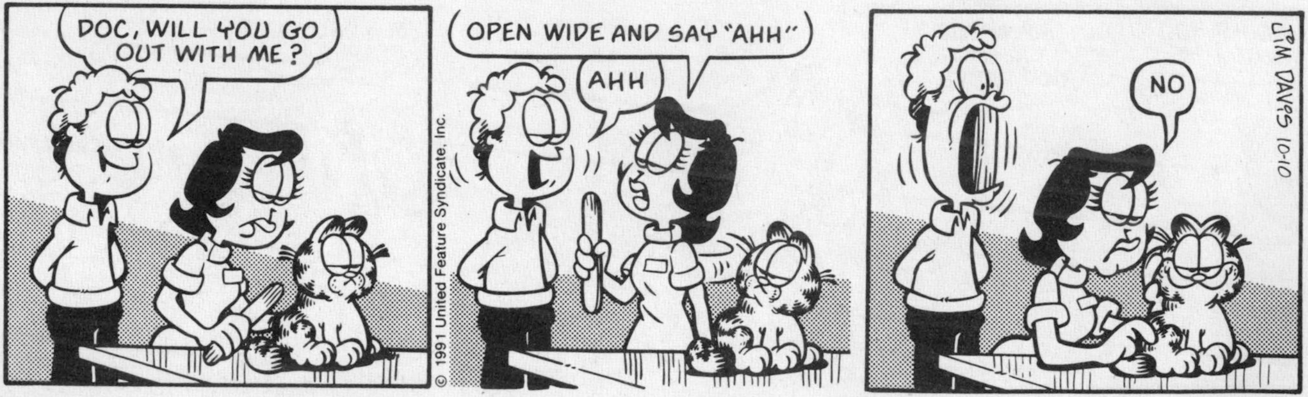
DOC, WILL YOU GO OUT WITH ME?
OPEN WIDE AND SAY "AHH"
AHH
NO
© 1991 United Feature Syndicate, Inc.
JIM DAVIS 10-10

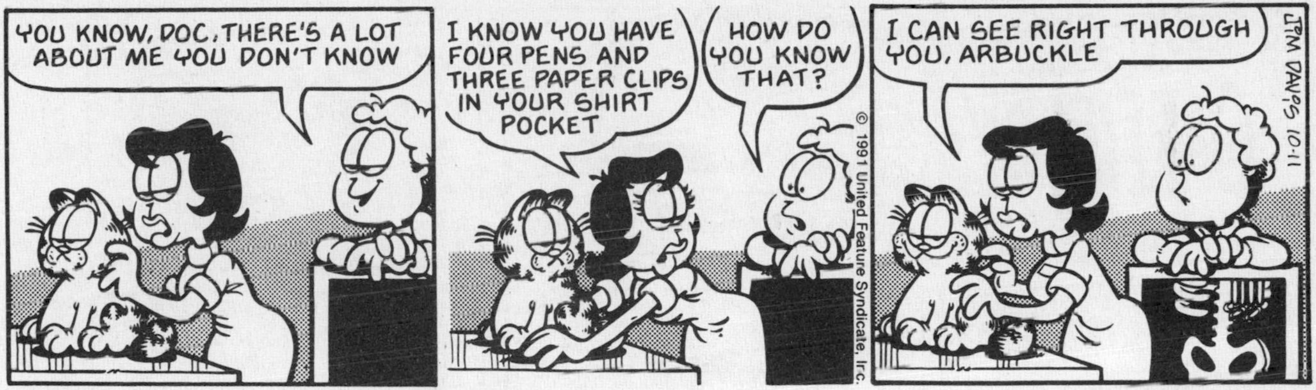
YOU KNOW, DOC, THERE'S A LOT ABOUT ME YOU DON'T KNOW
I KNOW YOU HAVE FOUR PENS AND THREE PAPER CLIPS IN YOUR SHIRT POCKET
HOW DO YOU KNOW THAT?
I CAN SEE RIGHT THROUGH YOU, ARBUCKLE
JIM DAVIS 10-11
© 1991 United Feature Syndicate, Inc.

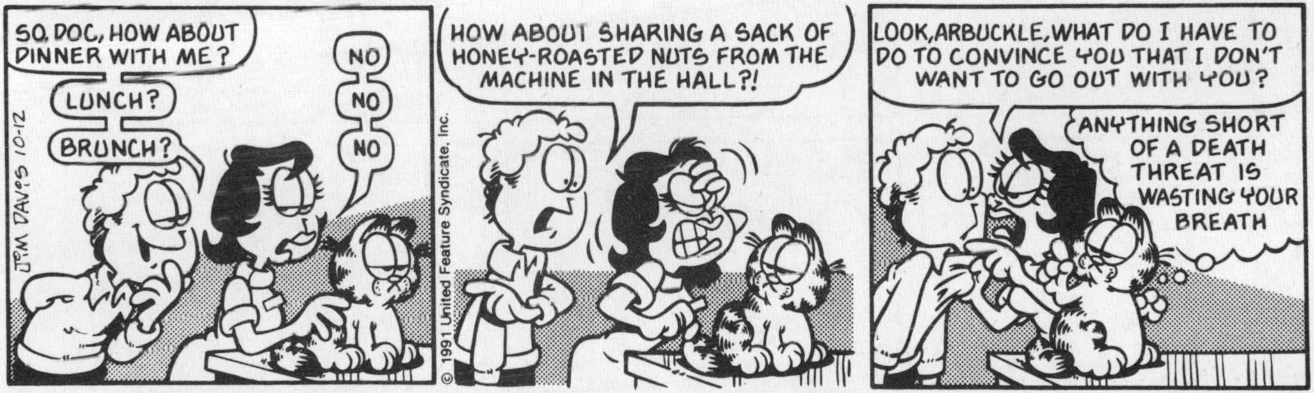
SO, DOC, HOW ABOUT DINNER WITH ME?
NO
LUNCH?
NO
BRUNCH?
NO
JIM DAVIS 10-12
© 1991 United Feature Syndicate, Inc.
HOW ABOUT SHARING A SACK OF HONEY-ROASTED NUTS FROM THE MACHINE IN THE HALL?!
LOOK, ARBUCKLE, WHAT DO I HAVE TO DO TO CONVINCE YOU THAT I DON'T WANT TO GO OUT WITH YOU?
ANYTHING SHORT OF A DEATH THREAT IS WASTING YOUR BREATH

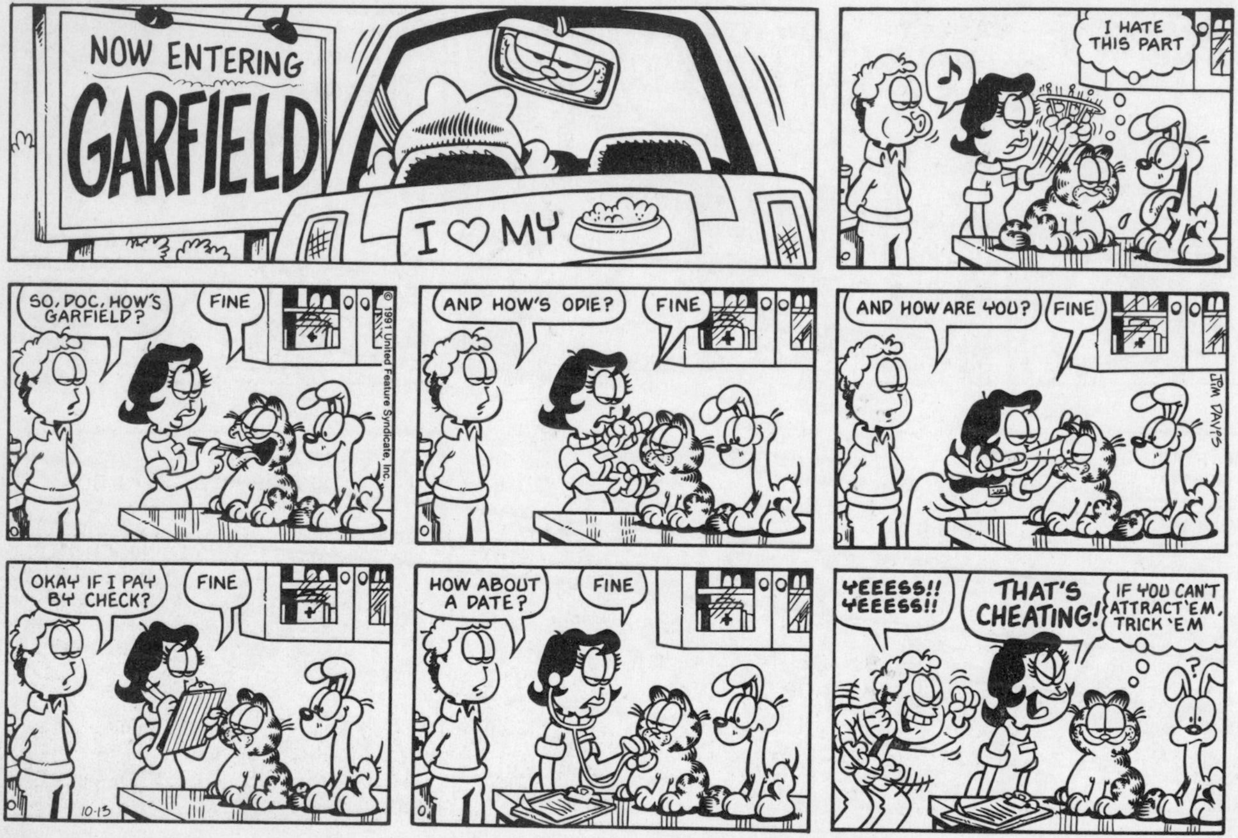
NOW ENTERING
GARFIELD
I ♥ MY
I HATE THIS PART
SO, DOC, HOW'S GARFIELD?
FINE
© 1991 United Feature Syndicate, Inc.
AND HOW'S ODIE?
FINE
AND HOW ARE YOU?
FINE
JIM DAVIS
OKAY IF I PAY BY CHECK?
FINE
10-13
HOW ABOUT A DATE?
FINE
YEEESS!! YEEESS!!
THAT'S CHEATING!
IF YOU CAN'T ATTRACT 'EM, TRICK 'EM
?

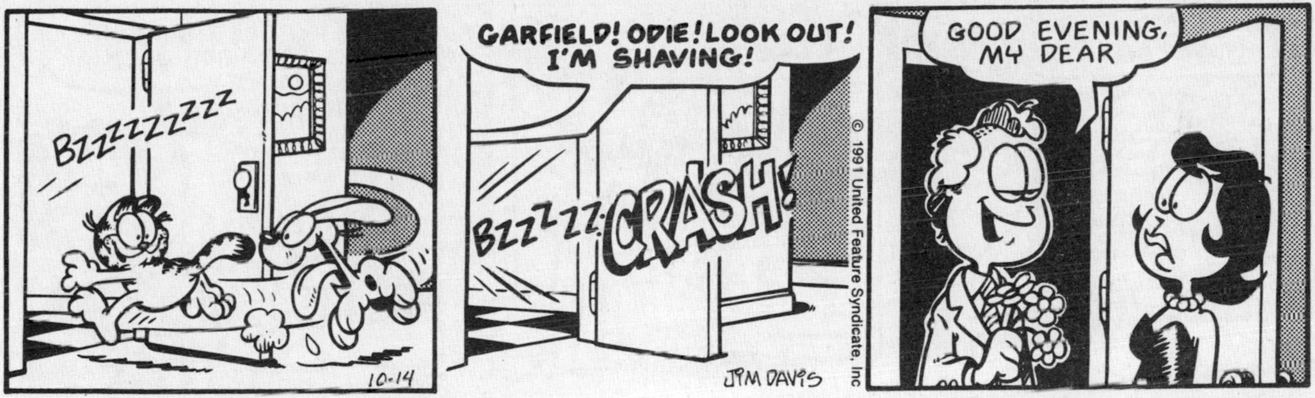
BZZZZZZZZZ
10-14
GARFIELD! ODIE! LOOK OUT! I'M SHAVING!
BZZZZZ
CRASH!
JIM DAVIS
© 1991 United Feature Syndicate, Inc
GOOD EVENING, MY DEAR

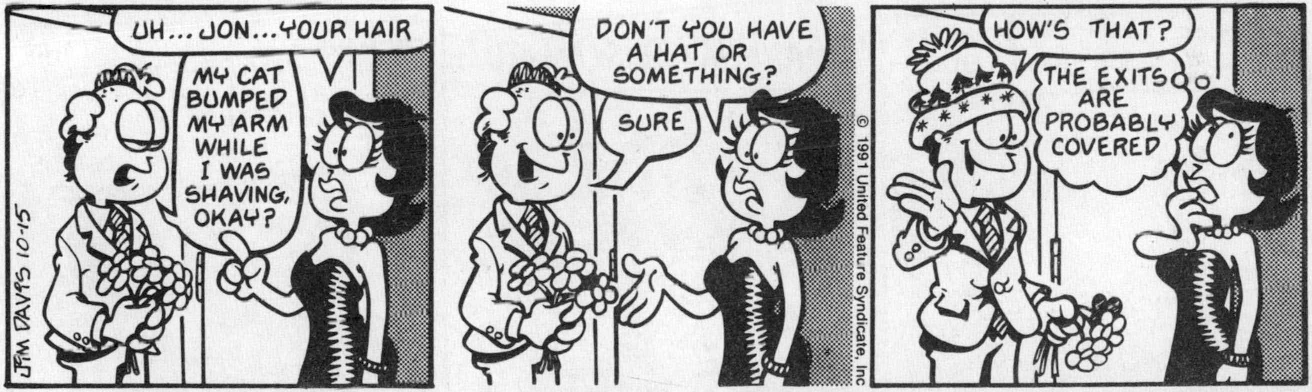
JIM DAVIS 10-15
UH... JON... YOUR HAIR
MY CAT BUMPED MY ARM WHILE I WAS SHAVING, OKAY?
DON'T YOU HAVE A HAT OR SOMETHING?
SURE
© 1991 United Feature Syndicate, Inc
HOW'S THAT?
THE EXITS ARE PROBABLY COVERED

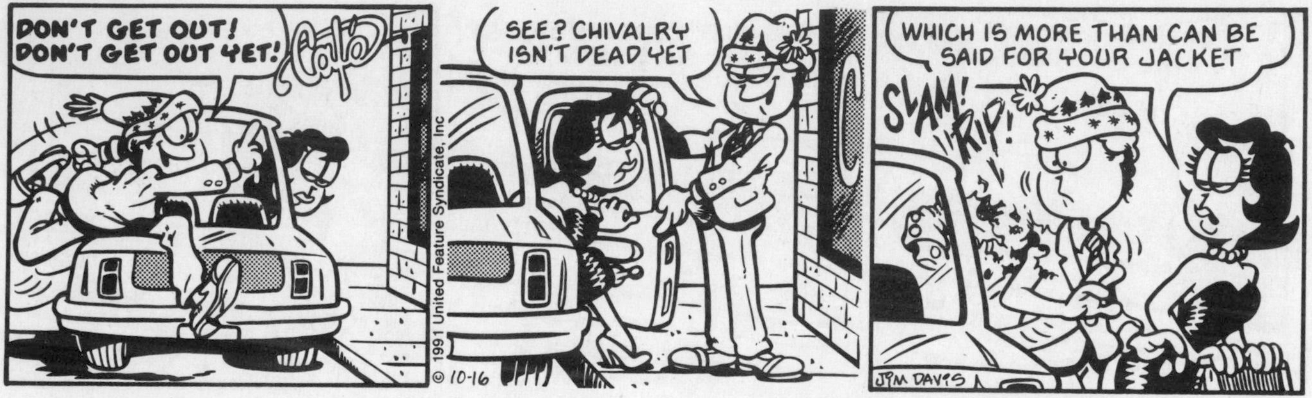
DON'T GET OUT!
DON'T GET OUT YET!
Café
SEE? CHIVALRY ISN'T DEAD YET
WHICH IS MORE THAN CAN BE SAID FOR YOUR JACKET
SLAM!
RIP!
© 1991 United Feature Syndicate, Inc
10-16
JIM DAVIS

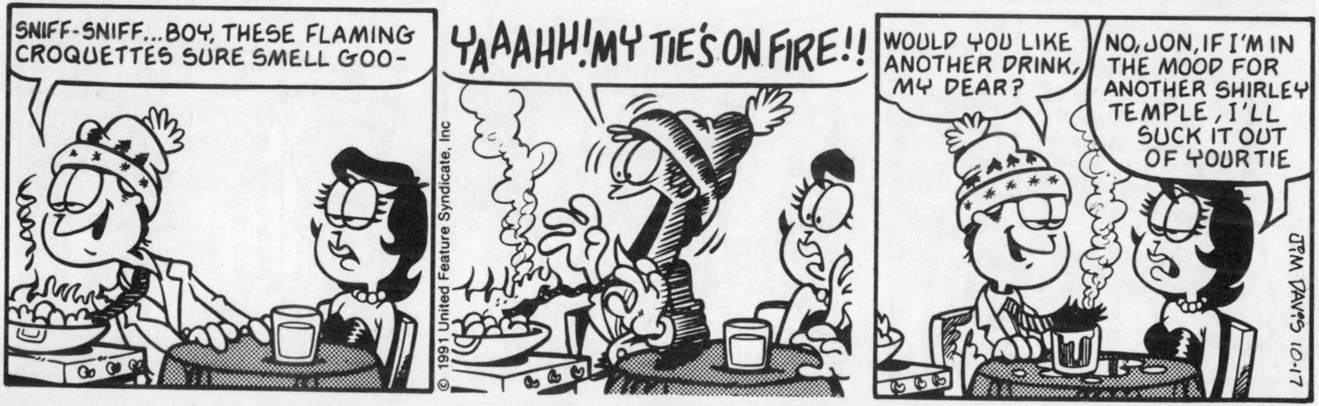
SNIFF-SNIFF... BOY, THESE FLAMING CROQUETTES SURE SMELL GOO-
YAAAHH! MY TIE'S ON FIRE!!
WOULD YOU LIKE ANOTHER DRINK, MY DEAR?
NO, JON, IF I'M IN THE MOOD FOR ANOTHER SHIRLEY TEMPLE, I'LL SUCK IT OUT OF YOUR TIE
© 1991 United Feature Syndicate, Inc
JIM DAVIS 10-17

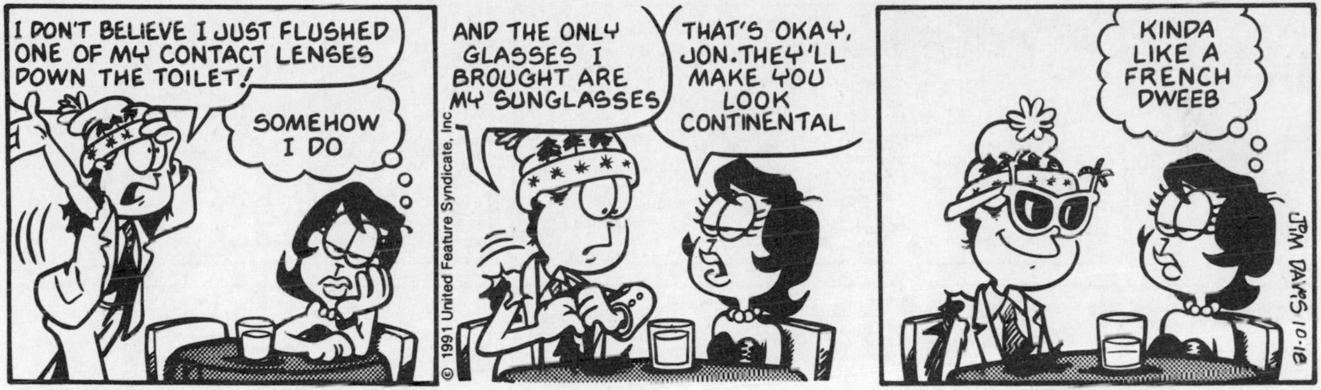
I DON'T BELIEVE I JUST FLUSHED ONE OF MY CONTACT LENSES DOWN THE TOILET!
SOMEHOW I DO
AND THE ONLY GLASSES I BROUGHT ARE MY SUNGLASSES
THAT'S OKAY, JON. THEY'LL MAKE YOU LOOK CONTINENTAL
KINDA LIKE A FRENCH DWEEB
© 1991 United Feature Syndicate, Inc
JIM DAVIS 10-18

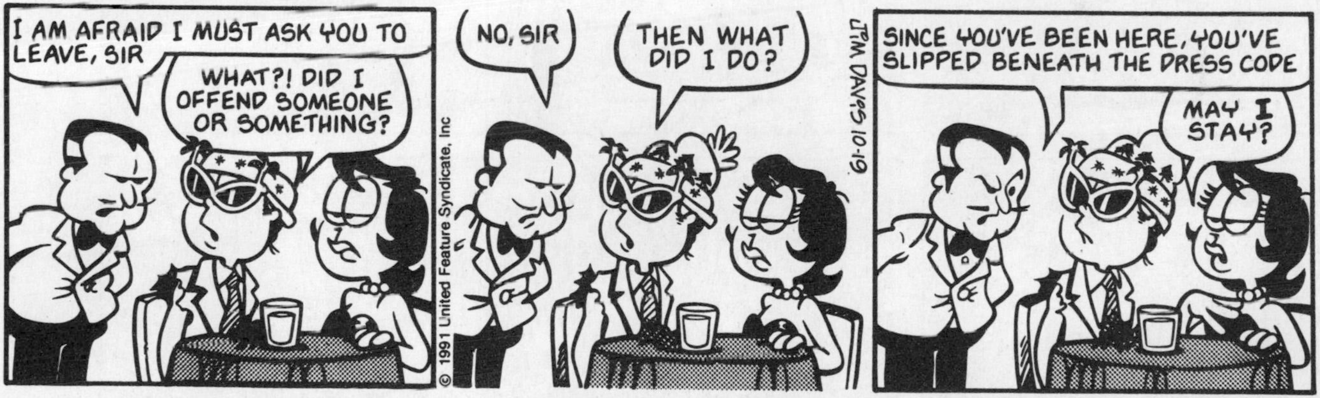
I AM AFRAID I MUST ASK YOU TO LEAVE, SIR
WHAT?! DID I OFFEND SOMEONE OR SOMETHING?
NO, SIR
THEN WHAT DID I DO?
SINCE YOU'VE BEEN HERE, YOU'VE SLIPPED BENEATH THE DRESS CODE
MAY I STAY?
© 1991 United Feature Syndicate, Inc
JIM DAVIS 10-19

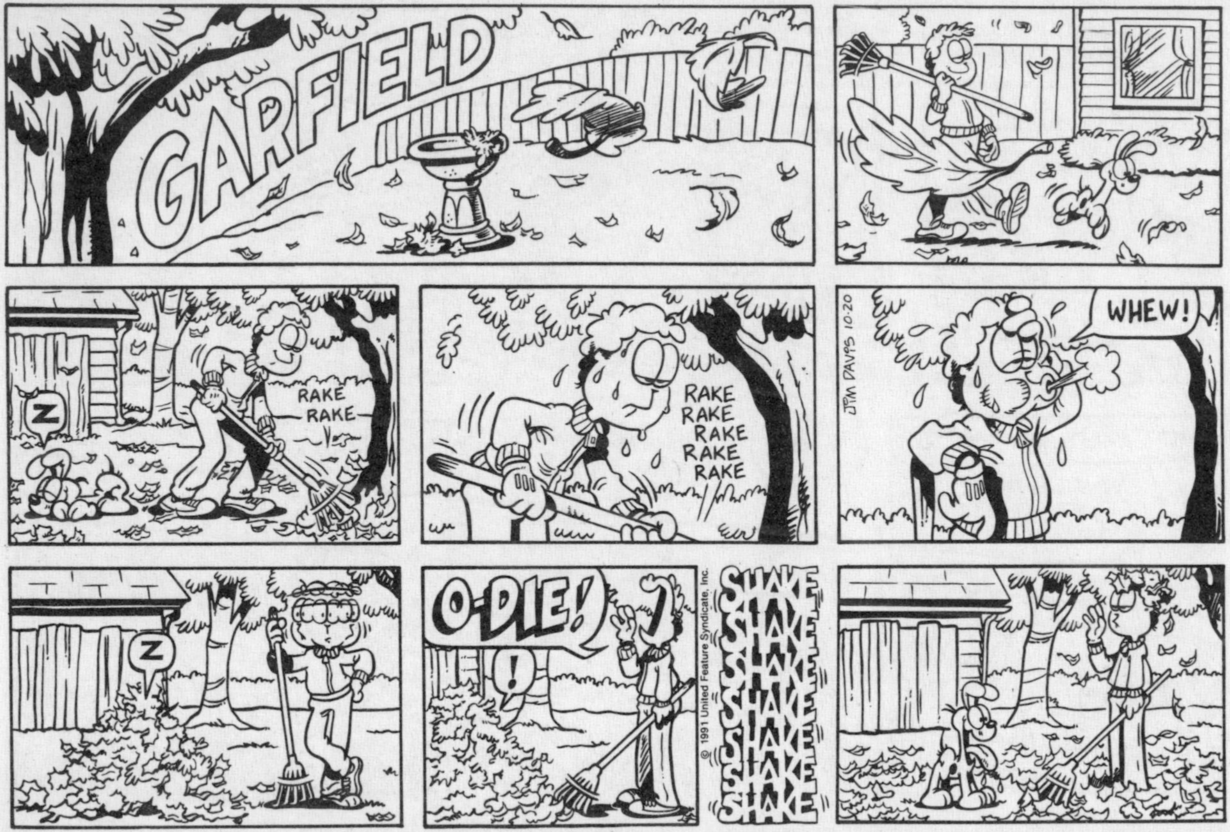

GARFIELD
RAKE RAKE
RAKE RAKE RAKE RAKE RAKE RAKE
JIM DAVIS 10-20
WHEW!
Z
O-DIE!
!
© 1991 United Feature Syndicate, Inc.
SHAKE SHAKE SHAKE SHAKE SHAKE SHAKE SHAKE SHAKE

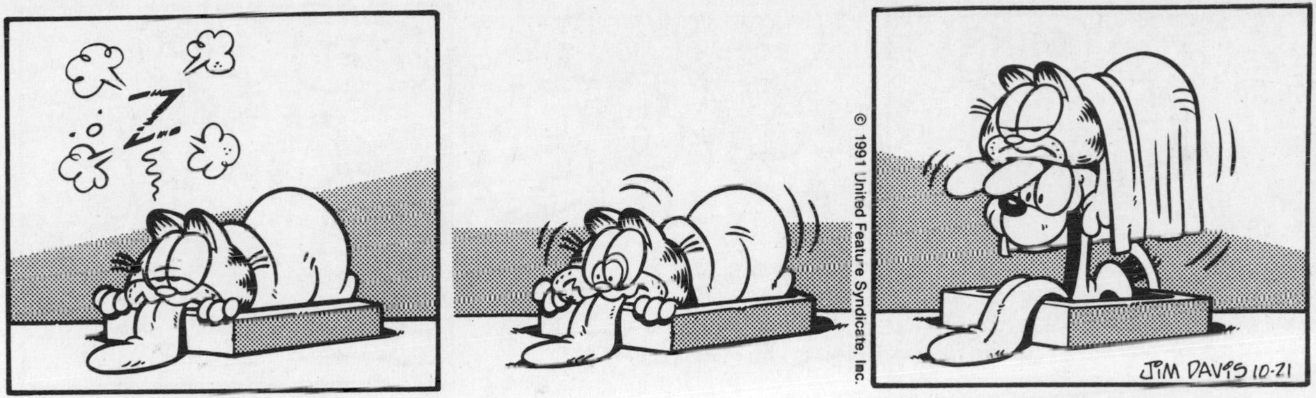
Z
JIM DAVIS 10-21

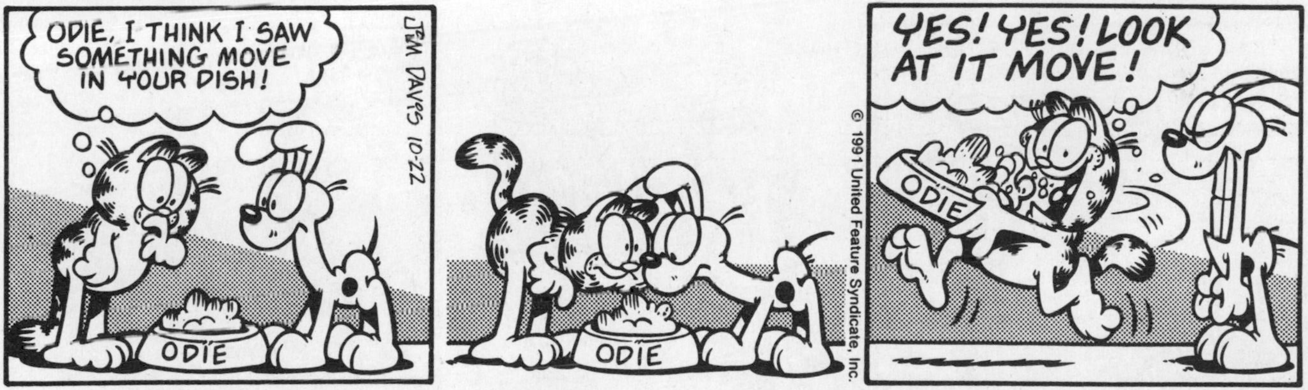
ODIE, I THINK I SAW SOMETHING MOVE IN YOUR DISH!
JIM DAVIS 10-22
ODIE
ODIE
YES! YES! LOOK AT IT MOVE!
ODIE

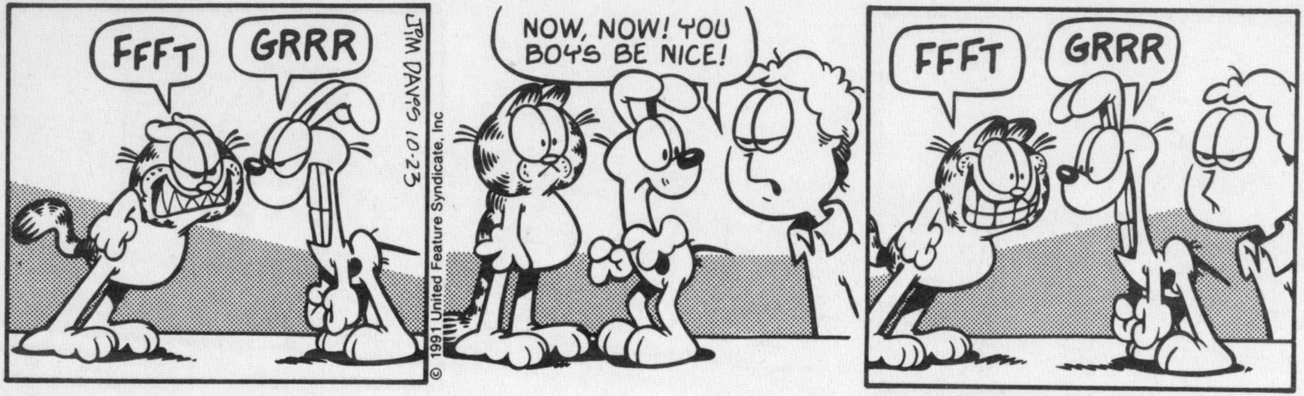
JIM DAVIS 10-23
© 1991 United Feature Syndicate, Inc
FFFT
GRRR
NOW, NOW! YOU BOYS BE NICE!
FFFT
GRRR

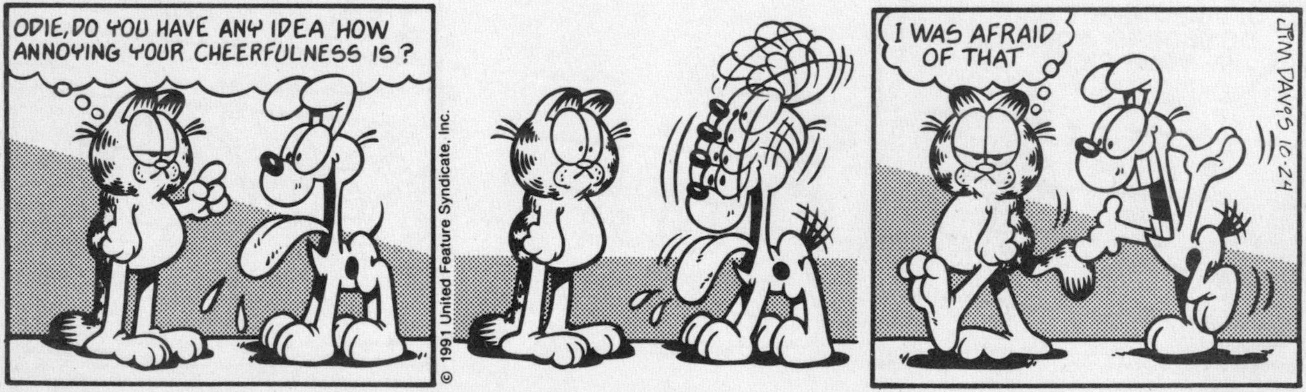
© 1991 United Feature Syndicate, Inc.
ODIE, DO YOU HAVE ANY IDEA HOW ANNOYING YOUR CHEERFULNESS IS?
I WAS AFRAID OF THAT
JIM DAVIS 10-24

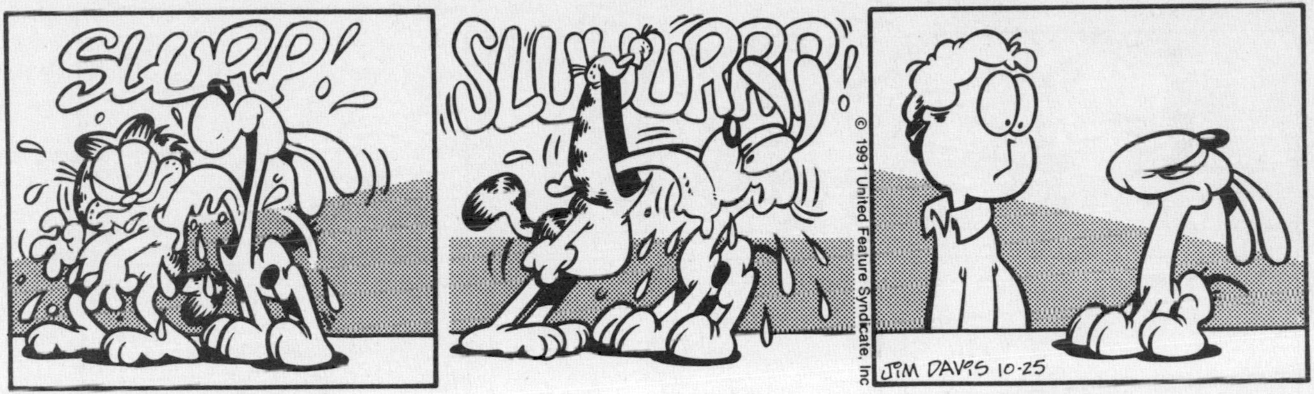
SLURP!
© 1991 United Feature Syndicate, Inc
JIM DAVIS 10-25

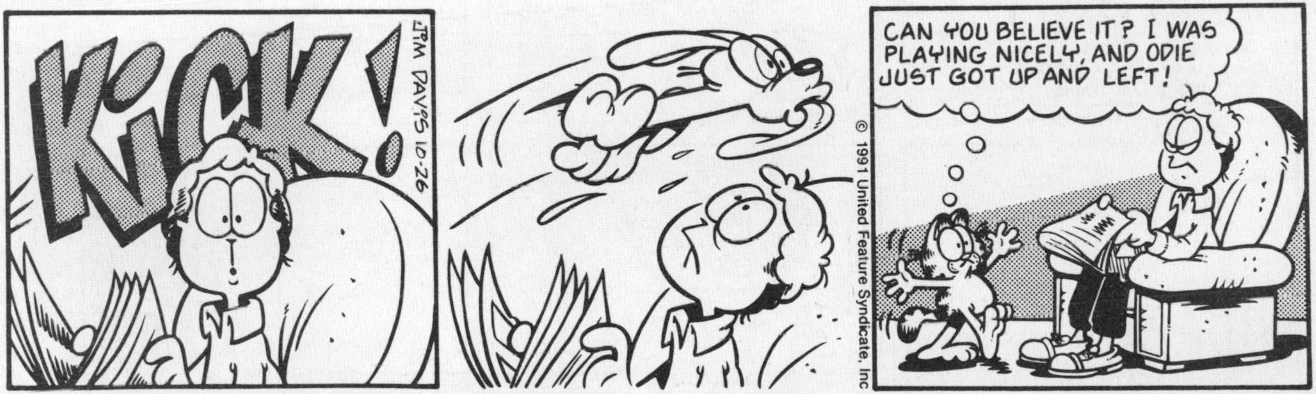
KICK!
JIM DAVIS 10-26
© 1991 United Feature Syndicate, Inc
CAN YOU BELIEVE IT? I WAS PLAYING NICELY, AND ODIE JUST GOT UP AND LEFT!

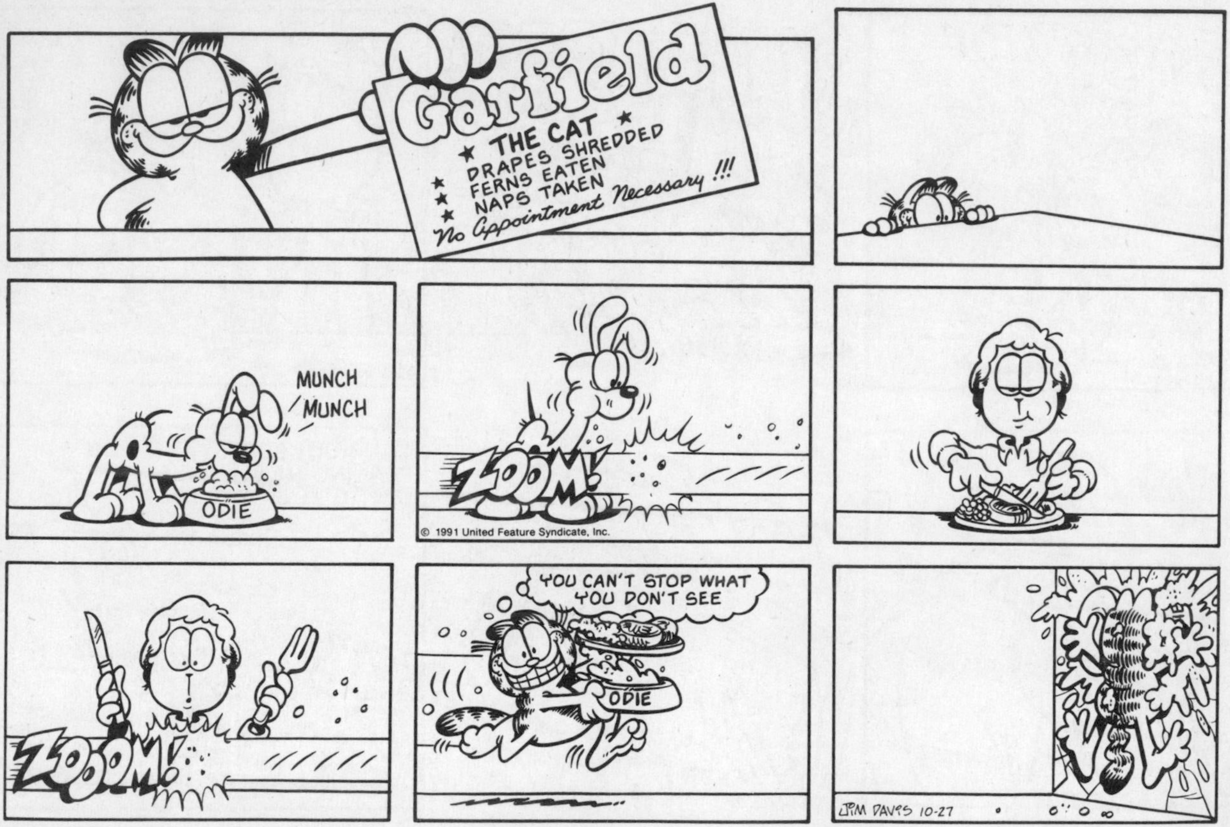
Garfield
★ THE CAT ★
DRAPES SHREDDED
FERNS EATEN
NAPS TAKEN
No Appointment Necessary !!!
MUNCH MUNCH
ODIE
ZOOM!
© 1991 United Feature Syndicate, Inc.
ZOOOM!
YOU CAN'T STOP WHAT YOU DON'T SEE
ODIE
JIM DAVIS 10-27

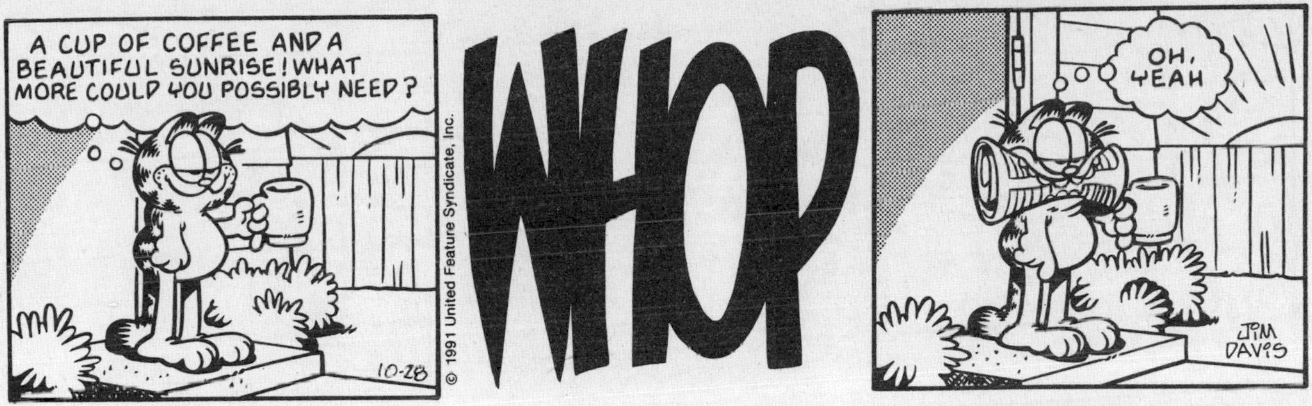
A CUP OF COFFEE AND A BEAUTIFUL SUNRISE! WHAT MORE COULD YOU POSSIBLY NEED?
10-28
© 1991 United Feature Syndicate, Inc.
WHOP
OH, YEAH
JIM DAVIS

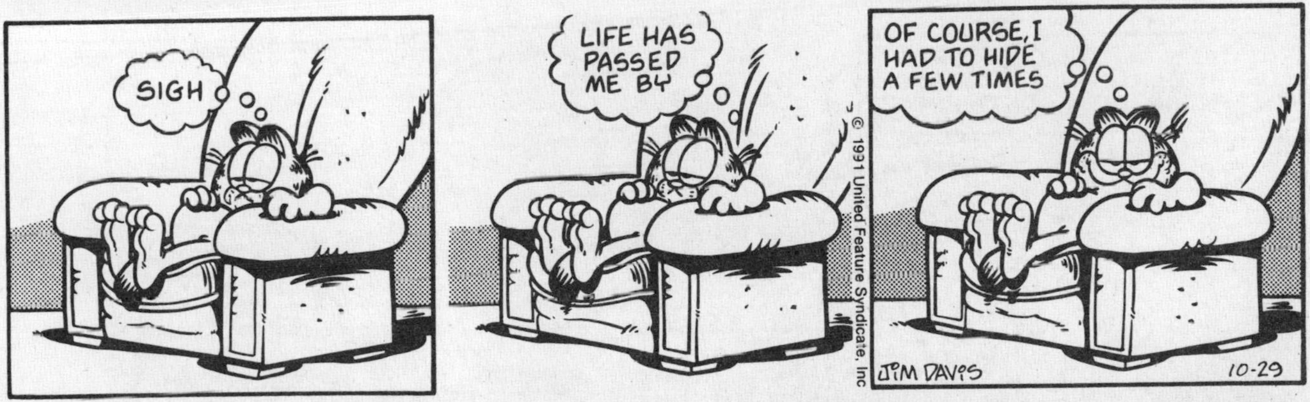
SIGH
LIFE HAS PASSED ME BY
© 1991 United Feature Syndicate, Inc
OF COURSE, I HAD TO HIDE A FEW TIMES
JIM DAVIS
10-29

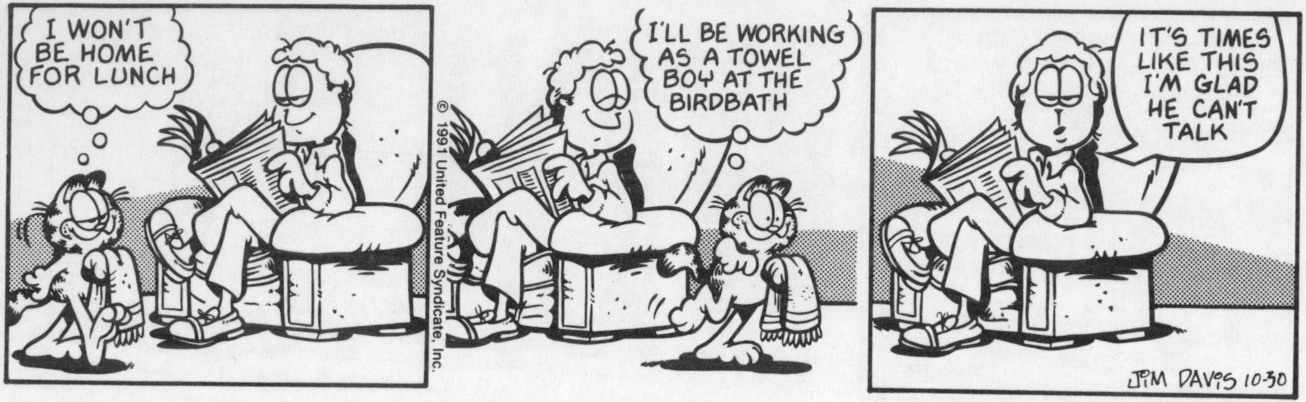
I WON'T BE HOME FOR LUNCH
© 1991 United Feature Syndicate, Inc.
I'LL BE WORKING AS A TOWEL BOY AT THE BIRDBATH
IT'S TIMES LIKE THIS I'M GLAD HE CAN'T TALK
JIM DAVIS 10-30

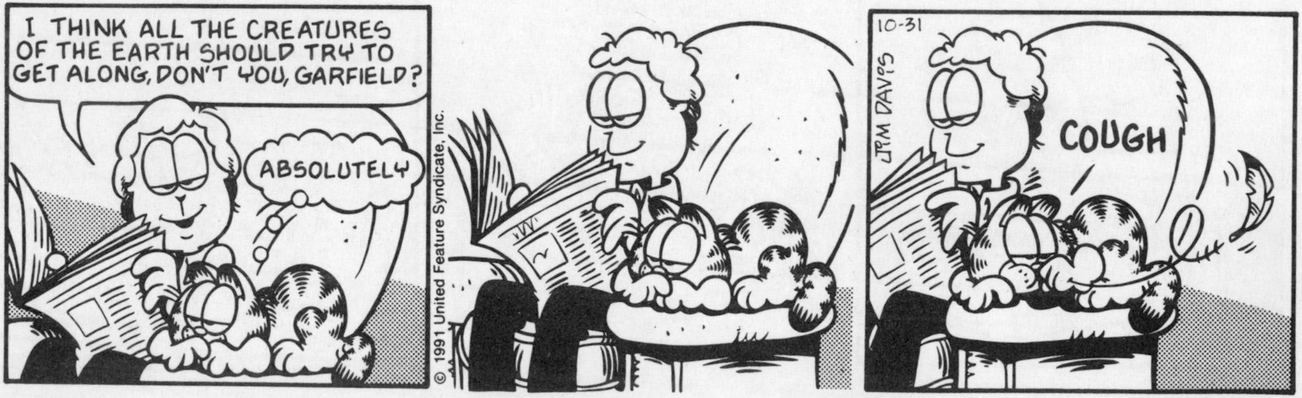
I THINK ALL THE CREATURES OF THE EARTH SHOULD TRY TO GET ALONG, DON'T YOU, GARFIELD?
ABSOLUTELY
© 1991 United Feature Syndicate, Inc.
JIM DAVIS 10-31
COUGH

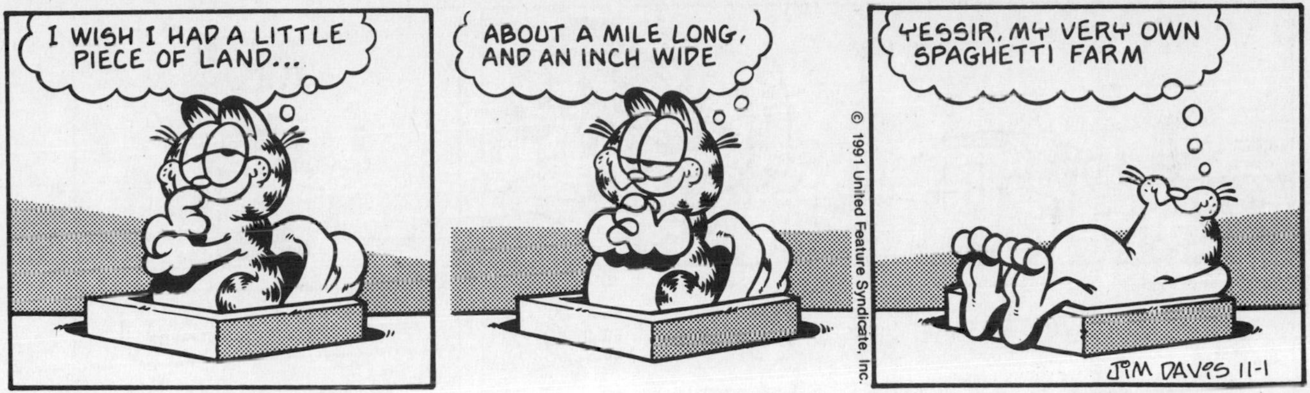
I WISH I HAD A LITTLE PIECE OF LAND...
ABOUT A MILE LONG, AND AN INCH WIDE
YESSIR, MY VERY OWN SPAGHETTI FARM
© 1991 United Feature Syndicate, Inc.
JIM DAVIS 11-1

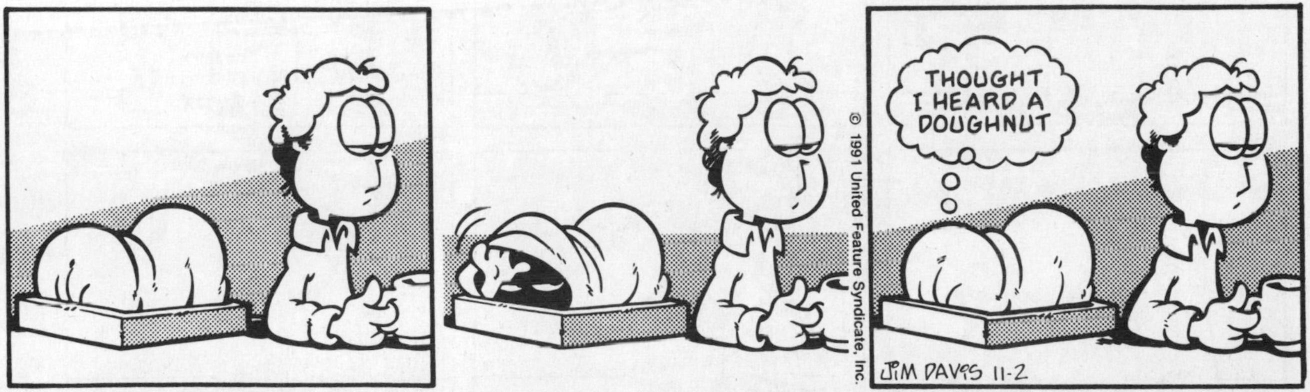
THOUGHT I HEARD A DOUGHNUT
© 1991 United Feature Syndicate, Inc.
JIM DAVIS 11-2

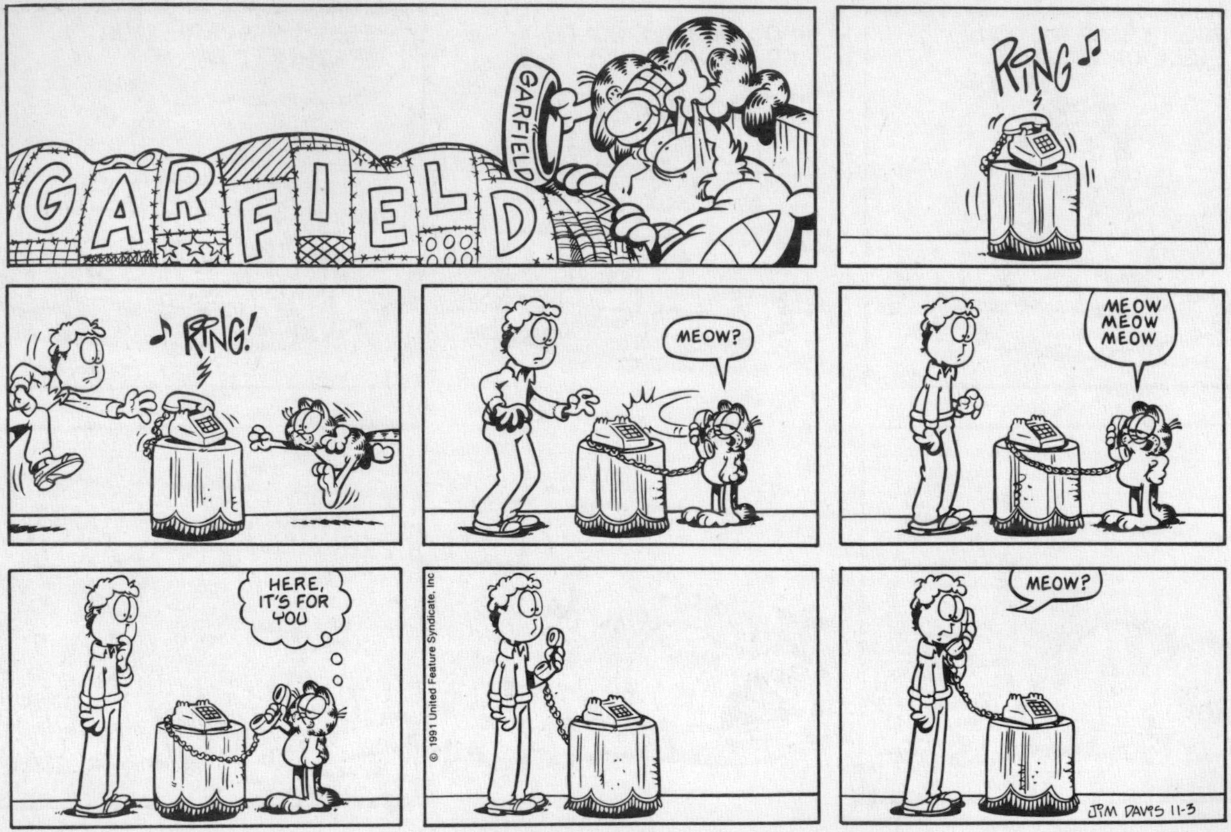
GARFIELD
GARFIELD
RING
RING!
MEOW?
MEOW MEOW MEOW
HERE, IT'S FOR YOU
© 1991 United Feature Syndicate, Inc
MEOW?
JIM DAVIS 11-3

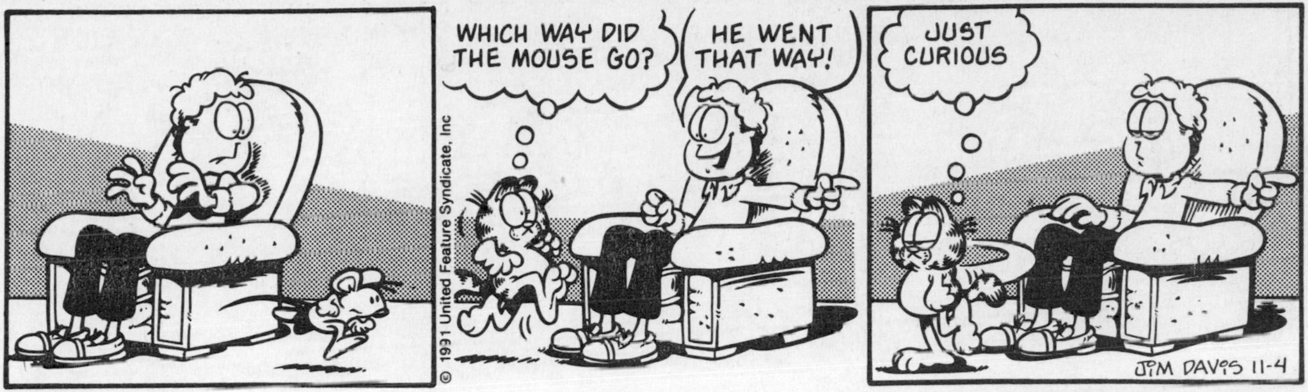
WHICH WAY DID THE MOUSE GO?
HE WENT THAT WAY!
JUST CURIOUS
© 1991 United Feature Syndicate, Inc
JIM DAVIS 11-4

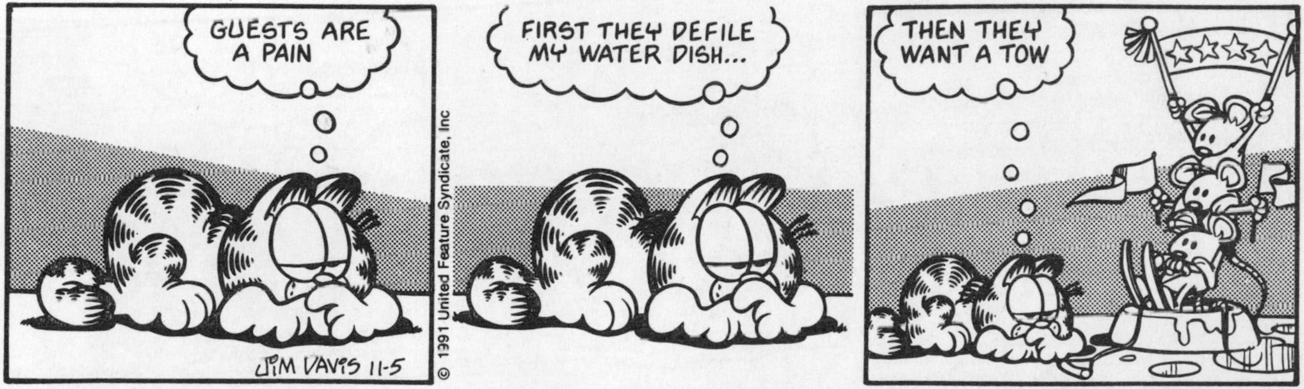
GUESTS ARE A PAIN
FIRST THEY DEFILE MY WATER DISH...
THEN THEY WANT A TOW
© 1991 United Feature Syndicate, Inc
JIM DAVIS 11-5

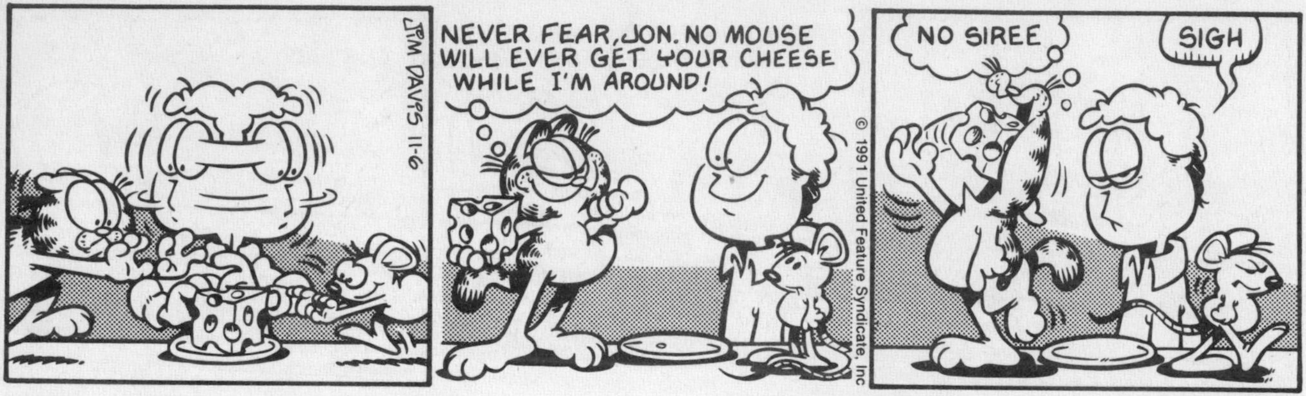
JIM DAVIS 11-6
NEVER FEAR, JON. NO MOUSE WILL EVER GET YOUR CHEESE WHILE I'M AROUND!
© 1991 United Feature Syndicate, Inc
NO SIREE
SIGH

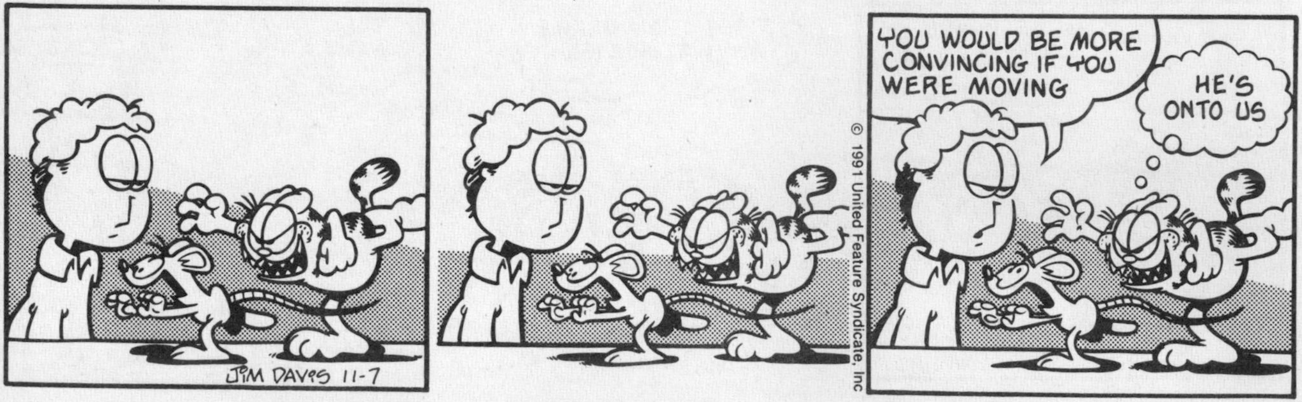
JIM DAVIS 11-7
© 1991 United Feature Syndicate, Inc
YOU WOULD BE MORE CONVINCING IF YOU WERE MOVING
HE'S ONTO US

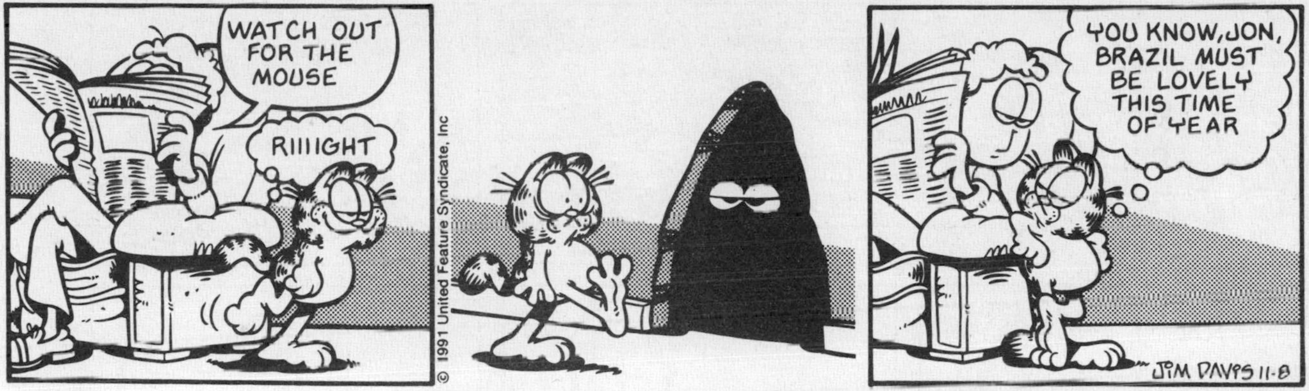
WATCH OUT FOR THE MOUSE
RIIIIGHT
© 1991 United Feature Syndicate, Inc
YOU KNOW, JON, BRAZIL MUST BE LOVELY THIS TIME OF YEAR
JIM DAVIS 11-8

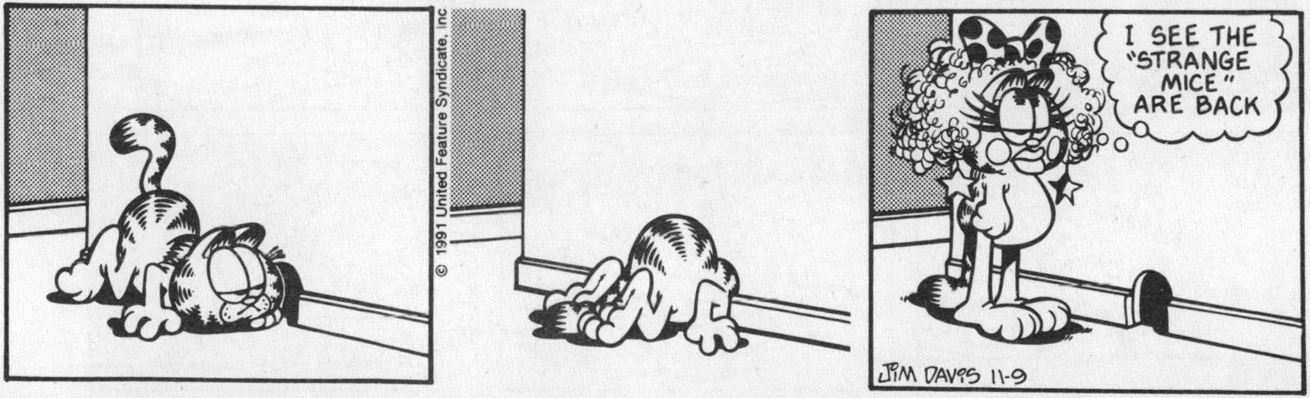
© 1991 United Feature Syndicate, Inc
I SEE THE "STRANGE MICE" ARE BACK
JIM DAVIS 11-9

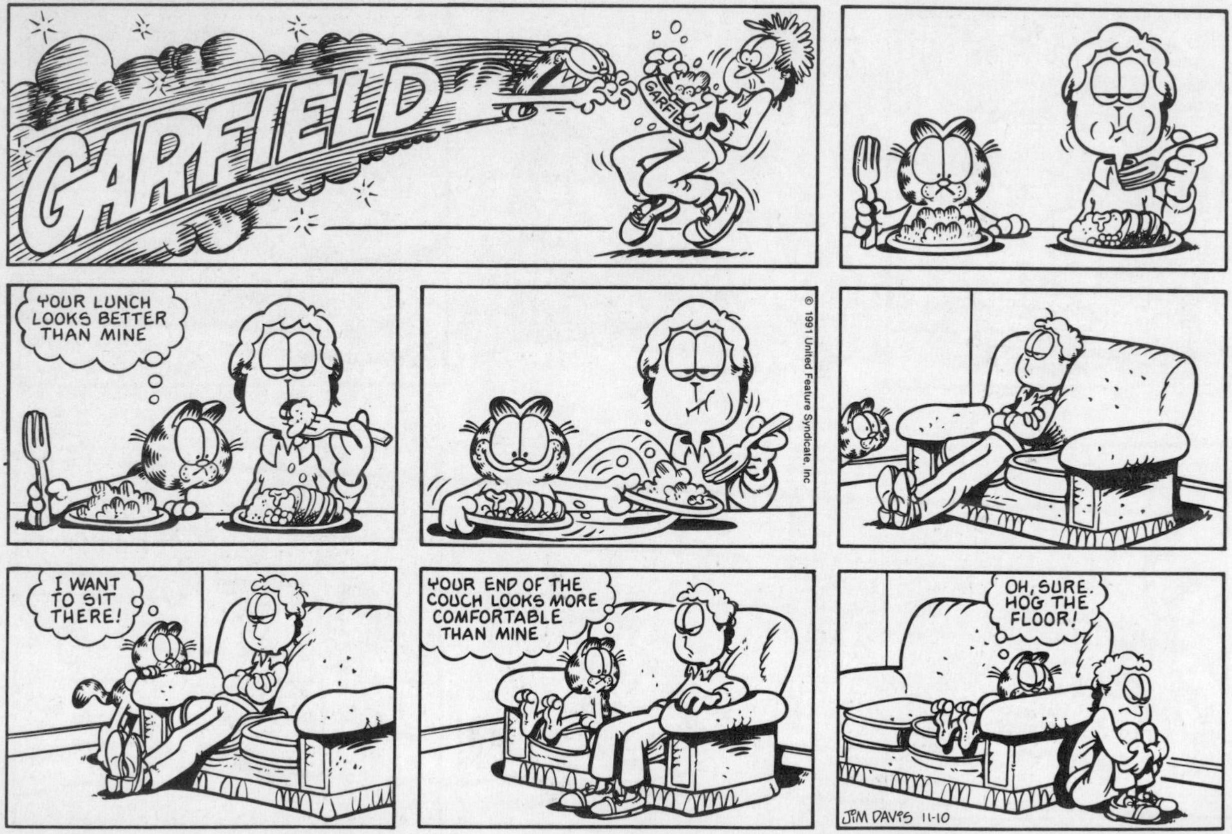
GARFIELD
GARFIELD
YOUR LUNCH LOOKS BETTER THAN MINE
© 1991 United Feature Syndicate, Inc
I WANT TO SIT THERE!
YOUR END OF THE COUCH LOOKS MORE COMFORTABLE THAN MINE
OH, SURE. HOG THE FLOOR!
JIM DAVIS 11-10

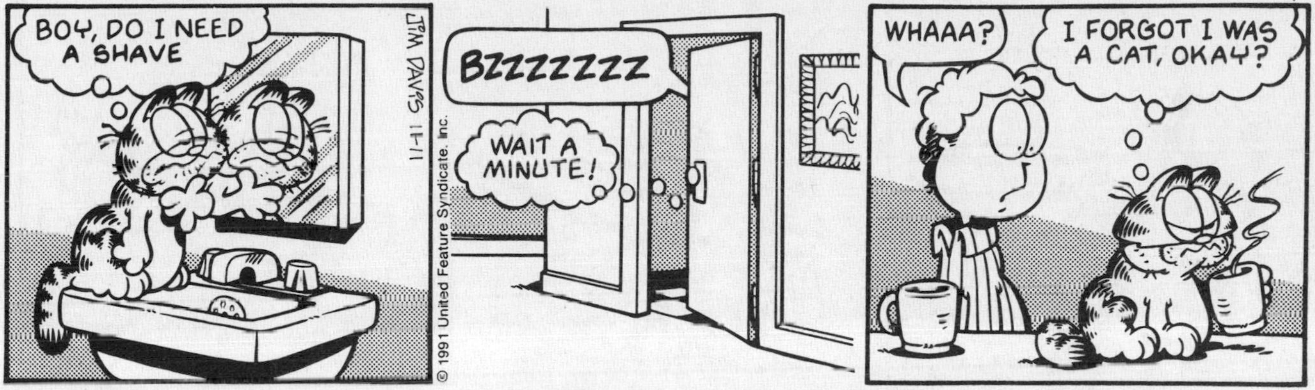
BOY, DO I NEED A SHAVE
JIM DAVIS 11-11
© 1991 United Feature Syndicate, Inc.
BZZZZZZZ
WAIT A MINUTE!
WHAAA?
I FORGOT I WAS A CAT, OKAY?

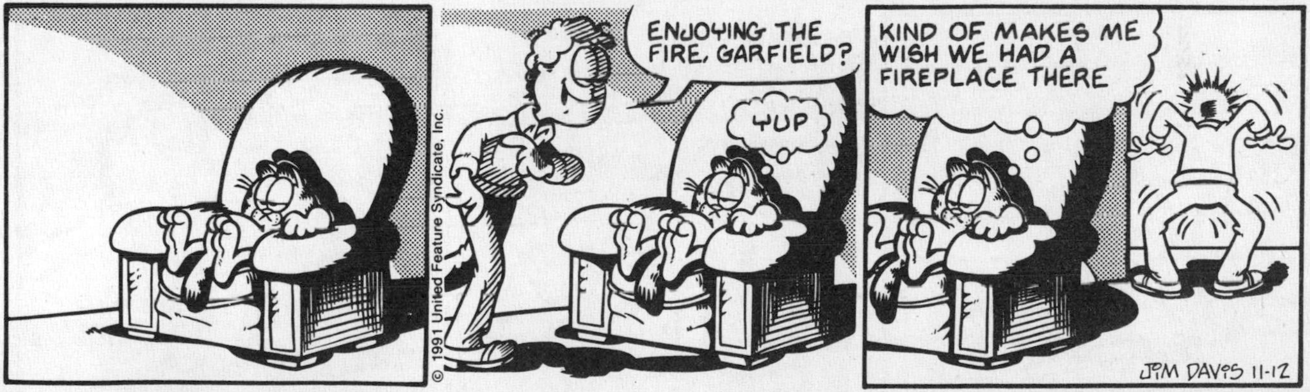
© 1991 United Feature Syndicate, Inc.
ENJOYING THE FIRE, GARFIELD?
YUP
KIND OF MAKES ME WISH WE HAD A FIREPLACE THERE
JIM DAVIS 11-12

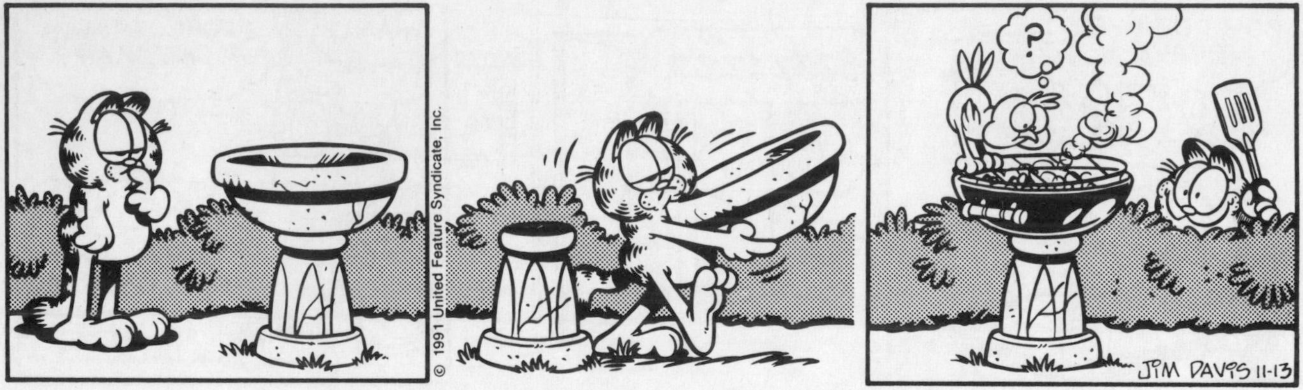
?
JIM DAVIS 11-13

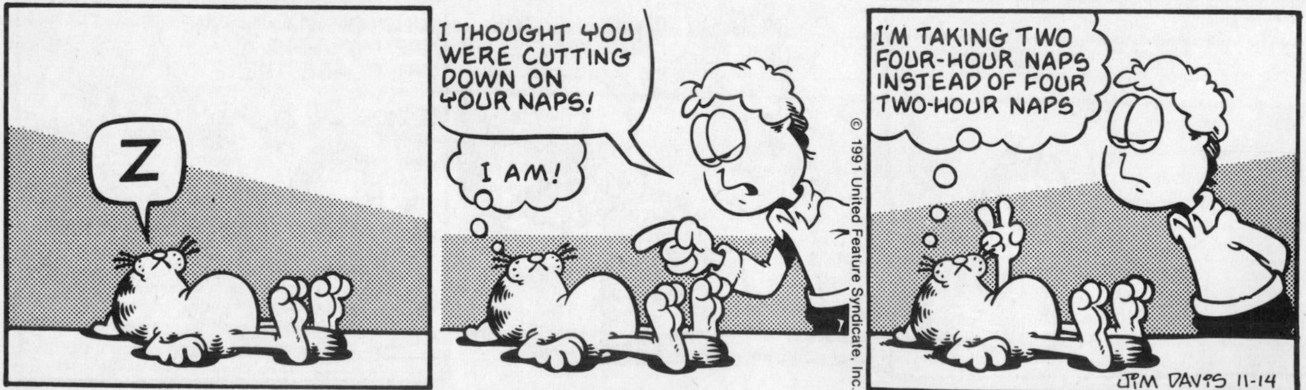
Z
I THOUGHT YOU WERE CUTTING DOWN ON YOUR NAPS!
I AM!
I'M TAKING TWO FOUR-HOUR NAPS INSTEAD OF FOUR TWO-HOUR NAPS
JIM DAVIS 11-14

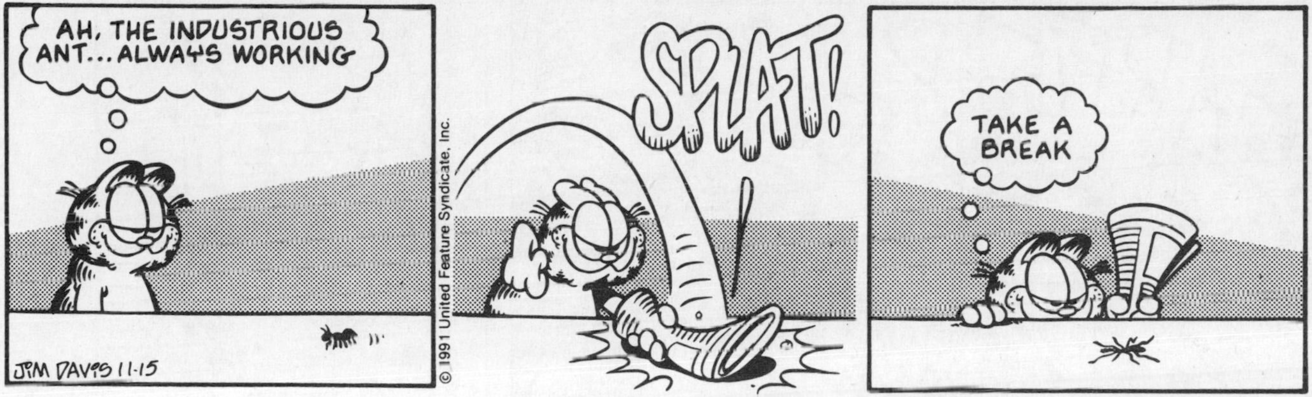
AH, THE INDUSTRIOUS ANT...ALWAYS WORKING
JIM DAVIS 11-15
© 1991 United Feature Syndicate, Inc.
SPLAT!
TAKE A BREAK

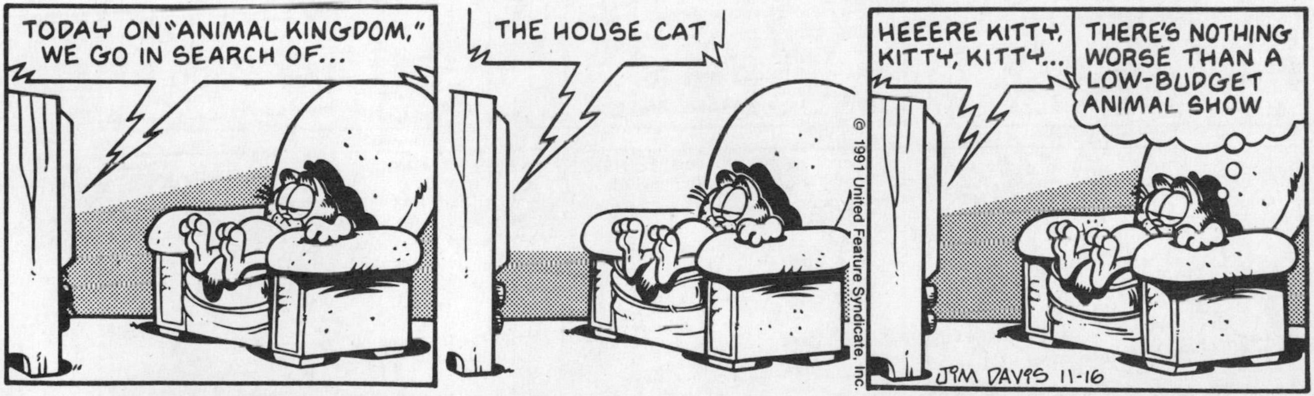
TODAY ON "ANIMAL KINGDOM," WE GO IN SEARCH OF...
THE HOUSE CAT
© 1991 United Feature Syndicate, Inc.
HEEERE KITTY, KITTY, KITTY...
THERE'S NOTHING WORSE THAN A LOW-BUDGET ANIMAL SHOW
JIM DAVIS 11-16

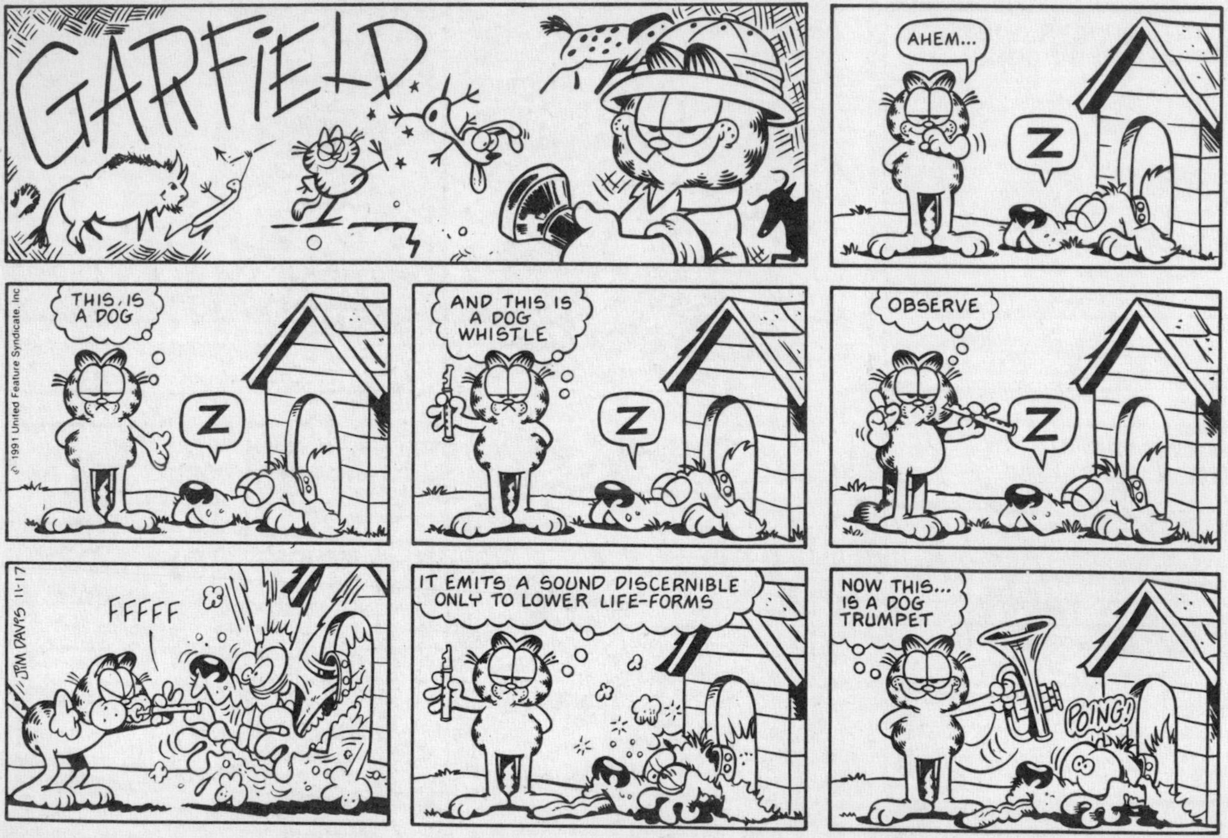
GARFIELD
AHEM...
Z
THIS IS A DOG
© 1991 United Feature Syndicate, Inc
Z
AND THIS IS A DOG WHISTLE
Z
OBSERVE
Z
JIM DAVIS 11-17
FFFFF
IT EMITS A SOUND DISCERNIBLE ONLY TO LOWER LIFE-FORMS
NOW THIS... IS A DOG TRUMPET
POING!

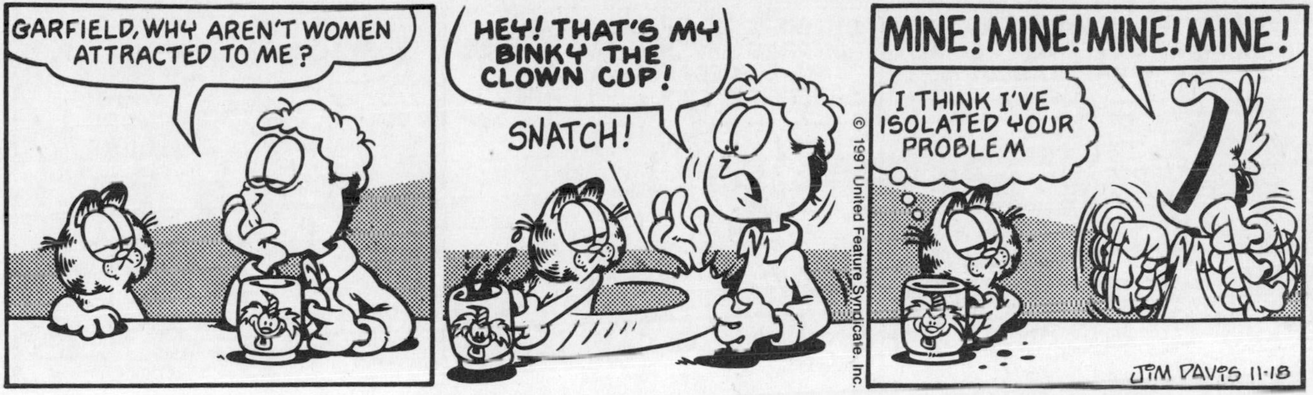
GARFIELD, WHY AREN'T WOMEN ATTRACTED TO ME?
HEY! THAT'S MY BINKY THE CLOWN CUP!
SNATCH!
© 1991 United Feature Syndicate, Inc.
MINE! MINE! MINE! MINE!
I THINK I'VE ISOLATED YOUR PROBLEM
JIM DAVIS 11-18

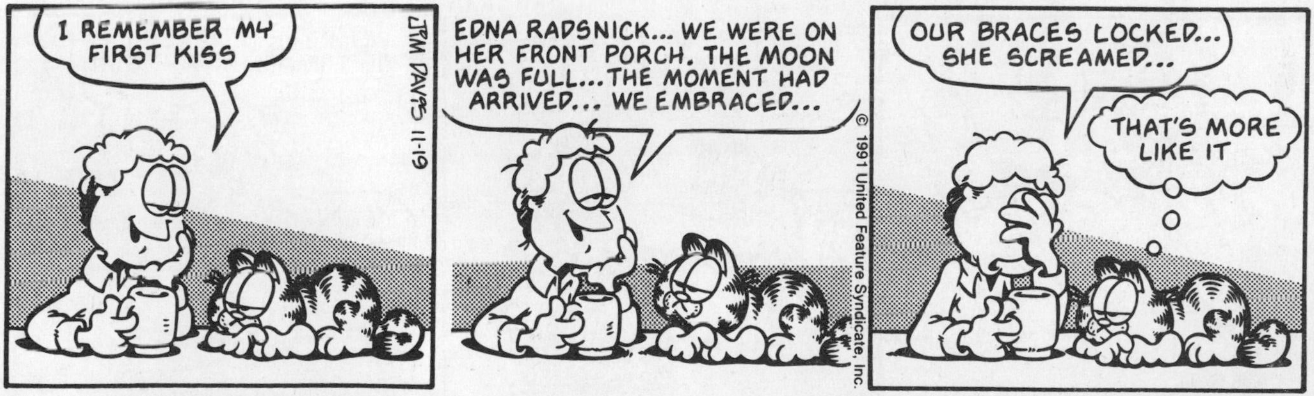
I REMEMBER MY FIRST KISS
JIM DAVIS 11-19
EDNA RADSNICK... WE WERE ON HER FRONT PORCH. THE MOON WAS FULL... THE MOMENT HAD ARRIVED... WE EMBRACED...
© 1991 United Feature Syndicate, Inc.
OUR BRACES LOCKED... SHE SCREAMED...
THAT'S MORE LIKE IT

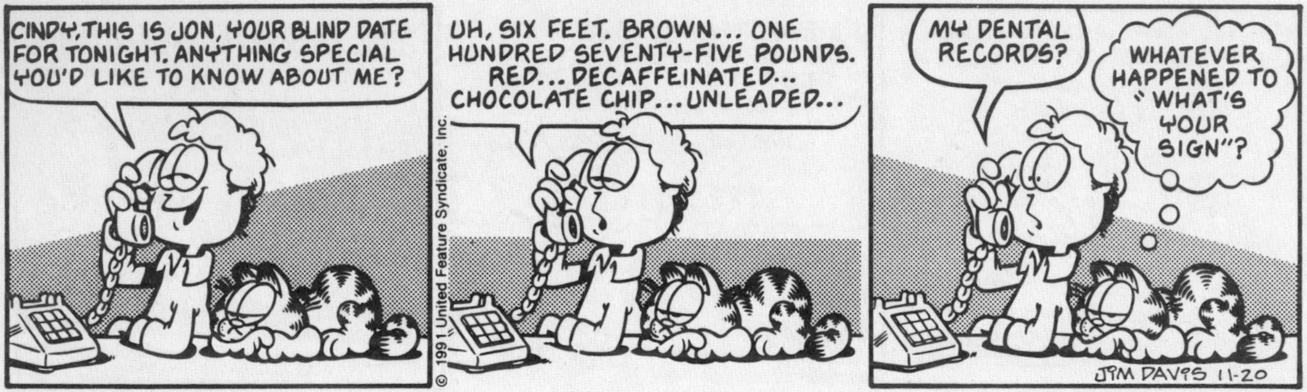
CINDY, THIS IS JON, YOUR BLIND DATE FOR TONIGHT. ANYTHING SPECIAL YOU'D LIKE TO KNOW ABOUT ME?
© 1991 United Feature Syndicate, Inc.
UH, SIX FEET. BROWN... ONE HUNDRED SEVENTY-FIVE POUNDS. RED... DECAFFEINATED... CHOCOLATE CHIP... UNLEADED...
MY DENTAL RECORDS?
WHATEVER HAPPENED TO "WHAT'S YOUR SIGN"?
JIM DAVIS 11-20

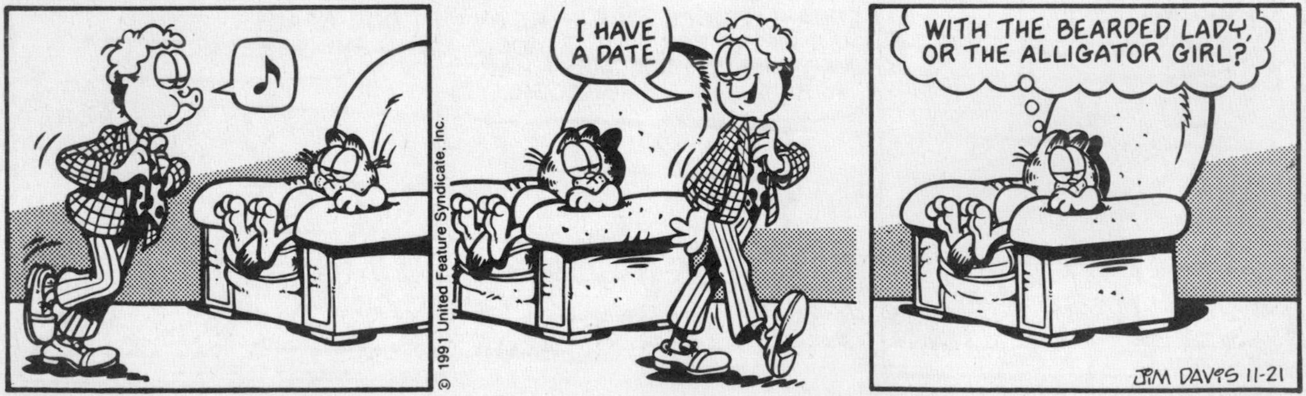
♪
© 1991 United Feature Syndicate, Inc.
I HAVE A DATE
WITH THE BEARDED LADY, OR THE ALLIGATOR GIRL?
JIM DAVIS 11-21

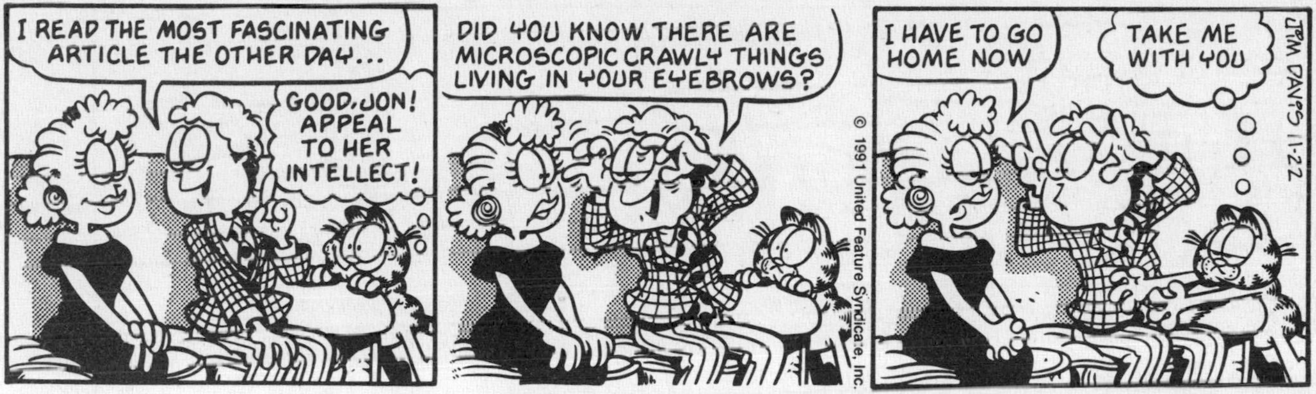
I READ THE MOST FASCINATING ARTICLE THE OTHER DAY...
GOOD, JON! APPEAL TO HER INTELLECT!
DID YOU KNOW THERE ARE MICROSCOPIC CRAWLY THINGS LIVING IN YOUR EYEBROWS?
I HAVE TO GO HOME NOW
TAKE ME WITH YOU
JIM DAVIS 11-22
© 1991 United Feature Syndicate, Inc.

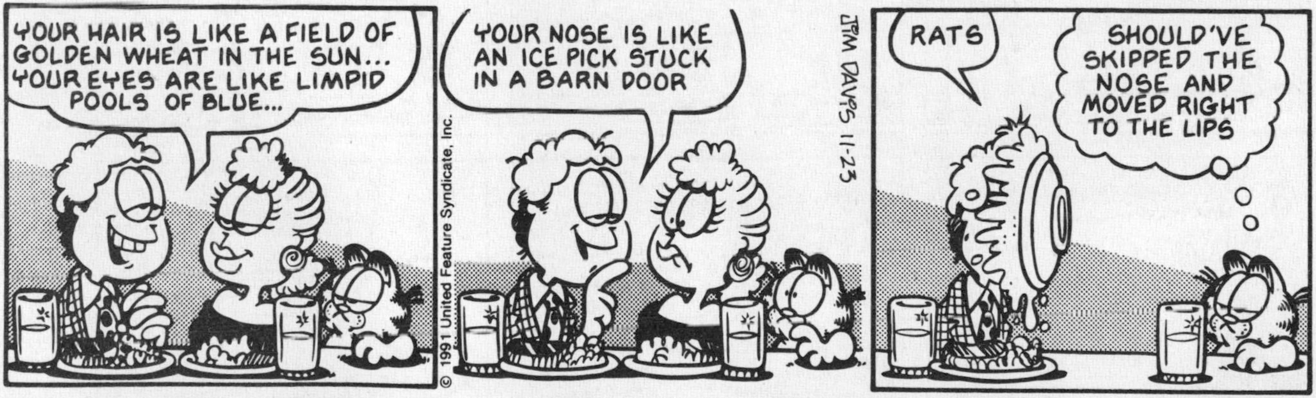
YOUR HAIR IS LIKE A FIELD OF GOLDEN WHEAT IN THE SUN... YOUR EYES ARE LIKE LIMPID POOLS OF BLUE...
YOUR NOSE IS LIKE AN ICE PICK STUCK IN A BARN DOOR
RATS
SHOULD'VE SKIPPED THE NOSE AND MOVED RIGHT TO THE LIPS
JIM DAVIS 11-23
© 1991 United Feature Syndicate, Inc.

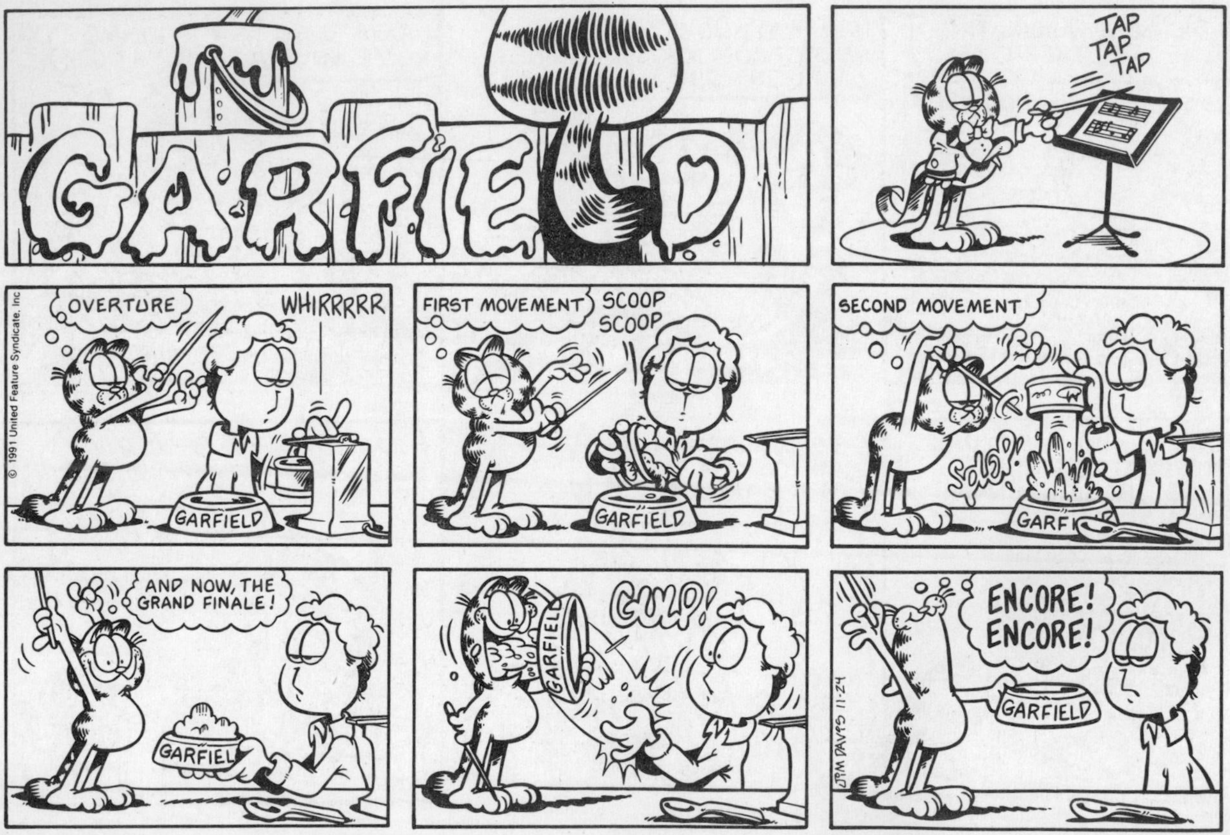
GARFIELD
TAP TAP TAP
OVERTURE
WHIRRRRR
GARFIELD
FIRST MOVEMENT
SCOOP SCOOP
GARFIELD
SECOND MOVEMENT
GARF
AND NOW, THE GRAND FINALE!
GARFIEL
GULP!
GARFIEL
ENCORE! ENCORE!
GARFIELD
JPM DAVIS 11-24

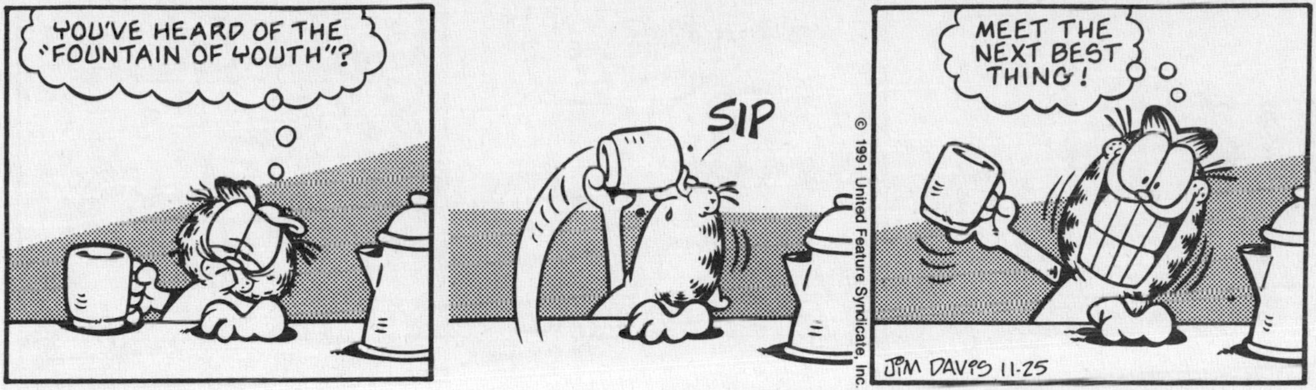

YOU'VE HEARD OF THE "FOUNTAIN OF YOUTH"?
SIP
MEET THE NEXT BEST THING!
© 1991 United Feature Syndicate, Inc.
JIM DAVIS 11-25

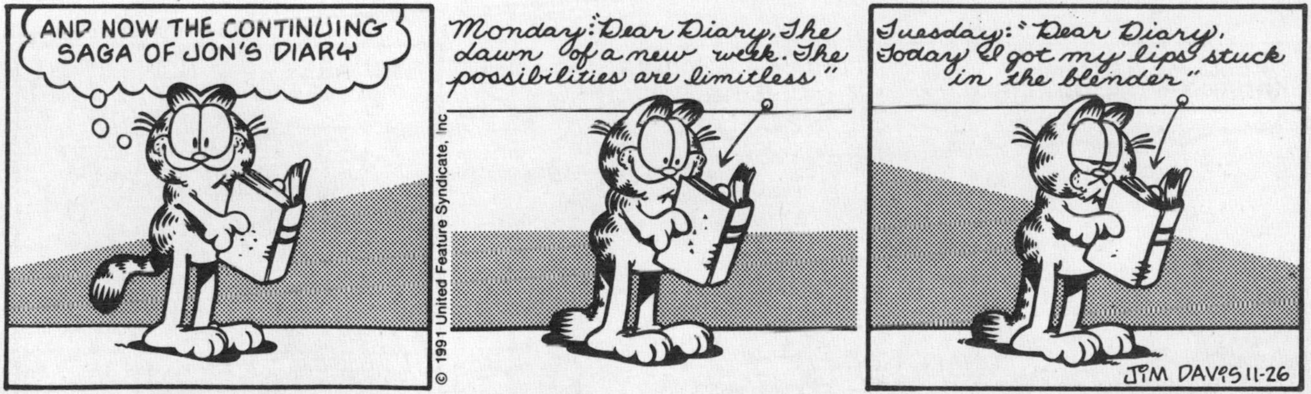

AND NOW THE CONTINUING SAGA OF JON'S DIARY
© 1991 United Feature Syndicate, Inc.
Monday: "Dear Diary, The dawn of a new week. The possibilities are limitless"
Tuesday: "Dear Diary, Today I got my lips stuck in the blender"
JIM DAVIS 11-26

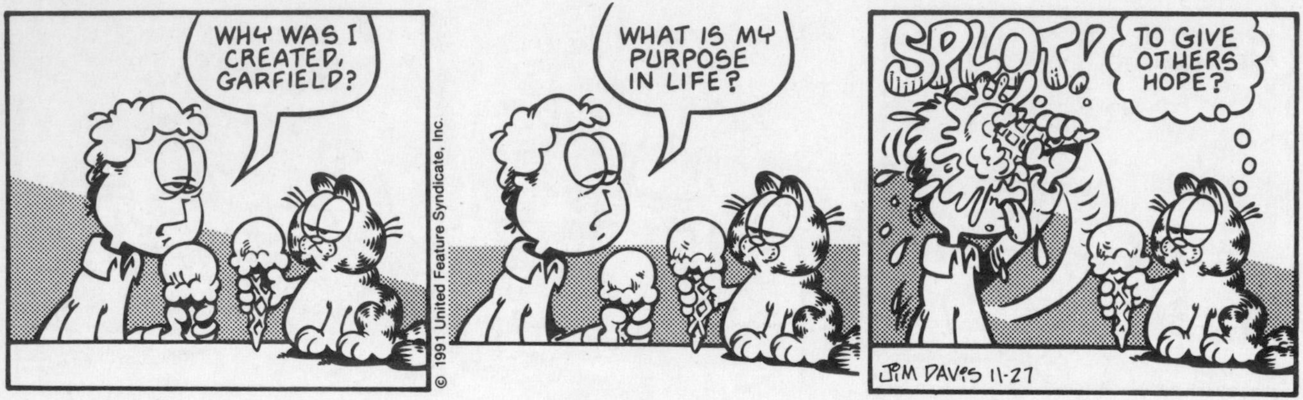
WHY WAS I CREATED, GARFIELD?
WHAT IS MY PURPOSE IN LIFE?
SPLOT!
TO GIVE OTHERS HOPE?
© 1991 United Feature Syndicate, Inc.
JIM DAVIS 11-27

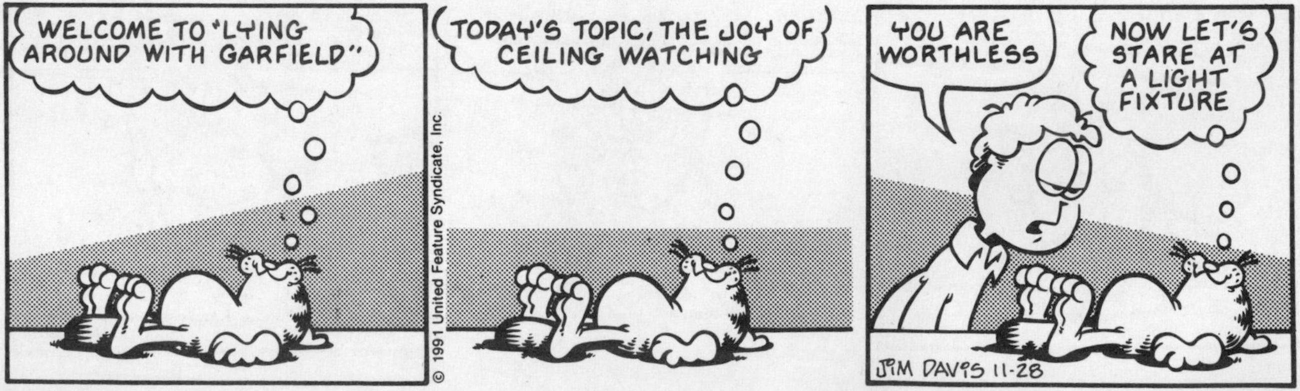
WELCOME TO "LYING AROUND WITH GARFIELD"
TODAY'S TOPIC, THE JOY OF CEILING WATCHING
YOU ARE WORTHLESS
NOW LET'S STARE AT A LIGHT FIXTURE
© 1991 United Feature Syndicate, Inc.
JIM DAVIS 11-28

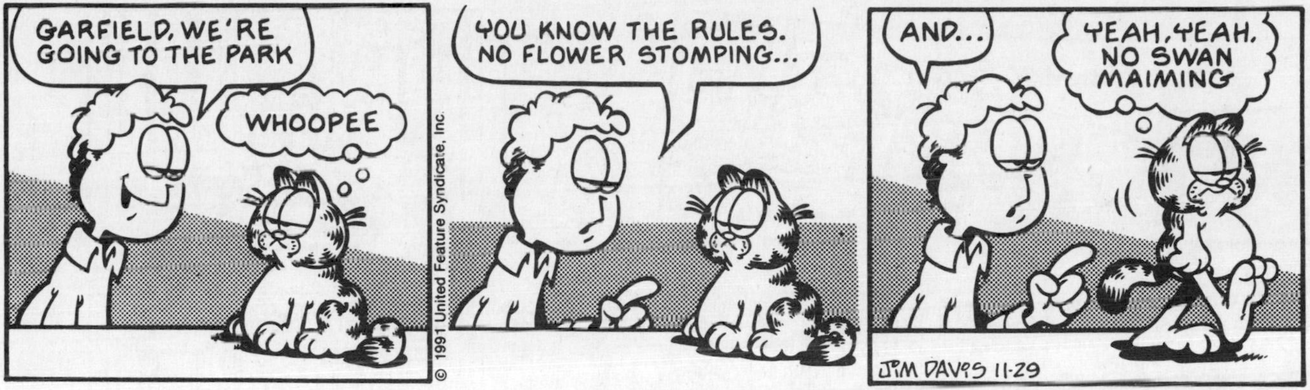
GARFIELD, WE'RE GOING TO THE PARK
WHOOPEE
YOU KNOW THE RULES. NO FLOWER STOMPING...
AND...
YEAH, YEAH, NO SWAN MAIMING
JIM DAVIS 11-29
© 1991 United Feature Syndicate, Inc.

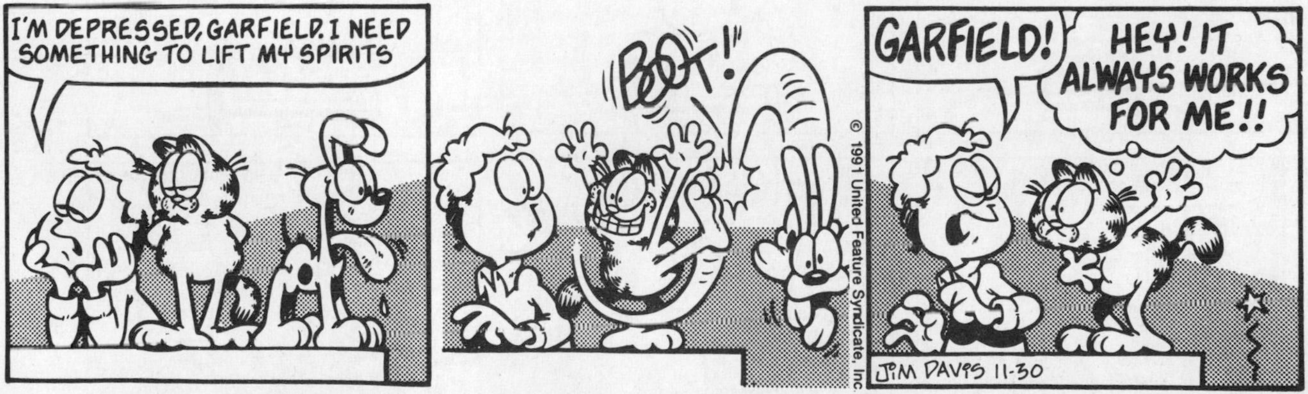
I'M DEPRESSED, GARFIELD. I NEED SOMETHING TO LIFT MY SPIRITS
BOO!
GARFIELD!
HEY! IT ALWAYS WORKS FOR ME!!
JIM DAVIS 11-30
© 1991 United Feature Syndicate, Inc.

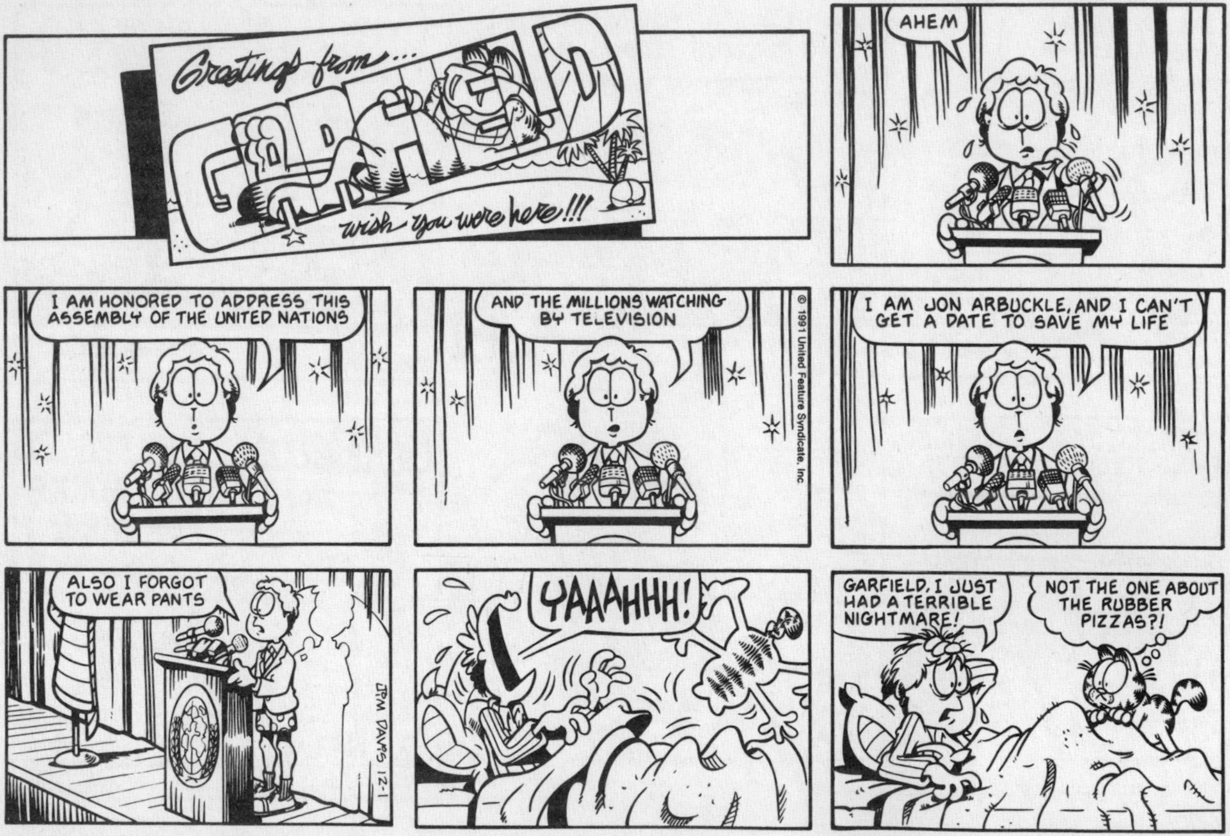
Greetings from...
GARFIELD
wish you were here!!!
AHEM
I AM HONORED TO ADDRESS THIS ASSEMBLY OF THE UNITED NATIONS
AND THE MILLIONS WATCHING BY TELEVISION
© 1991 United Feature Syndicate, Inc.
I AM JON ARBUCKLE, AND I CAN'T GET A DATE TO SAVE MY LIFE
ALSO I FORGOT TO WEAR PANTS
JIM DAVIS 12-1
YAAAHHH!
GARFIELD, I JUST HAD A TERRIBLE NIGHTMARE!
NOT THE ONE ABOUT THE RUBBER PIZZAS?!

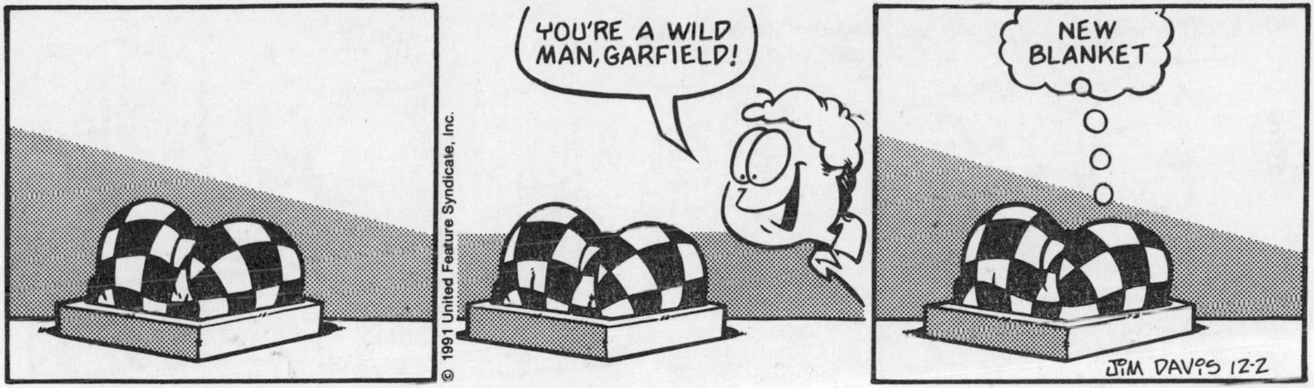
YOU'RE A WILD MAN, GARFIELD!
NEW BLANKET
JIM DAVIS 12-2
© 1991 United Feature Syndicate, Inc.

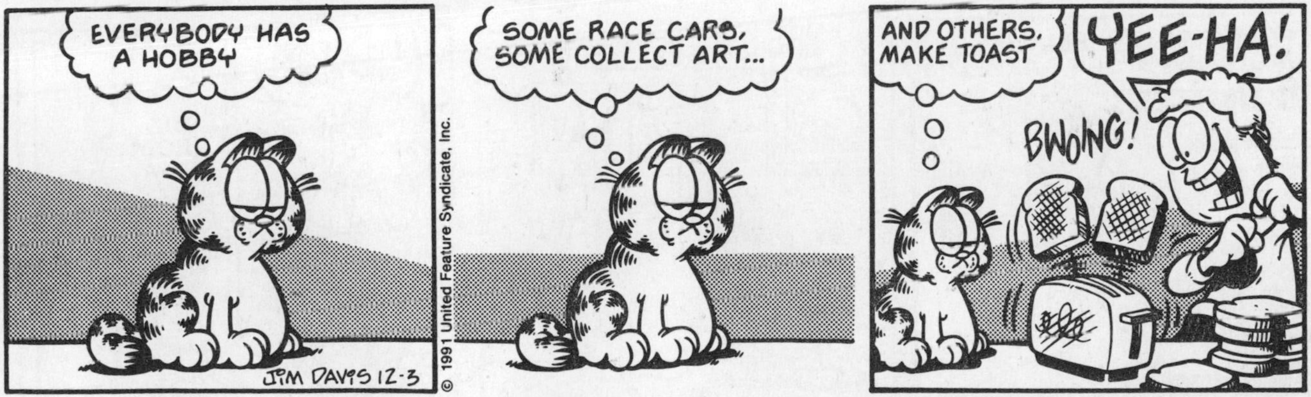
EVERYBODY HAS A HOBBY
SOME RACE CARS, SOME COLLECT ART...
AND OTHERS, MAKE TOAST
YEE-HA!
BWOING!
JIM DAVIS 12-3
© 1991 United Feature Syndicate, Inc.

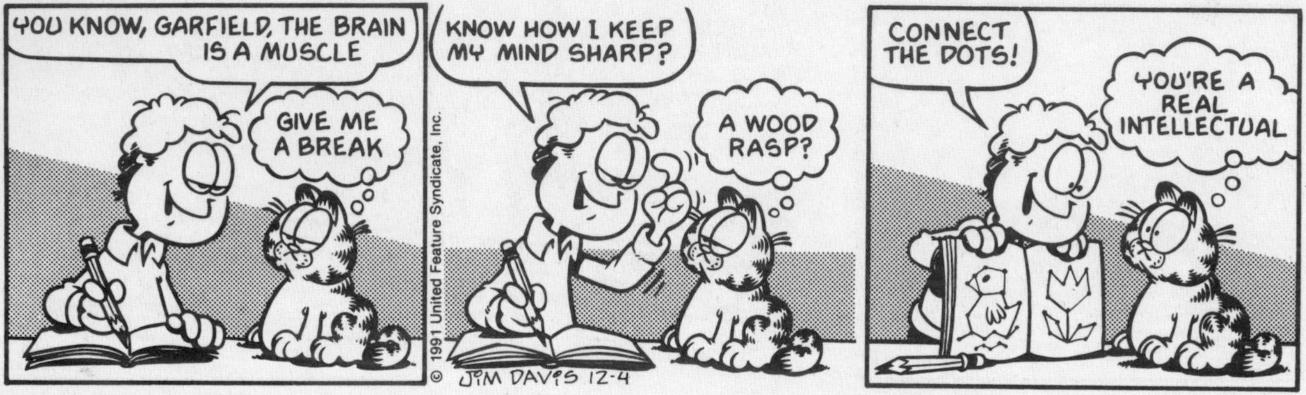
YOU KNOW, GARFIELD, THE BRAIN IS A MUSCLE
GIVE ME A BREAK
KNOW HOW I KEEP MY MIND SHARP?
A WOOD RASP?
CONNECT THE DOTS!
YOU'RE A REAL INTELLECTUAL
© 1991 United Feature Syndicate, Inc.
JIM DAVIS 12-4

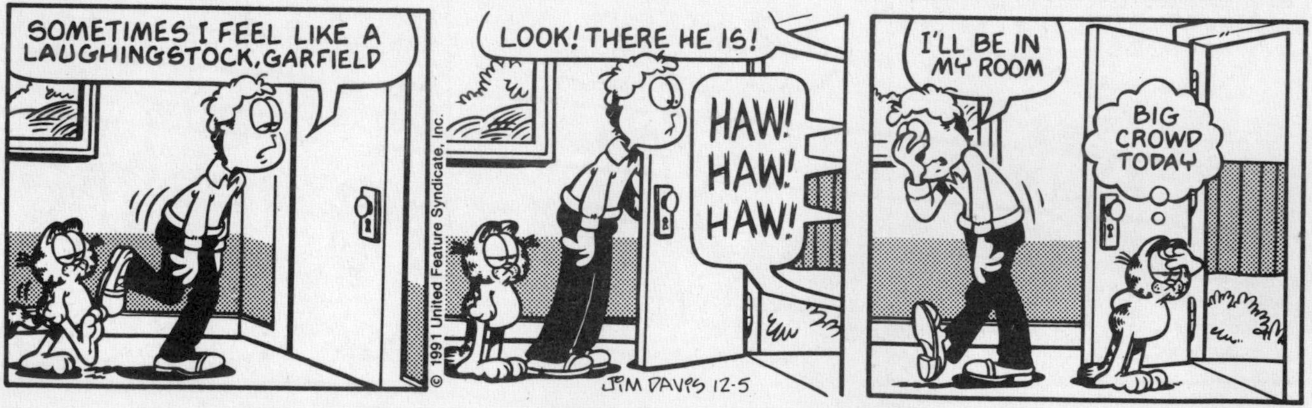
SOMETIMES I FEEL LIKE A LAUGHINGSTOCK, GARFIELD
LOOK! THERE HE IS!
HAW! HAW! HAW!
I'LL BE IN MY ROOM
BIG CROWD TODAY
© 1991 United Feature Syndicate, Inc.
JIM DAVIS 12-5

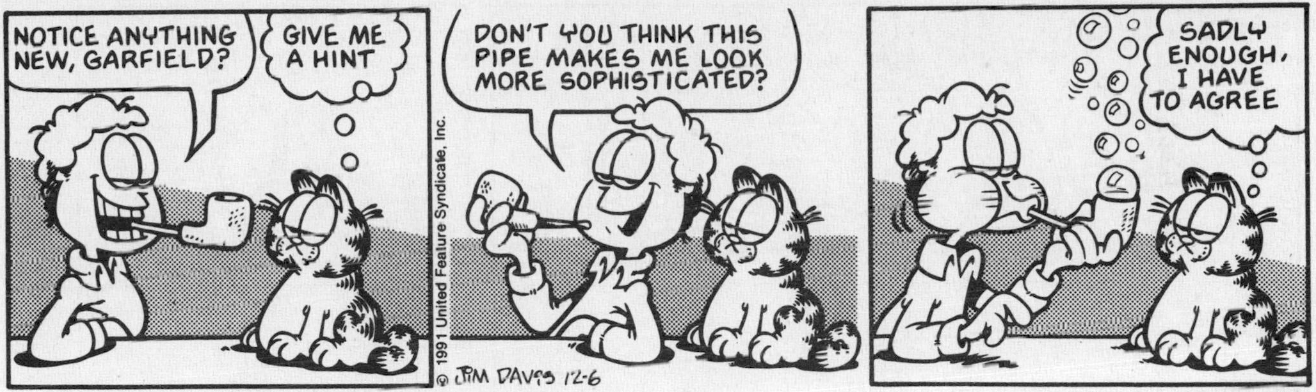
NOTICE ANYTHING NEW, GARFIELD?
GIVE ME A HINT
DON'T YOU THINK THIS PIPE MAKES ME LOOK MORE SOPHISTICATED?
SADLY ENOUGH, I HAVE TO AGREE
© 1991 United Feature Syndicate, Inc.
JIM DAVIS 12-6

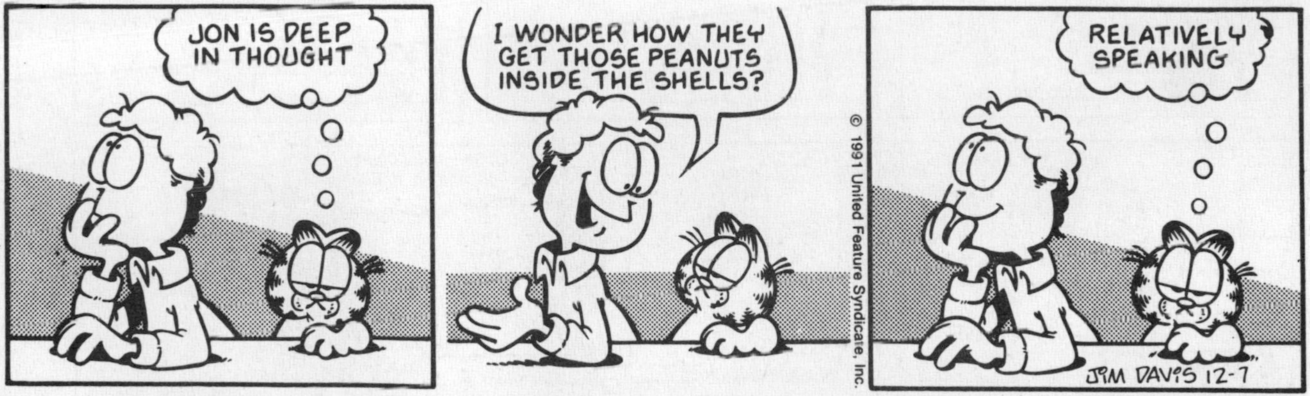
JON IS DEEP IN THOUGHT
I WONDER HOW THEY GET THOSE PEANUTS INSIDE THE SHELLS?
RELATIVELY SPEAKING
© 1991 United Feature Syndicate, Inc.
JIM DAVIS 12-7

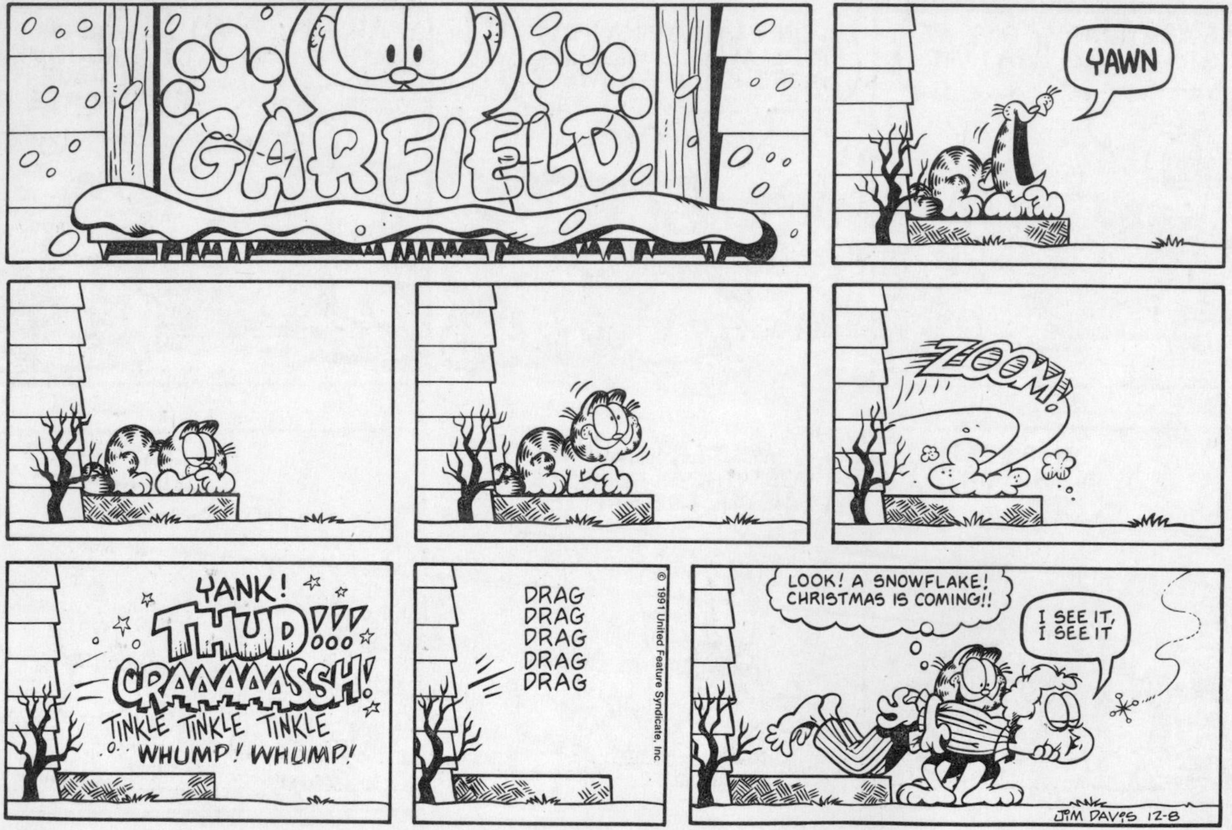
GARFIELD
YAWN
ZOOM!
YANK!
THUD!!!
CRAAAAASSH!
TINKLE TINKLE TINKLE
WHUMP! WHUMP!
DRAG
DRAG
DRAG
DRAG
DRAG
© 1991 United Feature Syndicate, Inc.
LOOK! A SNOWFLAKE! CHRISTMAS IS COMING!!
I SEE IT, I SEE IT
JIM DAVIS 12-8

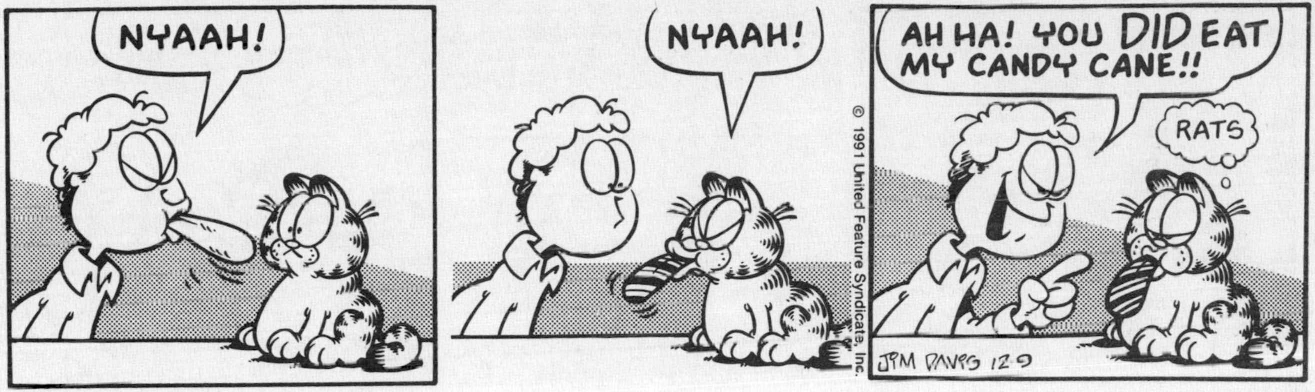
NYAAH!
NYAAH!
© 1991 United Feature Syndicate, Inc.
AH HA! YOU DID EAT MY CANDY CANE!!
RATS
JIM DAVIS 12-9

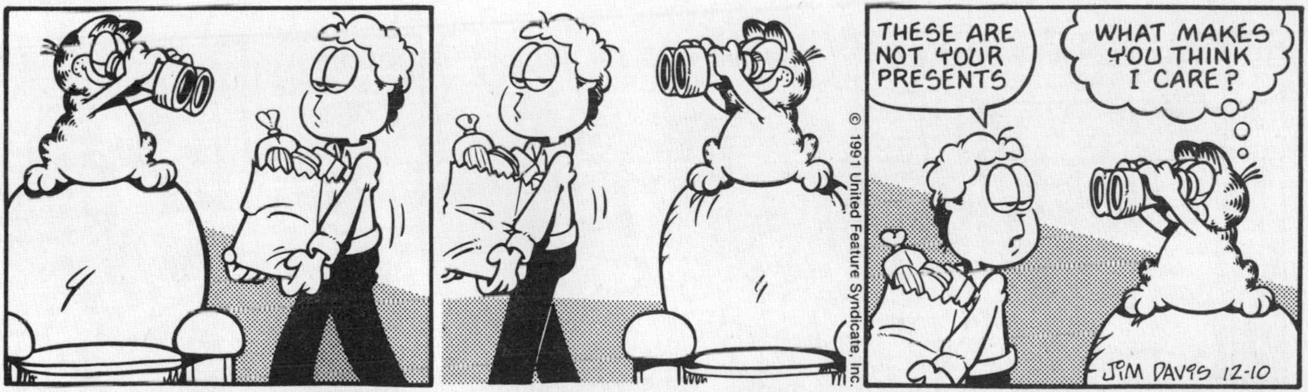
© 1991 United Feature Syndicate, Inc.
THESE ARE NOT YOUR PRESENTS
WHAT MAKES YOU THINK I CARE?
JIM DAVIS 12-10

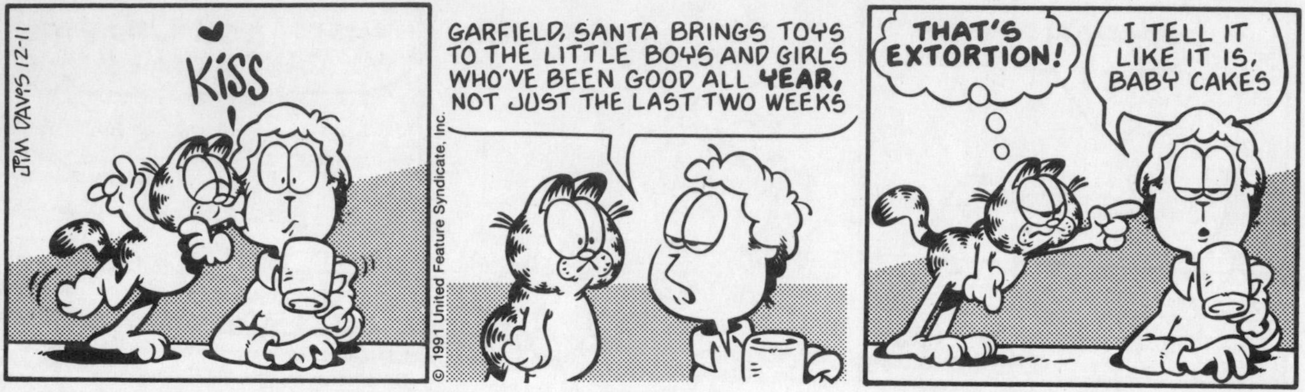
JIM DAVIS 12-11
KISS
© 1991 United Feature Syndicate, Inc.
GARFIELD, SANTA BRINGS TOYS TO THE LITTLE BOYS AND GIRLS WHO'VE BEEN GOOD ALL **YEAR**, NOT JUST THE LAST TWO WEEKS
THAT'S EXTORTION!
I TELL IT LIKE IT IS, BABY CAKES

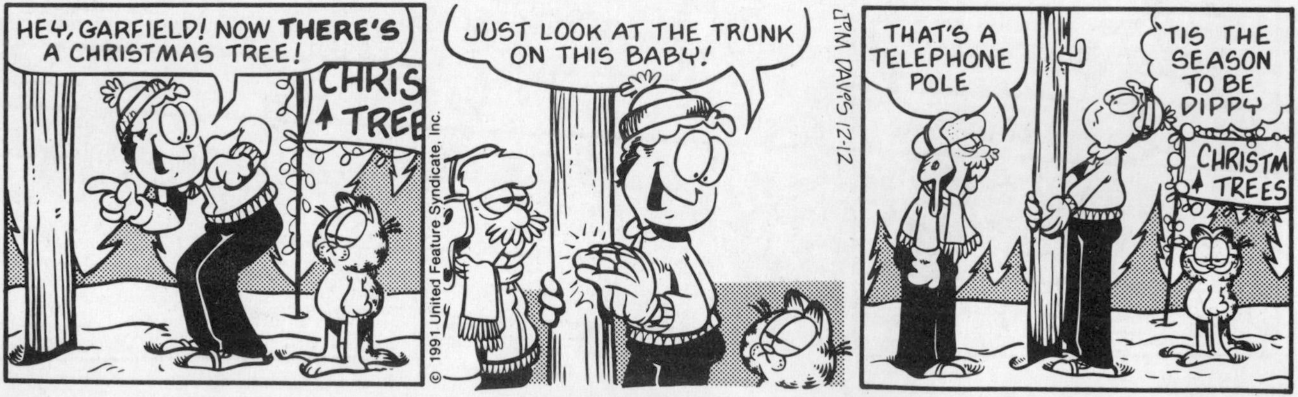
HEY, GARFIELD! NOW **THERE'S** A CHRISTMAS TREE!
CHRIS
TREE
© 1991 United Feature Syndicate, Inc.
JUST LOOK AT THE TRUNK ON THIS BABY!
JIM DAVIS 12-12
THAT'S A TELEPHONE POLE
'TIS THE SEASON TO BE DIPPY
CHRISTM
TREES

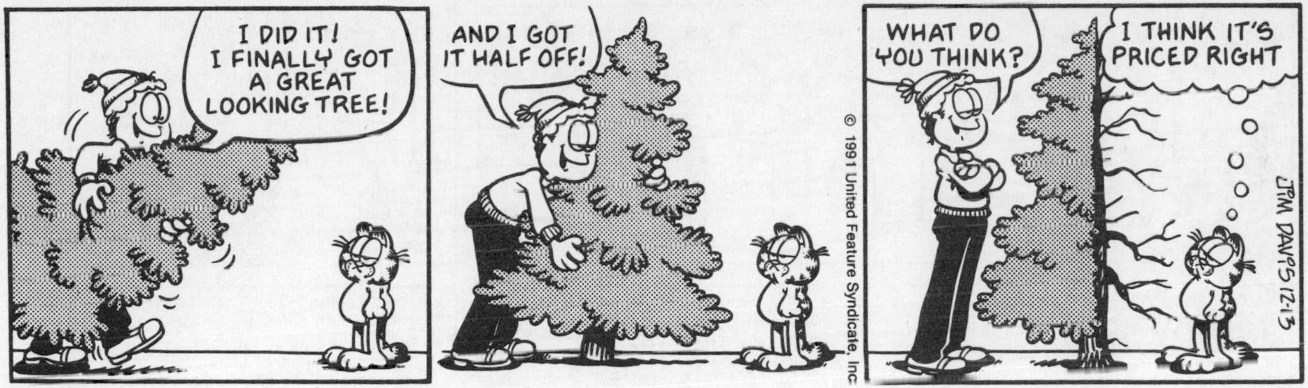
I DID IT! I FINALLY GOT A GREAT LOOKING TREE!
AND I GOT IT HALF OFF!
© 1991 United Feature Syndicate, Inc
WHAT DO YOU THINK?
I THINK IT'S PRICED RIGHT
JIM DAVIS 12-13

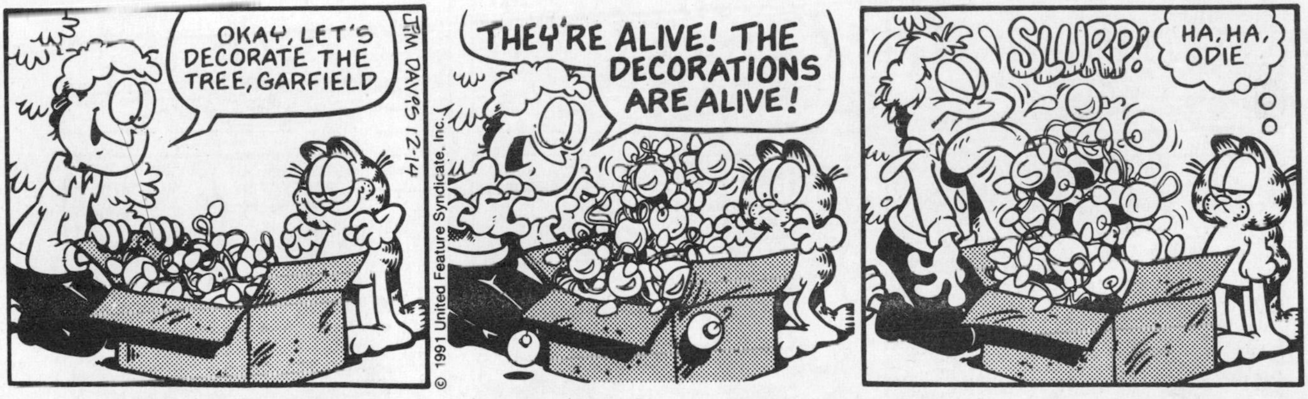
OKAY, LET'S DECORATE THE TREE, GARFIELD
JIM DAVIS 12-14
© 1991 United Feature Syndicate, Inc.
THEY'RE ALIVE! THE DECORATIONS ARE ALIVE!
SLURP!
HA, HA, ODIE

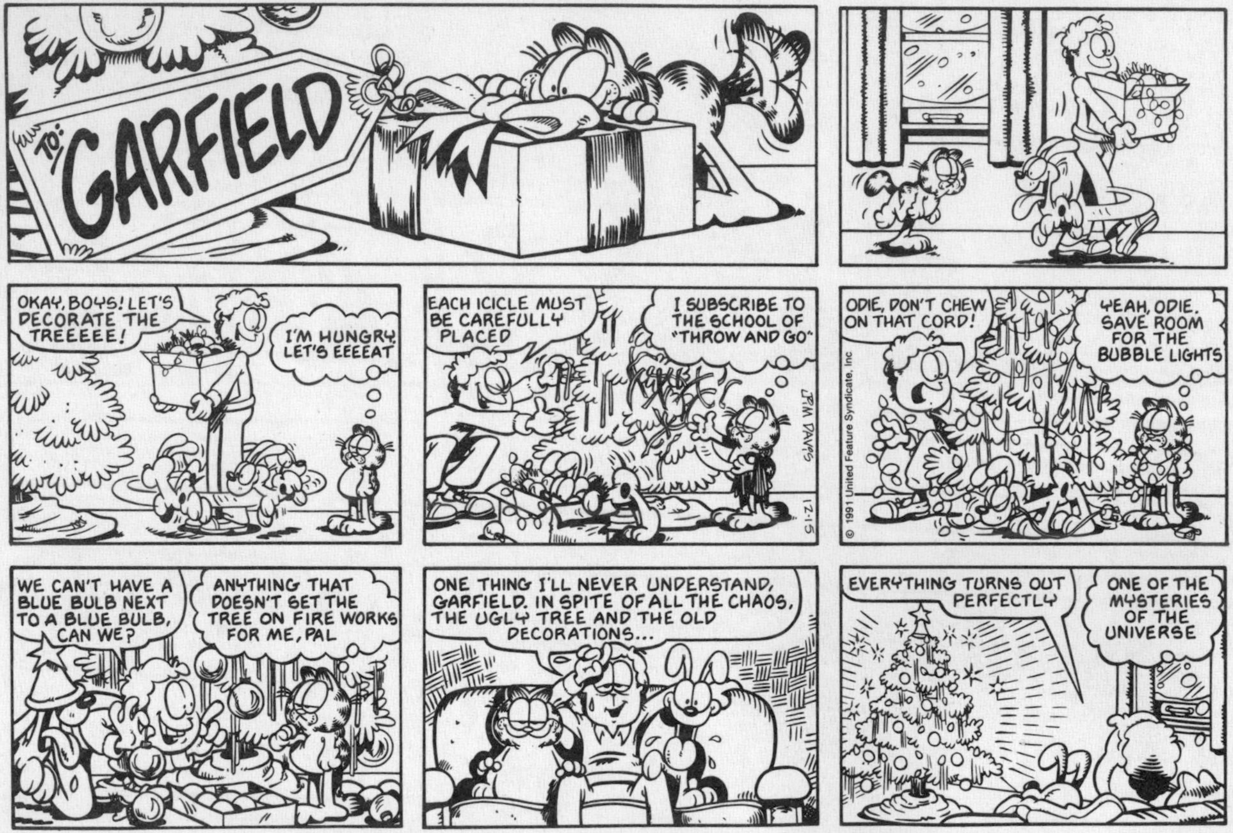
TO: GARFIELD
OKAY, BOYS! LET'S DECORATE THE TREEEEE!
I'M HUNGRY. LET'S EEEEAT
EACH ICICLE MUST BE CAREFULLY PLACED
I SUBSCRIBE TO THE SCHOOL OF "THROW AND GO"
JPM DAVPS 12-15
© 1991 United Feature Syndicate, Inc
ODIE, DON'T CHEW ON THAT CORD!
YEAH, ODIE. SAVE ROOM FOR THE BUBBLE LIGHTS
WE CAN'T HAVE A BLUE BULB NEXT TO A BLUE BULB, CAN WE?
ANYTHING THAT DOESN'T SET THE TREE ON FIRE WORKS FOR ME, PAL
ONE THING I'LL NEVER UNDERSTAND, GARFIELD. IN SPITE OF ALL THE CHAOS, THE UGLY TREE AND THE OLD DECORATIONS...
EVERYTHING TURNS OUT PERFECTLY
ONE OF THE MYSTERIES OF THE UNIVERSE

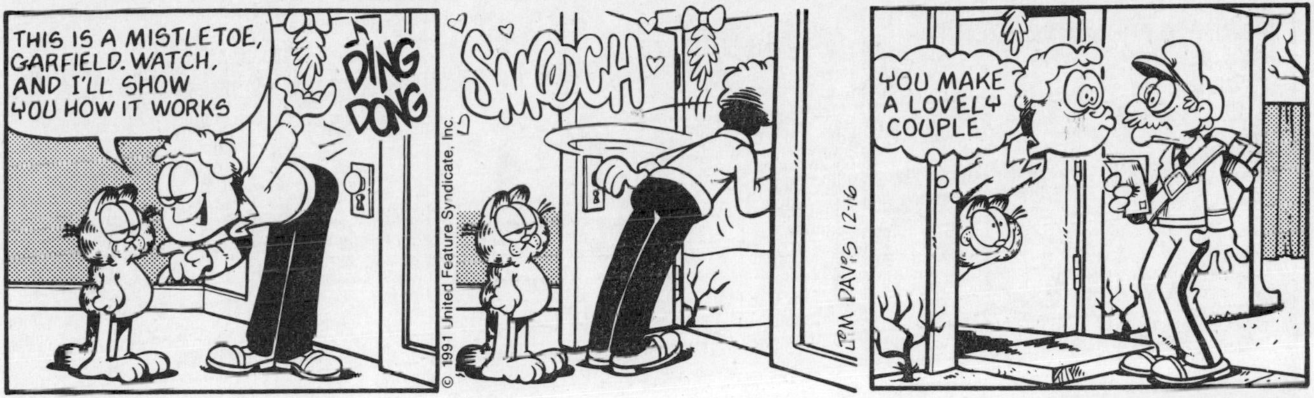
THIS IS A MISTLETOE, GARFIELD. WATCH, AND I'LL SHOW YOU HOW IT WORKS
DING DONG
SMOOCH
© 1991 United Feature Syndicate, Inc.
JIM DAVIS 12-16
YOU MAKE A LOVELY COUPLE

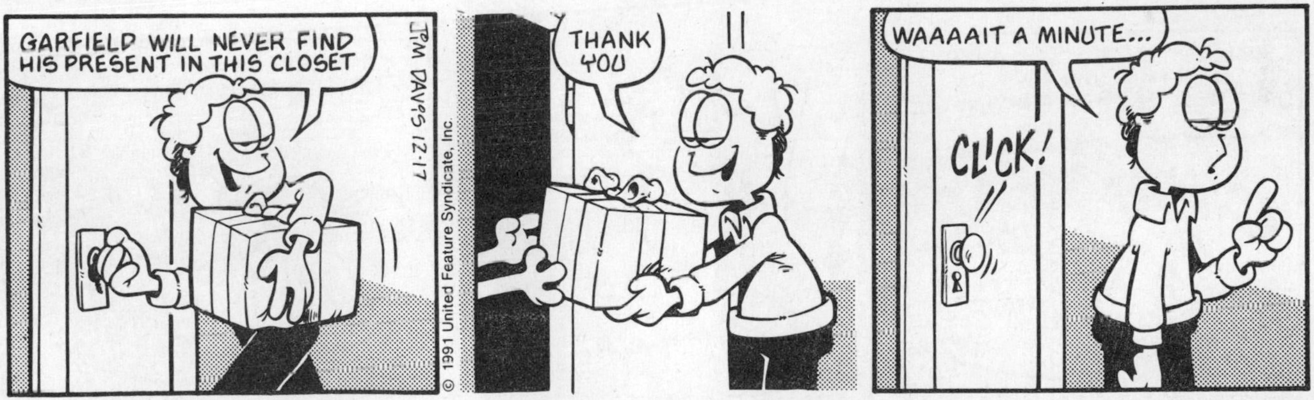
GARFIELD WILL NEVER FIND HIS PRESENT IN THIS CLOSET
JIM DAVIS 12-17
© 1991 United Feature Syndicate, Inc.
THANK YOU
WAAAAIT A MINUTE...
CLICK!

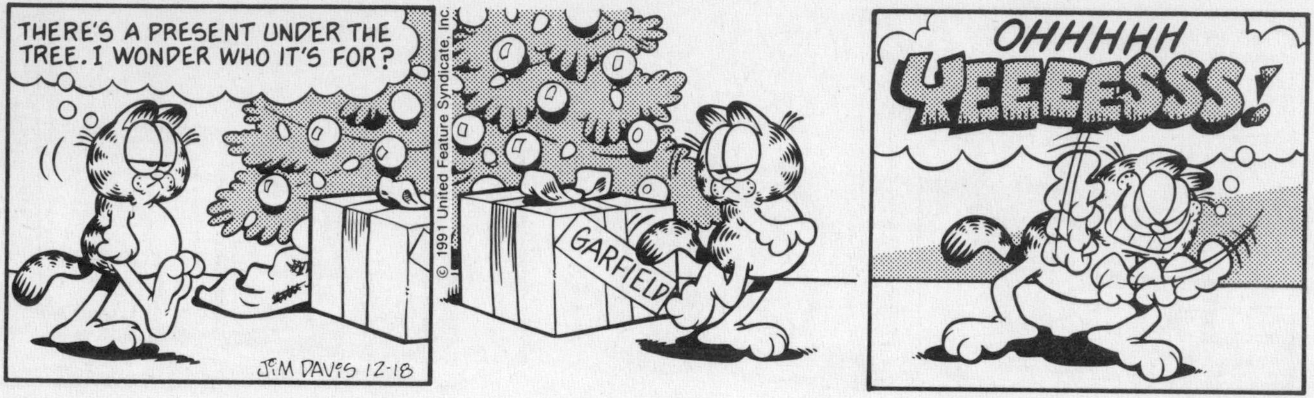
THERE'S A PRESENT UNDER THE TREE. I WONDER WHO IT'S FOR?
© 1991 United Feature Syndicate, Inc.
GARFIELD
OHHHHH YEEEESSS!
JIM DAVIS 12-18

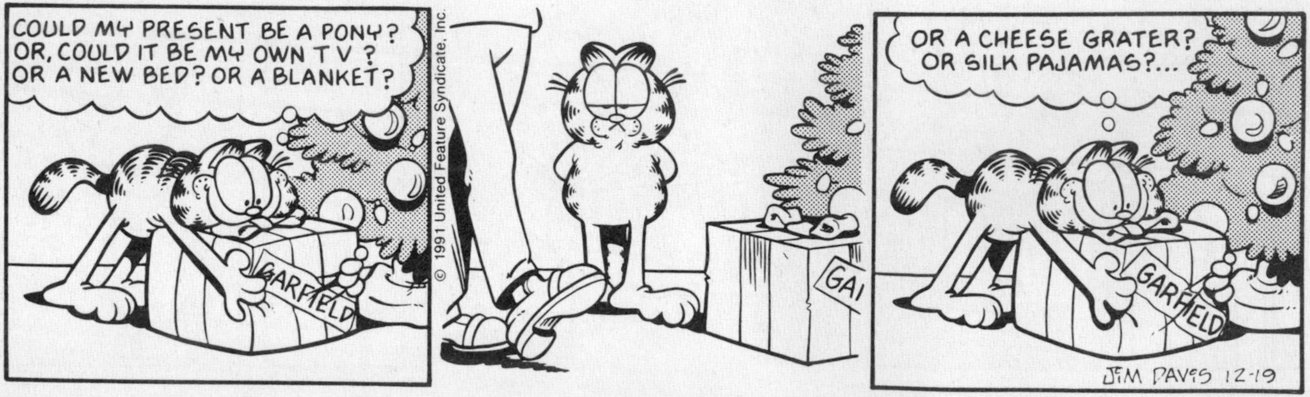
COULD MY PRESENT BE A PONY? OR, COULD IT BE MY OWN TV? OR A NEW BED? OR A BLANKET?
GARFIELD
© 1991 United Feature Syndicate, Inc.
GAI
OR A CHEESE GRATER? OR SILK PAJAMAS?...
GARFIELD
JIM DAVIS 12-19

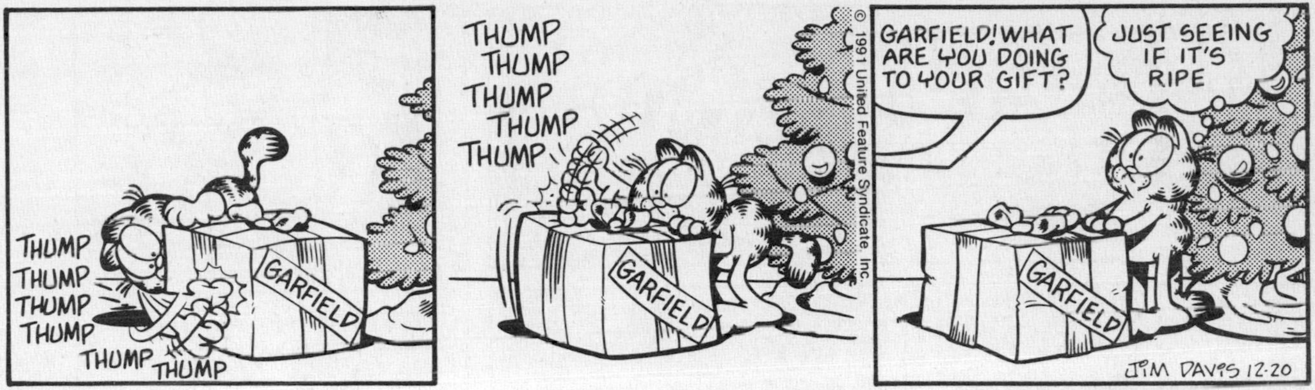
THUMP
THUMP
THUMP
THUMP
THUMP THUMP
GARFIELD
THUMP
THUMP
THUMP
THUMP
THUMP
GARFIELD
© 1991 United Feature Syndicate, Inc.
GARFIELD! WHAT ARE YOU DOING TO YOUR GIFT?
JUST SEEING IF IT'S RIPE
GARFIELD
JIM DAVIS 12-20

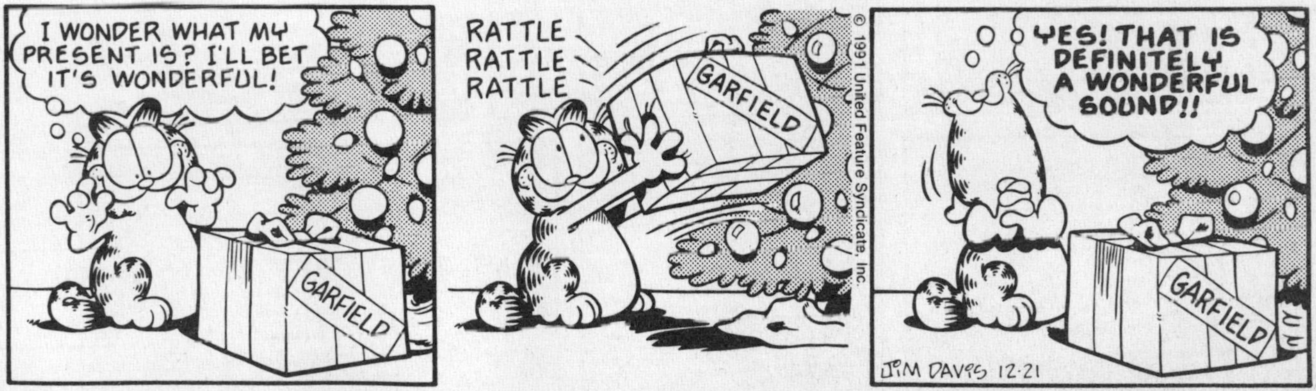
I WONDER WHAT MY PRESENT IS? I'LL BET IT'S WONDERFUL!
GARFIELD
RATTLE
RATTLE
RATTLE
GARFIELD
© 1991 United Feature Syndicate, Inc.
YES! THAT IS DEFINITELY A WONDERFUL SOUND!!
GARFIELD
JIM DAVIS 12-21

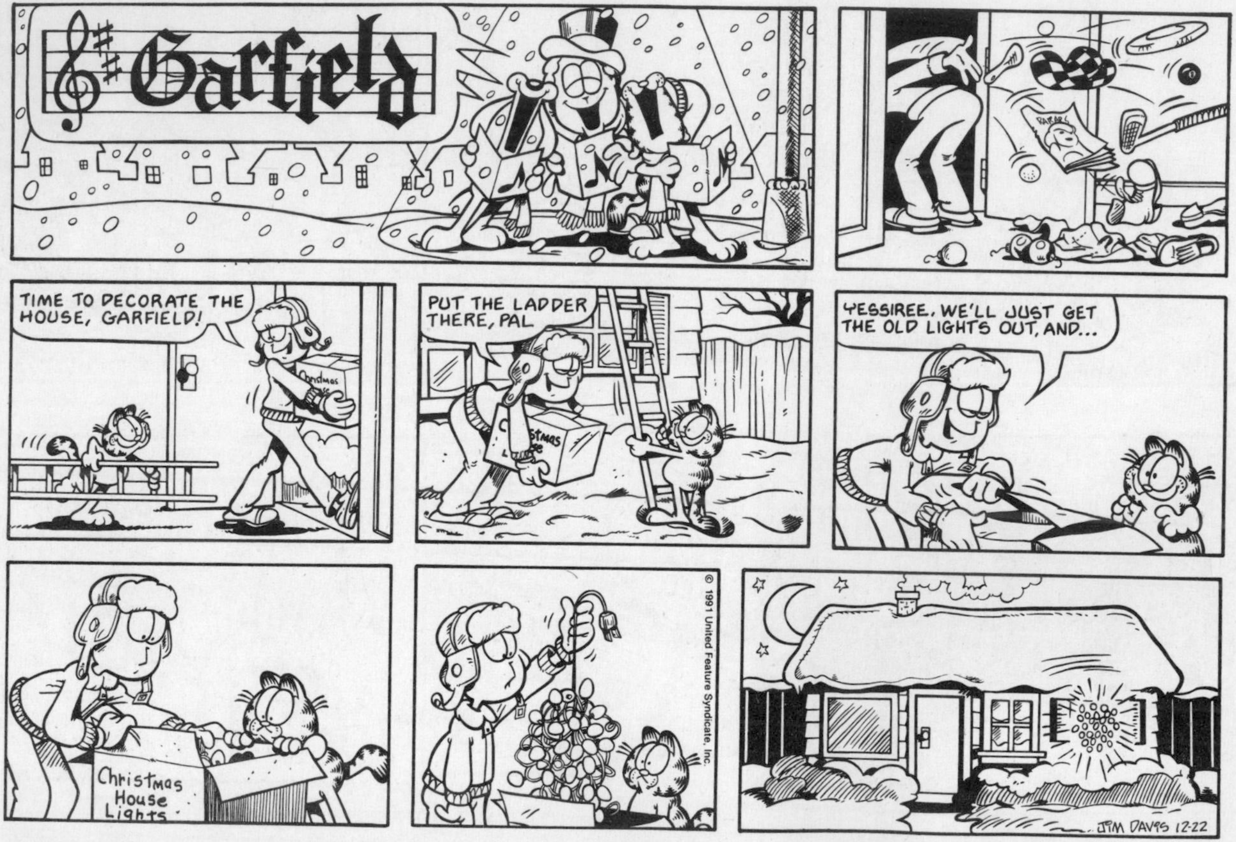
Garfield
TIME TO DECORATE THE HOUSE, GARFIELD!
PUT THE LADDER THERE, PAL
YESSIREE. WE'LL JUST GET THE OLD LIGHTS OUT, AND...
Christmas House Lights
© 1991 United Feature Syndicate, Inc.
JIM DAVIS 12-22

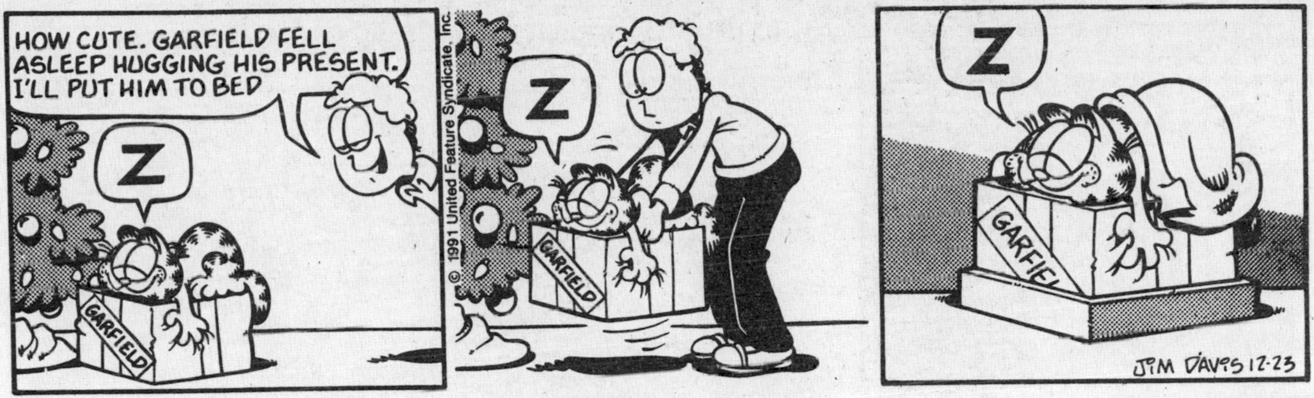
HOW CUTE. GARFIELD FELL ASLEEP HUGGING HIS PRESENT. I'LL PUT HIM TO BED
Z
GARFIELD
© 1991 United Feature Syndicate, Inc.
Z
GARFIELD
Z
GARFIELD
JIM DAVIS 12-23

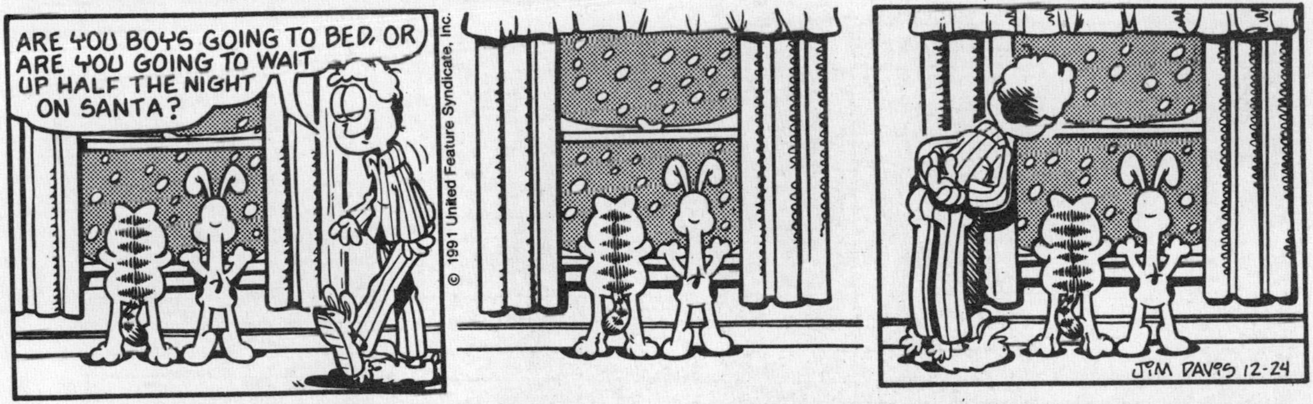
ARE YOU BOYS GOING TO BED, OR ARE YOU GOING TO WAIT UP HALF THE NIGHT ON SANTA?
© 1991 United Feature Syndicate, Inc.
JIM DAVIS 12-24

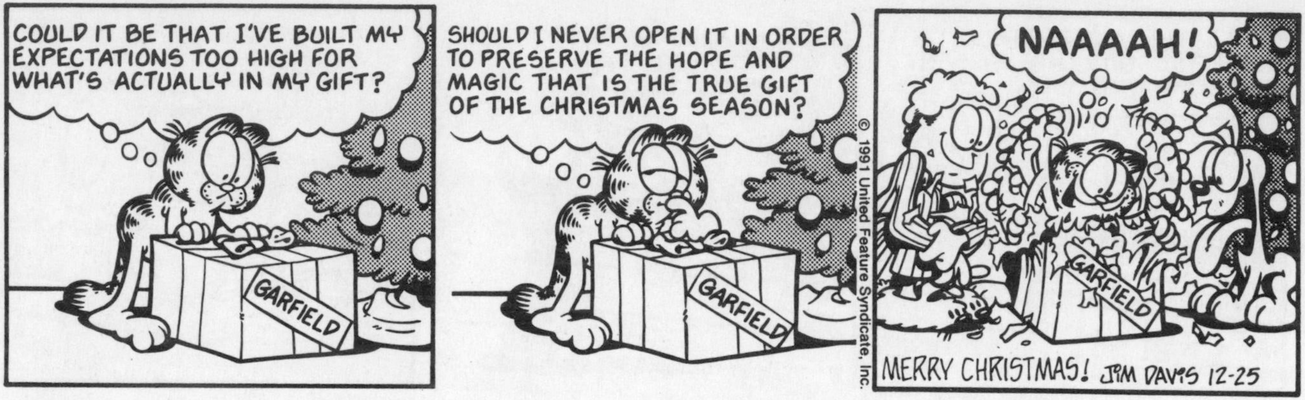
COULD IT BE THAT I'VE BUILT MY EXPECTATIONS TOO HIGH FOR WHAT'S ACTUALLY IN MY GIFT?
GARFIELD
SHOULD I NEVER OPEN IT IN ORDER TO PRESERVE THE HOPE AND MAGIC THAT IS THE TRUE GIFT OF THE CHRISTMAS SEASON?
GARFIELD
© 1991 United Feature Syndicate, Inc.
NAAAAH!
GARFIELD
MERRY CHRISTMAS! JIM DAVIS 12-25

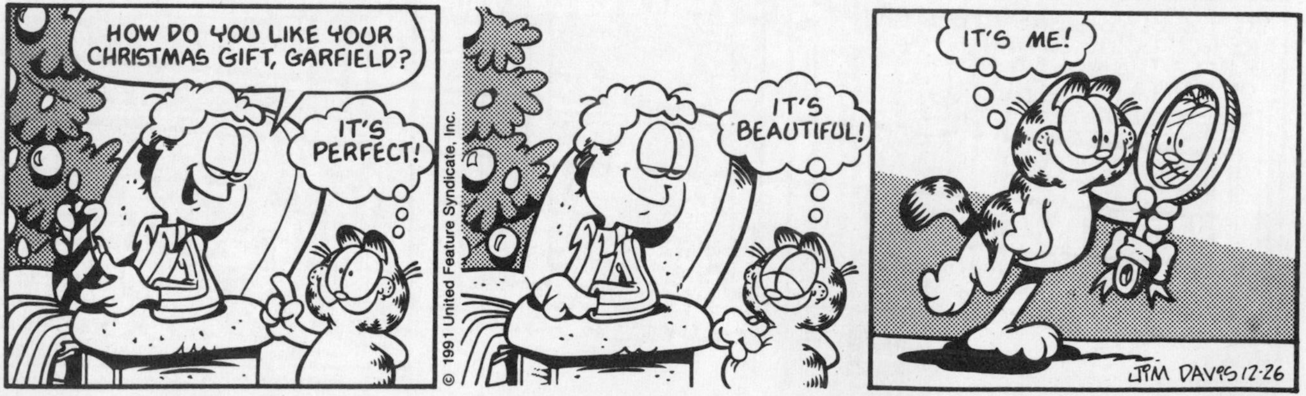
HOW DO YOU LIKE YOUR CHRISTMAS GIFT, GARFIELD?
IT'S PERFECT!
© 1991 United Feature Syndicate, Inc.
IT'S BEAUTIFUL!
IT'S ME!
JIM DAVIS 12-26

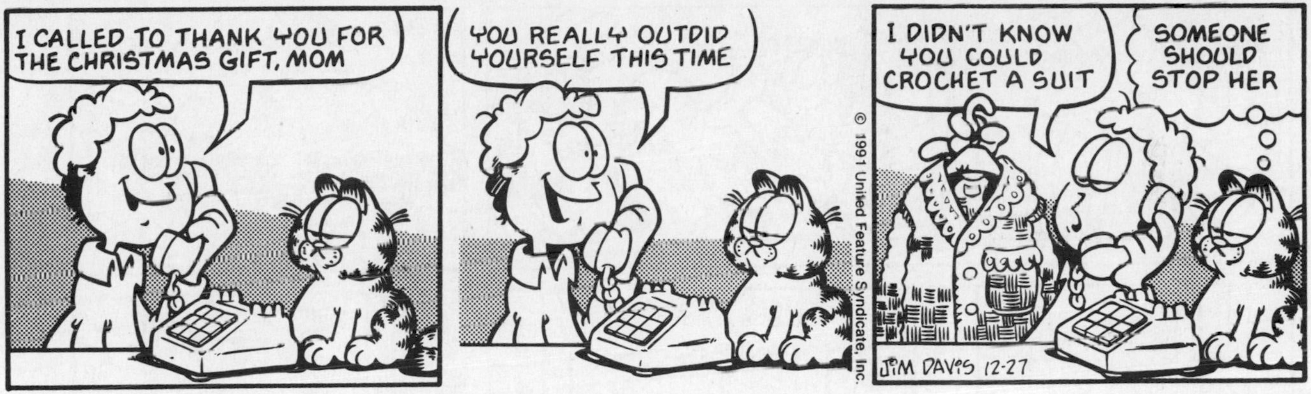
I CALLED TO THANK YOU FOR THE CHRISTMAS GIFT, MOM
YOU REALLY OUTDID YOURSELF THIS TIME
© 1991 United Feature Syndicate, Inc.
I DIDN'T KNOW YOU COULD CROCHET A SUIT
SOMEONE SHOULD STOP HER
JIM DAVIS 12-27

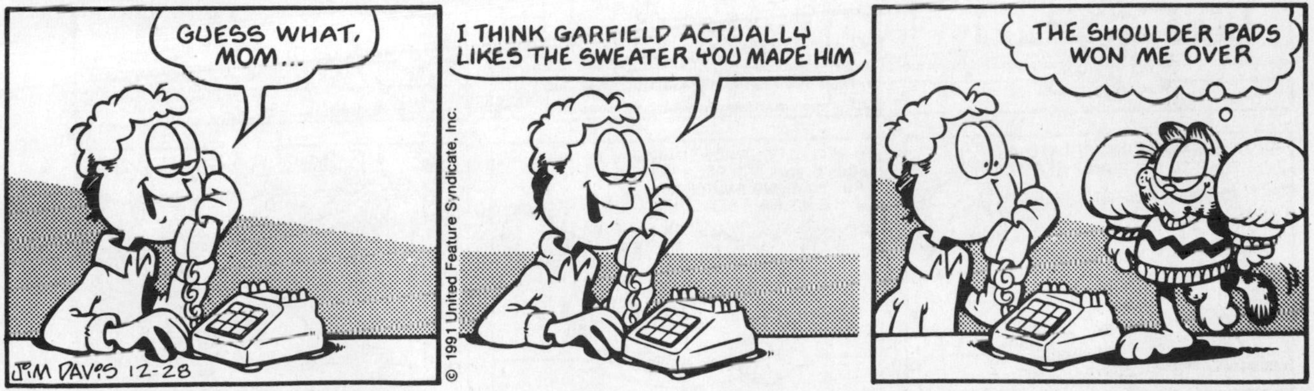
GUESS WHAT, MOM...
JIM DAVIS 12-28
© 1991 United Feature Syndicate, Inc.
I THINK GARFIELD ACTUALLY LIKES THE SWEATER YOU MADE HIM
THE SHOULDER PADS WON ME OVER

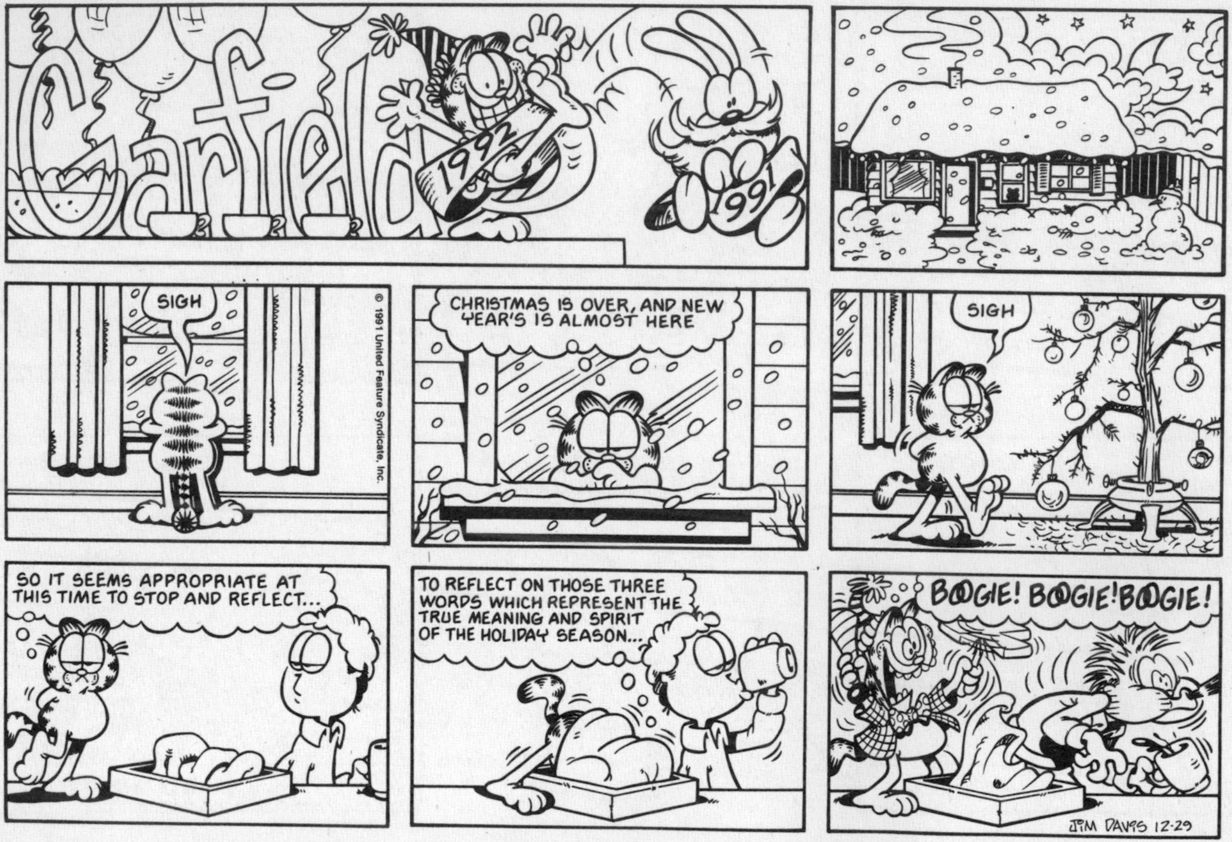
Garfield
1992
1991
SIGH
© 1991 United Feature Syndicate, Inc.
CHRISTMAS IS OVER, AND NEW YEAR'S IS ALMOST HERE
SIGH
SO IT SEEMS APPROPRIATE AT THIS TIME TO STOP AND REFLECT...
TO REFLECT ON THOSE THREE WORDS WHICH REPRESENT THE TRUE MEANING AND SPIRIT OF THE HOLIDAY SEASON...
BOOGIE! BOOGIE! BOOGIE!
JIM DAVIS 12-29

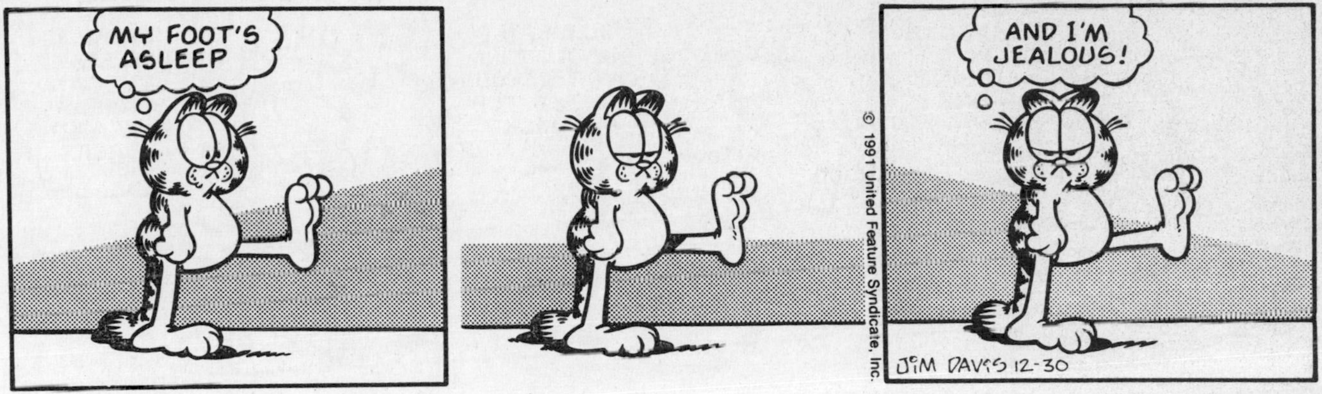
MY FOOT'S ASLEEP
AND I'M JEALOUS!
JIM DAVIS 12-30

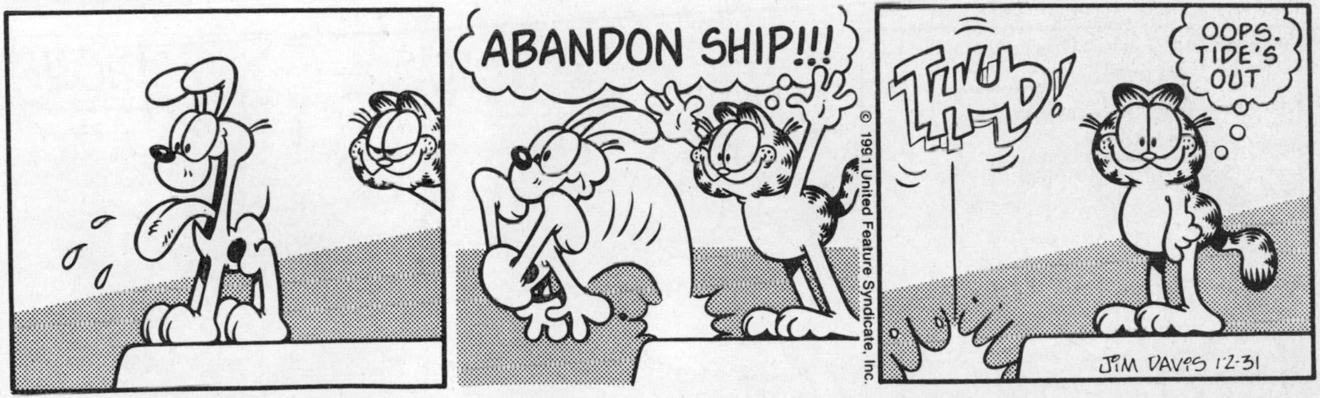
ABANDON SHIP!!!
THUD!
OOPS. TIDE'S OUT
JIM DAVIS 12-31

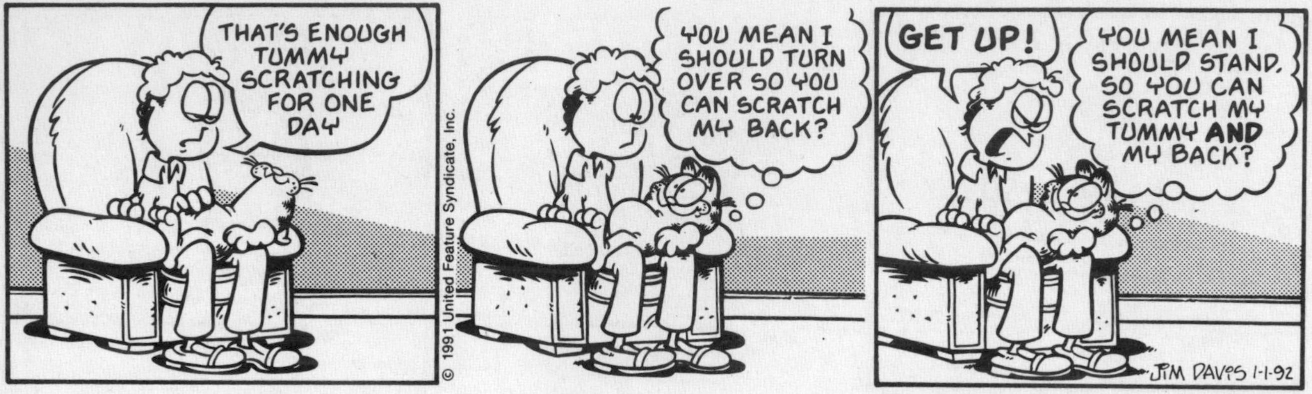
THAT'S ENOUGH TUMMY SCRATCHING FOR ONE DAY
© 1991 United Feature Syndicate, Inc.
YOU MEAN I SHOULD TURN OVER SO YOU CAN SCRATCH MY BACK?
GET UP!
YOU MEAN I SHOULD STAND, SO YOU CAN SCRATCH MY TUMMY **AND** MY BACK?
JIM DAVIS 1-1-92

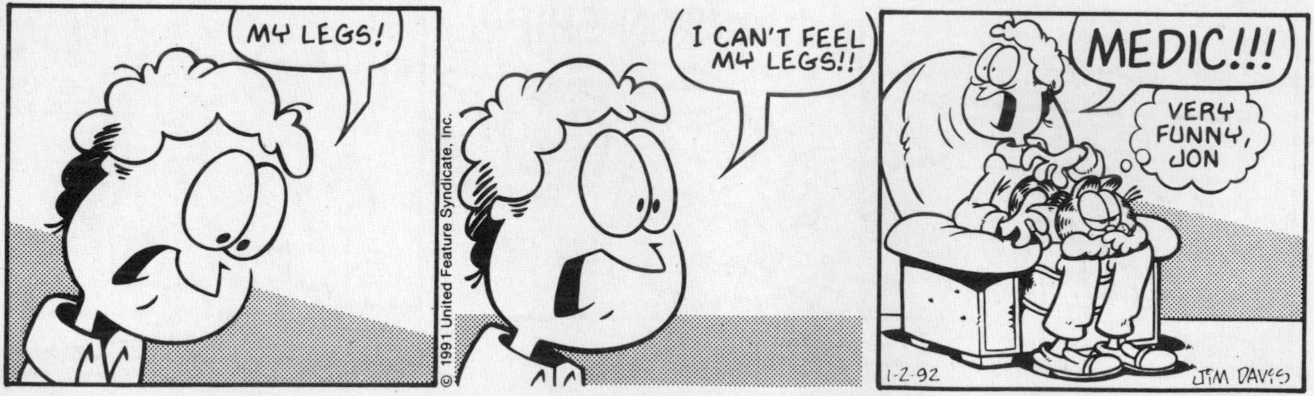
MY LEGS!
© 1991 United Feature Syndicate, Inc.
I CAN'T FEEL MY LEGS!!
MEDIC!!!
VERY FUNNY, JON
1-2-92
JIM DAVIS

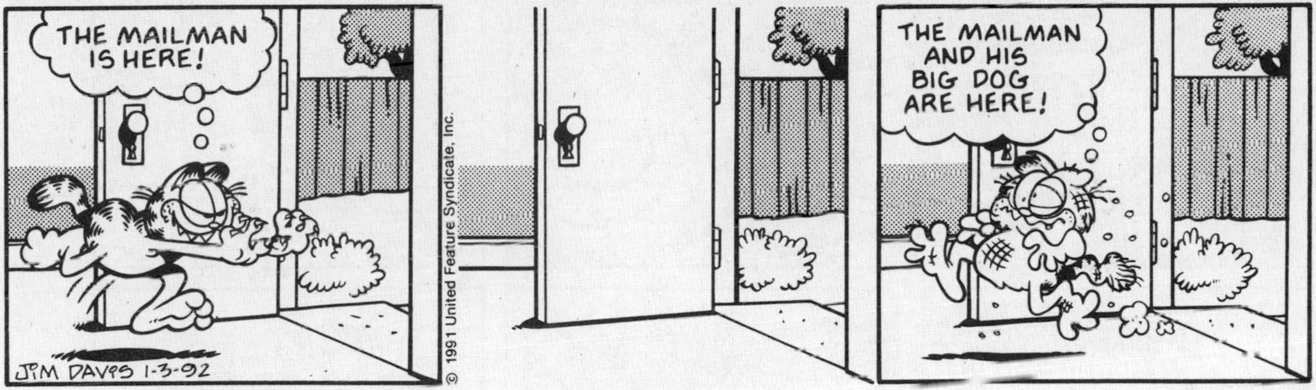
THE MAILMAN IS HERE!
JIM DAVIS 1-3-92
THE MAILMAN AND HIS BIG DOG ARE HERE!

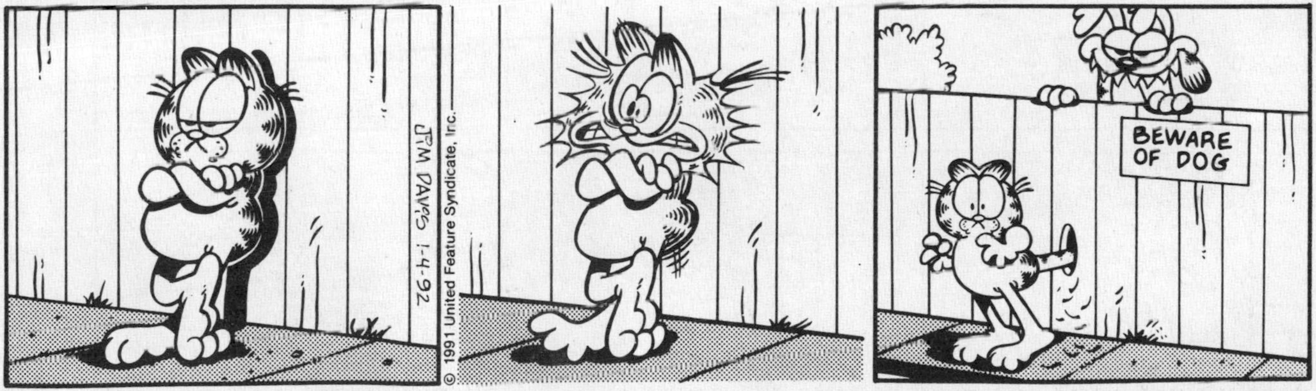
JIM DAVIS 1-4-92
BEWARE OF DOG

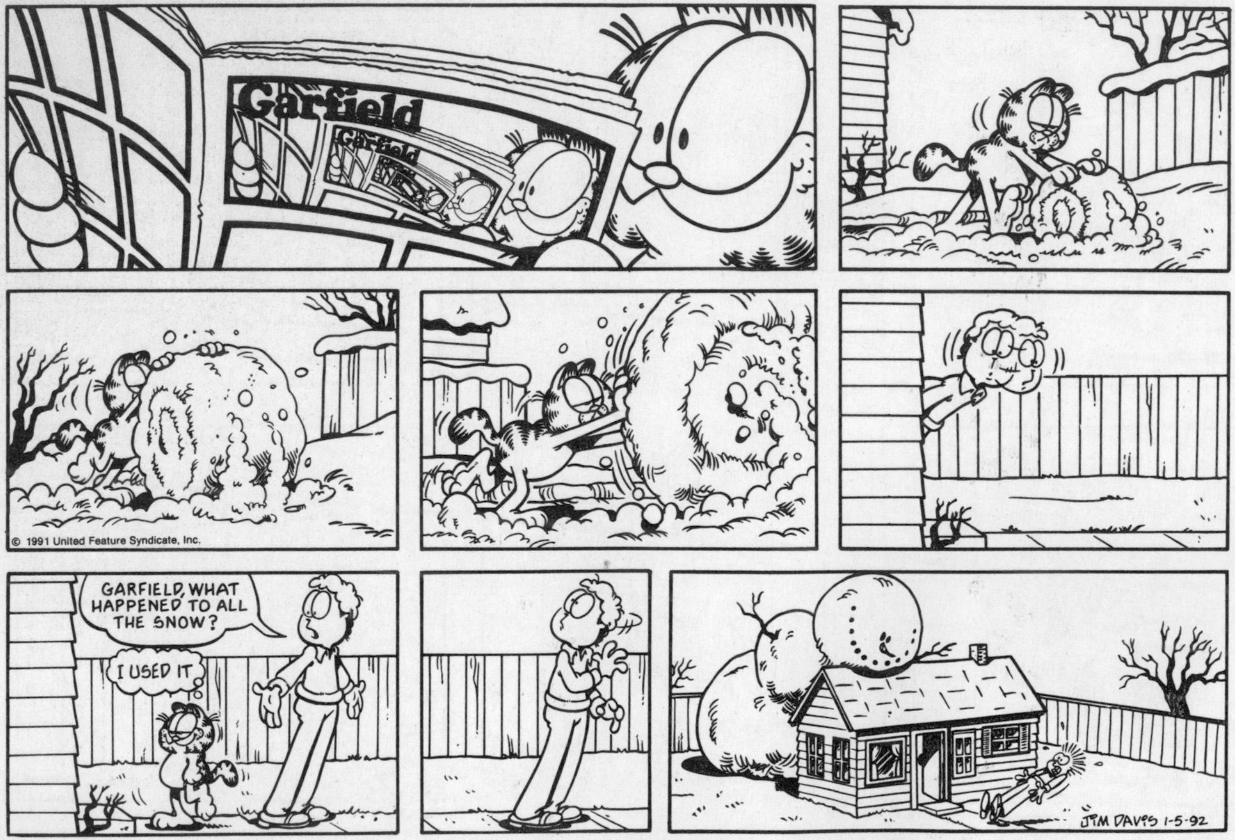
Garfield
Garfield
© 1991 United Feature Syndicate, Inc.
GARFIELD, WHAT HAPPENED TO ALL THE SNOW?
I USED IT
JIM DAVIS 1-5-92

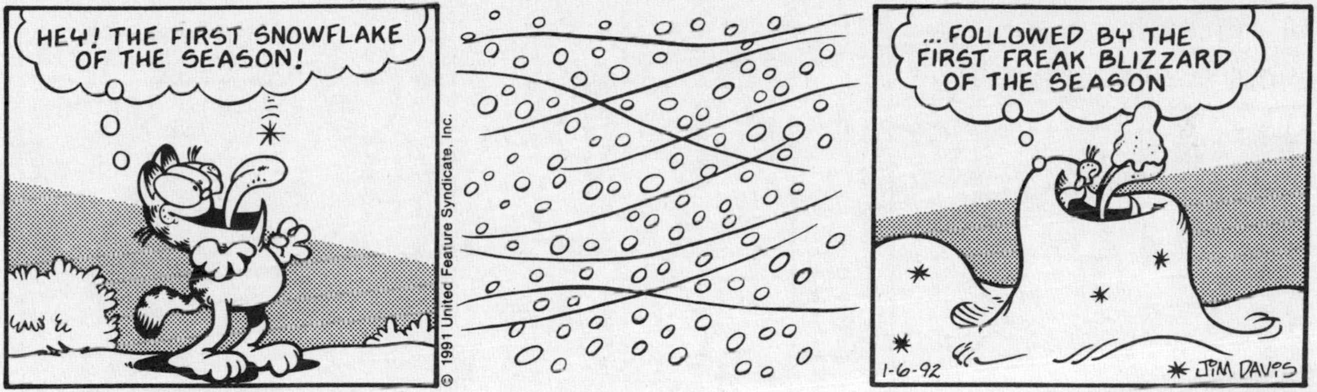
HEY! THE FIRST SNOWFLAKE OF THE SEASON!
© 1991 United Feature Syndicate, Inc.
... FOLLOWED BY THE FIRST FREAK BLIZZARD OF THE SEASON
1-6-92
JIM DAVIS

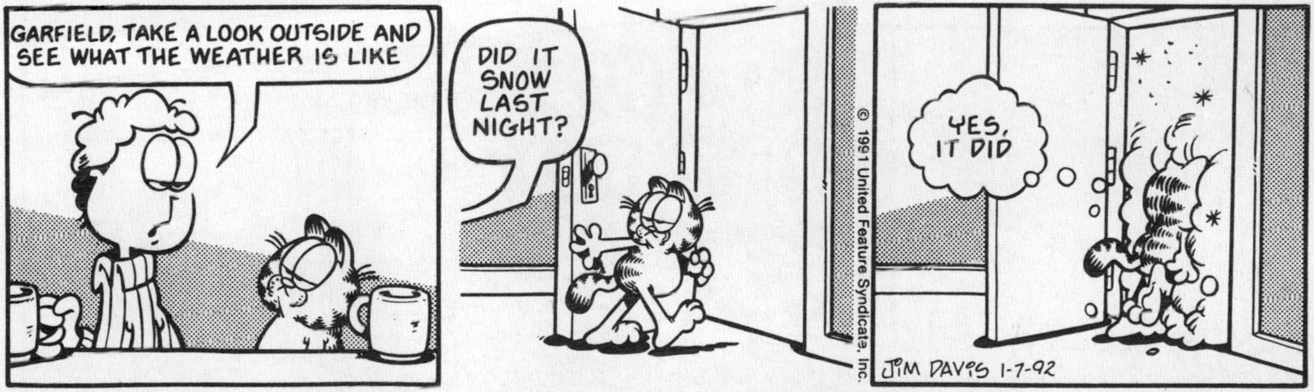
GARFIELD, TAKE A LOOK OUTSIDE AND SEE WHAT THE WEATHER IS LIKE
DID IT SNOW LAST NIGHT?
© 1991 United Feature Syndicate, Inc.
YES, IT DID
JIM DAVIS 1-7-92

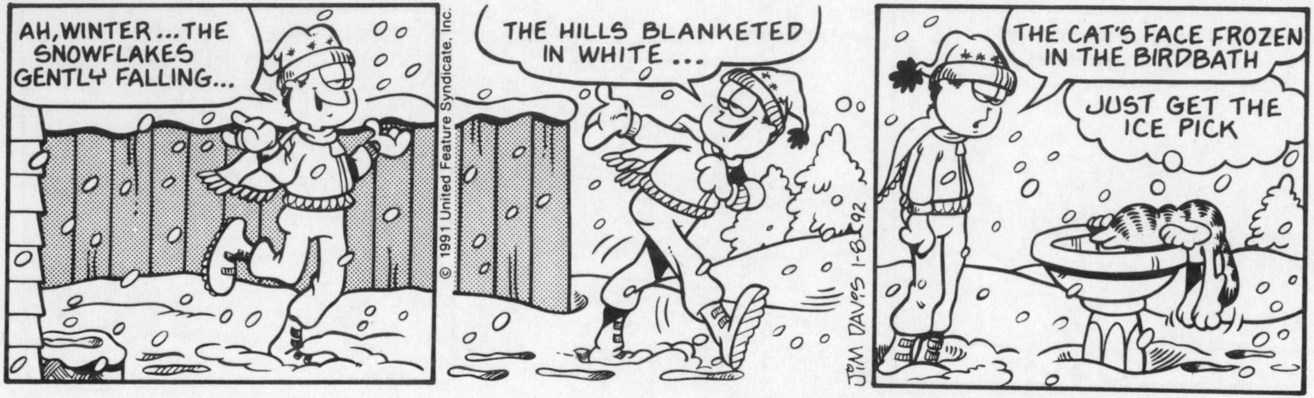
AH, WINTER ... THE SNOWFLAKES GENTLY FALLING...
© 1991 United Feature Syndicate, Inc.
THE HILLS BLANKETED IN WHITE ...
JIM DAVIS 1-8-92
THE CAT'S FACE FROZEN IN THE BIRDBATH
JUST GET THE ICE PICK

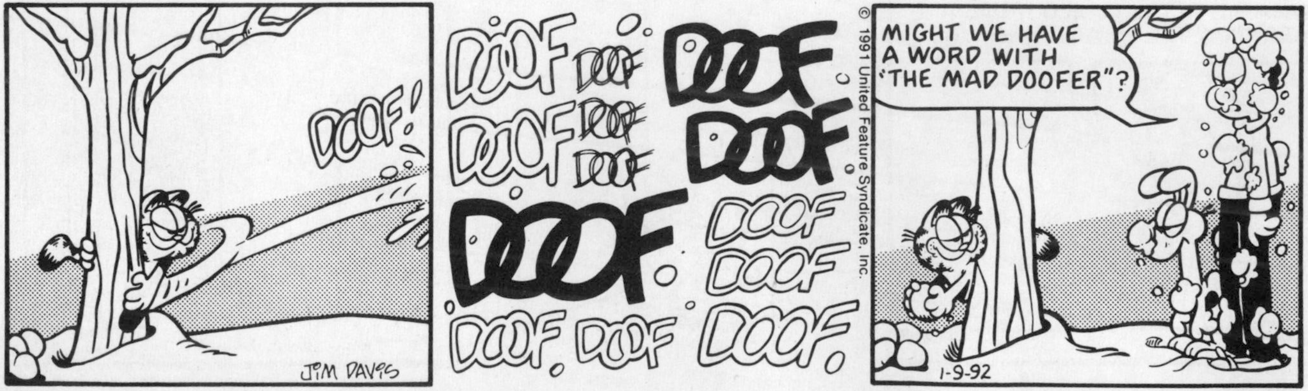
DOOF!
JIM DAVIS
DOOF DOOF DOOF DOOF DOOF DOOF DOOF DOOF DOOF DOOF DOOF DOOF DOOF DOOF
© 1991 United Feature Syndicate, Inc.
MIGHT WE HAVE A WORD WITH "THE MAD DOOFER"?
1-9-92

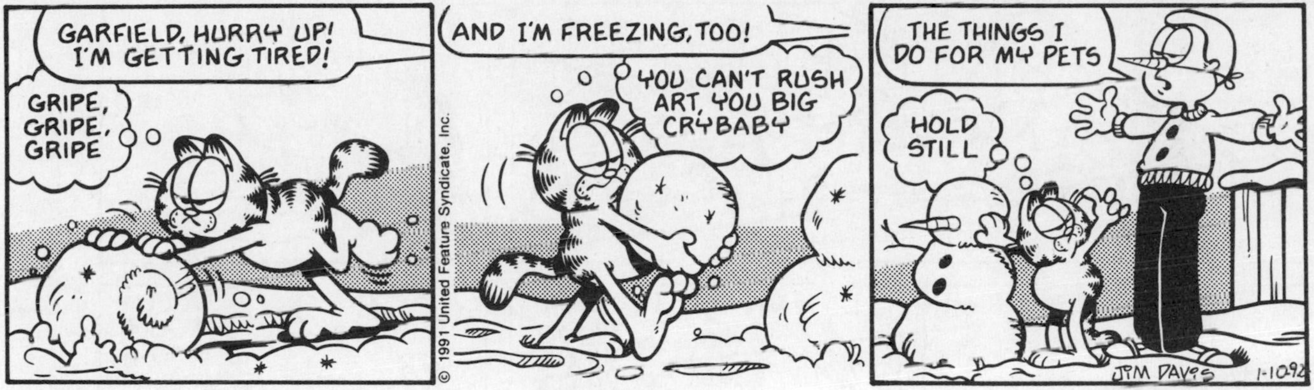
GARFIELD, HURRY UP! I'M GETTING TIRED!
GRIPE, GRIPE, GRIPE
AND I'M FREEZING, TOO!
YOU CAN'T RUSH ART, YOU BIG CRYBABY
THE THINGS I DO FOR MY PETS
HOLD STILL
JIM DAVIS 1-10-92
© 1991 United Feature Syndicate, Inc.

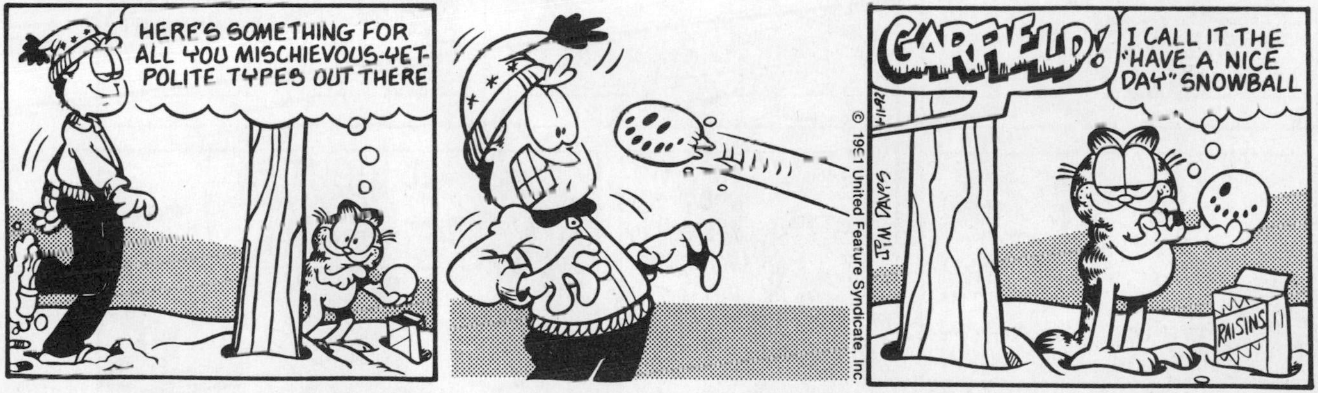
HERE'S SOMETHING FOR ALL YOU MISCHIEVOUS-YET-POLITE TYPES OUT THERE
GARFIELD!
I CALL IT THE "HAVE A NICE DAY" SNOWBALL
RAISINS
JIM DAVIS 1-11-92
© 1991 United Feature Syndicate, Inc.

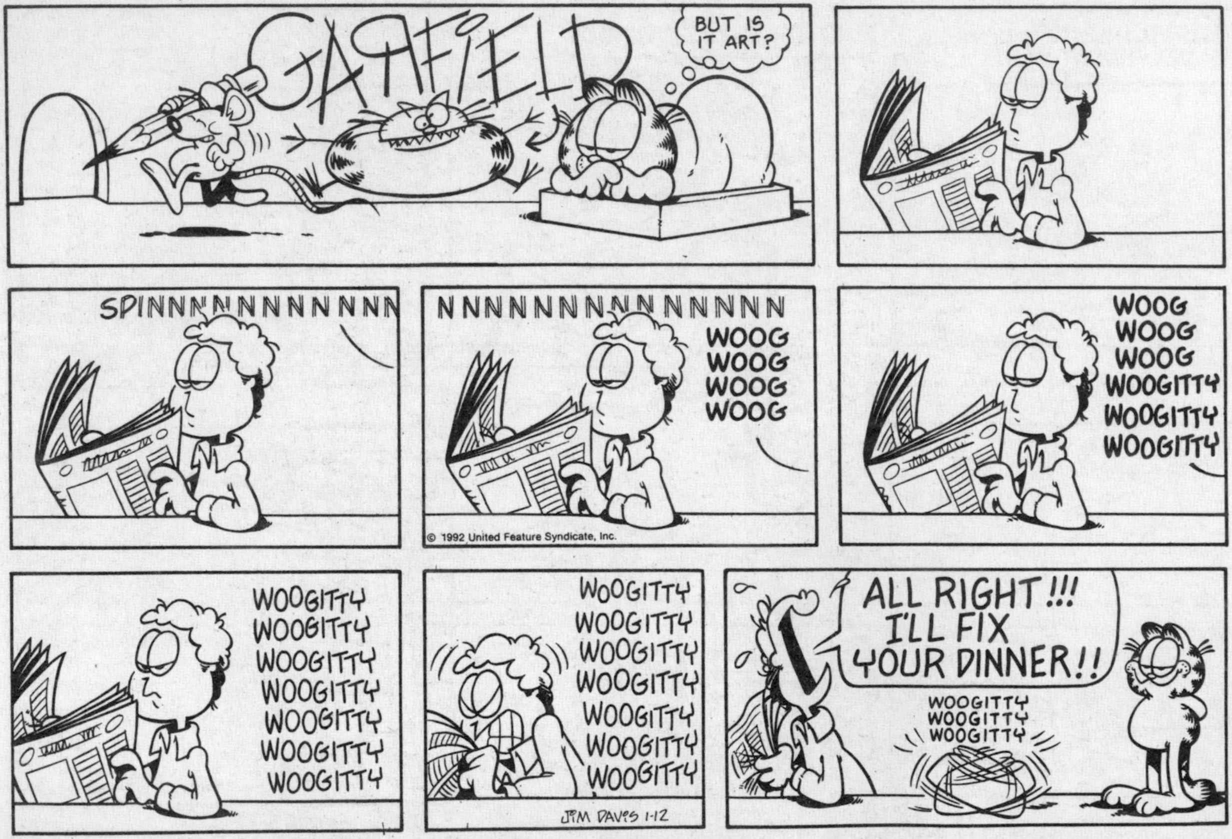
GARFIELD
BUT IS IT ART?
SPINNNNNNNNNNNNN
NNNNNNNNNNNNNNN
WOOG WOOG WOOG WOOG
WOOG WOOG WOOG WOOGITTY WOOGITTY WOOGITTY
© 1992 United Feature Syndicate, Inc.
WOOGITTY WOOGITTY WOOGITTY WOOGITTY WOOGITTY WOOGITTY WOOGITTY
WOOGITTY WOOGITTY WOOGITTY WOOGITTY WOOGITTY WOOGITTY WOOGITTY
JIM DAVIS 1-12
ALL RIGHT!!! I'LL FIX YOUR DINNER!!
WOOGITTY WOOGITTY WOOGITTY

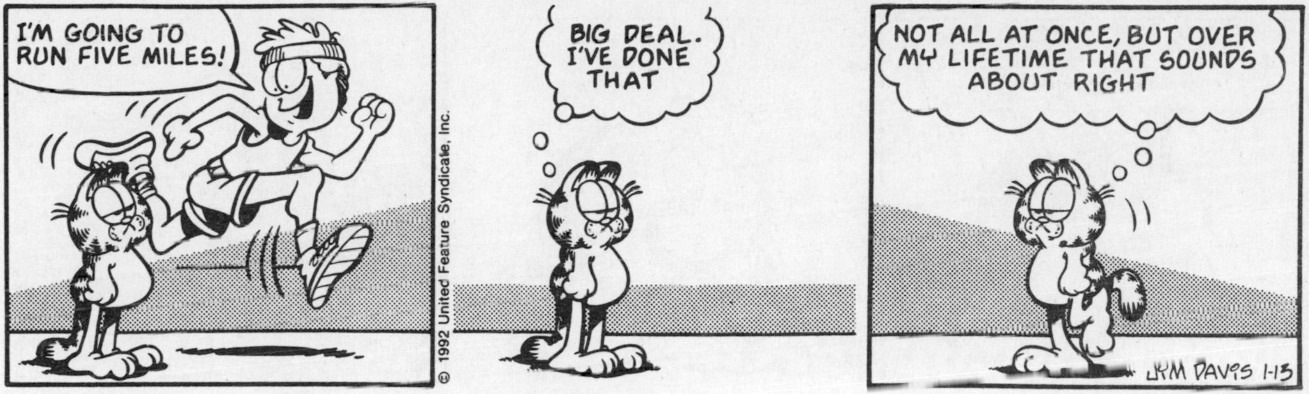
I'M GOING TO RUN FIVE MILES!
BIG DEAL. I'VE DONE THAT
NOT ALL AT ONCE, BUT OVER MY LIFETIME THAT SOUNDS ABOUT RIGHT
JIM DAVIS 1-13

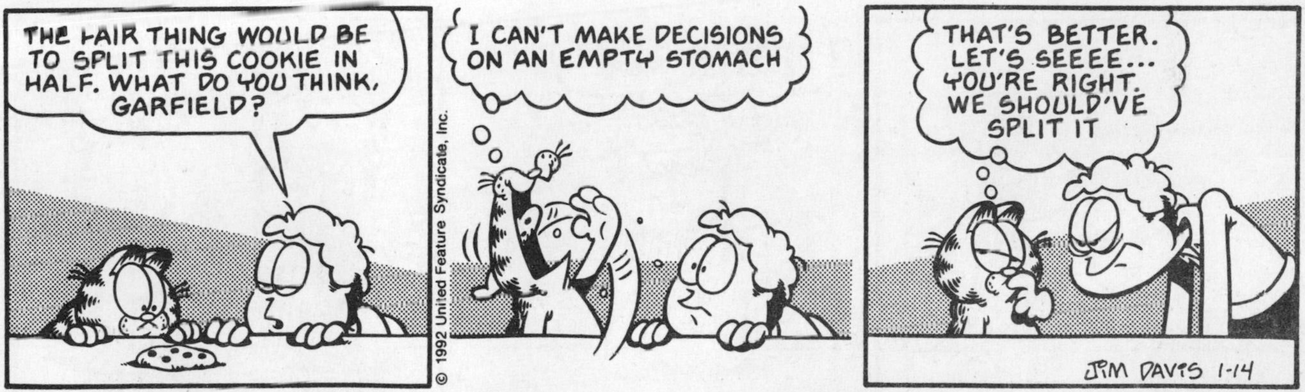
THE FAIR THING WOULD BE TO SPLIT THIS COOKIE IN HALF. WHAT DO YOU THINK, GARFIELD?
I CAN'T MAKE DECISIONS ON AN EMPTY STOMACH
THAT'S BETTER. LET'S SEEEE... YOU'RE RIGHT. WE SHOULD'VE SPLIT IT
JIM DAVIS 1-14

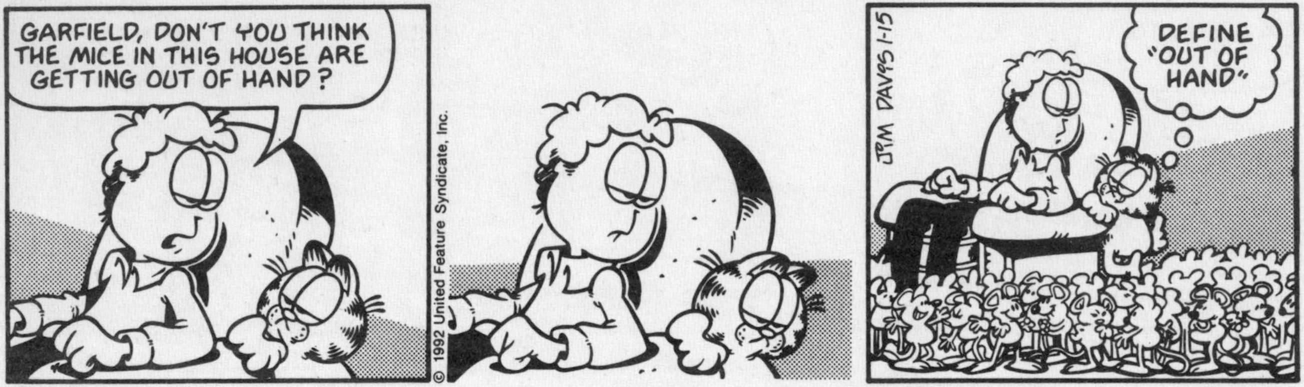
GARFIELD, DON'T YOU THINK THE MICE IN THIS HOUSE ARE GETTING OUT OF HAND?
© 1992 United Feature Syndicate, Inc.
JIM DAVIS 1-15
DEFINE "OUT OF HAND"

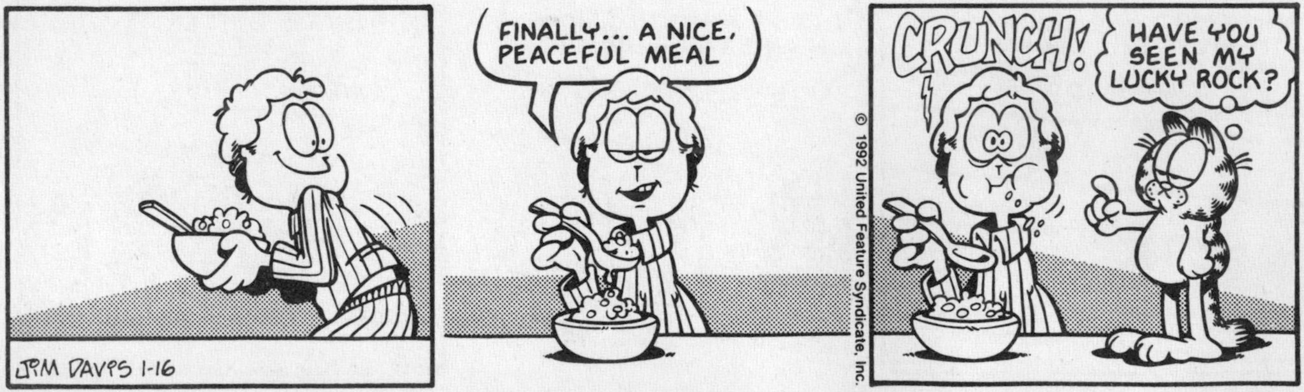
JIM DAVIS 1-16
FINALLY... A NICE, PEACEFUL MEAL
© 1992 United Feature Syndicate, Inc.
CRUNCH!
HAVE YOU SEEN MY LUCKY ROCK?

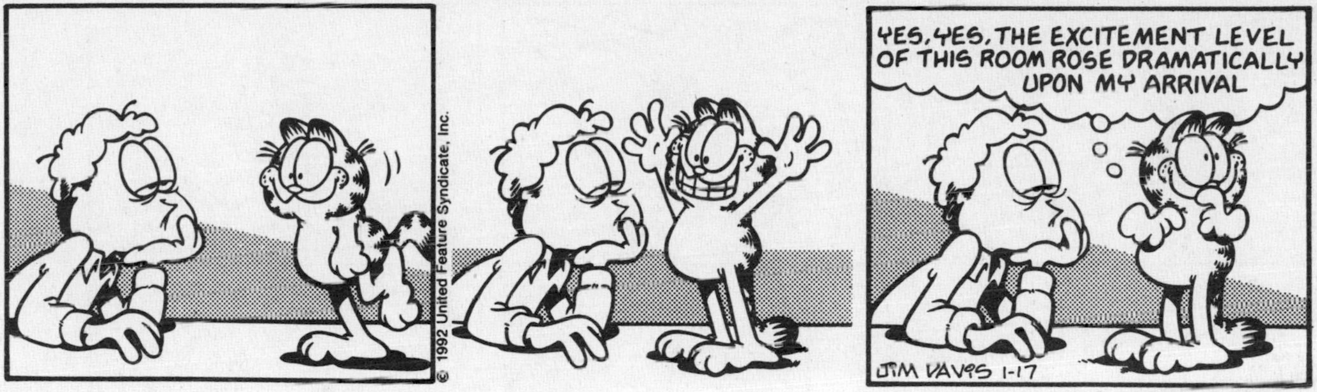
© 1992 United Feature Syndicate, Inc.
YES, YES, THE EXCITEMENT LEVEL OF THIS ROOM ROSE DRAMATICALLY UPON MY ARRIVAL
JIM DAVIS 1-17

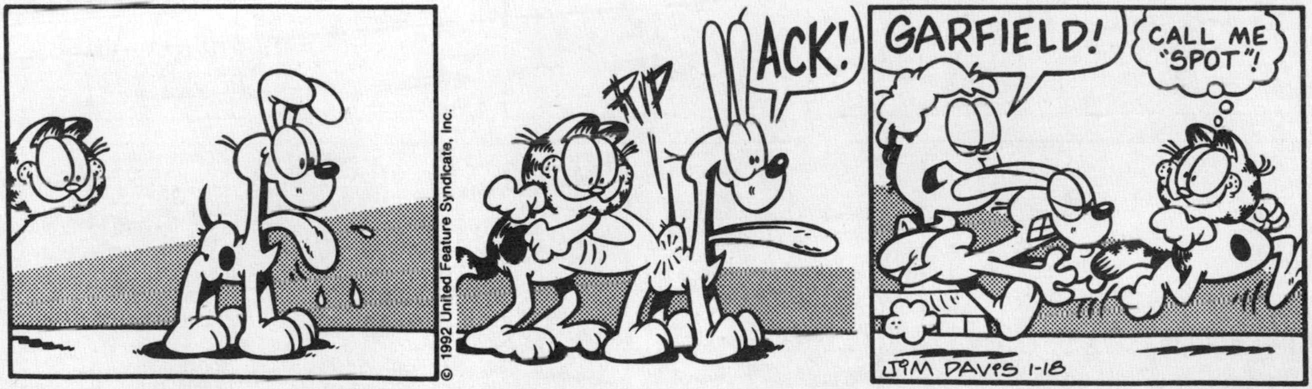
© 1992 United Feature Syndicate, Inc.
RIP
ACK!
GARFIELD!
CALL ME "SPOT"!
JIM DAVIS 1-18

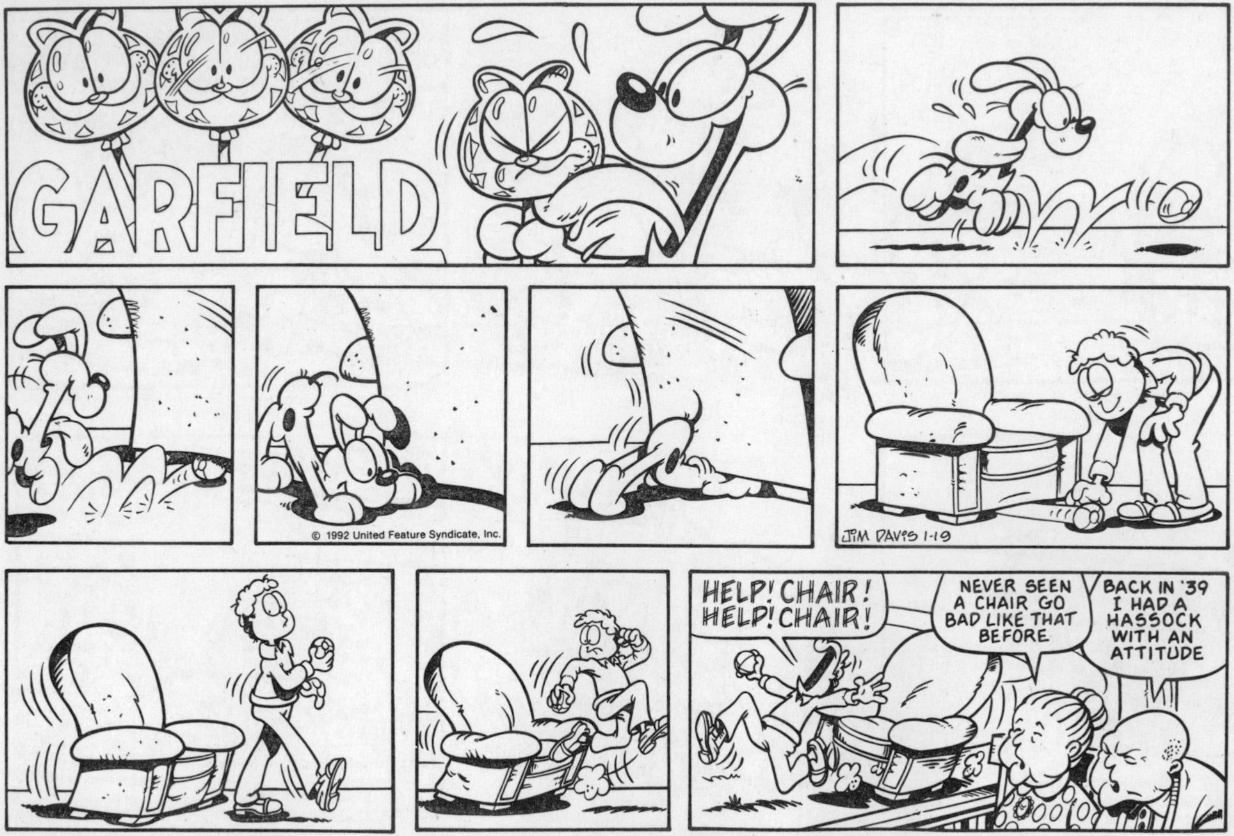

GARFIELD
© 1992 United Feature Syndicate, Inc.
JIM DAVIS 1-19
HELP! CHAIR! HELP! CHAIR!
NEVER SEEN A CHAIR GO BAD LIKE THAT BEFORE
BACK IN '39 I HAD A HASSOCK WITH AN ATTITUDE

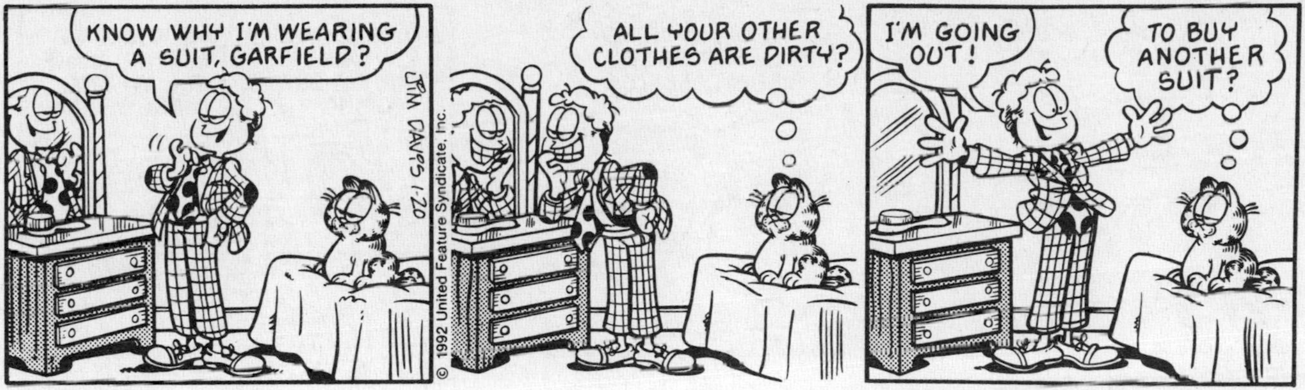
KNOW WHY I'M WEARING A SUIT, GARFIELD?
JIM DAVIS 1-20
© 1992 United Feature Syndicate, Inc.
ALL YOUR OTHER CLOTHES ARE DIRTY?
I'M GOING OUT!
TO BUY ANOTHER SUIT?

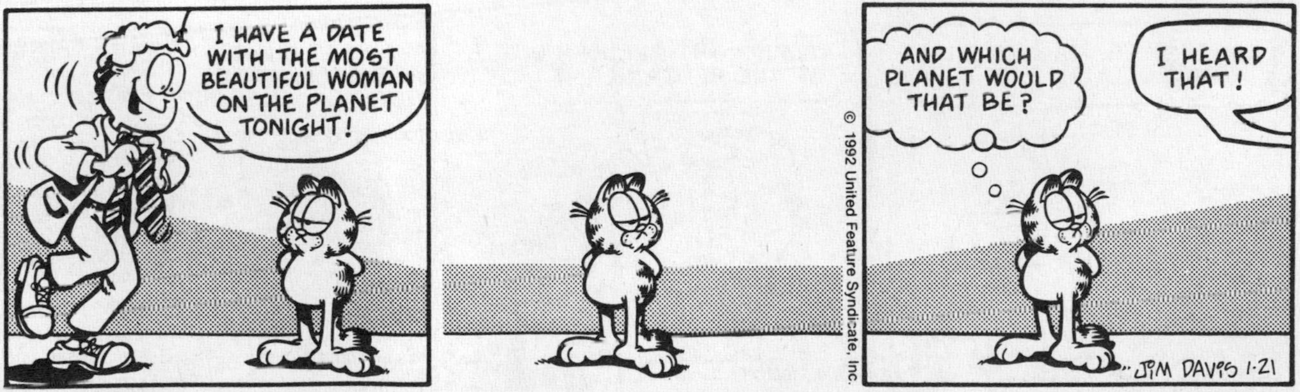
I HAVE A DATE WITH THE MOST BEAUTIFUL WOMAN ON THE PLANET TONIGHT!
© 1992 United Feature Syndicate, Inc.
AND WHICH PLANET WOULD THAT BE?
I HEARD THAT!
JIM DAVIS 1-21

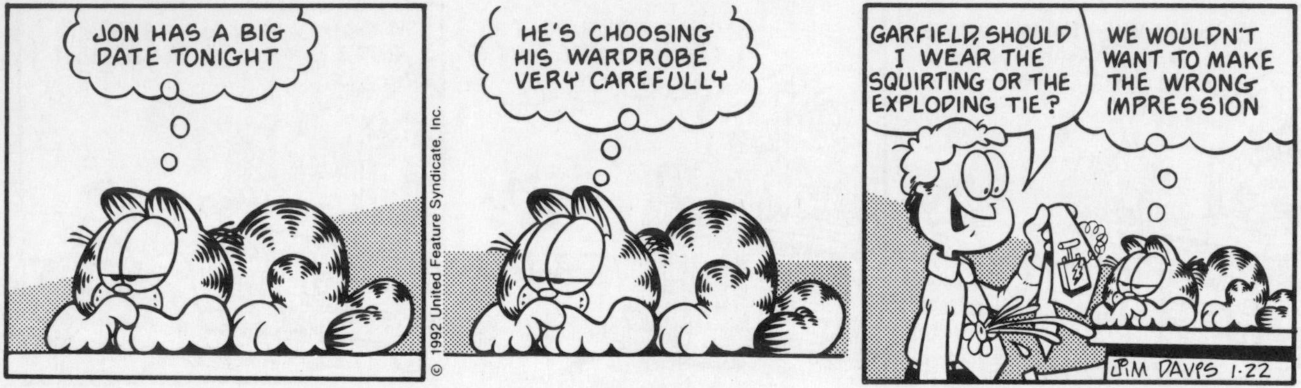
JON HAS A BIG DATE TONIGHT
HE'S CHOOSING HIS WARDROBE VERY CAREFULLY
GARFIELD, SHOULD I WEAR THE SQUIRTING OR THE EXPLODING TIE?
WE WOULDN'T WANT TO MAKE THE WRONG IMPRESSION
© 1992 United Feature Syndicate, Inc.
JIM DAVIS 1-22

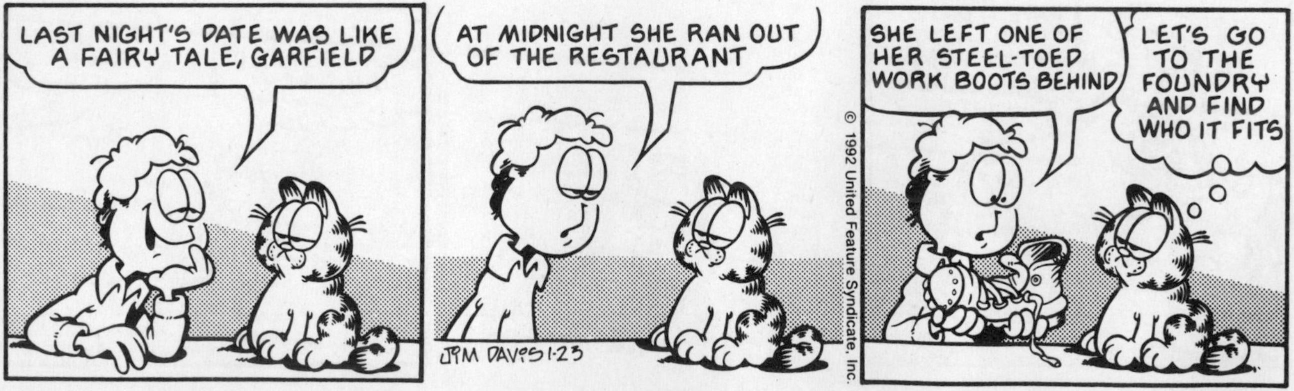
LAST NIGHT'S DATE WAS LIKE A FAIRY TALE, GARFIELD
AT MIDNIGHT SHE RAN OUT OF THE RESTAURANT
SHE LEFT ONE OF HER STEEL-TOED WORK BOOTS BEHIND
LET'S GO TO THE FOUNDRY AND FIND WHO IT FITS
© 1992 United Feature Syndicate, Inc.
JIM DAVIS 1-23

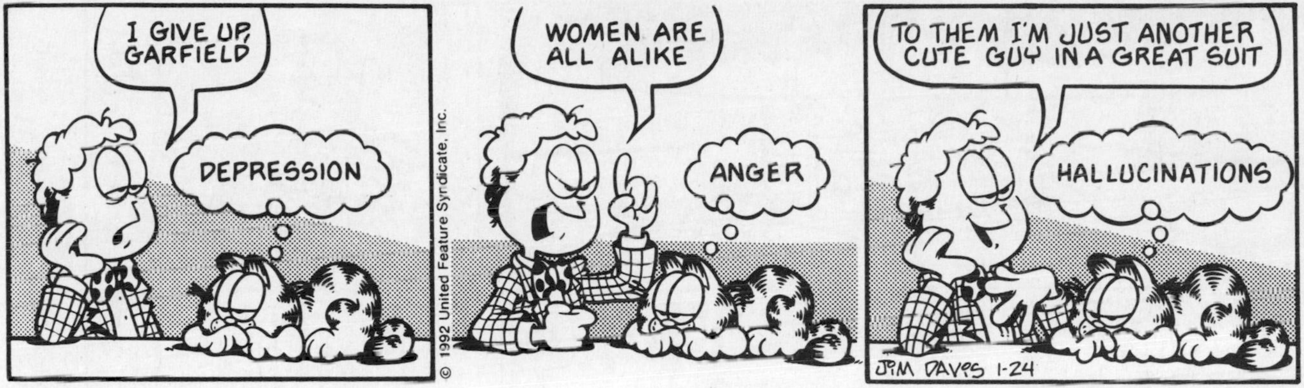
I GIVE UP, GARFIELD
DEPRESSION
WOMEN ARE ALL ALIKE
ANGER
TO THEM I'M JUST ANOTHER CUTE GUY IN A GREAT SUIT
HALLUCINATIONS
© 1992 United Feature Syndicate, Inc.
JIM DAVIS 1-24

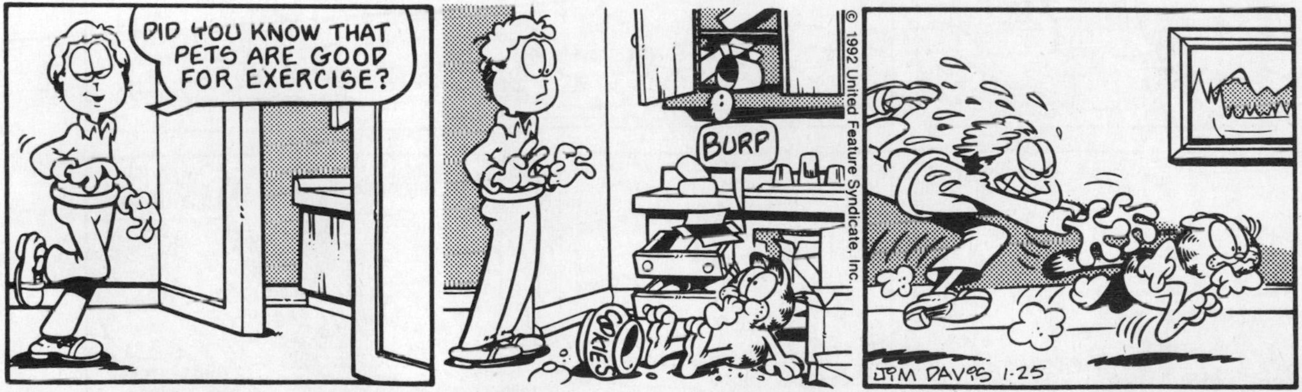
DID YOU KNOW THAT PETS ARE GOOD FOR EXERCISE?
BURP
COOKIES
© 1992 United Feature Syndicate, Inc.
JIM DAVIS 1-25

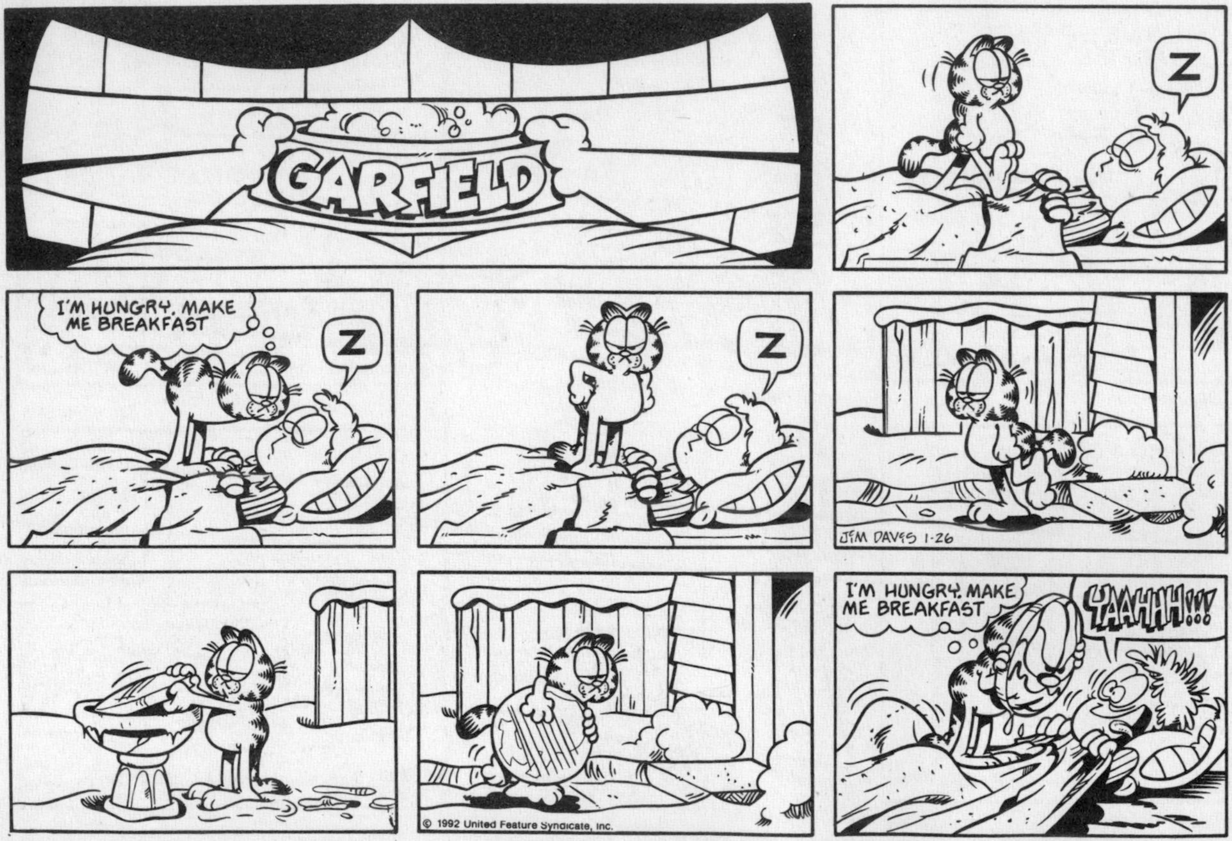
GARFIELD
Z
I'M HUNGRY. MAKE ME BREAKFAST
Z
Z
JIM DAVIS 1-26
© 1992 United Feature Syndicate, Inc.
I'M HUNGRY. MAKE ME BREAKFAST
YAAHHH!!!

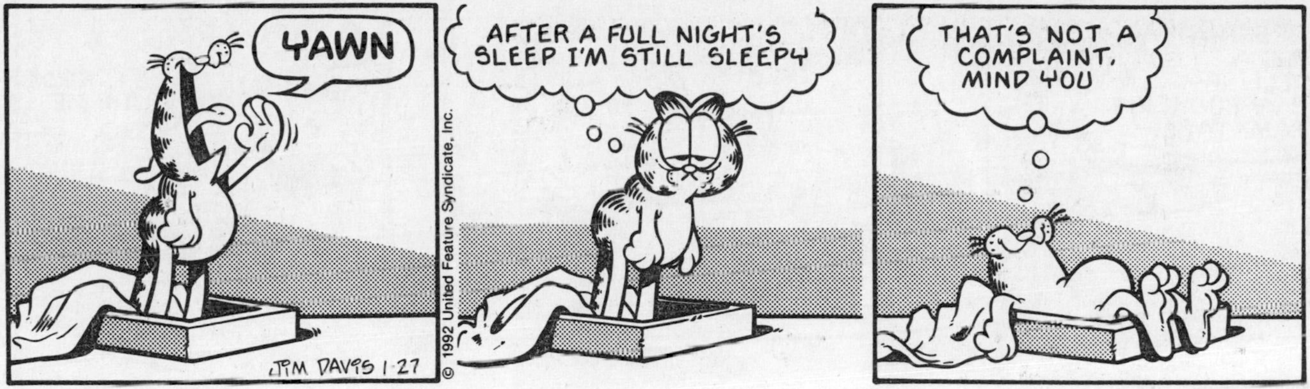
YAWN
JIM DAVIS 1-27
© 1992 United Feature Syndicate, Inc.
AFTER A FULL NIGHT'S SLEEP I'M STILL SLEEPY
THAT'S NOT A COMPLAINT, MIND YOU

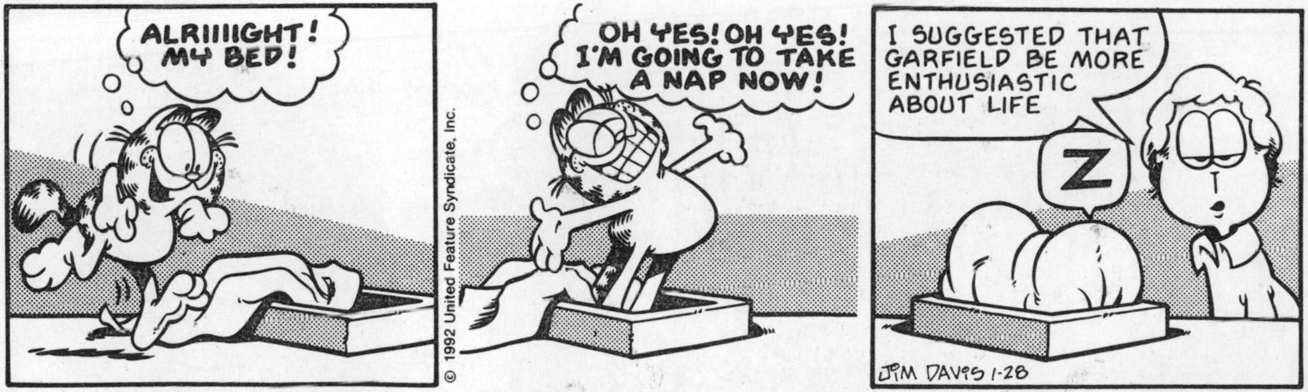
ALRIIIIGHT! MY BED!
© 1992 United Feature Syndicate, Inc.
OH YES! OH YES! I'M GOING TO TAKE A NAP NOW!
I SUGGESTED THAT GARFIELD BE MORE ENTHUSIASTIC ABOUT LIFE
Z
JIM DAVIS 1-28

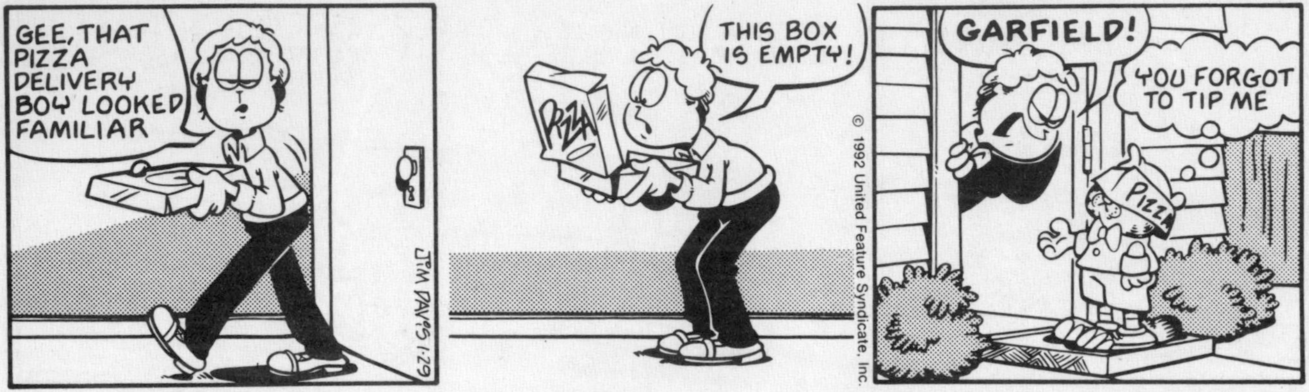
GEE, THAT PIZZA DELIVERY BOY LOOKED FAMILIAR
JIM DAVIS 1-29
THIS BOX IS EMPTY!
© 1992 United Feature Syndicate, Inc.
GARFIELD!
YOU FORGOT TO TIP ME
PIZZA

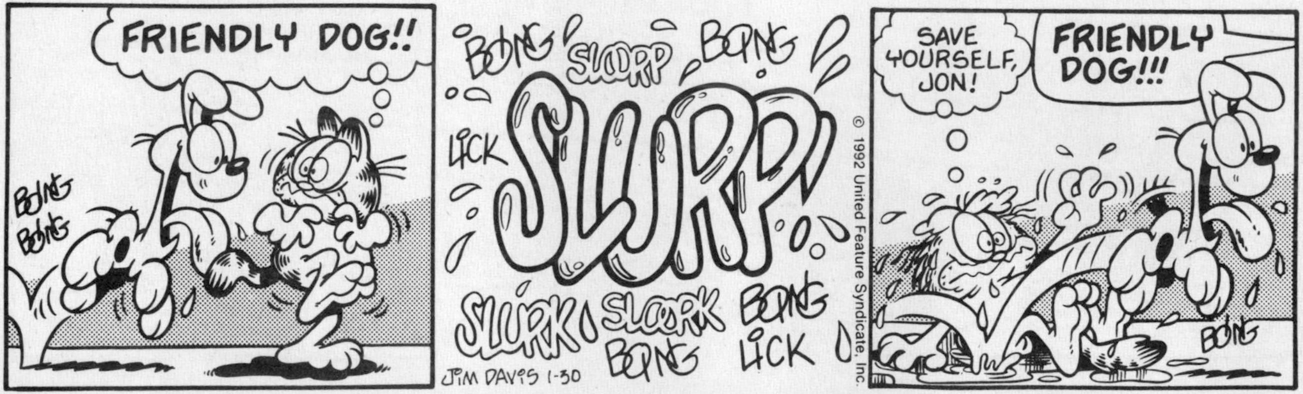
FRIENDLY DOG!!
BOING
BOING
BOING
SLOORP
BOING
LICK
SLURP!
SLURK
SLOORK
BOING
BOING
LICK
JIM DAVIS 1-30
© 1992 United Feature Syndicate, Inc.
SAVE YOURSELF, JON!
FRIENDLY DOG!!!
BOING

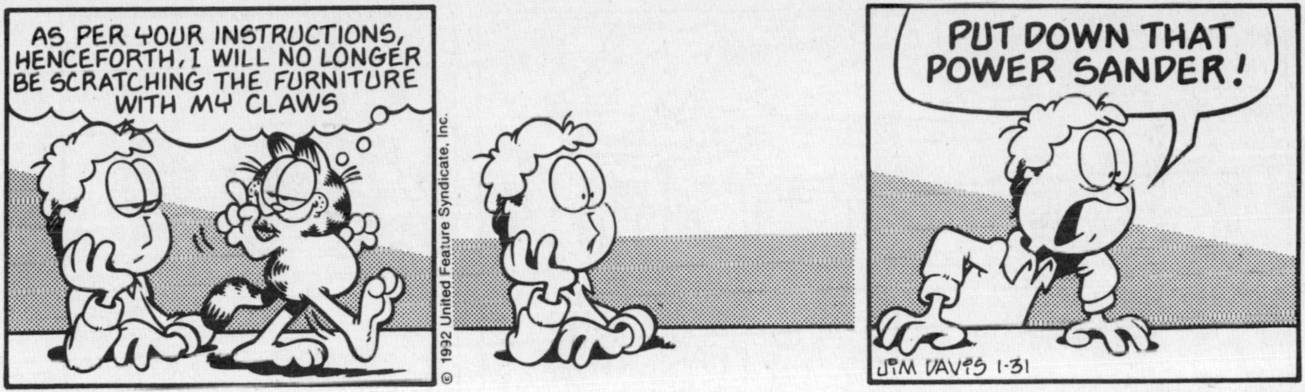
AS PER YOUR INSTRUCTIONS, HENCEFORTH, I WILL NO LONGER BE SCRATCHING THE FURNITURE WITH MY CLAWS
© 1992 United Feature Syndicate, Inc.
PUT DOWN THAT POWER SANDER!
JIM DAVIS 1-31

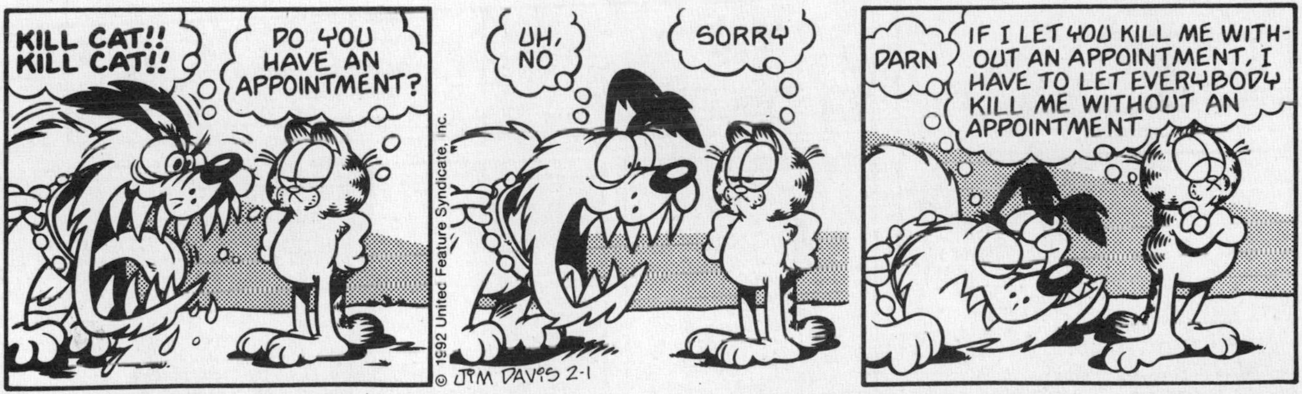
KILL CAT!! KILL CAT!!
DO YOU HAVE AN APPOINTMENT?
© 1992 United Feature Syndicate, Inc.
UH, NO
SORRY
JIM DAVIS 2-1
DARN
IF I LET YOU KILL ME WITHOUT AN APPOINTMENT, I HAVE TO LET EVERYBODY KILL ME WITHOUT AN APPOINTMENT

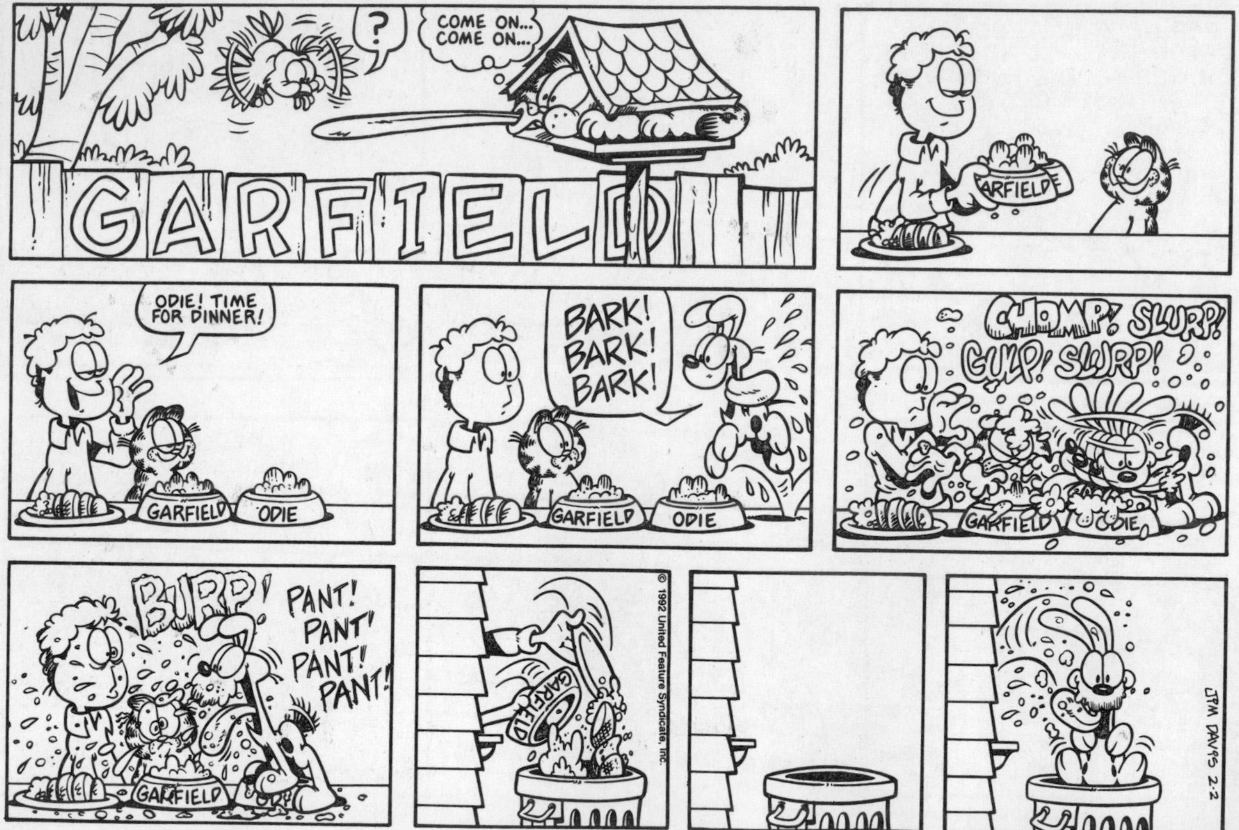

GARFIELD
?
COME ON... COME ON...
ODIE! TIME FOR DINNER!
GARFIELD
ODIE
BARK! BARK! BARK!
CHOMP! SLURP! GULP! SLURP!
BURP!
PANT! PANT! PANT! PANT!
© 1992 United Feature Syndicate, Inc.
JPM DAVIS 2-2

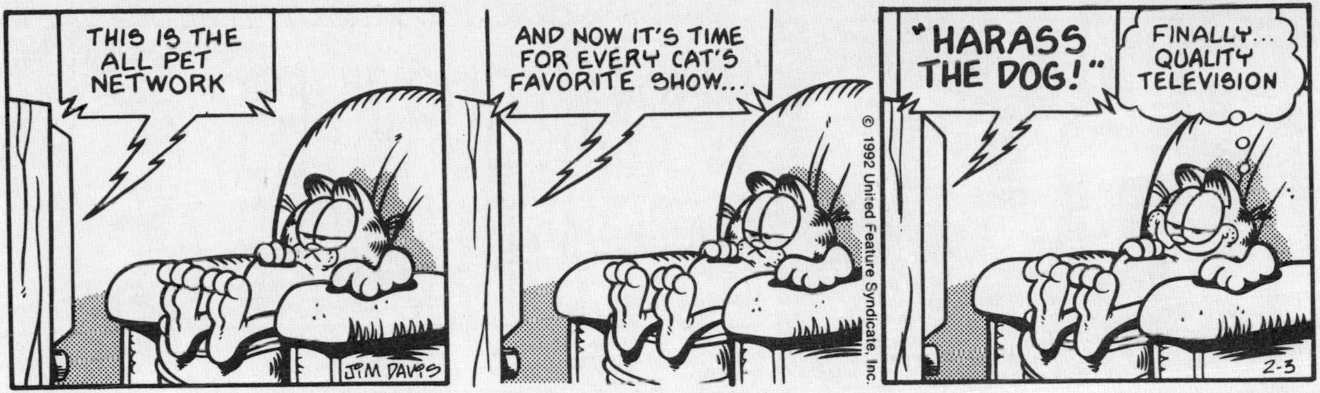
THIS IS THE ALL PET NETWORK
AND NOW IT'S TIME FOR EVERY CAT'S FAVORITE SHOW...
"HARASS THE DOG!"
FINALLY... QUALITY TELEVISION
JIM DAVIS
© 1992 United Feature Syndicate, Inc.
2-3

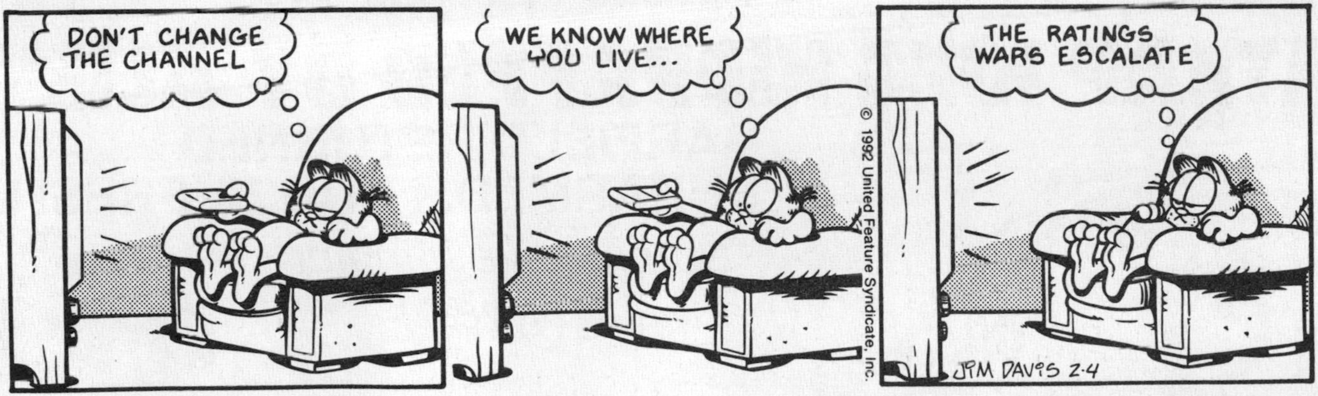
DON'T CHANGE THE CHANNEL
WE KNOW WHERE YOU LIVE...
THE RATINGS WARS ESCALATE
JIM DAVIS 2-4
© 1992 United Feature Syndicate, Inc.

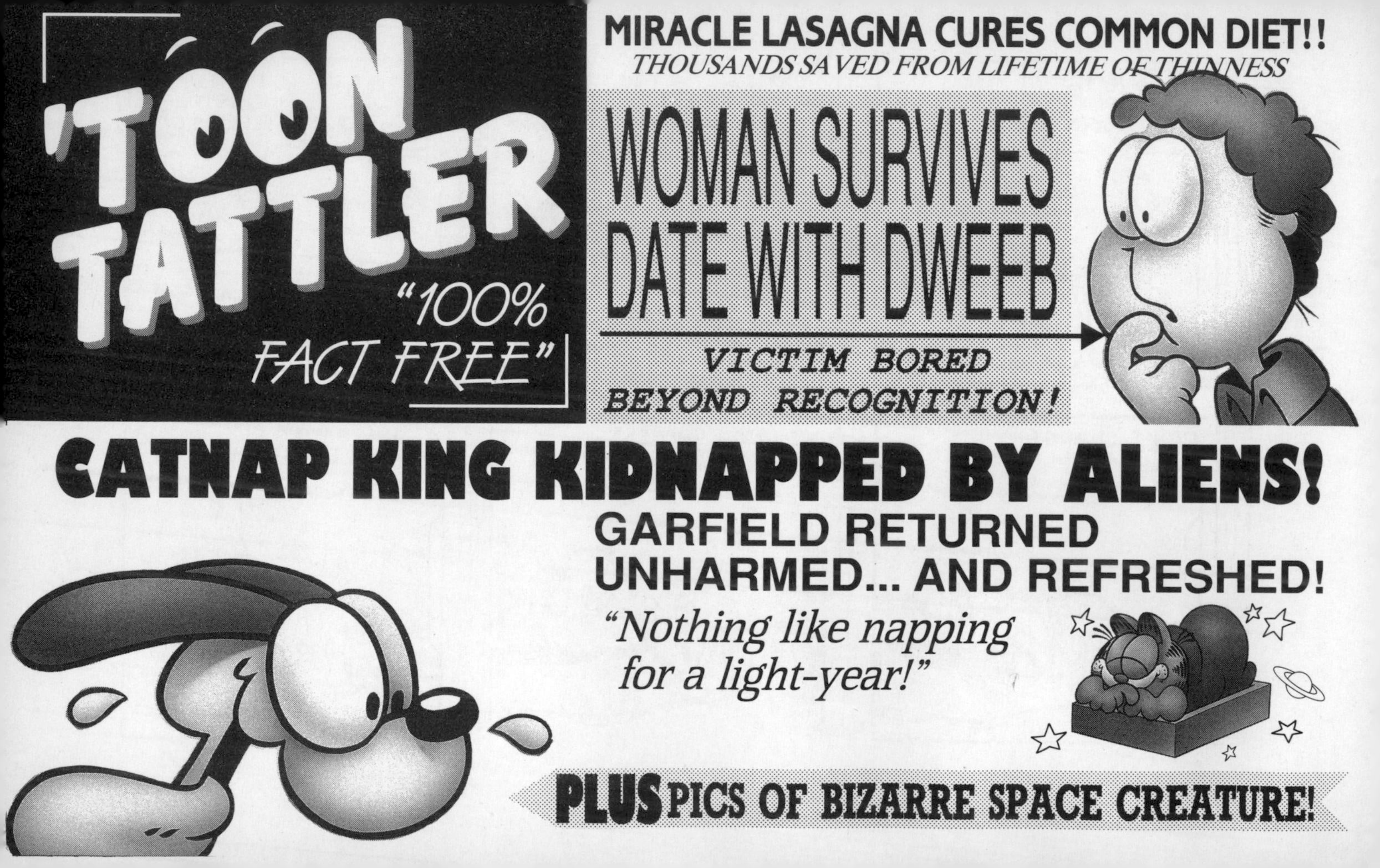
'TOON TATTLER
"100% FACT FREE"
MIRACLE LASAGNA CURES COMMON DIET!!
THOUSANDS SAVED FROM LIFETIME OF THINNESS
WOMAN SURVIVES DATE WITH DWEEB
VICTIM BORED BEYOND RECOGNITION!
CATNAP KING KIDNAPPED BY ALIENS!
GARFIELD RETURNED UNHARMED... AND REFRESHED!
"Nothing like napping for a light-year!"
PLUS PICS OF BIZARRE SPACE CREATURE!

Garfield
takes
his licks

BY: JIM DAVIS

TOP TEN REASONS TO OWN A CAT INSTEAD OF A DOG

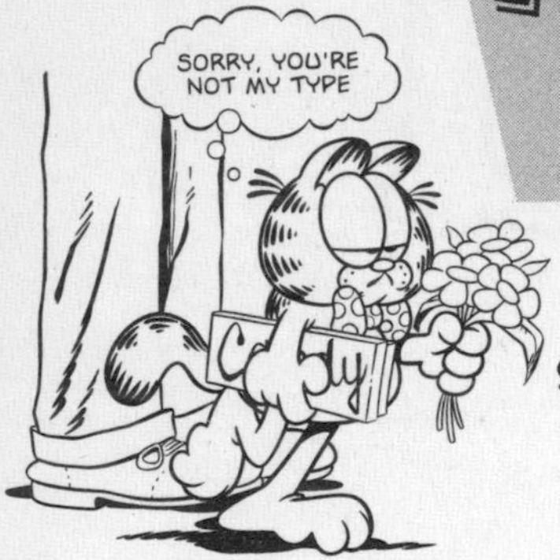
SORRY, YOU'RE NOT MY TYPE

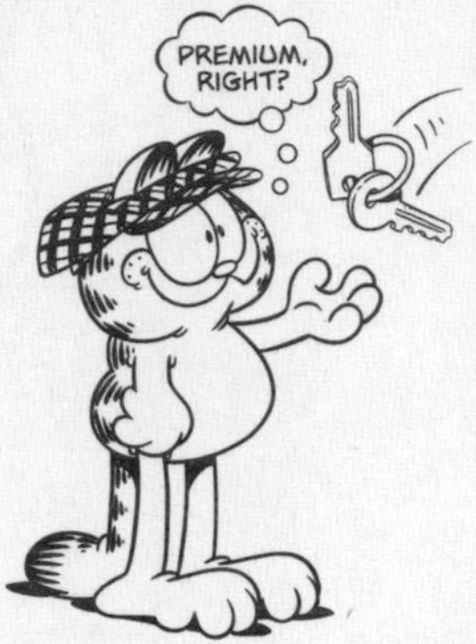
PREMIUM, RIGHT?

10. No need to drool-proof your home

9. Cat has absolutely no romantic interest in your leg

8. Nothing spooks a burglar like stepping on a cat

7. Dog breath actually killed a guy in Utah

6. Cat always returns your car with a full tank

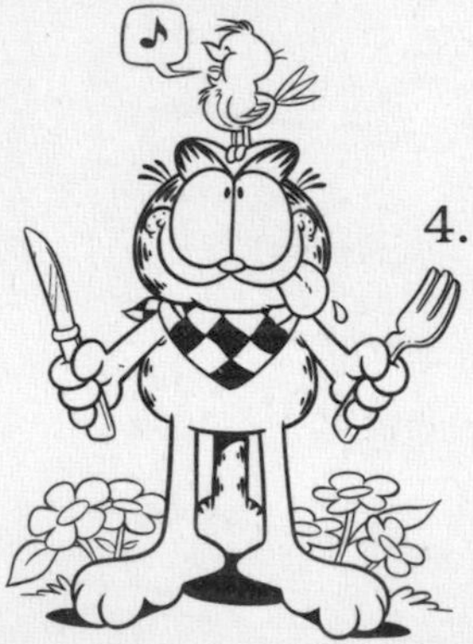

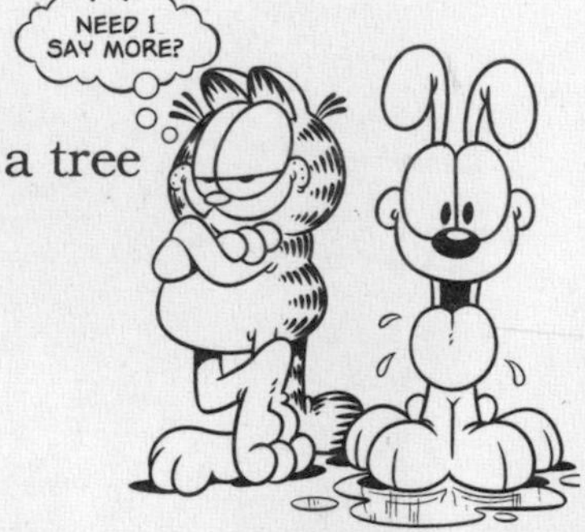
NEED I SAY MORE?

5. Cat will keep yard free of pesky songbirds

4. Cat won't drag you out into blizzard just to piddle on a tree

3. Ever seen **Cujo**?

2. Dogs... Fetch, roll over, sit up and beg;
Cats... Drive, balance checkbook, give CPR

1. Garfield. Odie. Case closed

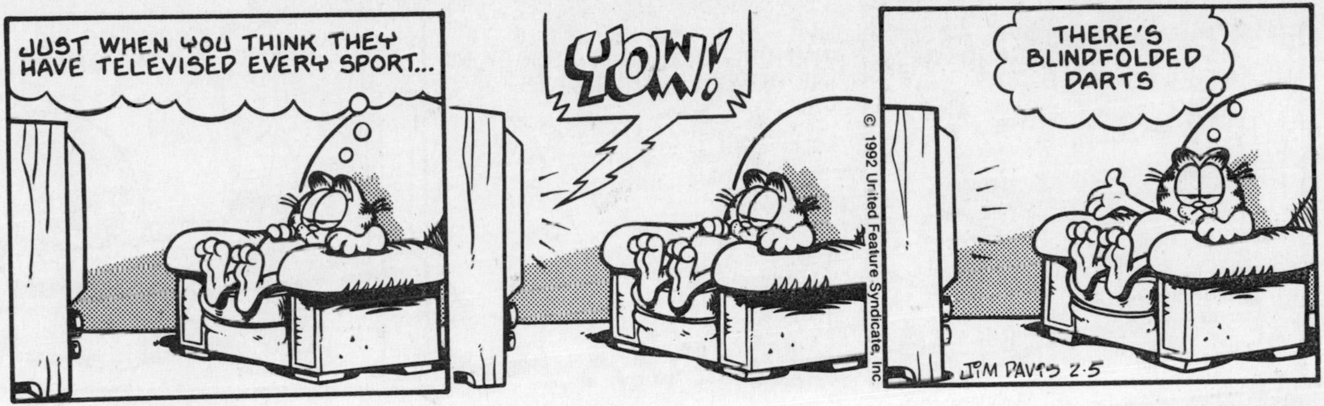
JUST WHEN YOU THINK THEY HAVE TELEVISED EVERY SPORT...
YOW!
© 1992 United Feature Syndicate, Inc.
THERE'S BLINDFOLDED DARTS
JIM DAVIS 2·5

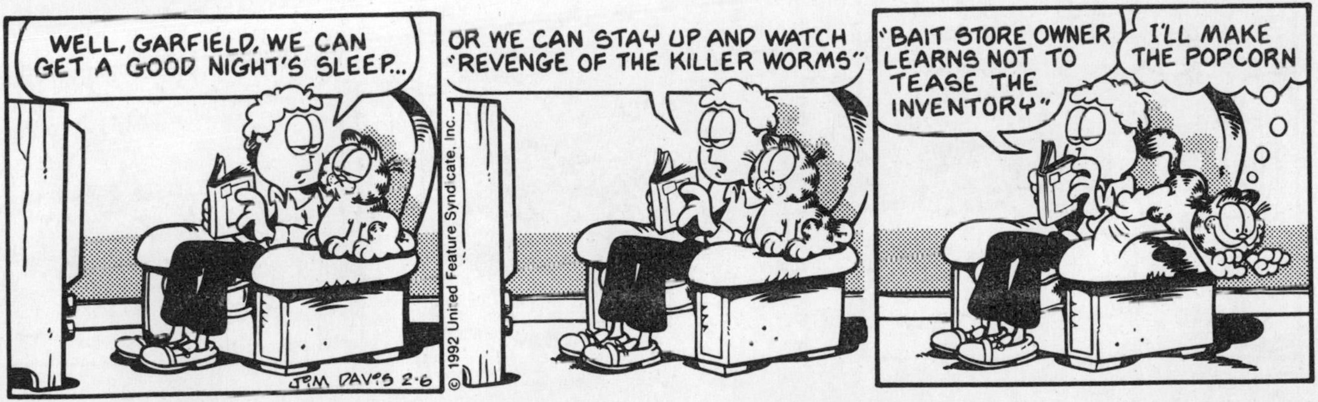
WELL, GARFIELD, WE CAN GET A GOOD NIGHT'S SLEEP...
JIM DAVIS 2·6
© 1992 United Feature Syndicate, Inc.
OR WE CAN STAY UP AND WATCH "REVENGE OF THE KILLER WORMS"
"BAIT STORE OWNER LEARNS NOT TO TEASE THE INVENTORY"
I'LL MAKE THE POPCORN

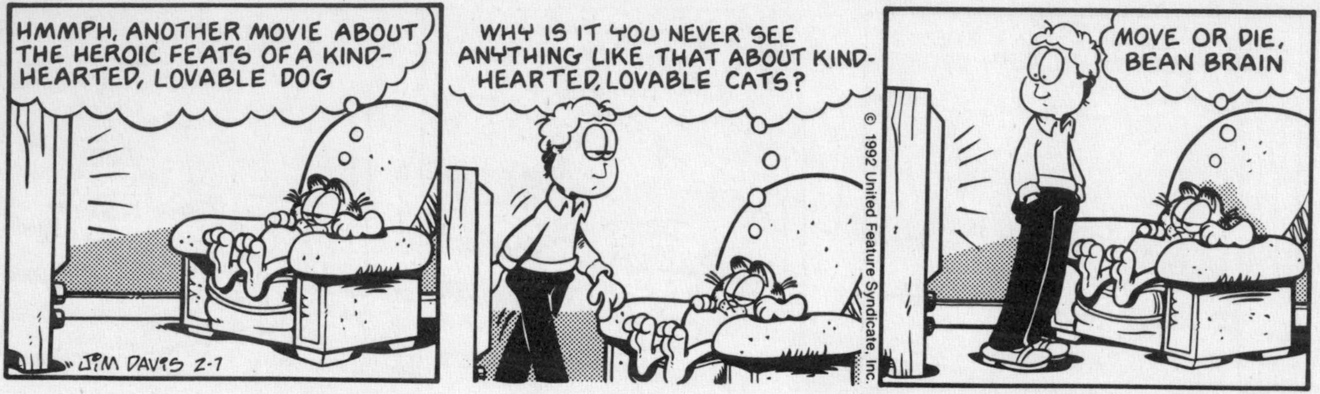
HMMPH, ANOTHER MOVIE ABOUT THE HEROIC FEATS OF A KIND-HEARTED, LOVABLE DOG
JIM DAVIS 2-7
WHY IS IT YOU NEVER SEE ANYTHING LIKE THAT ABOUT KIND-HEARTED, LOVABLE CATS?
© 1992 United Feature Syndicate, Inc.
MOVE OR DIE, BEAN BRAIN

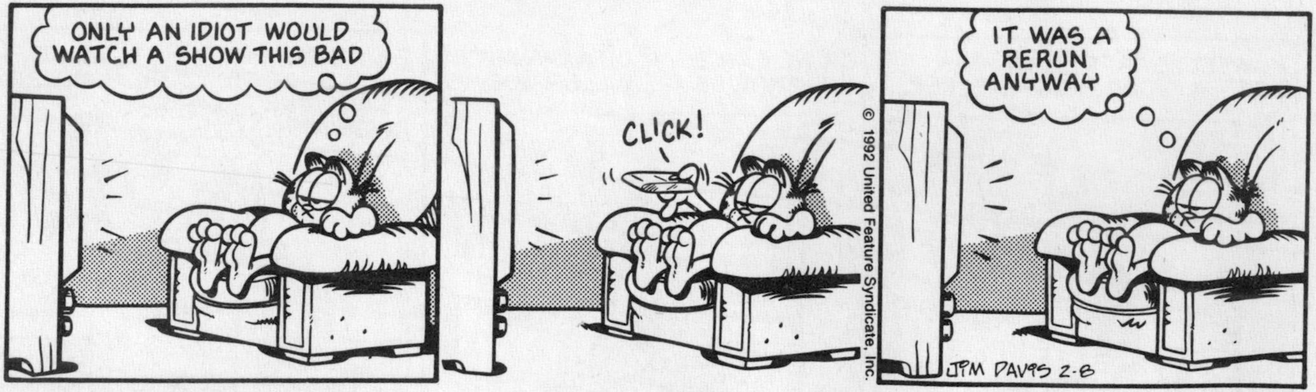
ONLY AN IDIOT WOULD WATCH A SHOW THIS BAD
CLICK!
© 1992 United Feature Syndicate, Inc.
IT WAS A RERUN ANYWAY
JIM DAVIS 2-8

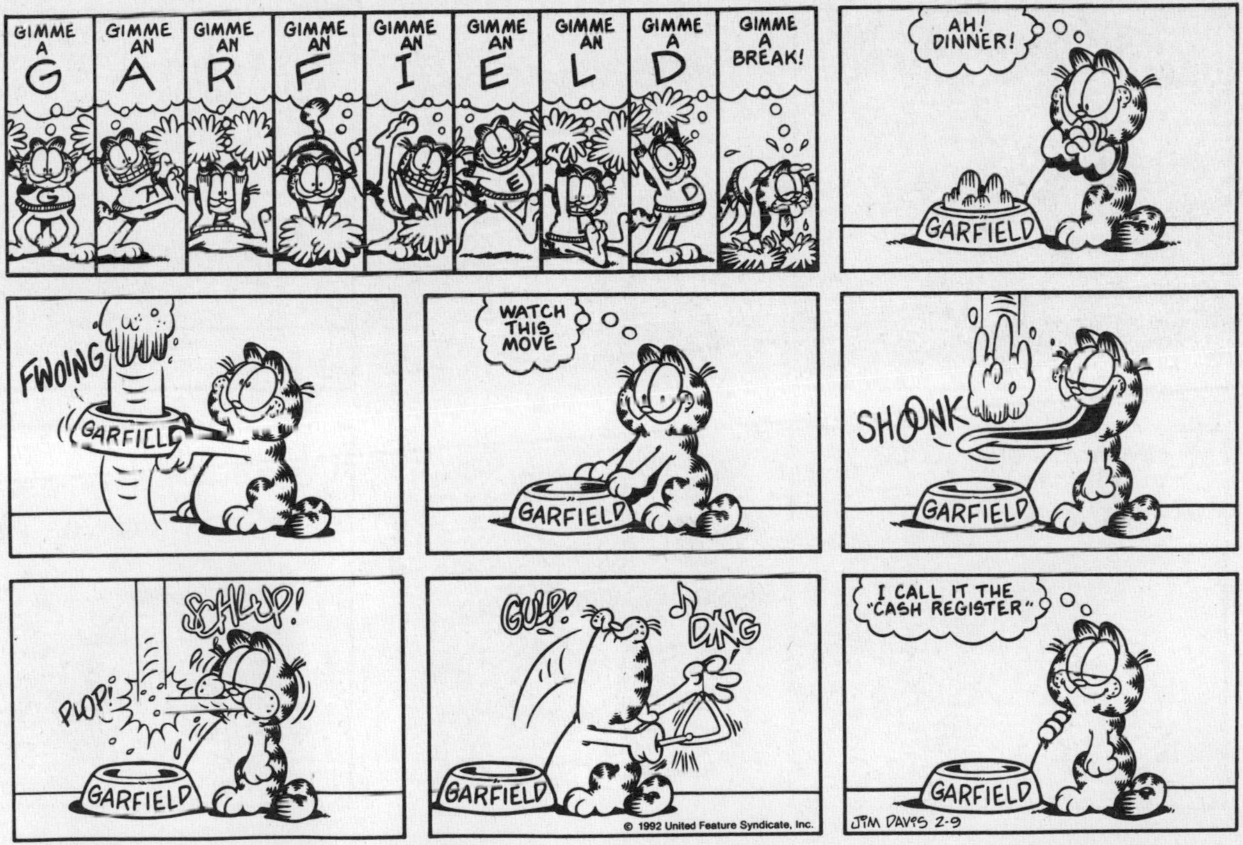
GIMME A G
GIMME AN A
GIMME AN R
GIMME AN F
GIMME AN I
GIMME AN E
GIMME AN L
GIMME A D
GIMME A BREAK!
AH! DINNER!
FWOING
WATCH THIS MOVE
SHOONK
SCHLUP!
PLOP!
GULP!
DING
I CALL IT THE "CASH REGISTER"
GARFIELD
© 1992 United Feature Syndicate, Inc.
JIM DAVIS 2-9

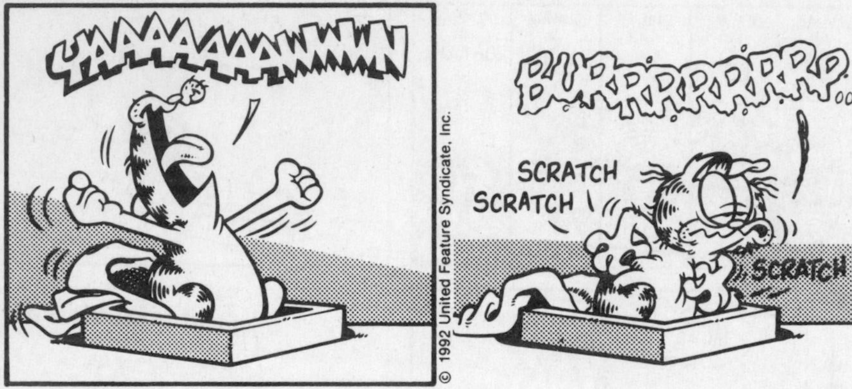
YAAAAAAAWWWN
© 1992 United Feature Syndicate, Inc.
BURRRRRRRRP...
SCRATCH
SCRATCH
SCRATCH
HAAAACK
KOFF
KOFF
KOFF
CATS SAY THE CUTEST THINGS
JIM DAVIS 2-10

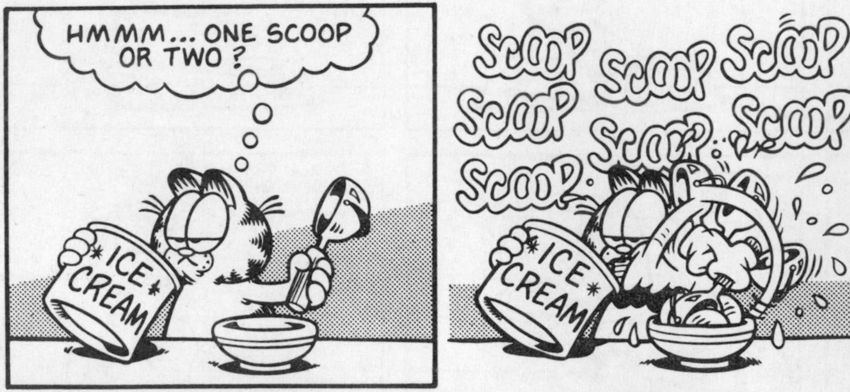
HMMM... ONE SCOOP OR TWO ?
ICE CREAM
SCOOP SCOOP SCOOP
SCOOP SCOOP SCOOP
SCOOP
© 1992 United Feature Syndicate, Inc.
I'LL LEAVE **ONE** SCOOP
JIM DAVIS 2-11

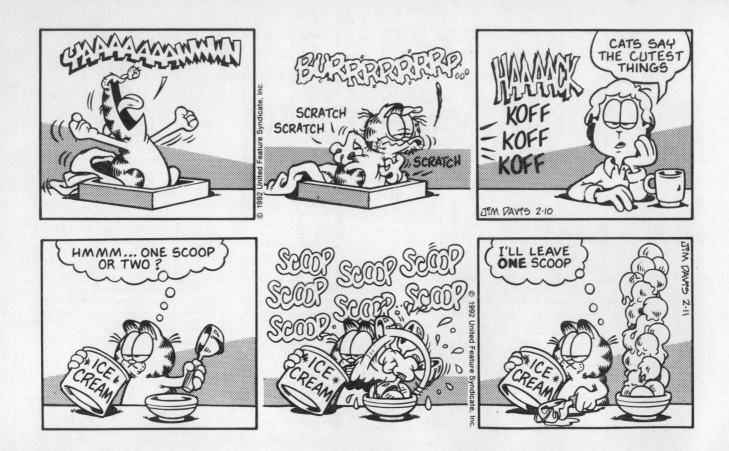

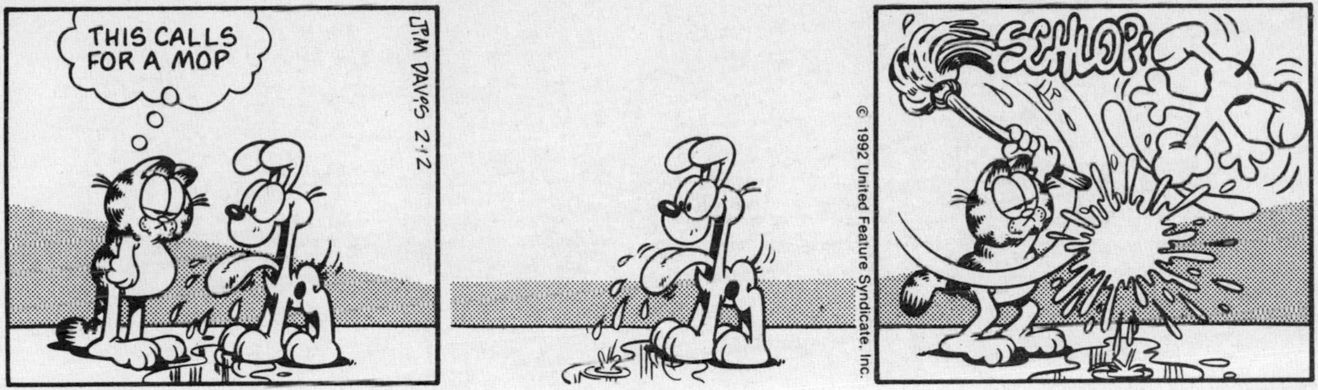
THIS CALLS FOR A MOP
JIM DAVIS 2-12
SCHLOP!
© 1992 United Feature Syndicate, Inc.

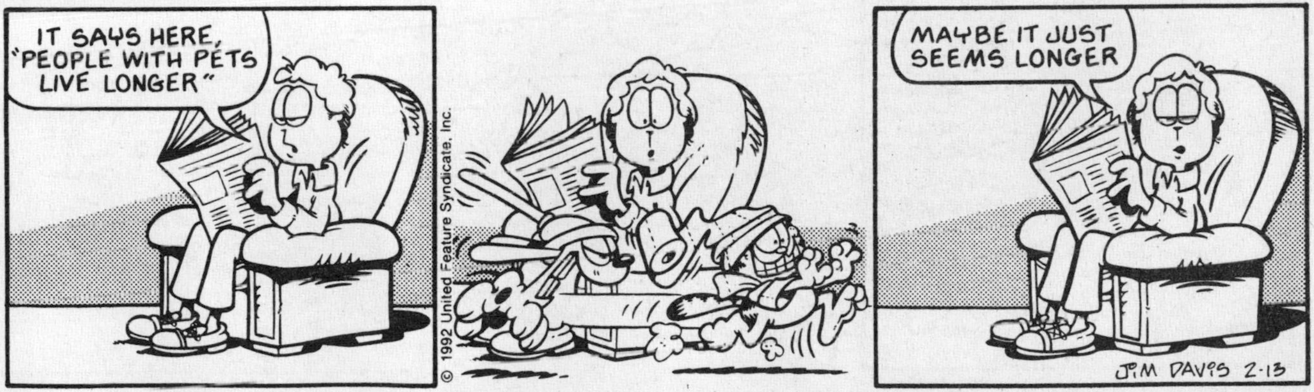
IT SAYS HERE, "PEOPLE WITH PETS LIVE LONGER"
© 1992 United Feature Syndicate, Inc.
MAYBE IT JUST SEEMS LONGER
JIM DAVIS 2-13

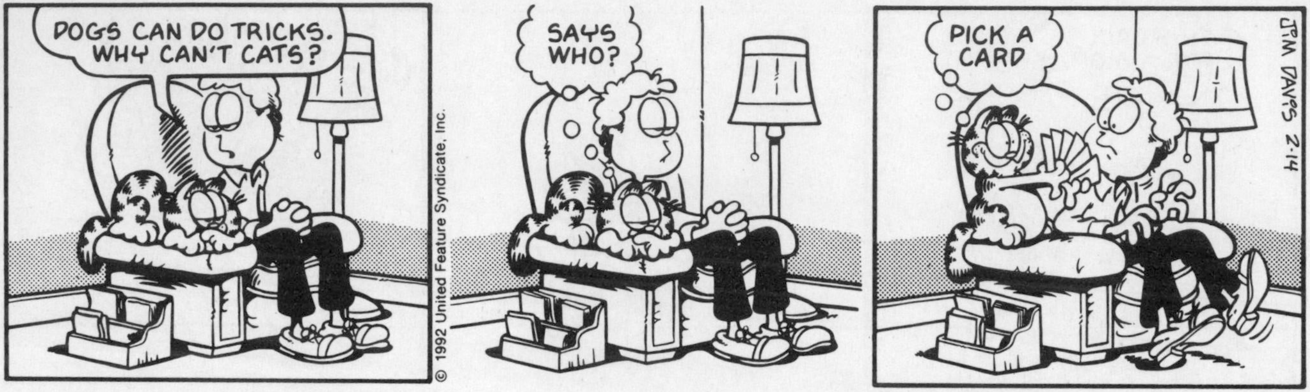
DOGS CAN DO TRICKS. WHY CAN'T CATS?
SAYS WHO?
PICK A CARD
JIM DAVIS 2-14
© 1992 United Feature Syndicate, Inc.

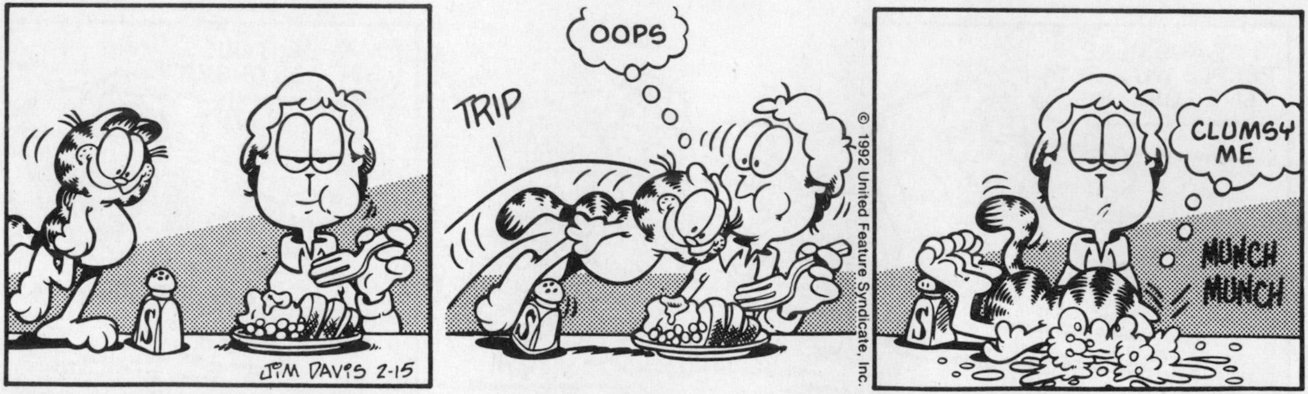
JIM DAVIS 2-15
TRIP
OOPS
CLUMSY ME
MUNCH MUNCH
© 1992 United Feature Syndicate, Inc.

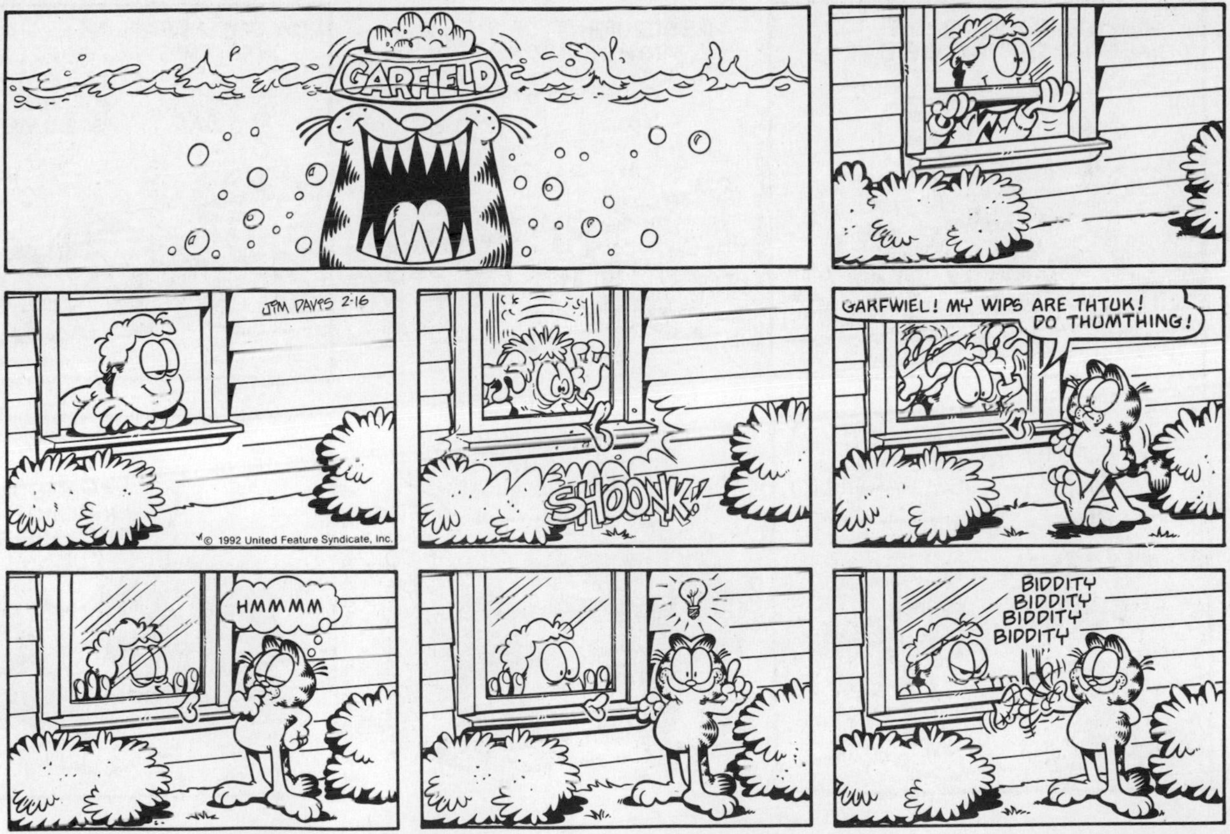
GARFIELD
JIM DAVIS 2·16
© 1992 United Feature Syndicate, Inc.
SHOONK!
GARFWIEL! MY WIPS ARE THTUK! DO THUMTHING!
HMMMM
BIDDITY
BIDDITY
BIDDITY
BIDDITY

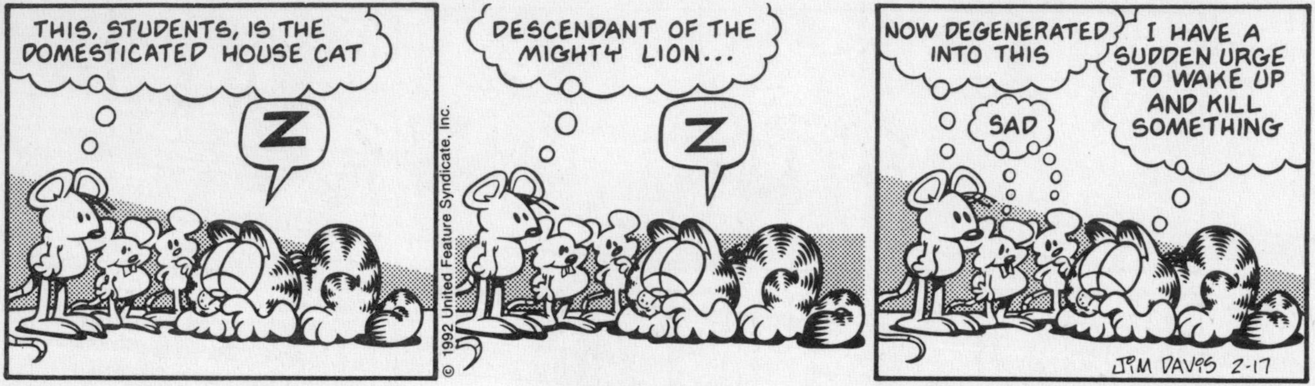
THIS, STUDENTS, IS THE DOMESTICATED HOUSE CAT
Z
DESCENDANT OF THE MIGHTY LION...
Z
NOW DEGENERATED INTO THIS
SAD
I HAVE A SUDDEN URGE TO WAKE UP AND KILL SOMETHING
JIM DAVIS 2-17
© 1992 United Feature Syndicate, Inc.

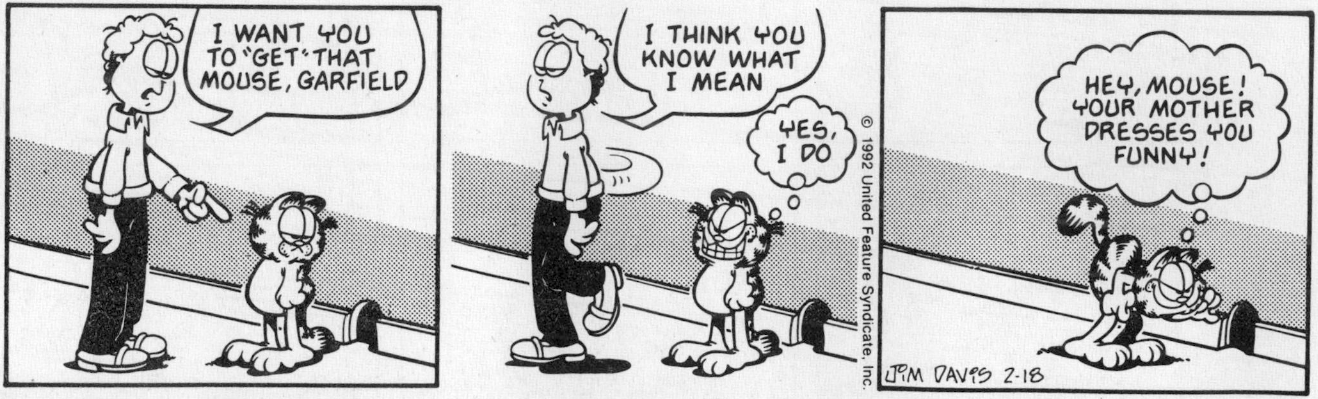
I WANT YOU TO "GET" THAT MOUSE, GARFIELD
I THINK YOU KNOW WHAT I MEAN
YES, I DO
HEY, MOUSE! YOUR MOTHER DRESSES YOU FUNNY!
JIM DAVIS 2-18
© 1992 United Feature Syndicate, Inc.

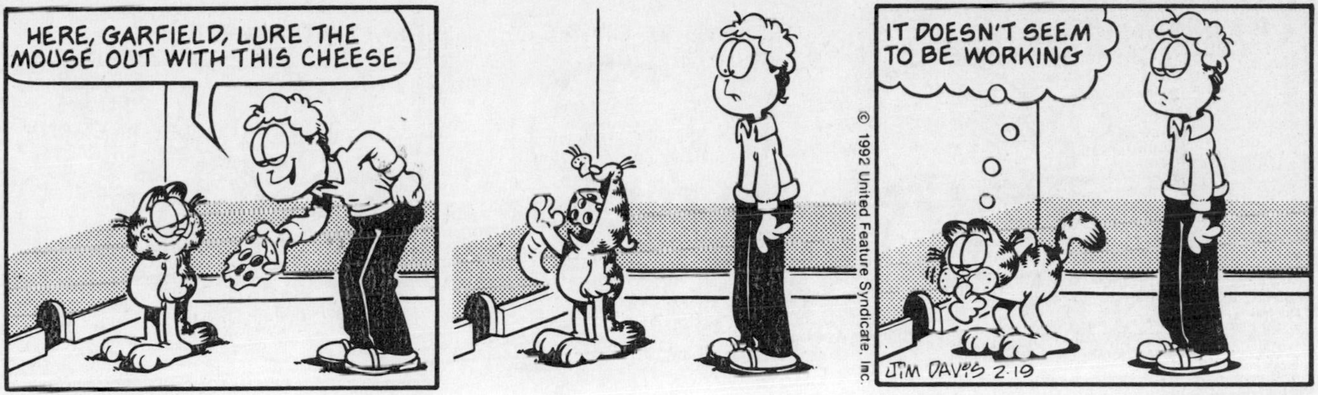
HERE, GARFIELD, LURE THE MOUSE OUT WITH THIS CHEESE
IT DOESN'T SEEM TO BE WORKING
© 1992 United Feature Syndicate, Inc.
JIM DAVIS 2-19

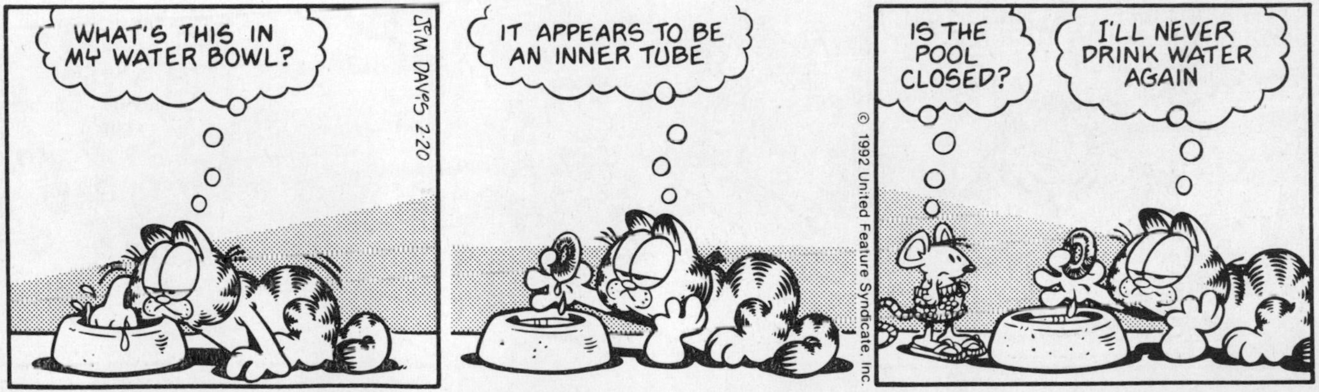
WHAT'S THIS IN MY WATER BOWL?
JIM DAVIS 2-20
IT APPEARS TO BE AN INNER TUBE
IS THE POOL CLOSED?
I'LL NEVER DRINK WATER AGAIN
© 1992 United Feature Syndicate, Inc.

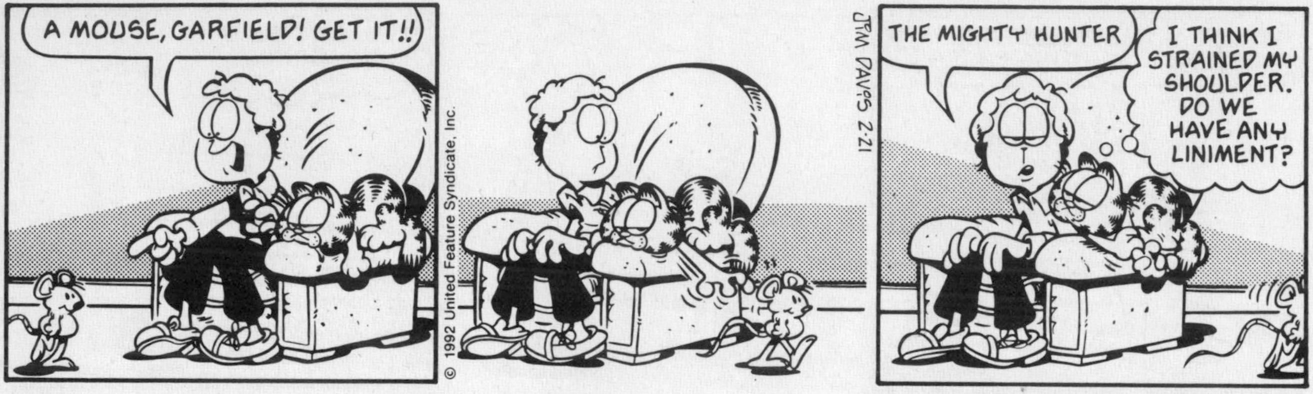
A MOUSE, GARFIELD! GET IT!!
THE MIGHTY HUNTER
I THINK I STRAINED MY SHOULDER. DO WE HAVE ANY LINIMENT?
JIM DAVIS 2·21
© 1992 United Feature Syndicate, Inc.

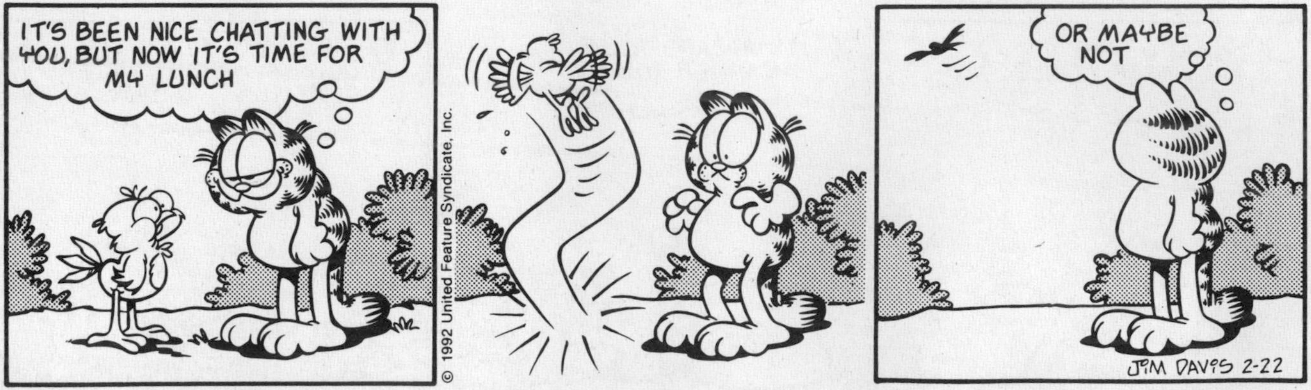
IT'S BEEN NICE CHATTING WITH YOU, BUT NOW IT'S TIME FOR MY LUNCH
OR MAYBE NOT
JIM DAVIS 2-22
© 1992 United Feature Syndicate, Inc.

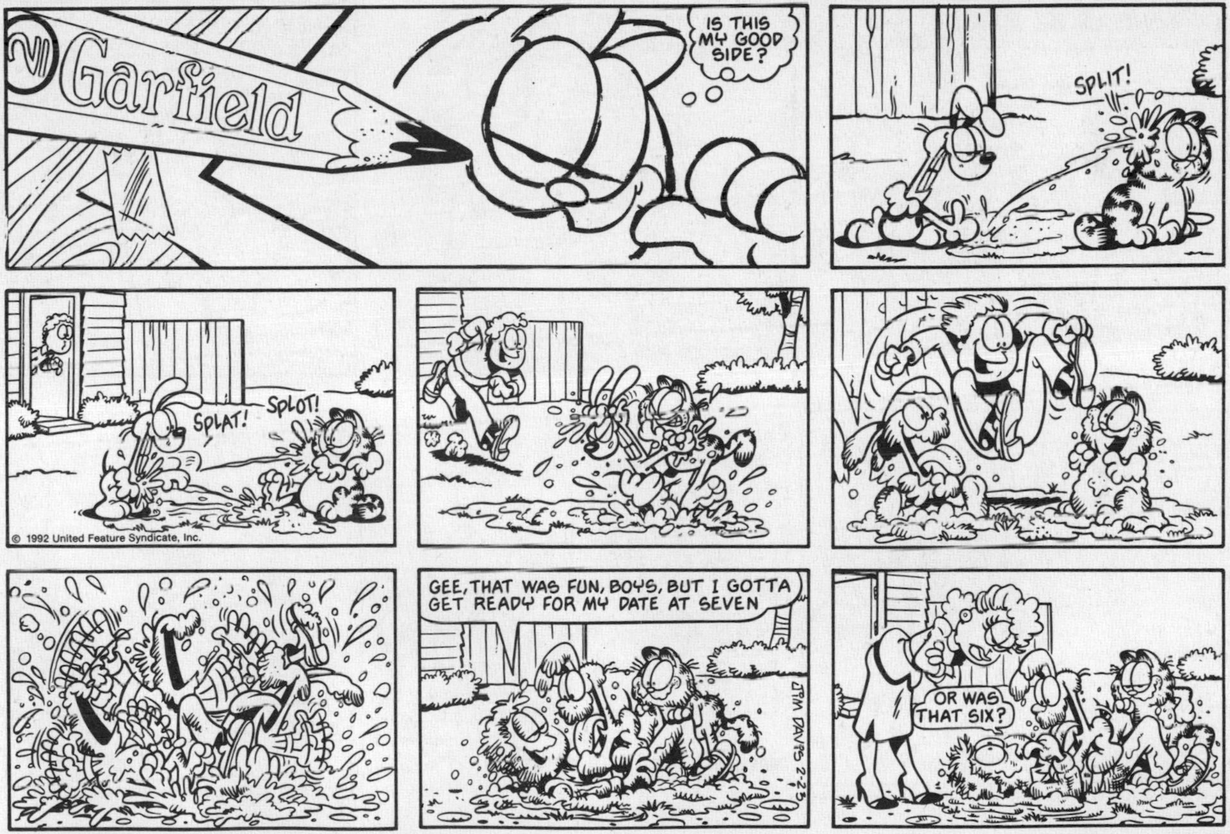

Garfield
IS THIS MY GOOD SIDE?
SPLIT!
SPLAT!
SPLOT!
© 1992 United Feature Syndicate, Inc.
GEE, THAT WAS FUN, BOYS, BUT I GOTTA GET READY FOR MY DATE AT SEVEN
JIM DAVIS 2-23
OR WAS THAT SIX?

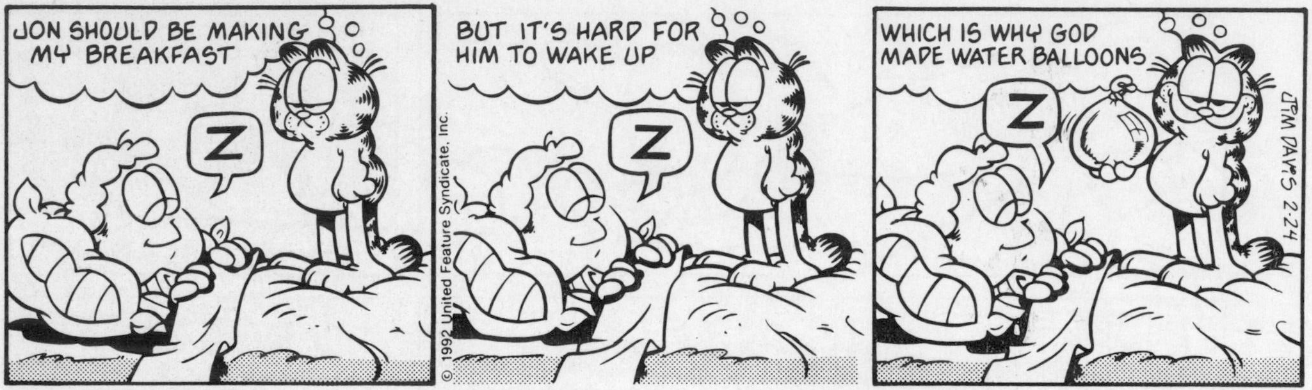
JON SHOULD BE MAKING MY BREAKFAST
Z
BUT IT'S HARD FOR HIM TO WAKE UP
Z
© 1992 United Feature Syndicate, Inc.
WHICH IS WHY GOD MADE WATER BALLOONS
Z
JIM DAVIS 2-24

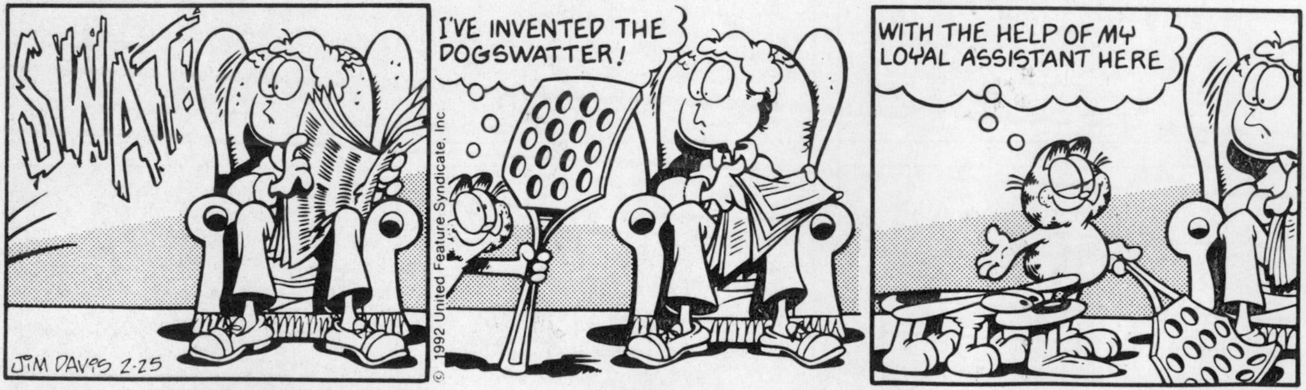
SWAT!
JIM DAVIS 2-25
© 1992 United Feature Syndicate, Inc
I'VE INVENTED THE DOGSWATTER!
WITH THE HELP OF MY LOYAL ASSISTANT HERE

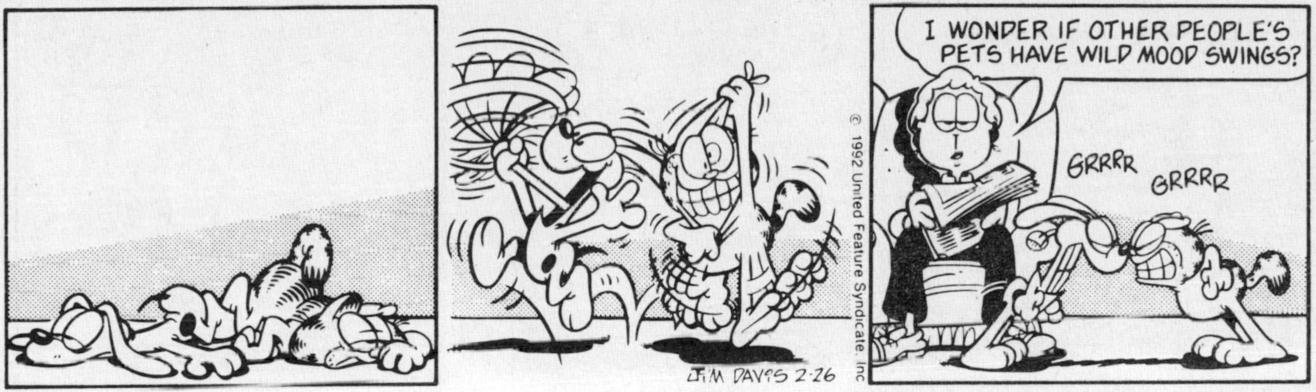
I WONDER IF OTHER PEOPLE'S PETS HAVE WILD MOOD SWINGS?
GRRRR
GRRRR
JIM DAVIS 2-26
© 1992 United Feature Syndicate, Inc.

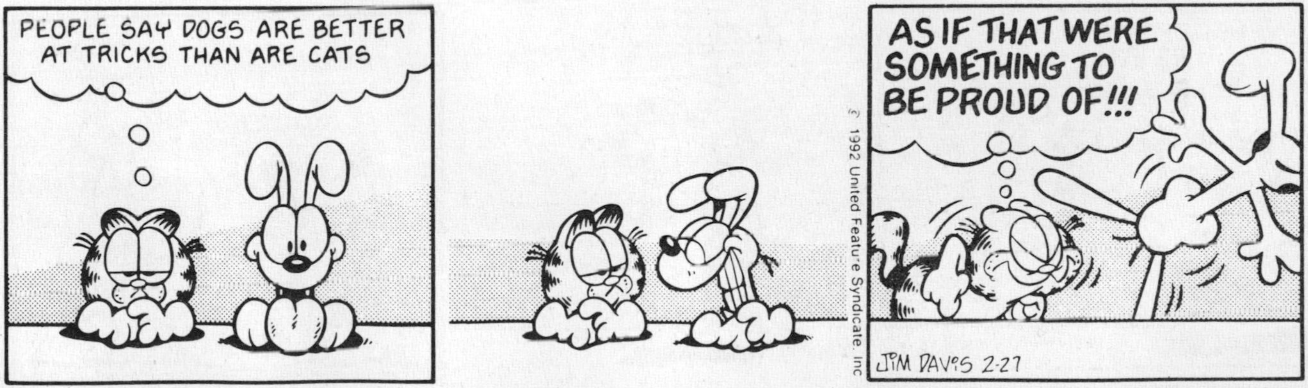
PEOPLE SAY DOGS ARE BETTER AT TRICKS THAN ARE CATS
AS IF THAT WERE SOMETHING TO BE PROUD OF!!!
JIM DAVIS 2-27
© 1992 United Feature Syndicate, Inc.

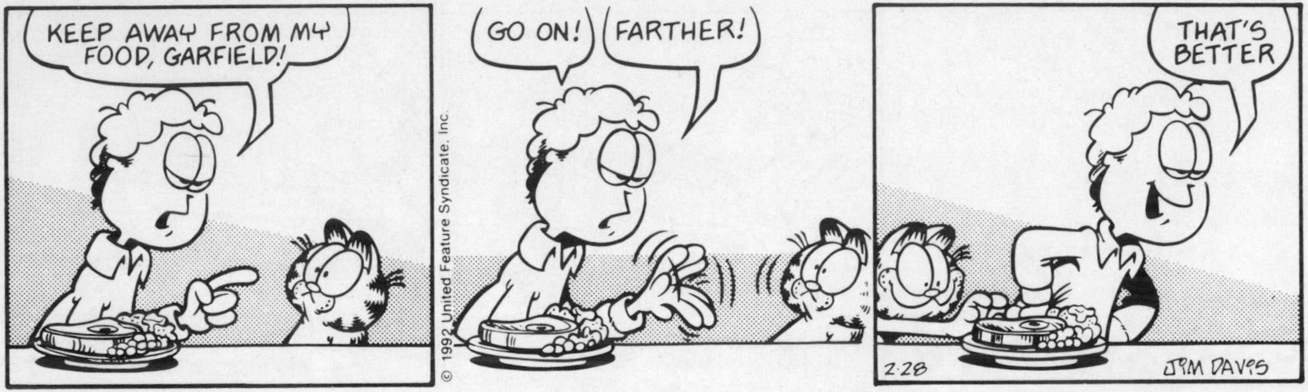
KEEP AWAY FROM MY FOOD, GARFIELD!
GO ON!
FARTHER!
THAT'S BETTER
© 1992 United Feature Syndicate, Inc.
2·28
JIM DAVIS

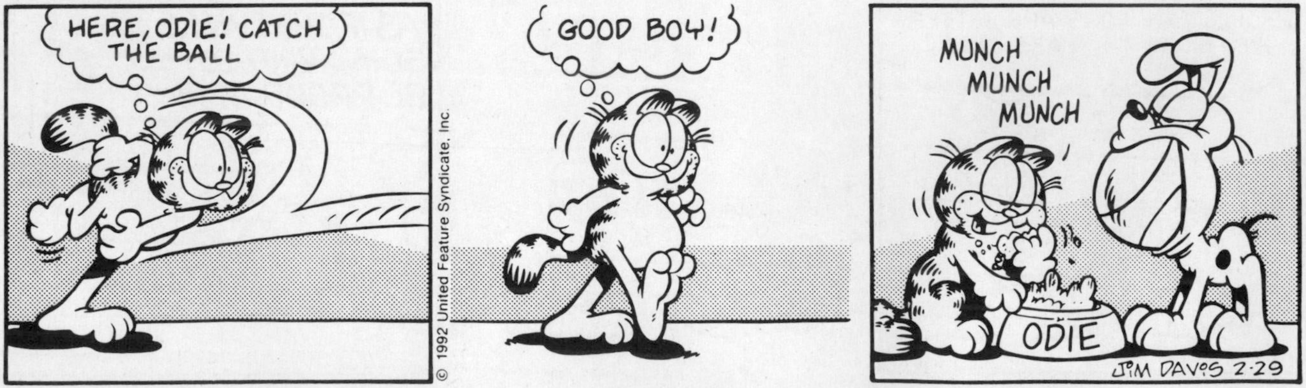
HERE, ODIE! CATCH THE BALL
GOOD BOY!
MUNCH MUNCH MUNCH
ODIE
© 1992 United Feature Syndicate, Inc.
JIM DAVIS 2·29

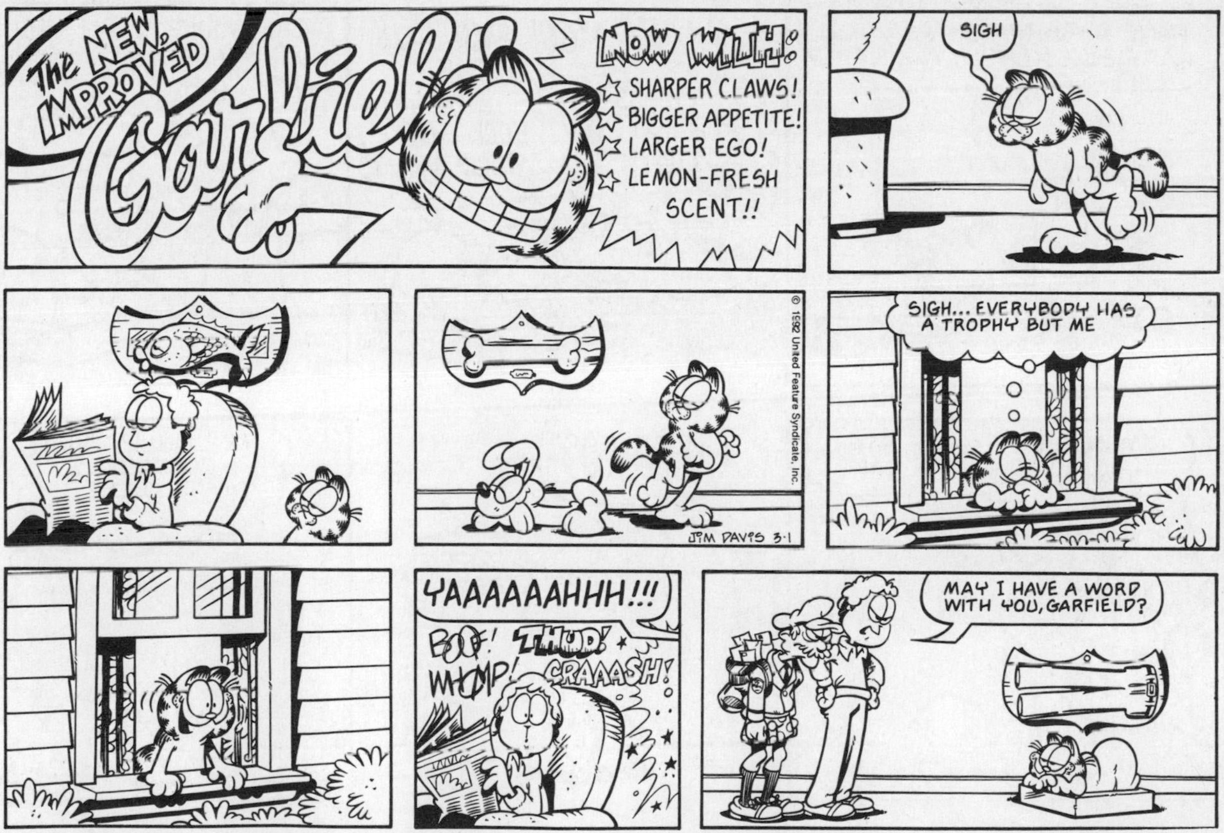

The NEW, IMPROVED Garfield
NOW WITH:
SHARPER CLAWS!
BIGGER APPETITE!
LARGER EGO!
LEMON-FRESH SCENT!!
SIGH
© 1992 United Feature Syndicate, Inc.
JIM DAVIS 3-1
SIGH... EVERYBODY HAS A TROPHY BUT ME
YAAAAAAHHH!!!
BOOF! THUD! WHOMP! CRAAASH!
MAY I HAVE A WORD WITH YOU, GARFIELD?

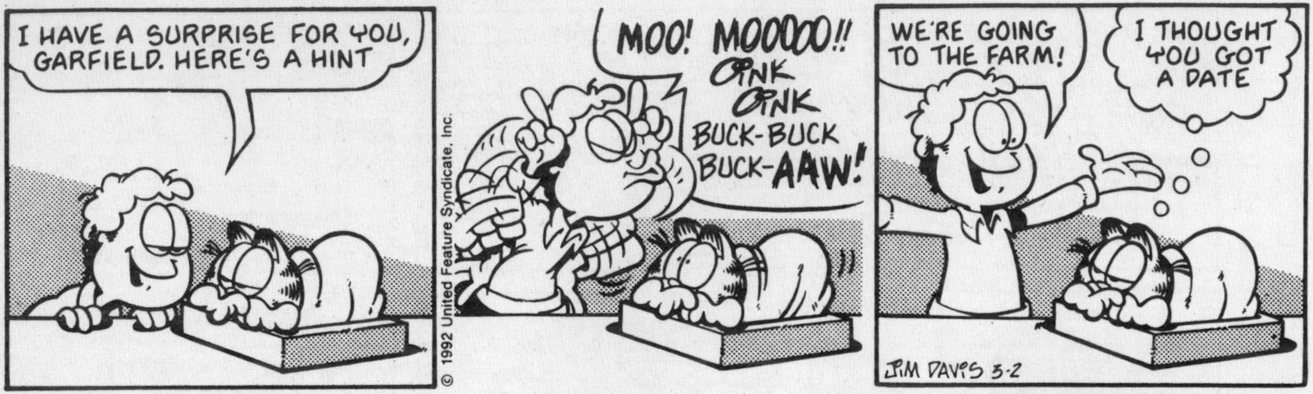
I HAVE A SURPRISE FOR YOU, GARFIELD. HERE'S A HINT
© 1992 United Feature Syndicate, Inc.
MOO! MOOOOO!!
OINK OINK
BUCK-BUCK BUCK-AAW!
WE'RE GOING TO THE FARM!
I THOUGHT YOU GOT A DATE
JIM DAVIS 3-2

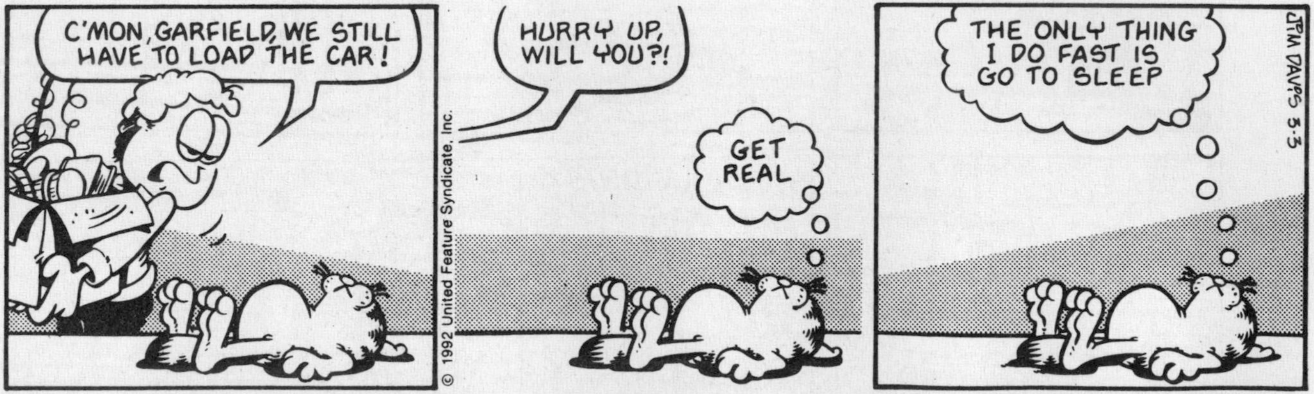
C'MON, GARFIELD, WE STILL HAVE TO LOAD THE CAR!
© 1992 United Feature Syndicate, Inc.
HURRY UP, WILL YOU?!
GET REAL
THE ONLY THING I DO FAST IS GO TO SLEEP
JIM DAVIS 3-3

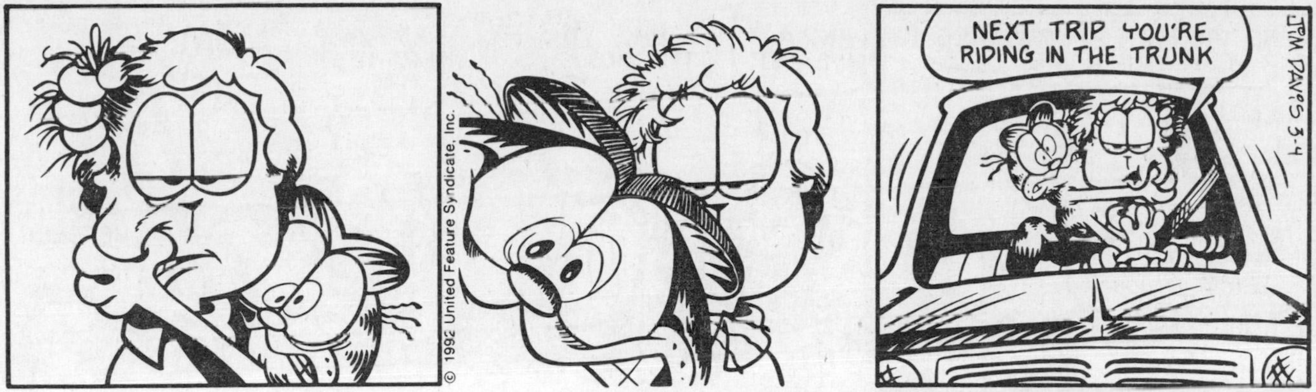
NEXT TRIP YOU'RE RIDING IN THE TRUNK
JIM DAVIS 3-4
© 1992 United Feature Syndicate, Inc.

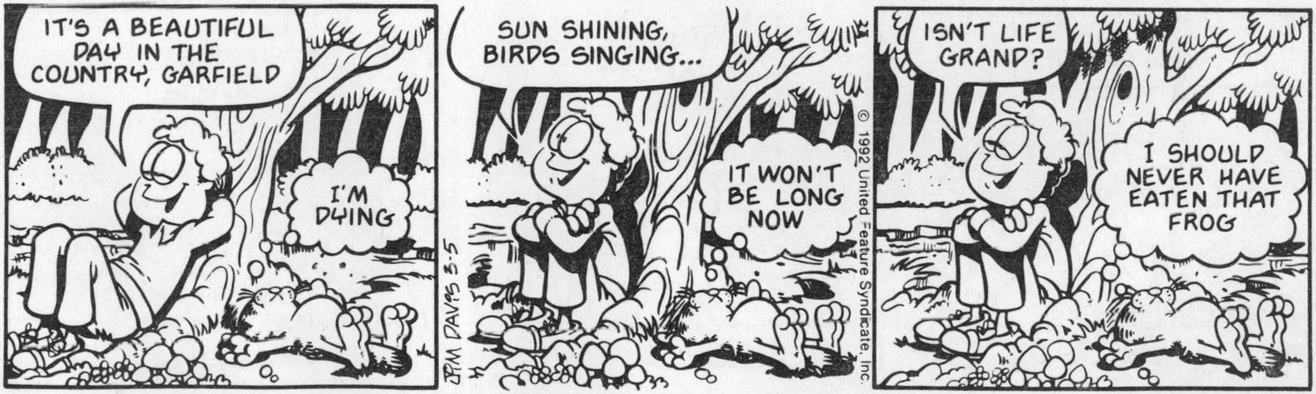
IT'S A BEAUTIFUL DAY IN THE COUNTRY, GARFIELD
I'M DYING
SUN SHINING, BIRDS SINGING...
IT WON'T BE LONG NOW
ISN'T LIFE GRAND?
I SHOULD NEVER HAVE EATEN THAT FROG
JIM DAVIS 3-5
© 1992 United Feature Syndicate, Inc.

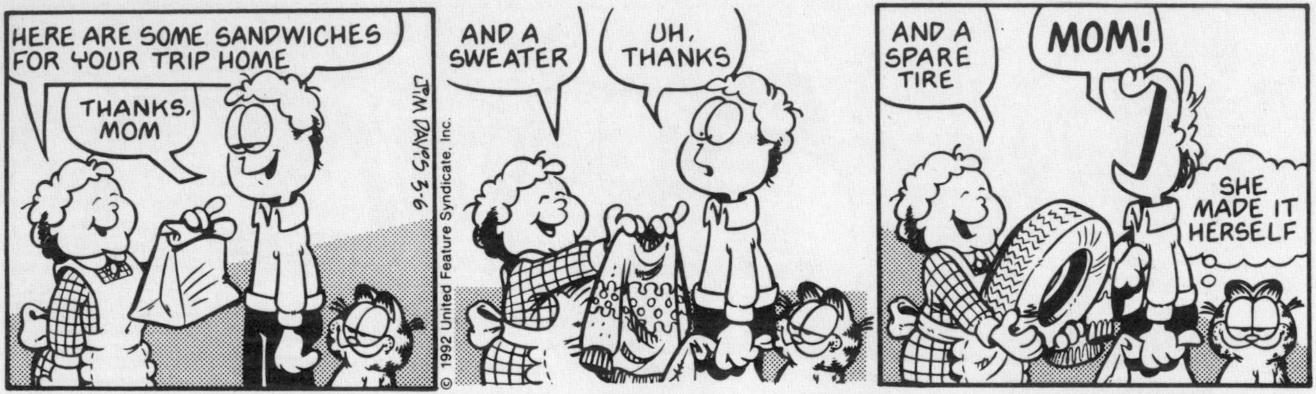
HERE ARE SOME SANDWICHES FOR YOUR TRIP HOME
THANKS, MOM
JIM DAVIS 3-6
© 1992 United Feature Syndicate, Inc.
AND A SWEATER
UH, THANKS
AND A SPARE TIRE
MOM!
SHE MADE IT HERSELF

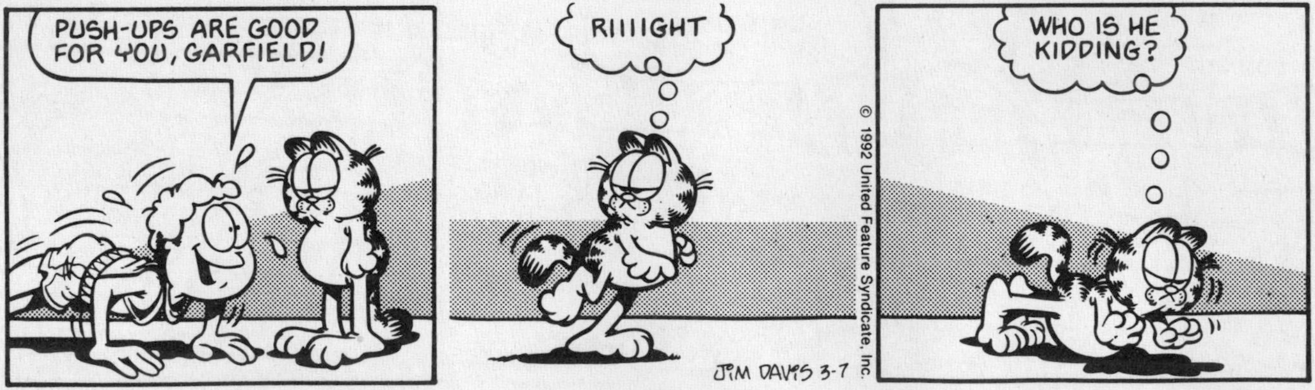
PUSH-UPS ARE GOOD FOR YOU, GARFIELD!
RIIIIGHT
JIM DAVIS 3-7
© 1992 United Feature Syndicate, Inc.
WHO IS HE KIDDING?

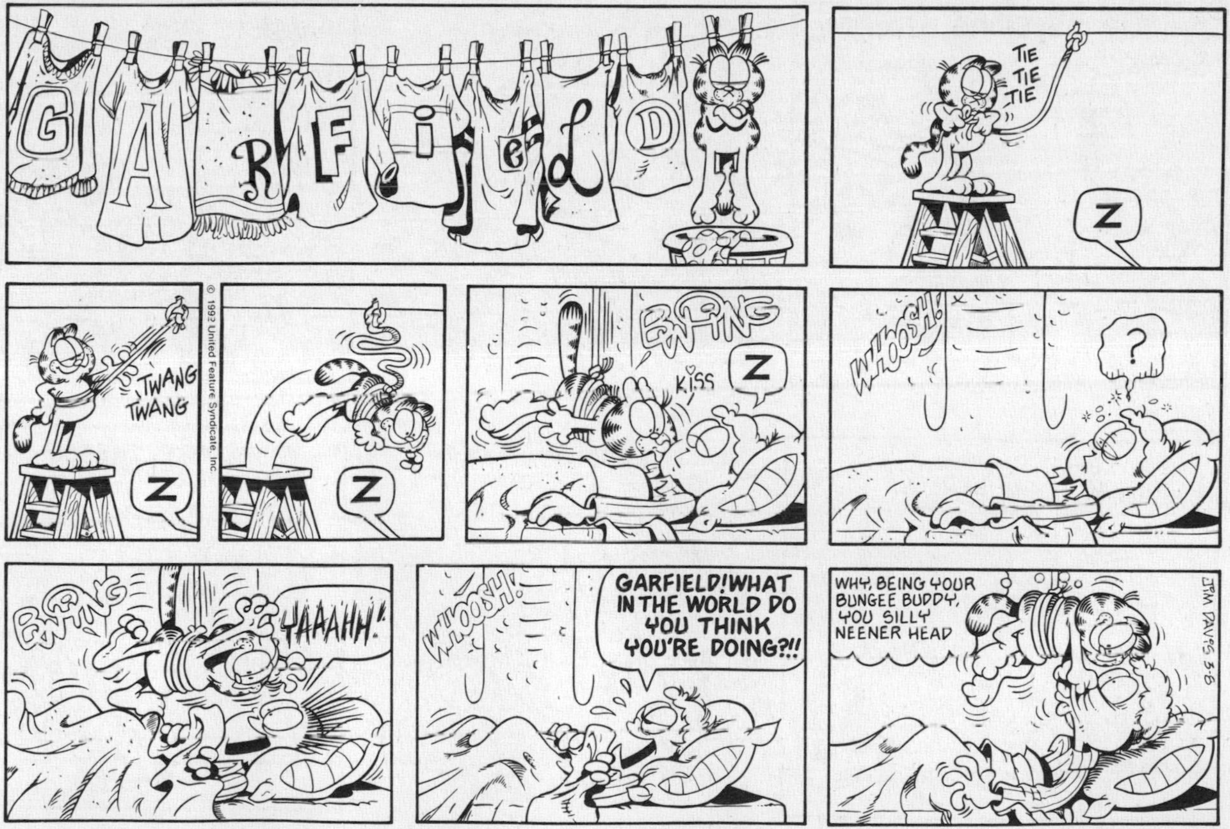
GARFIELD
TIE TIE TIE
Z
TWANG TWANG
Z
© 1992 United Feature Syndicate, Inc.
Z
BOING
KISS
Z
WHOOSH!
?
BOING
YAAAHH!
WHOOSH!
GARFIELD! WHAT IN THE WORLD DO YOU THINK YOU'RE DOING?!!
WHY, BEING YOUR BUNGEE BUDDY, YOU SILLY NEENER HEAD
JIM DAVIS 3-8

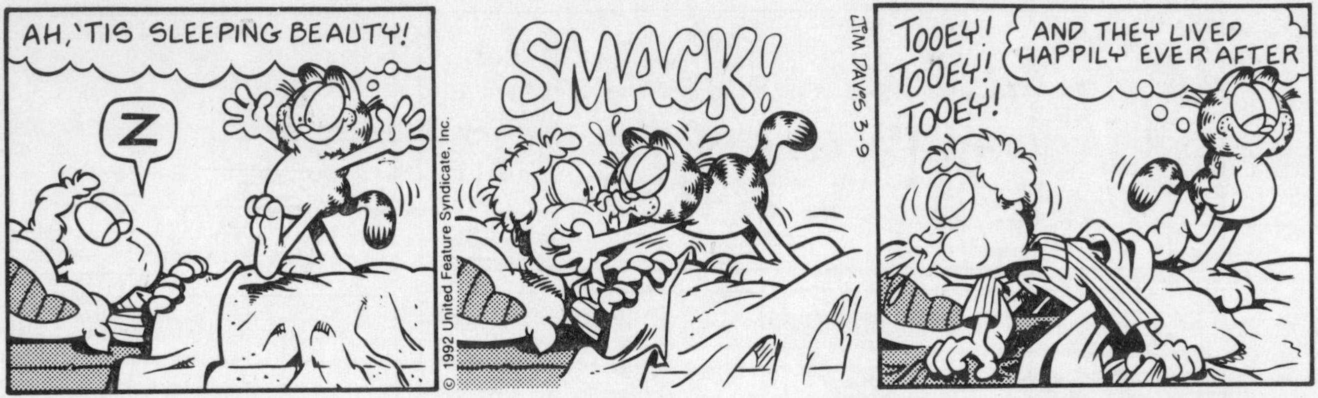
AH, 'TIS SLEEPING BEAUTY!
Z
SMACK!
TOOEY! TOOEY! TOOEY!
AND THEY LIVED HAPPILY EVER AFTER
© 1992 United Feature Syndicate, Inc.
JIM DAVIS 3-9

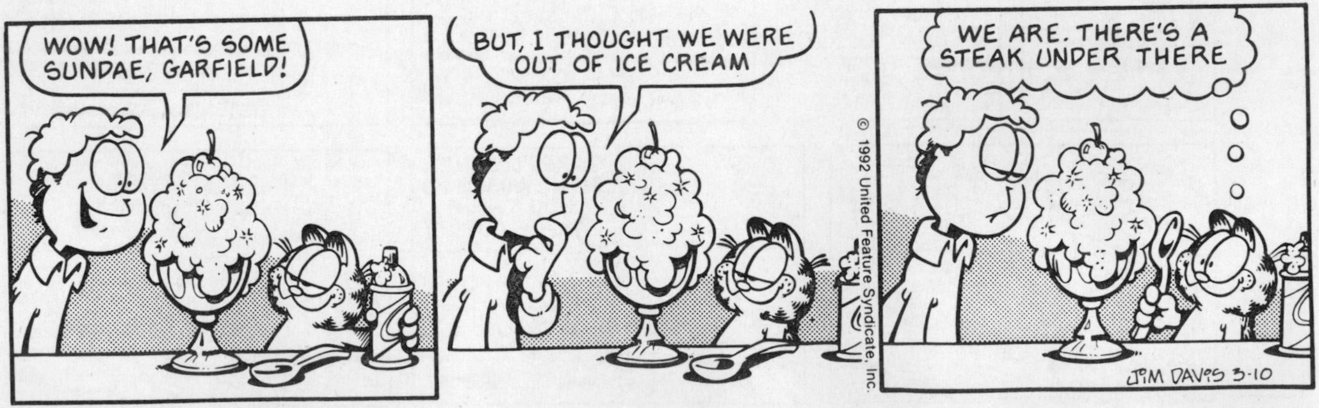
WOW! THAT'S SOME SUNDAE, GARFIELD!
BUT, I THOUGHT WE WERE OUT OF ICE CREAM
WE ARE. THERE'S A STEAK UNDER THERE
© 1992 United Feature Syndicate, Inc.
JIM DAVIS 3-10

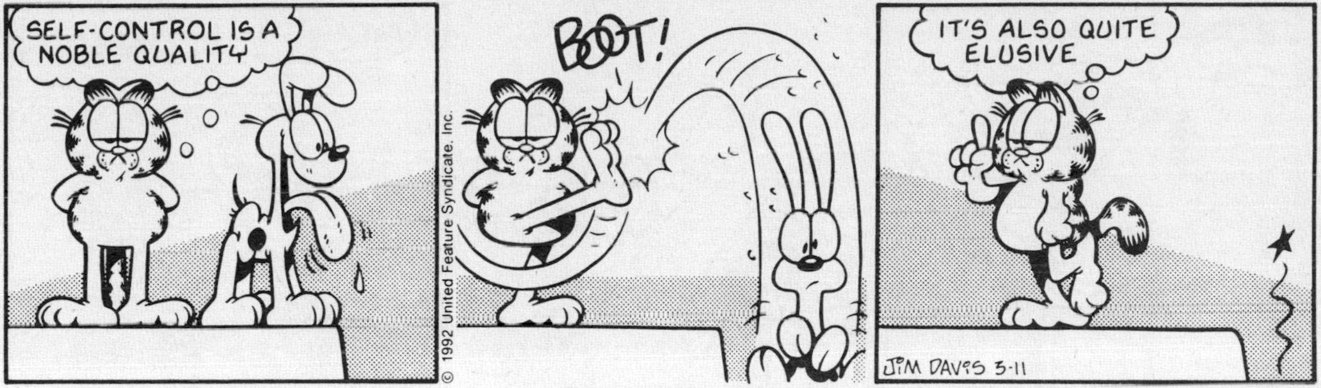
SELF-CONTROL IS A NOBLE QUALITY
BOOT!
IT'S ALSO QUITE ELUSIVE
© 1992 United Feature Syndicate, Inc.
JIM DAVIS 3-11

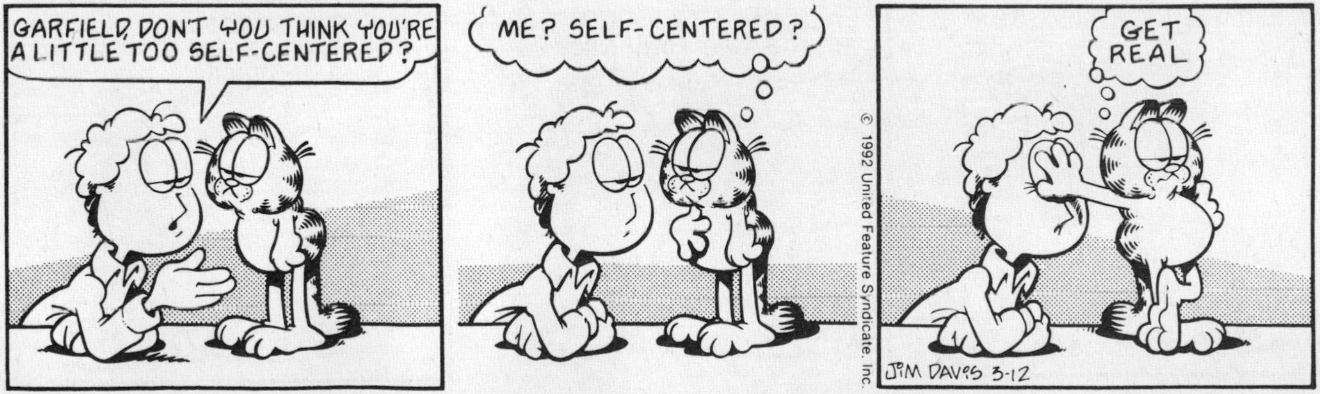
GARFIELD, DON'T YOU THINK YOU'RE A LITTLE TOO SELF-CENTERED?
ME? SELF-CENTERED?
GET REAL
© 1992 United Feature Syndicate, Inc.
JIM DAVIS 3-12

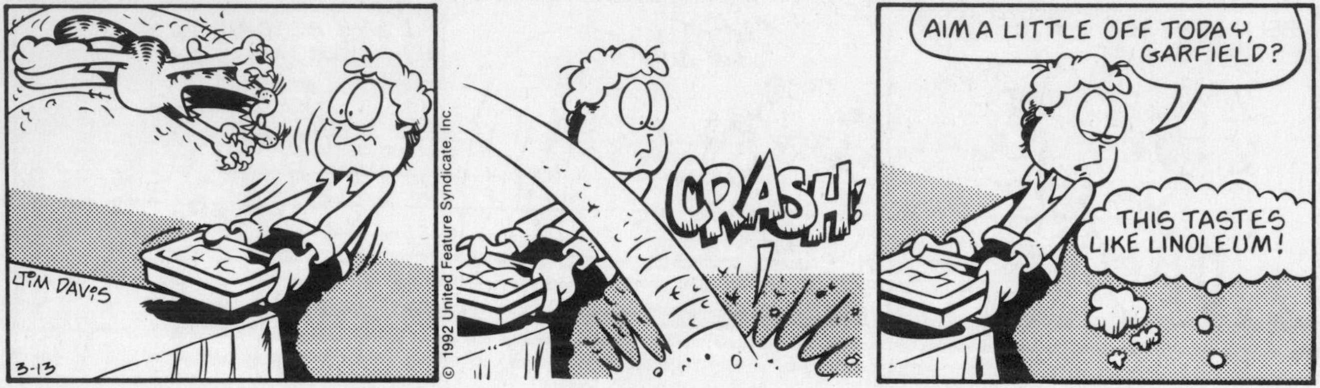
JIM DAVIS
3-13
© 1992 United Feature Syndicate, Inc.
CRASH!
AIM A LITTLE OFF TODAY, GARFIELD?
THIS TASTES LIKE LINOLEUM!

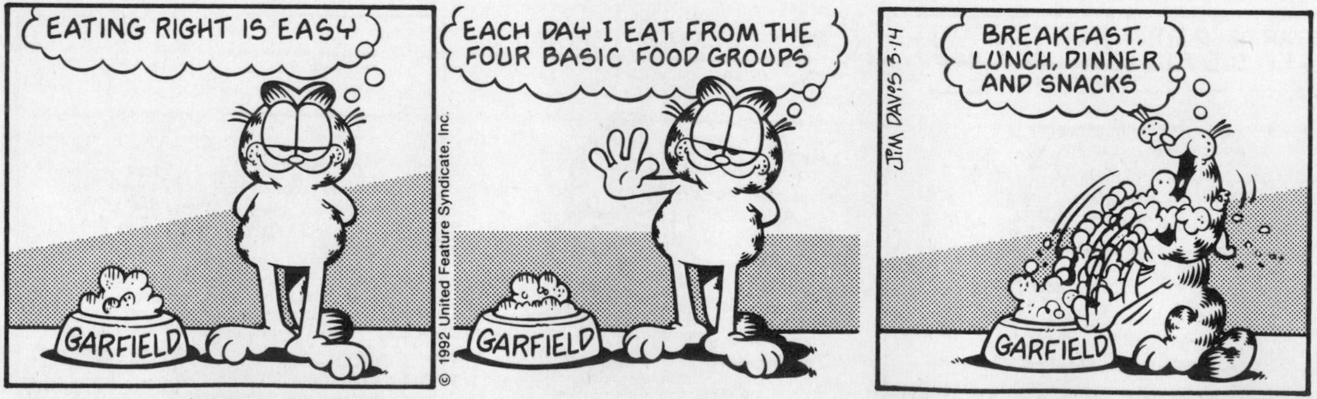
EATING RIGHT IS EASY
GARFIELD
© 1992 United Feature Syndicate, Inc.
EACH DAY I EAT FROM THE FOUR BASIC FOOD GROUPS
GARFIELD
JIM DAVIS 3-14
BREAKFAST, LUNCH, DINNER AND SNACKS
GARFIELD

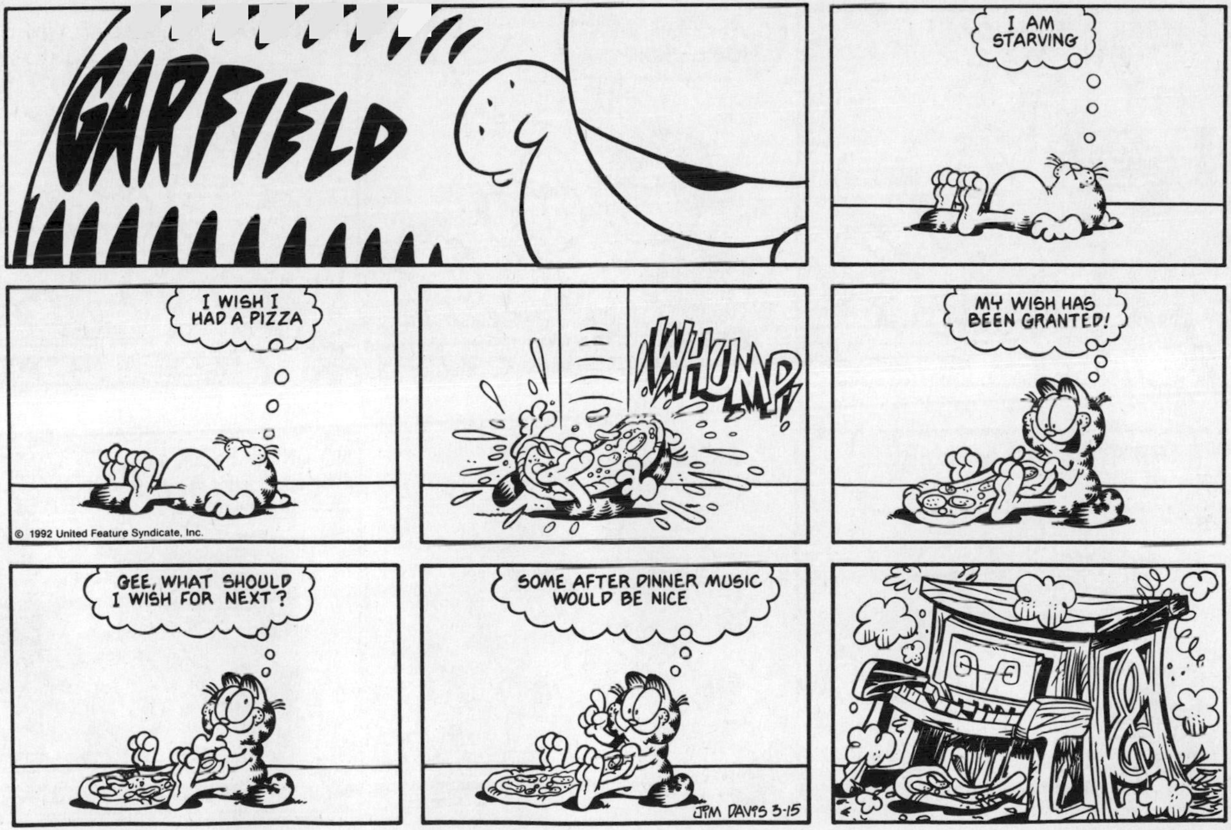
GARFIELD
I AM STARVING
I WISH I HAD A PIZZA
WHUMP
MY WISH HAS BEEN GRANTED!
GEE, WHAT SHOULD I WISH FOR NEXT?
SOME AFTER DINNER MUSIC WOULD BE NICE
JIM DAVIS 3-15
© 1992 United Feature Syndicate, Inc.

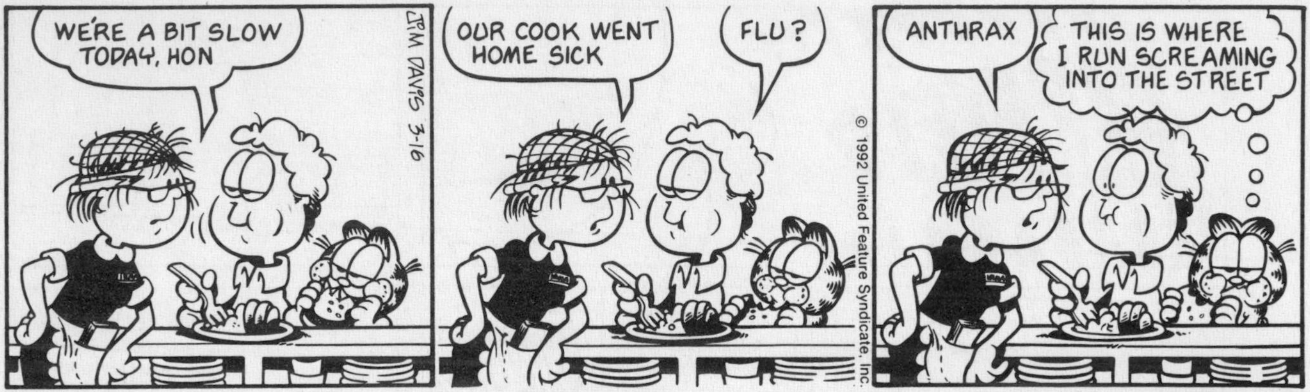
WE'RE A BIT SLOW TODAY, HON
JIM DAVIS 3-16
OUR COOK WENT HOME SICK
FLU?
© 1992 United Feature Syndicate, Inc.
ANTHRAX
THIS IS WHERE I RUN SCREAMING INTO THE STREET

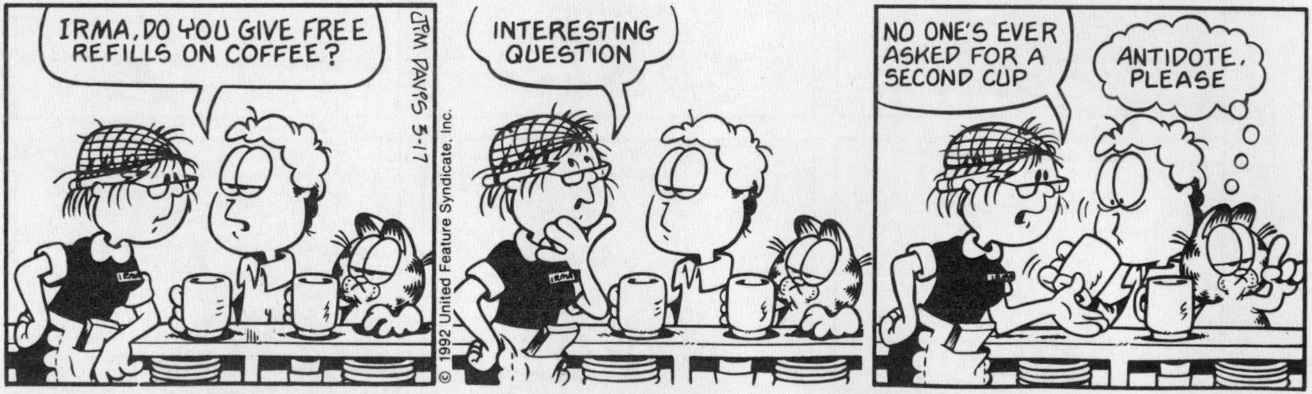
IRMA, DO YOU GIVE FREE REFILLS ON COFFEE?
JIM DAVIS 3-17
© 1992 United Feature Syndicate, Inc.
INTERESTING QUESTION
NO ONE'S EVER ASKED FOR A SECOND CUP
ANTIDOTE, PLEASE

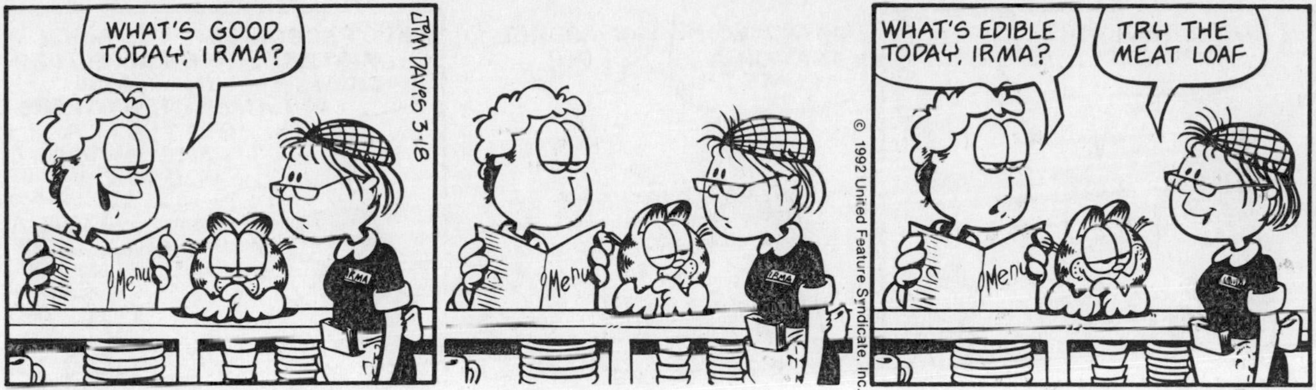
WHAT'S GOOD TODAY, IRMA?
JPM DAVPS 3-18
WHAT'S EDIBLE TODAY, IRMA?
TRY THE MEAT LOAF
© 1992 United Feature Syndicate, Inc.

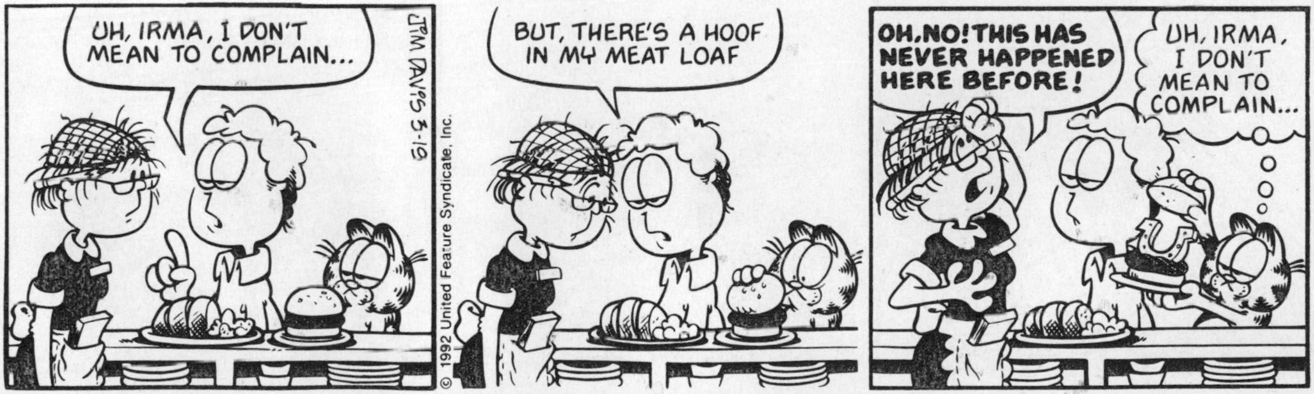
UH, IRMA, I DON'T MEAN TO COMPLAIN...
JPM DAVPS 3-19
© 1992 United Feature Syndicate, Inc.
BUT, THERE'S A HOOF IN MY MEAT LOAF
OH, NO! THIS HAS NEVER HAPPENED HERE BEFORE!
UH, IRMA, I DON'T MEAN TO COMPLAIN...

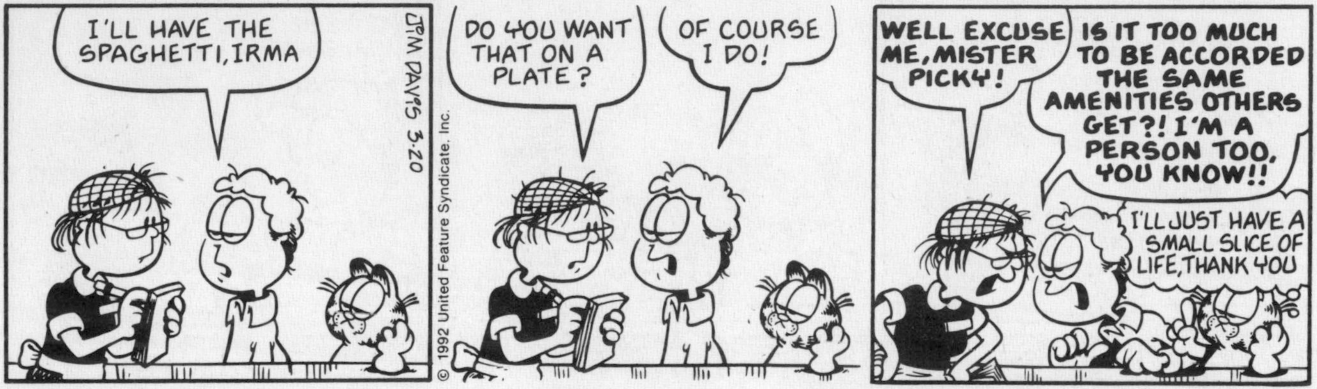
I'LL HAVE THE SPAGHETTI, IRMA
JIM DAVIS 3-20
© 1992 United Feature Syndicate, Inc.
DO YOU WANT THAT ON A PLATE?
OF COURSE I DO!
WELL EXCUSE ME, MISTER PICKY!
IS IT TOO MUCH TO BE ACCORDED THE SAME AMENITIES OTHERS GET?! I'M A PERSON TOO, YOU KNOW!!
I'LL JUST HAVE A SMALL SLICE OF LIFE, THANK YOU

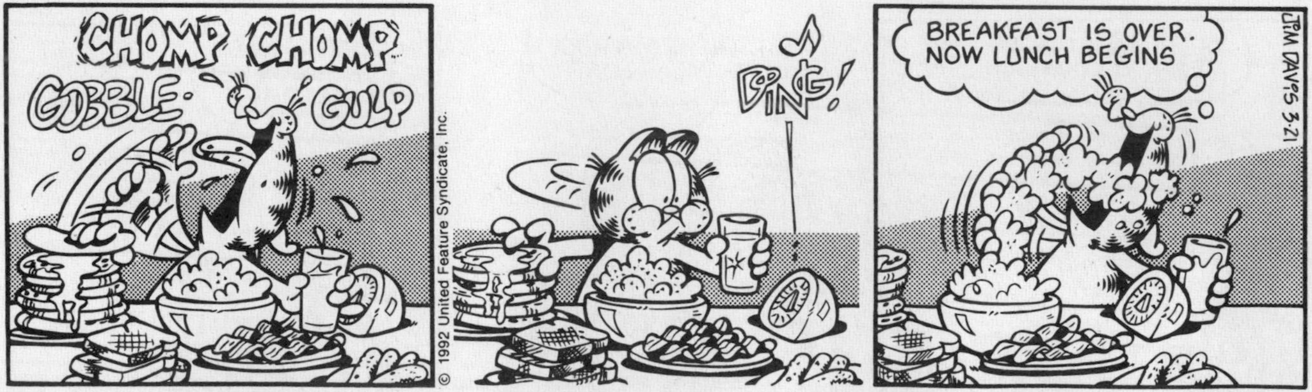
CHOMP CHOMP
GOBBLE
GULP
© 1992 United Feature Syndicate, Inc.
DING!
BREAKFAST IS OVER. NOW LUNCH BEGINS
JIM DAVIS 3-21

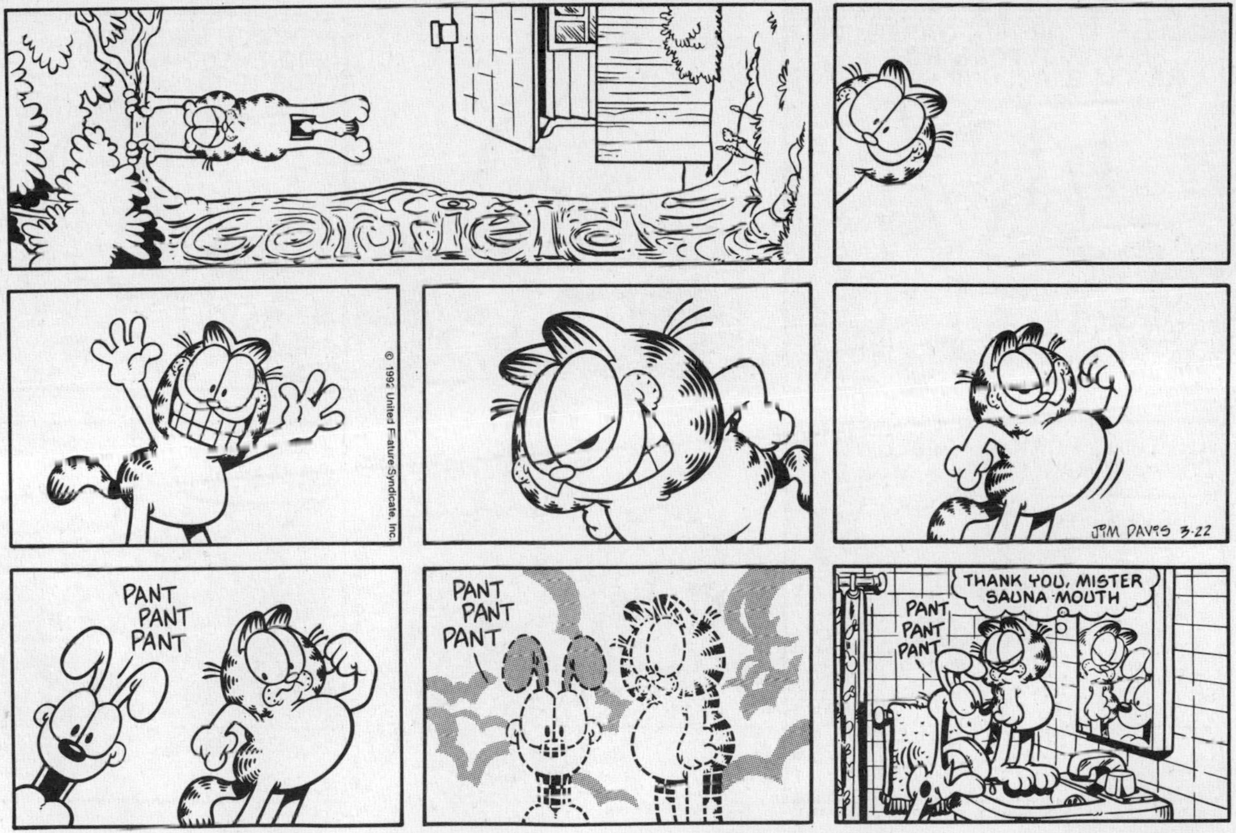
Garfield
© 1992 United Feature Syndicate, Inc.
JIM DAVIS 3-22
PANT
PANT
PANT
PANT
PANT
PANT
PANT
PANT
PANT
THANK YOU, MISTER SAUNA-MOUTH

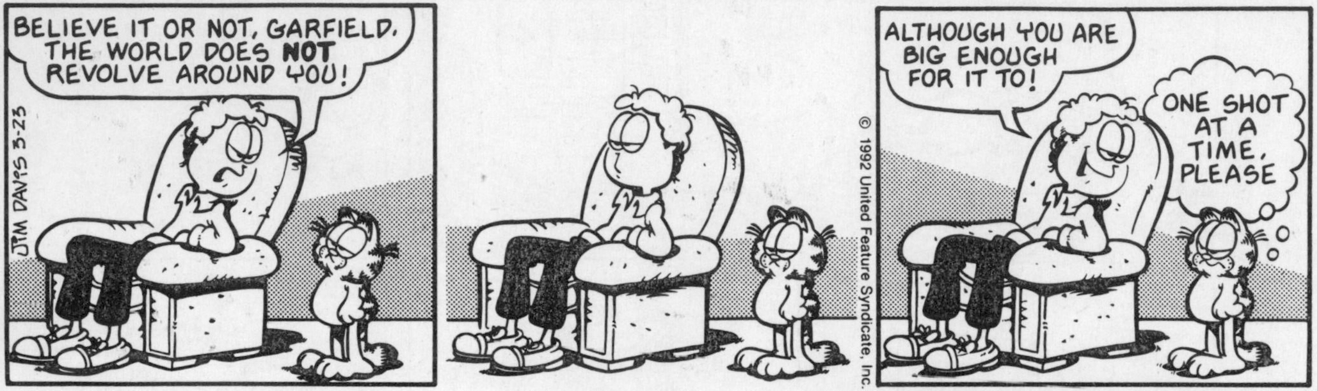
BELIEVE IT OR NOT, GARFIELD, THE WORLD DOES **NOT** REVOLVE AROUND YOU!
JIM DAVIS 3-23
ALTHOUGH YOU ARE BIG ENOUGH FOR IT TO!
ONE SHOT AT A TIME, PLEASE
© 1992 United Feature Syndicate, Inc.

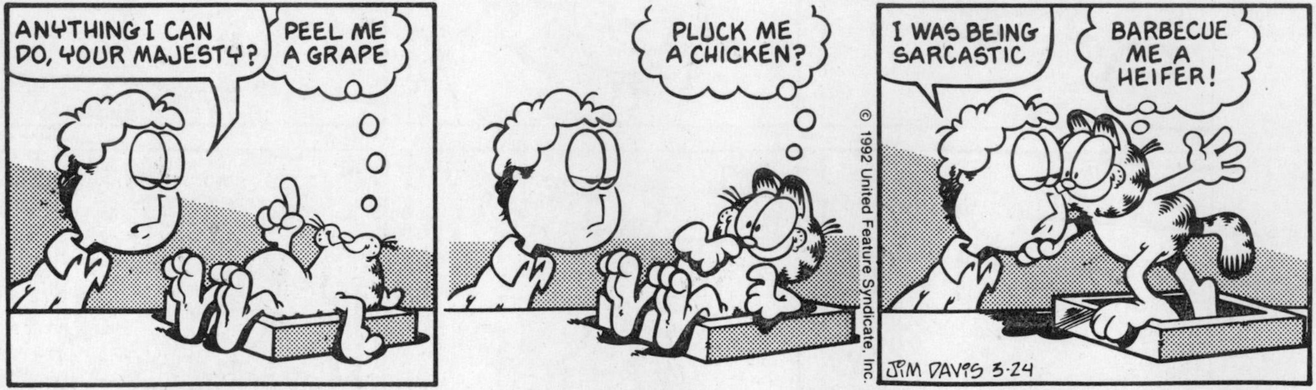
ANYTHING I CAN DO, YOUR MAJESTY?
PEEL ME A GRAPE
PLUCK ME A CHICKEN?
I WAS BEING SARCASTIC
BARBECUE ME A HEIFER!
JIM DAVIS 3·24
© 1992 United Feature Syndicate, Inc.

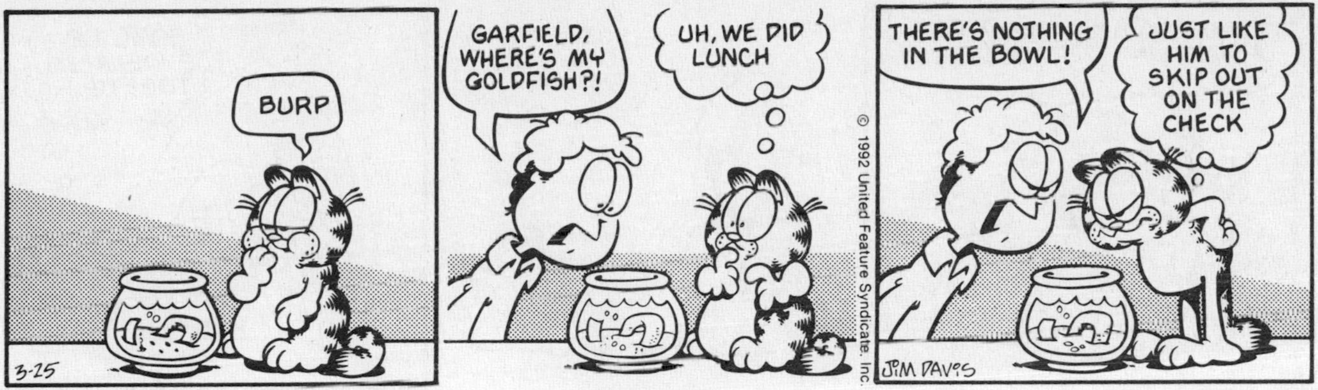
BURP
GARFIELD, WHERE'S MY GOLDFISH?!
UH, WE DID LUNCH
THERE'S NOTHING IN THE BOWL!
JUST LIKE HIM TO SKIP OUT ON THE CHECK
© 1992 United Feature Syndicate, Inc.
3-25
JIM DAVIS

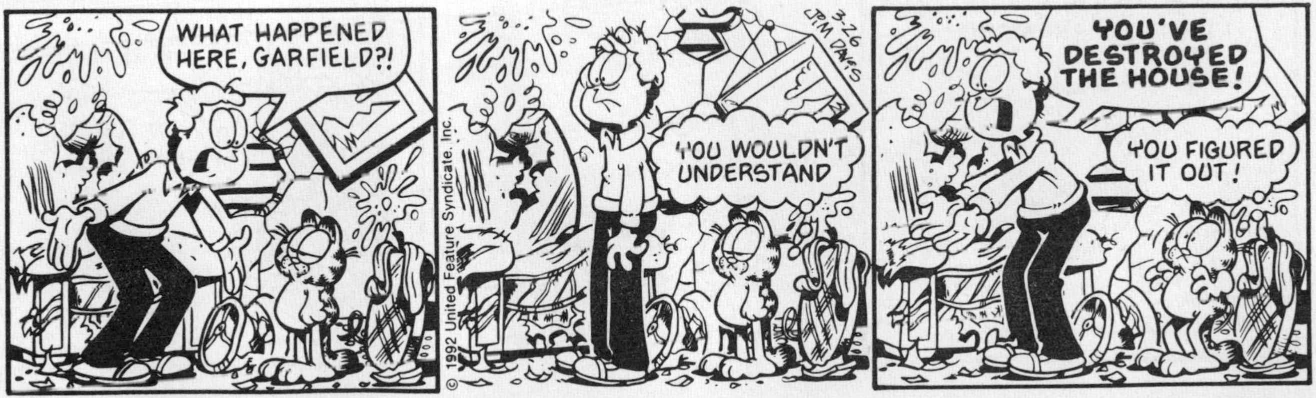
WHAT HAPPENED HERE, GARFIELD?!
YOU WOULDN'T UNDERSTAND
YOU'VE DESTROYED THE HOUSE!
YOU FIGURED IT OUT!
© 1992 United Feature Syndicate, Inc.
3-26
JIM DAVIS

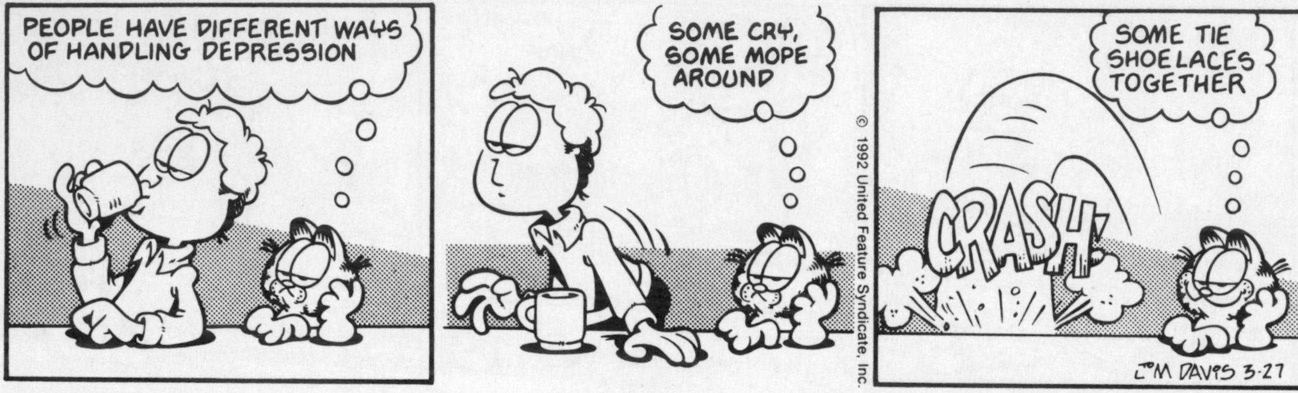
PEOPLE HAVE DIFFERENT WAYS OF HANDLING DEPRESSION
SOME CRY, SOME MOPE AROUND
© 1992 United Feature Syndicate, Inc.
SOME TIE SHOELACES TOGETHER
CRASH!
JIM DAVIS 3-27

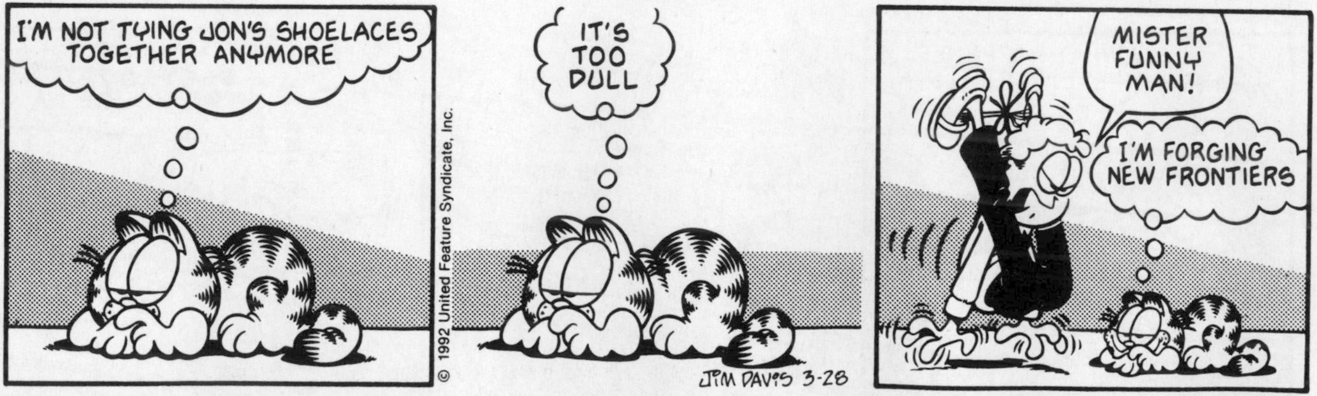
I'M NOT TYING JON'S SHOELACES TOGETHER ANYMORE
© 1992 United Feature Syndicate, Inc.
IT'S TOO DULL
JIM DAVIS 3-28
MISTER FUNNY MAN!
I'M FORGING NEW FRONTIERS

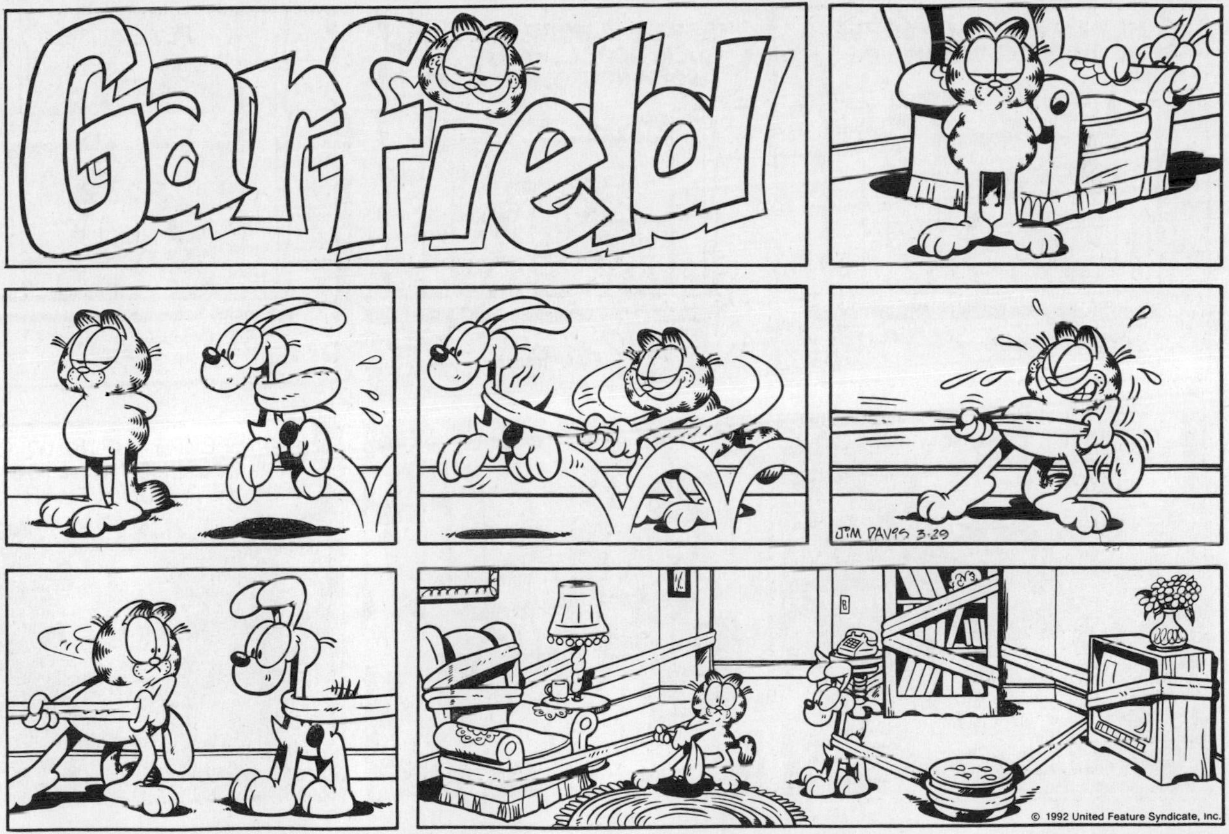
Garfield
JIM DAVIS 3-29
© 1992 United Feature Syndicate, Inc.

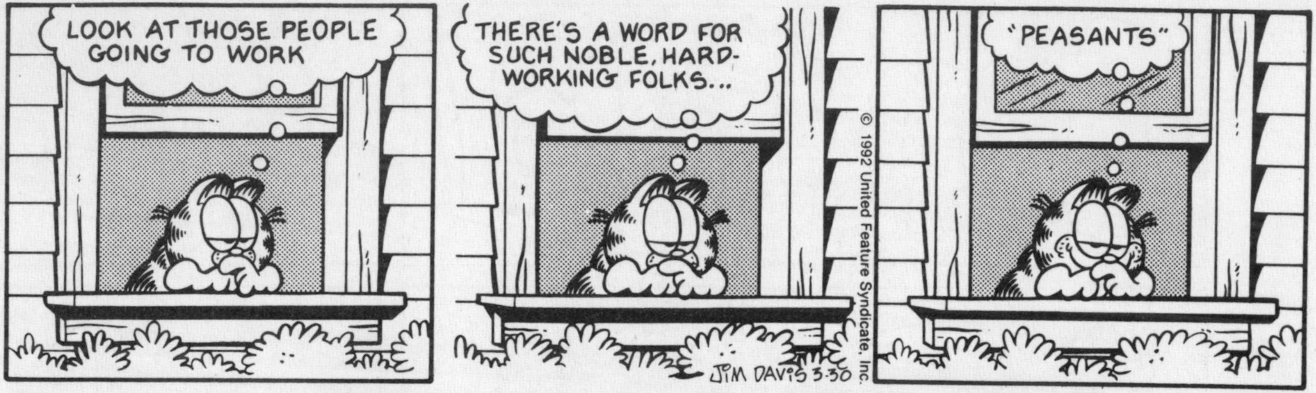
LOOK AT THOSE PEOPLE GOING TO WORK
THERE'S A WORD FOR SUCH NOBLE, HARD-WORKING FOLKS...
"PEASANTS"
JIM DAVIS 3-30
© 1992 United Feature Syndicate, Inc.

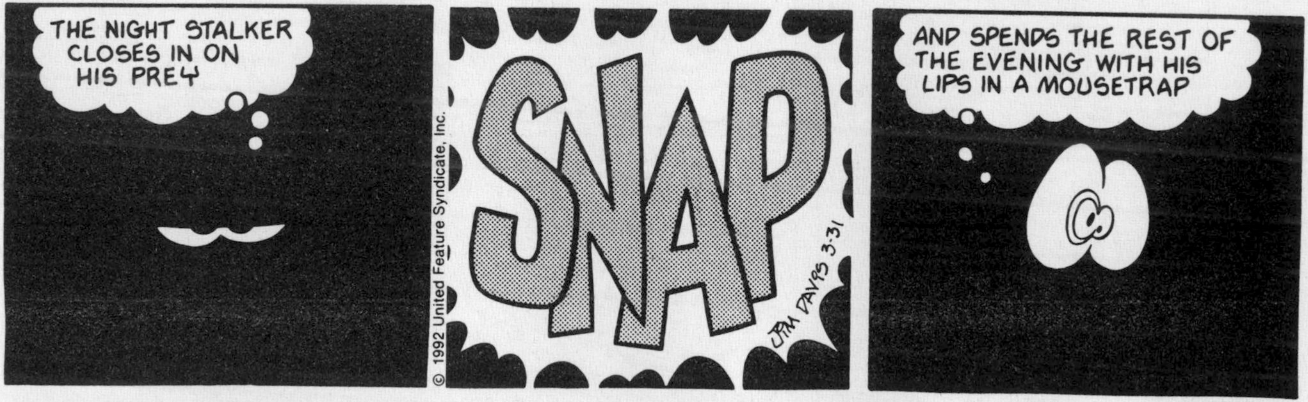
THE NIGHT STALKER CLOSES IN ON HIS PREY
SNAP
AND SPENDS THE REST OF THE EVENING WITH HIS LIPS IN A MOUSETRAP
JIM DAVIS 3-31
© 1992 United Feature Syndicate, Inc.

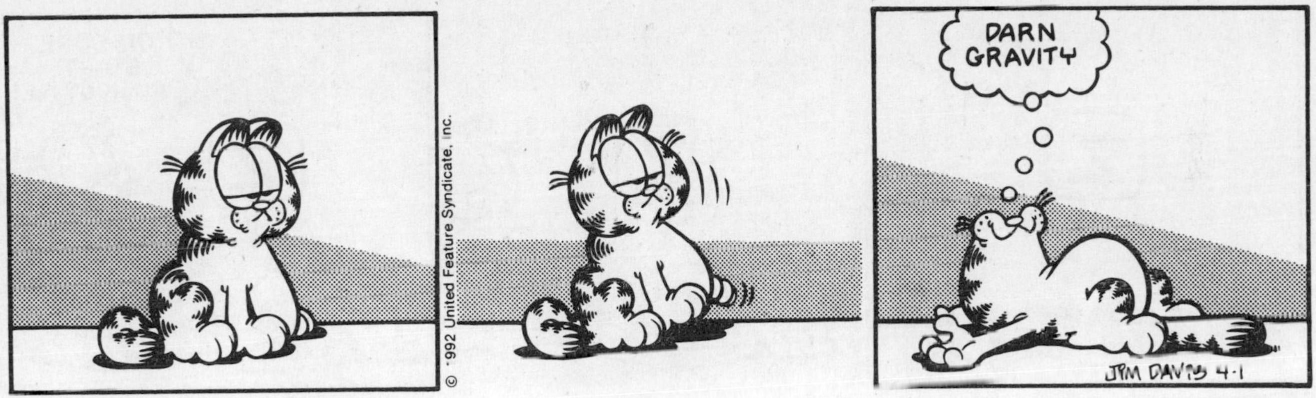
© 1992 United Feature Syndicate, Inc.
DARN GRAVITY
JIM DAVIS 4-1

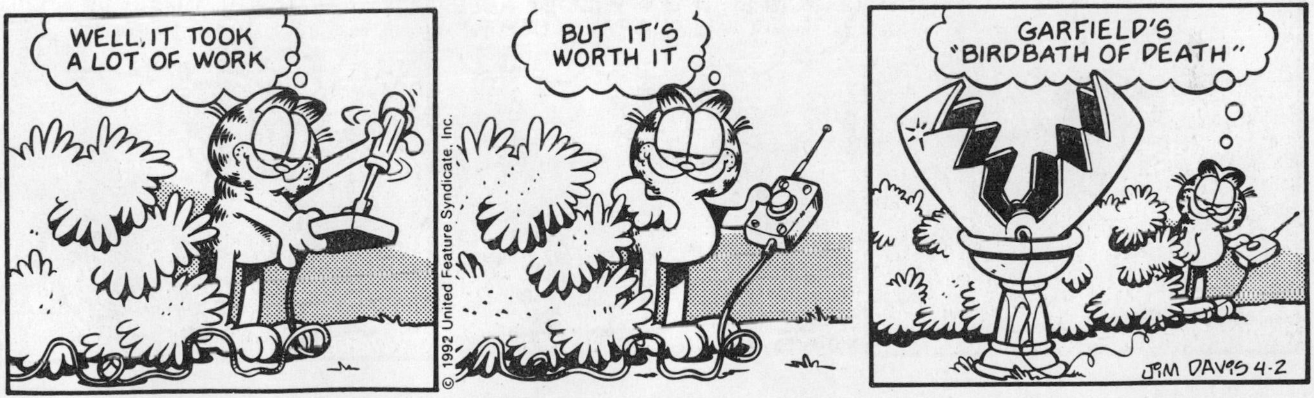
WELL, IT TOOK A LOT OF WORK
© 1992 United Feature Syndicate, Inc.
BUT IT'S WORTH IT
GARFIELD'S "BIRDBATH OF DEATH"
JIM DAVIS 4-2

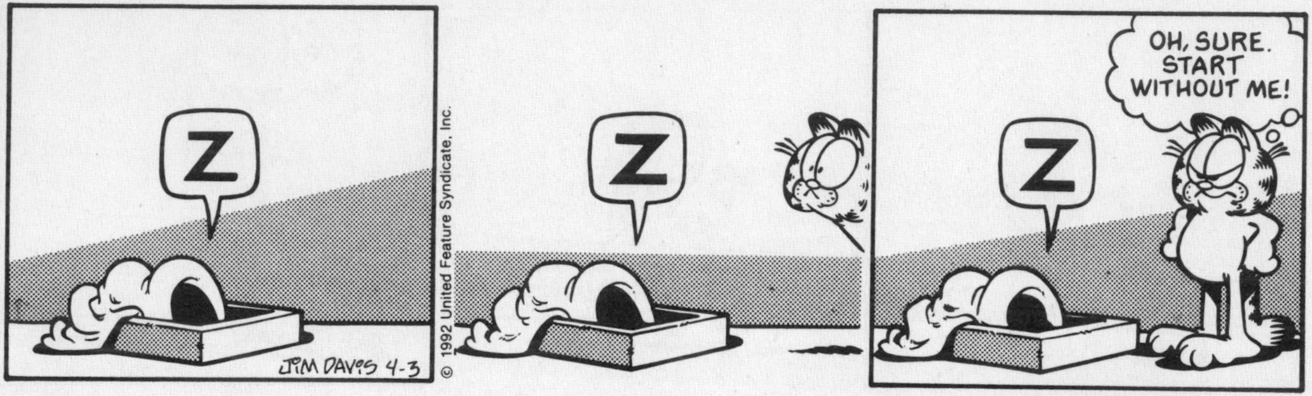
Z
JIM DAVIS 4-3
© 1992 United Feature Syndicate, Inc.
Z
Z
OH, SURE. START WITHOUT ME!

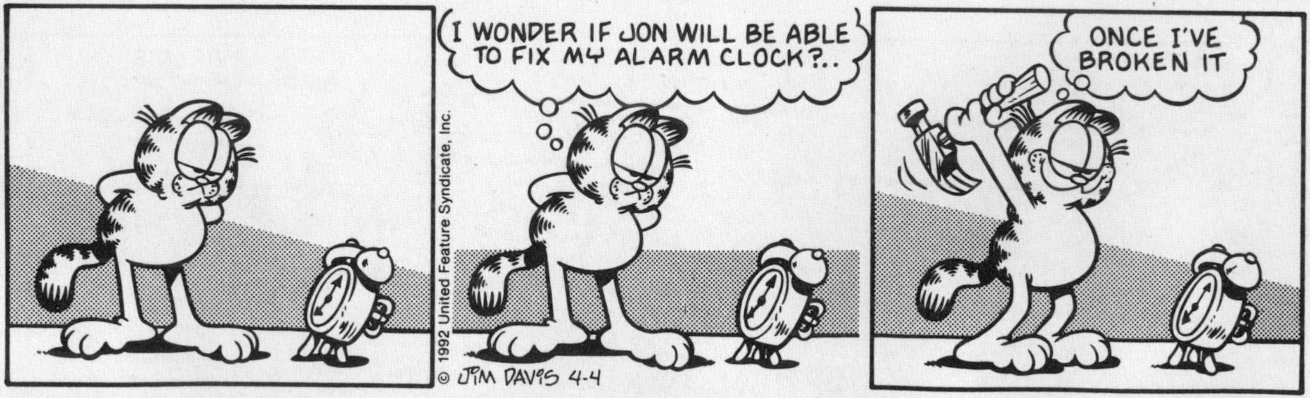
© 1992 United Feature Syndicate, Inc.
I WONDER IF JON WILL BE ABLE TO FIX MY ALARM CLOCK?..
JIM DAVIS 4-4
ONCE I'VE BROKEN IT

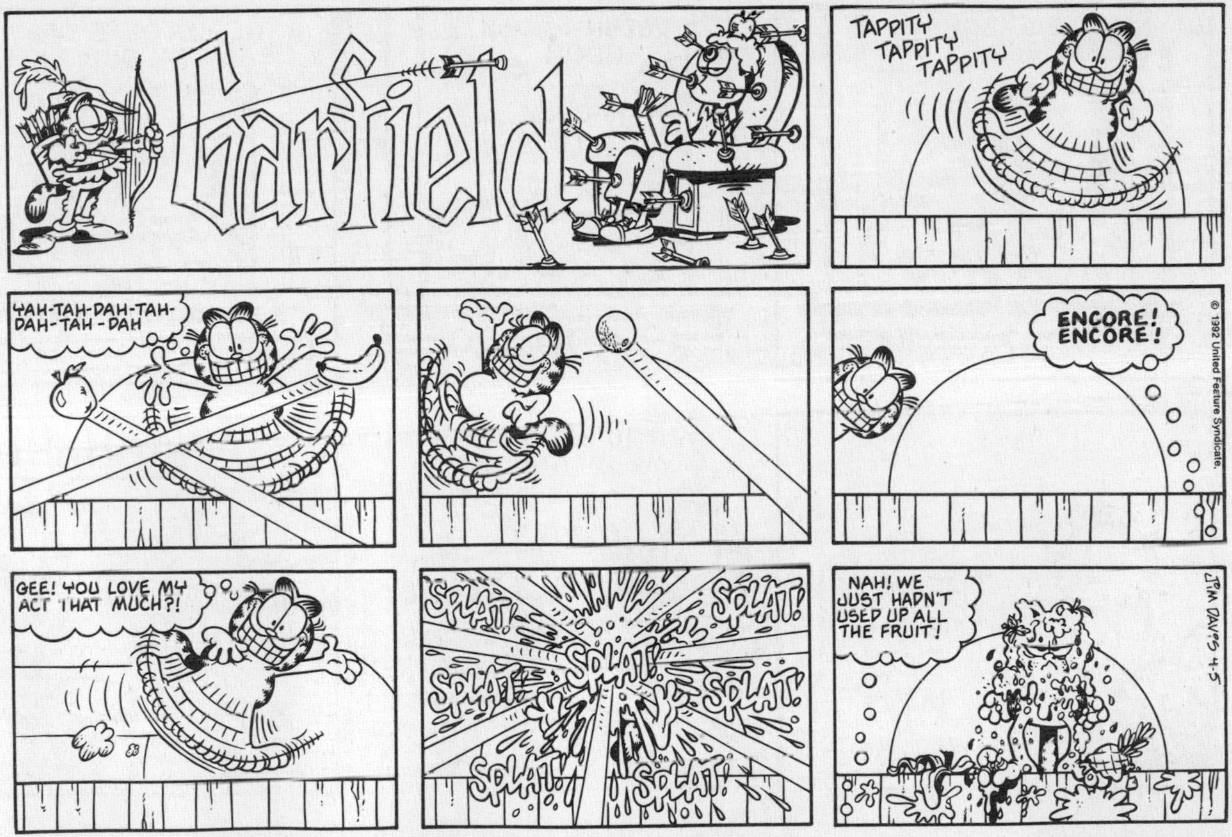
Garfield
TAPPITY TAPPITY TAPPITY
YAH-TAH-DAH-TAH-DAH-TAH-DAH
ENCORE! ENCORE!
© 1992 United Feature Syndicate.
GEE! YOU LOVE MY ACT THAT MUCH?!
SPLAT! SPLAT! SPLAT! SPLAT! SPLAT! SPLAT! SPLAT!
JIM DAVIS 4-5
NAH! WE JUST HADN'T USED UP ALL THE FRUIT!

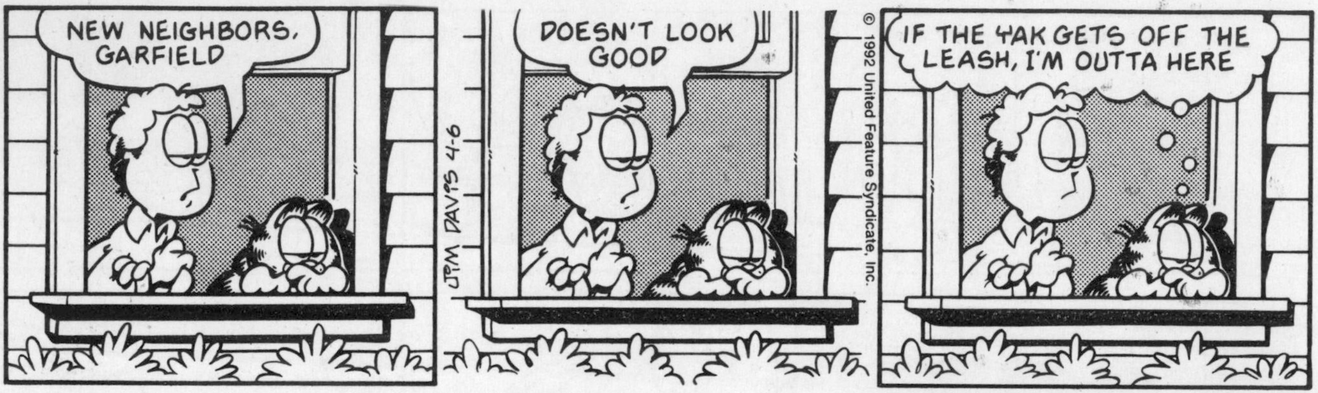
NEW NEIGHBORS, GARFIELD
DOESN'T LOOK GOOD
IF THE YAK GETS OFF THE LEASH, I'M OUTTA HERE
© 1992 United Feature Syndicate, Inc.

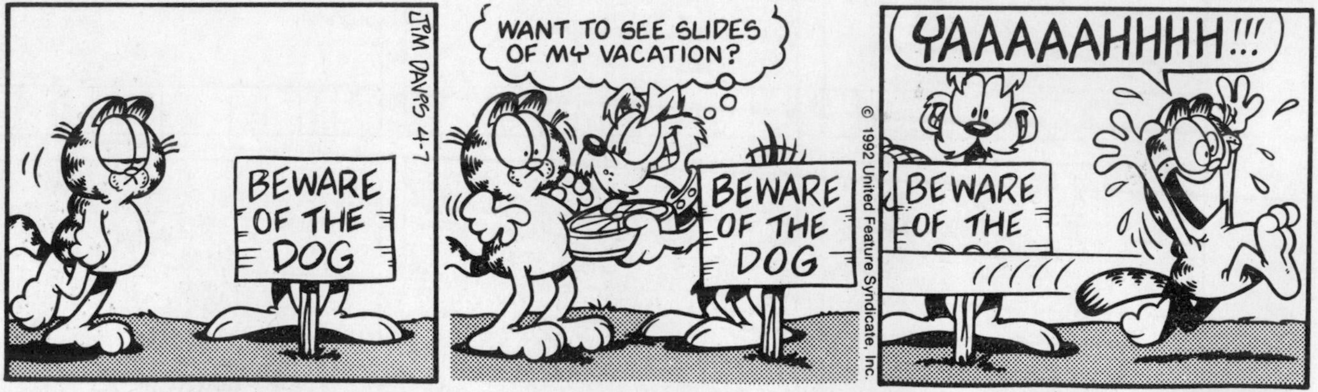
BEWARE OF THE DOG
WANT TO SEE SLIDES OF MY VACATION?
BEWARE OF THE DOG
YAAAAAHHHH!!!
BEWARE OF THE
© 1992 United Feature Syndicate, Inc.

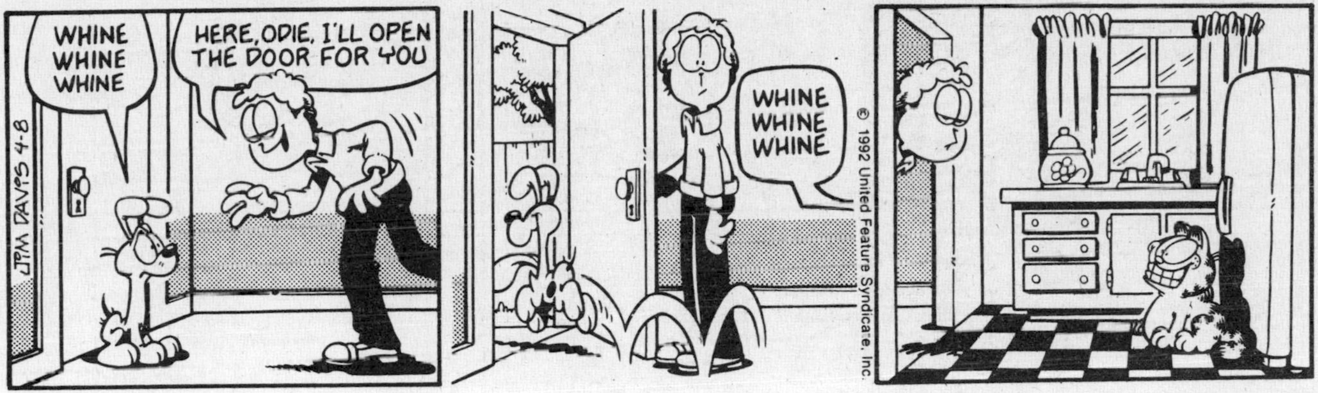
JIM DAVIS 4-8
WHINE WHINE WHINE
HERE, ODIE, I'LL OPEN THE DOOR FOR YOU
WHINE WHINE WHINE
® 1992 United Feature Syndicate, Inc.

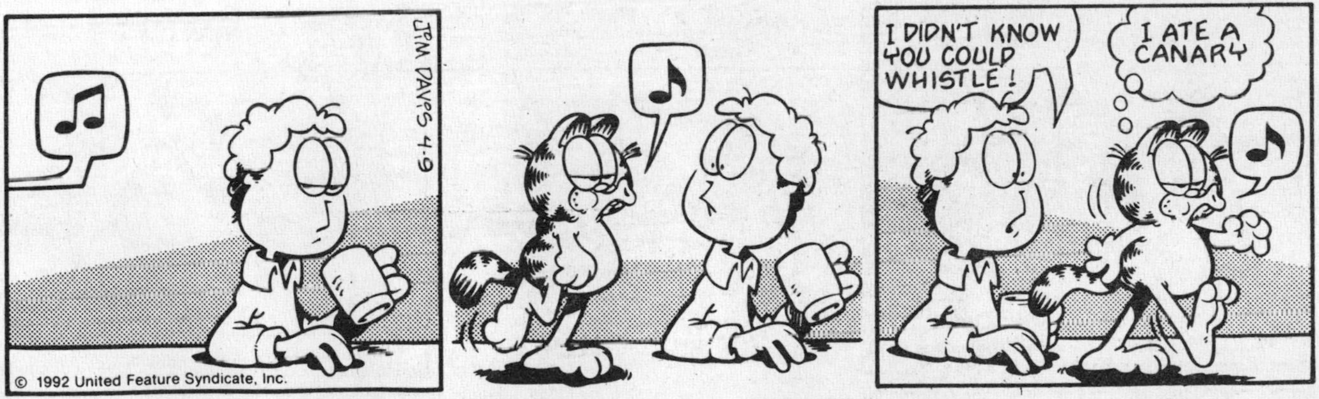
JIM DAVIS 4-9
© 1992 United Feature Syndicate, Inc.
I DIDN'T KNOW YOU COULD WHISTLE!
I ATE A CANARY

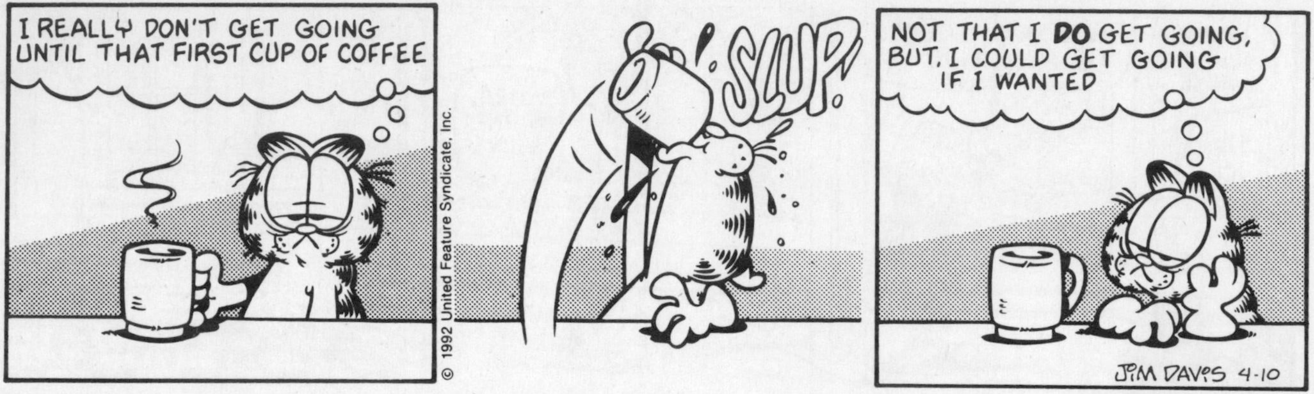
I REALLY DON'T GET GOING UNTIL THAT FIRST CUP OF COFFEE
© 1992 United Feature Syndicate, Inc.
SLUP
NOT THAT I **DO** GET GOING, BUT, I COULD GET GOING IF I WANTED
JIM DAVIS 4-10

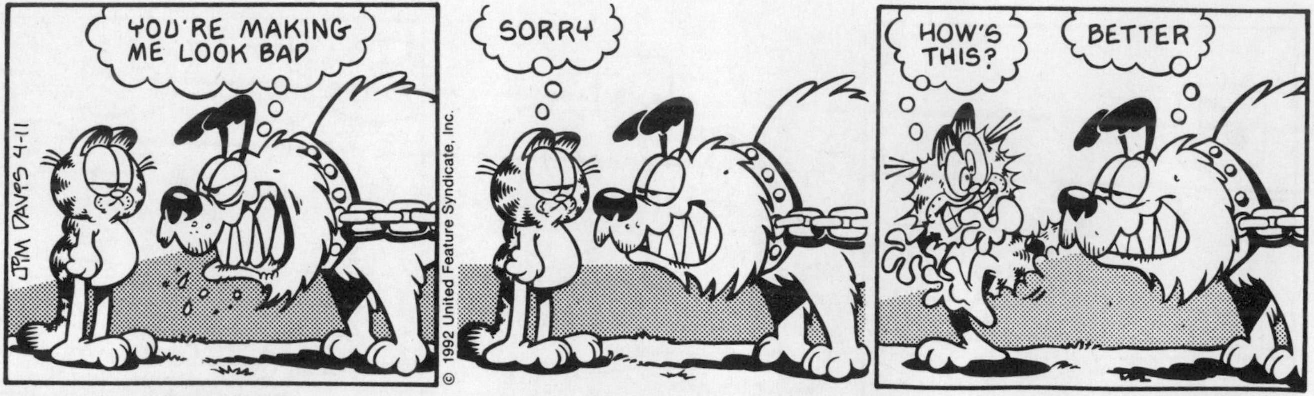
JIM DAVIS 4-11
YOU'RE MAKING ME LOOK BAD
© 1992 United Feature Syndicate, Inc.
SORRY
HOW'S THIS?
BETTER

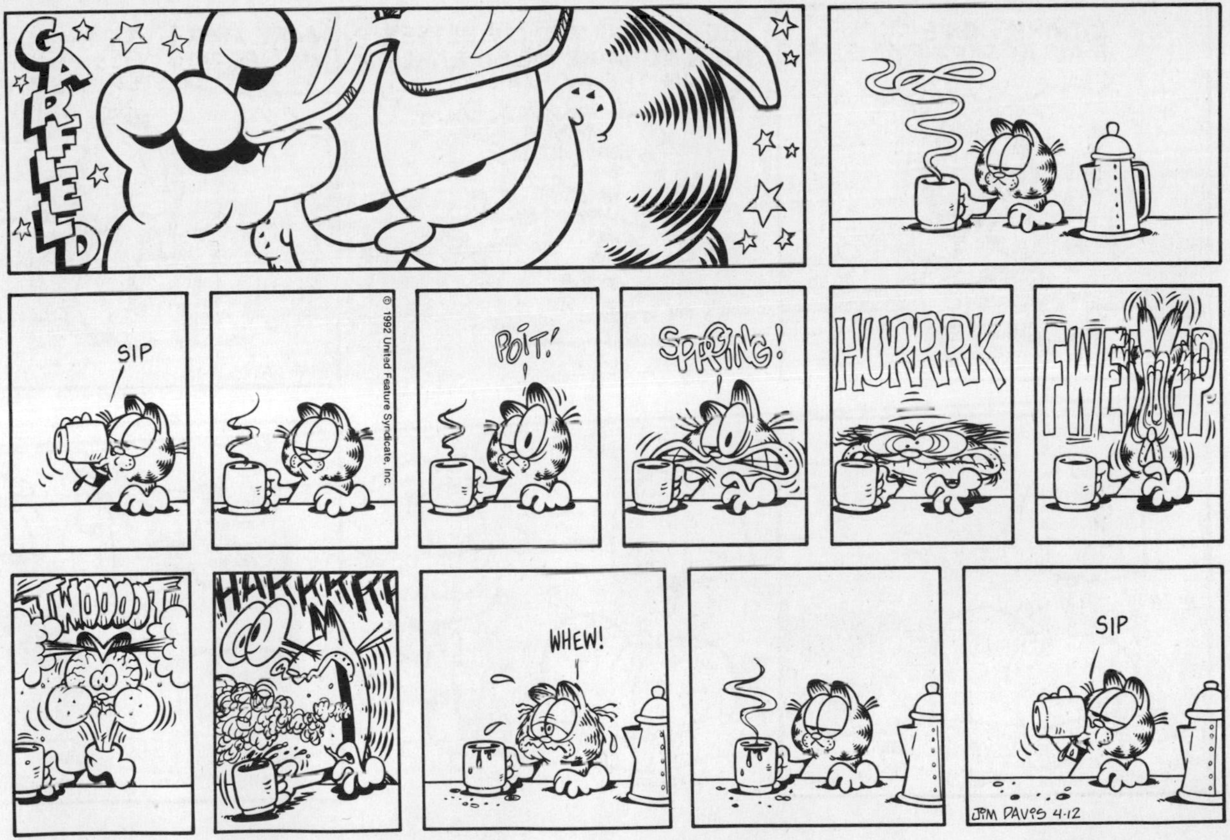
GARFIELD
SIP
© 1992 United Feature Syndicate, Inc.
POIT!
SPROING!
HURRRK
TWOOOOT
WHEW!
SIP
JIM DAVIS 4-12

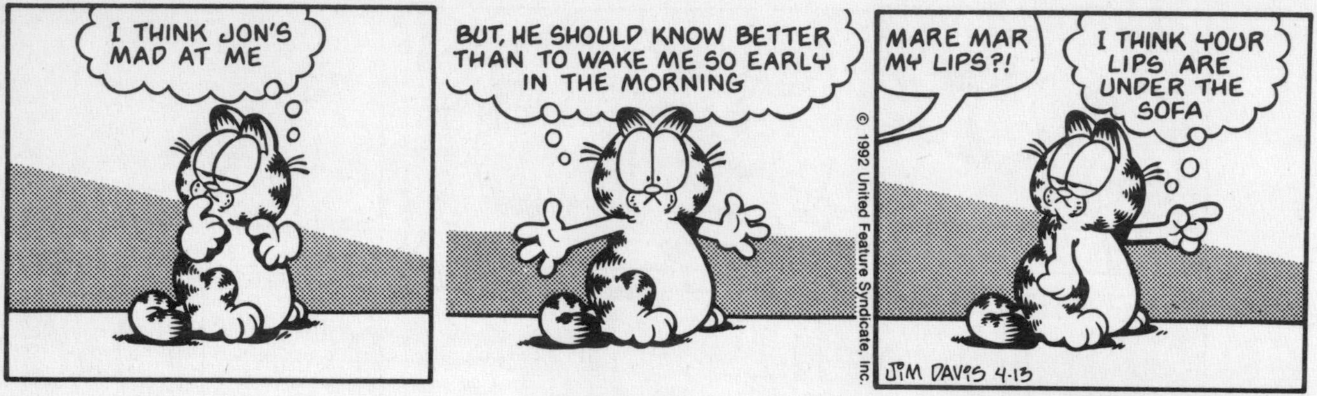
I THINK JON'S MAD AT ME
BUT, HE SHOULD KNOW BETTER THAN TO WAKE ME SO EARLY IN THE MORNING
MARE MAR MY LIPS?!
I THINK YOUR LIPS ARE UNDER THE SOFA
© 1992 United Feature Syndicate, Inc.
JIM DAVIS 4-13

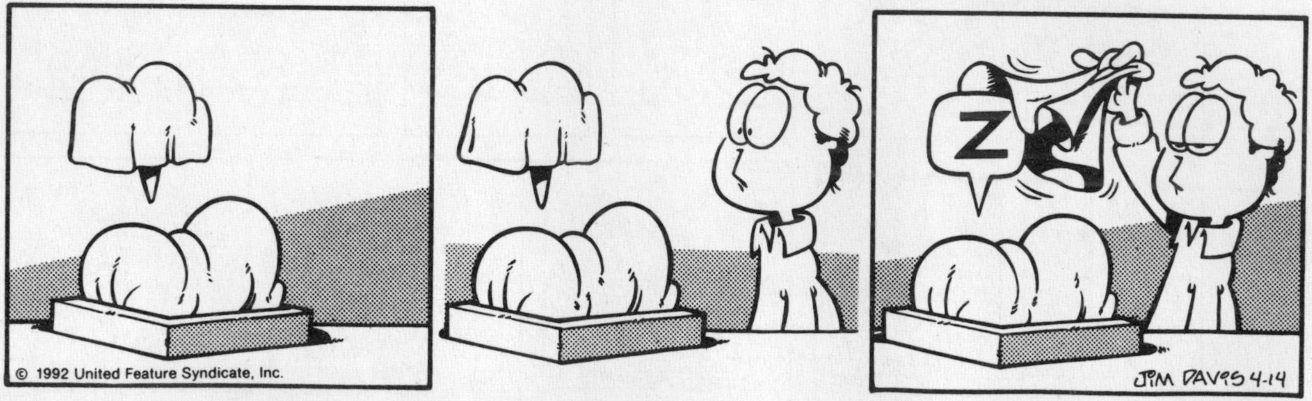
Z
© 1992 United Feature Syndicate, Inc.
JIM DAVIS 4-14

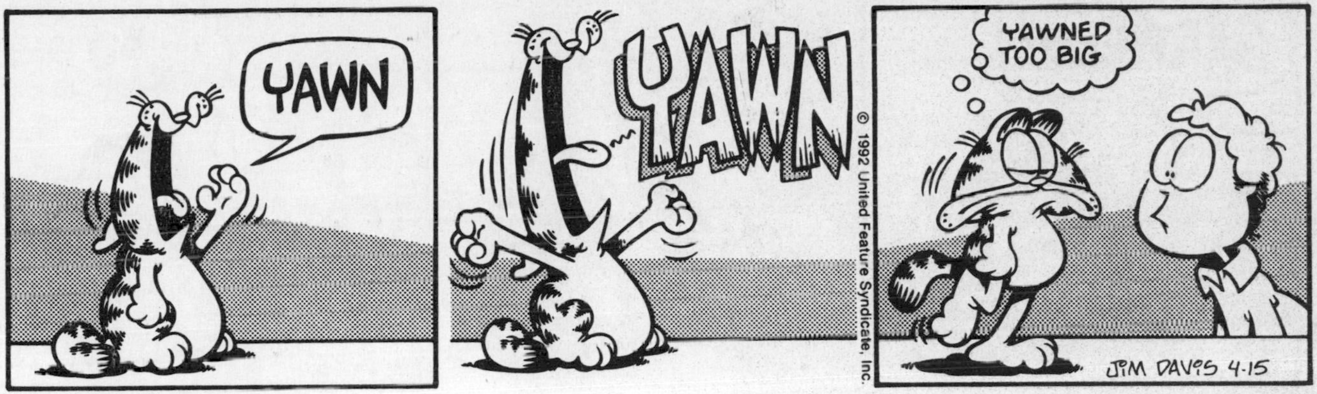
YAWN
YAWN
© 1992 United Feature Syndicate, Inc.
YAWNED TOO BIG
JIM DAVIS 4-15

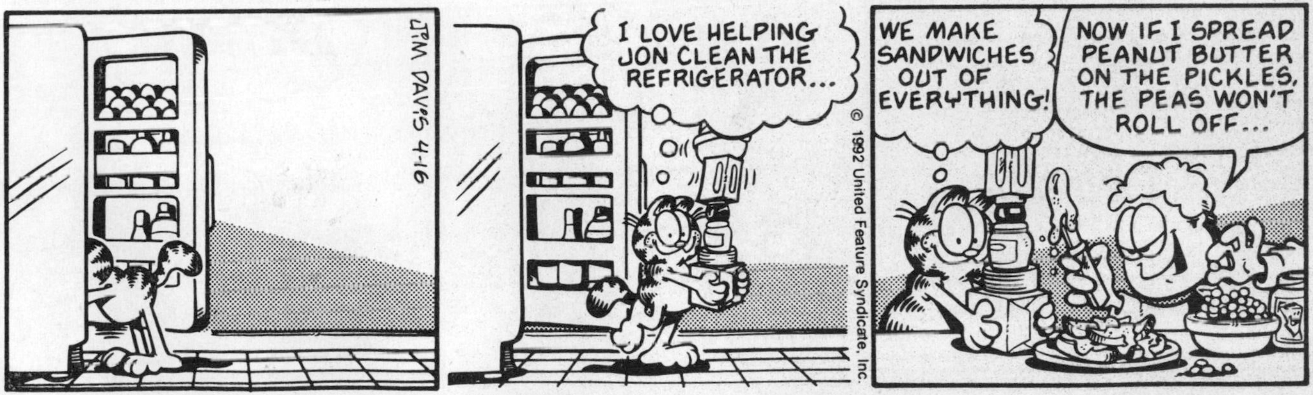
JIM DAVIS 4-16
I LOVE HELPING JON CLEAN THE REFRIGERATOR...
© 1992 United Feature Syndicate, Inc.
WE MAKE SANDWICHES OUT OF EVERYTHING!
NOW IF I SPREAD PEANUT BUTTER ON THE PICKLES, THE PEAS WON'T ROLL OFF...

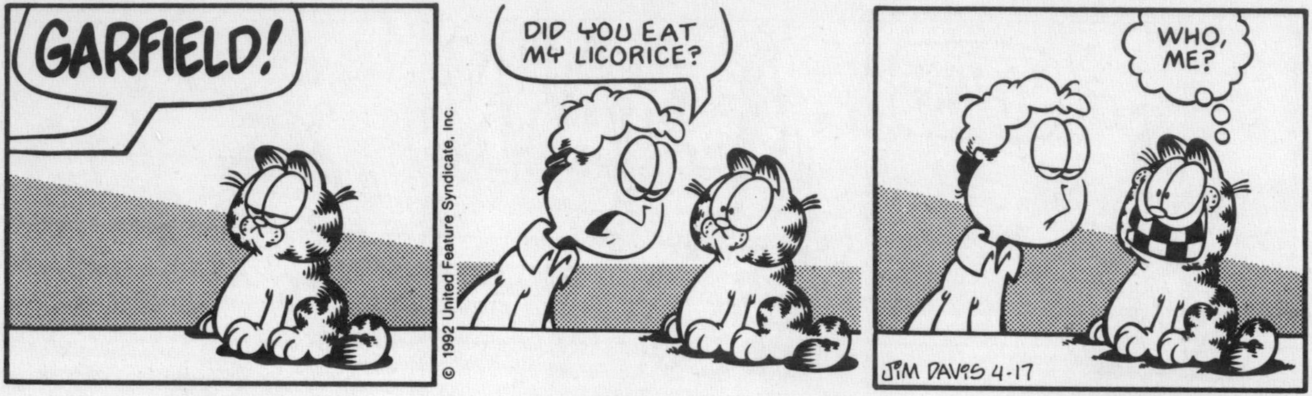
GARFIELD!
DID YOU EAT MY LICORICE?
WHO, ME?
© 1992 United Feature Syndicate, Inc.
JIM DAVIS 4-17

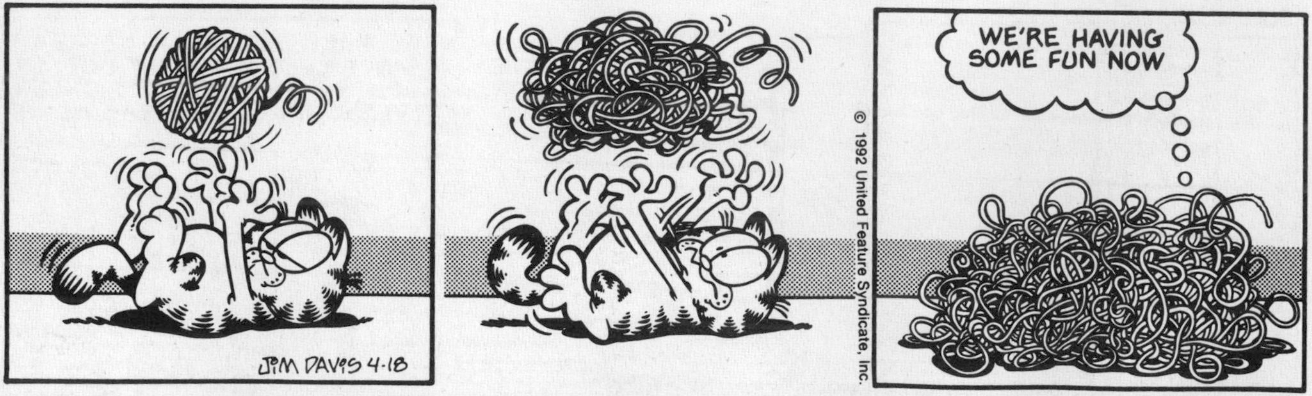
WE'RE HAVING SOME FUN NOW
© 1992 United Feature Syndicate, Inc.
JIM DAVIS 4-18

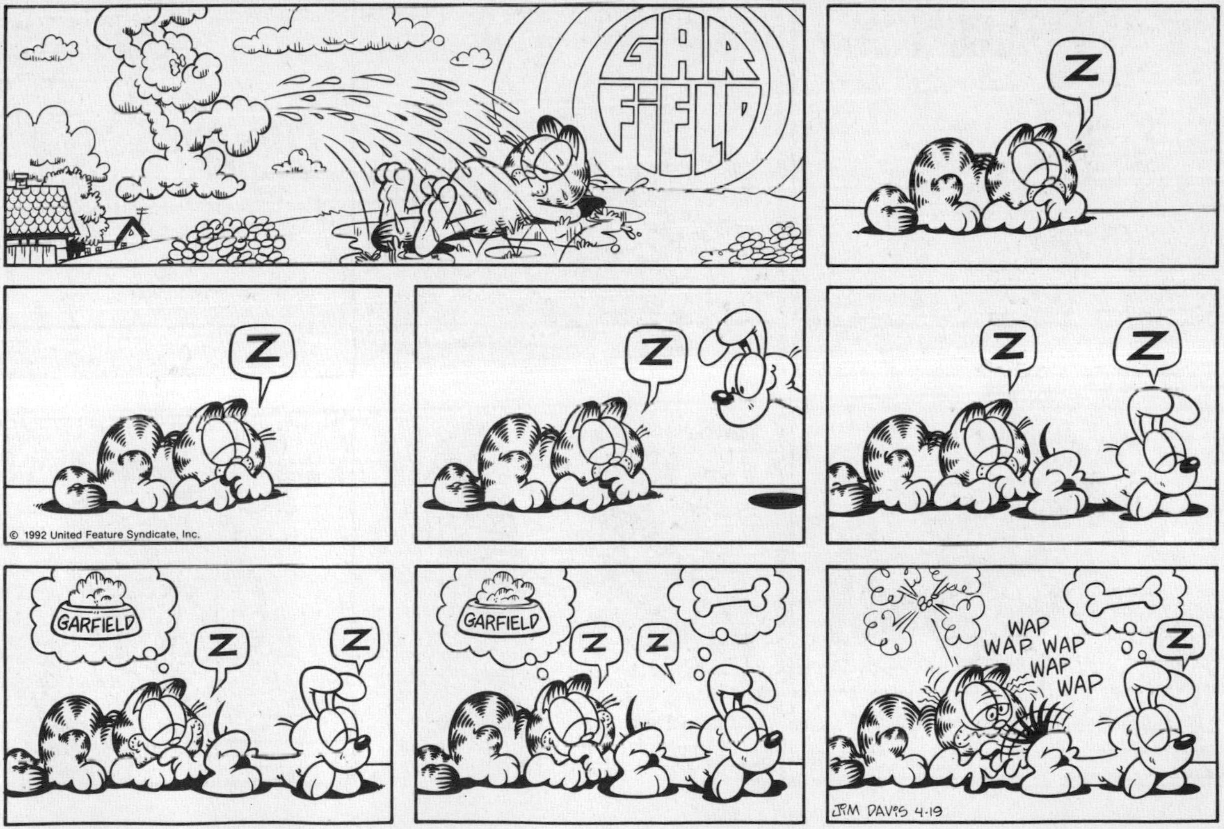
GARFIELD
Z
Z
Z
Z
Z
GARFIELD
Z
Z
GARFIELD
Z
Z
WAP
WAP WAP
WAP
WAP
Z
© 1992 United Feature Syndicate, Inc.
JIM DAVIS 4-19

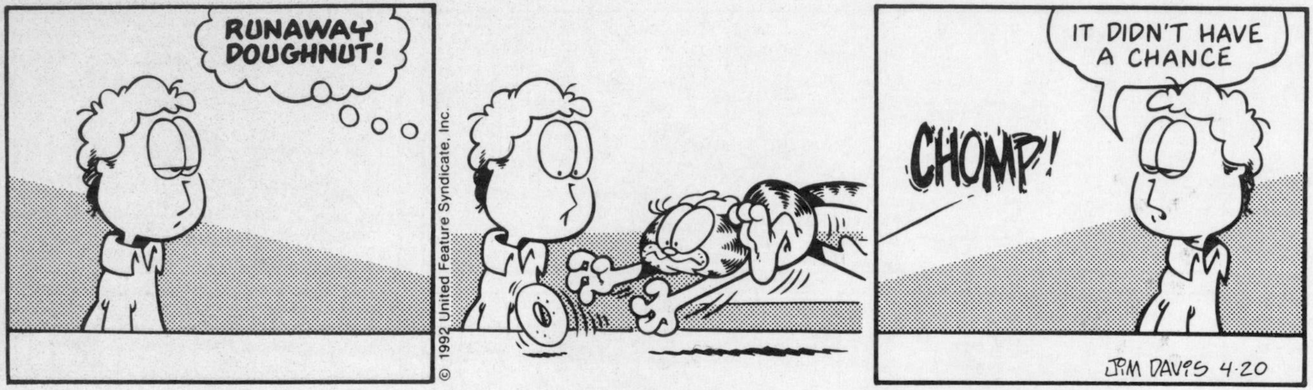
RUNAWAY DOUGHNUT!
© 1992 United Feature Syndicate, Inc.
CHOMP!
IT DIDN'T HAVE A CHANCE
JIM DAVIS 4·20

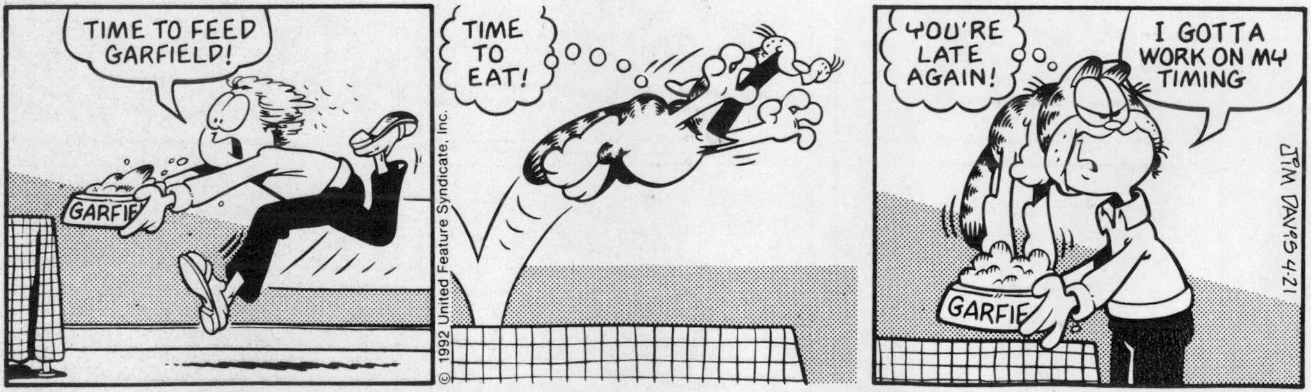
TIME TO FEED GARFIELD!
GARFIE
© 1992 United Feature Syndicate, Inc.
TIME TO EAT!
YOU'RE LATE AGAIN!
I GOTTA WORK ON MY TIMING
GARFIE
JIM DAVIS 4·21

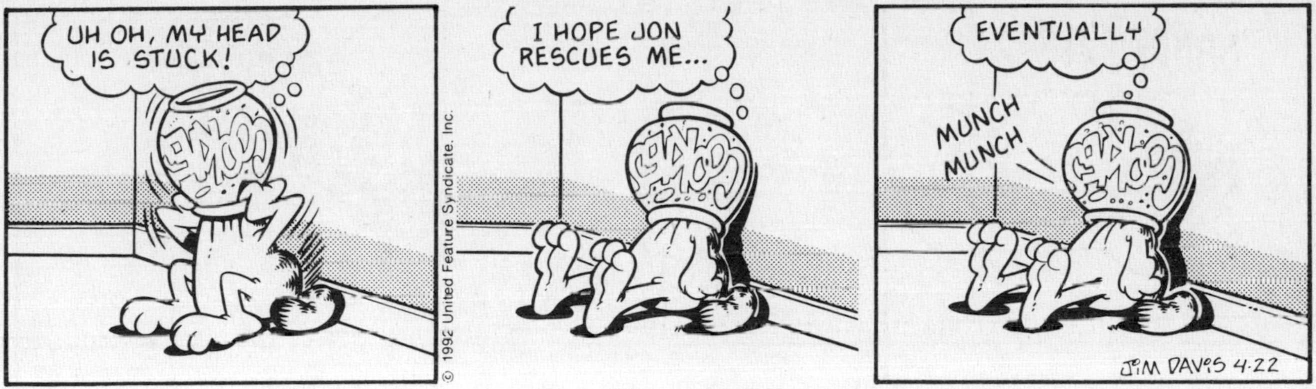
UH OH, MY HEAD IS STUCK!
I HOPE JON RESCUES ME...
EVENTUALLY
MUNCH MUNCH
JIM DAVIS 4-22

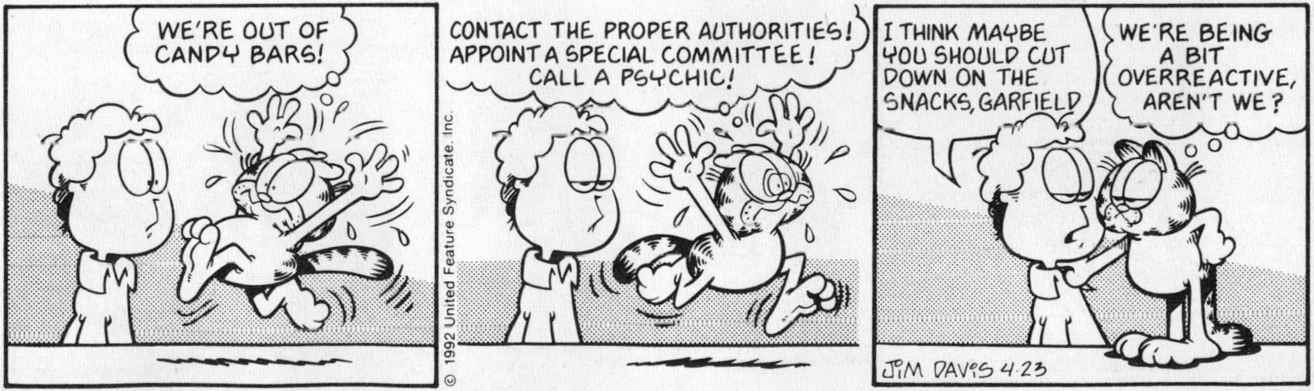
WE'RE OUT OF CANDY BARS!
CONTACT THE PROPER AUTHORITIES! APPOINT A SPECIAL COMMITTEE! CALL A PSYCHIC!
I THINK MAYBE YOU SHOULD CUT DOWN ON THE SNACKS, GARFIELD
WE'RE BEING A BIT OVERREACTIVE, AREN'T WE?
JIM DAVIS 4-23

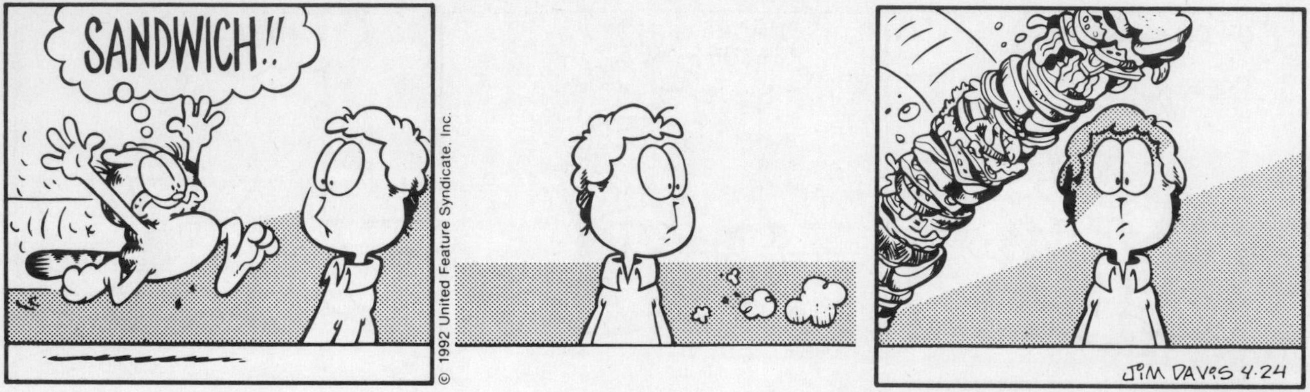
SANDWICH!!
© 1992 United Feature Syndicate, Inc.
JIM DAVIS 4·24

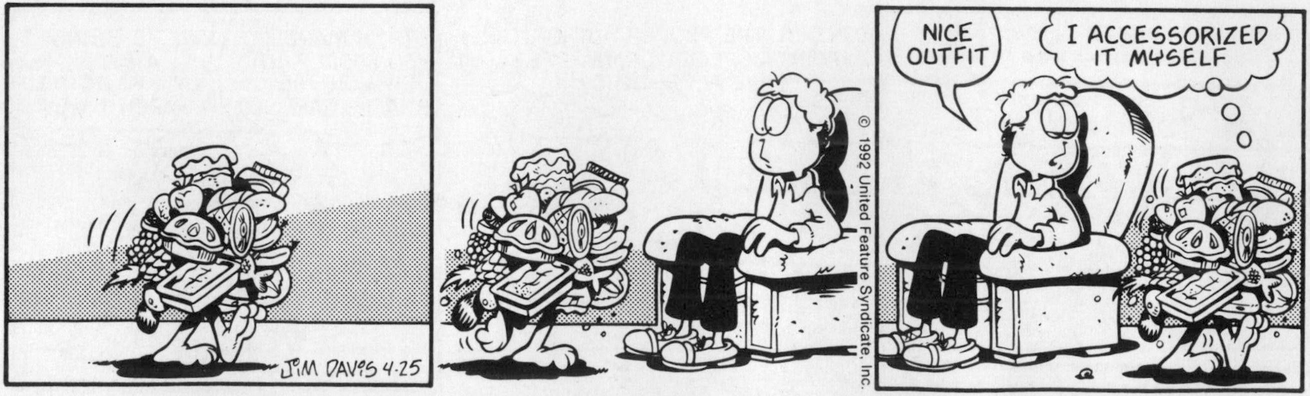
JIM DAVIS 4·25
© 1992 United Feature Syndicate, Inc.
NICE OUTFIT
I ACCESSORIZED IT MYSELF

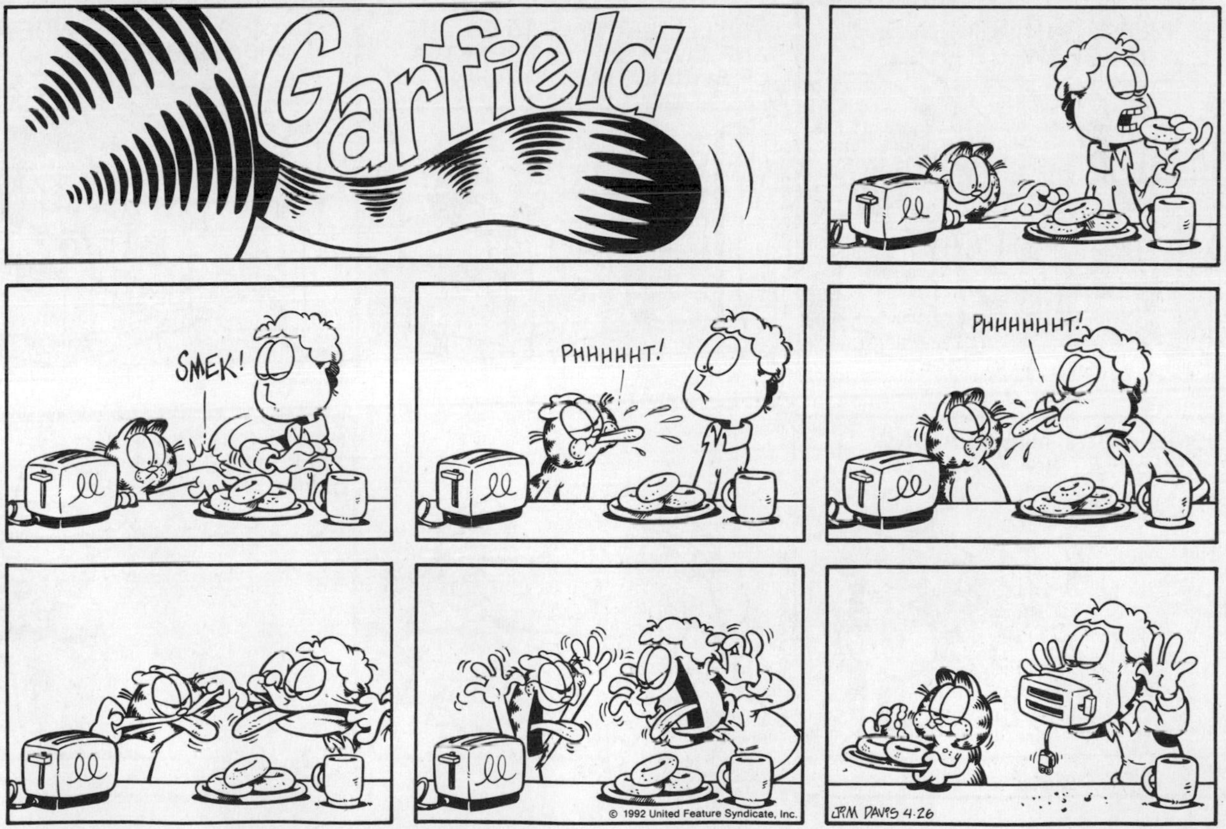
Garfield
SMEK!
PHHHHHT!
PHHHHHHT!
© 1992 United Feature Syndicate, Inc.
JIM DAVIS 4-26

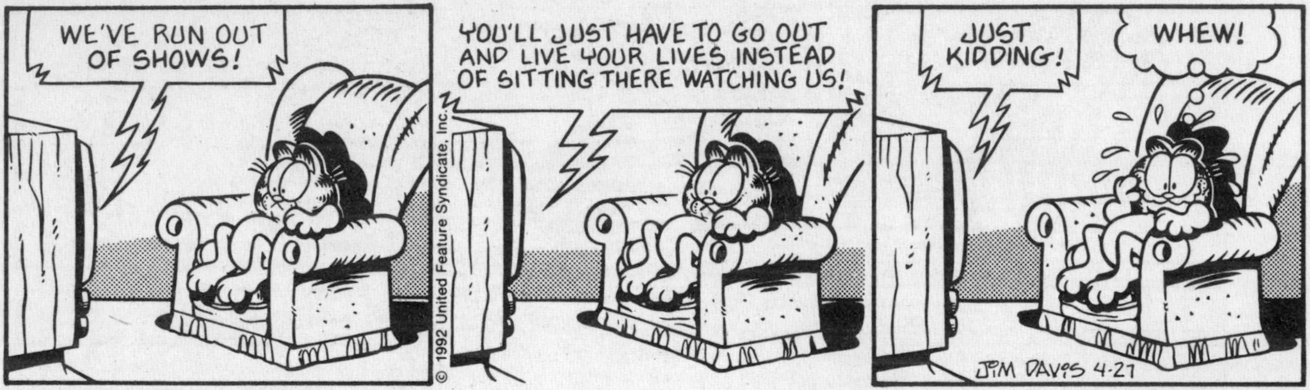
WE'VE RUN OUT OF SHOWS!
YOU'LL JUST HAVE TO GO OUT AND LIVE YOUR LIVES INSTEAD OF SITTING THERE WATCHING US!
JUST KIDDING!
WHEW!
JIM DAVIS 4-27
© 1992 United Feature Syndicate, Inc.

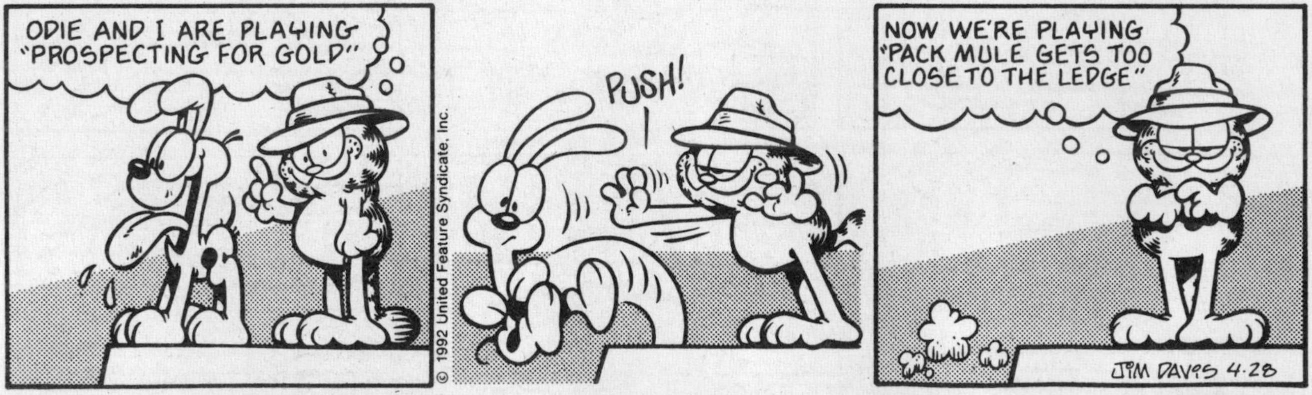
ODIE AND I ARE PLAYING "PROSPECTING FOR GOLD"
PUSH!
NOW WE'RE PLAYING "PACK MULE GETS TOO CLOSE TO THE LEDGE"
JIM DAVIS 4-28
© 1992 United Feature Syndicate, Inc.

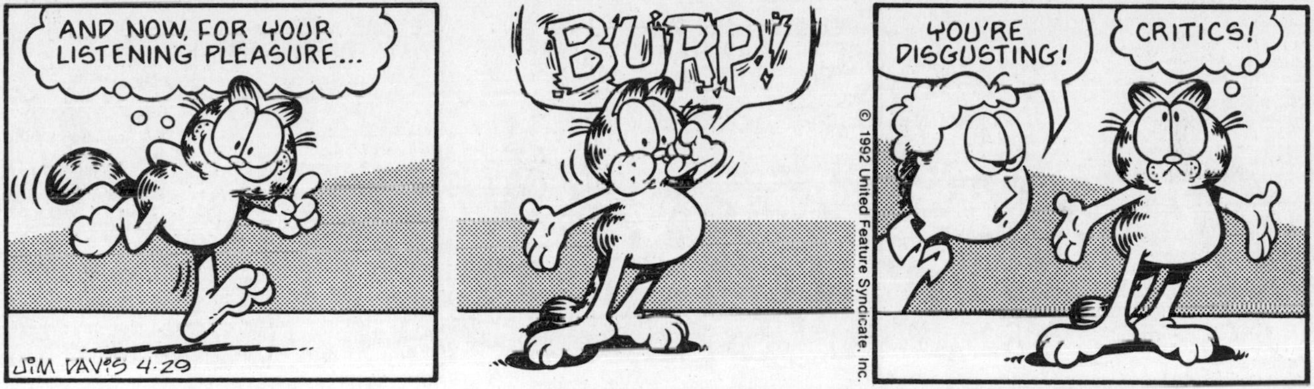
AND NOW, FOR YOUR LISTENING PLEASURE...
JIM DAVIS 4-29
BURP!
YOU'RE DISGUSTING!
CRITICS!

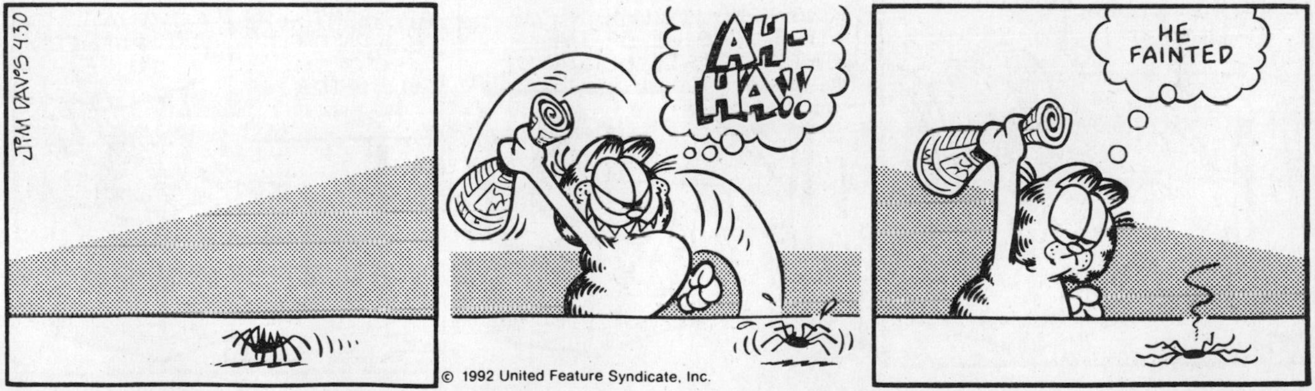
JIM DAVIS 4-30
AH-HA!!
HE FAINTED

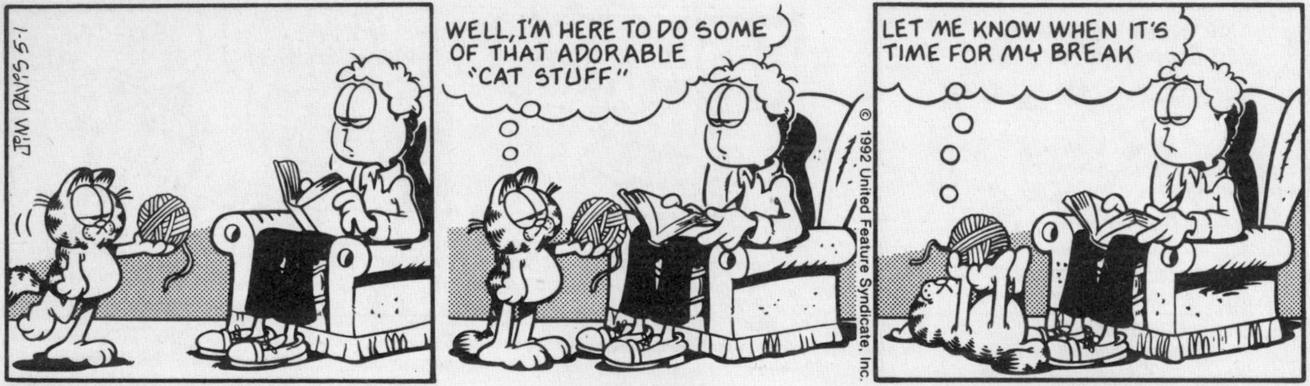
JIM DAVIS 5-1
WELL, I'M HERE TO DO SOME OF THAT ADORABLE "CAT STUFF"
© 1992 United Feature Syndicate, Inc.
LET ME KNOW WHEN IT'S TIME FOR MY BREAK

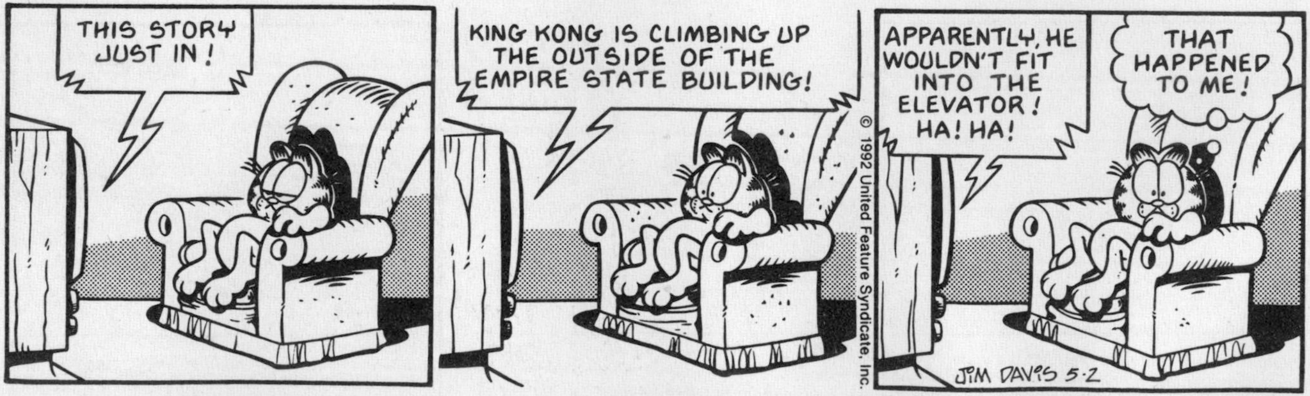
THIS STORY JUST IN!
KING KONG IS CLIMBING UP THE OUTSIDE OF THE EMPIRE STATE BUILDING!
© 1992 United Feature Syndicate, Inc.
APPARENTLY, HE WOULDN'T FIT INTO THE ELEVATOR! HA! HA!
THAT HAPPENED TO ME!
JIM DAVIS 5-2

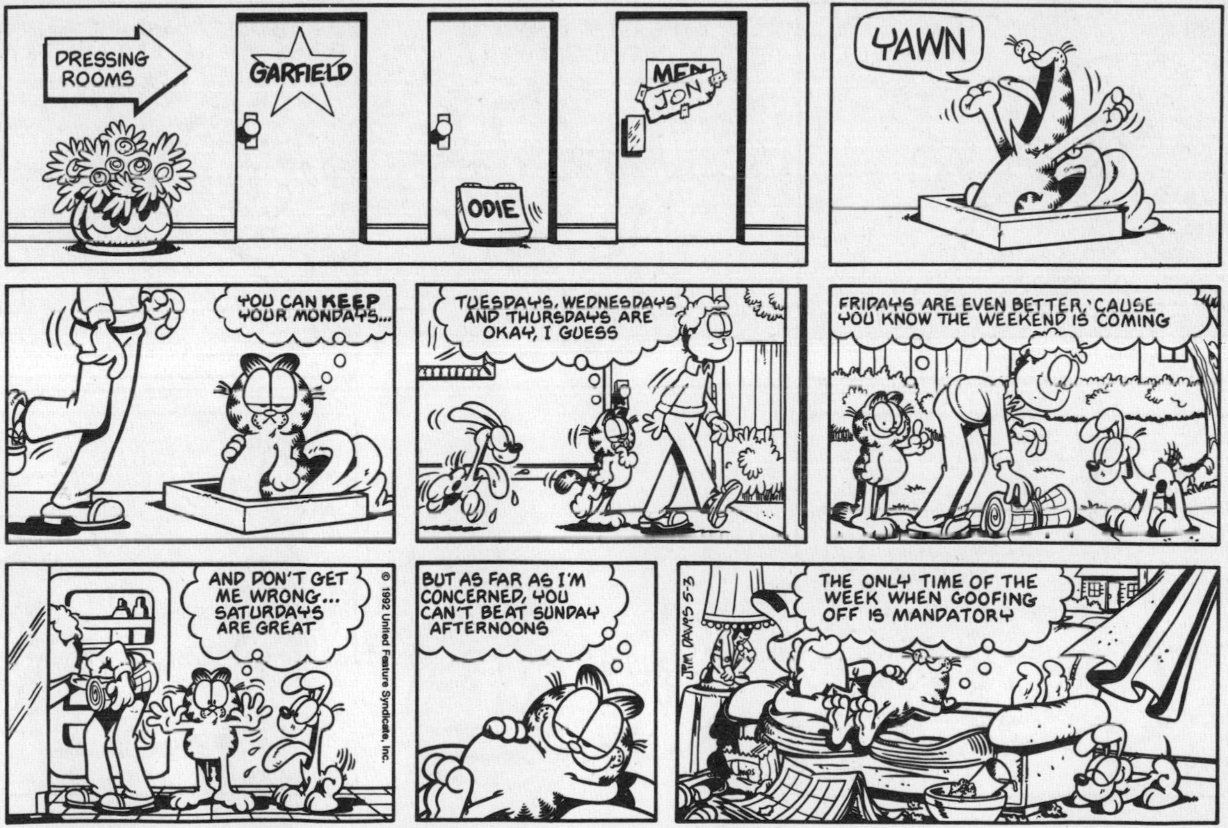
DRESSING ROOMS
GARFIELD
ODIE
MEN
JON
YAWN
YOU CAN KEEP YOUR MONDAYS...
TUESDAYS, WEDNESDAYS AND THURSDAYS ARE OKAY, I GUESS
FRIDAYS ARE EVEN BETTER, 'CAUSE YOU KNOW THE WEEKEND IS COMING
AND DON'T GET ME WRONG... SATURDAYS ARE GREAT
© 1992 United Feature Syndicate, Inc.
BUT AS FAR AS I'M CONCERNED, YOU CAN'T BEAT SUNDAY AFTERNOONS
JIM DAVIS 5-3
THE ONLY TIME OF THE WEEK WHEN GOOFING OFF IS MANDATORY

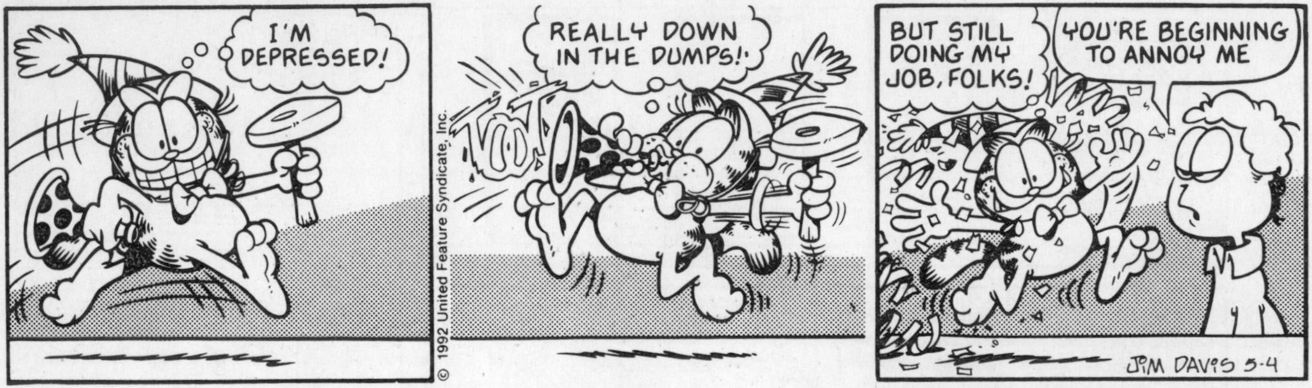
I'M DEPRESSED!
© 1992 United Feature Syndicate, Inc.
REALLY DOWN IN THE DUMPS!
TOOT
BUT STILL DOING MY JOB, FOLKS!
YOU'RE BEGINNING TO ANNOY ME
JIM DAVIS 5-4

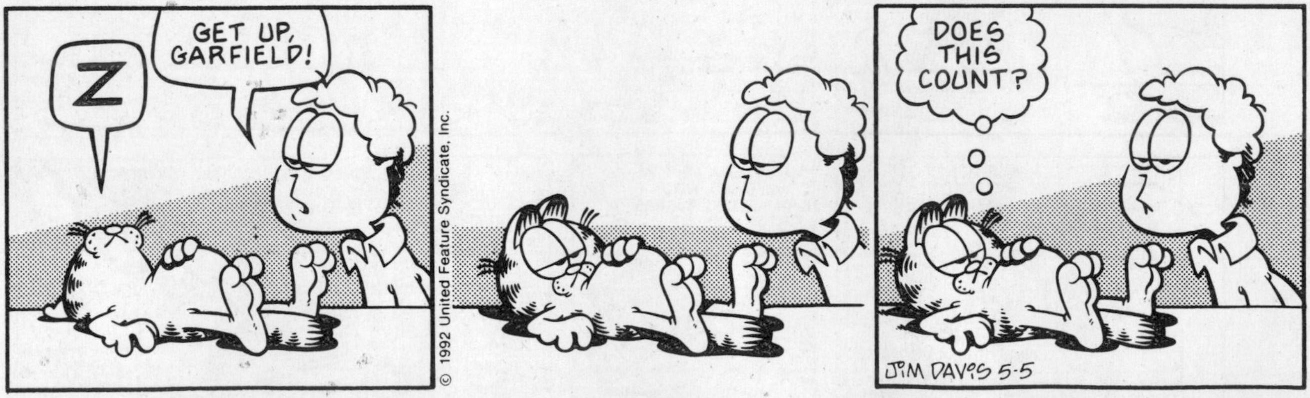
Z
GET UP, GARFIELD!
© 1992 United Feature Syndicate, Inc.
DOES THIS COUNT?
JIM DAVIS 5-5

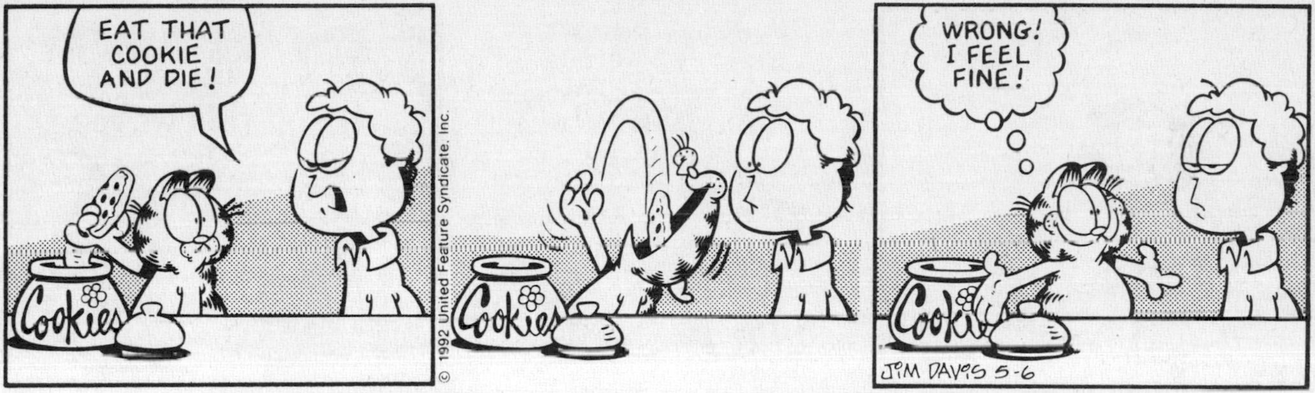
EAT THAT COOKIE AND DIE!
© 1992 United Feature Syndicate, Inc.
WRONG! I FEEL FINE!
JIM DAVIS 5-6

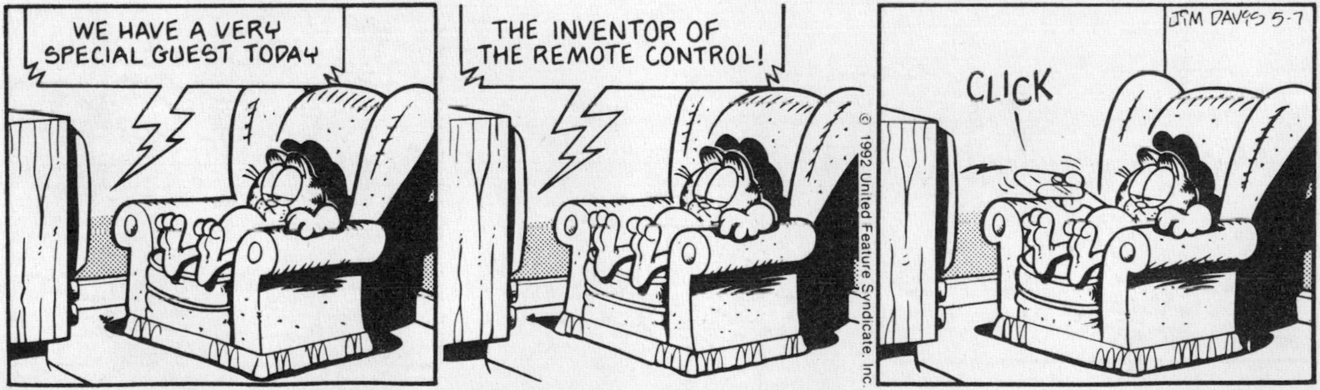
WE HAVE A VERY SPECIAL GUEST TODAY
THE INVENTOR OF THE REMOTE CONTROL!
© 1992 United Feature Syndicate, Inc.
JIM DAVIS 5-7
CLICK

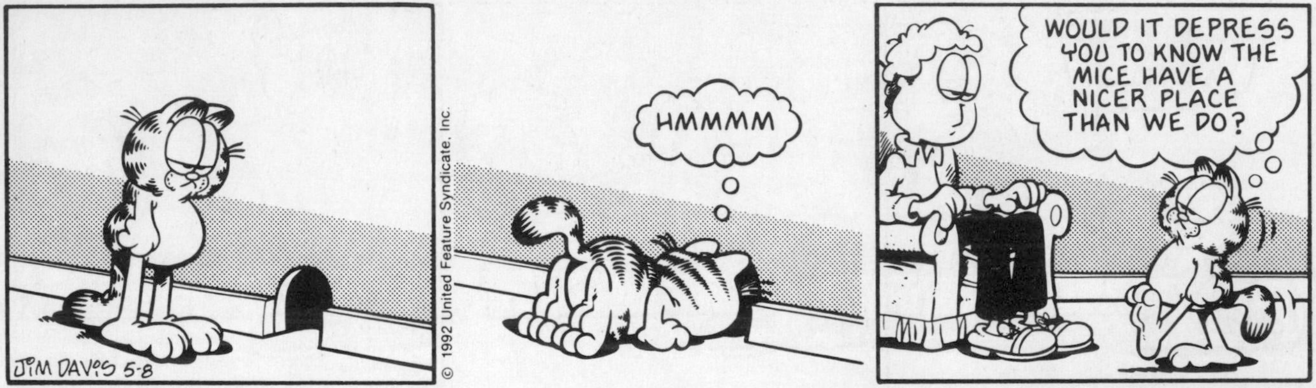
JIM DAVIS 5-8
© 1992 United Feature Syndicate, Inc.
HMMMM
WOULD IT DEPRESS YOU TO KNOW THE MICE HAVE A NICER PLACE THAN WE DO?

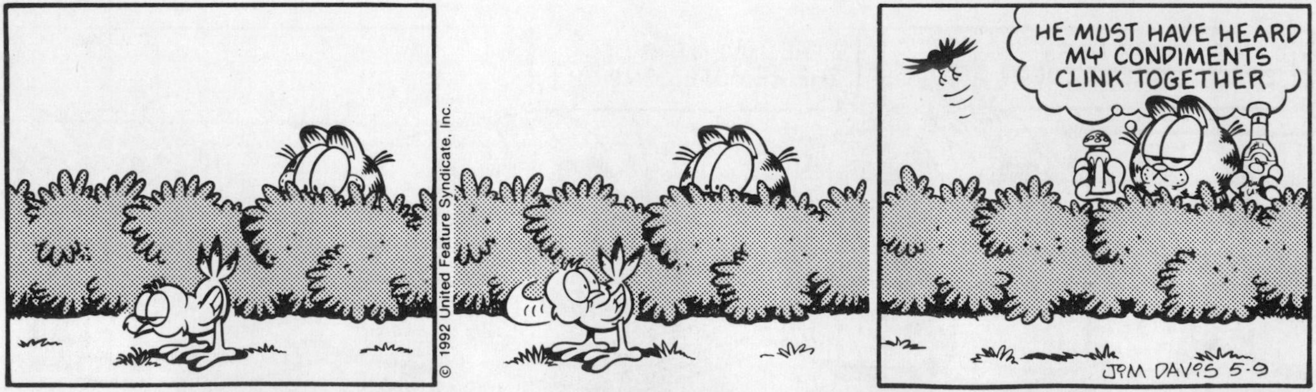
© 1992 United Feature Syndicate, Inc.
HE MUST HAVE HEARD MY CONDIMENTS CLINK TOGETHER
JIM DAVIS 5-9

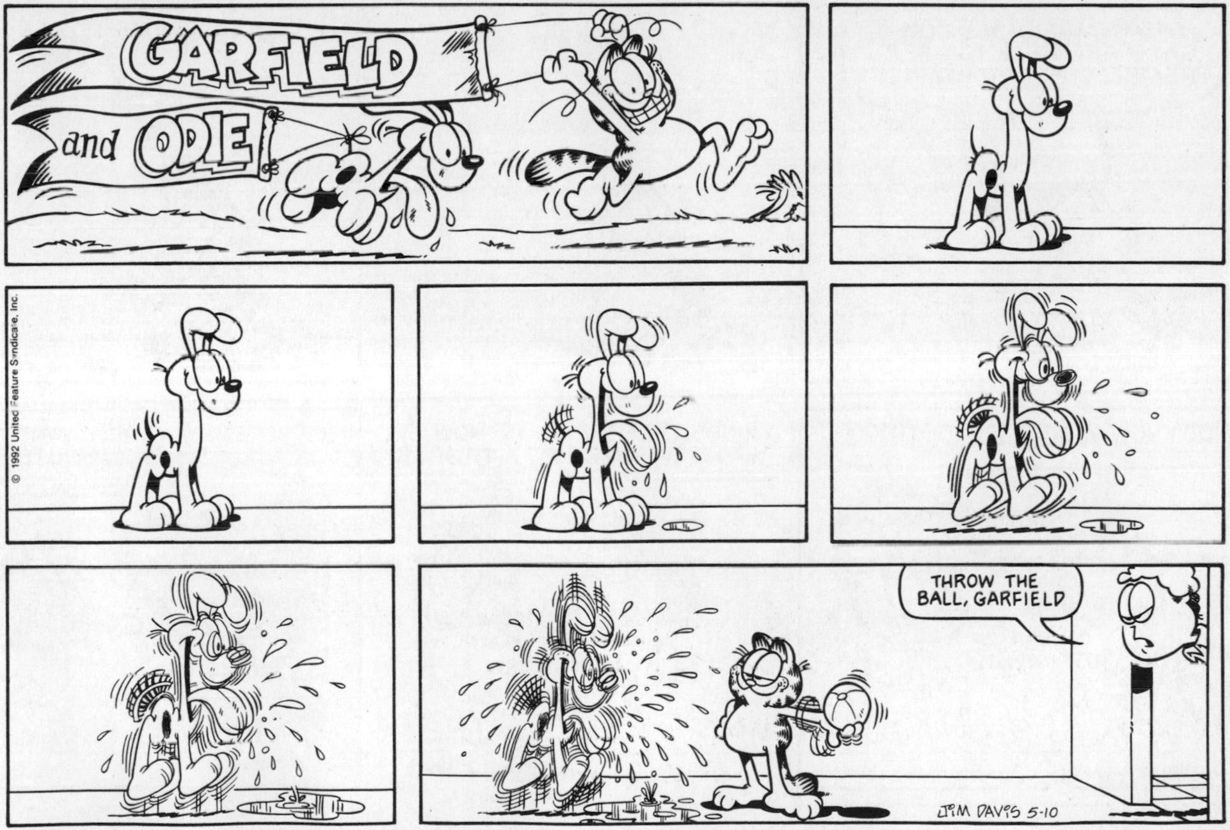
GARFIELD
and ODIE
© 1992 United Feature Syndicate, Inc.
THROW THE BALL, GARFIELD
JIM DAVIS 5-10

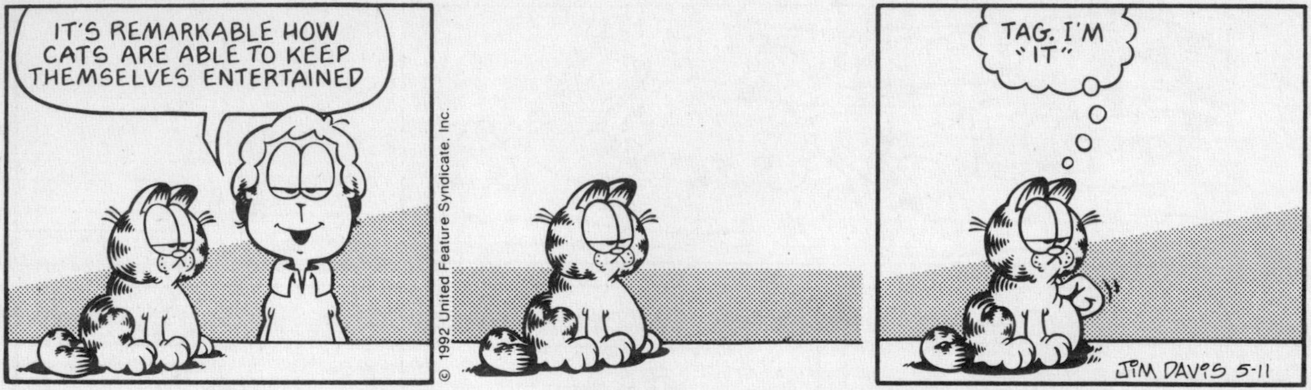
IT'S REMARKABLE HOW CATS ARE ABLE TO KEEP THEMSELVES ENTERTAINED
© 1992 United Feature Syndicate, Inc.
TAG. I'M "IT"
JIM DAVIS 5-11

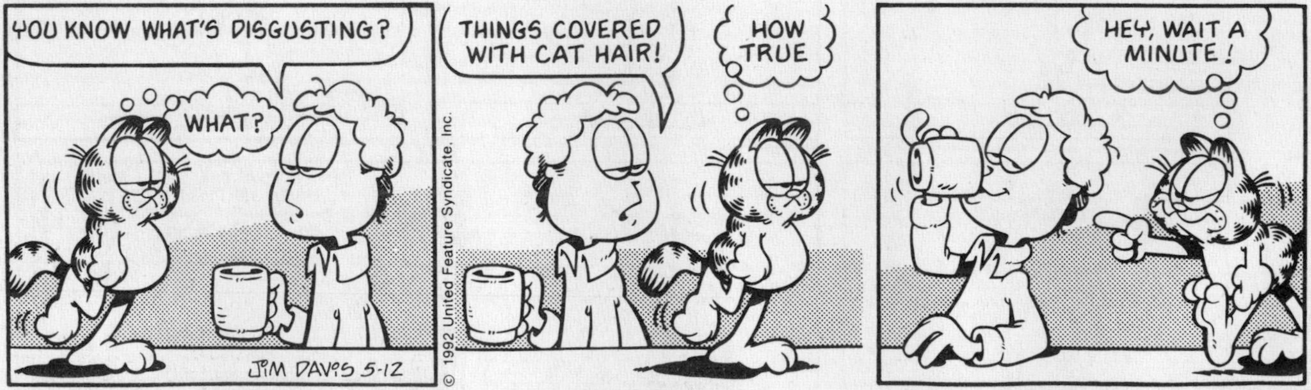
YOU KNOW WHAT'S DISGUSTING?
WHAT?
JIM DAVIS 5-12
© 1992 United Feature Syndicate, Inc.
THINGS COVERED WITH CAT HAIR!
HOW TRUE
HEY, WAIT A MINUTE!

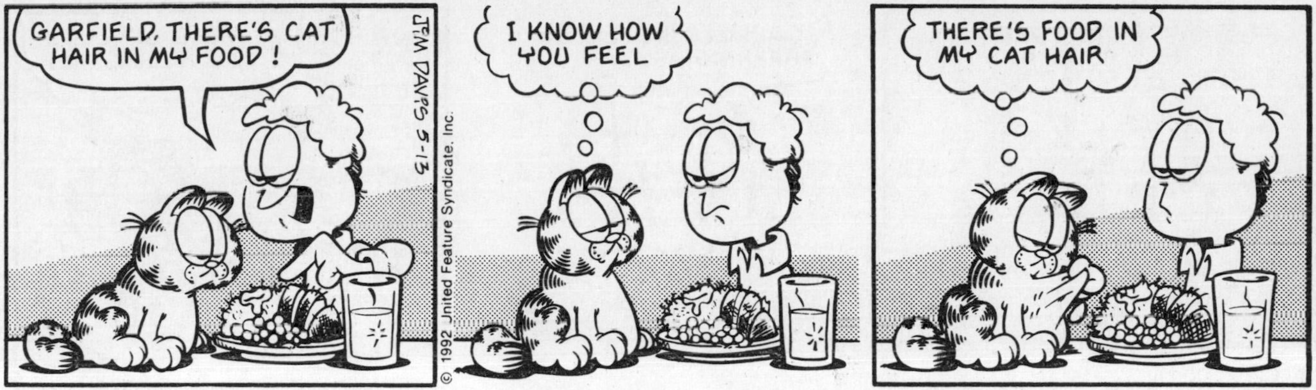
GARFIELD, THERE'S CAT HAIR IN MY FOOD!
I KNOW HOW YOU FEEL
THERE'S FOOD IN MY CAT HAIR
JIM DAVIS 5-13
© 1992 United Feature Syndicate, Inc.

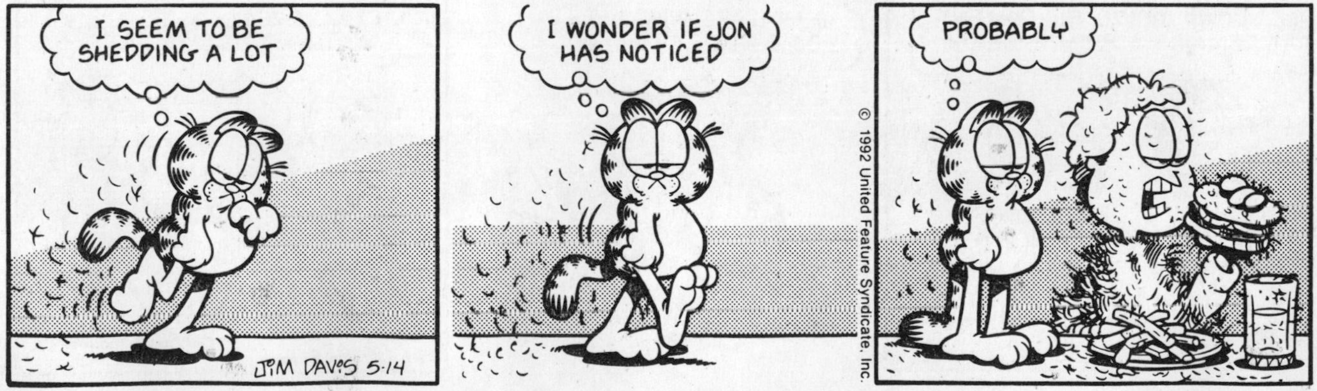
I SEEM TO BE SHEDDING A LOT
I WONDER IF JON HAS NOTICED
PROBABLY
JIM DAVIS 5-14
© 1992 United Feature Syndicate, Inc.

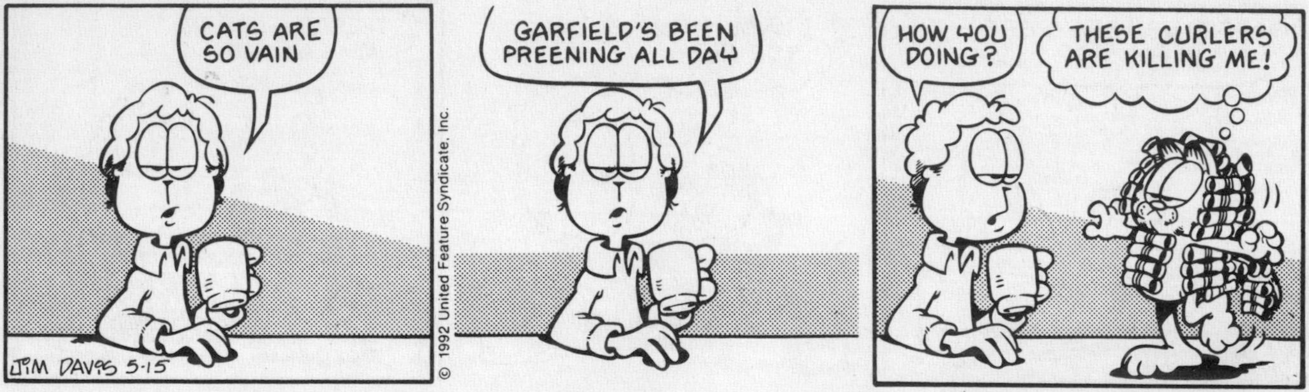
CATS ARE SO VAIN
GARFIELD'S BEEN PREENING ALL DAY
© 1992 United Feature Syndicate, Inc.
HOW YOU DOING?
THESE CURLERS ARE KILLING ME!
JIM DAVIS 5-15

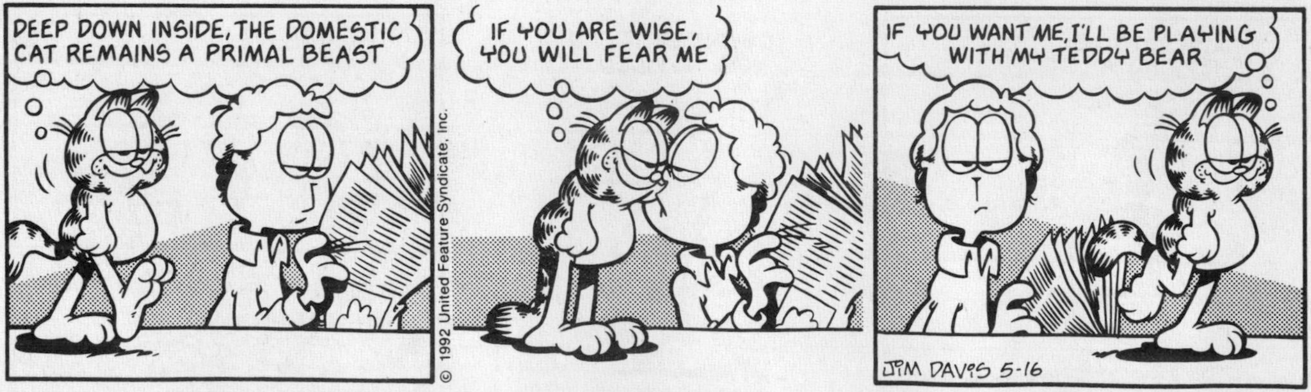
DEEP DOWN INSIDE, THE DOMESTIC CAT REMAINS A PRIMAL BEAST
IF YOU ARE WISE, YOU WILL FEAR ME
© 1992 United Feature Syndicate, Inc.
IF YOU WANT ME, I'LL BE PLAYING WITH MY TEDDY BEAR
JIM DAVIS 5-16

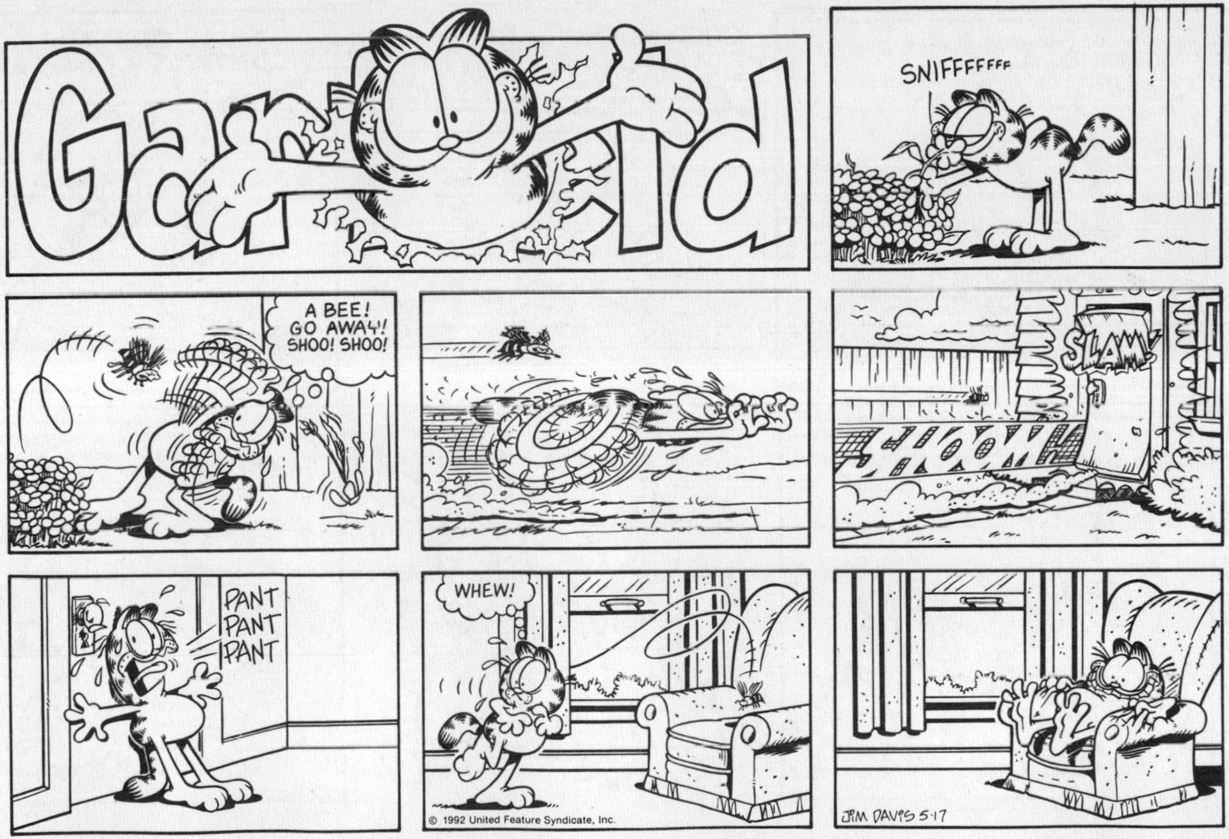
Garfield
SNIFFFFFFF
A BEE! GO AWAY! SHOO! SHOO!
SLAM
SHOOWH
PANT
PANT
PANT
WHEW!
© 1992 United Feature Syndicate, Inc.
JIM DAVIS 5-17

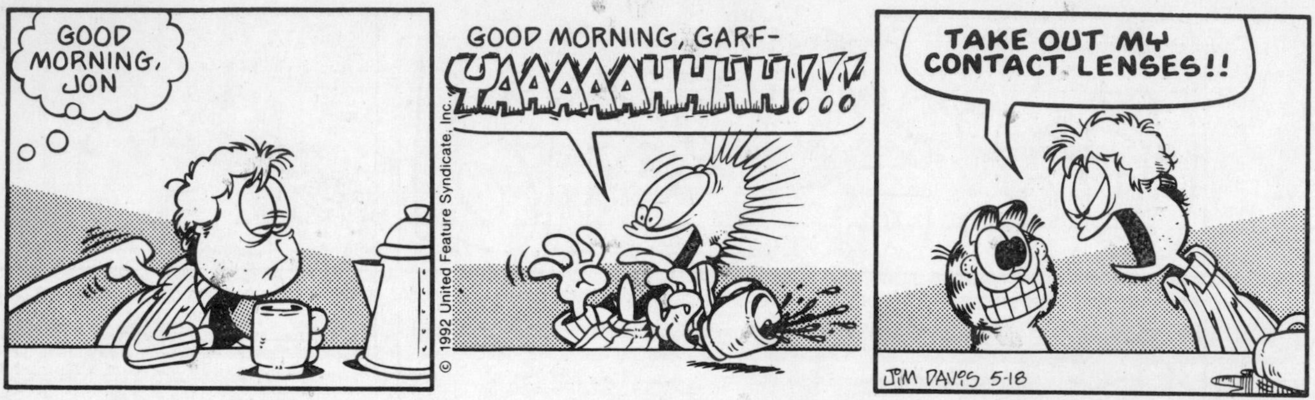
GOOD MORNING, JON
GOOD MORNING, GARF-
YAAAAAHHHH!!!
TAKE OUT MY CONTACT LENSES!!
© 1992 United Feature Syndicate, Inc.
JIM DAVIS 5-18

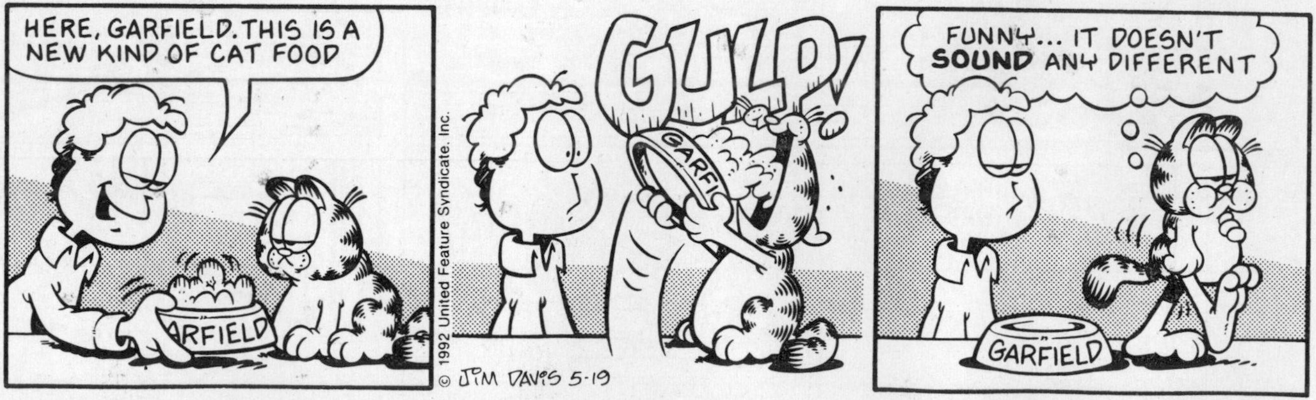
HERE, GARFIELD. THIS IS A NEW KIND OF CAT FOOD
ARFIELD
GULP!
GARFI
FUNNY... IT DOESN'T **SOUND** ANY DIFFERENT
GARFIELD
© 1992 United Feature Syndicate, Inc.
JIM DAVIS 5-19

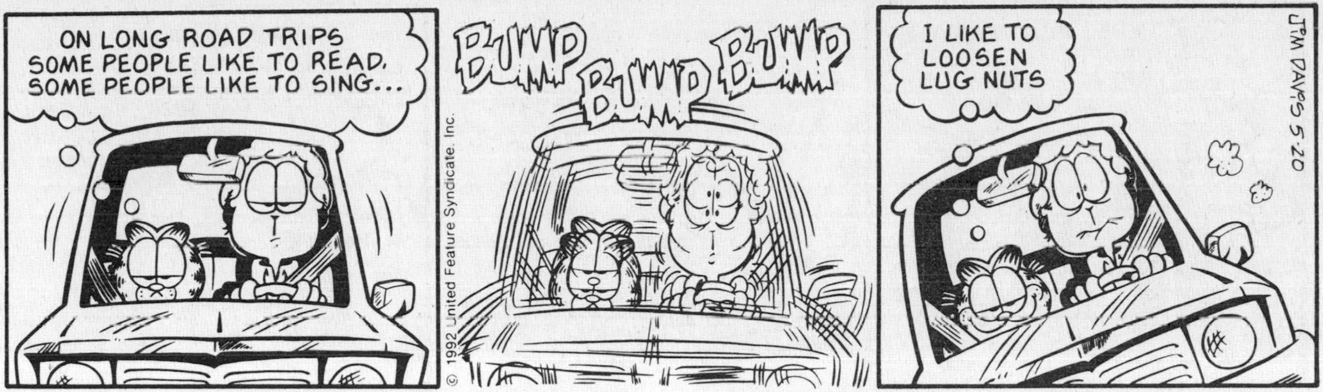
ON LONG ROAD TRIPS SOME PEOPLE LIKE TO READ, SOME PEOPLE LIKE TO SING...
BUMP BUMP BUMP
I LIKE TO LOOSEN LUG NUTS
JIM DAVIS 5-20
© 1992 United Feature Syndicate, Inc.

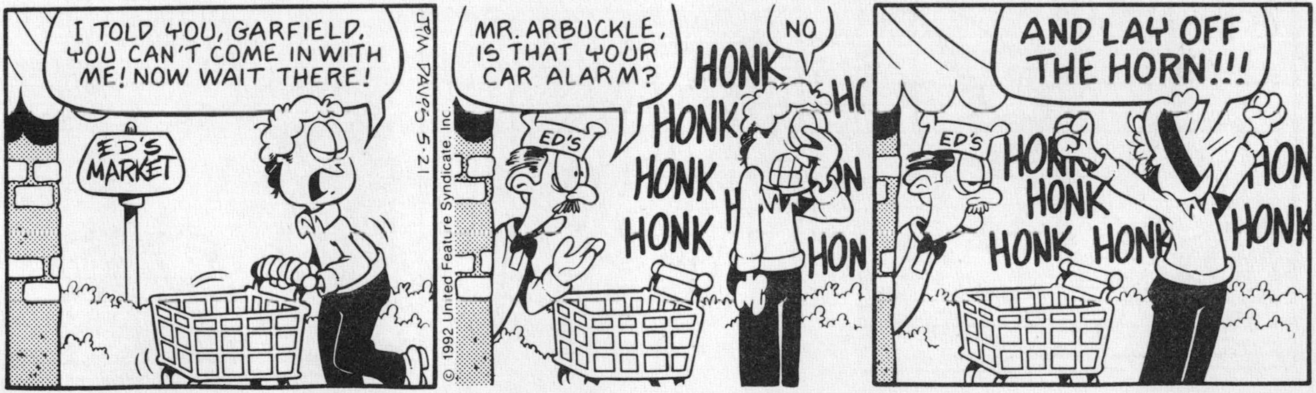
I TOLD YOU, GARFIELD. YOU CAN'T COME IN WITH ME! NOW WAIT THERE!
ED'S MARKET
JIM DAVIS 5-21
© 1992 United Feature Syndicate, Inc.
MR. ARBUCKLE, IS THAT YOUR CAR ALARM?
NO
HONK HONK HONK HONK
ED'S
AND LAY OFF THE HORN!!!
HONK HONK HONK HONK HONK

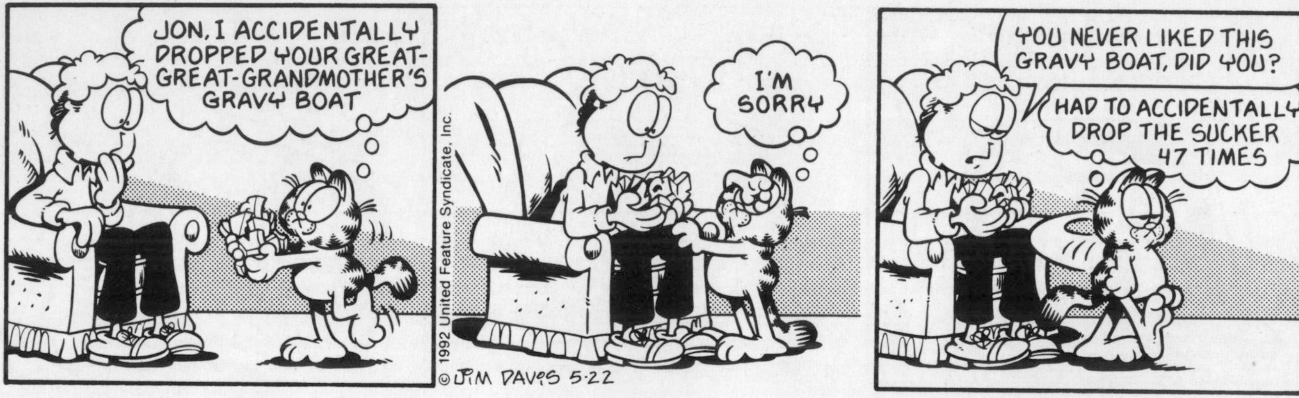
JON, I ACCIDENTALLY DROPPED YOUR GREAT-GREAT-GRANDMOTHER'S GRAVY BOAT
I'M SORRY
YOU NEVER LIKED THIS GRAVY BOAT, DID YOU?
HAD TO ACCIDENTALLY DROP THE SUCKER 47 TIMES
© 1992 United Feature Syndicate, Inc.
JIM DAVIS 5-22

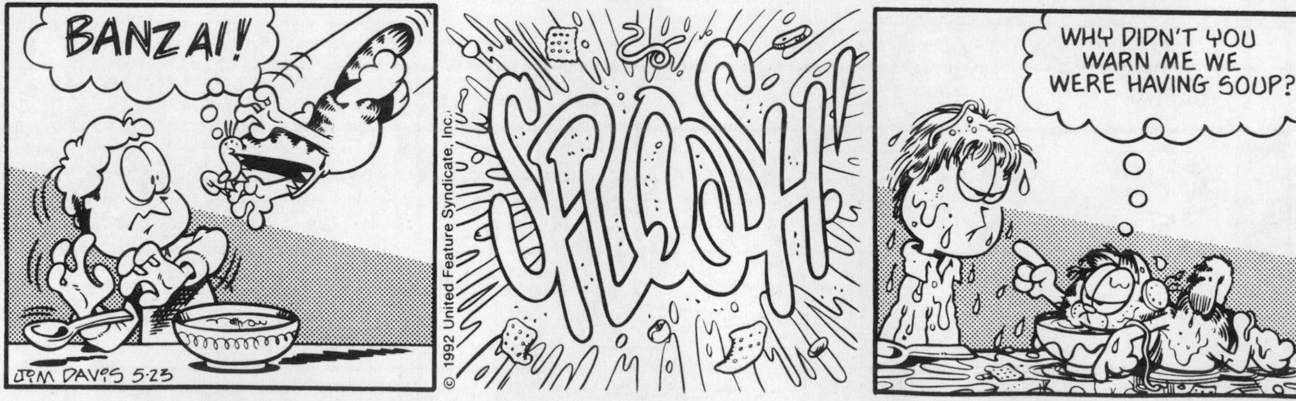
BANZAI!
JIM DAVIS 5-23
© 1992 United Feature Syndicate, Inc.
SPLOOSH!
WHY DIDN'T YOU WARN ME WE WERE HAVING SOUP?

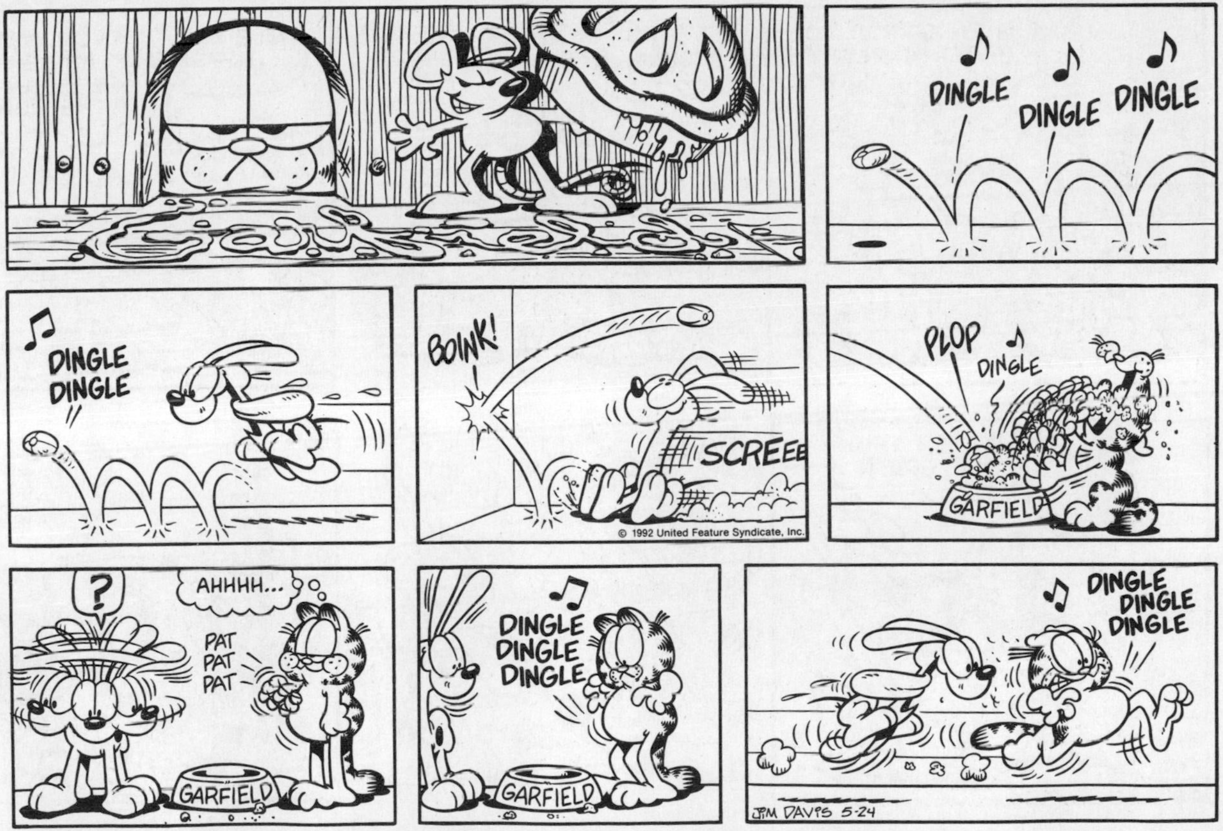

DINGLE
DINGLE
DINGLE
DINGLE DINGLE
BOINK!
SCREEee
© 1992 United Feature Syndicate, Inc.
PLOP
DINGLE
GARFIELD
?
AHHHH...
PAT PAT PAT
GARFIELD
DINGLE DINGLE DINGLE
GARFIELD
DINGLE DINGLE DINGLE
JIM DAVIS 5-24

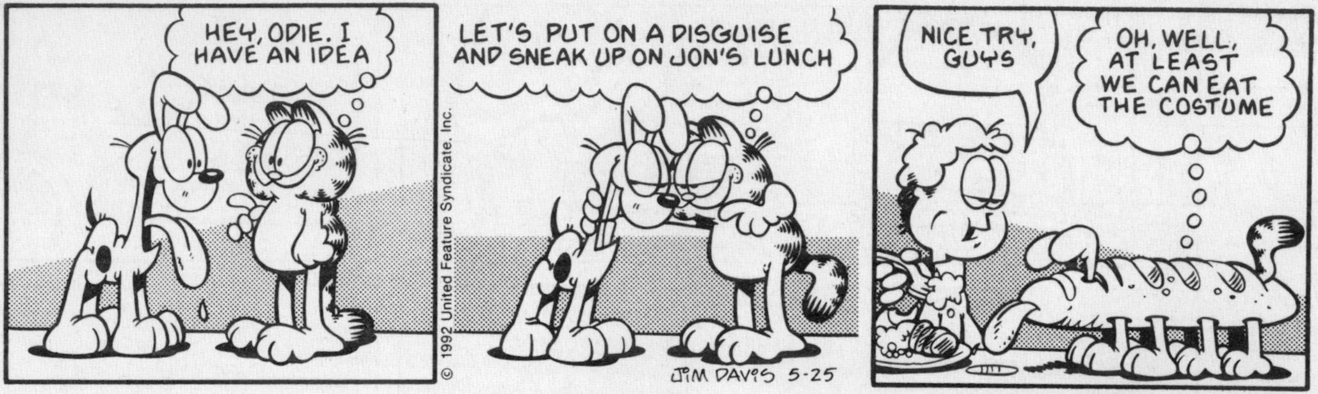
HEY, ODIE. I HAVE AN IDEA
LET'S PUT ON A DISGUISE AND SNEAK UP ON JON'S LUNCH
© 1992 United Feature Syndicate, Inc.
JIM DAVIS 5-25
NICE TRY, GUYS
OH, WELL, AT LEAST WE CAN EAT THE COSTUME

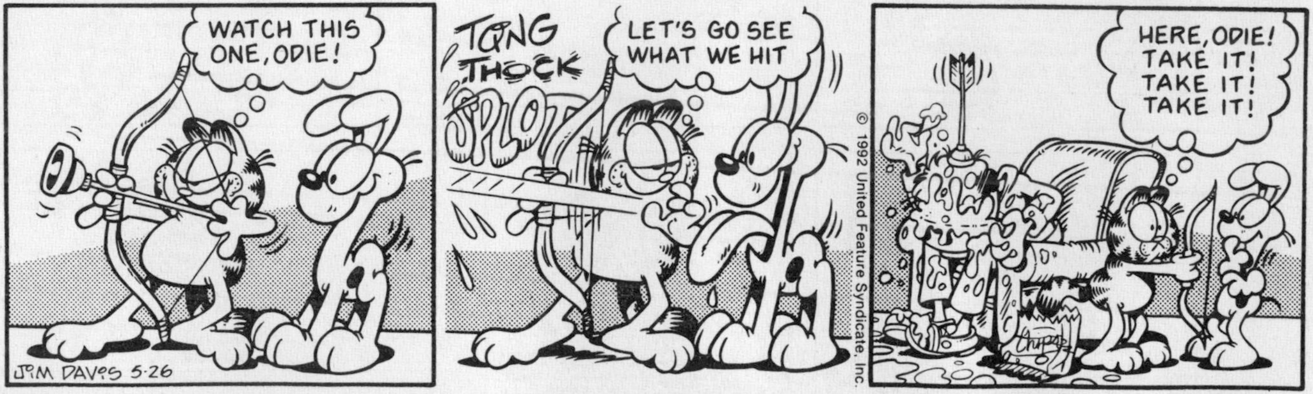
WATCH THIS ONE, ODIE!
JIM DAVIS 5-26
TANG
THOCK
SPLOT
LET'S GO SEE WHAT WE HIT
© 1992 United Feature Syndicate, Inc.
HERE, ODIE! TAKE IT! TAKE IT! TAKE IT!

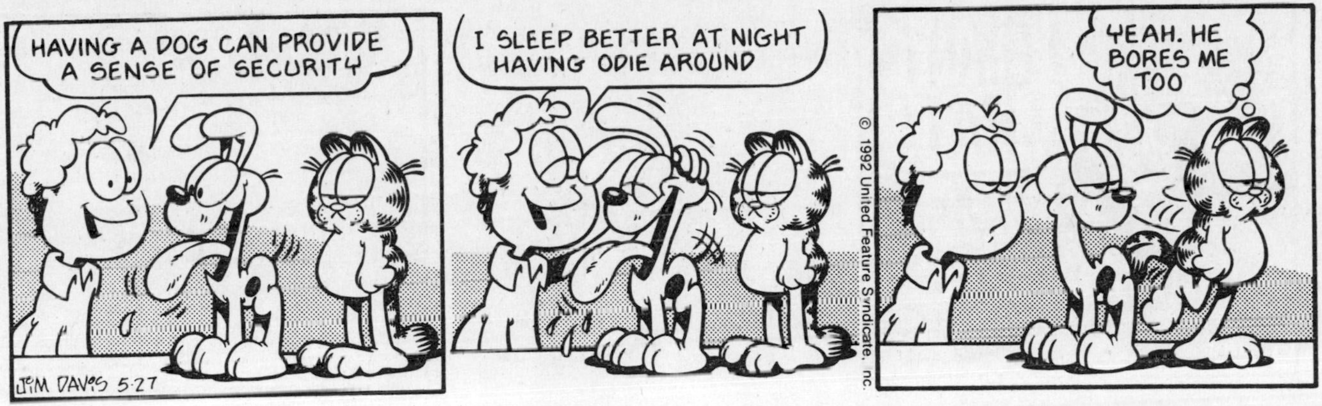
HAVING A DOG CAN PROVIDE A SENSE OF SECURITY
JIM DAVIS 5-27
I SLEEP BETTER AT NIGHT HAVING ODIE AROUND
YEAH. HE BORES ME TOO

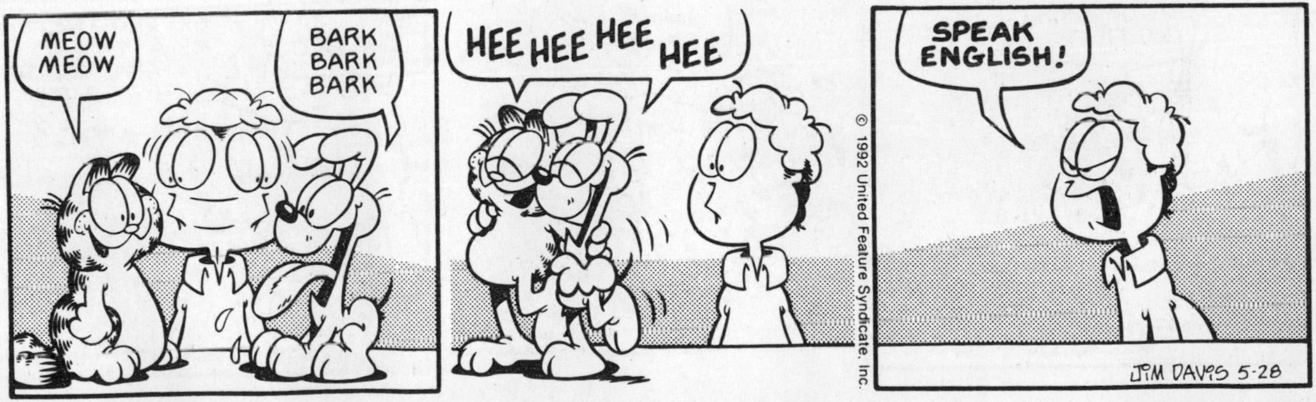
MEOW MEOW
BARK BARK BARK
HEE HEE HEE HEE
SPEAK ENGLISH!
JIM DAVIS 5-28

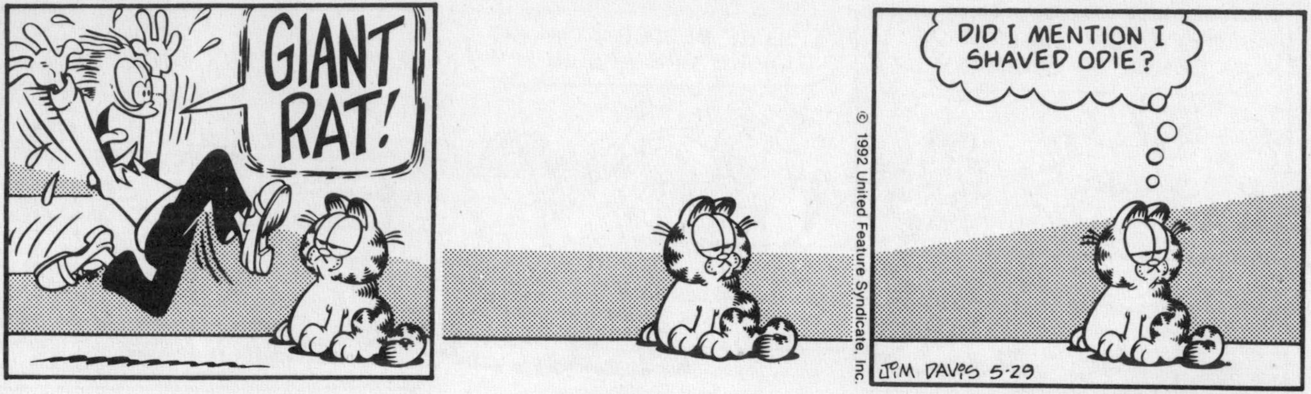
GIANT RAT!
DID I MENTION I SHAVED ODIE?
© 1992 United Feature Syndicate, Inc.
JIM DAVIS 5-29

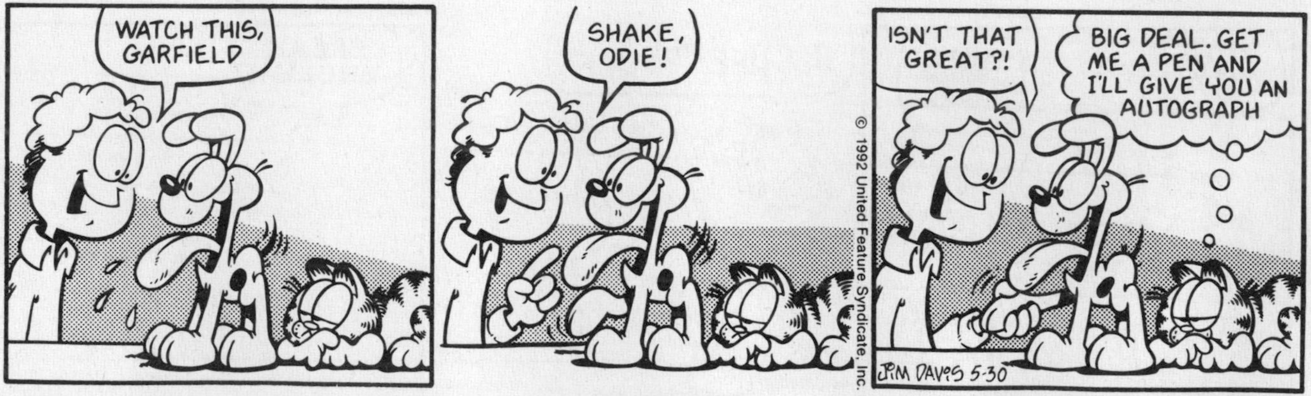
WATCH THIS, GARFIELD
SHAKE, ODIE!
ISN'T THAT GREAT?!
BIG DEAL. GET ME A PEN AND I'LL GIVE YOU AN AUTOGRAPH
© 1992 United Feature Syndicate, Inc.
JIM DAVIS 5-30

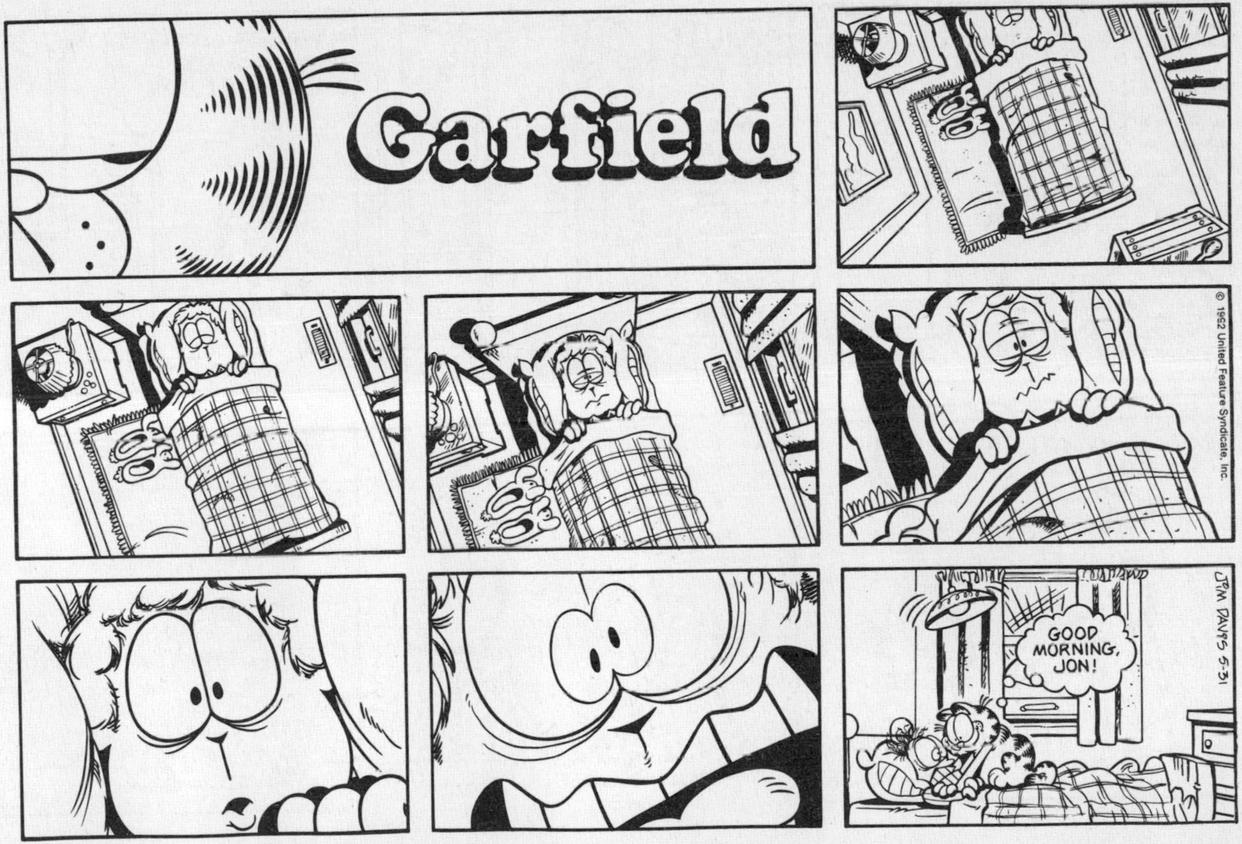
Garfield
© 1982 United Feature Syndicate, Inc.
JIM DAVIS 5-31
GOOD MORNING, JON!

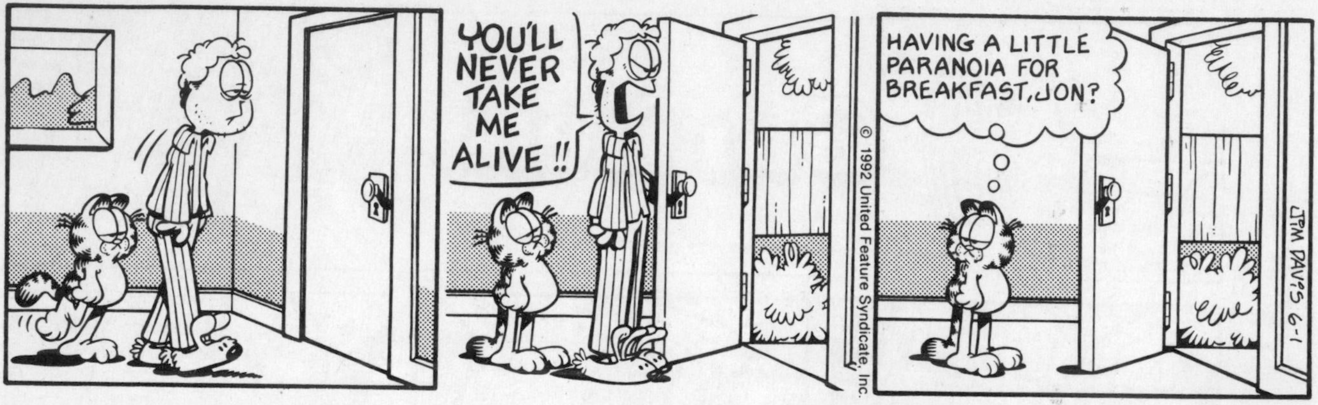
YOU'LL NEVER TAKE ME ALIVE !!
HAVING A LITTLE PARANOIA FOR BREAKFAST, JON?
© 1992 United Feature Syndicate, Inc.
JIM DAVIS 6-1

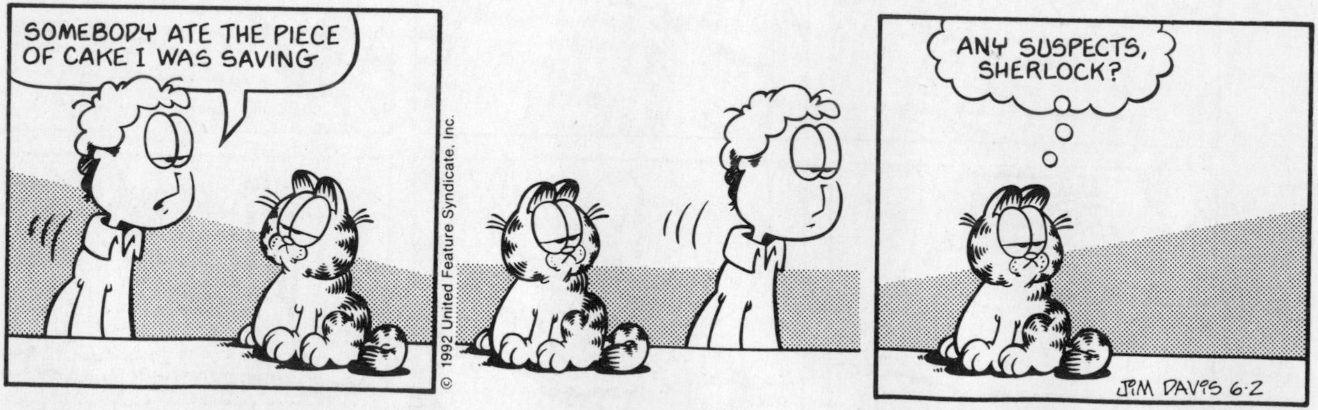
SOMEBODY ATE THE PIECE OF CAKE I WAS SAVING
ANY SUSPECTS, SHERLOCK?
© 1992 United Feature Syndicate, Inc.
JIM DAVIS 6-2

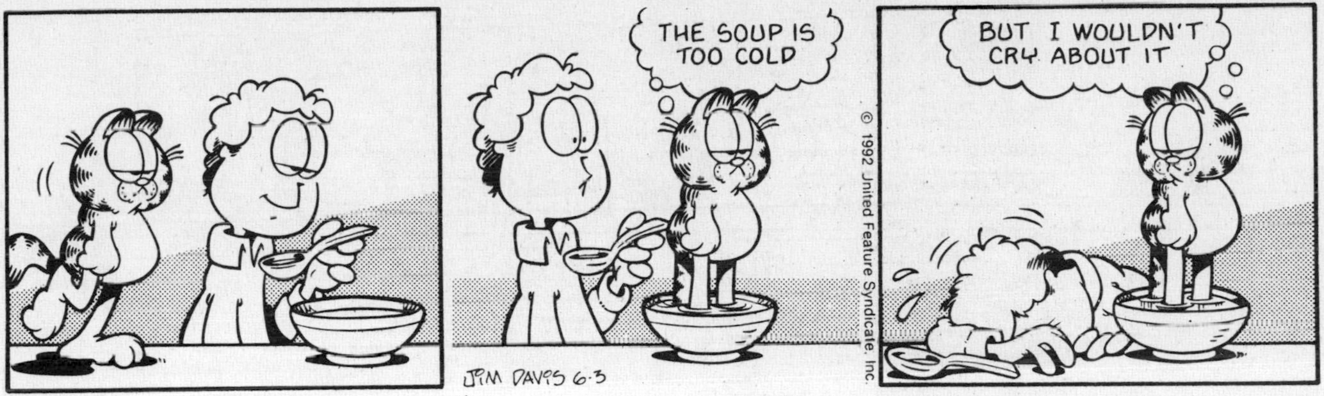
THE SOUP IS TOO COLD
BUT I WOULDN'T CRY ABOUT IT
JIM DAVIS 6·3
© 1992 United Feature Syndicate, Inc.

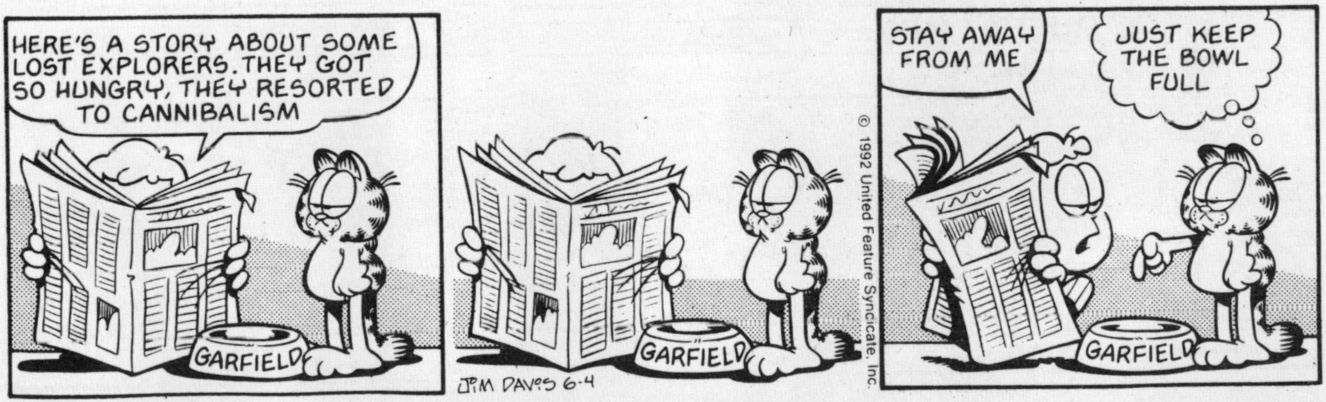
HERE'S A STORY ABOUT SOME LOST EXPLORERS. THEY GOT SO HUNGRY, THEY RESORTED TO CANNIBALISM
GARFIELD
GARFIELD
STAY AWAY FROM ME
JUST KEEP THE BOWL FULL
GARFIELD
JIM DAVIS 6·4
© 1992 United Feature Syndicate, Inc.

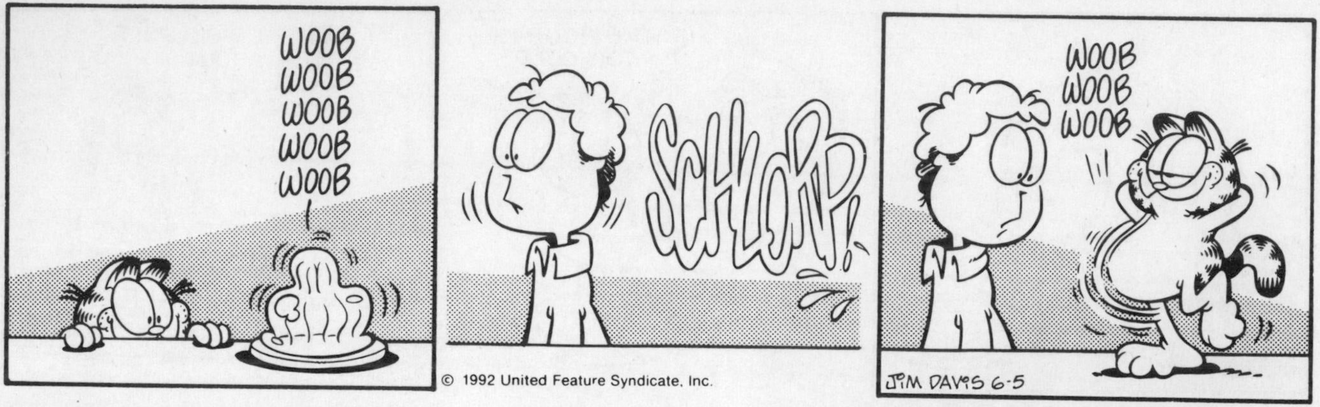
WOOB
WOOB
WOOB
WOOB
WOOB
SCHLORP!
WOOB
WOOB
WOOB
JIM DAVIS 6-5

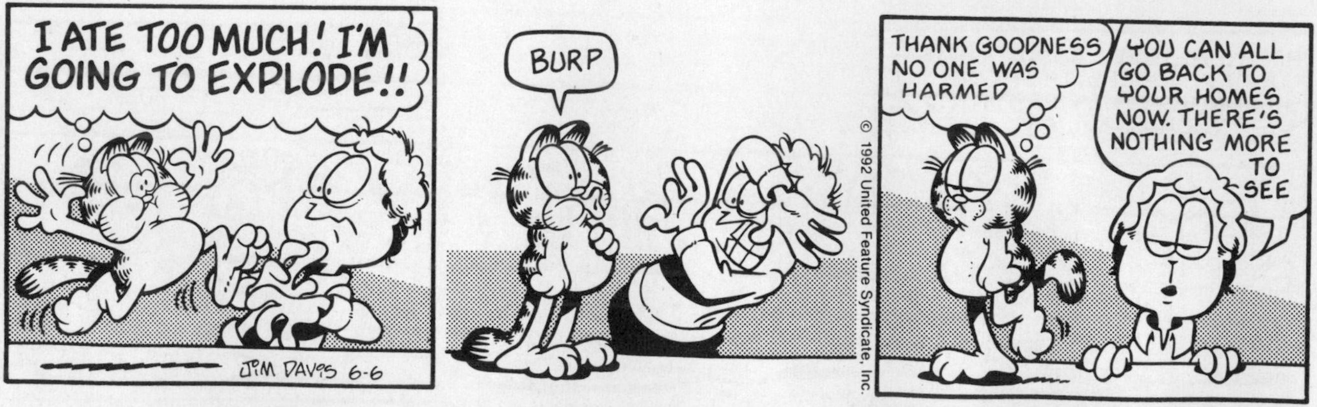
I ATE TOO MUCH! I'M GOING TO EXPLODE!!
JIM DAVIS 6-6
BURP
THANK GOODNESS NO ONE WAS HARMED
YOU CAN ALL GO BACK TO YOUR HOMES NOW. THERE'S NOTHING MORE TO SEE

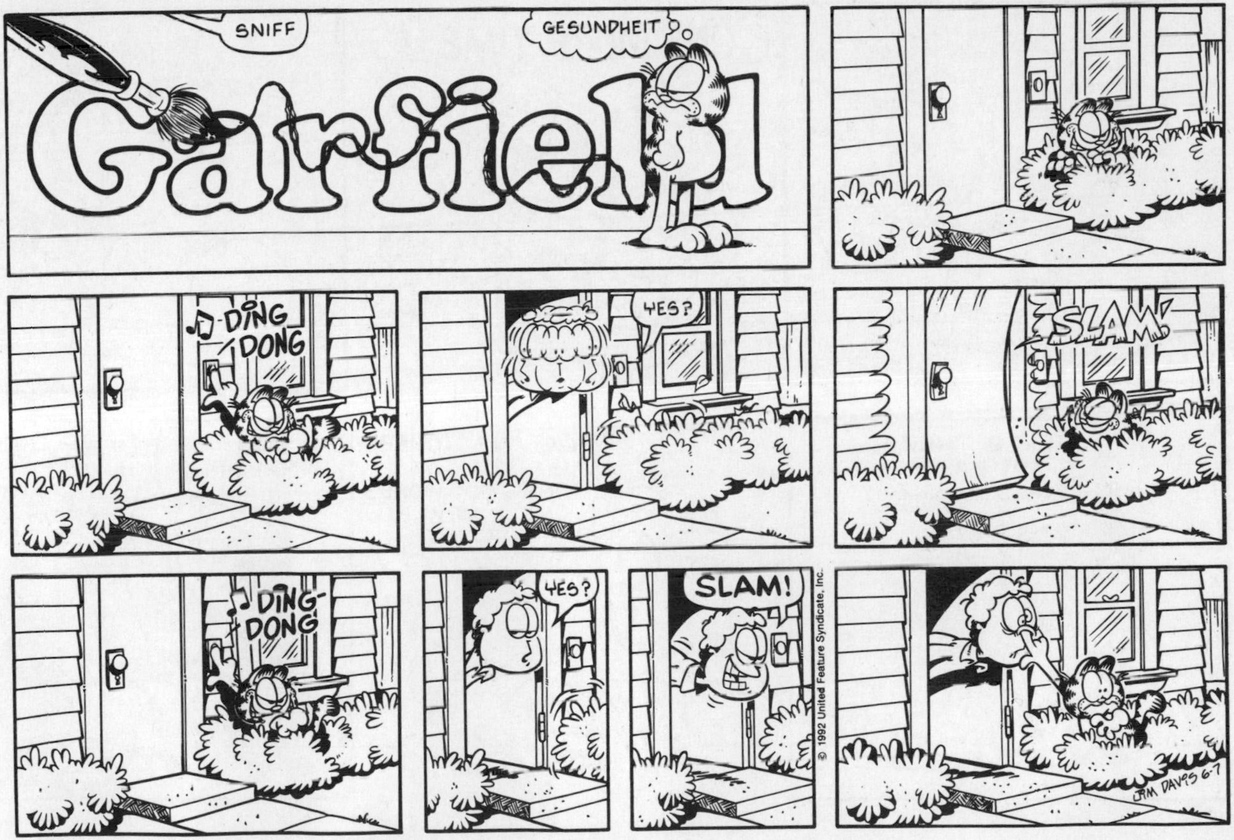
SNIFF
GESUNDHEIT
Garfield
DING DONG
YES?
SLAM!
DING DONG
YES?
SLAM!
© 1992 United Feature Syndicate, Inc.
JIM DAVIS 6-7

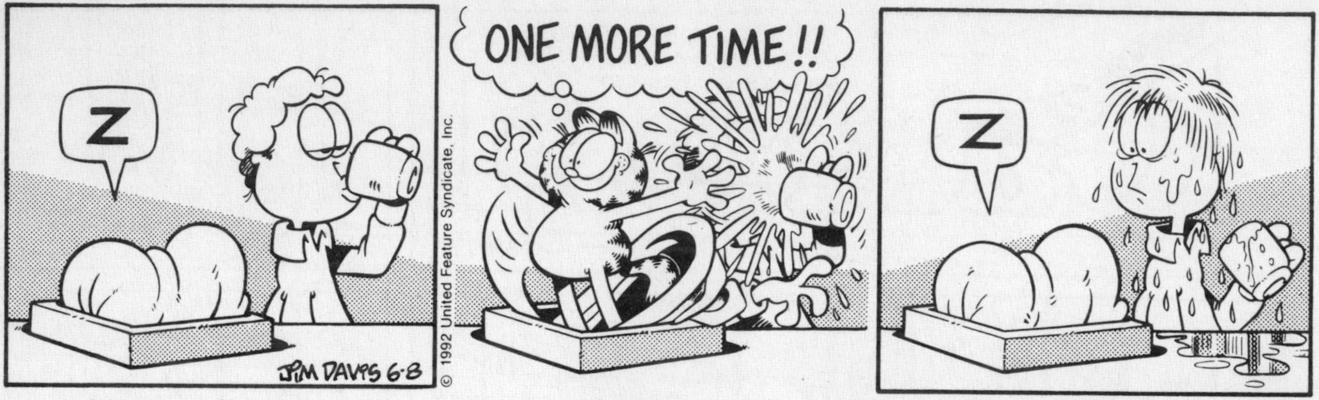
Z
JIM DAVIS 6-8
© 1992 United Feature Syndicate, Inc.
ONE MORE TIME!!
Z

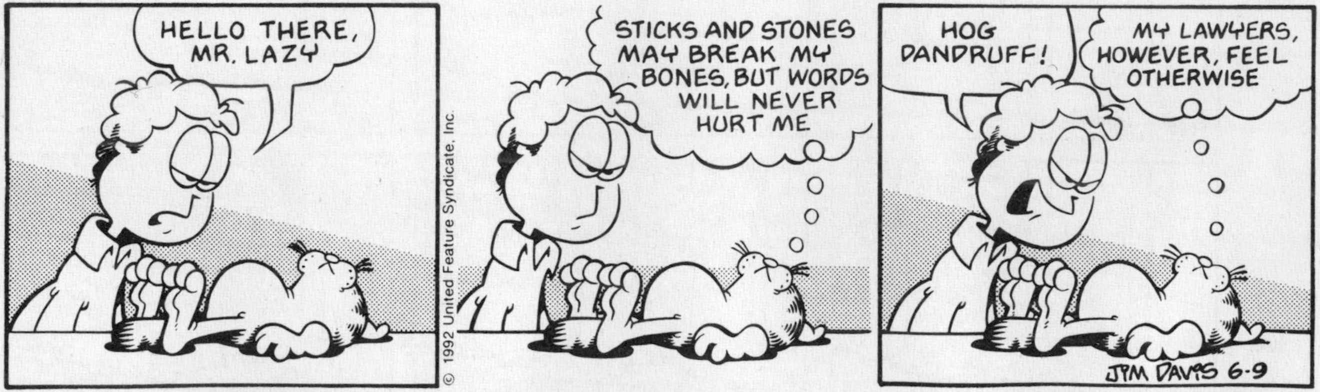
HELLO THERE, MR. LAZY
© 1992 United Feature Syndicate, Inc.
STICKS AND STONES MAY BREAK MY BONES, BUT WORDS WILL NEVER HURT ME
HOG DANDRUFF!
MY LAWYERS, HOWEVER, FEEL OTHERWISE
JIM DAVIS 6-9

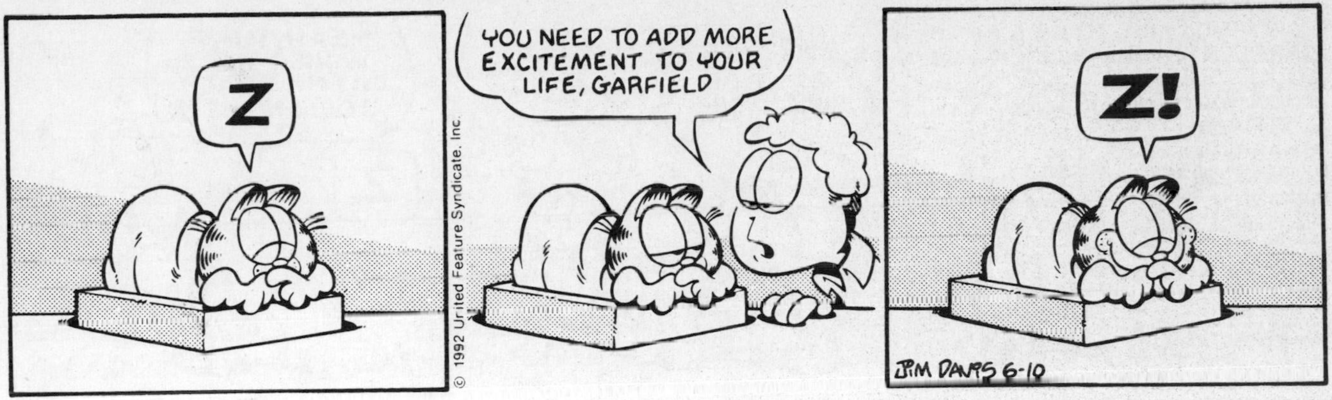
Z
YOU NEED TO ADD MORE EXCITEMENT TO YOUR LIFE, GARFIELD
Z!
© 1992 United Feature Syndicate, Inc.
JIM DAVIS 6-10

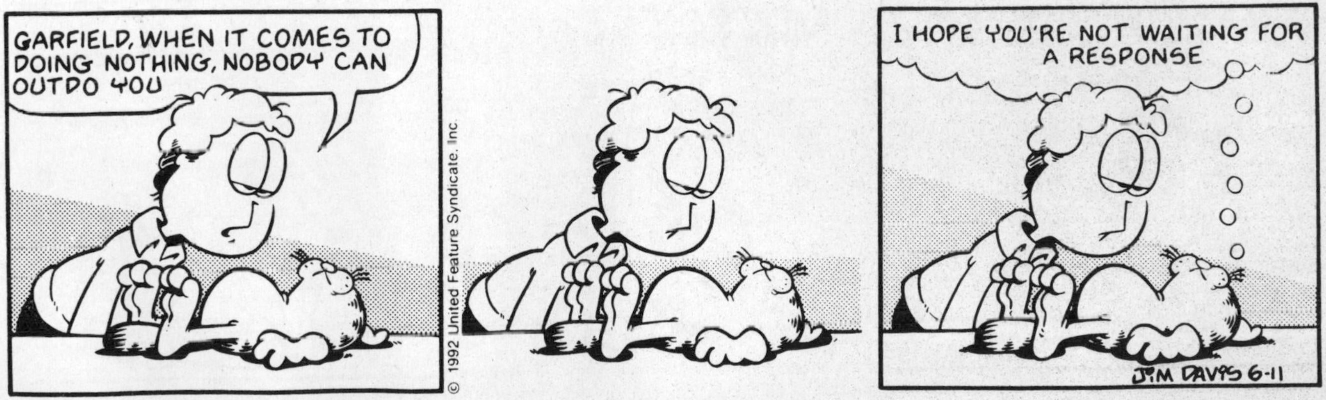
GARFIELD, WHEN IT COMES TO DOING NOTHING, NOBODY CAN OUTDO YOU
I HOPE YOU'RE NOT WAITING FOR A RESPONSE
© 1992 United Feature Syndicate, Inc.
JIM DAVIS 6-11

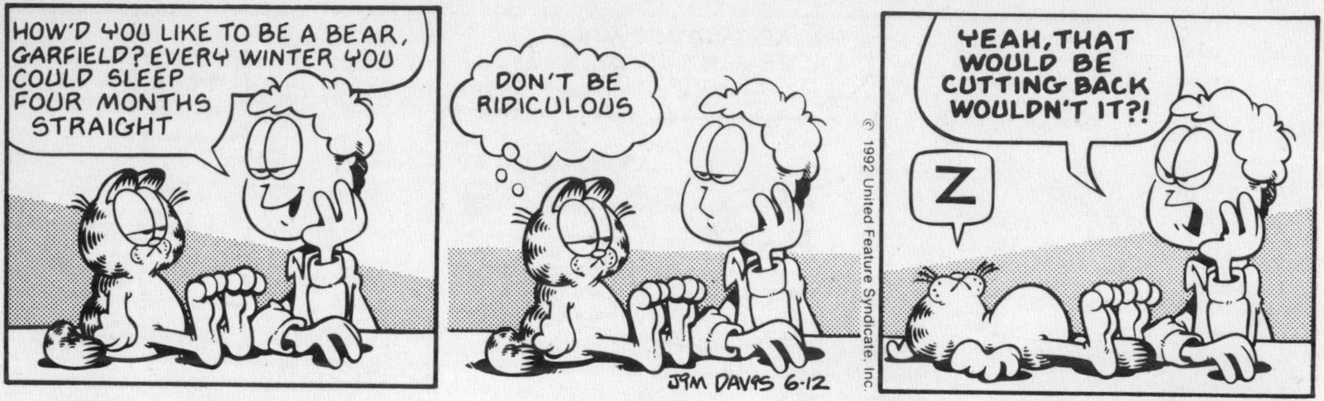
HOW'D YOU LIKE TO BE A BEAR, GARFIELD? EVERY WINTER YOU COULD SLEEP FOUR MONTHS STRAIGHT
DON'T BE RIDICULOUS
JIM DAVIS 6-12
Z
YEAH, THAT WOULD BE CUTTING BACK WOULDN'T IT?!

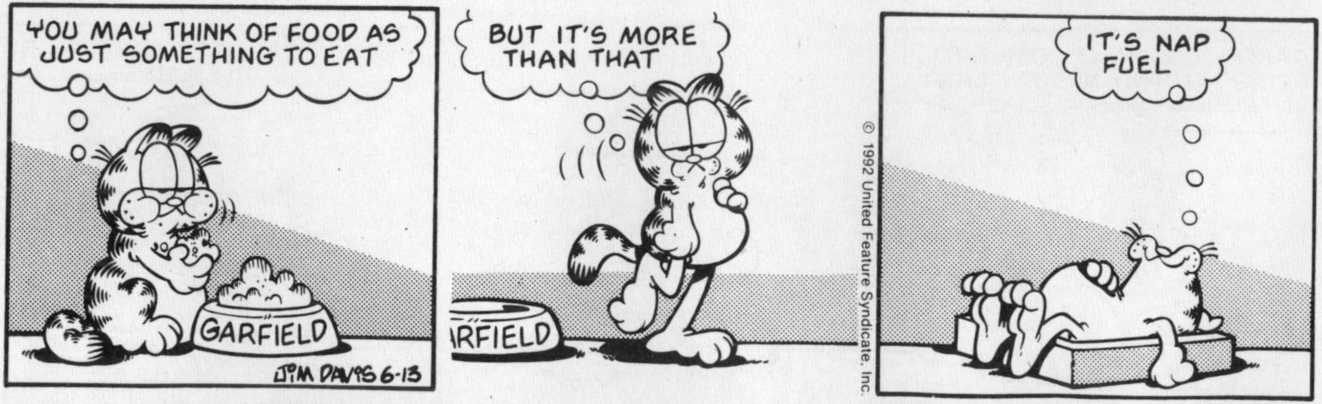
YOU MAY THINK OF FOOD AS JUST SOMETHING TO EAT
GARFIELD
JIM DAVIS 6-13
BUT IT'S MORE THAN THAT
ARFIELD
IT'S NAP FUEL

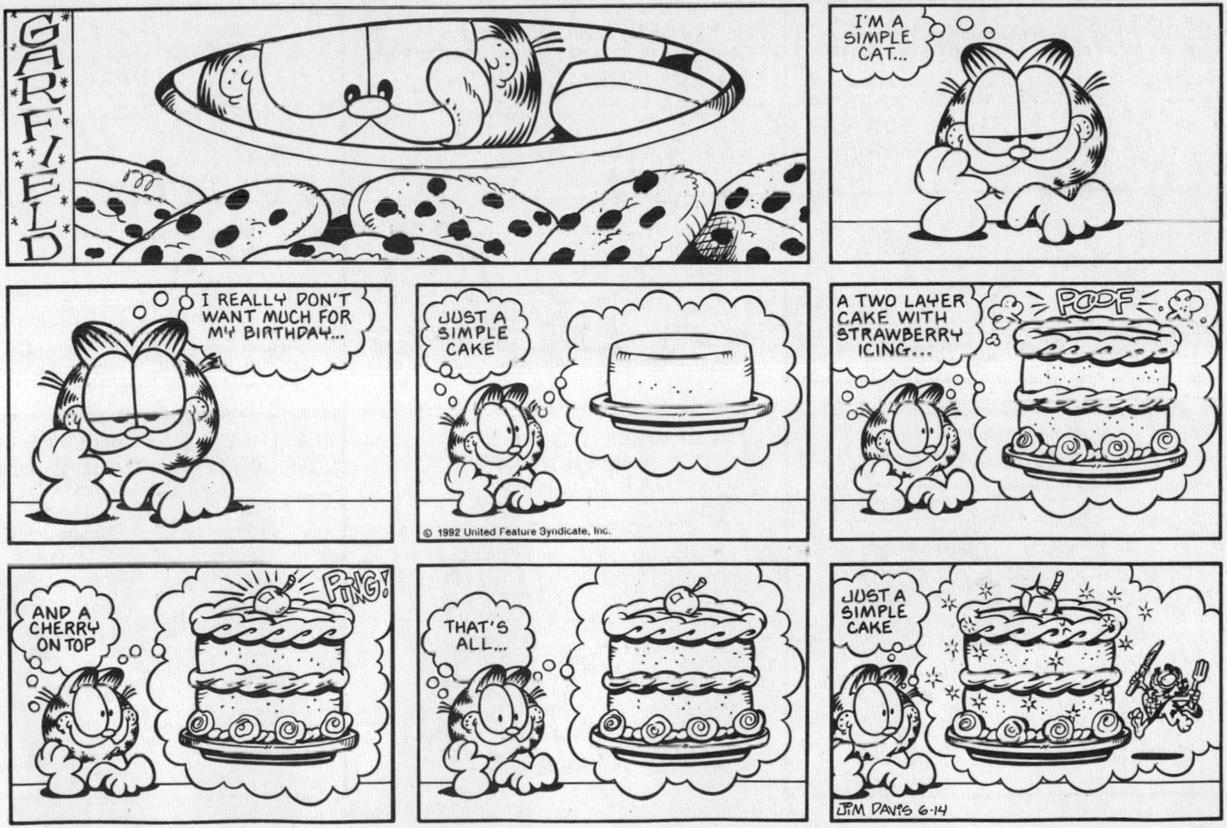
GARFIELD
I'M A SIMPLE CAT...
I REALLY DON'T WANT MUCH FOR MY BIRTHDAY...
JUST A SIMPLE CAKE
A TWO LAYER CAKE WITH STRAWBERRY ICING...
POOF
AND A CHERRY ON TOP
PING!
THAT'S ALL...
JUST A SIMPLE CAKE
JIM DAVIS 6-14
© 1992 United Feature Syndicate, Inc.

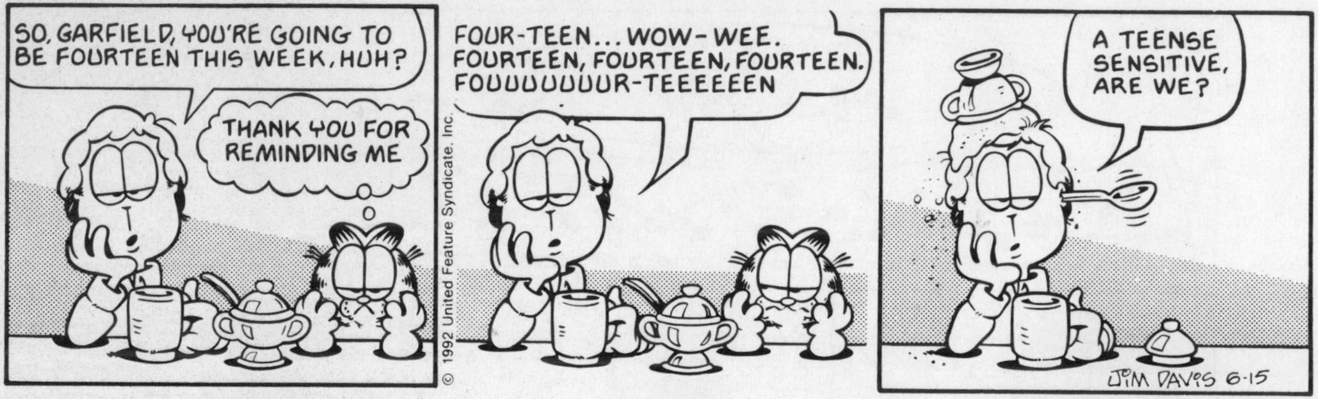
SO, GARFIELD, YOU'RE GOING TO BE FOURTEEN THIS WEEK, HUH?
THANK YOU FOR REMINDING ME
FOUR-TEEN... WOW-WEE. FOURTEEN, FOURTEEN, FOURTEEN. FOUUUUUUUR-TEEEEEEN
A TEENSE SENSITIVE, ARE WE?
JIM DAVIS 6-15

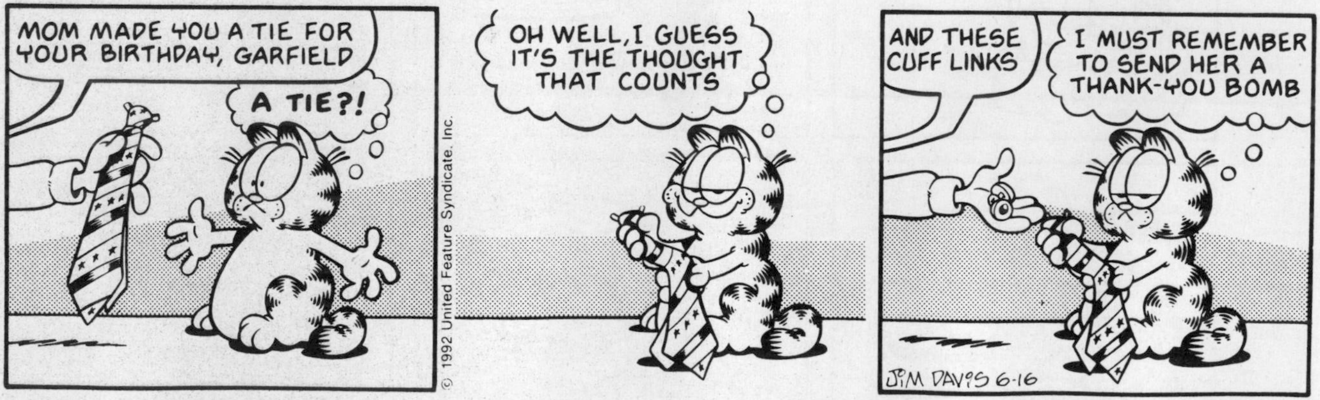
MOM MADE YOU A TIE FOR YOUR BIRTHDAY, GARFIELD
A TIE?!
OH WELL, I GUESS IT'S THE THOUGHT THAT COUNTS
AND THESE CUFF LINKS
I MUST REMEMBER TO SEND HER A THANK-YOU BOMB
JIM DAVIS 6-16

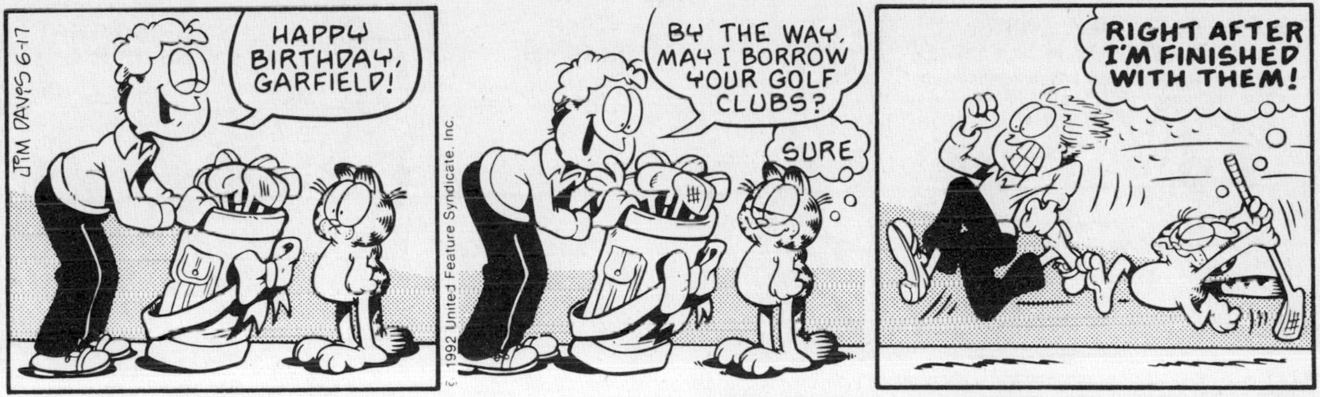
JIM DAVIS 6-17
HAPPY BIRTHDAY, GARFIELD!
© 1992 United Feature Syndicate, Inc.
BY THE WAY, MAY I BORROW YOUR GOLF CLUBS?
SURE
RIGHT AFTER I'M FINISHED WITH THEM!

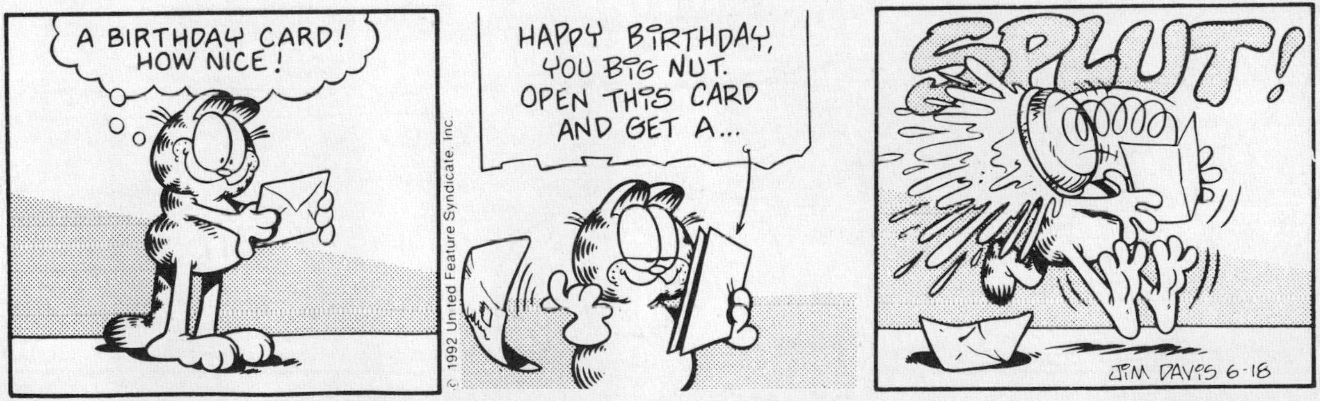
A BIRTHDAY CARD! HOW NICE!
© 1992 United Feature Syndicate, Inc.
HAPPY BIRTHDAY, YOU BIG NUT. OPEN THIS CARD AND GET A...
SPLUT!
JIM DAVIS 6-18

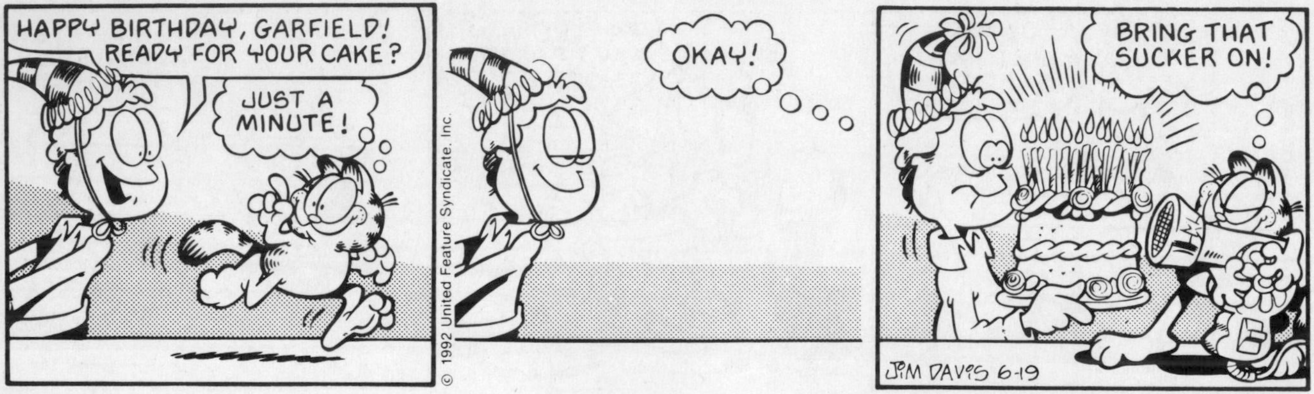
HAPPY BIRTHDAY, GARFIELD! READY FOR YOUR CAKE?
JUST A MINUTE!
OKAY!
BRING THAT SUCKER ON!
JIM DAVIS 6-19
© 1992 United Feature Syndicate, Inc.

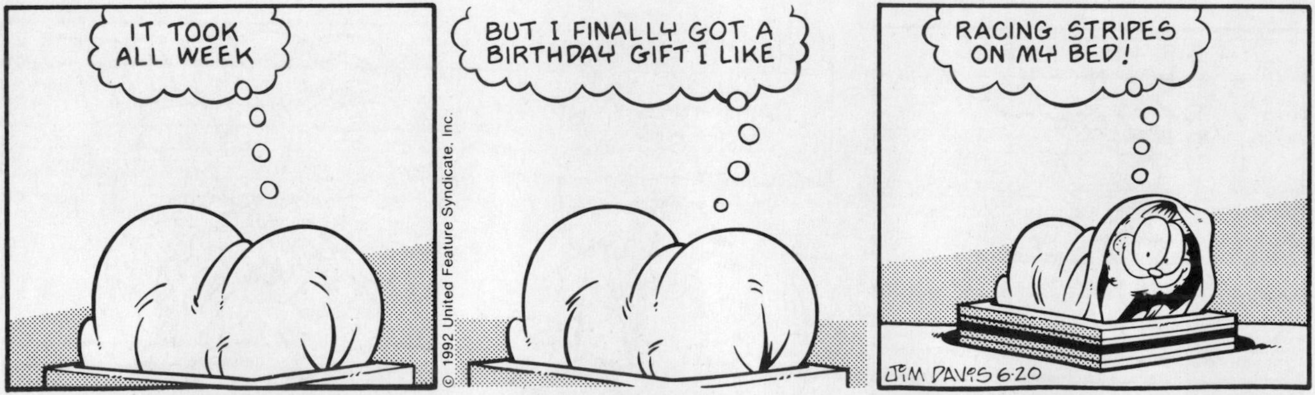
IT TOOK ALL WEEK
BUT I FINALLY GOT A BIRTHDAY GIFT I LIKE
RACING STRIPES ON MY BED!
JIM DAVIS 6-20
© 1992 United Feature Syndicate, Inc.

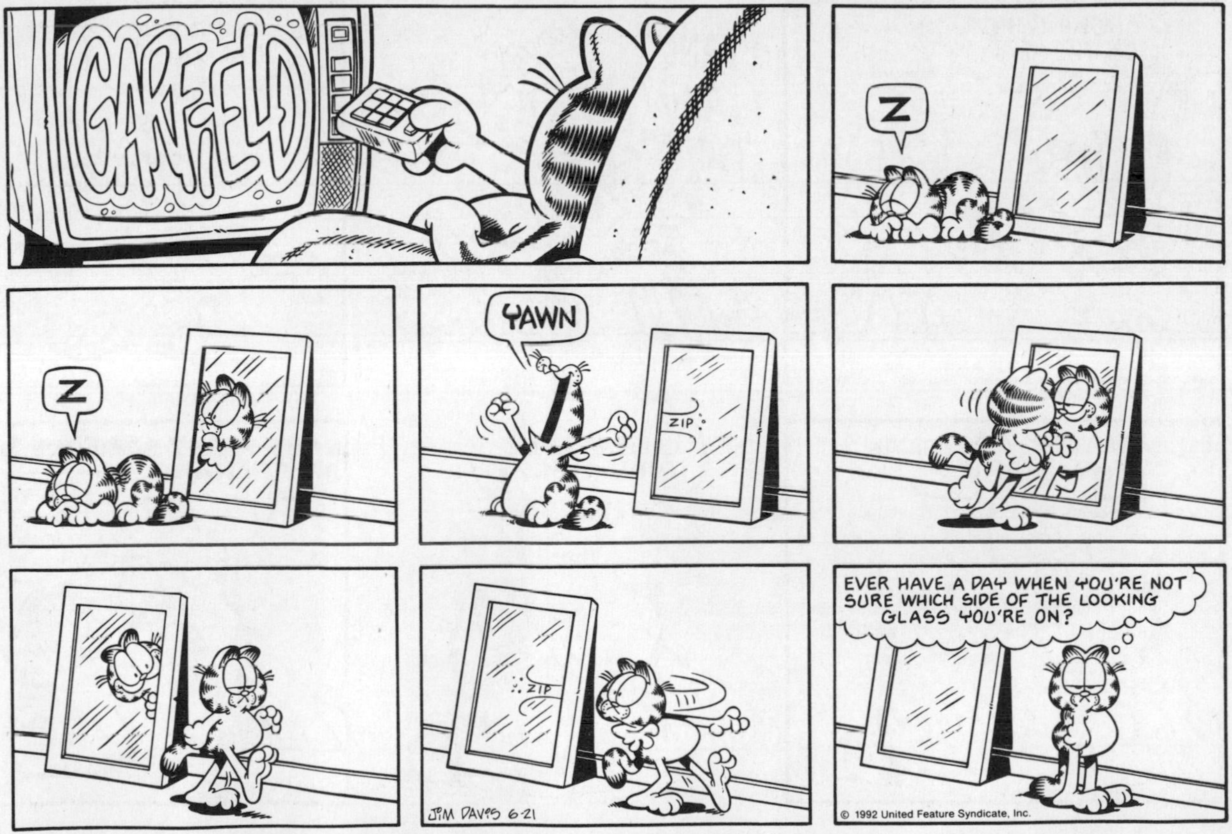
GARFIELD
Z
Z
YAWN
ZIP
ZIP
EVER HAVE A DAY WHEN YOU'RE NOT SURE WHICH SIDE OF THE LOOKING GLASS YOU'RE ON?
JIM DAVIS 6-21
© 1992 United Feature Syndicate, Inc.

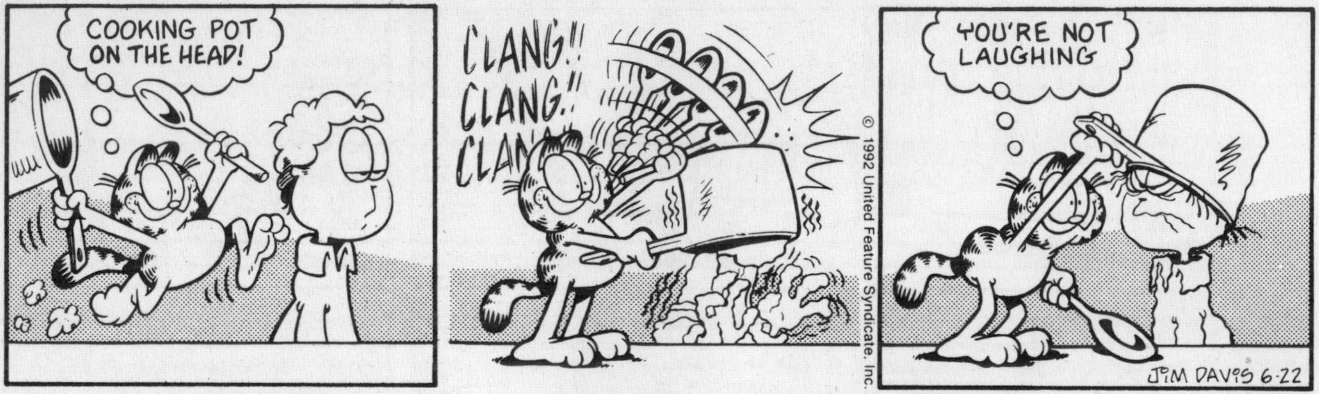
COOKING POT ON THE HEAD!
CLANG!!
CLANG!!
YOU'RE NOT LAUGHING
JIM DAVIS 6-22

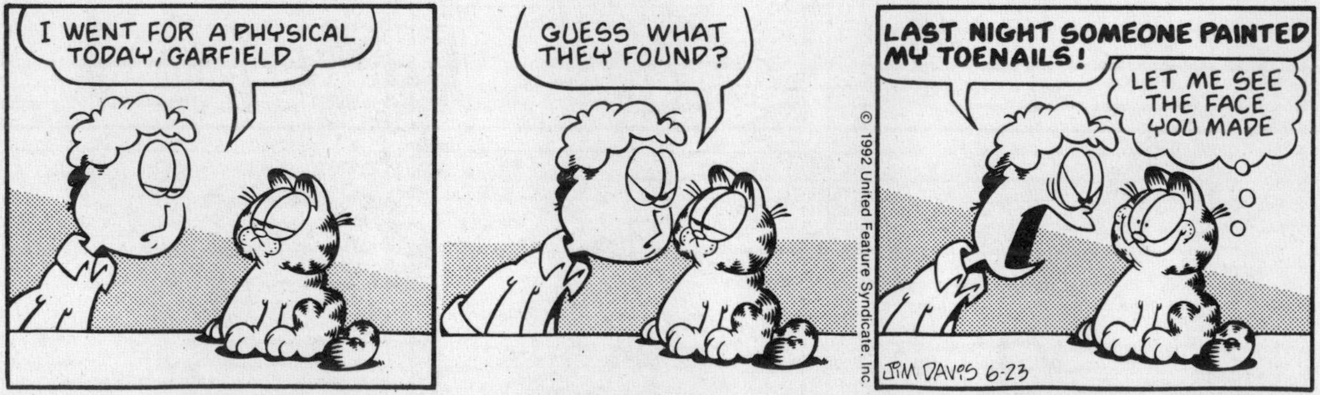
I WENT FOR A PHYSICAL TODAY, GARFIELD
GUESS WHAT THEY FOUND?
LAST NIGHT SOMEONE PAINTED MY TOENAILS!
LET ME SEE THE FACE YOU MADE
JIM DAVIS 6-23

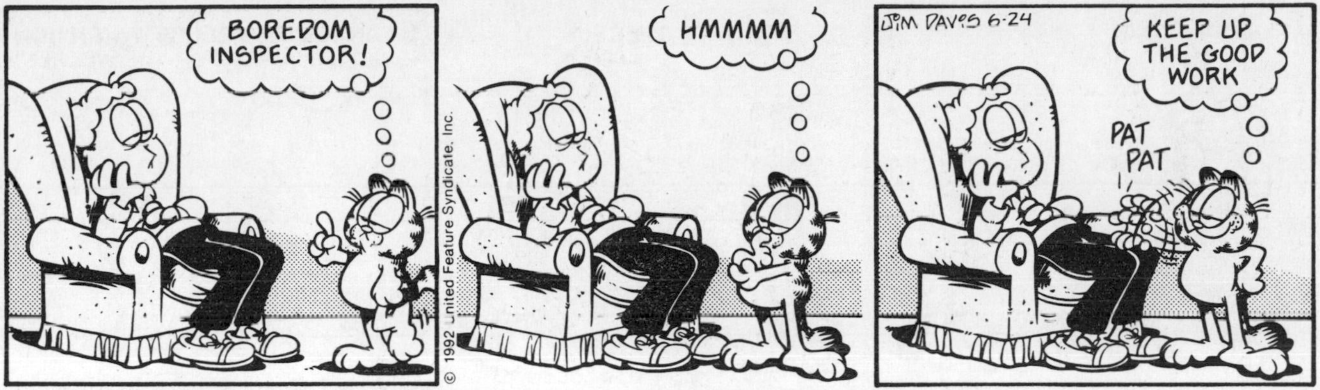
BOREDOM INSPECTOR!
HMMMM
JIM DAVIS 6-24
KEEP UP THE GOOD WORK
PAT PAT

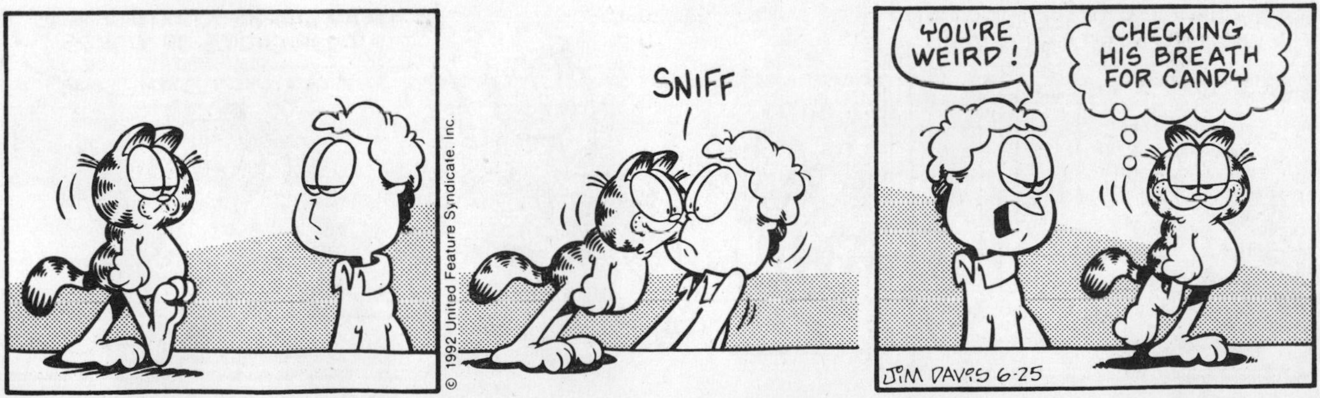
SNIFF
YOU'RE WEIRD!
CHECKING HIS BREATH FOR CANDY
JIM DAVIS 6-25

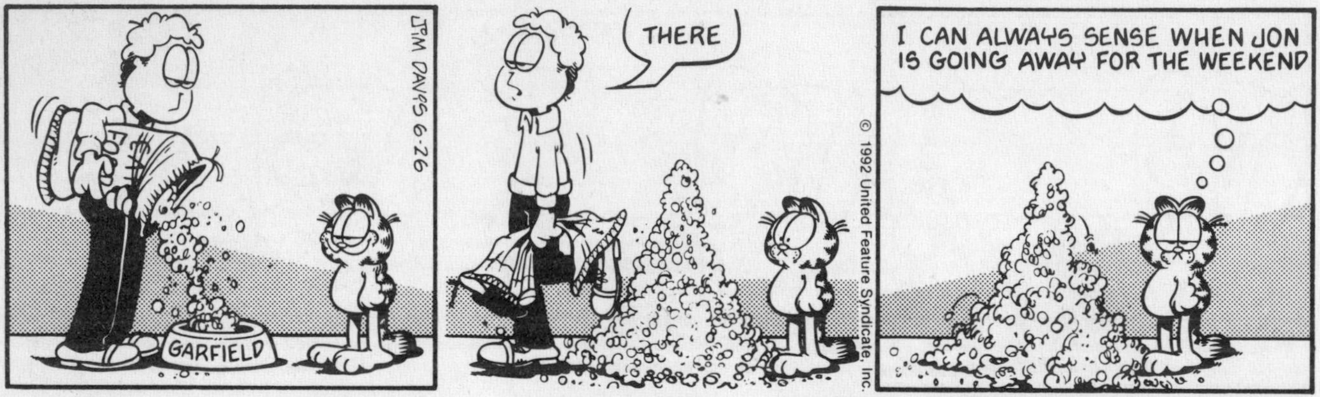
JIM DAVIS 6-26
GARFIELD
THERE
I CAN ALWAYS SENSE WHEN JON IS GOING AWAY FOR THE WEEKEND
© 1992 United Feature Syndicate, Inc.

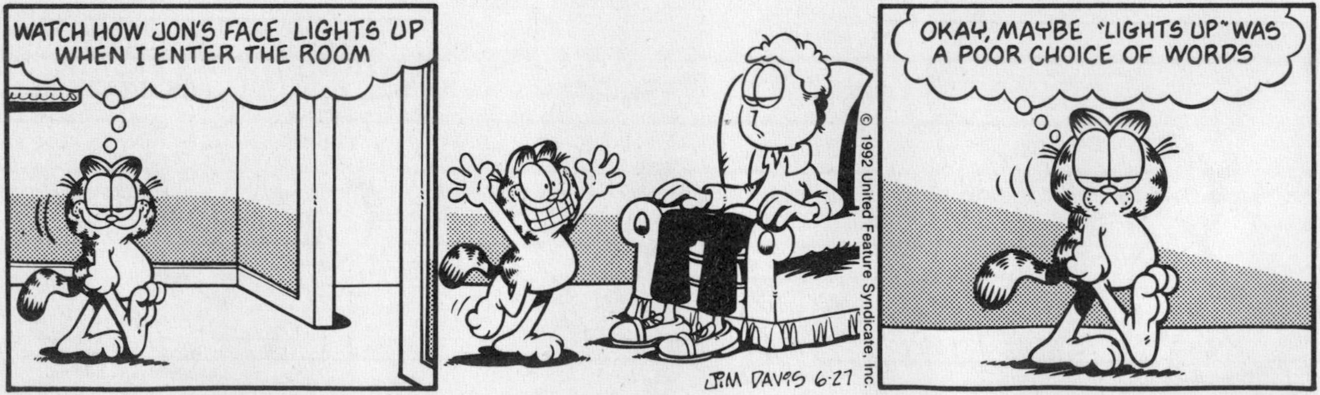
WATCH HOW JON'S FACE LIGHTS UP WHEN I ENTER THE ROOM
OKAY, MAYBE "LIGHTS UP" WAS A POOR CHOICE OF WORDS
JIM DAVIS 6-27
© 1992 United Feature Syndicate, Inc.

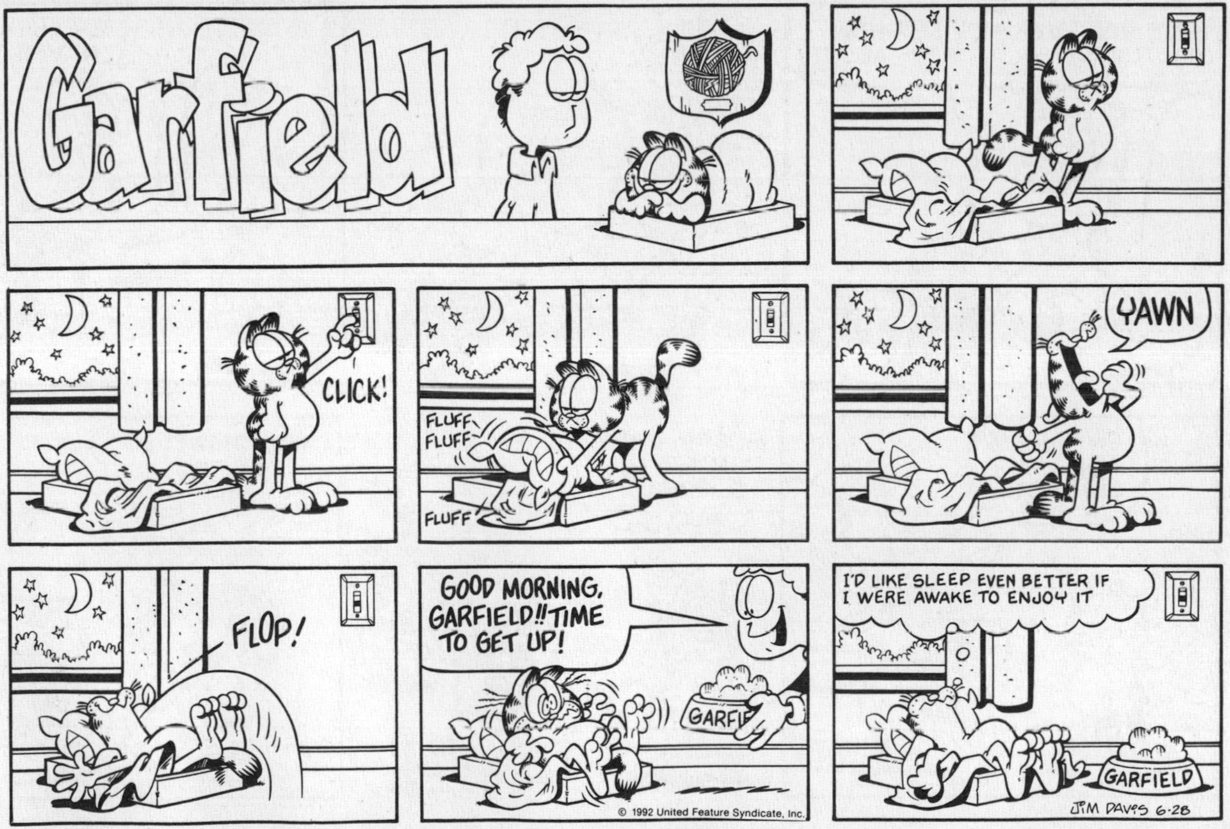
Garfield
CLICK!
FLUFF
FLUFF
FLUFF
YAWN
FLOP!
GOOD MORNING, GARFIELD!! TIME TO GET UP!
GARFI
I'D LIKE SLEEP EVEN BETTER IF I WERE AWAKE TO ENJOY IT
GARFIELD
© 1992 United Feature Syndicate, Inc.
JIM DAVIS 6-28

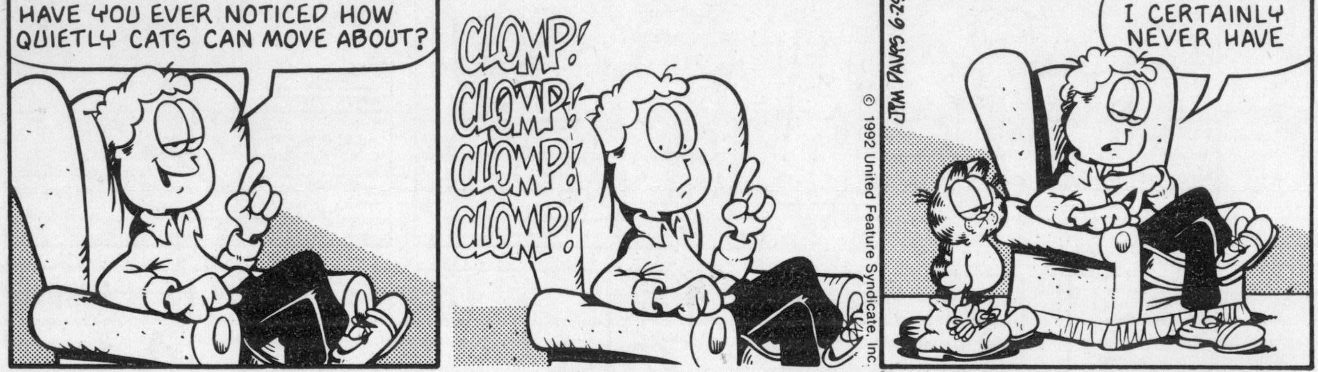
HAVE YOU EVER NOTICED HOW QUIETLY CATS CAN MOVE ABOUT?
CLOMP! CLOMP! CLOMP! CLOMP!
JIM DAVIS 6·29
© 1992 United Feature Syndicate, Inc.
I CERTAINLY NEVER HAVE

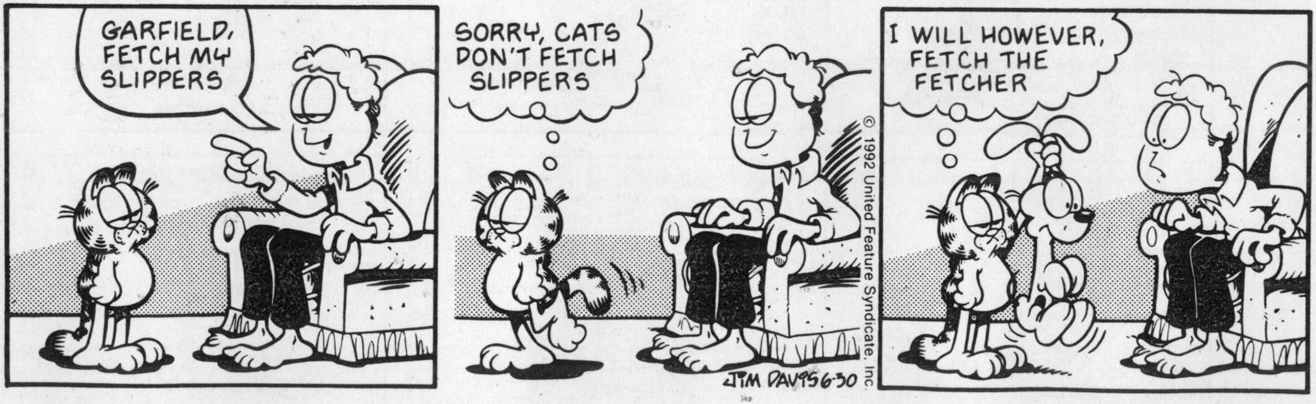
GARFIELD, FETCH MY SLIPPERS
SORRY, CATS DON'T FETCH SLIPPERS
JIM DAVIS 6·30
© 1992 United Feature Syndicate, Inc.
I WILL HOWEVER, FETCH THE FETCHER

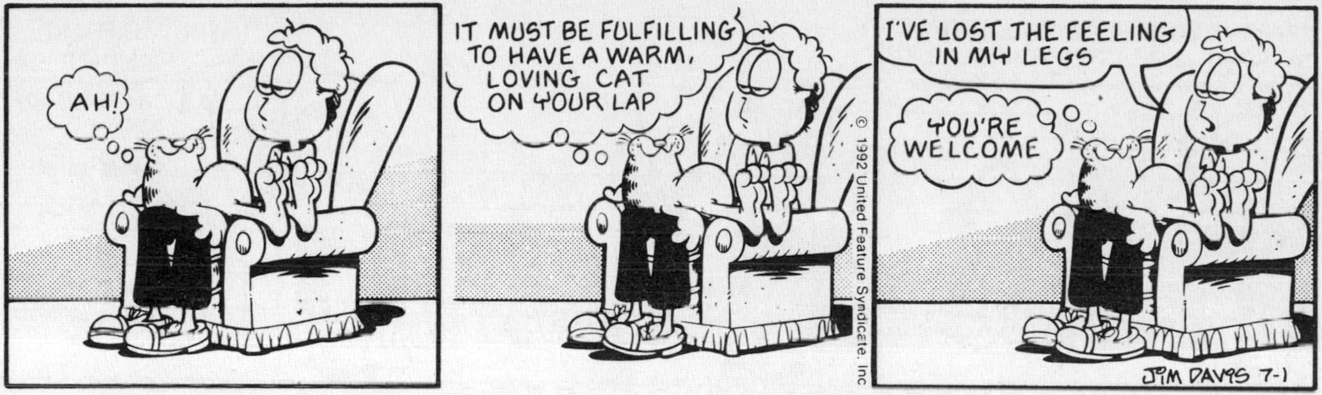
AH!
IT MUST BE FULFILLING TO HAVE A WARM, LOVING CAT ON YOUR LAP
© 1992 United Feature Syndicate, Inc.
I'VE LOST THE FEELING IN MY LEGS
YOU'RE WELCOME
JIM DAVIS 7-1

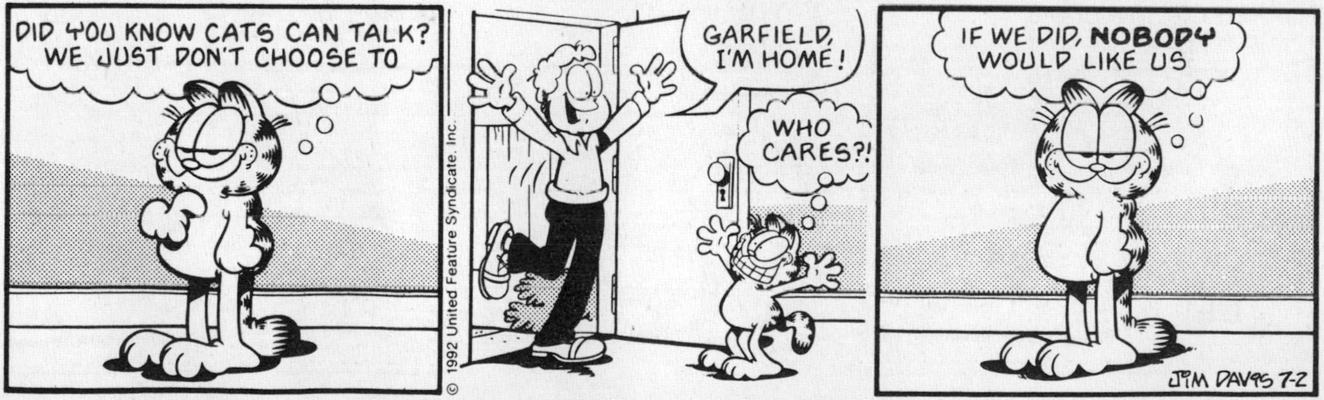
DID YOU KNOW CATS CAN TALK? WE JUST DON'T CHOOSE TO
© 1992 United Feature Syndicate, Inc.
GARFIELD, I'M HOME!
WHO CARES?!
IF WE DID, **NOBODY** WOULD LIKE US
JIM DAVIS 7-2

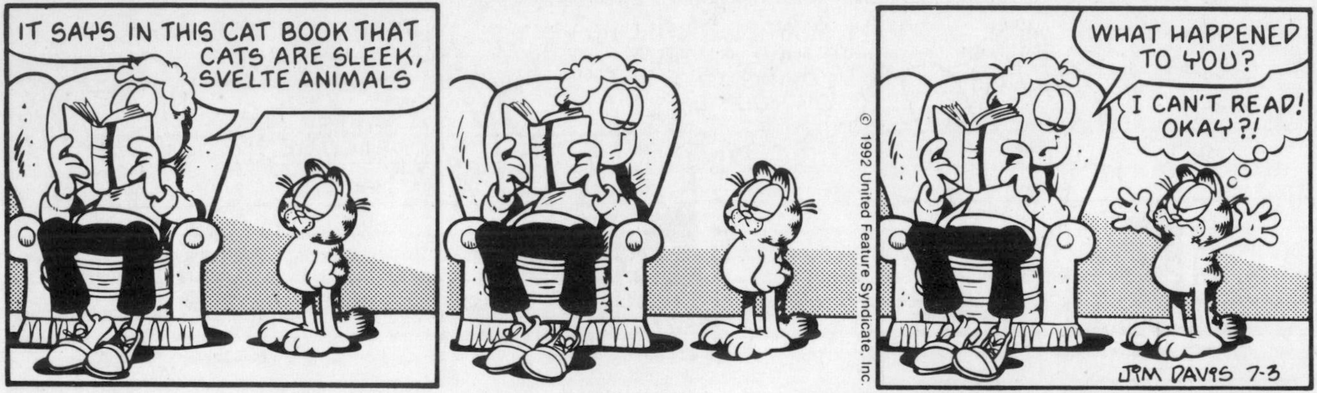
IT SAYS IN THIS CAT BOOK THAT CATS ARE SLEEK, SVELTE ANIMALS
WHAT HAPPENED TO YOU?
I CAN'T READ! OKAY?!
JIM DAVIS 7-3
© 1992 United Feature Syndicate, Inc.

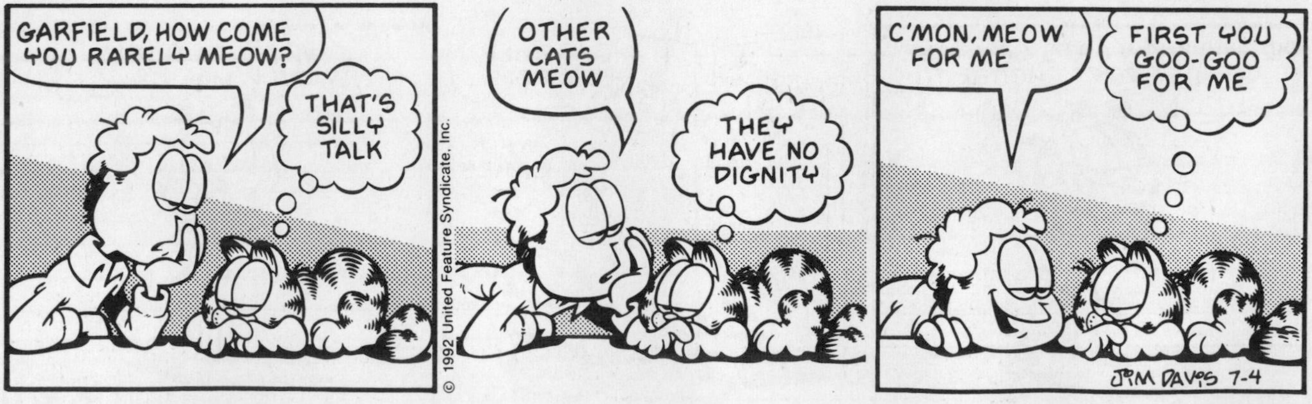
GARFIELD, HOW COME YOU RARELY MEOW?
THAT'S SILLY TALK
OTHER CATS MEOW
THEY HAVE NO DIGNITY
C'MON, MEOW FOR ME
FIRST YOU GOO-GOO FOR ME
JIM DAVIS 7-4
© 1992 United Feature Syndicate, Inc.

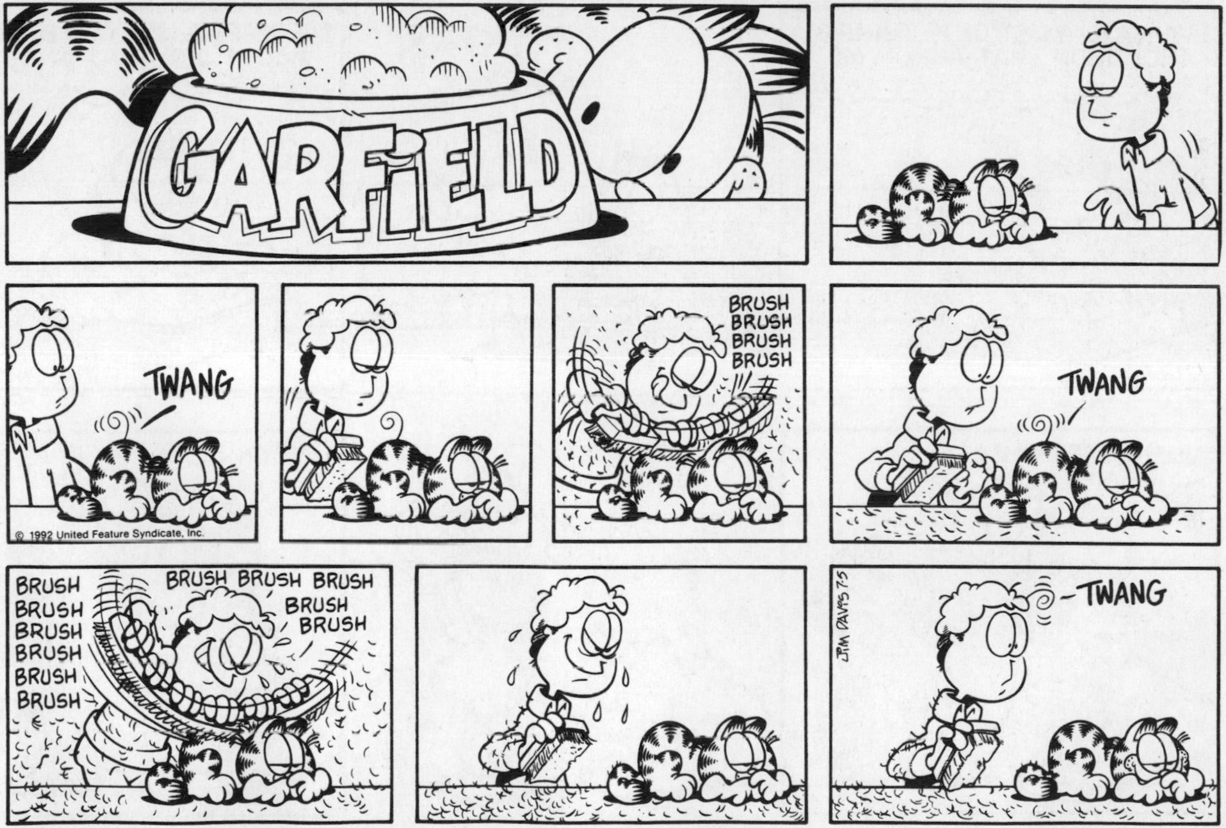
GARFIELD
TWANG
© 1992 United Feature Syndicate, Inc.
BRUSH BRUSH BRUSH BRUSH
TWANG
BRUSH BRUSH BRUSH BRUSH BRUSH BRUSH
BRUSH BRUSH BRUSH
BRUSH BRUSH
JPM DAVPS 7-5
TWANG

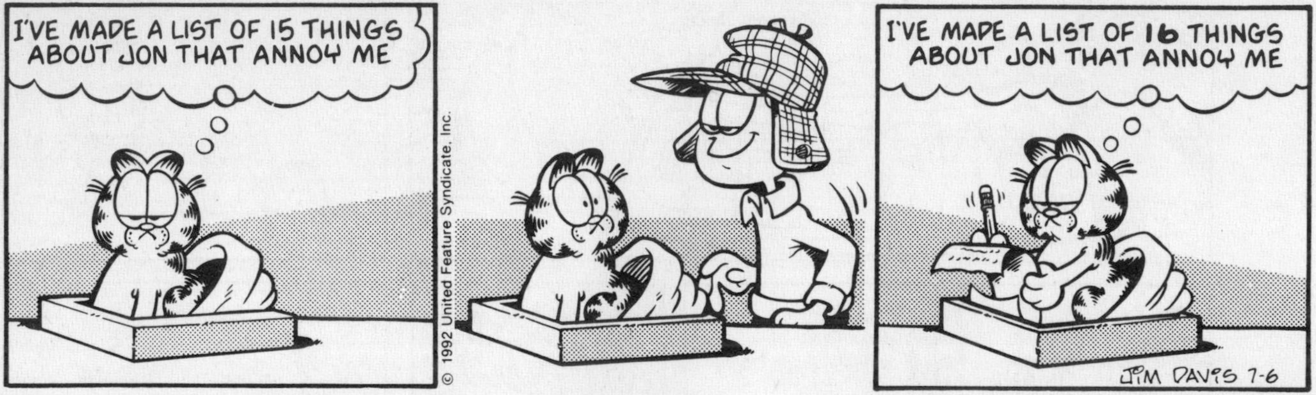
I'VE MADE A LIST OF 15 THINGS ABOUT JON THAT ANNOY ME
I'VE MADE A LIST OF 16 THINGS ABOUT JON THAT ANNOY ME
© 1992 United Feature Syndicate, Inc.
JIM DAVIS 7-6

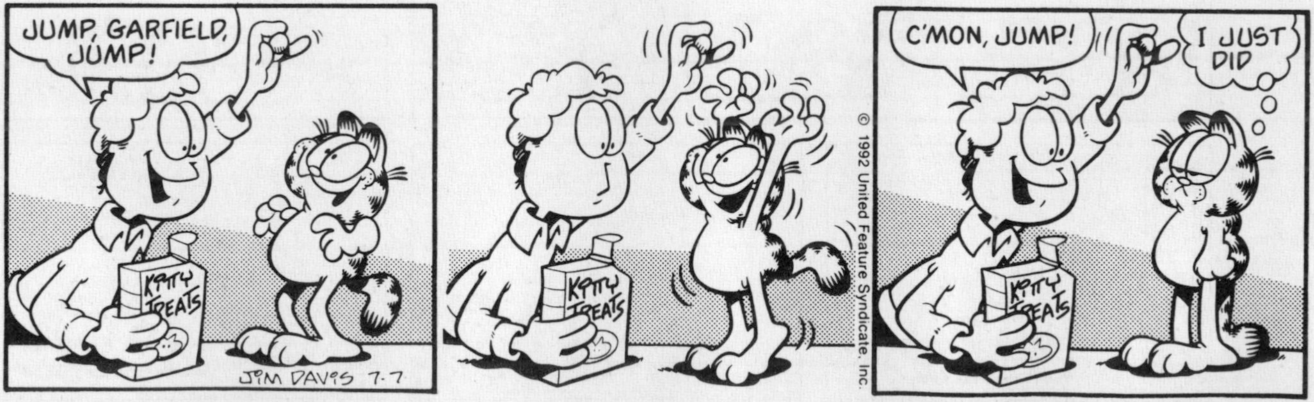
JUMP, GARFIELD, JUMP!
KITTY TREATS
JIM DAVIS 7-7
C'MON, JUMP!
I JUST DID
© 1992 United Feature Syndicate, Inc.

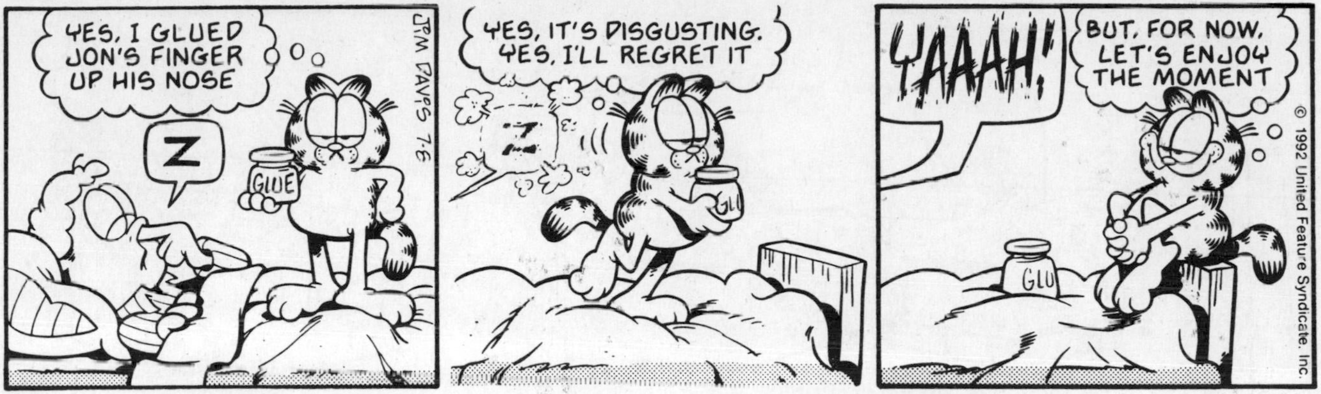
YES, I GLUED JON'S FINGER UP HIS NOSE
GLUE
JIM DAVIS 7-6
YES, IT'S DISGUSTING. YES, I'LL REGRET IT
GLU
YAAAH!
BUT, FOR NOW, LET'S ENJOY THE MOMENT
GLU
© 1992 United Feature Syndicate, Inc.

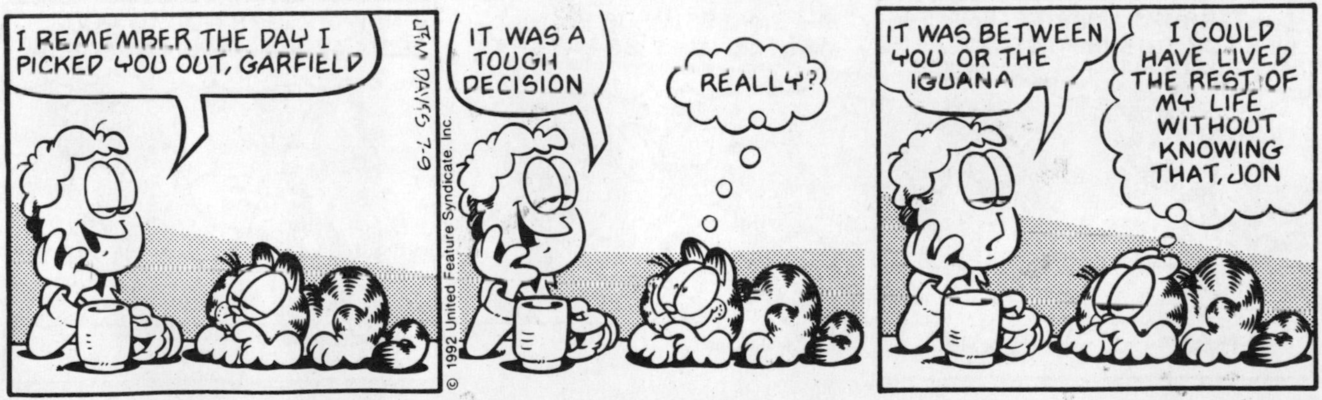
I REMEMBER THE DAY I PICKED YOU OUT, GARFIELD
JIM DAVIS 7-9
© 1992 United Feature Syndicate, Inc.
IT WAS A TOUGH DECISION
REALLY?
IT WAS BETWEEN YOU OR THE IGUANA
I COULD HAVE LIVED THE REST OF MY LIFE WITHOUT KNOWING THAT, JON

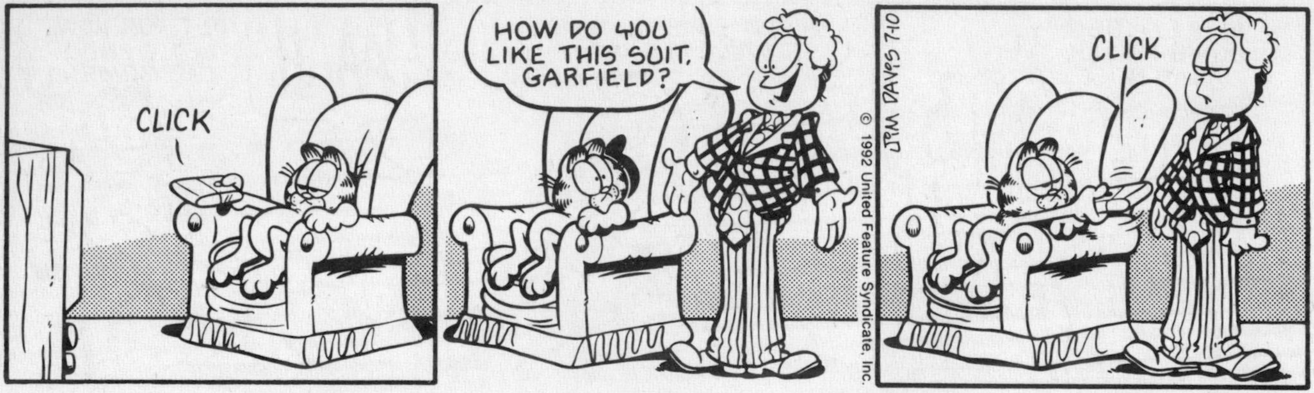
CLICK
HOW DO YOU LIKE THIS SUIT, GARFIELD?
CLICK
JIM DAVIS 7-10
© 1992 United Feature Syndicate, Inc.

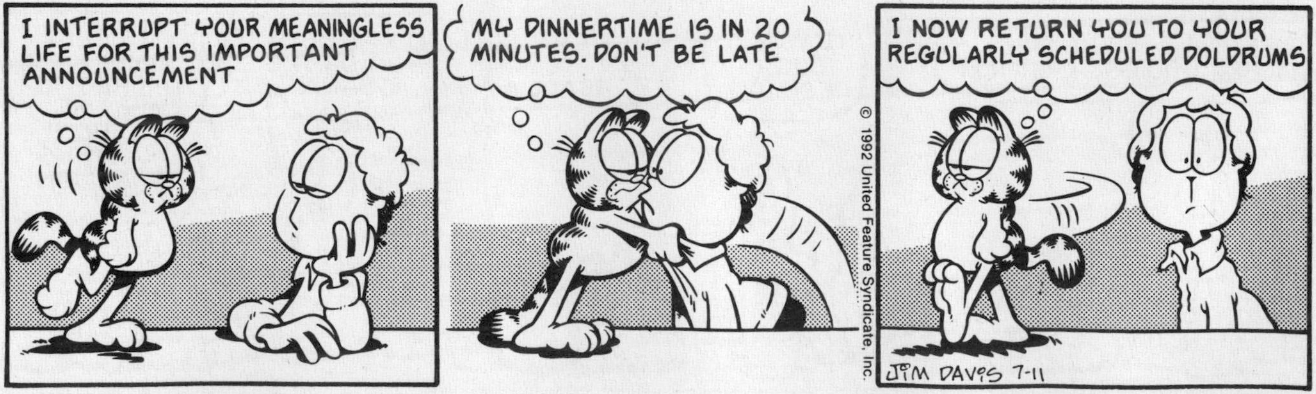
I INTERRUPT YOUR MEANINGLESS LIFE FOR THIS IMPORTANT ANNOUNCEMENT
MY DINNERTIME IS IN 20 MINUTES. DON'T BE LATE
I NOW RETURN YOU TO YOUR REGULARLY SCHEDULED DOLDRUMS
JIM DAVIS 7-11
© 1992 United Feature Syndicate, Inc.

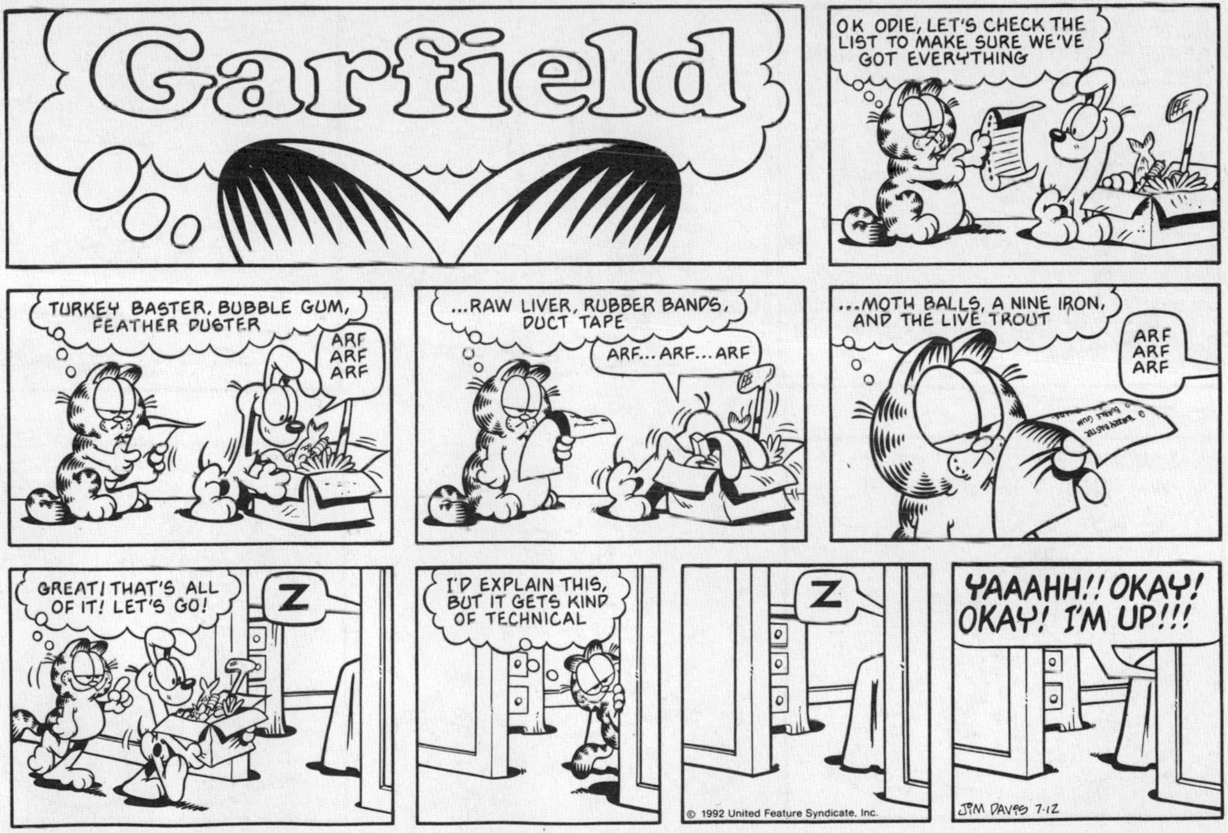
Garfield
OK ODIE, LET'S CHECK THE LIST TO MAKE SURE WE'VE GOT EVERYTHING
TURKEY BASTER, BUBBLE GUM, FEATHER DUSTER
ARF ARF ARF
...RAW LIVER, RUBBER BANDS, DUCT TAPE
ARF... ARF... ARF
...MOTH BALLS, A NINE IRON, AND THE LIVE TROUT
ARF ARF ARF
GREAT! THAT'S ALL OF IT! LET'S GO!
Z
I'D EXPLAIN THIS, BUT IT GETS KIND OF TECHNICAL
Z
© 1992 United Feature Syndicate, Inc.
YAAAHH!! OKAY! OKAY! I'M UP!!!
JIM DAVIS 7-12

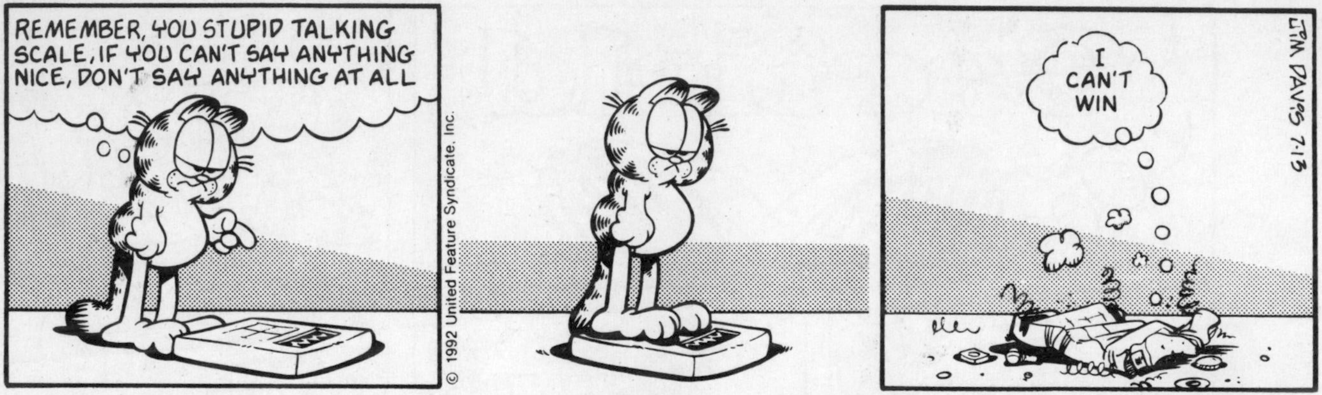
REMEMBER, YOU STUPID TALKING SCALE, IF YOU CAN'T SAY ANYTHING NICE, DON'T SAY ANYTHING AT ALL
© 1992 United Feature Syndicate, Inc.
I CAN'T WIN
JIM DAVIS 7-13

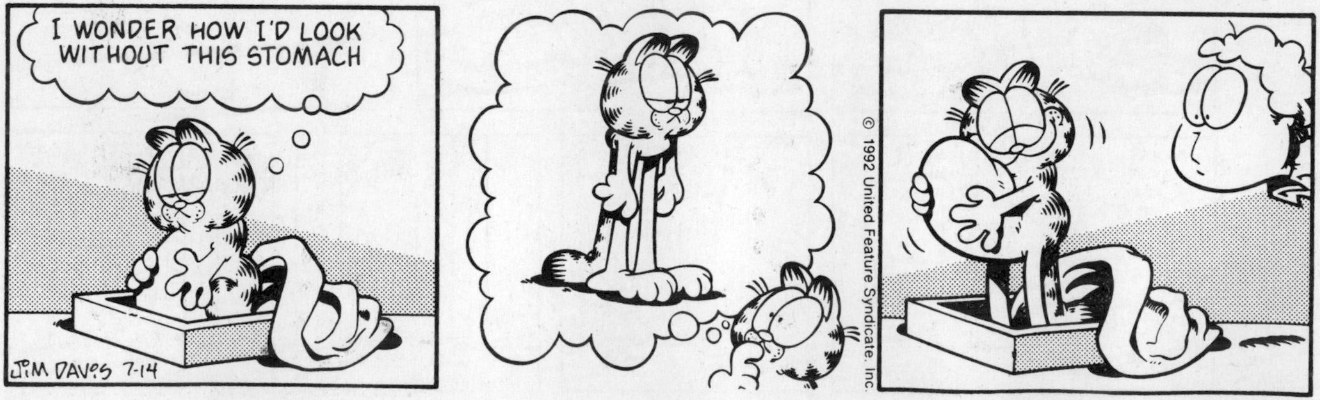
I WONDER HOW I'D LOOK WITHOUT THIS STOMACH
JIM DAVIS 7-14
© 1992 United Feature Syndicate, Inc.

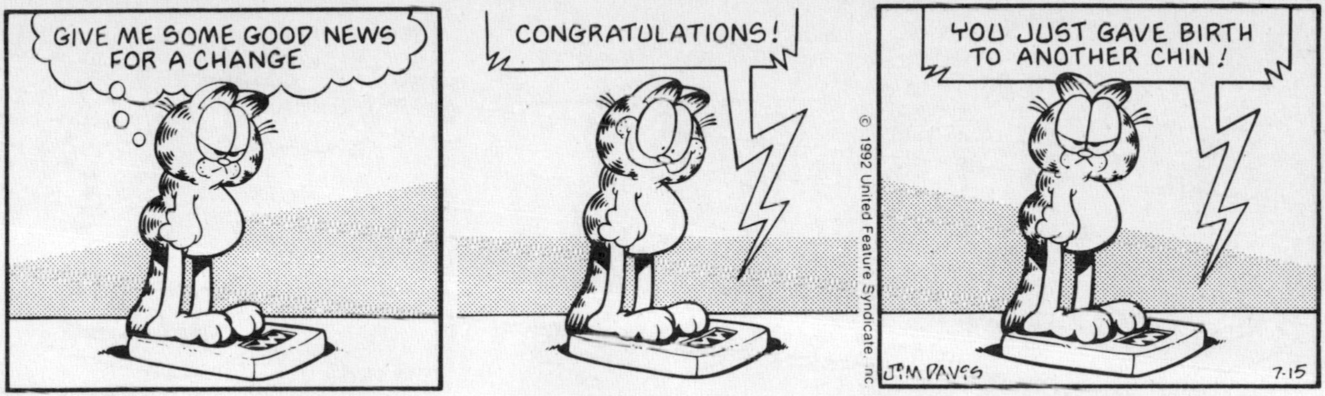
GIVE ME SOME GOOD NEWS FOR A CHANGE
CONGRATULATIONS!
YOU JUST GAVE BIRTH TO ANOTHER CHIN!
© 1992 United Feature Syndicate, Inc
JIM DAVIS 7-15

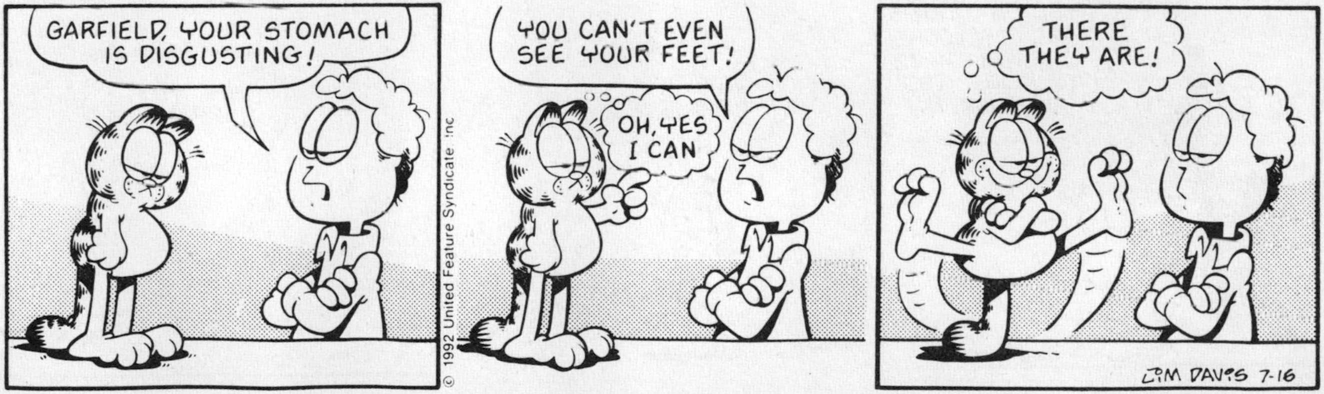
GARFIELD, YOUR STOMACH IS DISGUSTING!
YOU CAN'T EVEN SEE YOUR FEET!
OH, YES I CAN
THERE THEY ARE!
© 1992 United Feature Syndicate Inc
JIM DAVIS 7-16

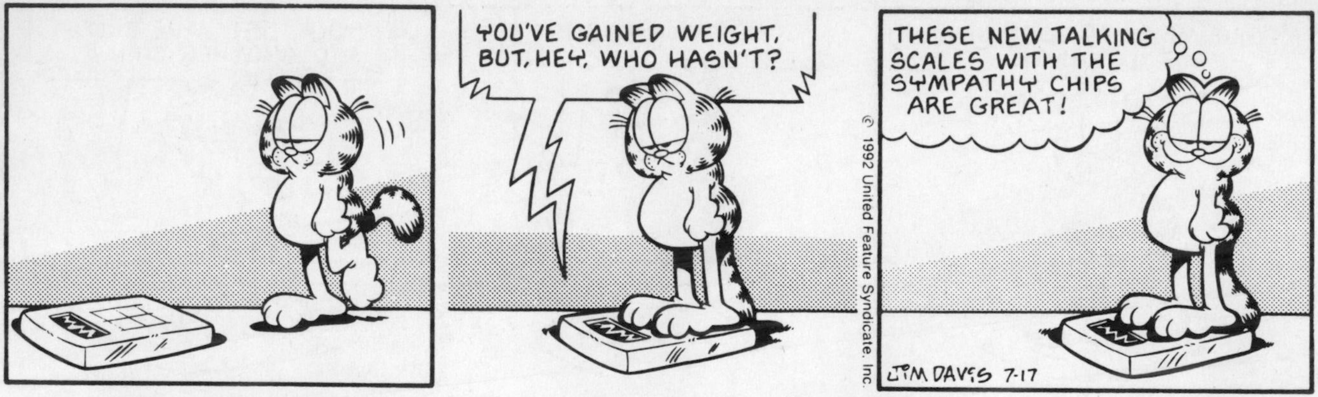
YOU'VE GAINED WEIGHT, BUT, HEY, WHO HASN'T?
THESE NEW TALKING SCALES WITH THE SYMPATHY CHIPS ARE GREAT!
© 1992 United Feature Syndicate, Inc.
JIM DAVIS 7-17

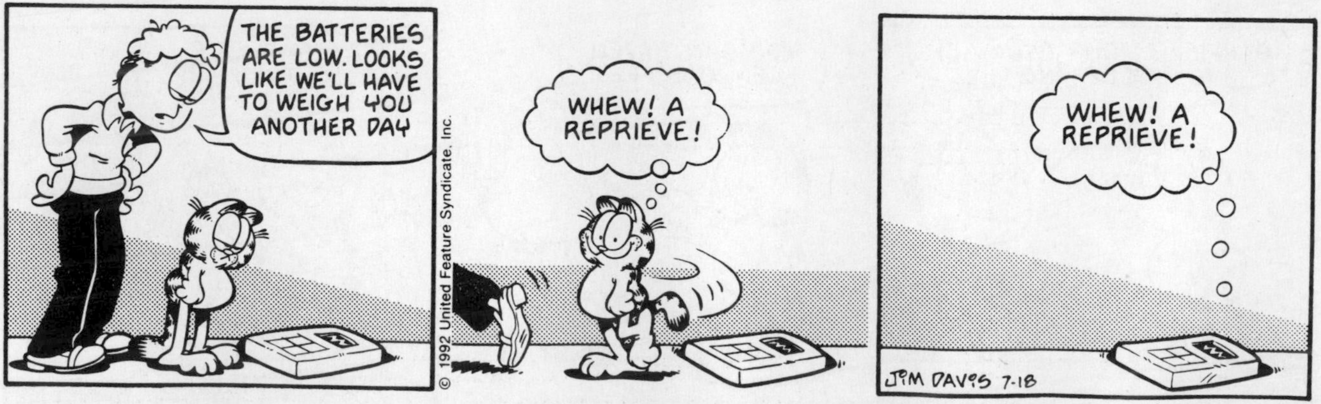
THE BATTERIES ARE LOW. LOOKS LIKE WE'LL HAVE TO WEIGH YOU ANOTHER DAY
© 1992 United Feature Syndicate, Inc.
WHEW! A REPRIEVE!
WHEW! A REPRIEVE!
JIM DAVIS 7-18

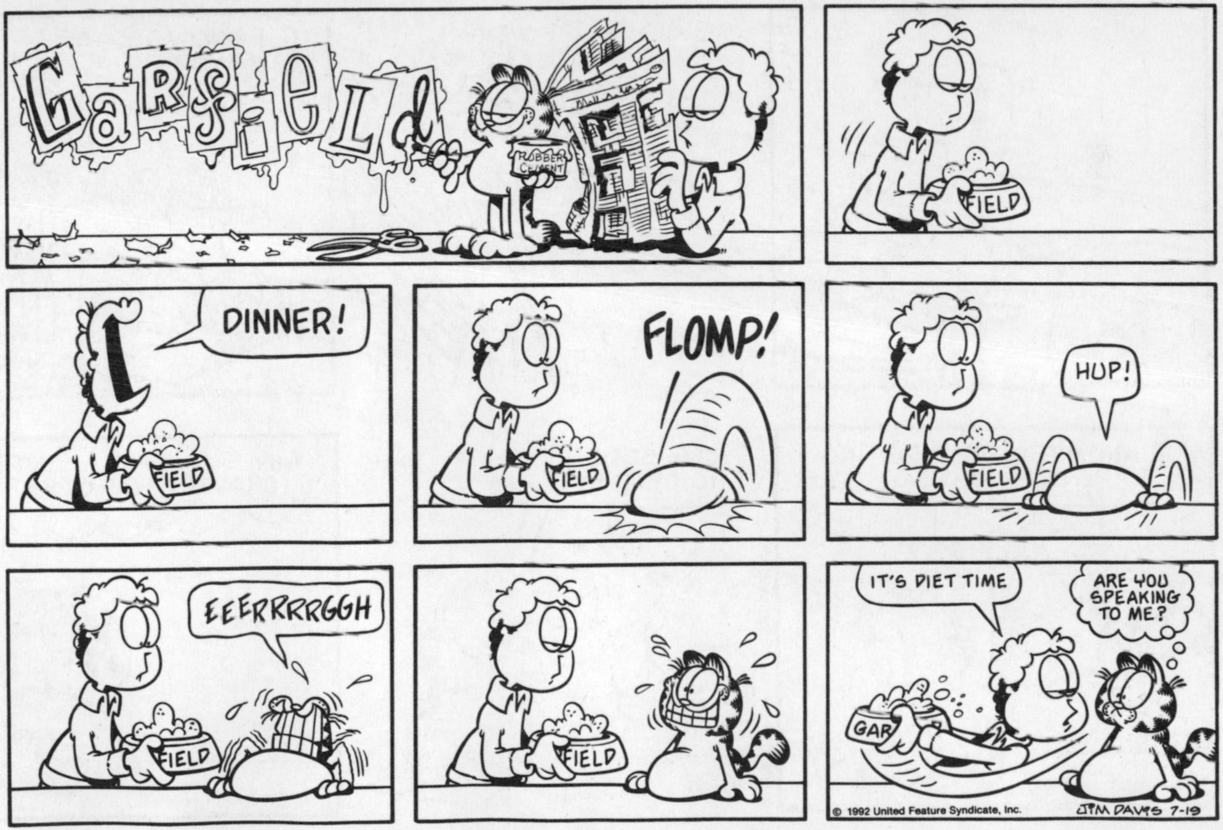
GARFIELD
RUBBER CEMENT
FIELD
DINNER!
FLOMP!
HUP!
EEERRRRGGH
IT'S DIET TIME
ARE YOU SPEAKING TO ME?
GAR
© 1992 United Feature Syndicate, Inc.
JIM DAVIS 7-19

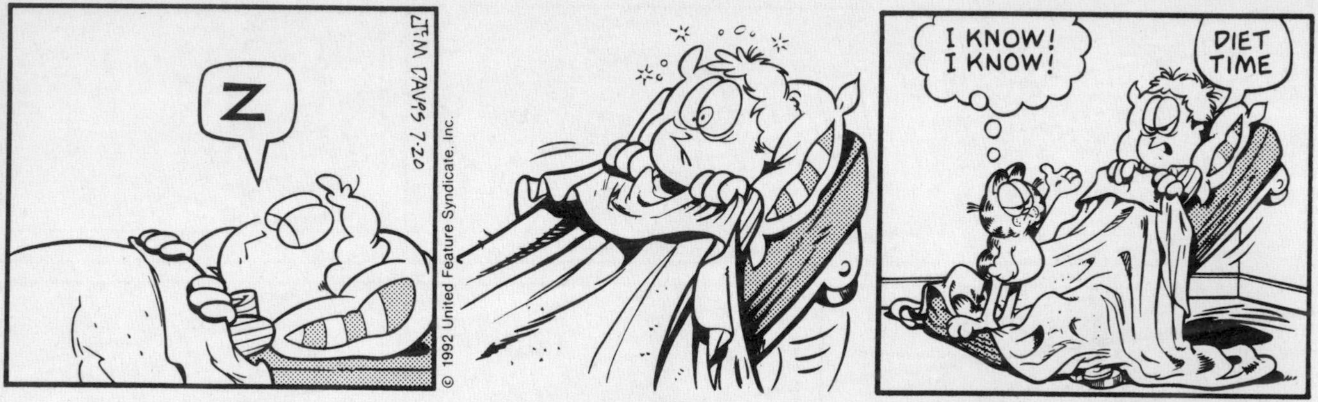
JIM DAVIS 7-20
© 1992 United Feature Syndicate, Inc.
Z
I KNOW! I KNOW!
DIET TIME

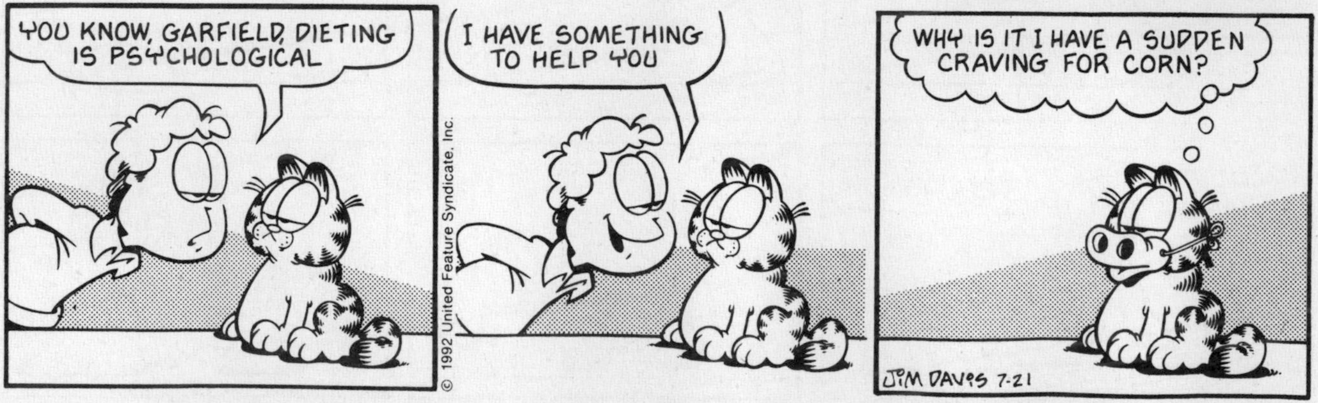
© 1992 United Feature Syndicate, Inc.
YOU KNOW, GARFIELD, DIETING IS PSYCHOLOGICAL
I HAVE SOMETHING TO HELP YOU
WHY IS IT I HAVE A SUDDEN CRAVING FOR CORN?
JIM DAVIS 7-21

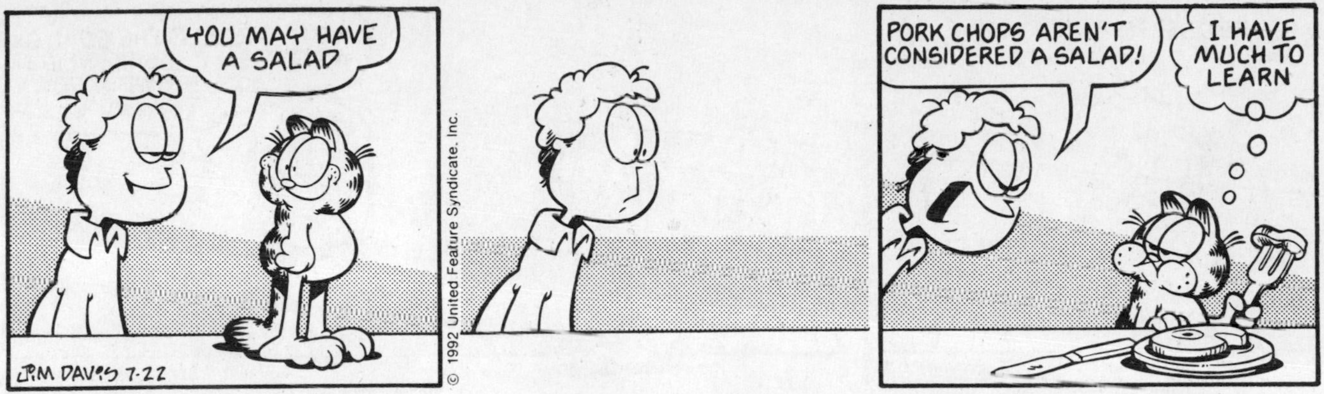
YOU MAY HAVE A SALAD
PORK CHOPS AREN'T CONSIDERED A SALAD!
I HAVE MUCH TO LEARN
JIM DAVIS 7-22
© 1992 United Feature Syndicate, Inc.

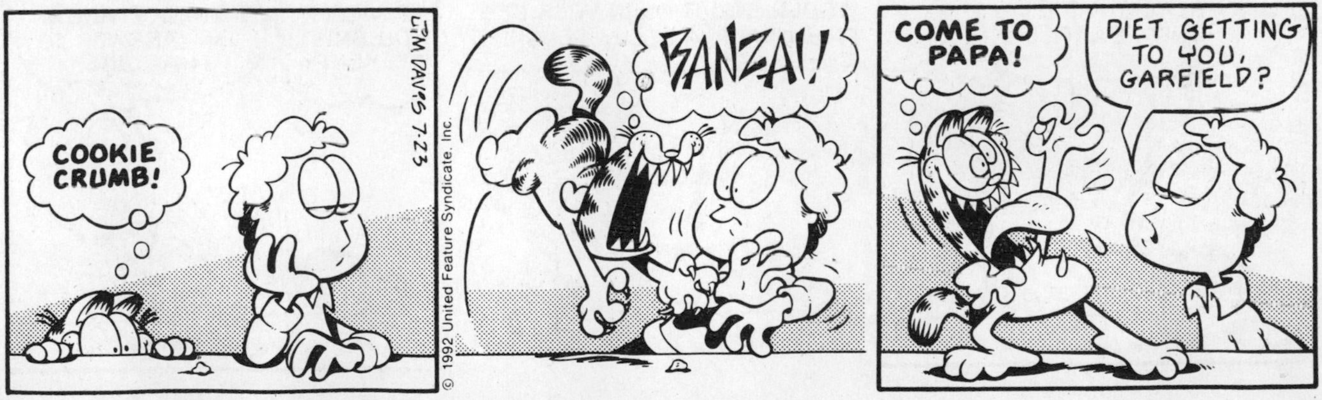
COOKIE CRUMB!
BANZAI!
COME TO PAPA!
DIET GETTING TO YOU, GARFIELD?
JIM DAVIS 7-23
© 1992 United Feature Syndicate, Inc.

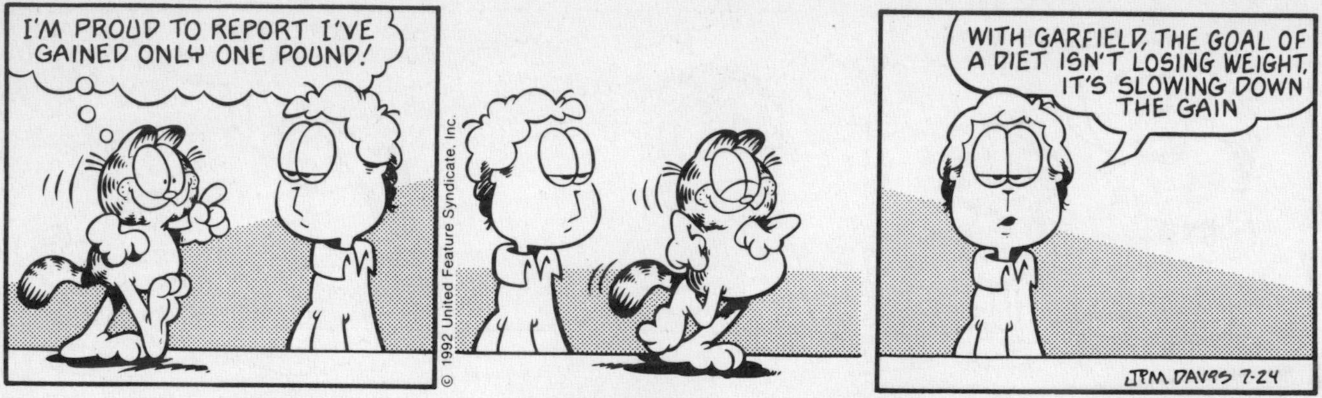
I'M PROUD TO REPORT I'VE GAINED ONLY ONE POUND!
© 1992 United Feature Syndicate, Inc.
WITH GARFIELD, THE GOAL OF A DIET ISN'T LOSING WEIGHT, IT'S SLOWING DOWN THE GAIN
JPM DAVPS 7-24

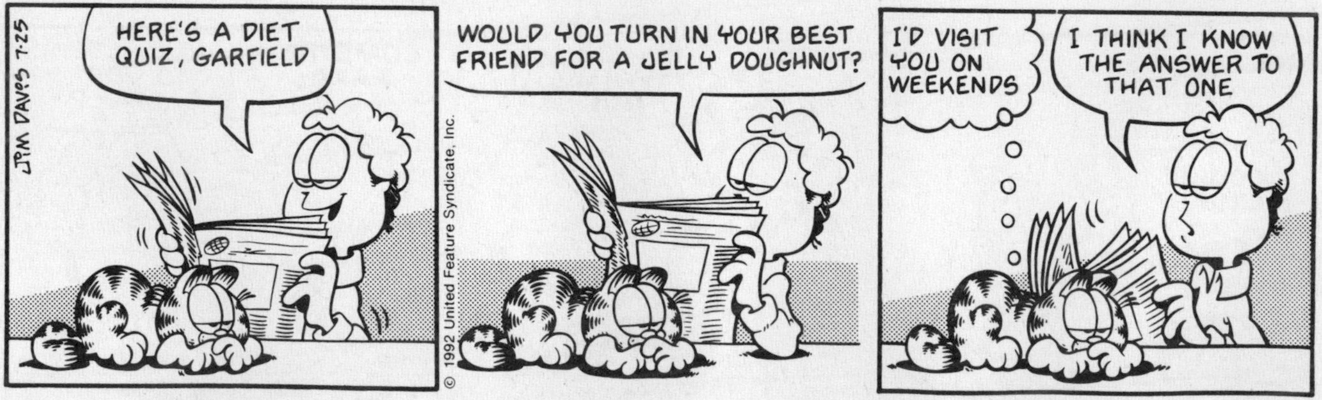
JPM DAVPS 7-25
HERE'S A DIET QUIZ, GARFIELD
© 1992 United Feature Syndicate, Inc.
WOULD YOU TURN IN YOUR BEST FRIEND FOR A JELLY DOUGHNUT?
I'D VISIT YOU ON WEEKENDS
I THINK I KNOW THE ANSWER TO THAT ONE

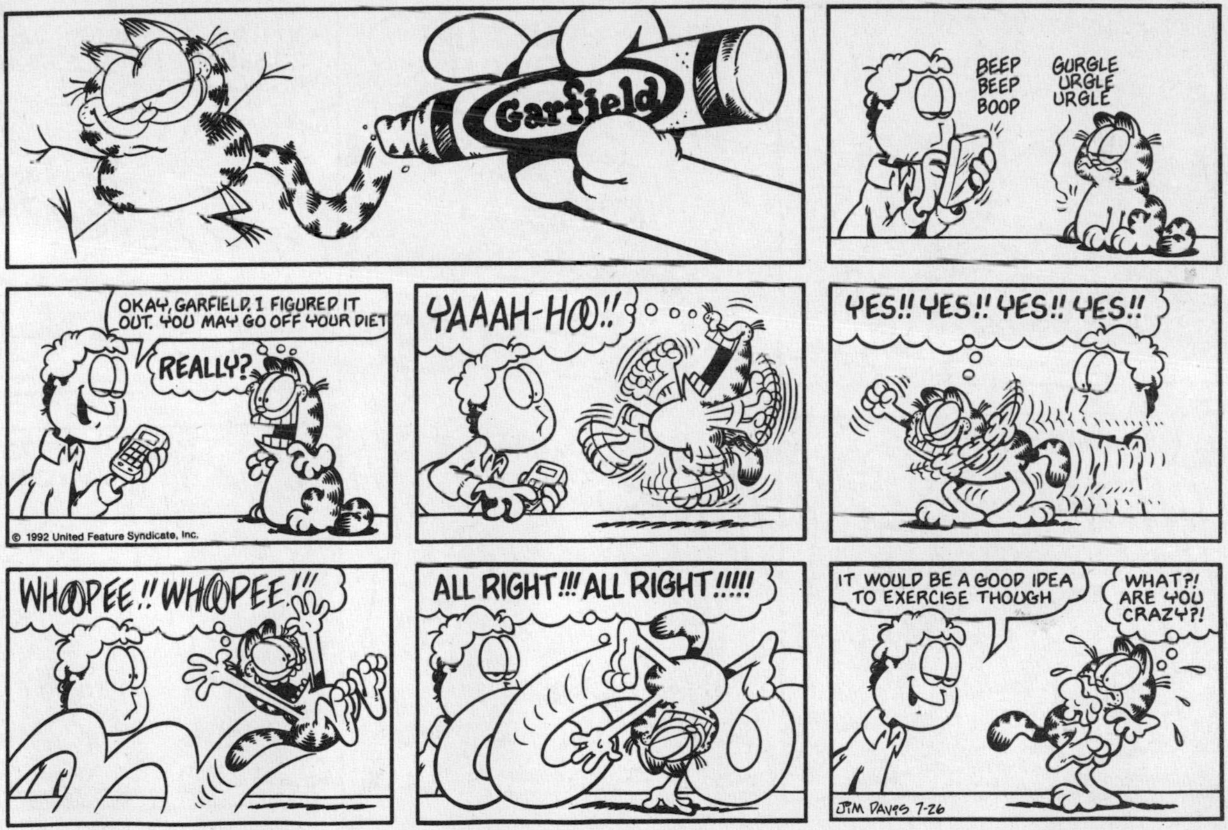
Garfield
BEEP BEEP BOOP
GURGLE URGLE URGLE
OKAY, GARFIELD, I FIGURED IT OUT. YOU MAY GO OFF YOUR DIET
REALLY?
YAAAH-HOO!!
YES!! YES!! YES!! YES!!
WHOOPEE!! WHOOPEE!!
ALL RIGHT!!! ALL RIGHT!!!!!
IT WOULD BE A GOOD IDEA TO EXERCISE THOUGH
WHAT?! ARE YOU CRAZY?!
© 1992 United Feature Syndicate, Inc.
JIM DAVIS 7-26

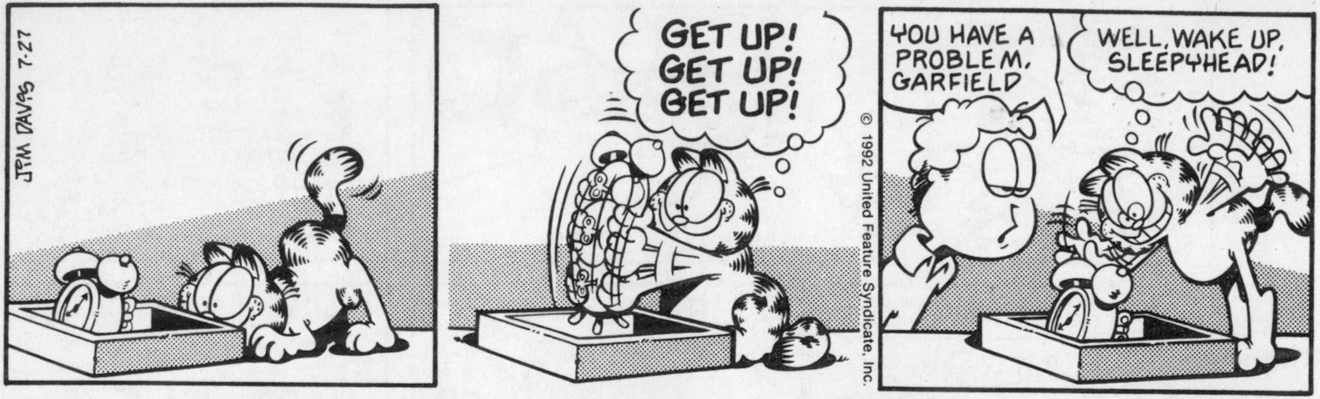
JIM DAVIS 7-27
GET UP! GET UP! GET UP!
© 1992 United Feature Syndicate, Inc.
YOU HAVE A PROBLEM, GARFIELD
WELL, WAKE UP, SLEEPYHEAD!

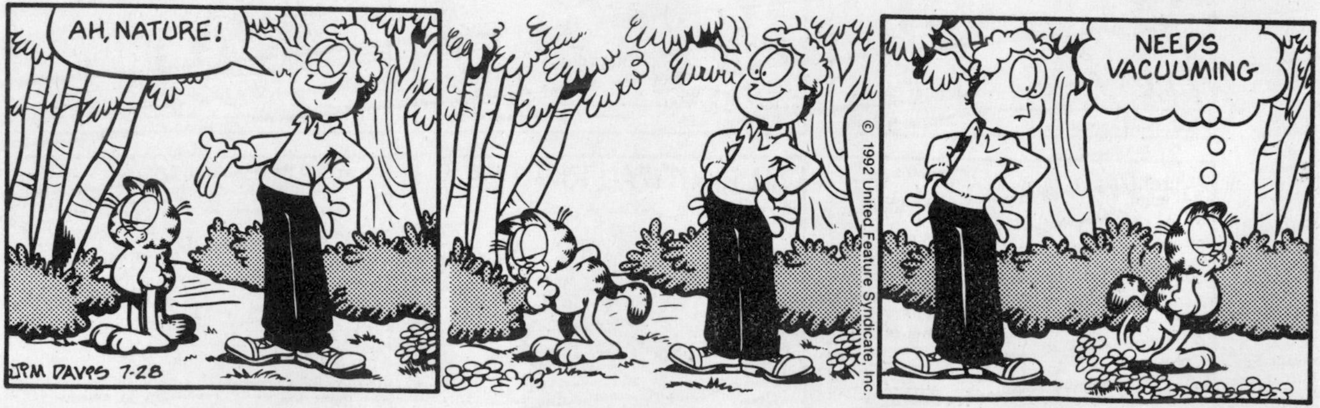
AH, NATURE!
JIM DAVIS 7-28
© 1992 United Feature Syndicate, Inc.
NEEDS VACUUMING

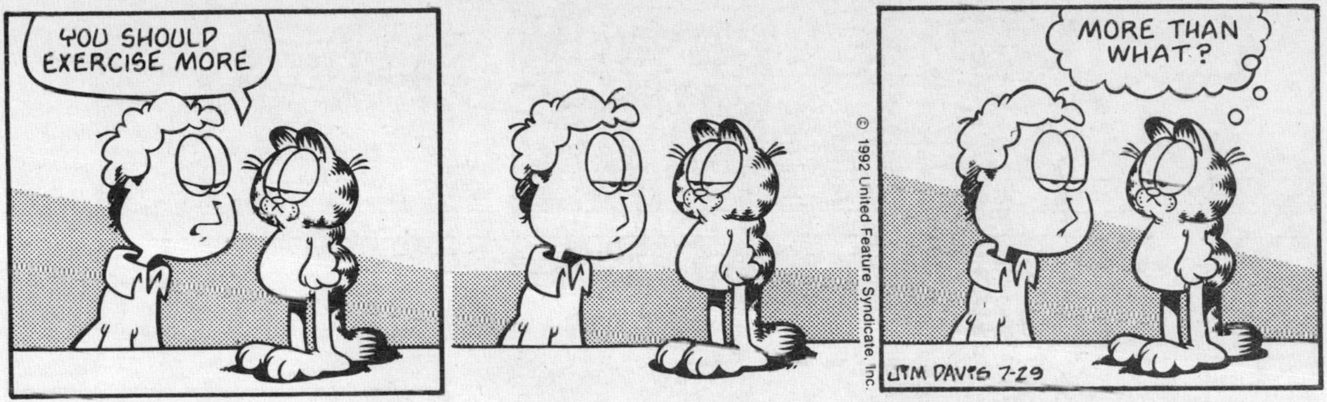
YOU SHOULD EXERCISE MORE
MORE THAN WHAT?
© 1992 United Feature Syndicate, Inc.
JIM DAVIS 7-29

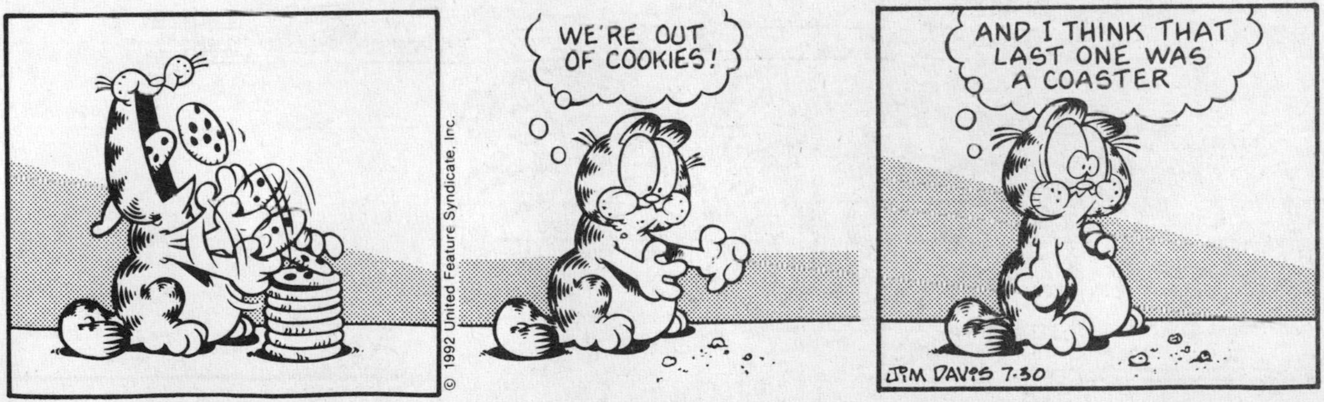
WE'RE OUT OF COOKIES!
AND I THINK THAT LAST ONE WAS A COASTER
© 1992 United Feature Syndicate, Inc.
JIM DAVIS 7-30

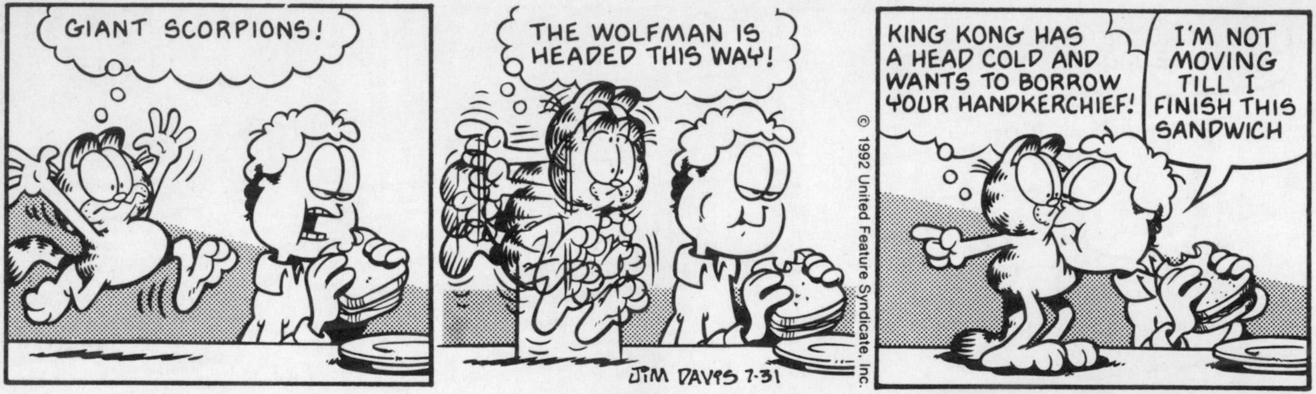
GIANT SCORPIONS!
THE WOLFMAN IS HEADED THIS WAY!
JIM DAVIS 7-31
© 1992 United Feature Syndicate, Inc.
KING KONG HAS A HEAD COLD AND WANTS TO BORROW YOUR HANDKERCHIEF!
I'M NOT MOVING TILL I FINISH THIS SANDWICH

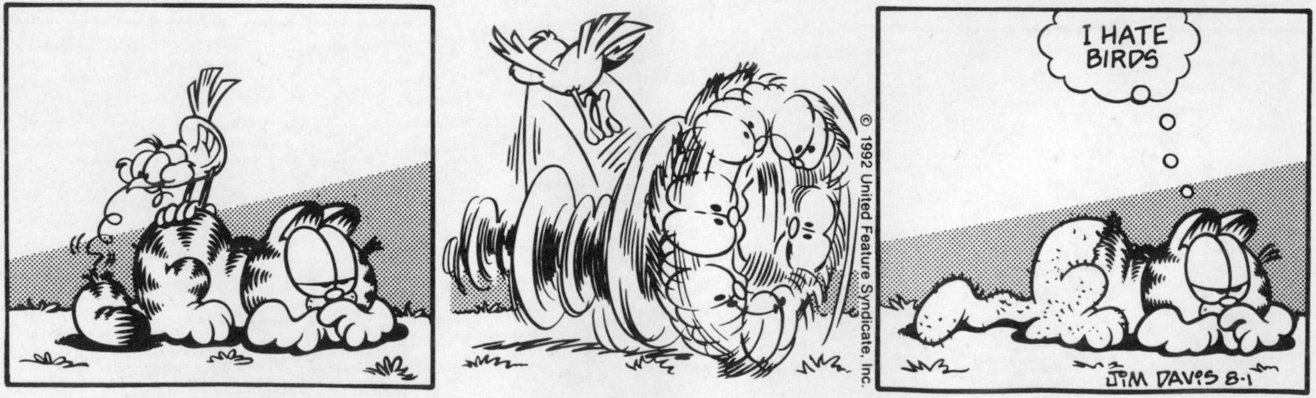
© 1992 United Feature Syndicate, Inc.
I HATE BIRDS
JIM DAVIS 8-1

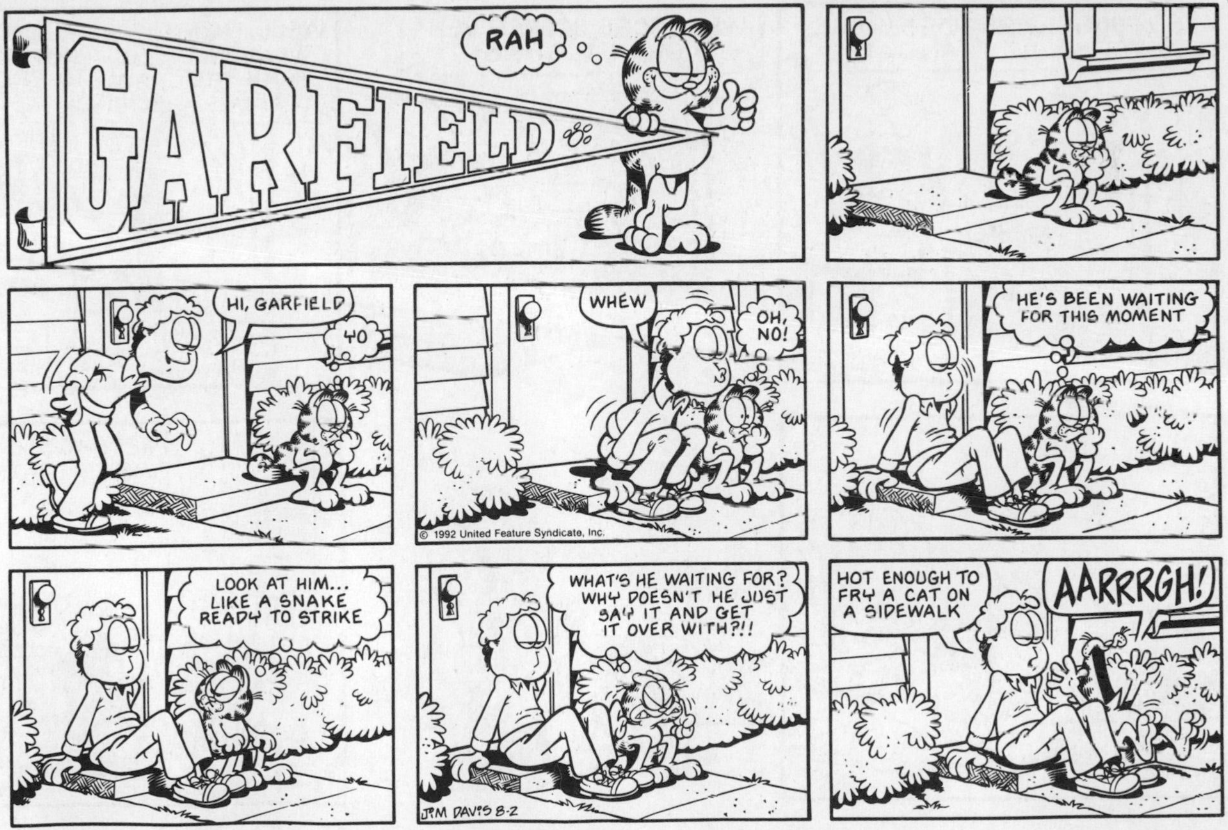
GARFIELD
RAH
HI, GARFIELD
YO
WHEW
OH, NO!
© 1992 United Feature Syndicate, Inc.
HE'S BEEN WAITING FOR THIS MOMENT
LOOK AT HIM... LIKE A SNAKE READY TO STRIKE
WHAT'S HE WAITING FOR? WHY DOESN'T HE JUST SAY IT AND GET IT OVER WITH?!!
JIM DAVIS 8-2
HOT ENOUGH TO FRY A CAT ON A SIDEWALK
AARRRGH!

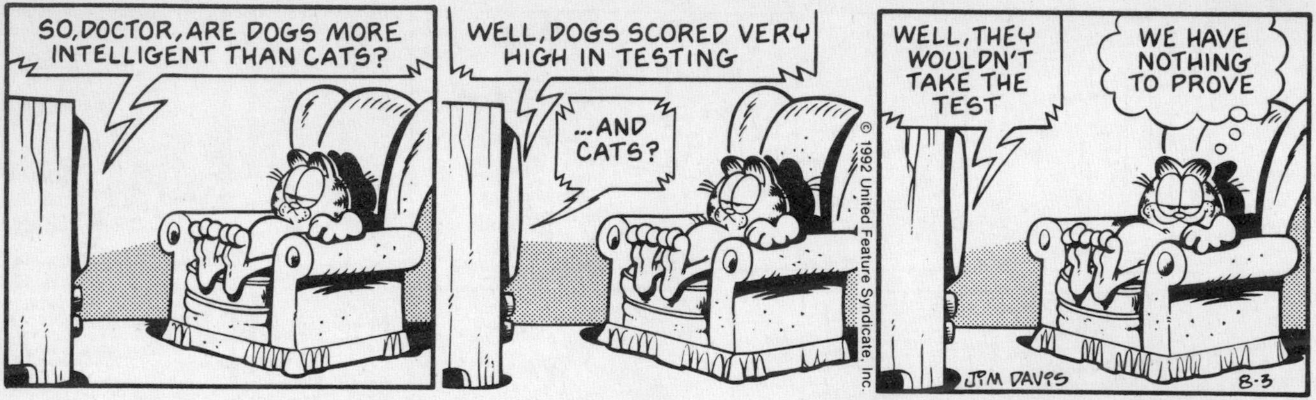
SO, DOCTOR, ARE DOGS MORE INTELLIGENT THAN CATS?
WELL, DOGS SCORED VERY HIGH IN TESTING
...AND CATS?
© 1992 United Feature Syndicate, Inc.
WELL, THEY WOULDN'T TAKE THE TEST
WE HAVE NOTHING TO PROVE
JIM DAVIS
8-3

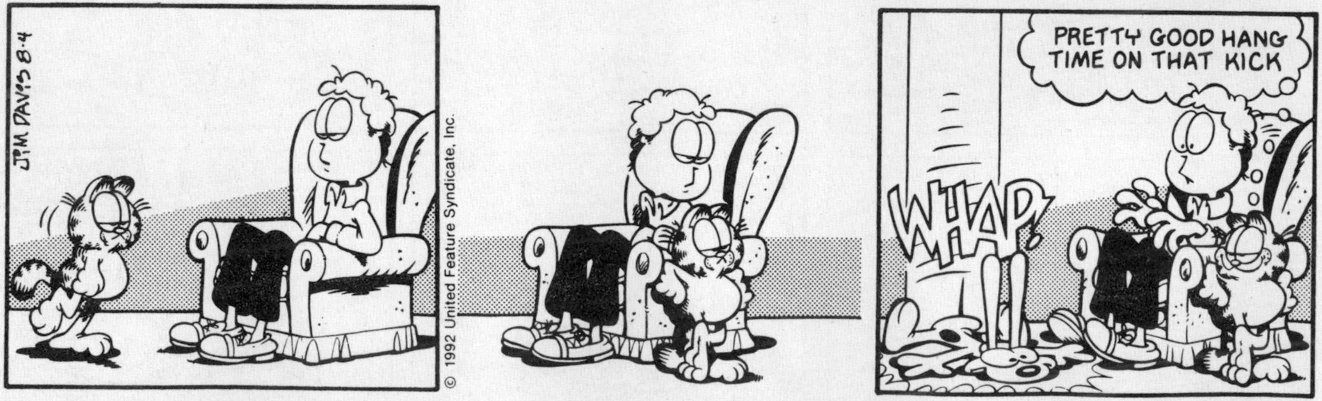
JIM DAVIS 8-4
© 1992 United Feature Syndicate, Inc.
WHAP!
PRETTY GOOD HANG TIME ON THAT KICK

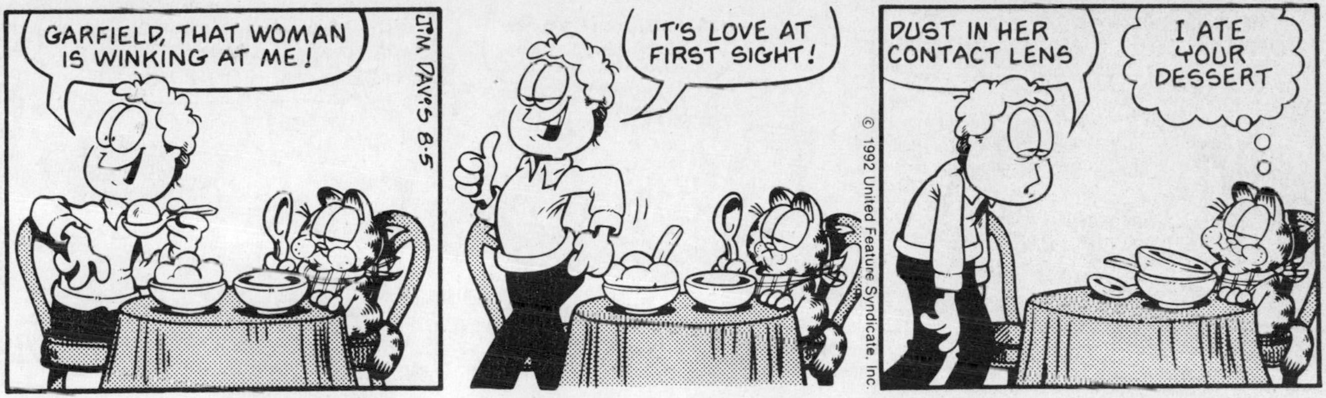
GARFIELD, THAT WOMAN IS WINKING AT ME!
JIM DAVIS 8-5
IT'S LOVE AT FIRST SIGHT!
© 1992 United Feature Syndicate, Inc.
DUST IN HER CONTACT LENS
I ATE YOUR DESSERT

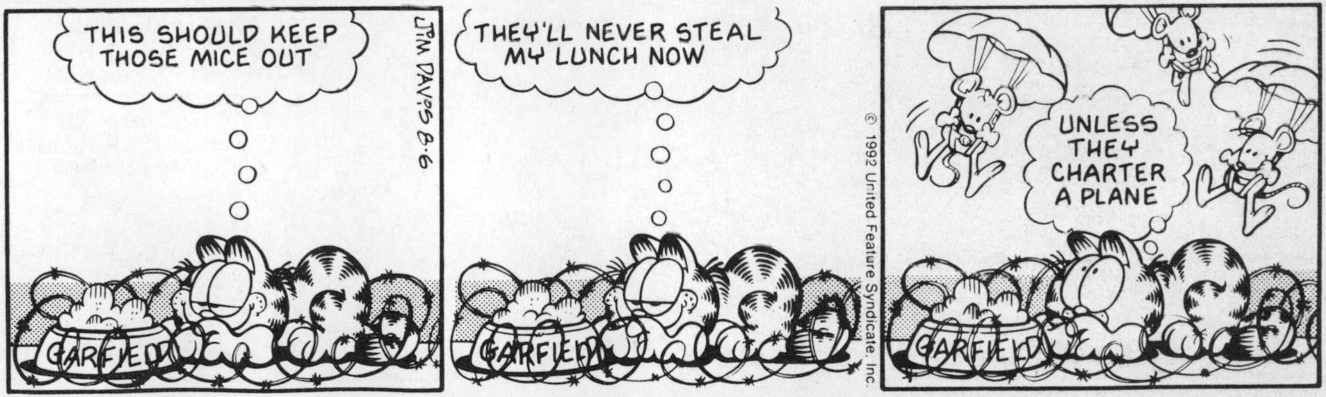
THIS SHOULD KEEP THOSE MICE OUT
JIM DAVIS 8-6
THEY'LL NEVER STEAL MY LUNCH NOW
© 1992 United Feature Syndicate, Inc.
UNLESS THEY CHARTER A PLANE
GARFIELD
GARFIELD
GARFIELD

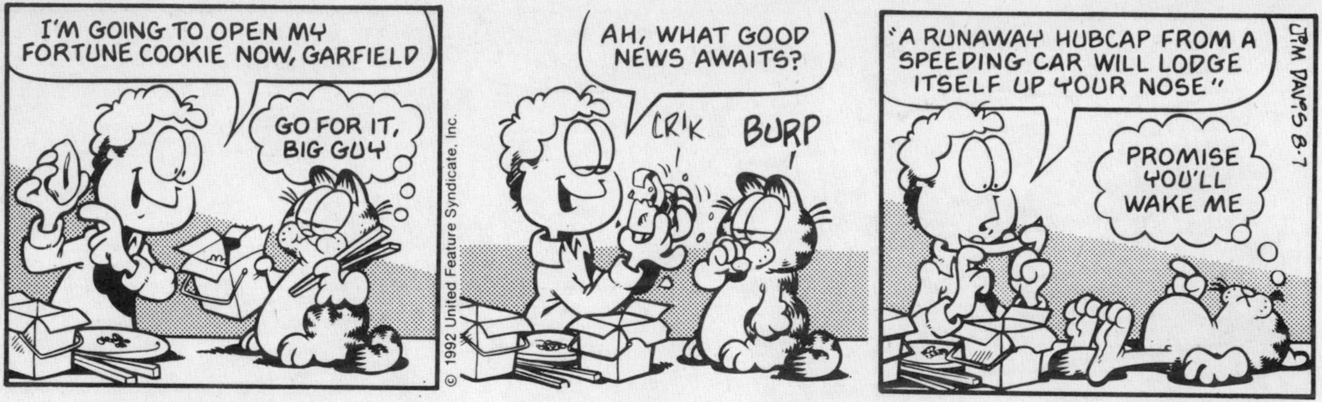
I'M GOING TO OPEN MY FORTUNE COOKIE NOW, GARFIELD
GO FOR IT, BIG GUY
© 1992 United Feature Syndicate, Inc.
AH, WHAT GOOD NEWS AWAITS?
CR'K
BURP
"A RUNAWAY HUBCAP FROM A SPEEDING CAR WILL LODGE ITSELF UP YOUR NOSE"
PROMISE YOU'LL WAKE ME
JIM DAVIS 8-7

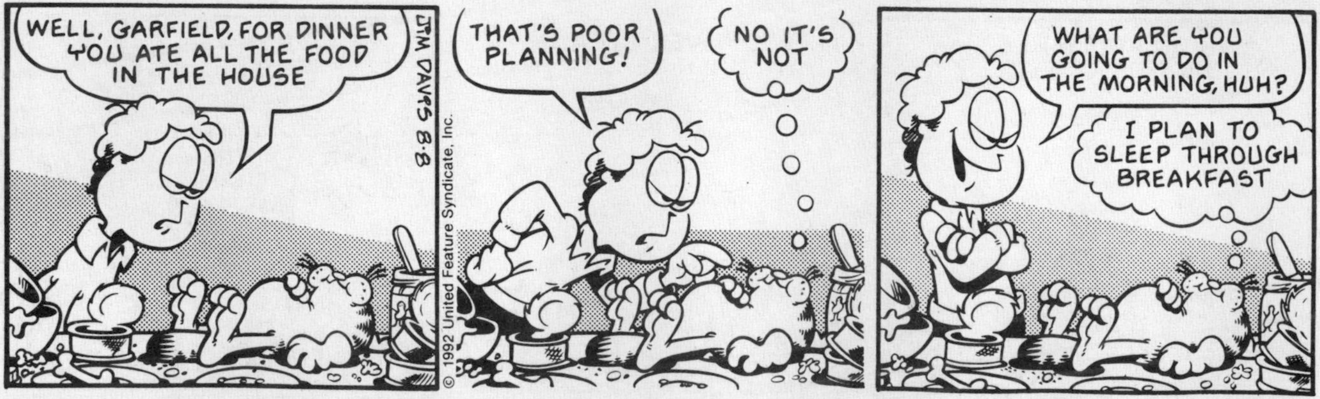
WELL, GARFIELD, FOR DINNER YOU ATE ALL THE FOOD IN THE HOUSE
JIM DAVIS 8-8
© 1992 United Feature Syndicate, Inc.
THAT'S POOR PLANNING!
NO IT'S NOT
WHAT ARE YOU GOING TO DO IN THE MORNING, HUH?
I PLAN TO SLEEP THROUGH BREAKFAST

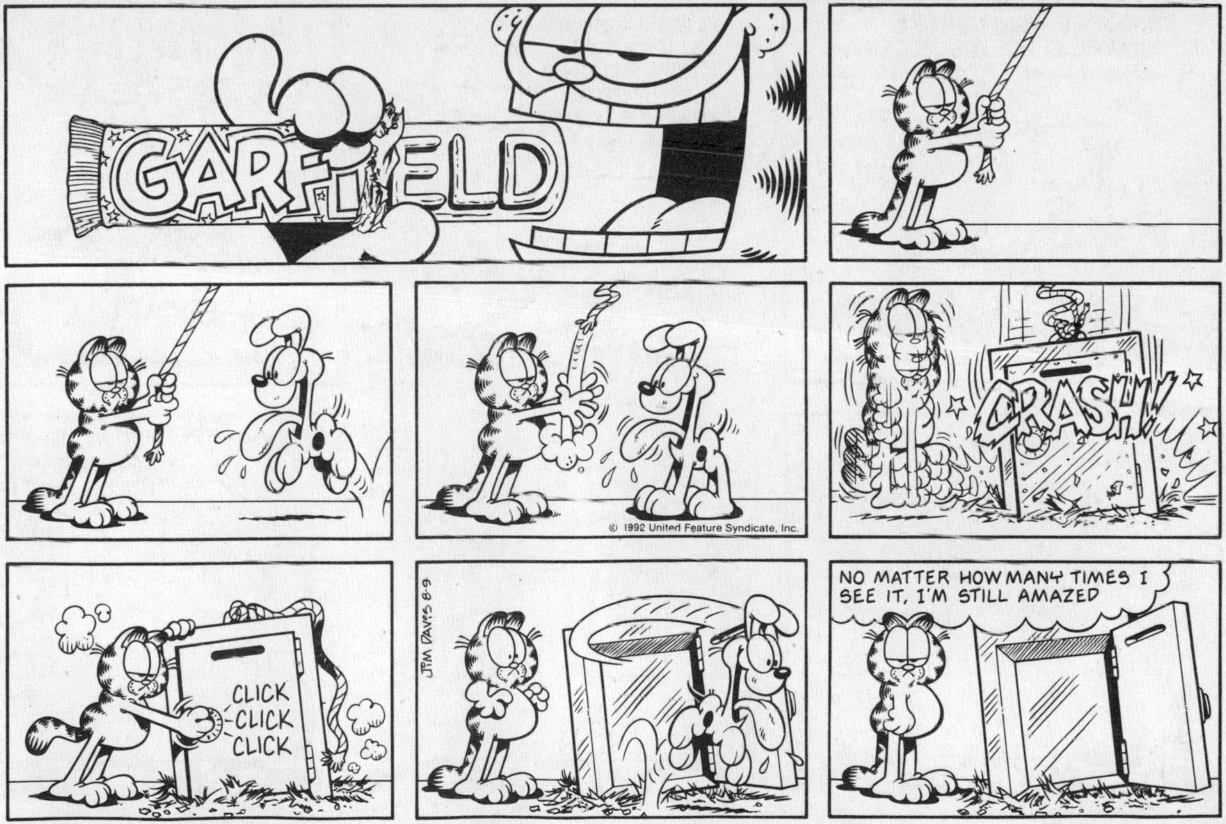
GARFIELD
CRASH!
© 1992 United Feature Syndicate, Inc.
CLICK
CLICK
CLICK
JIM DAVIS 8-9
NO MATTER HOW MANY TIMES I SEE IT, I'M STILL AMAZED

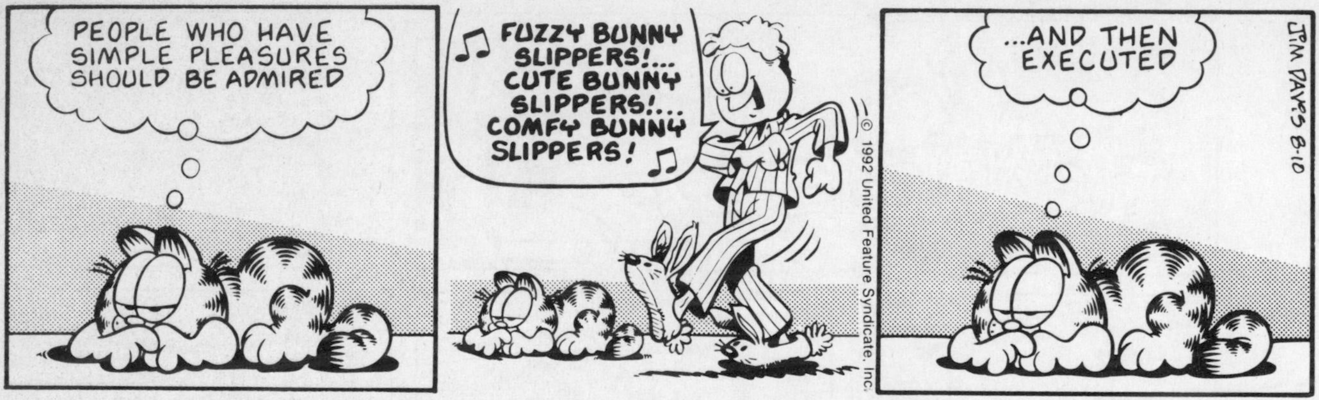
PEOPLE WHO HAVE SIMPLE PLEASURES SHOULD BE ADMIRED
FUZZY BUNNY SLIPPERS!... CUTE BUNNY SLIPPERS!... COMFY BUNNY SLIPPERS!
© 1992 United Feature Syndicate, Inc.
...AND THEN EXECUTED
JIM DAVIS 8-10

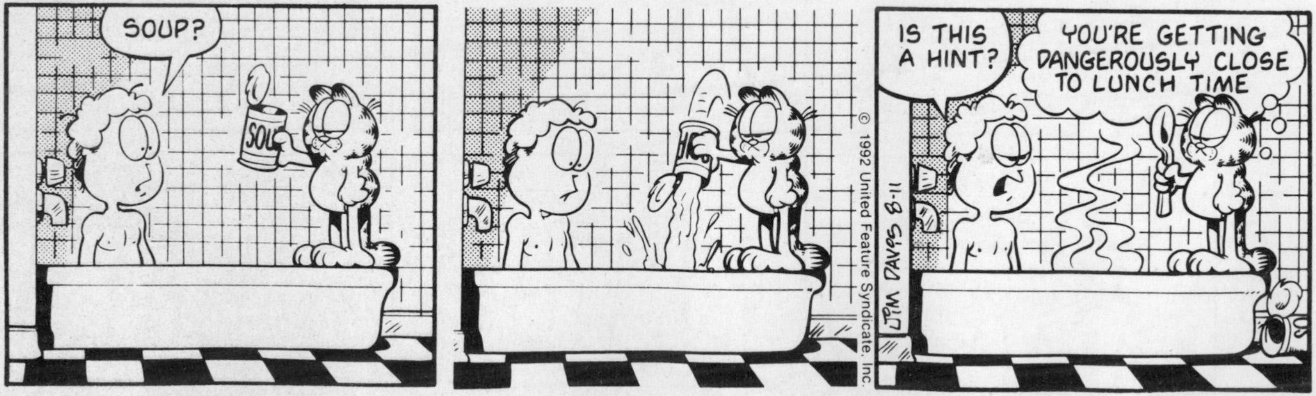
SOUP?
© 1992 United Feature Syndicate, Inc.
JIM DAVIS 8-11
IS THIS A HINT?
YOU'RE GETTING DANGEROUSLY CLOSE TO LUNCH TIME

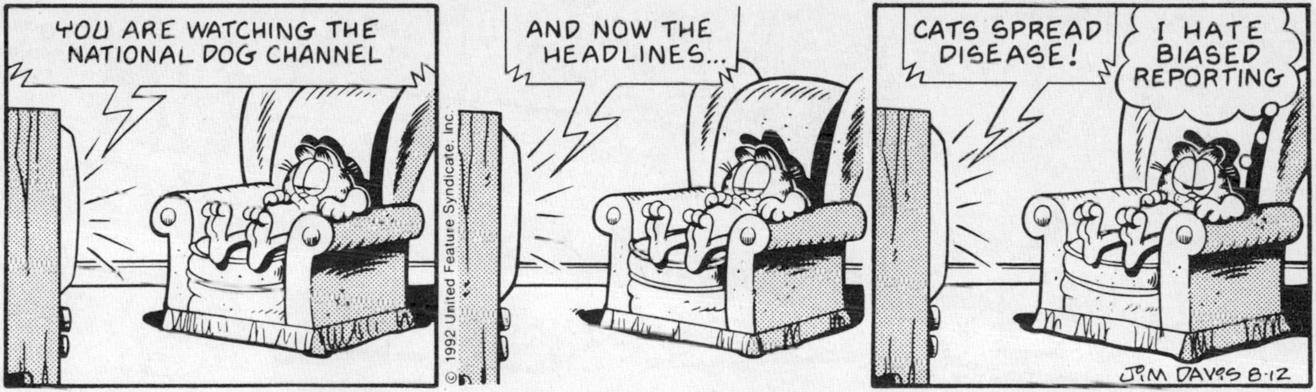
YOU ARE WATCHING THE NATIONAL DOG CHANNEL
AND NOW THE HEADLINES...
CATS SPREAD DISEASE!
I HATE BIASED REPORTING
© 1992 United Feature Syndicate, Inc.
JIM DAVIS 8-12

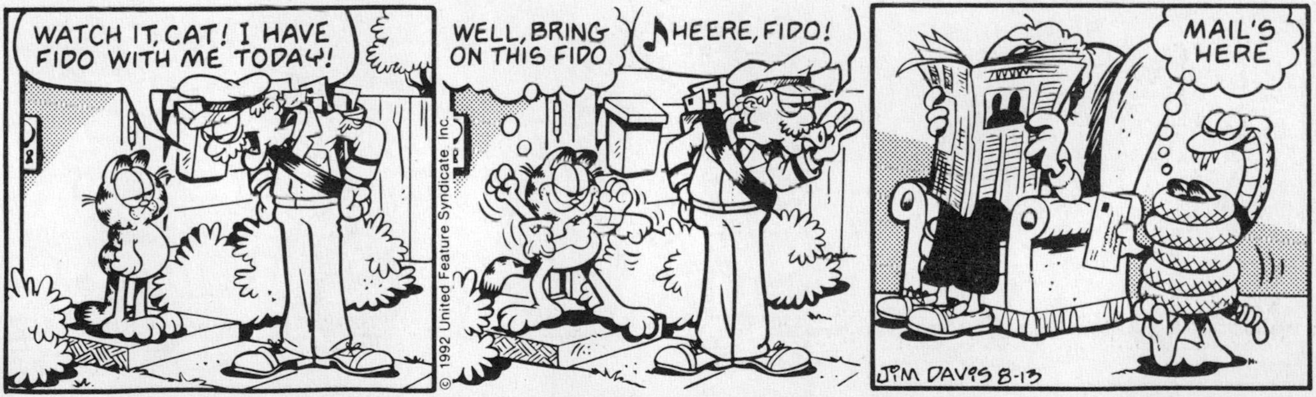
WATCH IT, CAT! I HAVE FIDO WITH ME TODAY!
WELL, BRING ON THIS FIDO
♪HEERE, FIDO!
MAIL'S HERE
© 1992 United Feature Syndicate, Inc.
JIM DAVIS 8-13

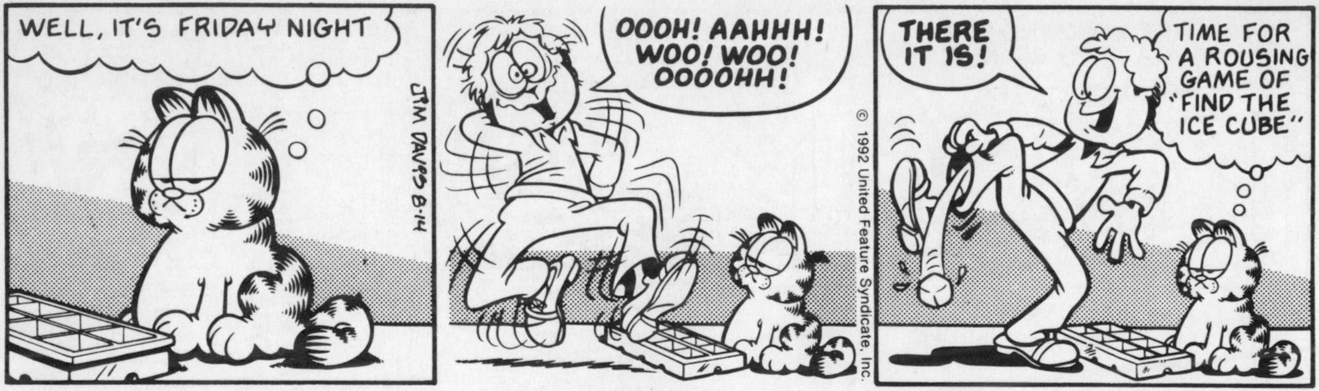
WELL, IT'S FRIDAY NIGHT
JIM DAVIS 8-14
OOOH! AAHHH! WOO! WOO! OOOOHH!
© 1992 United Feature Syndicate, Inc.
THERE IT IS!
TIME FOR A ROUSING GAME OF "FIND THE ICE CUBE"

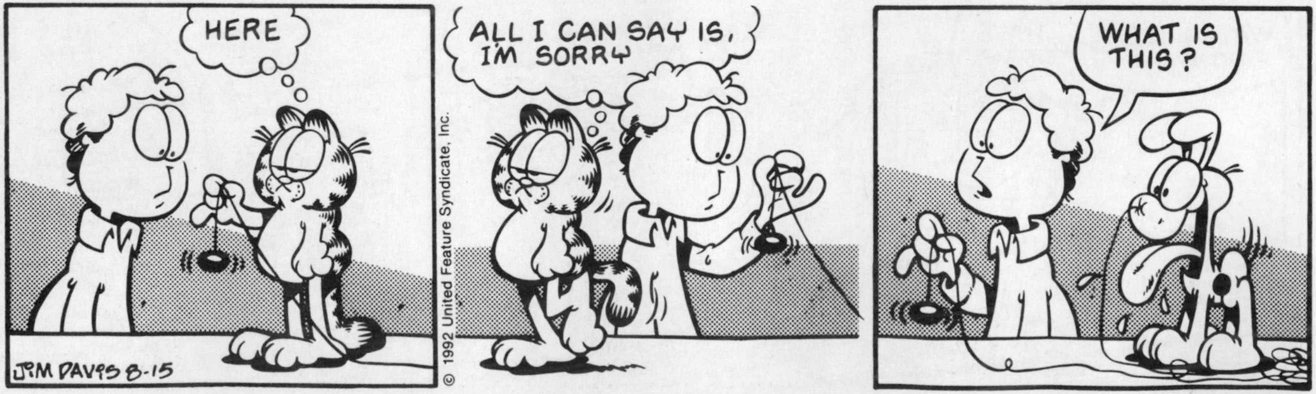
HERE
JIM DAVIS 8-15
© 1992 United Feature Syndicate, Inc.
ALL I CAN SAY IS, I'M SORRY
WHAT IS THIS?

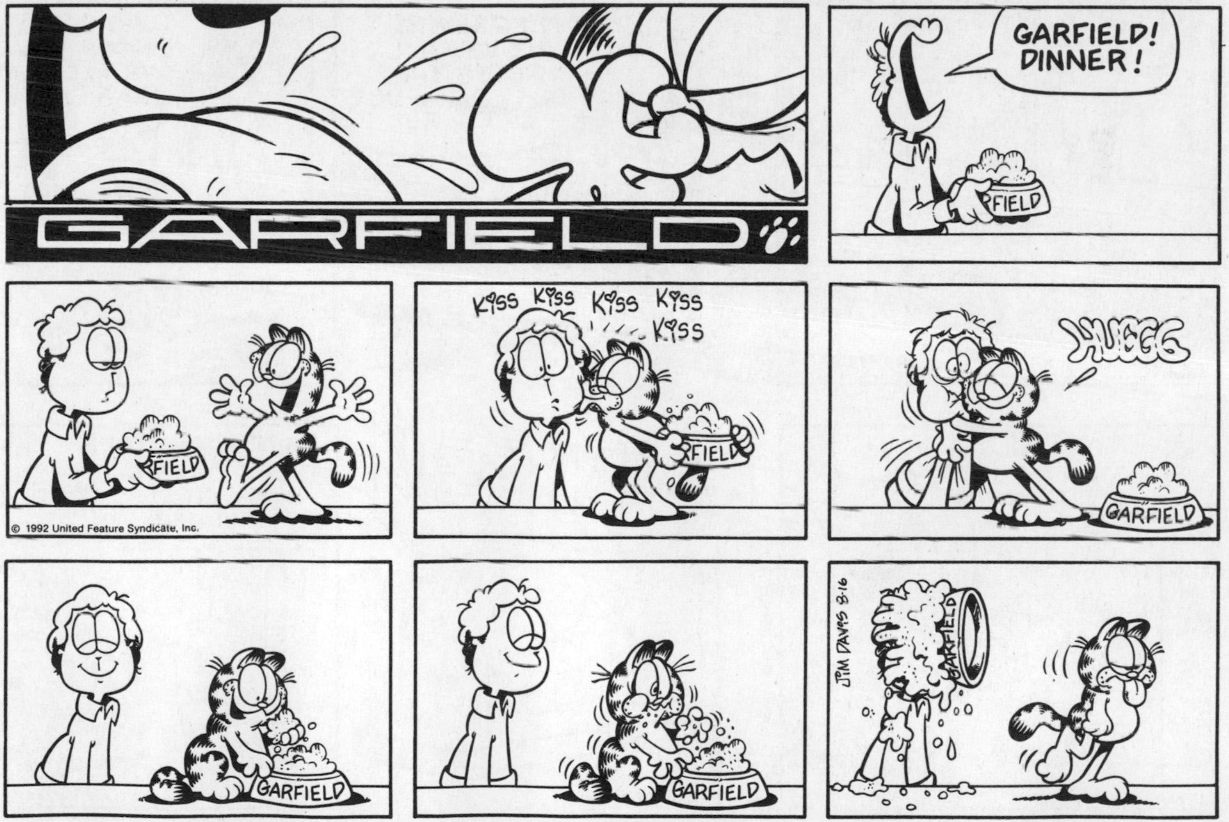
GARFIELD
GARFIELD! DINNER!
FIELD
FIELD
© 1992 United Feature Syndicate, Inc.
KISS KISS KISS KISS KISS
FIELD
HUGG
GARFIELD
GARFIELD
GARFIELD
GARFIELD
JIM DAVIS 8-16

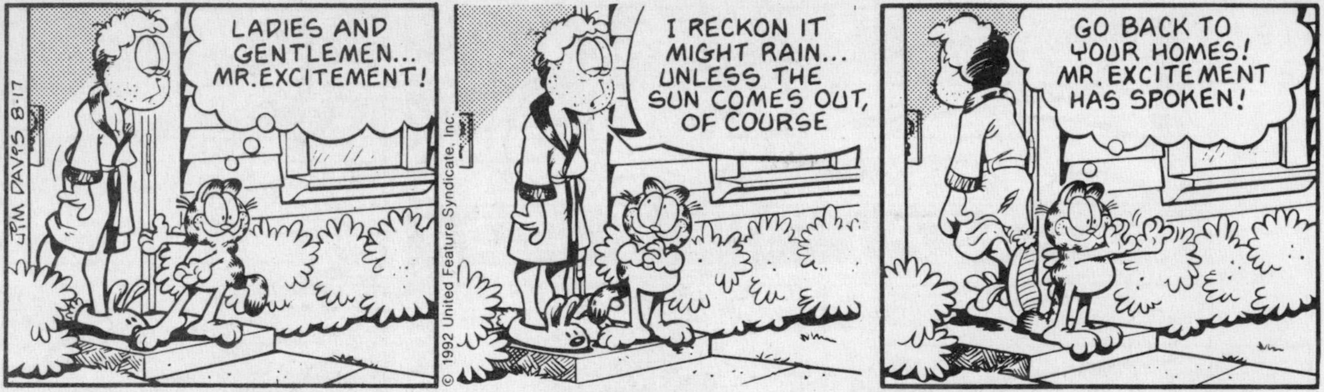
LADIES AND GENTLEMEN... MR. EXCITEMENT!
JIM DAVIS 8-17
© 1992 United Feature Syndicate, Inc.
I RECKON IT MIGHT RAIN... UNLESS THE SUN COMES OUT, OF COURSE
GO BACK TO YOUR HOMES! MR. EXCITEMENT HAS SPOKEN!

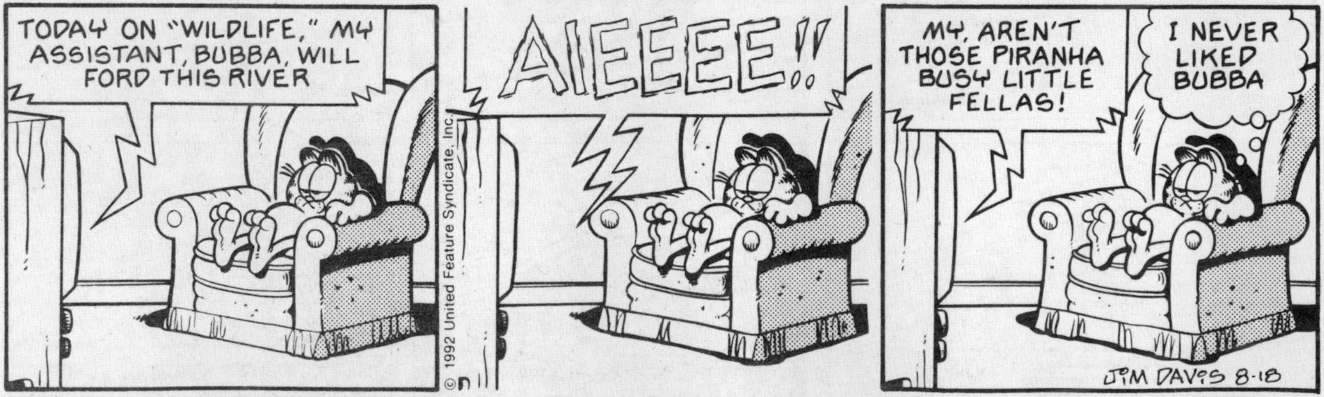
TODAY ON "WILDLIFE," MY ASSISTANT, BUBBA, WILL FORD THIS RIVER
© 1992 United Feature Syndicate, Inc.
AIEEEEE!!
MY, AREN'T THOSE PIRANHA BUSY LITTLE FELLAS!
I NEVER LIKED BUBBA
JIM DAVIS 8-18

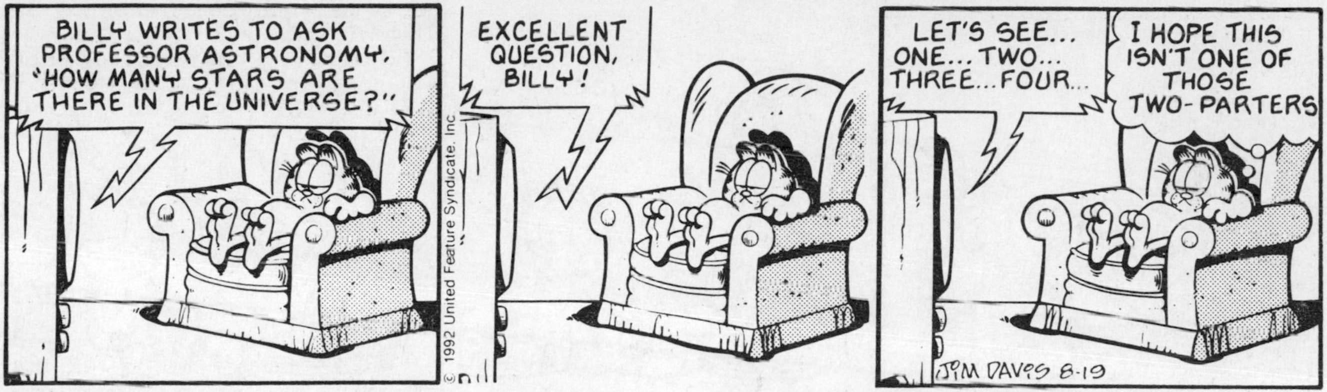
BILLY WRITES TO ASK PROFESSOR ASTRONOMY, "HOW MANY STARS ARE THERE IN THE UNIVERSE?"
EXCELLENT QUESTION, BILLY!
LET'S SEE... ONE... TWO... THREE... FOUR...
I HOPE THIS ISN'T ONE OF THOSE TWO-PARTERS
JIM DAVIS 8-19
© 1992 United Feature Syndicate, Inc.

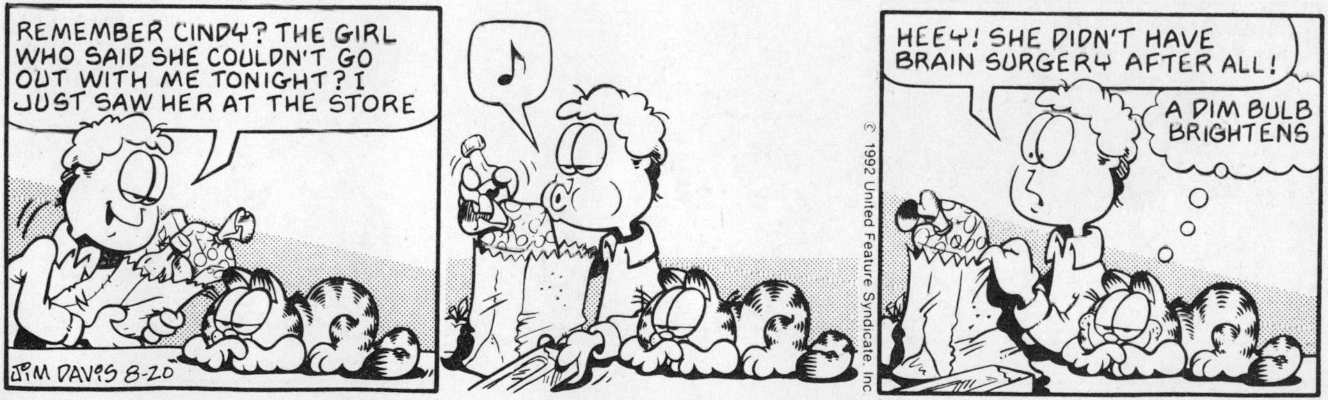
REMEMBER CINDY? THE GIRL WHO SAID SHE COULDN'T GO OUT WITH ME TONIGHT? I JUST SAW HER AT THE STORE
♪
HEEY! SHE DIDN'T HAVE BRAIN SURGERY AFTER ALL!
A DIM BULB BRIGHTENS
JIM DAVIS 8-20
© 1992 United Feature Syndicate, Inc.

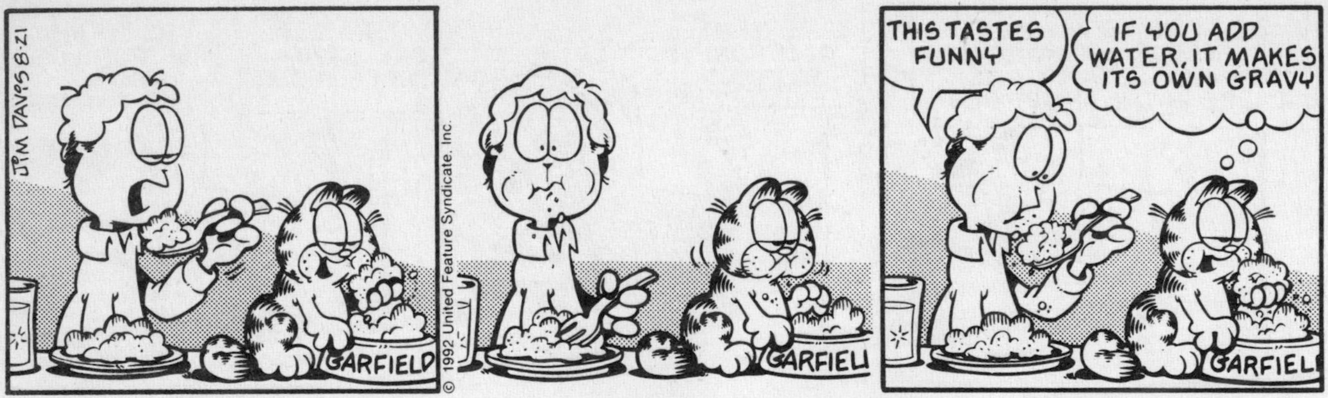
JIM DAVIS 8-21
© 1992 United Feature Syndicate, Inc.
GARFIELD
THIS TASTES FUNNY
IF YOU ADD WATER, IT MAKES ITS OWN GRAVY

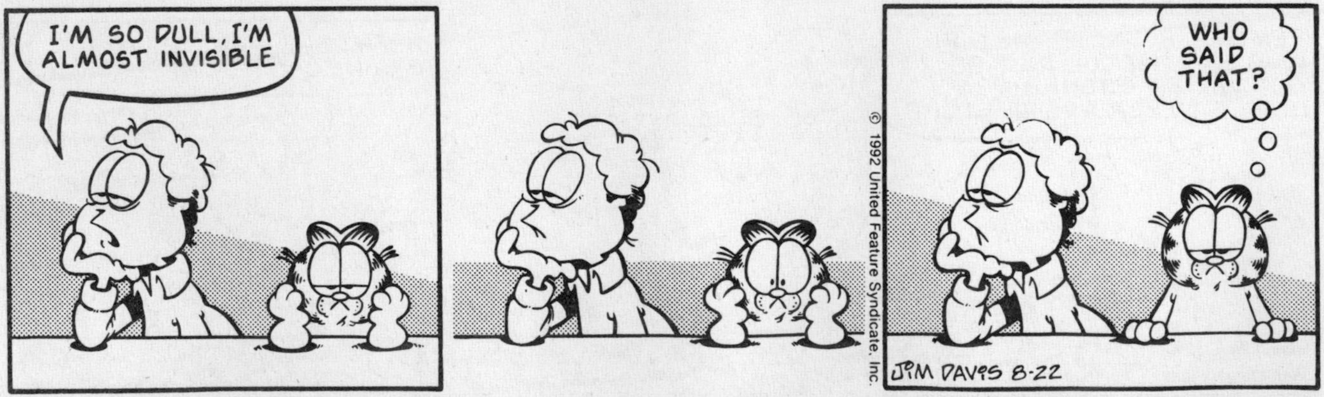
I'M SO DULL, I'M ALMOST INVISIBLE
© 1992 United Feature Syndicate, Inc.
WHO SAID THAT?
JIM DAVIS 8-22

Garfield

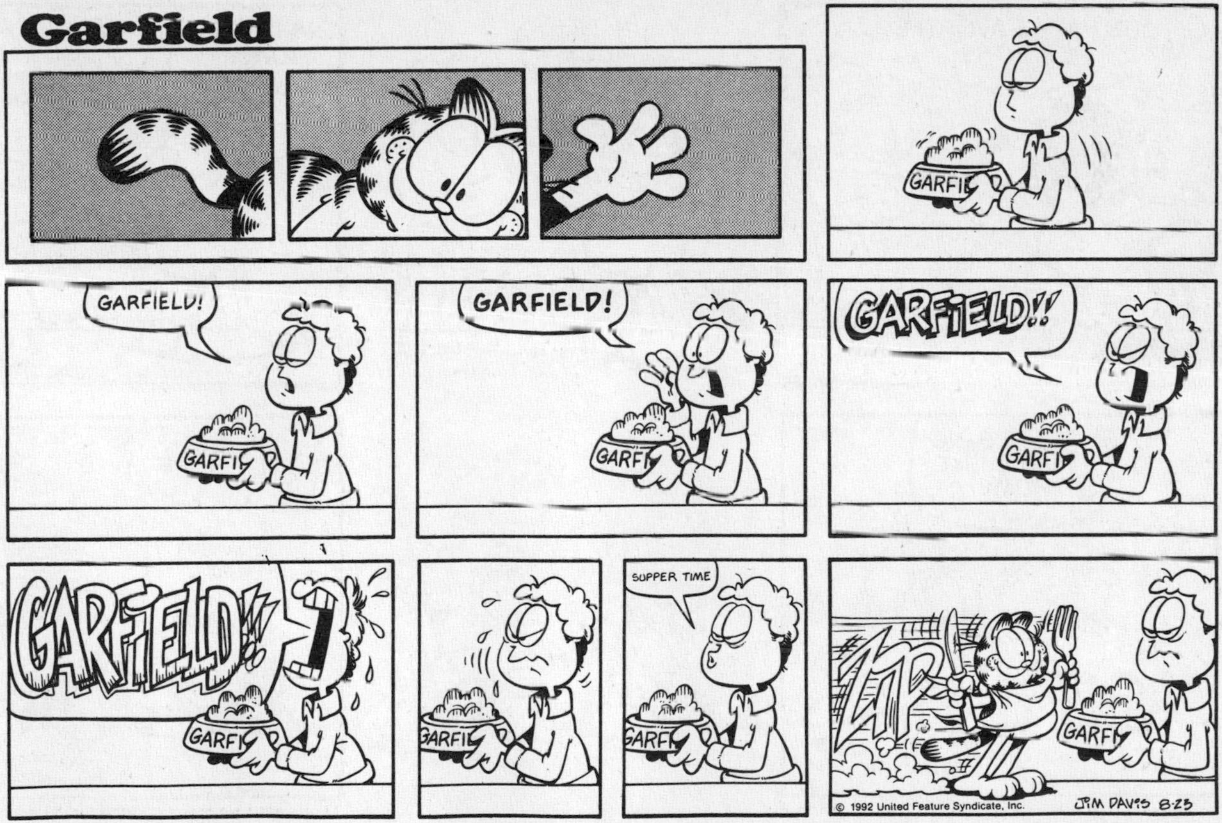
GARFI
GARFIELD!
GARFI
GARFIELD!
GARFI
GARFIELD!!
GARFI
GARFIELD!!
GARFI
GARFI
SUPPER TIME
GARFI
ZIP
GARFI
© 1992 United Feature Syndicate, Inc.
JIM DAVIS 8-23

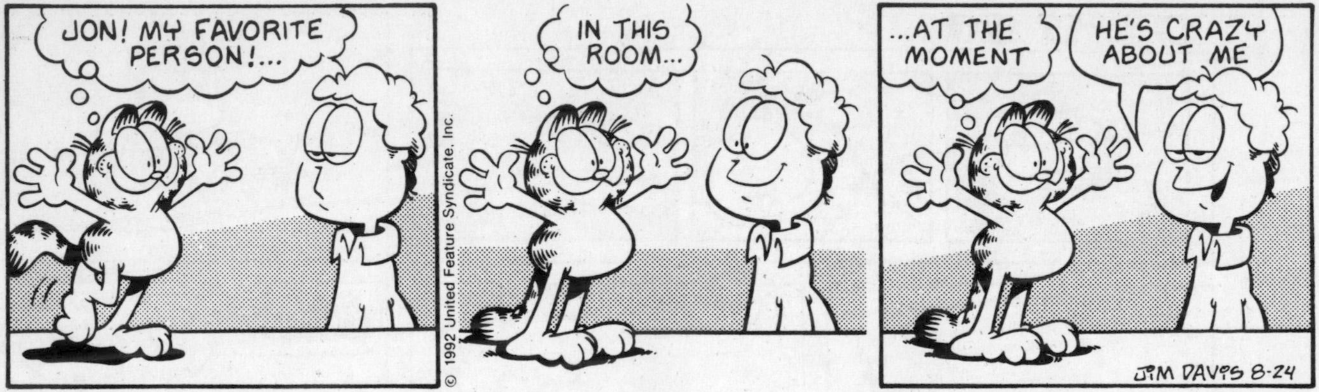
JON! MY FAVORITE PERSON!...
IN THIS ROOM...
...AT THE MOMENT
HE'S CRAZY ABOUT ME
JIM DAVIS 8-24
© 1992 United Feature Syndicate, Inc.

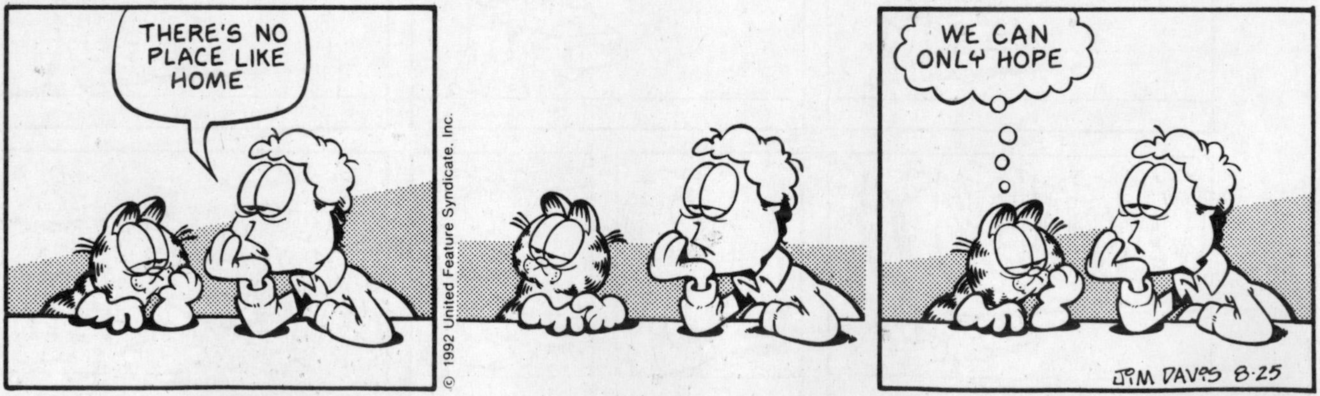
THERE'S NO PLACE LIKE HOME
WE CAN ONLY HOPE
JIM DAVIS 8-25
© 1992 United Feature Syndicate, Inc.

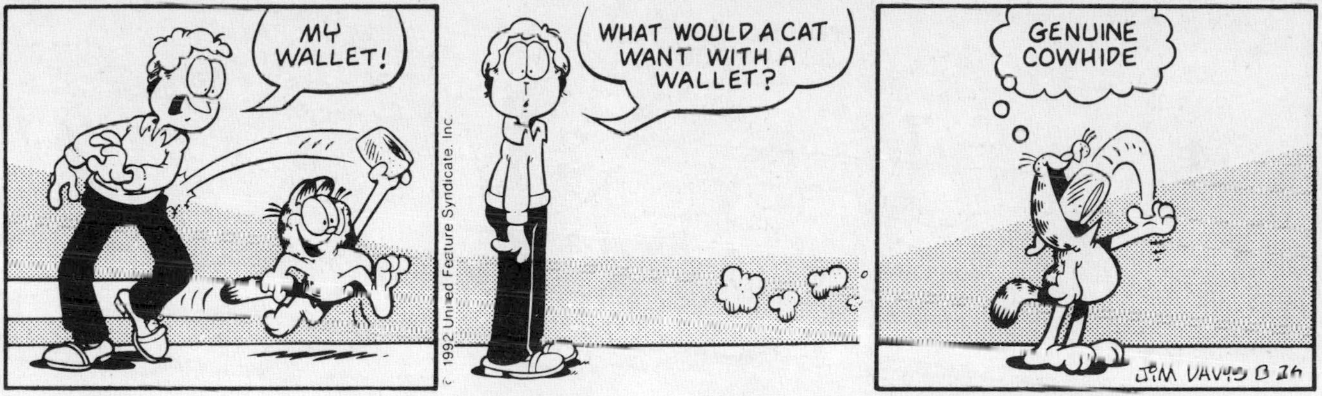
MY WALLET!
© 1992 United Feature Syndicate, Inc.
WHAT WOULD A CAT WANT WITH A WALLET?
GENUINE COWHIDE
JIM DAVIS 8-26

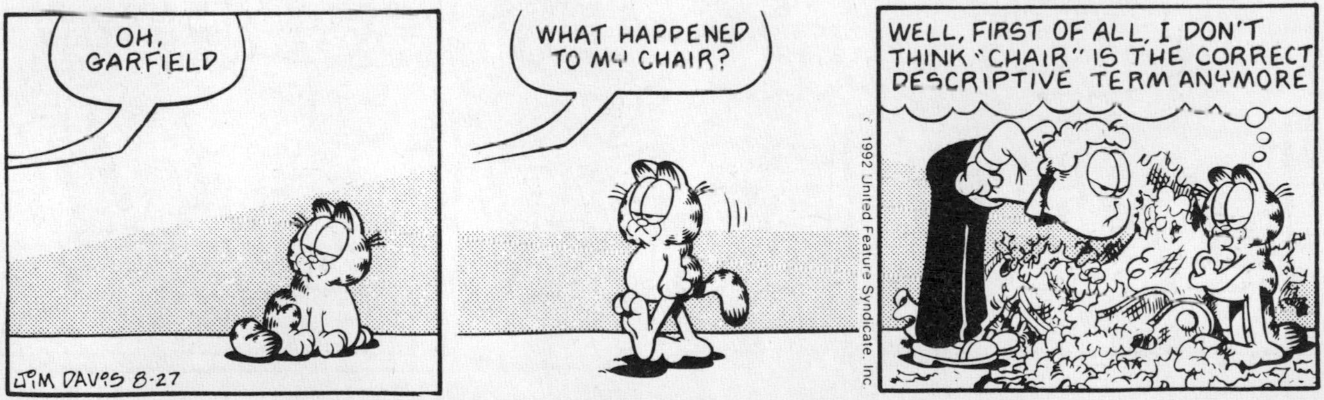
OH, GARFIELD
JIM DAVIS 8-27
WHAT HAPPENED TO MY CHAIR?
© 1992 United Feature Syndicate, Inc.
WELL, FIRST OF ALL, I DON'T THINK "CHAIR" IS THE CORRECT DESCRIPTIVE TERM ANYMORE

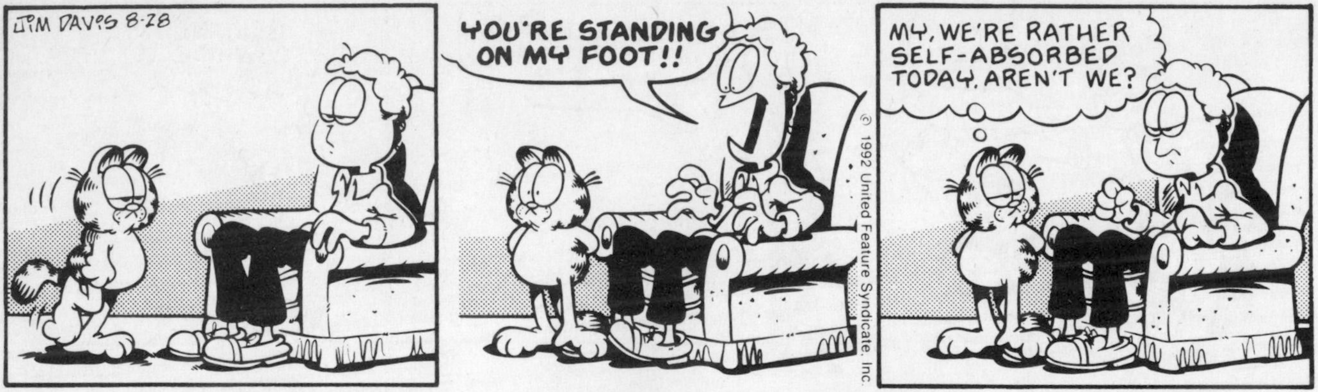
JIM DAVIS 8-28
YOU'RE STANDING ON MY FOOT!!
© 1992 United Feature Syndicate, Inc.
MY, WE'RE RATHER SELF-ABSORBED TODAY, AREN'T WE?

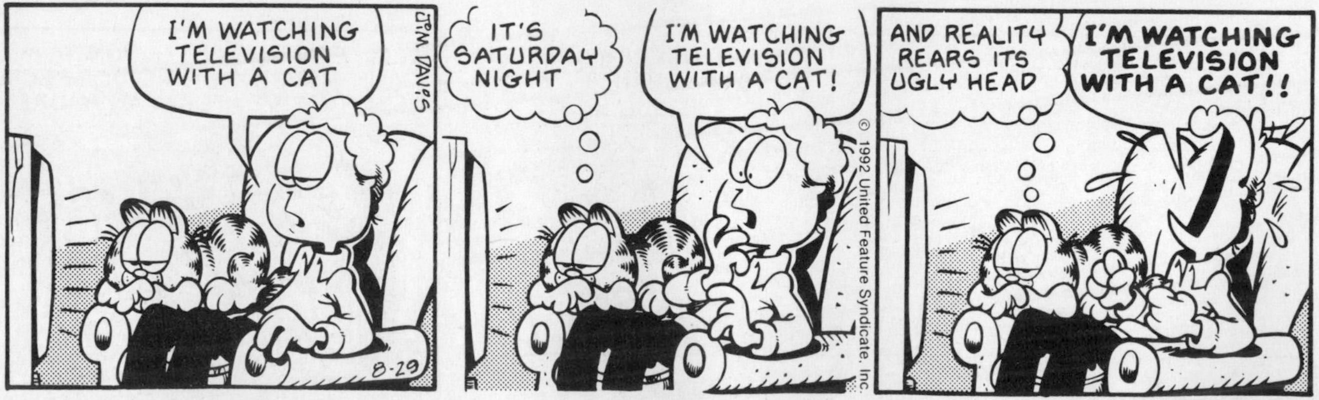
I'M WATCHING TELEVISION WITH A CAT
JIM DAVIS
8-29
IT'S SATURDAY NIGHT
I'M WATCHING TELEVISION WITH A CAT!
© 1992 United Feature Syndicate, Inc.
AND REALITY REARS ITS UGLY HEAD
I'M WATCHING TELEVISION WITH A CAT!!

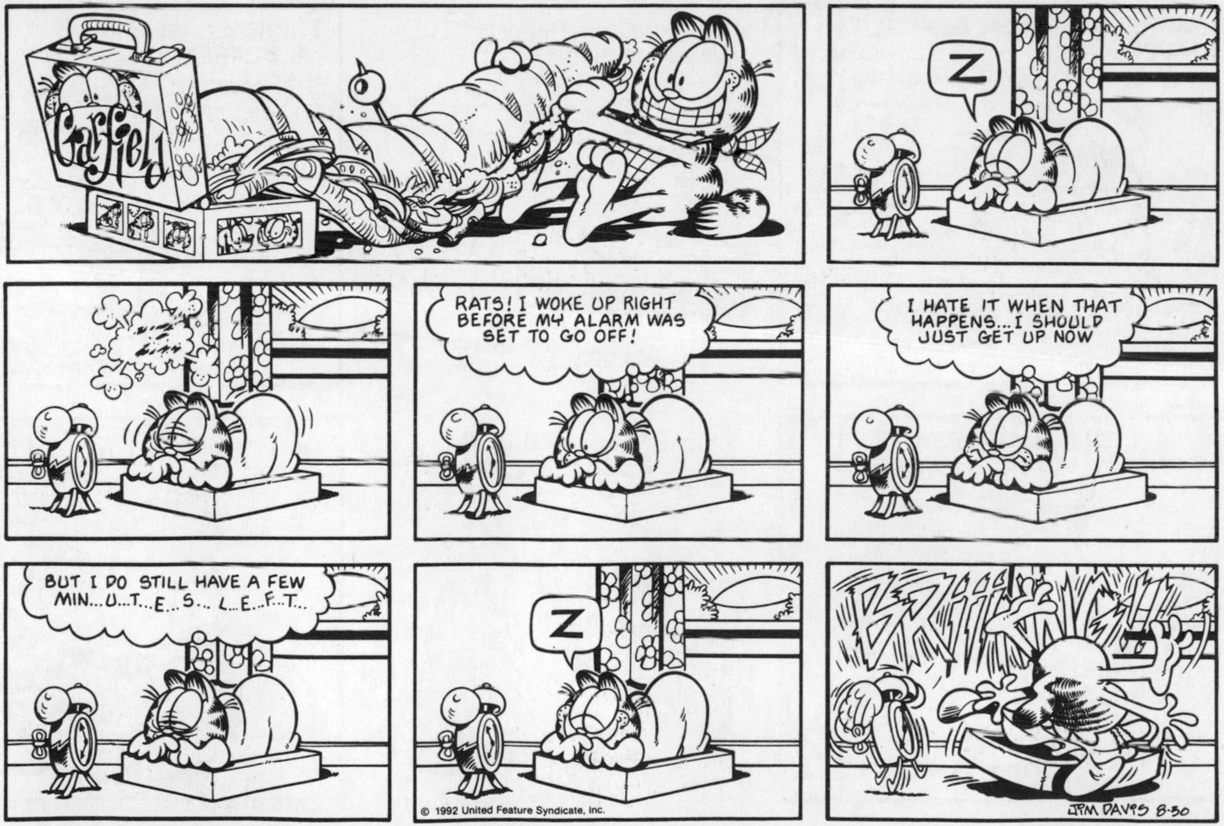
Garfield
Z
RATS! I WOKE UP RIGHT BEFORE MY ALARM WAS SET TO GO OFF!
I HATE IT WHEN THAT HAPPENS... I SHOULD JUST GET UP NOW
BUT I DO STILL HAVE A FEW MIN... U... T... E... S... L... E... F... T...
Z
© 1992 United Feature Syndicate, Inc.
JIM DAVIS 8-30

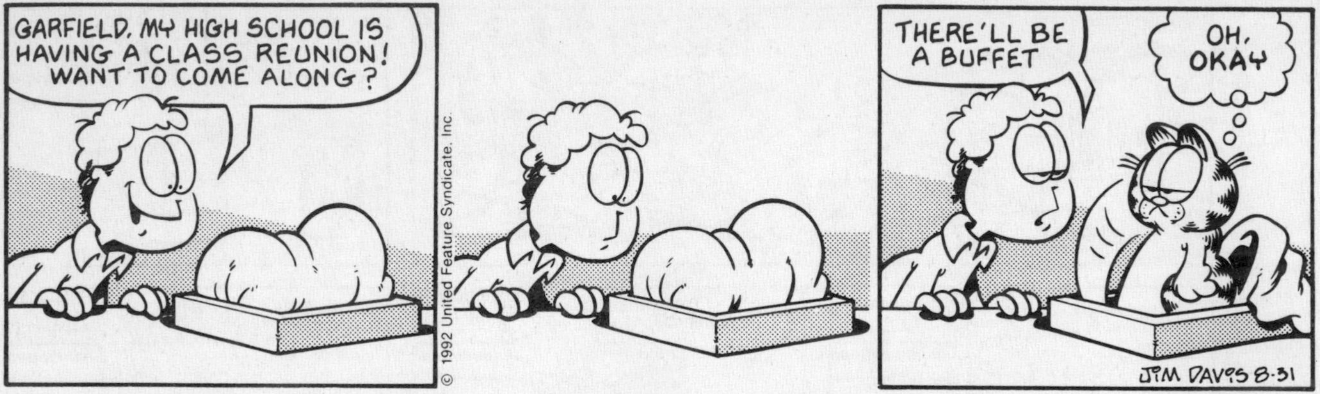
GARFIELD, MY HIGH SCHOOL IS HAVING A CLASS REUNION! WANT TO COME ALONG?
THERE'LL BE A BUFFET
OH, OKAY
JIM DAVIS 8-31
© 1992 United Feature Syndicate, Inc.

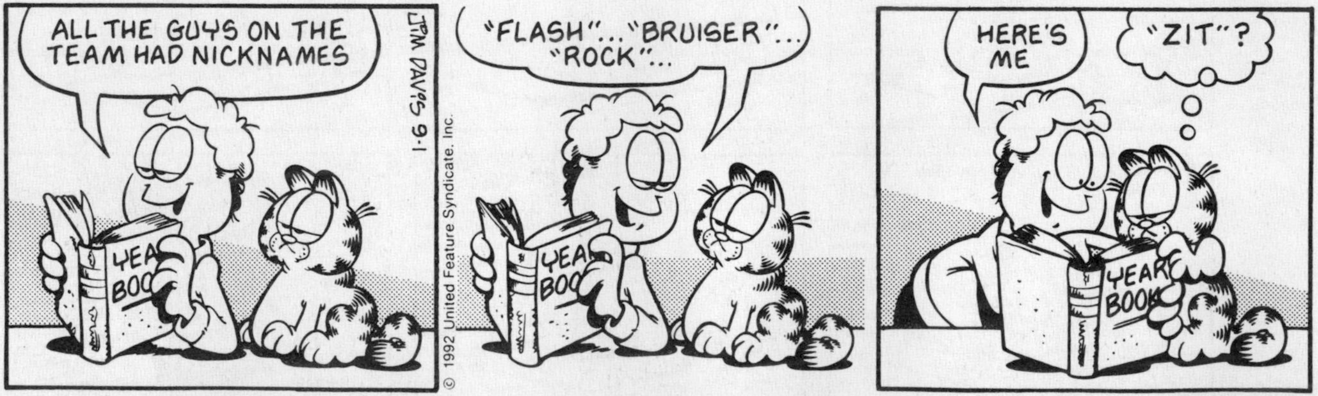
ALL THE GUYS ON THE TEAM HAD NICKNAMES
YEAR BOOK
"FLASH"... "BRUISER"... "ROCK"...
HERE'S ME
"ZIT"?
JIM DAVIS 9-1
© 1992 United Feature Syndicate, Inc.

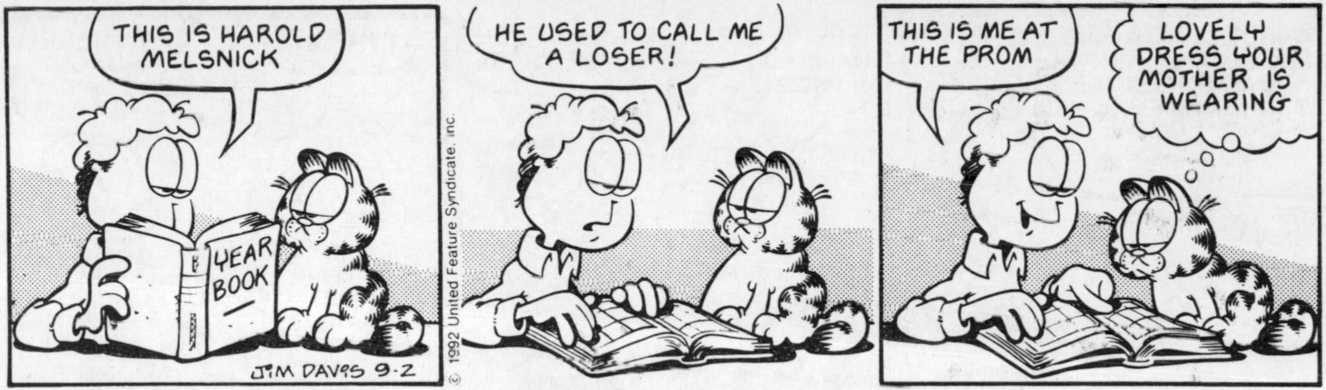
THIS IS HAROLD MELSNICK
YEAR BOOK
JIM DAVIS 9-2
© 1992 United Feature Syndicate, Inc.
HE USED TO CALL ME A LOSER!
THIS IS ME AT THE PROM
LOVELY DRESS YOUR MOTHER IS WEARING

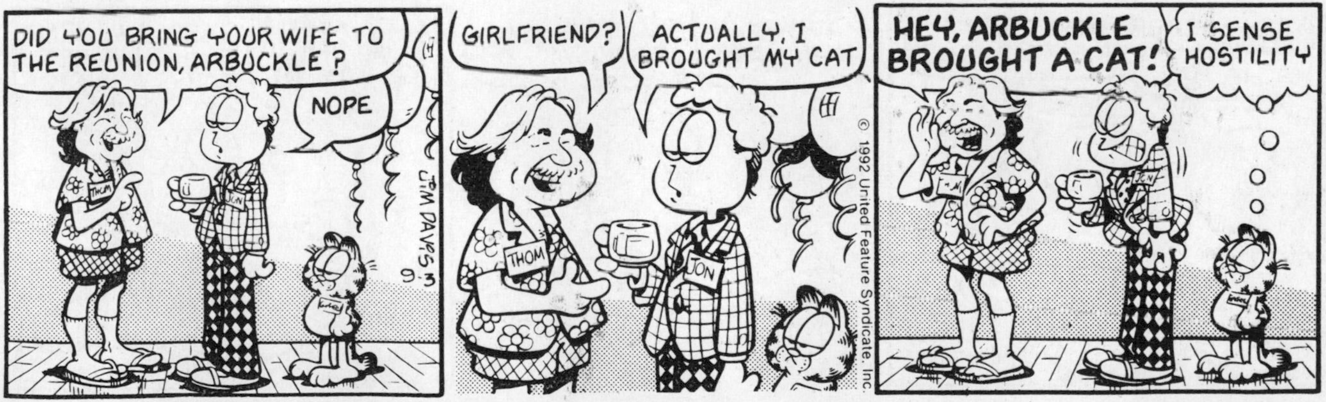
DID YOU BRING YOUR WIFE TO THE REUNION, ARBUCKLE?
NOPE
THOM
JON
JIM DAVIS 9-3
GIRLFRIEND?
ACTUALLY, I BROUGHT MY CAT
THOM
JON
© 1992 United Feature Syndicate, Inc.
HEY, ARBUCKLE BROUGHT A CAT!
I SENSE HOSTILITY

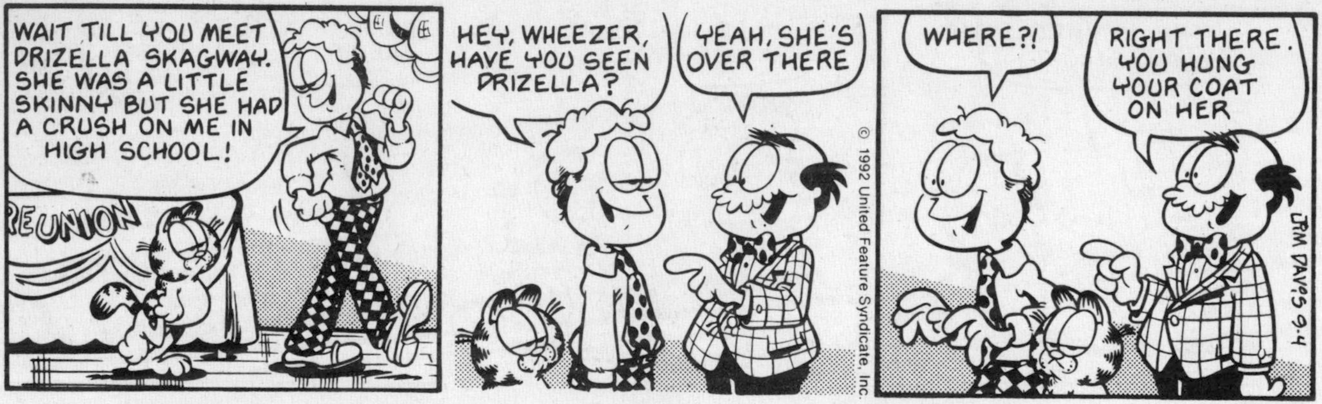
WAIT TILL YOU MEET DRIZELLA SKAGWAY. SHE WAS A LITTLE SKINNY BUT SHE HAD A CRUSH ON ME IN HIGH SCHOOL!
REUNION
HEY, WHEEZER, HAVE YOU SEEN DRIZELLA?
YEAH, SHE'S OVER THERE
© 1992 United Feature Syndicate, Inc.
WHERE?!
RIGHT THERE. YOU HUNG YOUR COAT ON HER
JIM DAVIS 9-4

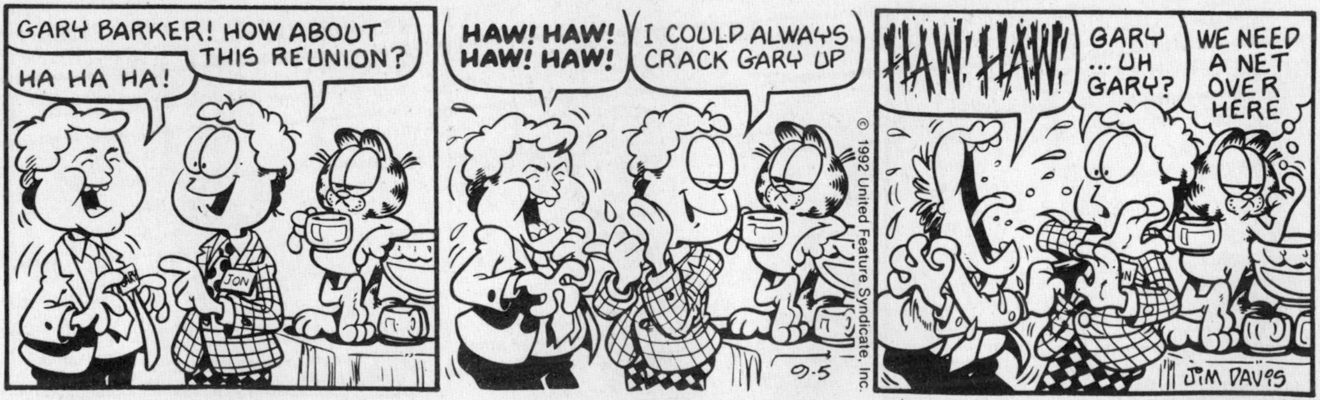
GARY BARKER! HOW ABOUT THIS REUNION?
HA HA HA!
JON
HAW! HAW! HAW! HAW!
I COULD ALWAYS CRACK GARY UP
9-5
© 1992 United Feature Syndicate, Inc.
HAW! HAW!
GARY ...UH GARY?
WE NEED A NET OVER HERE
JIM DAVIS

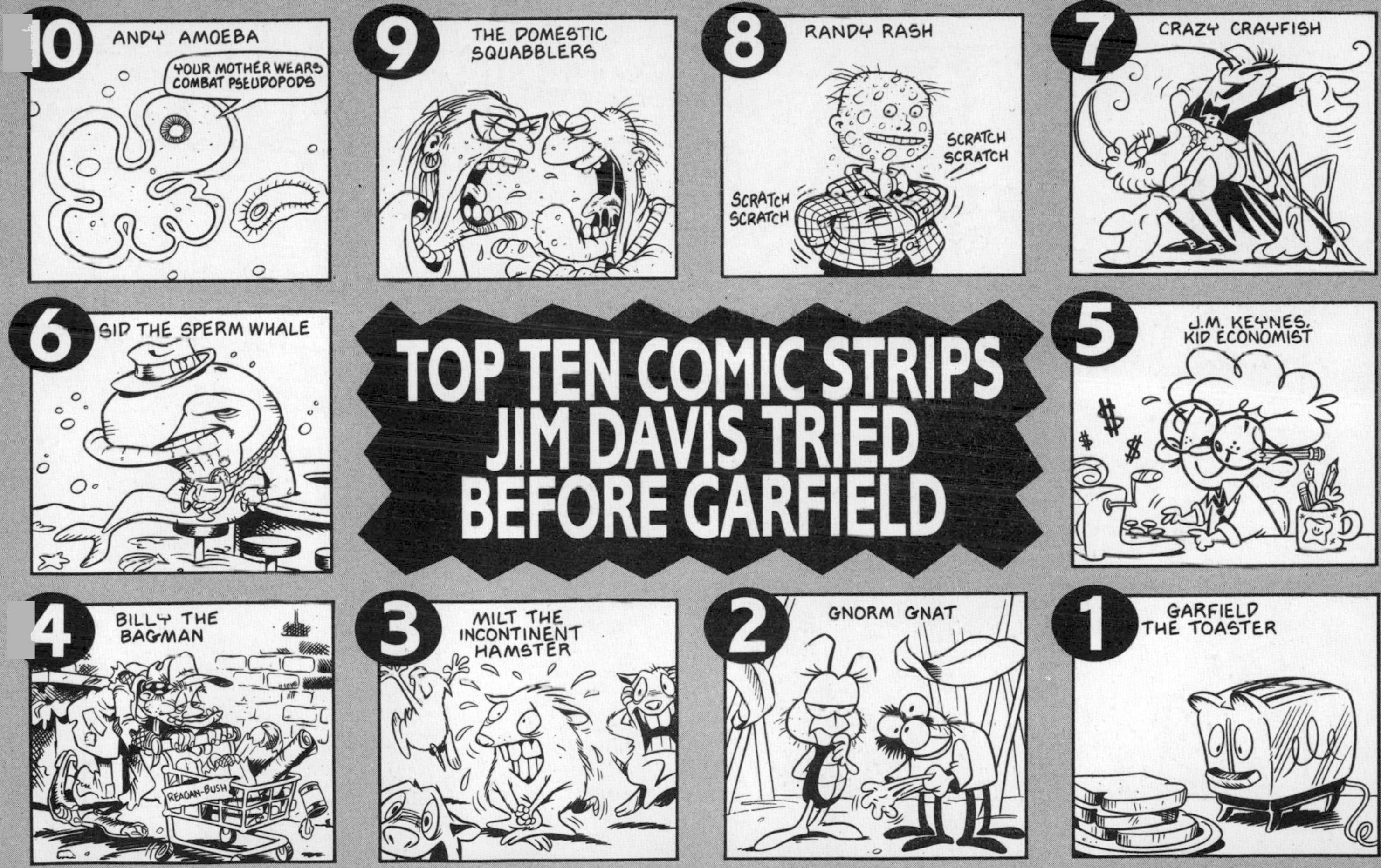
TOP TEN COMIC STRIPS JIM DAVIS TRIED BEFORE GARFIELD
10 ANDY AMOEBA
YOUR MOTHER WEARS COMBAT PSEUDOPODS
9 THE DOMESTIC SQUABBLERS
8 RANDY RASH
SCRATCH SCRATCH
SCRATCH SCRATCH
7 CRAZY CRAYFISH
6 SID THE SPERM WHALE
5 J.M. KEYNES, KID ECONOMIST
4 BILLY THE BAGMAN
REAGAN-BUSH
3 MILT THE INCONTINENT HAMSTER
2 GNORM GNAT
1 GARFIELD THE TOASTER

Like to get a **COOL CAT**alog stuffed with great **GARFIELD** products? Then just write down the information below, stuff it in an envelope and mail it back to us...or you can fill in the card on our website - **HTTP://www.GARFIELD.com**. We'll get one out to you in two shakes of a cat's tail!

Name:
Address:
City:
State:
Zip:
Phone:
Date of Birth:
Sex:

Please mail your information to:

Artistic Greetings
Dept. #02-7002
Elmira, NY 14925